SEA KAYAKING

A Guide for Sea Canoeists

PHILIP WOODHOUSE

BALBOA.
PRESS
A DIVISION OF HAY HOUSE

Balboa Press books may be ordered through booksellers or by contacting:

Balboa Press
A Division of Hay House
1663 Liberty Drive
Bloomington, IN 47403
www.balboapress.com.au
1-(877) 407-4847

ISBN: 978-1-4525-0848-1 (sc)
ISBN: 978-1-4525-0849-8 (e)

Printed in the United States of America

Balboa Press rev. date: 12/03/2013

Cover Photo: Paddling through a gauntlet at Cape Woolamai, Phillip Island, Victoria

Back Photo: Large surf (2.4 m–3.6 m, www.pofmlb.com.au nearby wave buoy) encountered by Todd Truscott and myself prior to landing at Rye back beach (ocean side) on March 6, 2006.

For Jacki, Christopher and Taryn

Preference

"The kayak is beyond comparison the best boat for single oarsman ever invented."

Fridtjof Nansen (1861—1930) Artic Explorer, Scientist,
Humanitarian, Nobel Peace Prize Laureate

ACKNOWLEDGEMENTS

I would like to thank the following people for their support and encouragement in compiling this manual over the years: Alan Woodhouse, Ian (Chalky) Thomas, Elizabeth (ET) Thomson, Tony Wennerbom, Rohan Klopfer (East Coast Kayaking), David Golightly (VSKC) and Paul Caffyn.

FOREWORD

Philip was introduced to canoeing in the 1970's through the New Zealand Boy Scouts. As a teenager he joined the Australian Army Reserve and upon leaving school joined the Royal Australian Air Force. One of his roles in the air force was that of an Adventure Trainer, where he organised and led adventure based activities for the development of junior officers and cadets as well as individual units.

Over the years, Philip has been a note taker, using his notebooks to prompt his memories. As a result this manual is a collection of his canoeing notes and is an on-going work written over the past 12 years about sea kayaking. It is his record of life's experiences.

The notes have been used by the Victorian Sea Kayaking Club (VSKC) as a principle reference source for sea kayaking, as well as by the Instructional staff and clients of East Coast Kayaking.

"These notes are invaluable to the keen sea kayaker. They are detailed, broad ranging and provide both experienced and novice sea kayakers with essential information for adventuring on the sea. A must have".

—Dr. Elizabeth Thomson, Ex-President NSW Sea Kayaking Club

TABLE OF CONTENTS

CHAPTER 1 PARTS OF A BOAT

"A ship is always referred to as 'she' because it costs so much to keep one in paint and powder."

Chester W. Nimitz

TERMINOLOGY

Deck features

The **deck** is a permanent covering over a compartment or hull of a boat. It can be described as the top covering of a kayak, which extends from side to side (gunwale to gunwale) and fore and aft. Deck profiles may be flat, ridged or curved. Ridged and curved forward decks have the advantage of shedding water, after a bow plunges through a wave.

Seam line refers to the join line between the hull and deck. It is desirable to have the seam sealed on both the inside and outside of composite material boats (e.g. fibreglass boats). Some manufactures do not believe external seams are required but experience in the VSKC has proven on several occasions that they are. The outer seam can be retro-fitted at any time.

Deck lines (aka *perimeter deck lines*) are cordage around the perimeter of the hull. They are required around the forward and aft decks. The suggested deck line diameter is 6 ± 1 mm. They are used when paddlers raft-up together or in rescue situations. Closer to the cockpit they are used to attach items like the removable deck compass or to secure items like a spare paddle bag to the aft deck.

Deck line fitting (aka *fairlead*) is either an integral (being formed into the deck during construction) or a separate fitting, fitted to the deck with bolts, washers and nuts (*fasteners*). Fairleads are used to run and secure the deck lines.

Shock cord (aka *bungee cord*) is elasticised cordage, made from rubber strands covered with a synthetic material sheath. It is used to hold items on to the deck. It should not, be solely trusted to keep items on the deck. If items are not attached by a lanyard, they will more likely than not,

become lost overboard from under the bungee cord when a powerful enough wave hits the deck.

Cleats are a deck fixture used to fasten the running-end of cordage. Several types and variations are found, but the common two types for kayaks are the jamming types and the cam types. Jamming cleats are used to hold tension on control lines, such as the drop-down rudder's deployment line. Cam-cleats are often used, for securing a sailing rig halyard.

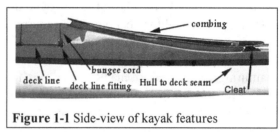

Figure 1-1 Side-view of kayak features

Hatches come in various shapes, types and sizes depending upon the make and model of the kayak. Hatches are the access points to the forward and aft compartments. Depending upon the quality and condition of the hatch covers, the compartments are either watertight or weather-tight. On selected designed kayaks, the aft hatch access point is behind the paddler's seat. It is advisable to have a lanyard attaching the hatch to the kayak. The Valley rubber hatches, which act somewhat like the sealing lids of kitchen storage containers, are most desirable; however, there are comparable brands used by various manufactures. Other designs are the use of a neoprene rubber cover, stretched over the hatch, with a fibreglass cover secured over the top. The fibreglass cover makes a useful table when camping. Rafter kayaks on the Sea-Leopard, effectively use strong rubber backed marine vinyl with a bungee gusset as covers, eliminating weight and excess items.

ⓘ **Note:** Day-hatches are not always accessible while at sea, depending upon the conditions. If you expect to encounter adverse conditions, you may need to consider carrying snacks, water and safety gear on your person, in a front deck bag or in the cockpit under the netting.

Day-hatch is normally the small compartment behind the cockpit. The hatch is offset from the centre-line, on the deck, to facilitate opening whilst seated in the kayak. The term can also be applied to the smaller forward cockpit hatch on some kayaks, which acts more like a car's 'glove-box'.

Skeg control if required is located on the topside of the deck, near or behind the cockpit. The control is usually a sliding knob connected to a cable. The cable runs back through the rear compartments to the skegs actuation mechanism. By varying the position of the control knob, the position (depth) of the skeg can be adjusted to suit the situation.

Rudder deployment control if required is usually located on the aft side of the cockpit or just behind. Some kayaks have the deployment control fitted behind the cockpit and it requires a bit of dexterity or fumbling around to find the deployment/retrieval knob. Often there is a jamming cleat fitted to enable the rudder to be locked down. However, paddlers often do not use the cleat or because of its location, fail to notice the rudder control line is not secured. This results in the rudder, not being fully deployed into the water, but left to trail along, in an inefficient position.

Toggles (aka *grab handles*) are attached to a kayak's bow and stern. They are required for portaging and manhandling the kayak. They assist in preventing a kayak slipping out of your grip.

Tow-points are the structurally sound securing points that may or may not be fitted to a kayak, when you buy it. If the manufacturer does not fit them, you will need to improvise and fit suitable tow points. They are used when you tow another kayak, and not when you are being towed.

Cockpit features

Spray deck (aka, *spray skirt, spray cover, skirt*) is the flexible and removable cockpit deck worn by the kayaker. Made originally from sea mammal skins, they are now made from neoprene synthetic rubber and other synthetic materials.

Cockpits are the part of a kayak, where the paddler or passenger sits. It is the aperture of the cockpit, which distinguishes a kayak from a *sit-on-top kayak*. Cockpits come in all sorts of shapes and sizes, depending upon the kayak and the manufacture's design preference. The top edge of the cockpit is surrounded by the *combing*, under which the elastic (known as the *rand*) from the skirt fits. The aperture shapes of cockpits vary, but broadly can be classified as either keyhole style or ocean style. Ocean style is based on the round Greenland Inuit kayak design and are often associated with low volume cockpits. Other shapes employed for the cockpit aperture are elliptical, round triangle and 'D' shape.

The point of interest to consider is: 'the cockpits required volume to fit a paddler in, verses excess space'. The less excess volume, the less water there is to remove if flooded. In addition, if you are snug and comfortable inside the cockpit, you have better control.

Being snug and comfortable inside the cockpit is a primary consideration. Kayaking is not about enduring pain, discomfort or numbness in the limbs, through poor ergonomics. If you are too loose you will slop around, even if it is only a small amount, and therefore you will not adequately transfer your energy and controlling forces into the boat.

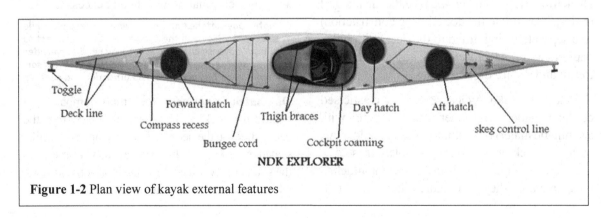

Figure 1-2 Plan view of kayak external features

Thigh braces are extensions on each side of a cockpit, for a paddler to brace their thighs against. In calm and or gentle sea conditions, a paddler can sit with their legs relaxed and have free play (slop) between their body and the boat. When required the paddler can brace (lock) their lower body into the boat through the thigh braces and remove any free play between themselves and the boat. Thigh braces assist in controlling the boat in a turn and or lean, by allowing the paddler to transfer their energy and controlling forces into the kayak. In rough water, they assist the paddler in controlling the kayak. In a roll, thigh braces assist in the transference of energy from the hips and thighs into the kayak, particularly during the 'hip-flick' phase.

The **seat** is one of the most important parts of a kayak. Seats are made from composite materials, fibreglass, foam rubber or a plastic like polyethylene. A poorly designed or ill-fitting seat is the source of great discomfort; obviously! In this situation, some paddlers tough it out, others look around and either get an ergonomically designed seat or make their own. Having a slightly raised forward portion on the seat, helps alleviate pressure on the buttock and thighs. Ensure your seat helps you maintain proper body posture for paddling, that is, you are sitting up straight and not slouching. Another seat term encountered is the *podded seat*. This refers to the back of the seat forming an aft bulkhead and can be associated with low volume cockpits.

Footrests are need for the paddler to maintain proper body posture and are vital to the transferring of power, from the legs on body rotation, when paddling. The paddler should be seated comfortably with their feet resting on the footrests. When required, the paddler can tension up, using the footrests, and brace themselves inside the boat in a snug position.

ⓘ **Note**: Like any mechanical piece of equipment, perform regular maintenance checks to ensure the equipment is serviceable, free from defects and functioning correctly.

Rudder pedals (aka *foot operated tillers*) come in a variety of configurations,  depending upon what the designer thought up and the manufacture sourced and fitted. The types of rudder pedals vary from the toe-flipper control type, to a tiller bar (aka rudder bar; like that of an aircraft) to the sliding foot-peg type.

Bulkheads are a structural member used to separate compartments inside your kayak and provide rigidity and strength into the kayak. They are also used to give shape and strength in ships and boats. In combination with the hatches, the bulkheads provide (hopefully) watertight compartments, which provide buoyancy, when the cockpit is flooded. Depending upon the design of the kayak there are generally two to three bulkheads. Polyethylene (aka plastic kayaks), usually have foam rubber bulkheads.

Bilge pump is a pump whose water inlet is located in the bilge and outlet is positioned to allow the water to be ejected overboard. There are two categories based on their mode of operation: manual and electrical.  Manual operated pumps can be sorted into two other categories of: hand and or foot operated. The best form of bilge pump is the hands free type. Hands free allow the paddler to paddle and brace while the cockpit is being emptied of water.

Hull Features

Hull refers to the main body of the boat and may be described as the shell of the vessel. The covering of the hull is called the skin, even though the material may be anything other than an animal's skin. The hull can be defined as the central concept in floating vessels, as it provides the buoyancy to keep the vessel afloat. There are three basic types of hulls *displacement, semi-displacement* and *planing*. Kayaks and canoes are displacement hull types. In kayaking, hull section and form, are often vociferously defended by the designer who favours a particular type or combination.

Features of the hull

Bilge refers to the lower part of the internal hull, where the topsides run to the keel. Kayaks do not have a keel but some, like skin-on-frame boats, have a keelson. A bilge's hardness or softness refers to the bilge's curvature (aka *turn of the bilge*), with small radii being described as *hard* and large radii as *soft*.

Chine is any corner or angle of the hull, as opposed to a curve in cross-section: *turn of the bilge*. Also described as the angular intersection between the bottom and side of a boat and may also be described as an angular shoulder. On a hull covered by a soft material, it is the longitudinal angular line, formed by an internal stringer over which a material is stretched. A *hard chine* has a turn radius over 45 degrees (Zimmerly, 1976). Other descriptive terms for a hard chine are: *small turn radius*, or *sharp turn of the bilge*. Boats may also be described as having a *soft chine*, where the chine (shoulder) is more smooth and curved rather than angular (aka *soft bilges*). *Moderate chine* falls in between hard and soft chine. *Multi chine* refers to several hard chines along a hull.

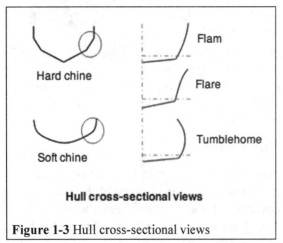

Hull cross-sectional views

Figure 1-3 Hull cross-sectional views

Flam is the convex shape of the hull above the waterline (Brewer, 1994). Particularly noticeable in the fore body, it imparts buoyancy when the vessel is heeled. Since there is no authoritative agreement about the term it is an ambiguously used term, and may be defined by some as, 'a part of hull flare'. Flam is also described as being 'the exaggerated outward curve right at the top of the flare'. For the same beam (compared to a boat with flare), flam has more reserve buoyancy, making the bow rise with and over a wave. It

is also incorporated into hull design to deflect spray and keep the foredeck *dry* in head seas.

Flare is the concave shape of a hull. It is the outwards spread and upwards curve or slant, of the hull's sides from the waterline to the deck and is usually associated with the bow section. It is often used to describe the non-vertical sides. There is no standardised degree of angle of flare to define slightly flared, moderately flared, and sharply flared (Zimmerly, 1976). The opposite term is *tumblehome*.

For canoes, John Winters wrote:

Flared ends will turn waves away but encourage pitching, which slows the canoe, while the increased beam caused by flare forces the paddler to reach further out with each stroke. As yet, no universally perfect shape has evolved . . .

Tumblehome refers to the upward and inward curvature of the hull, from the waterline to the deck. It is the opposite to flare. Some kayak designers on wide kayaks use a tumblehome design, meaning the sides actually curve inward as they come up creating a narrower beam on the deck. This structural design feature becomes an ergonomic design feature enabling the paddler to more easily reach the water, while still having the stability of a wider kayak. However, another designer will say that tumblehome 'allows more slop to come in and reduces the ultimate stability' (Winters, ibid.).

Hull form shows the plan view of the hulls shape. For kayaks, there are three basic types of hull form (plan shape): *symmetrical, Swede form* and *fish form*. Fish form and Swede form are collectively referred to as asymmetrical hulls. According to John Winters, they tend to pitch less in waves. The advantages and disadvantages of each type of form vary between designers. What is the best shape? See Design Caveat.

Symmetrical *form*—is the name given to the hull form shape, which has a greater underwater volume at midships.

Swede form—is the name given to the hull form shape which has a greater underwater volume aft of the midships.

Fish form—is the name given to the hull form shape which has a greater underwater volume forward of the midships.

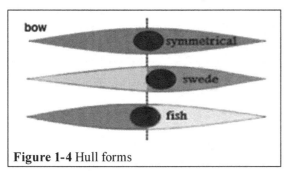

Figure 1-4 Hull forms

Hull section shows the hull's cross-sectional shape. For kayaks, the three basic types range from round bottomed (A), flat-bottomed (B), and V-bottomed (C and D), with variations of each in between.

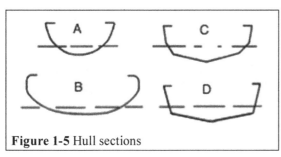

Figure 1-5 Hull sections

Figures A and B are soft turn of the bilge hulls; also known as soft chine. Cross-section A is representative of a narrow hull and typical of racing sprint kayaks. They have a small wetted surface area but this brings with it stability penalties. Cross-section B is representative of broad, flat-bottomed hulls. These types of hull have a greater wetted surface area than the narrower and rounded hull shown at figure A, but are more stable. The broadness of the hull's beam may be 55 centimetres for a sea kayak and around 60 centimetres for a touring kayak and even broader for a recreation/fishing kayak.

Cross-sections C and D are hard turn of the bilge hulls; also known as hard chine. Cross-section C shows a multi-chine hull. Cross-section D shows a hull with flared sides. Having flared sides produces increased buoyancy as a boat is loaded. When a boat is loaded, it sinks down into the water. This creates a larger wetted surface area on the hull and 'foot print' in the water. However, it takes more cargo to

sink it one inch (pounds per inch), than a kayak having straighter sides. The flare increases the buoyancy that is; it resists sinking under the weight of the cargo.

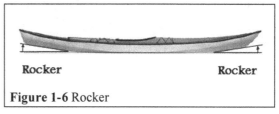

Figure 1-6 Rocker

Rocker refers to the upward curve built into the kayaks keelson from bow to stern. The greater the amount of rocker the more responsive the boat is, but this is at the sacrifice of tracking. *Tracking* is the ability of the kayak to travel in a straight line without directional correction paddle strokes. In a following sea, a kayak with too much rocker has the tendency to broach. In play boats, having a lot of rocker is an advantage because the boat becomes very manoeuvrable. Depending upon the purpose of the boat, the designer will determine how much or how little, rocker to incorporate.

Rudders and Skegs

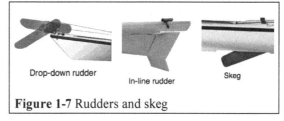

Figure 1-7 Rudders and skeg

The **rudder** is a controversial piece of equipment fitted to many kayaks. To the 'Purists' the use of a rudder and its advocates are anathema! However, leaving the purists to their myopic and insular arguments, we shall press on. The purpose of a rudder is to counteract all disturbing influences, whatever the source, that would tend to cause the kayak to move (slue) around its horizontal axis (i.e. yaw). Turning of a kayak is performed with body and boat lean in addition with paddle strokes. There are several types of rudder configuration on the market, with the drop down type (aka over stern rudder) being the most popular. Kayaks like the Mirage sea kayaks and Epic 18X have in-line rudders.

The **skeg** is a device used to improve a kayak's tracking ability and unlike rudders do not rotate around an axis point. Skegs can be deployed partially or fully depending upon the circumstances. A manual control cable normally deploys skegs but there are skeg units on the market that can be deployed hydraulically. A disadvantage with a skeg is that the housing can, on some kayaks, take up storage space in the aft hatch. Another is sand or fine pebbles jamming up the skeg inside the housing after a beach launch and thereby hindering or preventing the deployment of the skeg.

CHAPTER 2 CANOE AND PADDLE DESIGN

"Even today, canoes are rarely designed; they're more often adaptations or modifications of earlier shapes."

John Winters

DESIGN TERMINOLOGY

Design caveat

When talking about kayak speed one should differentiate between sea kayaks designed for touring and those designed for racing. Kayak design theory is subjective mainly because the monetary outlay verses returns for research and development (e.g. tank testing) is prohibitive.

Designers have, therefore, relied upon subjective evaluations of boats to determine performance values. This is neither reliable nor consistent. Test paddlers carry with them an extraordinary amount of baggage including personal and aesthetic bias, moods swings, the inability to duplicate test protocols and the more obvious inability to quantify or even sense performance variations in any reliable manner. This and the absence of formal design training for most designers results in a wide range of hull forms and little consensus on what is good or bad. Almost every shape has its proponents and detractors (Lazaukas, L and Winters, J, 1997).

The major influence on a sea kayak's performance is the kayaker. However, the application of hydrodynamic and hydrostatic design principles can produce a useful tool in comparing boats. The following terminology has been included to assist the reader in 'boat-speak' encountered in literature and during social conversations with other canoeists.

Classes of hull

Displacement hulls are a hull that is supported exclusively or predominately by buoyancy. Displacement hulls travel through the water at a limited rate, which is defined by their waterline length; and they do not obtain lift from their speed. Their maximum speed/length ratio

(S/L) is 1.34 (knots/feet) whereby the hull rides a single wave. The forward crest supports the bow section and the aft crest supports the stern section; see Figure 2-7. Exceeding the S/L causes the crest of the stern section wave to move aft of the hull's after-body and therefore, not support the stern. Thereby allowing the stern to squat down. At the same time, the bow rises as it tries to climb up the bow wave. This results in an exponential increase in wave making resistance with increasing speed.

In terms of economy, it is not practical to reach, let alone exceed, the S/L of 1.34 (knots/feet). When a displacement hull operates in the S/L range of 0 to 0.7 the rate at which the resistance increases is relatively slow and increases roughly according to the square of speed.[1] This means when speed is doubled, total resistance increases four times (e.g. at 2 knots speed the total resistance is 15 lb. then at 4 knots the resistance increases to 60 lb.). During the S/L range, wave-making resistance is negligible and speed depends mainly upon (skin) friction resistance generated from the wetted surface area and hull smoothness. The next S/L range between ~0.7 to ~1.1 shows wave making resistance starting to have a steadily increasing effect on hull speed. Above S/L 1.1 the rate of resistance increase is rapid and shows up as a sharp incline on a graph. Whereas below S/L 0.7 resistance increased to the second power of velocity (V^2) it has been shown, through modelling, that resistance increases to the third (V^3), fourth (V^4), fifth (V^5) or even sixth power of velocity (V^6) for heavy displacement keel boats. Increases in speed are then limited by design, structural and material considerations. These hulls may often be heavier than planing hulls, but not always. Typical displacement hulls are found on ocean liners, tugs, trawlers, sailboats, canoes, kayaks and rowboats.

Semi-displacement hulls (aka *semi-planing hulls*) are hulls that have features of both planing and displacement hulls.[2] The hull form is capable of developing a moderate amount of dynamic lift; however, the craft's weight is still supported through buoyancy. They have a maximum hull design speed. Exceeding this speed can result in erratic handling and unstable operation. Some general characteristics of a semi-displacement hull are: a pronounced chine forward; rounded bilges and a transom wide enough to provide some lift from the water flow under the hull; the versatility of combining speed with sea-worthiness; and the capability of high speeds having a maximum S/L ratio around 1.5 to 2.5 (knots/feet). Types of boats that fit in the general category of semi-displacement hulls are certain lightweight fast dinghies, day-sailers, lobster-boats and other power cruisers (Brewer, 1994).

Planing refers to aquaplaning and hulls that have speed/length ratios (knots/feet) over 2.5 up to 10 or higher.[3] True planing hull designs, use the concept of hydrodynamic lift developed from its own power-plant, as opposed to surfing on the energy of a wave. As is well known, one way to increase speed is to reduce the wetted surface area. To achieve this, the hull is designed to act as a hydroplane. The aim is to get as much of the hull as possible to rise out of the water, when at cruising speed.

To overcome the disadvantages of the displacement hull's resistance to increases in speed, the planing hull was designed and built. The purpose of the design is to develop dynamic pressure, thereby decreasing the boats draft with increasing speed (i.e. the hull lifts upwards and hydroplanes on the water). The hull design (shape) does not limit the maximum attainable speed but does affect the power required to get the hull to plane (i.e. hydroplaning). Planing hulls are characterized by hard chines and wide transoms. The two categories of planing hull are: hulls having little or no deadrise for high efficiency on calm water; and hulls having substantial deadrise for a smoother ride in rough water.

The degree of the angle of the 'V' is called *deadrise*. Deadrise in the deep V-hull application is the angle between the hulls surface (when looking at it in a cross-section) and a horizontal plane extending laterally from the baseline, forming an angle of 20 degrees or more. To improve the planing hulls performance in choppy and rough water, the deep V-hull and its variants were developed, to cut through the waves and reduce impact shocks. Another form of planing hull is the *tunnel bottom* (aka

hydroplanes) as seen on the Formula One racing boats. These hulls are designed to trap a cushion of air beneath the hull, to lift the boat and hence reduce total resistance on the outside hulls.

Canoe/kayak hulls are displacement types and do not plane in the true application of the term for hull design. This is because a person (i.e. the power-plant) cannot provide the power (kilowatts) required to support the hull through dynamic loading. However, in a simplistic way, it is said that under certain conditions and designs, some kayaks will plane (aquaplane) or at least display some characteristics of planing, while they are surfing. High speed in kayaks is achieved through the combination of excellent displacement/length ratios and narrow beams. These two factors develop very small waves, which are the major form of drag (resistance) at speeds above a speed/length ratio (S/L) of 1.34 (Winters, Pt2, Residual Resistance, Displacement/Length Ratio).

Figure 2-1 Flyak

One type of kayak, which truly hydroplanes under the propulsion of the paddler, is the *Flyak*. Designed by Einar Rasmussen, a Norwegian and former Olympian kayaker, the Flyak has two hydrofoil fins below the surface of the water that can produce lift with the correct application of power and ability from the paddler. The hull rises approximately 15 centimetres above the surface of the water and is reportedly able to travel twice as fast (~27 km/h, 7.6 m/s) as a conventional sprint kayak.

Coefficients

Coefficients are used to compare hull forms because they are non-dimensional and therefore comparisons between different hull types can be easily made. The commonly referred to coefficients found in kayaking literature are the block coefficient and prismatic coefficient.

Block coefficient (C_B)—is the volumetric ratio between the volume of the immersed hull portion and that of the volume of a solid block. Block coefficient is an important indicator of a kayaks directional stability. The *block* refers to a rectangular solid that has the identical measurements of the: beam at waterline (B_{WL}), waterline length (L_{WL}) and depth equal to the draft (T) of the immersed portion of the hull. It differs from the prismatic coefficients prism, which mimics the shape of the widest part of the immersed hull's beam.

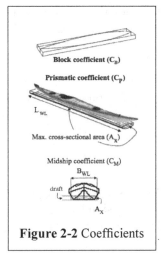

Figure 2-2 Coefficients

The block coefficient is used as a factor in resistance (drag) calculations. It also correlates with a kayaks tracking ability (Sea Kayaker Magazine. 2008, Kayak Review Information). Generally, the block coefficient lies between 0.35 for very fine hulls (usually V-shaped) and 0.5 for full form hulls (Winters, 2005).

The block coefficient is expressed as the volume (V) divided by the waterline length (L_{WL}) multiplied by the beam at waterline (B_{WL}) multiplied by the draft (T) written as:

$$C_B = V/L_{WL} \times B_{WL} \times T$$

Prismatic coefficient (C_P) (aka *longitudinal coefficient*) is a measure of the distribution of volume along a hull's length and is used to evaluate the distribution of the hull's volume. The prismatic coefficient has a major effect on wave making resistance. It is the ratio of the kayak's displacement compared to the volume of an identical prism. The prism mimics the same maximum cross-sectional beam (A_x) at the waterline (B_{WL}) and whose length is identical to the kayaks waterline length (L_{WL}). Written as

$$C_P = V/L_{WL} \times A_x$$

Prismatic coefficient differs from the block coefficients 'block', which is a rectangular solid. Since hulls are different shapes and sizes, the prism and therefore the prismatic coefficient makes a standard measure for comparison of the distribution of volume along a hull's length. If a craft displaces 48 per cent of the volume of the prism then the prismatic coefficient is 0.48. This is a rough measure used to look at the fineness or fullness of a hull. Fine end hulls have a C_P around 0.48 while full end hulls have a C_P around 0.63.

A kayak with a low prismatic coefficient has less volume in its ends and therefore less wetted surface area (S_W). A smaller wetted surface area contributes to efficiency at low speeds. The fine ends at higher speeds do not create a bow wave as far forward as a fuller ended (higher C_P) boat would and therefore create a shorter wave of transition. The shorter wave of translation results in a lower top speed but this is offset, to some degree, by the lower S_W assisting in making the kayak easier to paddle at cruising speed.

A kayak with a higher C_P has more volume in its ends and therefore a greater wetted surface area (S_W) and greater frictional resistance (R_F) (i.e. skin friction and therefore drag). This is offset to some degree at higher speeds by the fact that a full end kayak will develop a longer wave of translation and therefore with the right application of effort, can theoretically attain a higher top speed (Sea Kayaker Magazine 2008, Kayak Review Information).

Measurements

The following terms are associated with kayak hulls. Further terms can be found in the glossary.

Beam

Beam (B) (aka *breath*) is the width of the hull. Transverse measurement is a term that refers to the measurement of a kayak's beam (i.e. width). The following terms are used in relation to beam (aka *width in design*):

Beam overall (B_{OA}) is the width at the widest point of the hull.

Beam at waterline (B_{WL}) refers to the widest (maximum) part of the kayak's beam, at the waterline. It is the primary determinant of initial stability (Guillemot, Kayak Design Terms).

Depth and draught

Depth (D) is the vertical distance from the base line to the lowest part of the freeboard deck. Depth is the measure of the inside roominess of a hull. The measure is taken at the point of maximum beam up to the sheer line. It may also be referred to as *depth to sheer*. Depth is the most un-standardised measurement used in regard to kayaks, making comparisons between types difficult. The above measurement method is the recommended one (Zimmerly, 1976).

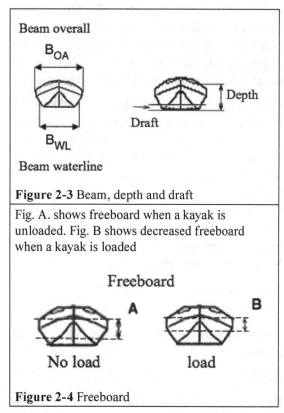

Figure 2-3 Beam, depth and draft

Fig. A. shows freeboard when a kayak is unloaded. Fig. B shows decreased freeboard when a kayak is loaded

Figure 2-4 Freeboard

Draught (d or T) (aka *draft*) refers to the depth of water, the hull is displacing, as measured from the keel (base line) to waterline. It does not include rudders or retractable skegs. Draught is linked to displacement.

Displacement (Δ) is the weight of water equivalent to the immersed volume of the hull and is the total weight of a boat. The Greek capital letter delta is the symbol used in equations. Displacement leads us to the concept of freeboard.

Freeboard (FB) is a dynamic measure (i.e. it varies), of the vertical distance from the waterline

to sheer. The amount of freeboard decreases as weight increases. **Least freeboard** is the lowest portion of freeboard.

Length

There are several measures for length used in naval architecture. The common ones used in kayak design are below. Further terms can be found in the glossary.

① **Note:** length alone does not indicate or make a fast kayak.

Load waterline (L_{WL})—is the length of a boat at the design loaded waterline. Waterline length is the prime factor in boat performance, but this is in conjunction with displacement (Winters, Speaking Good Boat Pt 1). Other variations to the meaning of the abbreviation L_{WL} are *Length at Waterline* and *Length Waterline Load*.

Length overall (L_{OA})—is the extreme length parallel to the design loaded waterline, from the foremost part of the hull to the aftermost part of the hull; excluding appendages.

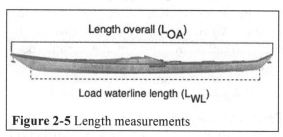

Figure 2-5 Length measurements

Resistance

Resistance is the term used to describe *drag*. In fluid dynamics, drag (which may also be called air resistance or fluid resistance) refers to forces that oppose the relative motion of an object through a fluid (i.e. a liquid or gas). Since the kayak is a human powered boat, reducing resistance to the bare minimum is a goal of designers. To quote Lazauskas and Winters:

The main force resisting the forward motion of kayaks is the drag of water on the hull. In a recent examination of Olympic racing kayaks Jackson (1995) estimated that this hydrodynamic resistance accounts for more than 90% of the total drag on the boat (The other 10% is mainly composed of aerodynamic drag on the crew and hull topside).

In naval architecture William Froude put forth that the resistance of a floating body in motion is the sum of two parts frictional resistance (R_F) and residual resistance (R_R) and both could be analysed separately; to a point.

Frictional resistance (R_F) is *skin friction,* which occurs between the hull's skin and the water. Frictional resistance takes into account the total effect of the hull's wetted surface (S_W), load waterline (L_{WL}) length, surface condition (smooth or rough) and speed.

Skin friction is far greater in water than in air because, water is approximately 835 times denser than air. As a hull travels through water it develops what is called the *boundary layer.* The boundary layer is a calculable thickness along the hull that increases towards the stern and travels at the same speed as the hull. The water on the outside of the boundary layer travels at a slower speed. It is within the boundary layer that frictional resistance acts. As the boundary layer becomes thicker, there is a greater mass of water receiving the hull's momentum and therefore a greater energy loss (i.e. greater the drag). Along the hull (for approximately 20 per cent of the boats overall length) the boundary layer is of laminar flow, until it reaches a critical value and a transition point is reached, whereby the flow becomes turbulent. This is why surface imperfections are removed from racing boats, since they create further turbulent flow. Designers attempt to keep the flow laminar along the hull as long as possible through hull design and delay the point of separation as far as possible. As the boundary layer separates from the hull, at or near the stern, a new form of drag is created and termed *eddy-current making resistance* (Marchaj, 1964). Despite the efforts of designers, damage accumulated by a sea kayak's hull can easily offset any design attempt to reduce skin friction. A year's damage can cause a 50 per cent reduction in the coefficient of friction (C_F) (i.e. increase in drag, without the paddler even noticing) (Winters, Speaking Good Boat Pt 1).

Wave making resistance (R_W)—is a type of drag, which affects the hull of a kayak and reflects the energy required to push the water away from the hull (i.e. hydrodynamic drag).

In small boats, wave-making resistance is the major source of drag. For all displacement type hulls, the system of waves produced by speed becomes an unavoidable trap.

As a hull moves through the water, it creates two forms of waves termed *divergent waves* and *transverse waves.* Divergent waves fan out from the bow and stern with little significance because, they do not combine. Transverse waves from the bow and stern have crests and troughs at right angles to the direction of hull travel. These waves can and do combine creating resistance (drag). However in some circumstances, the waves partially cancel each other out.

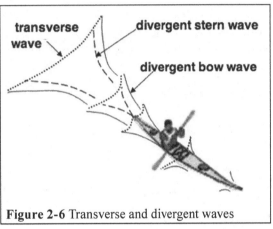

Figure 2-6 Transverse and divergent waves

Transverse waves are an indication of energy loss, as the bow pushes water out of the way and the stern sucks it back in. Prior to wave propagation speed the wave rapidly dissipates at the sides. As hull speed increases so does the wave making effect as the water piles up at the bow. This is because the water cannot escape fast enough, as it is limited by gravity and viscosity.[4] At the speed/length ratio (S/L) of 1.34—knots to feet—as defined by Froude, the hull has developed a large crest at the bow and another at the stern, with a trough at midships. In some references, this wave system is termed the *wave of translation.*

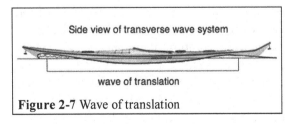

Figure 2-7 Wave of translation

Hull speed

Continuing on from wave making resistance, the boat is now at what is termed 'hull speed' and is riding its own wave, as measured from the transverse waves crest to crest. At the same time its longitudinal trim changes with the bow rising. As it attempts to exceed this speed, it finds itself literally trying to climb a hill of water. Increasing speed from this point results in an exponential increase in resistance (i.e. it requires a lot more effort for a small increase in speed).

Trim and **sinkage**—if the speed length ratio is increased the stern crest will move to the after-body of the hull (moves right to the back of the hull), causing the stern to *squat* excessively. Since the distribution of displacement along the water line length depends on wave profile, the hull at this speed is being sucked down below its intended waterline.

Table 2-1 Transverse wave length formed by a moving body

V_s in kn	1	2	3	4	5	6	7	8
λ in ft	0.56	2.23	5.01	8.9	13.9	20.06	27.3	35.6

Transverse waves have variable lengths (wavelengths–λ, Greek symbol Lambda) depending upon the hull speed therefore, the wavelength can be calculated if hull speed is known or vice versa; see Table 2-1.

Hull speed is not the final limit on a boat's speed; it is just the point whereby wavelength equals the boats waterline length. Any increase in speed after this point comes at an exponential increase in the requirement of power (e.g. to go faster, you have to paddler a lot harder for a small increase in speed).

Hulls and surfing

Surfing is a term that tends to be misinterpreted as planing and linked to planing hulls. Canoes and kayaks are displacement type hulls. Therefore, by their very nature, they cannot hydroplane. This is because the power-plant (i.e. the paddler) cannot develop the necessary kilowatts (power) to hydroplane. For a hull to *plane*, it requires the adequate application of power and then it will continue to plane regardless of the sea conditions.

However, a human powered boat (e.g. skis, canoes, kayaks, surfboards etc.) will experience a similar effect to planing when power is derived from the energy of a wave (i.e. surfing). Human powered boats experience aquaplaning when surfing, but in terms of boat design the hulls are not 'planing hulls'. Some manufactures produce wave skis and surfing kayaks based on the principles of planing hulls (broad transoms, flat hulls and hard chines), but the energy required for the boat to plane, comes from the wave the boat is on and not from the power-plant. As a result, when the wave has expended its energy, the paddler then has to manoeuvre the displacement hull, which is advertised as a planing hull, back out into the surf take-off zone. At no time could a paddler plane the boat back out to the take-off zone under human power.

STABILITY

The ultimate stability of a canoe, unlike other types of boats, lies with the passenger and a successful design will take this into account.

John Winters

Floating bodies

Any object will float if the volume of water it displaces weighs more than the object.

Density

The buoyancy of an object (i.e. its ability to float) is determined by its density (mass/volume). An object that is less dense than its surrounding medium will float and is said to have positive buoyancy. An object that is denser than its surrounding medium will sink, or have negative buoyancy. An object that floats in the middle is said to have neutral buoyancy.

For example—two 1 cm³ objects, one wood the other metal, are placed into fresh water, one floats the other sinks. In fresh water, an object with a density less than 1 g/m³ will float and if heavier it would sink.[5] Wood has a density around 0.8 g/cm³ and steel has around 8 g/cm³, so it is obvious, which will float and which would sink. This shows that whether an object floats or sinks depends upon both its weight and volume in relation to the liquid it is in.

Buoyancy

Buoyancy is an upward force exactly equal to a liquids own weight. An object submerged in a fluid has a force pushing up on it (upward thrust) that is equal to the weight of the fluid being displaced by the object. This is known as the buoyant force. This idea is known as Archimedes' Principle. Like the object, the force exerted by the fluid depends on its density. When a body of fixed volume (e.g. an empty boat), is immersed in water, it experiences an upward force (buoyancy, up-thrust). The size of the up-thrust increases until the body is fully submerged and after that, it does not change since the two forces are in equilibrium.

The shape of an object will affect the buoyant force against the object, since changing the shape changes the volume of the object. Changing the shape can cause the object to displace a greater or lesser amount of water, thereby changing the buoyancy. For example, a sheet of steel (8 g/cm^3) will sink in water, but shape it so that it displaces at least eight times its own volume then it will float. If it displaces 1000 times its own volume then it will be able to float and carry almost 1000 times its own weight of cargo as well.

A body immersed in water displaces some of the water. The more of the body that is under the water, the more water it displaces and the greater the up-thrust. Water (as considered within this frame of reference) is incompressible. When an object is placed in water, it makes a hole as it displaces the water. Remove the object and the hole fills back in; balance is restored. A boat is less dense than water and by virtue of its weight, will make a hole in the water (W = mg).

Floatation

When a body floats, it appears to lose all its weight. In this case, the up-thrust is equal to the weight of the body, but acting in the opposite direction to the weight. This is known as the law of flotation.

There are two forces at play, weight and buoyancy. A vessel has the force of weight (that is, it has gravity pulling its mass down), displacing water (i.e. making a hole). When the vessel has displaced its own weight in water, creating the hole, equilibrium is achieved through the counteracting upward force (buoyancy). When buoyancy equals or exceeds the weight of the vessel it will float.

Displacements

We know that the weight of the water displaced by a boat is the same weight as the floating boat. However, the boat's volume is greater than the volume of the water displaced. If the boat is moving, displacement is an on-going process requiring an appropriate amount of force. Water is both dense and heavy and it takes an appropriate amount of force to move it aside. The volume of water and speed of the boat will determine the force required. This is why to conserve energy, streamlining the boat is important.

When a boat is built with all its fittings, but before any items or cargo is loaded, it is known as *lightship displacement*. This does not change unless a major refit takes place. When cargo, stores and crew are added, it is known as *deadweight displacement* and can vary continuously. The combination of lightship displacement and deadweight displacement is known as *load displacement*.

Boat Stability

Stability is principally about staying upright and afloat. A boat has weight that acts vertically downwards under gravity. To prevent the downward force of gravity sinking the boat, an equal and opposite force acts vertically upwards, known as buoyancy. Buoyancy is derived from the displacement of water. To produce sufficient buoyancy to float, a boat needs to displace a weight of water equal to the weight of the boat. When this is achieved, the force of gravity, acting vertically downwards, equals the force of buoyancy acting vertically upwards.

Three cross sectional hull shapes 'U', 'V' and flat, all having the same displacement all experience pressure acting on their hulls, constituting a buoyant force acting upwards and increasing with depth (their draft). A narrow 'V' shape hull will sit lower in the water, and will therefore experience higher hull pressures as a function of depth; than a flat wide hull having the same displacement but floating higher towards the surface.

Stability is determined by the interaction between the two forces of gravity and buoyancy. Stability is not determined by the cross sectional shape of the hull being 'U', 'V' or flat, or the chines being hard or soft. Two kayaks having different cross sectional shapes, but similar water plane area, will have similar initial stability. Cross sectional shape has an effect, when the kayak is heeled to larger angles of inclination. In this situation, the shape of the hull changes whereby the kayak's topsides become the hull, causing the volume to change and the centre of buoyancy to move to a new position.[6]

Righting lever

Referring to Figure 2-8, when all the various stability factors—centre of gravity (G), centre of buoyancy (B) and metacentre (M) are all positioned along the centreline (CL), the vessel is stable and upright.[7]

Should the vessel heel (and assuming there is no loose cargo that can move), the centre of gravity (G) remains in the same position. The centre of buoyancy (B) moves off the centreline, to a new position, at the *geometric centre of the underwater shape* (i.e. hull) below the waterline (WL).

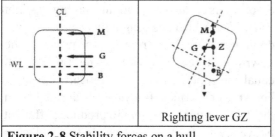

Righting lever GZ

Figure 2-8 Stability forces on a hull

The force of gravity, which always acts vertically downwards, acts from the unmoved centre of gravity point (G). The now displaced force of buoyancy (B), which always acts vertically upwards through the metacentre (at small angles of heel), creates what is known as the *righting lever* (aka *heeling arm, GZ lever*) between the two forces. The righting lever creates a righting moment. A *moment* being a measure of force applied to a lever arm.

The length of the righting lever is governed by: the distance the centre of gravity is below the metacentre (i.e. *metacentric height* (GM)) and the distance through displacement of the centre of buoyancy, from the centreline.

Righting moment

A righting moment (RM) is the restoring force that returns a vessel back to its stable position after a disturbing force (e.g. a wave) exerts an inclining moment. Do not confuse righting levers with righting moments, as they are not identical.

Basics for boat equilibrium

The three basic states of equilibrium are *stable*, *neutral* and *unstable*. Referring to Figure 2-9 when an external force inclines a boat and the centre of gravity (G) is below the metacentre (M), there is a *positive righting moment* set up by the righting arm (GZ). The boat will return to its former stable position (stable equilibrium), after the external force is removed.

For neutral equilibrium, the centre of gravity (G) is moved up to such a position that it is at the same position as the metacentre (M). When the boat is heeled, the buoyant forces, which always act vertically upwards, act inline through the centre of gravity. In this state of neutral equilibrium, there are no unbalanced forces of gravity and buoyancy. The boat has a zero moment arm (righting arm) and therefore zero moment. The boat will stay in this new position when the external force is removed, or until another external force moves it. In this condition, a boat is said to list (e.g. list to starboard).

For unstable equilibrium, move the centre of gravity (G) up to such a position, that when a boat is heeled, the centre of gravity is above the metacentre (M). The centre of gravity and therefore the force of gravity are outboard of the centre of buoyancy. In this situation, you create a state of unstable equilibrium. The two forces create a moment in the opposite direction (i.e. ZG), to that experienced for a stable equilibrium (i.e. GZ). The moment does not act in the direction that will restore the boat to the upright position, but rather, will cause it to incline further. The boat in this situation has a *negative righting moment* (capsizing moment) and a negative righting arm (ZG).

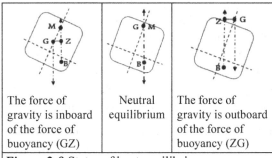

The force of gravity is inboard of the force of buoyancy (GZ)	Neutral equilibrium	The force of gravity is outboard of the force of buoyancy (ZG)

Figure 2-9 States of boat equilibrium

Transverse centre of buoyancy

The transverse (aka *athwartship,* side-to-side) centre of buoyancy is considered to be an important aspect of a vessel's stability. The transverse centre of buoyancy, affect a vessel's rolling moments. If a vessel is unable to recover from a disturbing force that causes it to roll (heel), it will capsize. When a vessel encounters a disturbing force, the hull shape changes. The centre of buoyancy will then move to a new position at the geometric centre of the new underwater section of the hull. The underwater hull section will change as a result of its design (shape) and the effects of heeling forces and pitching forces. Other factors that can affect a vessels underwater hull section are rising on to and off a plane when planing, changes to trim, weight and centre of gravity.

When a floating vessel with a fixed centre of gravity (G) is inclined, the centre of buoyancy (B) moves to a new position at the geometric centre of the underwater section of the hull. When it remains inboard of the centre of gravity (G), it creates a positive righting lever (GZ) and a righting moment. This will cause the vessel to recover itself to a stable upright position (i.e. stable equilibrium). If the centre of buoyancy moves off the centreline to a position whereby it is inline with the centre of gravity, the vessel will develop a permanent list (i.e. neutral equilibrium). If the centre of buoyancy is displaced by an inclining moment to a position

whereby it cannot establish itself at the geometric centre of the new hull underwater shape, the vessel will be unstable.

The strength of the righting lever (GZ), created by the displacement of the centre of buoyancy from the centre of gravity, will increase until the hull's underwater section reaches its maximum angle of heel. After this point the length of the righting lever (GZ) becomes smaller. The strength of the corresponding righting moment diminishes until it reaches zero (i.e. 0 Nm), which is known as the *angle of vanishing stability* (AVS) on the stability graph. At this point the vessel cannot right itself and after this point the righting moment is said to be a *negative righting moment* (ZG) whereby it assists in capsizing the vessel.

As a vessel heels towards it maximum righting lever angle, it passes the *danger angle*.[8] The danger angle is half the maximum righting angle. It is around this angle that a vessel can effectively operate and right itself. After the maximum angle of the righting lever (GZ) is reached, the vessel will soon be in a situation whereby it will flood its decks and possibly take on water. As freeboard is lost, the righting arm throughout the range of stability is reduced.

Movement of the centre of gravity

Movement of the centre of gravity (G) upwards reduces stability and moving it downwards increases stability. When the force of gravity, acting downwards from the centre of gravity (G), is inboard of the force of buoyancy, acting upwards from the centre of buoyancy (B), the boat will tend to resist a change in buoyancy (i.e. equilibrium). This is generally described as *initial stability*. When the centre of gravity is outboard of the centre of buoyancy (B), the boat is in an unstable position and depending upon the magnitude of the moment, will capsize if no corrective action is taken.

When paddling different kayaks of different hull shape, but similar water plane area and width, you experience a significant difference in initial stability. This will be due to the difference in the height position of the centre of gravity and its relationship with the centre of buoyancy. For example, this could be due to the difference in the height of the seat off the bilge.

Ignoring other human factors, between paddlers of different heights, a taller paddler (e.g. 6 ft 2 in) will have a higher body centre of gravity over a shorter paddler (e.g. 5 ft 2 in) and may find a particular boat more unstable, than the comparably skilled and experienced shorter paddler. This is because the sum of the overall centre of gravity is made up of the component centre of gravities.

Effect of weight on stability

Weight also affects the centre of gravity position. Adding items to a floating body will reposition the position of the centre of gravity (G). This is because the position of the centre of gravity (G) is the sum of the component parts. It is the positioning of the component parts in relationship to the entre of buoyancy that will determine if the boat is stable or unstable. An uneven transverse weight distribution is known as *list*. List is induced by load and or shifting weight. A boat will list if its centre of gravity (centre of weight distribution) is moved off the centreline. List may or may not affect transverse stability but it will affect paddling efficiency. Longitudinal weight distribution is known as *trim* and refers to the difference between the forward and aft draughts. A boat with a positive trim is said to be *down at the head* (bow) and one with a negative trim is *down by the stern*.

When draft increases the GZ righting levers are reduced throughout the entire range of stability. Another way of saying this is as freeboard decreases so to do the righting arms. When displacement increase a broad beam boat will develop a larger GZ righting lever over a narrow hull boat. Different weight paddlers in comparable boats will sit either higher or lower in the water. A 180 centimetre 70 kilogram paddler will sit higher in the water than a 100 kilogram person. The lighter paddler will produce and experience a longer righting arm (GZ) than the heavier paddler. This may be offset if there is any appreciable increase in hull displacement of the heavier paddlers boat. However the actual righting moment does not change as much as expected. Initial and secondary stability often

remain similar regardless of weight. (Schade, Kayak Stability, 2009).

Effect of beam on Stability

Shifting a boat's buoyancy requires effort and the boat will tend to oppose moving its centre of buoyancy. A vessel's beam will affect its stability because beam has a direct relationship with the outward movement of the centre of buoyancy as a boat heels. This affects the length (and therefore strength) of the righting lever. There is a formula naval architects use to determine the relationship between length and beam.

Judging transverse stability by beam alone can be misleading, as the entire waterplane area of the hull contributes to stability, not just the amidships cross sectional shape (A_x). Therefore, naval architects apply the theory of couples and heel to many sections of the hull to determine the total effect. A simplified rule to remember here is *stability increases with water plane area* (Winters, 2005).

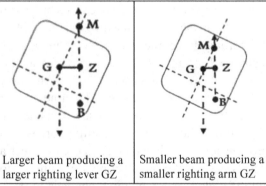

| Larger beam producing a larger righting lever GZ | Smaller beam producing a smaller righting arm GZ |

Figure 2-10 Effect of beam on stability

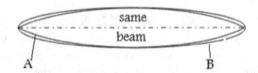

Two hull shapes with the same displacement and mid-section width but A (inside line drawing) has fine ends and B (outside line) has full ends. Stability increases with water plane area with shape B producing a greater righting arm moment than A at the forward ends.

Figure 2-11 Water plane area

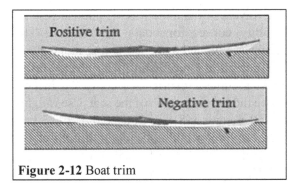

Figure 2-12 Boat trim

Longitudinal stability

Longitudinal stability (aka *trim*) refers to the stability of a vessel through the longitudinal plane (forward and aft). Due to a boat being many times longer than wide, there is more resistance to changes in longitudinal inclination (pitch) than in transverse inclination (roll). However, when loading sea kayaks, attention needs to be paid to the cargo being stowed fore and aft to ensure the longitudinal centre of gravity position, which acts in a similar manner as the effect of the centre of gravity and a transverse weight shift, but in a smaller magnitude.

Hull cross-sectional shape and beam seas

Wide beam kayaks (say ≥ 600 mm) are considered stable boats. This is because they possess greater form stability than a narrower hull kayak, in swell conditions, with non-breaking waves possessing greater than twice the kayaks beam. In these conditions, these wide beam hulls tend to follow the shape of the waves.

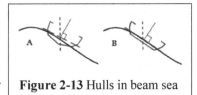

Figure 2-13 Hulls in beam sea

Unless the paddler is inattentive, the kayak should not capsize. In beam seas with waves around 1.5 times the boats beam and less than 10 times the wavelength in height, the kayak will try to follow the waves shortened surface, making it difficult for the paddler to heel the hull into the wave. At this point, a narrow beam boat (say ≤ 550 mm) will be much easier to heel into the body of the breaking wave.

At this juncture, it needs to be restated, that stability in a kayak is highly dependent upon the skill of the paddler. Case in point, I was once out in 25 knot increasing winds and a breaking beam sea, with a paddler who has greater skill levels than me. Chalky, who is around 1.83 metres tall and weighing 70 kilograms, was paddling a narrow (< 50 cm) hard chined boat (a down-river racer), while I, at 1.86 metres and weighing 100 kilograms, was paddling my 55 centimetre beam, soft chined boat. As we 'ran for cover', I felt quite comfortable in the conditions and the breaking beam sea, but Chalky later admitted, he was working hard to prevent himself from being capsized. Had I have been in Chalky's boat, I know I would have capsized. It was only his skills, which kept him upright, especially in the 35 knot plus gusts. My boat for my build and height provided me with enough stability in the conditions, for my skill level. Had I been in the small beam boat, my height would have raised the centre of gravity and the boat would have been extremely tippy (i.e. unstable), even though my weight would have increased the hull's displacement. I felt comfortable in my kayak because it felt stable through a lower centre of gravity and greater displacement. Having a low centre of gravity and increased displacement is known as, *low form stability.*

High form stability boats will tend to follow the surface of the wave and are prone to capsize in short, sharp beam seas. Conversely a narrow beam boat may be easier to heel into a breaking beam sea but there is still the risk of capsize through physical and mental fatigue, inattentiveness or some other human factor.

Quantifying stability

The stability graph

The stability graph (aka *GZ graph, static stability graph*) is an efficient way to quantify stability through the (static) *stability curve*. For all types of canoes, the ultimate form of stability lies with the paddler, so in order to determine a canoe's stability, several assumptions need to be made to limit the variations of paddlers. The dynamic variations introduced by a paddler are weight and height, which factor in to the centre of gravity. Individual stability curves show on the x-axis the angle of heel against the y-axis of either righting arm lengths in metres (m) or righting moments in newton-metres (Nm). The righting arms are not identical to righting moments.

Stability curve for a Valley Sea Kayaks, Rapier 20; adapted from Sea Kayaker Magazine June 2007

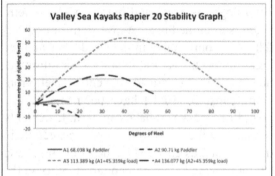

Note the effect of weight on stability.

Stability curve for a Epic 18x Sport; adapted from Sea Kayaker Magazine, October 2008

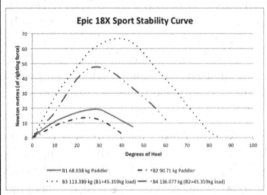

	VSK Rapier 20	Epic 18X Sport
L_{OA}	6.070 m	5.489 m
B_{OA}	0.450 m	0.555 m
Weight	19.958 kg	20.184 kg
Volume cubic metres	0.374 m³	0.410 m³
C/pit size	0.838 m x 0.381 m	0.857 m x 0.413 m
C/pit coaming height		
Fwd	0.346 m	0.292 m
Aft	0.191 m	0.210 m
Height of seat	0.022 m	0.015 m
HYDROSTATICS		
L_{WL}	5.979 m	5.397 m
B_{WL}	0.431 m	0.505 m
Draft	0.111 m	0.109 m
C_P	0.56	0.60
Wetted surface area in square metres	2.239 m²	2.222 m²
Centre of Buoyancy (B)	51%	50.4%

Figure 2-14 Stability curves

Sea Kayaker Magazine (SKM) publishes static stability curves for boats they review. The graphs are plotted against righting moments in foot-pounds of force. To normalise the test result SKM assume a centre of gravity, 10 inches, above the lowest portion of the seat. Use weights of 150 pounds (68 kg), 200 pounds (90.7 kg); then add 100 pounds (45.4 kg), to each of the original weights. The loaded test weights are 113.4 kilograms and 136 kilograms respectively. Other dynamic variables introduced by a paddler are flexibility, fitness, skill and knowledge. Stability curves are static. That is they assume the boat is floating on a millpond surface and not moving (i.e. not dynamic), and therefore remove the dynamic variations to produce a graph that can be used as a baseline to compare different boats.[9]

The purpose of the stability curve is to show the *righting force* (*righting moment*) required by a heeled boat to return itself back to a position of stable equilibrium. That is, a kayak resisting the heel motion and return back upright.

The stability is calculated by naval architects for angles of inclination (heel) above seven degrees. The static stability curve graph plots a line proportional to the horizontal distance, between the centre of gravity and the centre of buoyancy (i.e. GZ, for differing degrees of heel).[10] Another way of looking at the stability curve is through the metacentric height (GM).

The y-axis is the *righting moment* or *righting arm*. The righting moment plot represents the amount of force required by a disturbing force to heel the boat and therefore the opposing force required to counteract the disturbing force and return the boat back to a stable position. This is determined by multiplying a boat's total weight by the righting arm, which determines the total moment acting to return the boat to a stable position. The x-axis represents the *degrees of heel* (lean).

Points to remember when reading a stability curve: the boat's centre of gravity does not change as it is assumed to be fixed; the centre of buoyancy always moves to the geometric centre of the underwater portion of the hull; and the shape of the boat's underwater hull section changes with the angle of heel.

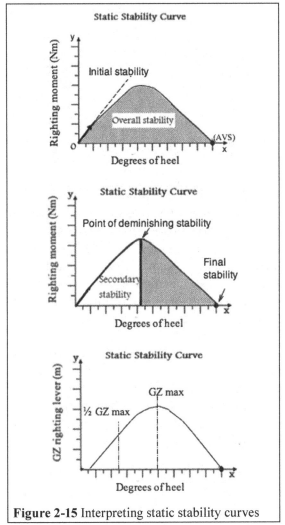

Figure 2-15 Interpreting static stability curves

The slope of the curve up to the apex indicates the resistance to further heel. Initial stability is represented by the rise of the curve's slope, from the zero point, along the smaller range of degrees of heel angles. The steeper the curve's slope, the higher the initial stability and the stiffer the boat will feel. This is explained by the small degrees of heel being counteracted by larger opposing forces. For example: 5 degrees heel being counteracted by 10-foot-pounds of force, then at 10 degrees heel being counteracted by 20-foot-pounds of force. This is as opposed to 5 degrees heel being counteracted by 5-foot-pounds and at 10 degrees heel counteracted by around 8-foot-pound of force. For initial stability, it takes a greater force to effect a small amount of change in heel.

The height of the curve generally relates to secondary stability. It tells how much force the boat is creating to return upright. The higher the curve as read from the y-axis righting moment or lever, the greater the righting moment (force). Kayaks with high stability curves will generally feel more stable. If two kayaks are heeled to the same angle (as shown along the x-axis), the kayak with the higher righting moment value (along the y-axis) will be hardest to heel. It will also be faster in returning back, to a stable condition.

For stability values greater than zero, a kayak will tend to come back upright if, no other forces are acting on it. If a kayak stability value is below the x-axis, it indicates a very 'tippy' boat. Refer to the Valley Sea Kayaks Rapier 20 stability curve plot A2 (90 kg paddler, no cargo), which is below the x-axis.[11] Positive stability moments shown at higher angles of heel indicate a more stable hull. The centre of gravity has remained inboard of the centre of buoyancy.

The apex of the curve represents where stability starts to diminish. The apex of the curve shows the maximum righting arm length or the maximum righting moment. After this point the length and therefore strength of the righting moment diminishes. As the curve slopes back down, it demonstrates positive righting moments until it reaches zero degrees of heel. This point is known as the *angle of vanishing stability*. At this point there is no positive righting lever (GZ). As the slope proceeds under the x-axis the righting levers become negative (ZG) and assist in capsizing the vessel.

The left hand side of the curve's apex represents secondary stability. The higher the apex, the greater resistance would be felt, when edging the boat. The farther the apex is to the right of the graph the greater the degree of heel you can apply to the kayak before the kayak's righting force is diminished. A broad apex indicates that a kayak will gradually enter a condition of instability and hence not catch the kayaker out by surprise. A sharp apex indicates that a kayak can suddenly capsize if the paddler is inattentive.

The right hand side of the curve's apex (back slope) shows a diminishing amount of righting force for given increases of heel. A kayak can be (very carefully) balanced (neutral equilibrium), at these increased angles. However, the slightest disturbance will cause it to capsize (unstable equilibrium) if no corrective action is taken (i.e. a bracing stroke). In this situation, the kayak is unable to return itself to a stable equilibrium, unless the paddler performs a corrective manoeuvre. The centre of gravity has been moved outboard of the centre of buoyancy. The boat is in the area where it has a negative righting moment.

The area under the curve indicates how much energy is absorbed by the boat when inclined. A large area under the curve indicates the requirement for a larger effort to heel the kayak; that is to push it over. It also indicates that if the kayak hits a large destabilising force, for example, a wave, that could cause it to capsize, it can absorb the force of the impact.

CONTROLLABILITY

Controllability is comprised of two separate parts: tracking (course stability) and manoeuvrability. It is a compromise between the two to suit a particular function of a boat. A white water boat is designed to be manoeuvrable, while a sprint kayak is designed to have good tracking, to ensure no energy is wasted on course correction strokes, (i.e. sweep strokes).

Tracking

Tracking refers to the ability of a boat to hold a course. This however is very subjective since the forward paddle stoke introduces a component of yaw. It then depends upon the skill of the paddler and their interpretation of how they consider a particular boat tracks. Then you introduce environmental considerations like waves and wind to temper the opinion. Tracking leads us into the notion of turning.

A boat in a turn, rotates around its centre of gravity with the bow scribing a smaller arc that the stern. It is somewhat like a car in a tail-out skid. Use of correction paddle strokes increases

lateral resistance forwards thereby increasing turn rate and decreasing turn radius.

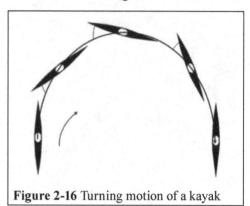

Figure 2-16 Turning motion of a kayak

From a design perspective, some general guidelines for factors that improve course stability are a lower block coefficient (C_B), increased length/beam ratio (L/B) and length/draft ratio (L/H), increased hull profile aft and stern-down trim. Factors with minimal affect are mid-section shape, waterline shape, location of the longitudinal centre of buoyancy (LCB) and the prismatic coefficient (C_P) within normal limits. It needs to be pointed out LCB and C_P extremes in either direction has a negative effect while mid-section and waterline shape on boats with fine ends produces a minimal positive effect (Winters, 2005).

Manoeuvrability

Manoeuvrability is a compromise against tracking and therefore the purpose of the boat and the target market are of concern to the designer. What is desirable to a novice paddler may be considered undesirable to an experienced paddler's preconceived ideas.

Concerning design and in no particular order of precedence, manoeuvrability is improved by: decreasing underwater profile, increasing vertical prismatic coefficient (C_{VP}), more 'U' Shaped sections, shorter waterline length, reducing draft (increasing the L/H ratio), increasing C_B, using harder bilges amidships, moving LCB aft, which improves forward turning only when heeled and angled relative to the water's flow. (Winters, 2005).

Manoeuvrability brings us to the notion of *turning*. By edging (i.e. tilting on its side), a kayak will turn in the opposite direction. Turning a kayak by edging will cause a kayak to turn faster than if you were to just use a series of paddle strokes on one side (as you would if rowing a dingy). By edging the kayak on to its side (e.g. starboard (right), by raising your left knee and dropping your right hip/buttock), you are creating less surface area on the opposite (i.e. port) side of the hull and therefore less wetted area. This in turn results in less water resistance against the hull. With boat lean and the combination of forward and reverse sweep strokes (depending upon the situation) a kayak can be quickly turned.

Wind and waves affect controllability

Wind from any direction except dead ahead or dead aft induces a turning moment on a boat's hull. A boat that turns into the direction of the wind is said to weathercock; a boat that turns downwind is said to lee cock.

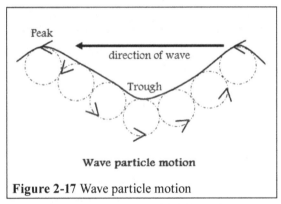

Figure 2-17 Wave particle motion

On a forward moving boat with no correction; as a crosswind acts on the bow section, *lateral pressure* is induced on the downwind side of the hull. Remembering that water is about 800 times more dense than air, as the lateral pressure build up (from the interaction of the underwater portion of the hull and the water) there is a higher pressure on the downwind side than on the upwind side of the hull. As a result, the bow on the upwind side tends to move towards the area of least pressure. With the stern being free to move downwind, the bow thus turns into the wind (windward) and is said to weathercock.

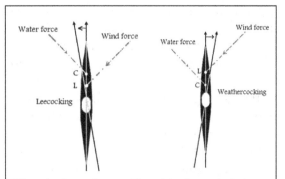

When the force of water (C) and the force of wind (L) coincide there is no turning moment. When L is forward of C the boat turns into the wind (weathercocks). When C is forward of L the boats turns downwind (lee cocks).

Figure 2-18 Lee cocking and Weathercocking

The amount of exposed bow to the wind is often a point of conversation. Looking at the bow windage (amount of bow section exposed to the effects of wind) and inferring that it would be hard to handle as it would get blown around, may not be a totally valid observation. Naval architects can employ what is termed *balance*. Balance, involves the interaction of the boat's shape above and below the water. Since water is considerably denser than air, a hull's bow can be offset by the shape of the hull underwater section (Schade, Kayak Stability, 2009).

When paddling in a following sea, the boat acts in response to waves from astern. If a boat's length is comparable to, and the speed practically the same as that of the waves, the boat may run for a considerable time along the crest of a wave. The wave lifts the stern diminishing directional stability (and possibly control depending upon skills) so that when the boat pitches, bow downwards, the combined effects of gravity and water flow, pushes the boat down the face of the wave. As the boat, surfs down the face of the wave directional stability may be further compromised (depending upon skills) and a violent yaw may suddenly develop.

In the trough, the yawing boat encounters the reverse flow pushing it back with the combined effects of the following wave pushing it forwards; both of which create a strong turning moment around the centre of gravity. As the stern swings around, the boat lies broadside to the following wave, in what is termed broaching.

When encountering quartering waves, the boat experiences the same effects as with following waves, whereby a strong turning moment is induced by the wave's behaviour. As the stern lifts, heave and roll are induced compounding to the turning moment. For design purposes, in general, soft bilges are of an advantage where directional stability is a priority. Design characteristics that are employed by naval architects to minimize control problems are 'V' sections aft, forward rocker and longitudinal centre of buoyancy (LCB) slightly (up to two per cent of the boat length) forward of amidships (Winters, 2005).

Waves from the side can cause what is known as *synchronisation*. Synchronisation is the term used to describe the roll period of a boat that coincides with the roll period of a wave causing the boat to move violently. In this situation alter course to change the period of encounter with the waves (chop) or alter the centre of gravity up or down; this can be achieved through design and or body posture. This changes the natural roll period of the boat and can reduce synchronisation.

For naval architects raising the centre of gravity reduces the roll motion. Flat bottom and wide beam hulls can be employed but are not as effective as popular wisdom dictates. To limit the boat from being pushed sideways the turn of the bilge has more of an effect. A hard chined hull resists sliding sideways over a soft chined hull; however, it is suggested, that a hard chined hull can 'trip' over its chine resulting in possible capsize.

DIRECTIONAL STABILITY

Rudders and skegs

According to John Winters, who is a naval architect that designs and builds canoes, designers usually make every effort to design controllability into the hull shape but he points out:

Rudders can provide subtle corrections to unbalanced forces due to waves, wind and currents, and trim variations as well as providing an additional method of primary control.

Two design features employed to assist in directional stability (aka course stability, tracking) are skegs and rudders. As seen previously, directional stability is achieved through low block coefficients, high length/beam ratios and a greater lateral area aft than forwards. Manoeuvrability can be designed in through the use of fore and aft rocker with most of it being in the fore section to reduce turning moments and all of which can be augmented by the use of a rudder. In real life, paddling a boat is subject to yaw, surge and pitch as well as the inputs from the paddler. For example, each paddle stroke introduces a component of yaw that varies with stroke mechanics. A wide sweeping stroke will develop a larger yaw effect than a higher upright stroke that follows closely to the hull (Lazaukas & Winters, 1997)

Many kayak rudders are a flat plate, constructed usually from either metal or plastic. The flat plate though effective in its purpose, is inefficient in terms of hydrodynamics, since the flat plate stalls at low angles of attack creating drag. Other inefficiencies that lead to the creation of drag can also be found in the sub-assemblies of the head and pivot assembly. These inefficiencies are designed out of rudder assemblies through the use of aerofoil shapes, streamlining into the hull and making the assembly rigid and free from play.

According to Greg Barton from Epic Kayaks:

A well designed rudder will add less than two per cent total drag to a kayak. In comparison, modifying your stroke to correct or maintain your course results in anywhere from 30 per cent to 70 per cent forward power loss. Very minor corrections will result in five per cent to ten per cent less power than a fully efficient forward stroke (Barton, 2009).

Paul Caffyn wrote in a kayak forum on May 5th, 2005:

Situations where I have found a rudder to be invaluable include: tight manoeuvring in congested sea ice or ice berg choked seas, ferry gliding across channels with fast tidal streams, coping with boils and eddies in overfalls, steering when the wind is too strong to paddle, fast manoeuvring in congested shipping lanes, hugging a reef fringed coast when paddling into a strong tidal stream flow, surfing in front of following seas. Another advantage of a sturdy deep draught, over-stern rudder is a surprising increase in overall boat stability.

In the dialogue, Caffyn highlights the inefficiencies of a poorly designed rudder system and describes how his over-stern rudder projects 12 inches below the keel line and that he has never broken a rudder only bent one and he remedied the situation by just bending it back into shape.

He also provided the following data to show how through the fitment of a rudder to his HM Nordkapp during his 1981-82 circumnavigation of Australia his daily mileage averages increased. He makes the comment:

It saved my life on several occasions, the most crucial being the overnighter along the Baxter Cliffs. The statistics show the benefit gained:

- *Melbourne to Sydney HM stern 30.6 miles per day.*

- *Sydney to Brisbane Skeg 34.3 miles per day.*

- *Brisbane to Cape York Rudder 39.2 miles per day* (Caffyn, 2005).

Since paddle strokes and boat lean are the effective means of turning a kayak, rudders have been described as trim tabs, correcting and unbalanced forces enabling all of the forward paddling effort to go into effective propulsion. However, Caffyn's view is:

I use my rudder for steering and the paddle for forward propulsion. When a paddle is used for corrective steering strokes, either sweep or paddling on one side, forward propulsion suffers and the normal paddling cycle is upset (Caffyn, 2005).

Between a skeg and a rudder, both Barton and Caffyn refer to the rudder being more efficient than the skeg. Barton notes that all top paddlers in flat water or open ocean races prefer and use a rudder over going rudderless or the option of a skeg. While skegs provide directional stability they can reduce

the usable storage volume in the aft hatch and can also be jammed with small pebbles on launch.

Skeg CLR Position	In this "not to scale" drawing, at position A the CLR is farther aft than at position B. At position B the skeg produces greater resistance (drag) than at A.
	Figure 2-19 CLR on a skeg

A retractable skeg can be designed into a boat that has the propensity to weather helm. The skegs deployment shifts the centre of lateral area aft to balance the turning moment at the bow. The farther aft a skeg is located the smaller it needs to be with its corresponding reduction in resistance. High aspect ratio skegs shaped like an aerofoil produce a greater lift component but this can be diminished by the resistance created by turbulence from the skeg trunk. If a skeg is mounted farther forwards towards the cockpit it acts more like a centreboard whereby it resist lateral motion and consequently reduce leeway and therefore the turning moment at the bow.[12] Being located farther forward the skeg needs to have a larger area to be effective and therefore incurs greater resistance.

Rudders on boats have been found in pre-history, with the earliest archaeological pictures showing the very prominent steering oars with wide rudder like blades held to the stern (Gillmer, Thomas C.; Johnson, Bruce, 1982). Russian fur traders fitted rudders to the Alaskan Eskimo's iqyax (baidarka). Rudder dynamics is an involved subject and if the reader desires to look into the subject refer to the reference cited. The rudder is a foil, and the terms used to describe the forces acting on a rudder and how a boat behaves, are described in the same terms as those used to describe the forces on an aircraft's wing.

Simplistically, if you observe a kayaks rudder in flat-water conditions, when it is moved to port, the water line rises along its length, on the side it is deflected to. On the opposite side (i.e. starboard), the water line appears to drop. With an increased wetted surface area on the portside and the reduced wetted surface area on the starboard side a greater force is applied to the portside rudder surface. This in turn causes the stern to move towards the area of less resistance on the starboard side.

For the end user, the choice between using and or not using a rudder or a skeg is purely a personal choice. It is your sport and enjoyment after all.

PADDLES

It becomes obvious that the paddle is just as important a selection as your boat, if not more so.

Greg Barton, Epic Kayaks

Paddles used in kayaking can be either single blade or double blade types. Verlen Kruger paddled from the Beaufort Sea in northern Canada, down to and around Cape Horn in South America, using a single blade paddle. Some paddlers, who use split paddles, carry only one-half of a spare paddle fitted with a removable T-handle piece on their boats. If they damage one blade of their double bladed paddle, they can replace the damaged section with the spare. If they lose their double bladed paddle they can utilise the spare single blade paddle. For those interested in single blade paddles for sea kayaking there is an article in Sea Kayaker Magazine, June 2007 titled *Single-Blade Canoe Paddles for Kayakers* by Brian Day. An interesting statement in the article is 'A bent-shaft marathon canoe paddle can help you cover long distances with less fatigue.' The article is well worth reading and thinking about. Since double bladed paddles are the *norm* for recreational sea kayakers, I will endeavour to focus on them instead of single bladed paddles.

For sea kayaking, paddles come in a wide variety. Some are replicas of those used by the Arctic Circle indigenous peoples through to the designs based on the latest technology and used in international competitive sport. A concept, which is gaining popular acceptance in some circles, is that you need paddles to match the type of boat you are paddling, the conditions you are facing and the type of paddling you expect to do. In other words, one style of paddle does not suit all; since people, for whatever reasons, have different paddling styles and preferences.

There are several considerations to consider when looking at paddles such as length, grip diameter, weight, blade size, purpose, efficiency, feel, personal preference, materials and budget. Leaving aside two big drivers for choice of a paddle, being personal preference and budget, I will attempt to provide some information that I have found useful.

For an explanation of the physics of paddle operation refer to John Winters' *The Shape of the Canoe, 2005*. In his opening statements, he writes a statement worth considering when talking about paddles:

There are very few studies of paddle design . . . the absence of concrete data explains the absence of uniformity in paddle shapes as well as the confusion surrounding how paddles function.

Efficiency

One Olympic kayaker described using a paddle to that of poles stuck into the water. The paddler leans forward and grasps the pole and rotates their torso, pulling against the fixed pole, then reaches out and grasps the pole on the other side. In such manner they pull themselves along. Paddle efficiency can be described as how much energy (force) is put into a stroke compared to how much work is being done. An efficient paddle is one that converts the paddler's energy into forward motion whilst eliminating and or minimising adverse variables like ventilation (aeration), flutter from disturbed flow, eddies and slippage. It needs to be pointed out, that there is no such thing as a 100 per cent efficient paddle but designers can attempt to come close. An efficient paddle for a paddler is one that allows them to achieve their aim effectively and without injury.

Through the very nature of the physical world, as soon as a paddle's blade is inserted and moved through the water and the other blade moves through the air, there are losses of energy supplied by the paddler (the power-plant). Ignoring the loss of energy of the blade moving through the air (through factors like blade and paddle weight, feather angle and paddling style), we will look at the inefficiencies of a paddle moving through the water since this is where we derive our thrust from.

First some basics; the study of motion of an object can be seen through Newton's three laws of motion and in particular, here, Newton's third law of motion which states:

Whenever one object exerts a force on a second object, the second object exerts an equal and opposite force on the first.

In analysing the forces at play, we can also discuss motion in terms of two quantities: *energy* and *momentum* (Schade, How a Paddle Works, n.d.). The importance of these two quantities is that they are constant that is, remain constant. Newton's third law of motion also relates to the law of the conservation of momentum, which states:

The total momentum of an isolated system of bodies remains constant. [13]

Momentum (p) is the product of mass (in kg) and velocity (in m/s) expressed as $p = mv$. This means for example, two boats travelling at different speeds but having the same mass have different momentums (mass x velocity). Another way of looking at this is, if you have 1 kg of water moving at 10 m/s and 10 kg of water moving at 1 m/s; both have the same amount of momentum:

$p_1 = 1$ kg x 10 m/s = 10 kg·m/s

$p_2 = 10$ kg x 1 m/s = 10 kg·m/s

From momentum, we are led into energy and in particular kinetic energy. Kinetic energy (energy in motion) is the amount of energy contained in a moving object. Kinetic energy (KE) is mass times velocity squared and written as $KE = mv^2$. According to this equation if you were to move a 1 kg mass of water at 10 m/s and another 10 kg mass at 1 m/s the lighter mass travelling faster, has 10 times more energy, than the heavier mass travelling slower; even though they have the same momentum of 10 kg·m/s. This can be shown as:

$KE_1 = 1$ kg x 10 m/s x 10 m/s = 100 kg·m/s^2

$KE_2 = 10$ kg x 1 m/s x 1 m/s = 10 kg·m/s^2

What this shows is, the amount of energy increases faster with an increase in velocity, than it does with an increase in mass. For a paddle stroke to be efficient, it needs to maximise the kinetic energy from the paddler into the kayak and minimise any losses into the water.

The purpose of a paddle is to push against the water, in order to propel the boat forward. This is Newton's third law of motion in action. By doing so, you are relying upon the resistance of the water to create a force to propel the boat forward. As the blade pushes against the water, the water starts to move and through the water's movement inefficiencies can be observed.

Water being a fluid, does not want to be pushed against. When disturbed, water wants to return to a state of equilibrium. As the paddle blade moves, it has an effect on a mass of water, according to the size of the blade and its velocity. This action creates an area of high pressure on the blade's power face. At the same time there is a lower pressure area acting on the blade's back face. The lower pressure allows water to find a path around the edges of the blade, from the high-pressure side to the low-pressure side, in order for the water to return itself to a state of equilibrium.

As the water moves around the edges of the blade, it creates vortices. This is a result of the water at the power face moving away from the blade and the water at the back face trying to follow the blade. This process is referred to as *slippage* as water moves around the edges of the blade creating a vortex. A vortex is another name for an eddy, vortices and or whirlpool, involving the circular motion of a fluid. At low velocities, the vortices remain attached to the blade, but at a certain increased speeds, they will alternatively break away from each side. These break away eddies, which can be seen trailing behind a stroke, are called a von Kármán vortex street and are responsible for paddle flutter (Winters, 2005).

Relating back to Newton's third law of motion and the law of the conservation of momentum. The paddle is used to impart momentum from the paddler into the boat, with any momentum imparted into the water is lost. The unavoidable presence of a vortex, as the water returns to equilibrium, is evidence of momentum flowing off from the sides of the blade and being lost. One way to maximise your efficiency is by minimising the velocity you impart into the water.

Minimising velocity can be achieved by fully immersing the blade into the water. This increases the blades surface area and decreases velocity. This therefore, affects the mass of water being moved. To a novice, the paddle may feel harder to move, but it is actually more effective since you use less energy to achieve the same result. This is also a reason to experiment with different blade sizes to match your power output.

Correct paddle placement into the water is important in order to minimise inefficiencies. You need a fast clean entry referred to as *catch*. In the next one hundredth of a second, to achieve the greatest power, the paddle is vertical and in line with the hulls centre-line. If you apply power too early and the blade is not fully submerged you will end up *splashing*. Splashing refers to moving a small amount of water too fast. If you apply power too late you will have lost the maximum effect of power and you will slow down and lose momentum if uncorrected.

Incorrect paddle entry can lead to *ventilation*. Ventilation can occur in two ways. When air is sucked down the back face of the blade from the surface, as you apply power, or when the blade on entry brings it down.[14] Ventilation can occur when quickly accelerating and the blade is overloaded in such a manner that its area cannot absorb the energy expended. The issue with ventilation is, air at the power face displaces and decreases the mass of water, you intended to use. Since air is compressible and decreases the mass of water, to achieve the same momentum you need to expend more energy. To avoid ventilation develop a clean entry and ensure the blade is fully immersed before applying power. The use of the blade's entire surface leads to a general principle concerning propulsion efficiencies, which as stated by Nick Schade in his article titled *How a Paddle Works* is:

It is more efficient to develop a propulsive force by pushing a large mass slowly than it is to push a small mass quickly.

Energy can also be lost through an inefficient blade exit from the water. If the blade is lifting water vertically upwards on the end of a stroke, you are wasting energy. Momentum is achieved with the blade in the water. Lifting water up into the air is just wasting energy.[15]

All of the above discussion is based on steady flow fluid dynamics. John Winters points out that a kayak's propulsion is derived from the impulse energy of the paddle and not steady motion. As a result he says:

We will have to accept that our understanding of paddles and paddle power is flawed or, at best, incomplete (Winters, 2005).

Blades

There are a variety of blade styles from the classic Inuit style through to racing wing paddles. As a result, of human nature rather than science, there are a multitude of opinions about the pros and cons. Here I will mention a few of the common terms used by people when talking about paddles.

The blade of a paddle consists of the *power face* and *back face*. The power face refers to the face of the blade that faces you on the forward stroke and does the work. The opposite face is termed the back face.

The majority of advertising literature gives a paddle's length and width, when the concerning issue is *blade area*. In many cases, due to the concaved shape of blades, length and width measurements do not provide us with the full data about a blade. The area of the blade relates to how much force is required to draw the foil through the water. Conventional wisdom is that a bigger blade results in more speed but this needs to be tempered with technique, fitness and condition of the paddler. Bigger blades do not necessarily translate into more speed as much as precise technique. A blade that is too big for an individual paddler with an inefficient forward stroke, can lead to fatigue and a repetitive strain injury (RSI). The efficient blade size for an individual paddler depends upon their physical conditioning, style of paddling and cadence.

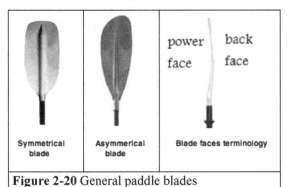

Figure 2-20 General paddle blades

The force developed by a paddle is a function of both area and velocity. Another important consideration to blade size is velocity. Velocity is linked to cadence and is a factor used in the formula to calculate the force being developed by a paddle. Thrust (force) squares with velocity; meaning if you double velocity you quadruple (increase by a factor of four i.e. four times) thrust. To increase thrust you can either double your paddles velocity or comparatively increase its area four times. Increasing area comes with weight and handling penalties and fatigue issues. Increasing cadence with a smaller area blade can theoretically, achieve the same comparative result as increasing area without the associated penalties. However, if your natural cadence is slow, a larger blade may be a viable option.

To get an understanding of what constitutes a small blade and what is a large blade, go to several paddle manufactures websites, to note and compare their definitions. As an example of the available data about different paddles, Table 2-2 has been included as a guide. The table shows three models of Brácsa paddles, two of which are commonly purchased by members of the VSKC. The Typhoon 60 utilises a 690 square centimetre blade compared to the other popular paddle the Hurricane 20 min, which has a blade size of 660 square centimetres. As the table shows, the Typhoon 60 has a more ridged shaft (less flex) than the Hurricane 20. Due to the composition make up of the shafts and blades, the Typhoon 60 is the lighter of the two. One of the clubs expedition paddlers uses a Hurricane 20 min paddle while another paddler of comparable

fitness and skills in the same type of boat uses a Typhoon 60. A subjective conclusion is that for kayak touring, there is little advantage in the extra 30 square centimetres of area and the approximate 100 grams weight saving for the extra monetary cost.

Table 2-2 Example of paddle and blade data

Brácsa Model	Blade colour	Blade size (sq.cm.)	Carbon content (%)		Shaft stiffness (mm)	Weight (g)
			Blade	Shaft		
Typhoon 60	black	690	75	60	3.2-3.4	~850
Hurricane 20 min	yellow	660	50	20	4.0-4.5	~950
Hurricane 20 max	yellow	720	50	20	4.0-4.5	~950

Asymmetrical blade shape

Asymmetrical blade shape refers to the removal of area (clipping) from the lower side end of the blade. The purpose (it is claimed) is to reduce torque along the shaft caused by the unequal pressure on each half of the blade as it enters and departs the water. The theory for clipping the lower outboard edge of the blade is to equalise the pressure between the lower half of the blade, which sits deeper in the water, to that of the upper half of the blade. The reduction of torque results in the paddler being able to maintain a relaxed grip on the shaft.

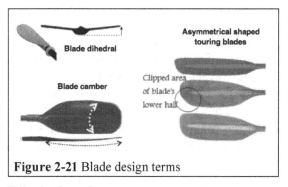

Figure 2-21 Blade design terms

Dihedral angle

Dihedral angle refers to the angling up of the blade's edges at the power face, so that in cross section it looks somewhat like an open book. Dihedral is associated with the reduction of *flutter* in some articles but other designers and instructors point out that flutter can be reduced through other design features and point out that in some cases, some blades with dihedral flutter excessively. Adding to the diversity of opinion, one paddle manufacture does not build any dihedral into any of their touring paddles only white-water. There are many manufactures in favour of dihedral in touring paddles but they at no time reference quantitative data or studies to support their theory or statements.

Camber

Camber in a paddle can be broken down into vertical camber and horizontal camber. Camber is noticeable by the curvature of the back face creating a concaved power face. John Winters points out that the claims made about camber on the back face as either increasing thrust or decreasing flutter are speculative having no evidence to support such claims.

Wing shape blades

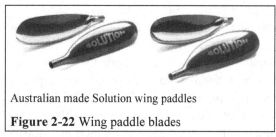

Australian made Solution wing paddles

Figure 2-22 Wing paddle blades

Wing shape blades along with efficient technique, can increase a boat's speed by seven to ten per cent, compared to using a conventional paddle with the same amount of effort (Epic Kayaks). Wing paddles are used by those interested in racing and are becoming popular with many touring kayakers. The downside to a wing paddle, for some in touring, is that when they execute a brace stroke they find the blade dives under the water resulting in capsize. However, practice tends to reduce the possibility of this happening. A positive comment about capsizing while using a wing paddle is that they are easy to roll with.

Feather and feather angle

Feather and feather angle refers to the angle of the blade (as taken from the chord line) relative to the direction of travel and the encountered free stream velocity. The purpose of blade feather is to reduce wind resistance on the airborne blade during a stroke. In general theory, a feathered

blade offers less of its back face surface area to the air (wind). Whereas an unfeathered blade offers its entire back face surface to the air, which depending upon its velocity, will induce varying degrees of resistance to the blades forward motion.

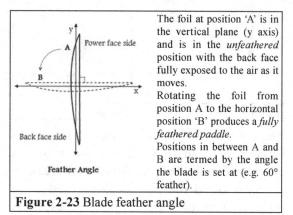

The foil at position 'A' is in the vertical plane (y axis) and is in the *unfeathered* position with the back face fully exposed to the air as it moves.
Rotating the foil from position A to the horizontal position 'B' produces a *fully feathered paddle*.
Positions in between A and B are termed by the angle the blade is set at (e.g. 60° feather).

Figure 2-23 Blade feather angle

The length of a paddle can be divided into two halves, the left hand side and the right hand side. If you are right handed the right hand side is the *control side* and vice versa for a left-handed person.[16] The hand used to control the angle of entry of the blade into the water is known as the *control hand*. On a feathered paddle on the control side, there will be a raised section at the handgrip area known as a *locator*. The locator allows the paddler to orientate their paddle forwards at the correct angle.

The angle of the blade will either be fixed from manufacture or can be adjusted by the paddler. Feather angle varies from 90 degrees through to around 45 degrees, but can be less depending upon person preference. Touring paddlers using feathered blades generally have them set from 60 to 45 degrees.

The feather angle is set by neutralising the control side at zero degrees, that is: the blade chord is in the vertical plane. In this position, all of the blade's back face area is offered to the air, like that of a fly swatter. Next, the non-control side blade's chord is positioned in the same vertical plane while ensuring both left and right blade faces are facing the same direction (i.e. both back faces facing forwards). With the control side held in the neutral (vertical) position the non-control blade's top edge is rotated forwards from its zero (vertical) position. The farther forward the blade is rotated from the vertical (y-axis) position down towards the horizontal (x-axis) position the less of its back face surface area is offered to the air. If the blade is rotated through 90 degrees, the blade is said to have a 90 degree feather angle with the non-control blade offering only its thickness to the air, providing the best efficiency for the returning blade. A paddle with a blade at 90 degrees feather is known as a *fully-feathered paddle*. However, there are issues to consider with feathered blades.

The blade becomes an aerofoil as it is feathered and so is subject to the effects of lift and drag as it moves through the air. In head winds, blades feathered less than 90 degrees (and most pronounced around 45 degrees feather) tend to dive on the control side and lift (is blown upwards) on the other side. In cross winds, the windward blade tends to lift (is blown upwards). This lifting is experienced more on blades with greater degrees of feather, since the camber of the blade at or near the horizontal plane allows the wind to act on the blade's tip.

A drawback with fully feathered or high angle feathered blades is the occurrence of repetitive strain injuries on the control side wrist. Some authors write that they and their colleagues have been paddling for decades with full-feathered paddles and have not suffered wrist RSI. However, it seems to be a complaint associated with weekend and infrequent paddlers, who quickly increase their paddle distance and frequency. Incorrect technique could also be included into the explanation. Eliminating the paddler as the cause, having a full-feathered paddle involves a higher degree of wrist action than blades with less feather. We see people who preferred a feathered blade select angles from 60 to 45 degrees feather. Those who do not like feathered paddles cite the advantage of less wrist rotation as one of the benefits of unfeathered paddles.

To feather or not feather is a personal choice. If you are looking to buy your first paddle try an adjustable paddle first and experiment.

Paddle length

The old school thought was that the appropriate size paddle for your height was determined by standing beside a paddle (in the vertical plane) with one arm extended up to the top of the blade and your fingers tips reaching over the top. The current thought is that a paddle's shaft needs to be long enough to reach the water. The paddles length will vary depending upon the type of paddling it was designed for (e.g. marathon, sprint, white water). Paddle length in the market place, refers to the overall length of the paddle and seldom if ever the shaft length. This is mentioned because blades come in various lengths and shapes, therefore the length of a blade influences the length of a paddle. When paddling, the join of the shaft to blade, needs to be just at the surface of the water. Therefore, the shaft's length is the consideration when considering ergonomics. The considerations for the length of a shaft are the matching of your body (torso) to the boat and include body height, the beam at the cockpit and seat height. The size (shape and area) of the blade will determine how much force is being generated and how much effort it would take you to use the paddle to propel yourself forward.

Table 2-3 Overall length paddle to height sizes

Low Angle Stroke Style		Boat's Beam (cm)					
		53-58 (21-23")	58.4 (≤23")	58-66 (23-26")	58-71 (23-28")	61-71 (24-28")	> 63 (> 25")
Paddle Height	< 5'		210		220		
	5'-5'6"		215		220		
	5'-5'10"	220					
	< 5'5"			210-220		230	
	5'5"-5'11"		220			230	
	5'6"-6'		220		220*		
	5'6"-6'2"			230*			
	≥ 6'		220		230	230-240	
	> 6' 3"						240

High Angle Stroke Style		Boats Beam	
		≤ 61cm (≤ 24")	≤ 66cm (≤ 26")
Paddle length	5'0"-5'10"	210	
	< 5'4"		205
	5'4"-6'		210
	5'6"-6'2"	215	
	> 6'		215
	Over 6'3"	220	

In 2008 Nigel Dennis came to Australia and gave a presentation about paddles to the VSKC. A salient point that came out of the workshop was:

The majority of touring paddlers use paddles that are too long.

Case in point: At 1.86 metres, I had been fitted up with a 222 centimetre paddle by an ex-Olympian paddler. After the workshop, a number of the participants including myself had our paddles reduced in length. From the table of sizes produced by Nigel and experimentation with differing size paddles and blade types I reduced my paddle down to 215 centimetre. This has enabled me to increase my cadence without a noticeable increase in effort. This is however subjective and possibly flawed as previously discussed in this chapter. Other tall expedition paddlers like Dave Winkworth and Peter Treby had already gone to shorter paddles, with Pete (~1.8 m tall) using a 210 centimetre paddle.

The current thinking for using a shorter paddle for touring is that you can increase your cadence easily when in windy conditions and make headway. These shorter paddles are indicative of a high angle stroke style. However, your personal touring style of paddling may be long, slow strokes (low angle stroke style), whereby the use of a longer paddle may be preferred. Visit the various paddle manufactures websites and use their programs to match your requirements to the type of paddle that suits you. After a bit of research you will get a better understanding of what to look for when you go to buy.

Swing weight

Swing weight refers to the weight of the blades as they swing through the air. The less weight you have to repetitiously lift and swing through the air results in energy savings and a delay or reduction in fatigue. Test paddles for balance by grasping the mid-section with one hand and rotate it around. You will soon feel the difference in differing paddles. However, this is only a very lose test and an 'on-water test paddle' may change your original assessment.

Overall weight

Overall weight depends upon materials and construction methods. The general opinion is, the lighter the better, but this is tempered against the designer's and end user's purpose for the paddle. For example, I would not willingly take an $800 dollar carbon/graphite paddle into a rock garden but I would take a trusty $180 fibreglass

shaft with a plastic blade in and use it to bash my way around the rocks.

The accompanying Table 2-3 has been compiled from three manufacturers sizing charts for sea kayak paddles. The second table shows two manufacturers recommendations for sea kayak paddles. Note how the recommendations are broad and if you are looking to buy your first paddle, consider purchasing an adjustable shaft paddle. One manufacturer even produces paddles that have both adjustable shafts and interchangeable blades.

Shaft stiffness

Shaft stiffness and *flex* are considerations often found in literature about paddles. Depending upon the style of paddling, sprint through to touring, results in varied preferences in paddle stiffness. Sprint racers are concerned about velocity and time, where touring paddlers paddle in varied conditions and are not concerned about tenths or hundredths of a second being reduced from their times through having a ridged paddle. One aspect of paddle flex is its link to paddle flutter and the associated loss of propulsion efficiency. Another consideration is the general public perception that associates stiff paddles (particularly carbon fibre shafts) to the likelihood of repetitive strain injuries (RSI); this however needs to be balanced against the paddler's technique and physical conditioning.

Shaft diameter

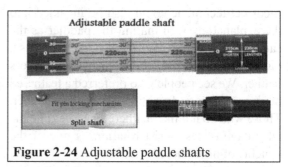

Figure 2-24 Adjustable paddle shafts

Obviously, people's hands are of different sizes. Having a grip size that is of incorrect diameter for your hand may lead to your gripping the shaft to tight, which can lead to early fatigue, discomfort and repetitive strain injuries like Tennis Elbow and Golfer's Elbow. Some manufacturers produce a one size fits all paddle shafts, while others produce shafts in two or more sizes to accommodate the variety in hand size. The best shaft diameter comes down to how it feels for you, so you need to borrow a few paddles whilst on different outings and experiment. Some manufactures websites have sizing charts and *Wizards* where you can enter your measurements into a program and it will advise you of the most appropriate size to look at.

Some articles suggest the best cross-sectional shape of the handgrip is not round; but designed to fit the natural shape of a *grasping* hand. This natural shape, it is claimed, allows the application of light pressure to hold the paddle in order to reduce fatigue and prevent over-use injuries. Concerning this point, while the principles of grip pressure are valid, John Winters refers to U.S. government research into the advantages of oval over round shafts, which concluded that: *There was no significant comfort advantage in oval over round* (shafts).

Types of shafts

There are several category choices available that are diversified by various features. The two major categories are the one-piece shaft or the two or multiple piece shafts. An advantage of the breakdown (pull apart) shafts is that they often have the capability to adjust the feather angle of the blades. This is useful when experimenting with what suits you and would be an asset for a first paddle. There may be a slight weight penalty depending upon the style of adjustable ferrule but of higher concern is how well balanced the paddle feels. Some of the adjustable paddles use a hole and pit-pin to hold the two shafts in place. While this is effective, after a while (depending upon how much paddling you do) the joint wears and introduces slight looseness into shaft.

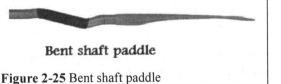

Bent shaft paddle

Figure 2-25 Bent shaft paddle

At the grip area, shafts can either be straight or bent shaft types. For whatever reason peculiar to individual paddlers, straight shaft paddles can result in the person cocking their wrist from side to side resulting in a repetitive strain injury (RSI). Aside from stroke technique correction, the use of the bent shaft paddle has been found to be beneficial to a great multitude of weekend paddlers. Originally designed for the purpose of reducing the amount of water lifted at the end of each stroke, it derives it efficiency from remaining vertical through the power phase of the stroke (Winters, 2005). At the same time, the wrist is not cocked off to one side, but held relatively straight throughout the movement of the stroke, thereby reducing the sideways cocking action and the possibility of wrist RSI. When using a straight shaft, to prevent cocking your wrist, use a light grip and loosen your outer fingers of the non-control hand.

There are a multitude of variations and names given to bent shaft paddles including natural bent shaft, crankshaft, double torque crank and modified crank. You need to read the manufacturer's literature/media to find out what the logic is behind their particular product and the shafts bend angles.

MATERIALS

There are a variety of materials used in the construction of kayaks and paddles from wood, canvas and aluminium through to the myriad of polymers and their trademark names.

Polymers

The term polymer covers an extremely broad spectrum of substances from proteins to Aramid fibres commonly known as Kevlar®. Restricting ourselves to the engineering world, scientists and engineers are always researching and developing better materials by manipulating the molecular structure that affects the final polymer produced. Manufacturers introduce various fillers, reinforcements, and additives into the base polymers, expanding product possibilities and variety. Polymers can be divided into two distinct groups: thermoplastics and thermosets (aka thermosetting plastics). Thermoplastics can be reheated and remoulded and include materials like: Acrylonitrile butadiene styrene (ABS), Polyvinyl Chloride (aka *Vinyl*) (PVC), polyethylene (PE). Thermosetting plastics refers to polymer materials that are irreversibly cured and include such materials as Epoxy resins, Polyester resins, Phenolic resins (Bakelite), Silicone and Vulcanised rubber.

The array of literature on thermoplastics is massive and can be quite confusing. Reasons for this are that the same chemical can be available in many different forms (i.e. at different molecular weights), which might have quite different physical properties. The same chemical can be referred to by many different trademarks (™), by different abbreviations in some cases; two chemical compounds can share the same name. So if you are confused by the advertising literature, do not feel too bad about it. Hopefully the information in the accompanying tables can assist you, when reading advertising literature.

Table 2-4 Plastics data

	Linear	Superlinear™	Crosslink	Xytec™
Density (g/cm³)	0.939	0.946	0.944	0.963
Impact (at 40°C)	41	56	82	69
Flexural Modulus	80 000	120 000	100 000	190 000
Heat Distortion	40	67	82	77
Tensile Strength	1160	3650	3000	3660

Plastic Boats

Plastic resins

Polyethylene resins are used in a plethora of household and every day products. In the recreational sporting goods market a wide variety of canoes, kayaks, paddles and sundry components are produced. The standard polyethylene kayak is described as durable and strong. Polyethylene is a vinyl polymer, made from the monomer ethylene. Polyethylene resins are simply labelled PE and are classified according to their density, branching structure as: High Density PE (HDPE), Medium Density PE (MDPE), Low Density PE (LDPE) and Linear Low Density PE (LLDPE). HDPE through the aid of a Zieglar-Natta catalyst has strong intermolecular forces and tensile strength. HDPE through its non-branching molecular structure is also referred to as linear polyethylene. It is much stronger than branch polyethylene (i.e. LDPE)

and can be welded. Mechanical properties of PE depend significantly on variables such as the extent and type of molecular branching, the crystal structure (e.g. semi-crystal for HDPE) and the molecular weight.[17] There are many polymers and trademark names given to plastics used in the construction of recreational kayaks. Table 2-5 lists some of them.

Cross-link refers to a covalent bond formed between polymer chains, either within or across chains. They are the characteristic property of thermosetting polymer materials. Polymers, which are branched but not cross-linked, are generally thermoplastic.

Cross-linking can be induced in materials that are normally thermoplastic through exposure to radiation. In most cases, cross-linking is irreversible, and the resulting thermosetting material will degrade or burn if heated, without melting. PEX is the common name for cross-linked high-density polyethylene.

Polycarbonate is also starting to be used in recreational boat construction and was pioneered by Tom Derrer of Eddyline kayaks. His Carbonlite 2000 is a thermocomposite of polycarbonate and acrylic blend.[18] Other construction methods involve the use of a polycarbonate for the exterior of the hull and an aramid fibre (Kevlar®) lay-up for the inside.

Polycarbonate boats fall between PE boats and glass reinforced plastic (fibreglass) boats for weight but this could change with new techniques and material designs. Polycarbonate has good scratch resistance compared to PE and has shown itself to be durable and UV resistant.

Polyacrylonitrile-*co*-butadiene-*co*—styrene (ABS) is one of several copolymers derived from polyacrylonitrile.[19] Polyacrylonitrile is a vinyl polymer, and a derivative of the acrylate family of polymers.

ABS is very strong and lightweight possessing good shock absorbing qualities and is used by the automotive industry to make vehicle body parts.

Plastic moulding techniques

There are three types of moulding techniques. The common two processes used to manufacture plastic recreational boats are rotational moulding and blow moulding.

Rotational moulding (aka *Rotomolding*) differs from other processing methods in that the heating, melting, shaping and cooling stages all occur after the polymer is placed in the mould, therefore no external pressure is applied during forming. The process starts with a good quality mould, which is placed in a moulding machine that has a loading, heating, and cooling area. Pre-measured plastic coloured resin is loaded into the mould, which is then placed into the oven and heated to around 288 degrees Celsius. Here the mould is slowly rotated on both the vertical and horizontal axis. The melting resin sticks to the hot mould and coats every surface evenly. The mould continues to rotate during the cooling cycle so the parts retain an even wall thickness. After about 20 minutes, once the component(s) or part(s) have cooled it is released from the mould. Throughout the process rotational speed, heating and cooling times are carefully controlled.

Blow moulding is a process whereby a blob (parison and/or perform) of molten polyethylene is injected with hot air into a cold mould, pressurised, allowed to cool and then removed in the shape of the desired product. A typical blow moulding process uses an extruded hot plastic resin parison and a compressed gas (usually hot air) to fill a chamber of a divided mould. The parison is a tube like piece of hot plastic with a hole in one end to allow compressed air to pass through. The gas blows the plastic resin against the sides of the mould and then pressurises the mould until the plastic cools. The two halves of the mould are separated and the finished product is released.

General characteristics of *plastic* boats are their robustness, durability, and impact absorption; however, they are not indestructible. Plastic boats are derided by some and attract the nickname '*Tupperware*' boats. However, since the early seventies when plastic white water boats came on to the market and especially since the nineties great advances have been made in materials and manufacturing processes.[20]

Table 2-5 Example of plastics used in manufacture of kayaks and canoes	
Carbonlite 2000	Eddyline Kayaks. A thermocomposite of polycarbonate and acrylic, the material combines the best of plastic and fiberglass.
Exolar™ resin	A newer plastic material that's being used in kayaks, is 40% stiffer and more durable than superlinear polyethylene.
HTP Polyethylene	Prijon Kayaks. **High Performance Thermoplastic.** HTP PE is used for the blow-molded construction. This material has an ultra-high molecular bond. HTP kayaks are UV stabilised, very abrasion resistant and virtually maintenance free.
Linear Select™	Necky Kayaks. Superlinear™ polyethylene
Methalacine SuperLinear PE Resin	Prijon Kayaks. Optimized Rotomold using Methalacine SuperLinear PE Resin.
Nitrylon™	Use on inflatable kayaks and rafts. A combination of tough, nylon fabric and a Nitrile/natural rubber coating.
Oltonar	Is Old Town's exclusive version of Uniroyal's Royalex®, a multi-laminate composed of ABS, ABS foam and crosslinked vinyl.
PolyLink3™	Old Town Canoe. Three-layer linear polyethylene technology that provides exceptional stiffness, low weight and built-in flotation
PolyLite™	Necky Kayaks. Necky PolyLite material optimizes stiffness, durability and impact resistance while keeping the overall weight of the kayak down.
Polyvinyl Chloride (PVC)	PVC is used on inflatable kayaks and rafts being a flexible, cloth like thermoplastic material possessing toughness and having good abrasion and puncture resistants.
Royalex®	Uniroyal. A multi-laminate composed of ABS, ABS foam and crosslinked vinyl that provides ultra-light weight, excellent strength and resiliency
Single Layer Linear Polyethylene	Excellent durable linear polyethylene at an affordable price
Superlinear resin **SUPERLINEAR™**	Kayaks that are rotomolded using Superlinear resin produce a product that is both extremely durable and rigid. The Superlinear polyethylene plastic is durable enough to handle years of abrasion and is 100% recyclable. Superlinear plastic also inhibits U.V.degradation providing exceptional colour and strength when exposed to the sun's harmful rays. A premium, high-density polyethylene that is very strong and provides bombproof durability.

Three Layer Superlinear	Old Town Canoes. A layer of closed cell foam sandwiched by layers of high-density polyethylene that provides strength, buoyancy and resiliency.
Xytec™	It's properties include, the stiffness of blow-molded plastic, impact resistance of cross-link polyethylene, and the repair-ability and recycle-ability of linear polyethylene

Plastic boats are generally heavier than their glass reinforced plastic counterpart but this is only an issue when you have to carry it to and from the water. With respect to the effect of a boats weight in the water, one needs to consider buoyancy and displacement, if you are going to make definitive statements about performance. There are paddlers out there who have plastic kayaks and can out paddle in both speed and distance other paddlers in 'fibreglass' kayaks. Plastic boats have been chosen by many adventures for expeditions around Cape Horn and circumnavigation of Tasmania. These boats are also said to flex when being paddled but, I have not seen any studies backing up the statement and I hazard a guess, that this statement may be a carryover from the twentieth century and based on the results of early materials and manufacturing methods. Also as a point of comparison, lightly laid-up composite boats will and do flex.

Composite Boats

Composite materials

Fibreglass kayaks are plastic boats too!

Glass Reinforced Plastic (GRP) also known as Glass Fibre Reinforced Plastic (GFRP) and Fiberglass Reinforced Plastic (FRP) are the names given to what is commonly called Fibreglass. All synthetic resins are man-made materials called *polymers,* and are categorised under the general description of plastics. Plastics lack the strength of metals and other structural materials. Thermoset resins are brittle and thermoplastic resins are relatively elastic. About the only way to make certain plastic resins strong and ridged is by combining them with a reinforcing material. One common reinforcing material is glass fibre. There are many types of glass fibre but for practical reinforcement only six types are produced in fibre form. Table 2-6 shows the five types of common glass fibre materials.

Glass fibre comes in various fibre sizes and forms from chopped strand, yarns and rovings through to woven cloths of varying weave patterns. These products are designed for a general application with considerations towards price, weight, strength and finish.

Chopped strand is referred to as *mat* (aka *chop strand mat*) and woven glass is referred to as *cloth*. Woven fabrics have higher strength than mats as reinforcement materials; as well, they provide consistency of uniform thickness and weight. When being used in the production of an item, different layers of cloth will be laid in such a manner against each other to form a *laminate* that will provide strength and rigidity for the plastic resin and final product.

Table 2-6 Glass Fibre Types

C glass	Chemical resistant	
E glass	Electrical grade	Excellent all round properties. Suits most applications.
R glass	Special high strength	Aerospace industry use.
S glass	Special high strength	Aerospace industry use. 30% stronger than E glass.
High modulus glass	Based on beryllia	Heavier and less elastic than other glasses.

Other composite fibres

There are three commonly used materials employed as alternative reinforcement materials to glass fibre: aramid fibre, carbon fibre and polyester fibre. All three are manufactured in woven fabric form.

Table 2-7 Types of Kevlar®

Kevlar® 29 (K29)	From the original family of product types having similar tensile properties available in many deniers and finishes. Applications include ropes, cables, personal and vehicular armour, protective apparel such as cut-resistant gloves and as rubber reinforcement in tires and automotive hoses.
Kevlar® 49 (K49)	High-modulus type used primarily in fibre optic cable, textile processing, plastic reinforcement, ropes, cables and composites for marine sporting goods and aerospace applications.
Kevlar® 100	Used in ropes and cables, tapes and strapping, gloves and other protective apparel, and sporting goods.

Kevlar® 119	Higher elongation, flexible fatigue-resistant yarn types found in mechanical rubber goods such as tires, automotive belts and hoses.
Kevlar® 129	High-tenacity type of yarns used in MRG, life protection such as ballistic vests and helmets, ropes and cables, and high-pressure hoses used in the oil and gas industry.
Nomex®	Blends of Nomex® and Kevlar® are used to make fireproof clothing.

Aramid fibres (aromatic polyamide) are fundamentally a type of nylon and are commonly known by their trademark names as Nomex®, Kevlar®, Twaron®, Technora® and Conex®. Aramid fibres tend to be difficult to corrode, resistant to heat and have no melting point. They also offer high strength to weight ratios and puncture resistance. Unfortunately most aramid yarns are affected by UV light, which alters the natural colour and degrades fibre strength upon prolonged exposure.

Kevlar® which is manufactured by DuPont™ is a commonly known and used aramid fibre and an alternative to glass fibre for laminates requiring high strength to low weight ratios. DuPont produces different types of Kevlar® for different applications, some of which are shown in Table 2-7. Kevlar® *49* (K49) is used in plastic reinforcement and composites for marine sporting goods and aerospace applications. K49 has been developed for optimum bonding characteristics with epoxy resin and current technology has produced finishes, which are suitable to be used with polyester resin.

Having said this, Epoxy resins make the best Kevlar laminates. As a simplified comparison, a laminate produced with Kevlar® is thicker, stronger and stiffer than GRP for the same weight. In some cases, a weight reduction of 30 to 40 per cent can also be achieved with an aramid compared to the same product made with GRP. However, weight is also a function of the amount of resin and material used, as well as, the manufacture process and skill of the tradesman.

Where aramid fibres do compare poorly to GRP is in compressive strength. An aramid fibre laminate can reduce weight and still produce the same or better tensile strength and impact resistance as GRP but it has less flexural strength to resist buckling loads. The Table 2-8 shows a comparison between different material and fibres.

Carbon fibre (aka graphite fibre, Carbon/Graphite fibre) is a polymer, which is a form of graphite. Graphite is a form of pure carbon. *Carbon/Graphite fibre* is a high tensile fibre that is made by heating rayon, polyacrylonitrile (PAN) fibres, or petroleum residues to appropriate temperatures.

Carbon (graphite) fibres are silky black, small diameter filaments made up of millions of long chained carbon atoms. Carbon fibres are produced by controlled oxidation and carbonisation. Using a precursor fibre called *polyacrylonitrile* (PAN), it is held under tension and heated from 1000 to 3000 degrees Celsius. The oxygen, hydrogen and nitrogen are removed from the precursor fibre leaving long chains of carbon atoms, which are aligned along their original axis due to the applied tension, which adds strength to the fibre.

During the heat treatment process, the fibres are typically over 90 per cent carbonised with the resulting graphite fibres having a higher specific tensile strength than steel. When used as a reinforcement material with epoxy resins, and or many other thermosetting materials, it becomes what is termed a *composite* material. As a composite, it is stronger and lighter than steel and can be used to replace metals in many applications. When carbon fibre is used as a composite, it can often produce products that are lighter and stronger than their contemporary made out of metal.

Carbon fibre is used in aerospace composite fabrics, sporting goods and racing auto frames to form structural and weight bearing components. The resulting structures are lightweight, very strong and highly resistant too. Carbon fibre is very strong when stretched or bent, but weak when compressed or exposed to high shock loads (e.g. impact). Lower quality carbon fibre is made from pitch (petroleum products) and rayon. Carbon fibres are developed, through heat treatment, into two common forms: *high strength* (HS) carbon and *high modulus* (HM) carbon.

Table 2-8 Plastics reinforcement materials data

Fibre	Density (g/cc) (Specific gravity)	Tensile strength N/m²	Tensile modulus N/m²	Specific tensile strength N/m²	Specific tensile modulus N/m²
Polyester	1.38	1.0	11	0.72	8
Kevlar 49	1.44	3.6	130	2.48	90
Carbon HS	1.74	3.1	227	1.77	130
Carbon HM	1.81	2.1	330	1.16	215
S-glass	2.48	4.0	86	1.57	34
E-glass	2.54	3.4	72	1.34	28

Density is also referred to as specific gravity.
Tensile strength column highest value represents the strongest material.
Tensile modulus refers to a material stiffness. The higher the value the stronger and stiffer the reinforcement properties.
Specific tensile strength is a measure of the tensile strength/weight ratio.
Specific tensile modulus is a measure of the stiffness/weight ratio. The higher the numbers the better the performance as a lightweight reinforcement. (Warring, 2003)
Source: (Bally Ribbon Mills, 2006)

	Density (g/cc)	Elongation at Break (%)	Breaking Tenacity (g/Denier)	Abrasion Resistance	1. Aging 2. Sunlight
Nylon	1.14	17 to 45	4.0 to 7.2	Excellent	1. Excellent 2. Degrades.
Polyester (PET)	1.38	15.3	9.2	Excellent	1. Excellent 2. Degrades
Polyethylene				Good to poor	1. ND 2. Degrades
Kevlar 49®	1.44	2.4	23.6	Fair to good	1. Excellent 2. Degrades
Carbon / Graphite	1.77	1	21.3		ND
S-glass	2.48	5.7	19.8	Good	Excellent
E-glass	2.54	4.8	15.3	Good	Excellent
Spectra®/ Dyneema®	0.97	2.7-3.5	26-34	Good	Excellent

Polyester fibre fabrics are employed where high impact strength is required in the product. Polyester fibre is the lightest of the reinforcement materials and is considered by some as the best material for laminate products requiring high impact resistance. However, polyester reinforced plastic laminates lack stiffness but this can be modified by the use of other reinforcement fabrics like fibreglass (i.e. Diolen® polyester/fibreglass).

Resins

One of the biggest improvements in plastic technology and its application to recreational canoes has been in the resin matrices. Polyester resins are now significantly tougher and for higher performance or lighter laminates, vinalesters and epoxies are now employed.[21]

Types of resins used for laminating glass fibre and other composites are: unsaturated polyester resins, epoxide (epoxy) resins, Furane resins, silicon resins, and phenolic resins. The common two types used in the recreational marine industry are unsaturated polyester resins and epoxy resins.

Unsaturated polyester resins

Unsaturated polyester resins (UPR) are the durable, resinous polymers derived from vinyl monomers; the most common being liquid styrene. The term *unsaturated* refers to the chemical bond of the styrene molecules. When an initiator, called a *catalyst*, is added to the resin a reaction takes place causing the substance to *cure,* from a liquid into a solid. Application of a catalyst like methyl ethyl ketone peroxide (MEKP), also known as butanone peroxide, is used to initiate the polymerization reaction (curing process), whereby the material becomes permanently set as a solid. There are many types of polyester resins having different characteristics and developed for specific application.[22]

The characteristics range from, when once cured, hard solids through to quite flexible materials. The majority of unsaturated polyester resins are developed for glass reinforced plastics application, while some of the others are developed for applications like casting, surface coatings, nut locks and thread sealants. Polyester resins have been developed for and are used in the recreational marine industry.

Epoxy resins

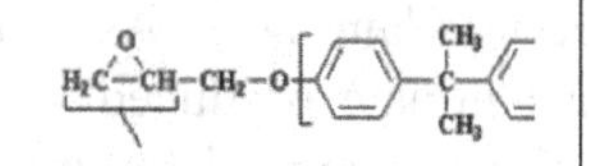

Epoxy resins are the other common type of resin used instead of polyester resins in laminated structures. Epoxy or polyepoxide is

Figure 2-26
Epoxy group molecules

a thermosetting epoxide polymer that cures (polymerizes and crosslinks) when mixed with a catalysing agent known as a *hardener.* Most common epoxy resins are produced from a reaction between epichlorohydrin and bisphenol-A to produce a low molecular weight polymer with a molecular structure containing *epoxy* groups at each of its ends; known as a *diepoxy.*

The second part of an epoxy resin, the hardener, has a molecular group termed a *diamine*. On mixing the diepoxy (resin) with the diamine (hardener) the two groups crosslink together forming one large molecule. When this happens, the result is a hard substance that can be very strong, but not processable.

The applications for epoxy based materials are extensive and include coatings, adhesives and composite materials such as those using carbon fibre and fibreglass reinforcements. The chemistry of epoxies and the range and variety of commercially available products allows cure polymers to be produced with a very broad range of properties, which means not all epoxies are suitable for marine use.

In general, epoxies are known for their excellent adhesion characteristics, chemical and heat resistance, good to excellent mechanical properties, and very good electrical insulating properties; but almost any property can be modified to suit a particular application. Epoxies are exceptional adhesives for wood, metal, glass, stone, and some plastics.[23] Their form can be flexible or rigid, transparent or opaque/coloured. Their setting times can be fast or extremely slow.

The advantages of epoxies for laminated structures over polyester resins are: low percentage of shrinkage, high strength to weight ratio, ability to provide a much more impervious barrier to the ingress of moisture, possessing better flexibility and having greater resistance to fatigue from vibration. Formulate epoxy resins are better suited for the purpose of laminating aramid fibres (e.g. Kevlar®).

Another type of resin that is associated with polyester resins is *Vinylester*. Vinylesters were developed later then polyester and epoxy resins with it having properties midway between the two. It is classified more as a polyester because of its similarities in cost, adhesive qualities and process' procedures. Vinylesters give good adhesion, impact resistance and possesses mechanical properties, which fall between those of epoxy and polyester. They reduce brittle failure and improve toughness because of their high elongation and some are enhanced with rubber to further enhance toughness. Additional weight is saved as a result of their lower density versus epoxy systems.

Gelcoat

Gelcoat is a resin used to provide an external protective barrier and cosmetic finish to a composite product. Most common gelcoats are either epoxy or unsaturated polyester based. They are formulated with stabilizers and additives to suit particular environments, applications and can be pigmented in a wide and variegated array of colours and patterns. Gelcoat cures in the absence of air and is applied to a mould in a liquid state before the reinforcement fibre and resin is laid over the top of it. The gelcoat cures to form a crosslinked polymer, which is backed up by the composite polymer matrices. On removal from the mould, the product presents its gelcoated external surface.

Gelcoat is damaged through wear and tear on your kayak, showing up as chips and scratches. Gelcoat is the sacrificial material in the laminate and it is there to protect the reinforcement fibres. Fine scratches in the gelcoat can be buffed out with a rotary polisher and car polish. Gouges and chips are easily repaired through the application of gelcoat or flowcoat. Flowcoat cures (sets) in the presence of air and can be brushed on to the repair.

For information about repairing composites and plastics, go to the chapter titled 'Seamanship'.

Laminates

Laminates is a term used to describe the process of laying reinforcing fabrics on top of each other and then having a resin applied. A glass laminate is one where by fibreglass mat sheets are used. Sometimes they are referred to by their construction of both the type of fabric and resin (e.g. glass/epoxy laminate). Table 2-9 has been included to show the different mechanical properties, different laminates produce using epoxy resins. The terms *woven* and *uniaxial* refers to the reinforcement fabric's construction.

Unidirectional mats have a fibre orientation running in one direction that provides strength in that direction. They are usually constructed of carbon/graphite materials. Bidirectional and or multidirectional refers to fibres which have an orientation in two or more directions and are usually woven together. These mats disperse the stresses along the multiple orientations. An example of a bidirectional fabric is *bidirectional Kevlar*.

Hybrid systems are made by combining two or more types of fibres in a single laminate (i.e. glass fibre with an aramid fibre). By using different fabrics, a laminate can be tailored to meet a specific function and specific performance requirements. The unique performance characteristics of one reinforcing material compared to another, when formed as a composite laminate, can be used to perform a function that neither could do independently. For example, to compensate for carbon fibres low impact strength, glass fibre can be employed. Developing an aramid/carbon laminate produces a composite, which is lighter than a comparable glass fibre reinforced plastic; combines the flexibility of Kevlar® with the stiffness of carbon; and has higher impact resistance and fracture toughness than an all carbon composite.

Table 2-9 Comparison of Fibre Reinforced Composites
Source: Building With Boat-Coat Australia's Reliable Marine Epoxy Systems, BoatCraft Pacific Pty. Ltd, 204, p.17

Fibre	Woven E-glass	Uniaxial E-glass	Uniaxial Carbon
Resin	Epoxy	Epoxy	Epoxy
Fibre content (%)	50-60	50-60	50-60
Tensile strength (MPa)	350	550	830
Compressive Strength (MPa)	275	415	620
Flexural Modulus (GPa)	23	30	95

Composite Build Methods

The purpose of the reinforcement material is to compensate for the deficiencies of the resin used and vice versa. Depending upon the type and quantity of material and resin used will impact on the weight of the boat. This is where engineering design and tradesman skills combine to hopefully produce a quality product for an intended use and meets customer's expectations. Using incorrect products or too

much (e.g. resin), can lead to a heavier product when a lighter product is just as capable of performing the intended function.

There are many industrial methods used in the manufacturing of products from composite materials. Some of the composite moulding methods are hand lay-up, vacuum bag moulding, pressure bag moulding and resin transfer moulding (RTM). The two common methods employed to manufacture canoes are *hand lay-up* and *vacuum bagging*.

Hand lay-up refers to the manufacturing process whereby the reinforcement fibre and resin are applied through manual (hand) methods. The *job* is then left to cure by itself through chemical reaction of the resin. Two terms used to describe hand lay-up methods is the *dry method* and the *wet method*. The dry method involves using a squeegee to spread the resin over and into the reinforcement material. The wet method involves the use of paint brushes or a roller to spread and work the resin into the fibre. The dry method differs from the wet method in the amount of resin remaining in the reinforcement material. The less remaining unnecessary resin results in a lighter lay-up.

Vacuum bag moulding (aka *vacuum bagging*) involves encapsulating the job, after it has been laid up with reinforcement material and resin, with a bag and then creating a vacuum inside the bag. Vacuum bagging has several advantages over the hand lay-up method. This method produces a better uniformity of lay-up and reduced material thickness. Less resin is required and what is used is worked thoroughly through the reinforcement material. During the process, the vacuum excludes the air and therefore removes air bubbles from the job. At the end of the process, the method produces a laminate with a better strength to weight ratio.

SPRAY SKIRTS

Spray skirts (aka *spray deck*, *spray cover*) have the function of preventing the cockpit from becoming flooded. The Greenland Inuit had two main types of spray skirts: the full jacket called a *tuilik* and the half jacket waist/torso band call an *akuilisaq*; with the latter having the form and function of the modern day spray skirt. The modern version of the tuilik in some cases is made out of neoprene synthetic rubber and is called a *tuiliusaq* (The British Museum).

Solution Passage Flexi-fit Nylon spray cover and Solution Eclipse spray cover

Figure 2-27 Two types of kayak spray skirts

The most common type of spray skirt, in Victoria, is the modern form of the akuilisaq style, consisting of a waist/torso band and bib (i.e. the removable cockpit deck) that secures to the cockpits coaming by the rand. The rand consists of around 6 to 10 millimetre shock cord (aka bungee cord). The types of materials used to make a skirt, depends upon the manufacture and the price the customer desires to pay. The akuilisaq style of spray skirt may or may not have braces to assist holding up the waistband. Other possible features are draw cords around the top of the waist/torso band, stowage pockets, attachment rings to hold a map case down and an access hole for a hand pump nozzle.

Spray skirt materials

Materials advertised as used in the construction of modern day spray skirts are nylon, neoprene, 4 millimetre Chloroprene rubber (superior quality neoprene), hybrid Kevlar® materials, waterproof 420 denier WaveTex™ fabrics, Aquatherm fabric et cetera

Nylon spray skirts are useful for flat water paddling with neoprene spray skirts being the most common type for sea kayaking. Having said that, Cordura® is a nylon product constructed in various deniers and textures. Nylon in its various fibre forms comes in various deniers, construction, textures and coatings of polyurethane, silicon, et cetera for different applications. It is often difficult to find out what the parent fibre (e.g. nylon, polyester etc.) is of a trademark material, but the denier number does provide some useful information.

Reed akuilisaq style spray skirt and Reed tuilik style spray skirt.

Figure 2-28 Modern day akuilisaq and tuilik

The term *denier* is a unit of measuring the thickness/weight of a thinly spun fibre. It indicates the material's durability, plus the fineness of both natural and synthetic fibre filaments and yarns. The higher the denier numbers the thicker the fibre and the lower the denier rating, the finer the fibre. For example, 1000 denier nylon is used to make rucksacks and 420 denier nylon pack-cloth is described as lightweight and being the *elephants hide* of outdoors fabrics; being as tough as leather or vinyl and offering superior water repellence under all weather conditions.

Neoprene spray skirts are durable but they do let water through, if not eventually. Spray skirts are usually made from 3 to 4 millimetre neoprene. Neoprene is the trade name given by DuPont, to the polymer polychloroprene, which is a type of synthetic rubber. Originally developed as an oil-resistant substitute for natural rubber, neoprene is classed as a synthetic rubber, designed to possess flexibly, durably and to resist breakdown by water. The basic chemical composition of neoprene synthetic rubber is polychloroprene, which through modification by copolymerization yields a family of materials with a broad range of chemical and physical properties, as well as different grades and thicknesses. It is through the manufactures correct selection of the class and grade of neoprene that will determine the quality of a spray skirt. Manufactures also mix neoprene fabrics with Kevlar® and other fabrics like Aquatherm to try and get the best qualities of each type of material and overcome the shortcomings of the other.

Aquatherm is a material developed and used by Reed Chill Cheater. The material is waterproof and has an outer shell made of polyurethane. Aquatherm deck fabric has 360 degree stretch, instant memory return, and has 80 per cent less volume and weight compared with traditional neoprene products. The fabric's outer surface is

20 times more abrasion resistant than neoprene; however Reed recommends if people are going to practice rescues and drag kayak bows up on to their spray decks, then they chose one of their other types of spray skirts. Reed Aquatherm spray skirts have become popular with many VSKC members.

---

1 C.A. Marchaj, op. cit., p.252. Information taken from the hydrodynamic resistance model results and converted to full scale results by the Stevens Institute of Technology, USA. The model was of the New York, a keeled yacht of: L_{OA}—45.50 ft, L_{WL}—32.26 ft, Beam—10.58 ft, Draft—6.56 ft, Displacement—25,500 lb.

2 This information even thought it does not apply to kayaks, has been included to complement the information on displacement and planing hulls.

3 Some sea kayaks are advertised as having a shallow-V hull and some surfing kayaks are advertised as having planing hulls. The information about planing hulls, even though it does not strictly apply to kayaks, has been included to give an understanding of what a planing hull is.

4 Waves travelling at a given velocity have a corresponding given speed (e.g. $V_s/\sqrt{L_{WL}} = 1.34$. Knots ≈ 1.34 x $\sqrt{L_{WL}}$ x ft)

5 The density of salt water can be up to 10% greater than fresh water (i.e. up to 1.1 g/cm^3). An egg will sink in fresh water but it will float in very salty water; the density of the egg is greater than the density of fresh water but less than the density of the very salty water. Pure fresh water has a density of one tonne per cubic metre and pure salt water is said to have 1.025 tonnes per cubic metre.

6 To simplify this topic about stability I have avoid using a kayak with a kayaker seated inside of it. The reason being, a paddler's body position, core strength, the mass of the head attached to the torso by the neck etc. have an effect on a kayaks stability. This is to say the paddler has the greatest effect on kayak stability. From the basic principles and concepts one has a base from which to apply further knowledge.

7 Note: The drawings have been exaggerated for clarity and explanation purposes. The metacentre is only valid for angles of inclination of 0° up to a range of 7° to 10° of heel and is therefore applicable to initial stability but is used here in the drawings to give a physical reference point as an aid to gain an understand of the concepts, which do not detract from the principles at larger angles of heel.

8 Refer www.marineenginering.org.uk

9 For further information on kayak stability go to Nick Schade's web page.

10 The static stability curve is also referred to as a GZ curve.

11 The two stability curves shown in Figure 2-22 were developed using an incorrect formula as reported by SKM in their December 2009 issue, Vol. 26, No. 5. These are two boats I was looking at to purchase and was using the data in consideration of which one to get. The point to be made in this comparison of the two graphs (compiled using the same formula pre December 2009) is how two comparable boats stability are affect by weight and how the stability curve can approach zero or even go below zero Newton metres (foot pounds) of righting force.

12 Re: www.qcckayaks.com/resources/controllability.asp accessed 1Jun09. This cited article is the only place I came across the term centre of lateral area (CLA) and is assumed by me to be a synonym for CLP. In his book: The Shape of the Canoe, 2005 the mentioning of CLA (i.e. CLP & CLR) and the description about the forces on a skeg has been omitted from Chapter 5, Motions, Factors Affecting Manoeuvrability, pp.29-31. Of interest are the statements by Marchaj and Brewer that CLP (and therefore CLR) and CE are only applicable terms to sailboats. The CE can only exist if there is a sail. This was borne out through Gillmer/Johnson, Introduction to Naval Architecture, 1982, which discussed ships and submarines, where no references were found for the aforementioned terms. In this reference, great detail is given about stability and controllability (e.g. factors affecting turning, rudders, effect of wind and water etc.). Of interest; Marchaj references sailing canoes when talking about induced resistance and notes from testing that "canoe's shallow draft hull can only contribute about 2.5 per cent towards the side force, and the hull proper may be described as a very inefficient hydrofoil." Sailing Theory and Practice, 1964, p.274. The information therefore has been included about skegs for the reader to gain an understanding of the principles of directional stability and controllability even though the terms may only be applicable to sailboats.

13 For every action there is an equal and opposite reaction.

14 People confuse ventilation (aeration) with cavitation. Ventilation involves the presence of air where cavitation involves a vacuum (absence of a gas or fluid).

15 Note I am not referring to residual water being flung off of the blades surface.

16 This is not an absolute statement. There is no advantage over a right hand control paddle to that of a left hand control. Also, in general, a right handed person can easily adapt to a left hand control paddle and vice versa. However, the majority of paddles made are right hand control.

17 Polyethylene terephthalate (PET, PETE) is a common plastic used for food, beverage and pharmaceutical containers. It should not be confused with polyethylene (PE) or polypropylene (PP).

18 Polycarbonate of bisphenol A is a clear thermoplastic used to make shatterproof windows and is made by General Electric as Lexan. Polycarbonate used in eyeglasses has been cross-linked and is a thermosetting plastic.

19 Clothing labelled as acrylic are made from a polyacrylonitrile copolymer.

20 Steve Crow, A Bit About Boat Building, Wavelength Magazine, Dec02/Jan03. In the 1970s Bill Masters designed a plastic white water boat for Perception.

21 The term matrix when used to describe composite materials or reinforced plastics refers to the resin system used as a cementing agent to bind the fibres giving it strength and the ability to transfer stress to surrounding structures.

22 One company alone develops over 100 different types of polyester resins.

23 A good Australian product is Bote-Cote which is designed for use on wooden boats but can also be used on fibreglass boats. I have used it with forming foam to make after market modification strengthening formers (running from the under-deck around the inside hull to the bilge) laminated against Kevlar.

Chapter 3 Kit Requirements and Suggestions

"A man who carries a cat by the tail learns something he can learn in no other way."

Mark Twain

① **Note:** In the following text the safety requirements of Marine Safety Victoria (MSV) have been referenced. Other country, state or territory equivalent marine safety authorities should be consulted in order to comply with their requirements. Website addresses can be found at Appendix 2.

The following is based on the requirements of the VSKC and has been developed from the collective knowledge of club members over thirty years. Many of the requirements also align with the requirements of Australian Canoeing and the NSWSKC.

Have serviceable and appropriate for the seasons, sea conditions, locations and state and territory law requirements appropriate: Sea Kayak, Personal Floatation Device (PFD), paddling clothing, Cockpit Accessible Items, First Aid Kit, Ancillary Gear Items, Camping Gear.

Sea Kayak

Must be a recognised sea kayak design and fitted out to VSKC standards and Law requirements.[1] It must be in a seaworthy condition and fitted out with:

Minimum volume cockpit, watertight bulkheads and hatch covers, including positive buoyancy.[2]

Deck lines: recommended five millimetre (5 mm) minimum diameter with carry toggles or loops at both ends.

Proper fit out, including foot, thigh and hip bracing.

Hands free pump, either electric or foot operation (see MSV requirements).

Sponge and or bailer (see MSV requirements).

Deck mounted compass (see MSV Requirements). The compass may be either fixed or removable.

Spray skirt that fits cockpit and paddler, with release strap.

Towing points.

Paddle and paddle leash as/if required.

Spare paddle (accessible from cockpit) (see MSV Requirements).

Rudder or skeg, if fitted is to be fully retractable (if applicable) and in proper working order.

Personal Flotation Device (PFD)

According to statics from the USCG Boating Safety division for 2011, 84 per cent of boating deaths by drowning were a result of people not wearing a PFD.

Wear an appropriate PFD type 1 (recognised by MSV as a lifejacket) or PFD type 2 or type 3 (a buoyancy vest) with a whistle. Most sea kayakers choose a type 2 PFD. Some wear a Type 1 *horse collar* inflatable PFD.

Cockpit Accessible items

① **Note:** Day hatches are not always accessible at sea.

When on the water, under certain conditions, your day-hatch is not accessible. With respect to survival equipment the motto is:

"If it is not on you, you do not have it."

Consider also carrying as applicable to the conditions, locations, situations and Law requirements:

Signal mirror

Rescue knife

Strobe light

Sea marker dye

EPIRB (see MSV Requirements).

Carry appropriate to location, situation, conditions seasons and Law requirements:

Smoke and Flares (see MSV Requirements)

Torch (see MSV Requirements). Waterproof head torches are best suited. A white light is the only acceptable colour. Strobing white lights are also unacceptable as they are used as a means of identifying a man-overboard.

Communication equipment (e.g. mobile phone and or marine VHF radio). Maritime New Zealand recommend kayakers carry two sources e.g. mobile phone and flares.

Emergency wind chill protection (e.g. large plastic rubbish bag, space blanket or emergency poncho). Carry two, one for patient and one for rescuer-supporter.

Mini first aid kit (e.g. to treat sea sickness, strains, cuts) and containing personal medications (e.g. Insulin, asthma pumps, anti-histamines etc.).

Spare hat and or beanie. Beanies are also very useful in summer and should be stowed.

Sun-cream; consider zinc cream and lip balm.

Fluids (i.e. minimum of two litres drinking water).

Food/snacks (e.g. high-energy snacks, chocolate, and fruit and nut bars).

Helmet for use during surf sessions, surf launches and landings.

① **Note:** Tow rope to be deployed from its storage container with the minimum possibility of entanglement.

Fifteen metre (15 m) tow rope made from 3–4 mm cordage with float and two small quick release fittings. It needs to be stowed in a bag or on a reel and be able to be deployed tangle free.

Securing line 1–1.25 metres long, of 5–6 mm cordage, with stainless steel clips at each end. Ensure the securing line can be deployed in a quick and efficient manner.

ANCILLARY GEAR ITEMS

Carry appropriate to situation, conditions and seasons:

Dry clothes

Footwear

Spare warm clothing

Wet weather/wind chill protection

Thermos or brew kit

Meals

Ground sheet

Repair kit.

Carry sufficient food and water for the time expected (i.e. lunch on day trips). On longer trips plan for contingencies (i.e. carry an extra days rations).

It is useful to carry a small ground sheet (1 m x 1.6 m) or carry a space blanket, which doubles as a ground sheet. Military ponchos also double as 'fly tents' (aka *hootchies*) and ground sheets.

TRIP LEADER ITEMS

The trip leader needs to carry or ensured is carried within the group:

Spare group warm clothing

Spare group beanie and hat

Group first aid kit

Spare paddle

Navigation equipment

Appropriate charts and maps

Note book and pencil

VSKC Indemnity Waiver Sheet

Copy of the float plan.

CLOTHING

On-water clothing

Dress using the layer principle and have as appropriate to the conditions and seasons:[3]

Head and face protection (e.g. hat, beanie, sunglasses). In any season, it is advisable to carry a beanie.

Paddling clothing. Avoid cotton garments and use synthetic materials (e.g. polyester, Aquatherm, fleeces etc.) garments as they dry quite fast.

- One piece suits such as 'Farmer John wet-suits' and paddling dry suits.

- Bottoms using materials like neoprene, lycra, Chill Cheater Aquatherm/ Aquafleece, board shorts, synthetic thermals et cetera.

- Tops using synthetic materials and having good UV protection ratings. Consider wearing long sleeve tops. Note rash vests tend to feel cold against the skin. Use thermal garments as a base layer. Do not wear cotton garments in winter and cold weather paddling. Polartech® Shark Skins and Reed Chill Cheater Aquatherm and Aquafleece products are well received by may paddlers and SCUBA divers. Ten-dollar polyester sloppy Joes' make great thermal tops.

Consider high visibility clothing (e.g. fluor-colours).

To reduce chaffing, wear thermals or inner garments inside out (have the bunched up seam of the garment away from your skin). Lanolin is also useful if you are prone to chaffing under the arms.

Appropriate outer-shell clothing (e.g. cag) or similar paddling/wind protection jacket.

Paddling gloves and/or UV resistant gloves. Gloves are useful after applying sunscreen to prevent the paddle slipping out of your hands.

Appropriate footwear. Appropriate footwear involves the feet being protected from cuts and abrasions but will not catch on any inside cockpit fittings and prevent egress (e.g. wetsuit booties).

Wet weather & wind chill protection on land

Wet weather gear and wind chill protection clothing may be one and the same thing or separate types of garments depending upon the products. To make it easier to differentiate the two types, here they are defined as:

Wet weather gear refers to waterproof jackets/ coats, over-pants, raincoats and ponchos. May also be referred to as outer shell clothing. Note these garments may keep you dry and the wind out but without warm garments underneath you may still be cold.

Wind chill protection clothing (aka *warm gear*) may consist of garments such as 'Gore Wind Stopper®' jackets/vests, fleeces and the like, which are not waterproof. Spray (e.g. nylon) jackets fall into this category.

Depending upon the weather forecast you may decide not to carry wet weather gear (e.g. rain coat and over-pants) however, wind chill is an issue if you need to land somewhere during the day other than the destination. If you have a waterproof coat and over-pants (Gortex®, or other techo-material), that can double as wind chill protection, it is advisable you carry them. A good inexpensive substitute to the expensive materials is the nylon/ plastic poncho and over pants.

Pack your wet weather and wind chill protection separate from your main dry clothes. Stow this last in your compartment so that it is easily and quickly accessible. Tag your dry bags with what is in them (e.g. warm clothes), not only for yourself, but primarily for someone who is assisting you if you are incapacitated (e.g. hypothermic).

Dry clothes

Dry clothes are your non-paddling clothes. Stow your 'dry clothes' in a dry bag. People tend to over pack with clothes for camping trips. Treat all the kayaks stowage space as if you were packing your 70 litre hiking pack for a hike.

It is advisable if you are sharing transport and there is a car shuffle, to pack your dry clothes in your kayak and not leave them back at the start point. People have stood around in wet kit, in winter, waiting for their dry kit to arrive! Do not forget and leave your land footwear behind in the car either!

DRY BAGS AND BAGS

If you do not have any dry bags do not rush out and buy inappropriate equipment (learn from our mistakes), contact a club member or me.

There are many manufacturers of dry bags but a common popular brand is the Sea to Summit (STS) dry bags. These bags are functional and crushable thereby taking up less storage space but do wear out after several years. Herculite dry bags are hard wearing but do not crush as easily as the STS dry bags. I use tapered Wxtex bags (x 1 small and x 1 medium), which are strong and durable but more expensive than the STS dry bags.

Not everything has to go into a dry bag. Dry bag size depends upon your hatch sizes. Many paddlers prefer to use separate dry bags for separate types of kit (e.g. warm gear, dry gear, sleeping bag etc.). A few paddlers like to use one big dry bag (e.g. STS XL dry bags) in each of their kayaks compartments in the same manner as a hiking pack liner. To load kit into kayaks with small hatches, these large dry bags need to be inserted empty through the hatch then loaded with kit. To portage all your gear in, acquire from the 'Two Dollar' shops the collapsible storage bags. Two medium size bags (approximately 52 cm x 60 cm x 20 cm) are easier to carry to a campsite than one large size bag.

CAMPING EQUIPMENT

The following is a basic list of camping equipment items that you will need to (or at least should consider) stowing in your kayak for a camping trip:

Hiking tent

Sleeping bag and mat

Cooking set and equipment

Matches and or a lighter

Cup, plate/bowl and utensils

Washing up kit and drying cloth

Gaiters

Sewing kit.

Personal equipment

The following personal equipment should be stowed in your kayak for a camping trip:

Personal medications

Toiletries

Towel.

There is a multitude of hiking tents on the market, look at the one or two man tents with a weight of around two kilograms.

Another consideration is to look at getting a stand-alone tent. Stand-alone hiking tents have become a popular choice with some kayakers, as they are easier to pitch on a sandy surface and potentially offer more reliability in windy conditions.

Put your sleeping bag in a dry bag. The sleeping mat does not need to be put in a dry bag but can be stowed in the far upper reaches of the bow or stern, depending upon how dry your cargo compartments are.

For a pillow you can use a dry bag stuffed with a coat and spare clothes. If you do use an inflatable pillow, to prevent chasing it around the tent during the night, glue (using contact cement) strips of Velcro to it and the sleeping mat. Alternatively, you can also do this on the dry/stuff bag you use as a pillow.

People have a bias towards different cooking systems (i.e. Trangia® methylated spirits burner verses gas cylinders and liquid fuel pressurised stoves like *Wisperlites*) and hence banter and in some cases dogma! The advantage of the Trangia style of liquid fuel burners is the absence of moving parts and the potential for foreign object damage and blockages, caused usually by sand. In winter when using methylated spirits as the fuel, they are slow to boil water. Another detractor, for some people, is the bulkiness of the system compared to some gas cylinder models. The Trangia two person cooking set is quite bulky and has a larger diameter than some hatches on kayaks. If you are sharing and splitting up kit between boats, then it is useful and can fit through the larger oval hatches.

Disposable gas cylinder effectiveness depends upon the brand but consider issues like corrosion, damage and blockages from foreign bodies. In winter, they boil water quickly but you do need to use care and perform maintenance on the O-ring seals and jets.

To reduce the risk of envenomisation from snake bite, carry and wear gaiters. For sewing thread, dental floss is very useful.

LOADING A KAYAK

Instead of tell people how to, here are some points to consider when kayak camping:

'Count every ounce, for every ounce counts'
Remember you may have to portage your kayak a long way!

A crew of four paddlers is ideal for trips with heavily laden kayaks for a four-man carry. Two tapes with handles used as carry straps passed under the hull make portage easier.

Pay attention to boat trim. This involves both lateral stability (i.e. one side is too heavy) and longitudinal stability (nose down or up). Put heavy items like water and tents close to the boat's centre of gravity.

Practice loading your boat before you arrive at the beach and then delay the launch because you do not have your kayak pack.

Need verses want:

Summer requirements differ from winter requirements in both food and clothing.

Do you require all the clothes you want to pack?

1 The VSKC does not consider a sit-on-top kayak as a sea kayak as of 2009. The NSWSKC as of May 2007 have the following sea kayak requirements:
A minimum overall length of 4.5 m
An enclosed cockpit
Permanent bulkheads or
Some form of buoyancy
A cockpit rim to fit a spray skirt
Is reasonably stable
Can be manoeuvred in rough seas.
For their club activities the NSWSKC do not consider the following types of kayaks as suitable for club ocean paddling:
'Sit-on-tops' (e.g. surf skis, wave skis, racing skis)
Estuary or river kayaks suitable for calm water only
Open canoes (i.e. Canadian canoes)
Inflatable kayaks; excluding folding kayaks that have inflatable sponsons
Multi-sport hybrid boats that are intended for multi-sports events or flat water racing (NSWSKC, 2007, pp. 17-18).
2 The NSWSKC in their NSWSKC Policy Guidelines and Standard Operating Procedures Ver. 1.5.2 of May 2007 State the following about positive buoyancy: floatation material inside the boat or bulkheads to displace water if the hull is flooded. These are in addition to bulkheads. Options include commercially made inflatable air bags through to foam, inflated wine bladders, dry bags etc. Note that equipment stored in dry bags inside the hull acts as positive buoyancy.
3 Pioneered and used by the 19th century Norwegian arctic explorer Fridtjof Nansen (1861-1930)

Chapter 4 Sea Kayaking Skills

"What one has not experienced, one will never understand in print."

Isadora Duncan

① **Note:** This chapter on paddling skills is a form of reference and revision after being shown correct techniques by an instructor. Practice and allow yourself to be critiqued by someone who has the knowledge, skills and attitude to assist you.

① **Note:** There are several good DVDs on the market showing and describing paddle techniques and even books with plenty of pictures. I would suggest you compliment these notes with aforementioned media.

Basic sea kayaking handling skills are:

Paddle strokes:

- Forward stroke
- Back (Reverse) stroke
- Emergency stop
- Forward sweep stroke
- Reverse sweep stroke
- Draw stroke
- Stern rudder
- Support strokes.

Braces:

- Slapping, both high and low
- Sculling, both high and low.

Low brace turns

Rafting-up

Wet exit

Self-rescue

Group rescue

Launching and landing techniques.

Holding the Paddle

"Hold your paddle like a fairy holds her wand, not how a witch holds her broomstick"

Derek Hutchinson

Depending upon the type of paddle you have, (feathered or unfeathered) and the make, there is a 'hand locator' on the shaft. If you are using a feathered paddle, and you are right-handed, the locator is on the right-hand side. When you grasp the shaft at the locator, your hand is known as the *'control hand'*.

With your control hand clasped around the paddle shaft locator, lightly grasp the other end of the shaft. Have the lengthwise centre of the paddle shaft central with your body's centreline. Position your hands slightly outside of your shoulder width. With the paddle in front of you, you can rotate it backwards and forwards with the control hand, while it slides around the inside of your other hand.

Paddle Strokes

Phase of the stroke

Paddle strokes can be divided into three phases of the:

Catch

Power

Recovery.

Since the forward stoke is the predominantly performed paddle stroke, we will discuss the three phases of a paddle stroke using the aforementioned stroke as an example.

The catch phase is the start of the stroke, when the water is caught by the planted blade. The blade needs to be 'square' to the water; if it is angled away the blade will slide outwards, and if angled inwards it will slide under the hull with both resulting in an inefficient stroke. The full blade needs to be submerged. The lower hand quickly spears the blade into the water and remains just above the water. The hand during the power phase follows the bow wave as it moves away from the hull. It does not run parallel to the hull during the stroke as this allows the arm to bend and results in a loss of power (Australian Canoeing, n.d.). The top hand does not push the blade into the water, but follows the paddle shaft's forward movement.

When planting the blade think of it as a pole in the water. You are reaching out and grabbing the pole and by rotating your body you pull yourself forward.

The power phase (aka drive phase) involves pulling yourself forward on the planted blade. The stroke is driven by torso rotation with the arms remaining in roughly the same plane.

Rotation when viewed from above sees the paddlers shoulders rotate around a stationary spine and head. As the pelvis is facing forward and the head is looking forward. Rotation is the key to an efficient and powerful stroke. Efficient rotation, allows a paddler to have an efficient catch at the beginning of the stroke and achieve their maximum power and acceleration from the stroke. Remember to rotate and not cycle your arms. The power phase ends when the blade is around the mid thigh to pelvis region. Note in sea conditions, the paddle can remain in the water in order to perform a ruddering stroke to maintain directional stability.

At this point the paddler enters the exit stage whereby the blade exits the water. The top hand extends forward, and still remains in its plane, around eye height. The lower arm bends and the hand moves upwards exiting the paddle out of the water to the side. The elbow remains relaxed, stays below the hand and away from the body.

The recovery phase takes place at the end of the power phase, after the exit stage and before the next catch. It is when the next drive stroke blade, is transferred from the completed stroke side, across the deck ready for the next catch phase. With the torso fully rotated the 'new drive' side shoulder is at its forward maximum position. Due to the torso rotation, the paddle is parallel to the kayaks centreline. The drive side is ready for the next catch phase on the opposite side. The paddle is then brought across the deck and speared down into the water.

Forward Strokes

Cruise forward stroke

The cruise forward stroke is the stroke that you will perform the most. Points to consider are:

Wrists are straight and relaxed. Not flexing side to side, or back and forth.

Upper hand has a relaxed grip. The back of your hand is in-line with the forearm. When paddling this hand is at chin level or lower, but not below the shoulder. Note this may be awkward with some sea kayak paddles. Ideally, the hand should be between the top of the head and chin. Experiment not crossing the centre-line of boat (this will allow the blade, in the water, to be out when level with the hip) however, adapt a style that is efficient for you.

Elbows are bent slightly throughout the stroke, to keep the paddle shaft away from and square with the torso. Do not use your arms in a cyclic motion.

Arms form a strong link between the torso and paddle. They do not drive the stroke; the torso does! Fully extend but do not over extend (i.e. straighten) the lower arm on the catch phase. During the power phase the lower arm should not be allowed to bend excessively. The top arm follows the paddle with the top hand stabilising the blade in the water.

Posture involves having an erect torso and bent slightly forward, maintaining the curvature of your back. The shoulders should be

Figure 4-1 Paddler's box	

Note how with body rotation the "paddler's box" is maintained and a more efficient and powerful stoke is developed that reduces fatigue and the risk of injury.	Note that there is no or little body rotation as the arms are being swept across the body. This causes stress and fatigue on the limbs joints leading to injury (e.g. Repetitive Strain Injury).

slightly in front of the hips. Head, neck and shoulders should be relaxed. Do not slouch, as this limits rotation, and may cause lower back muscle irritation. Have your head up, and looking around.

Legs are relaxed but in a position that allows knees and thighs to be instantly tensed, to lock you firmly in the cockpit.

Feet are resting on the foot pegs, and or foot rests.

Torso is kept square with the paddle shaft. Remember the *'paddler's box'* which is an imaginary *'box'* formed by the chest, arms and paddle shaft. Hold the paddle in front of your torso at chest/stomach height, with elbows bent at a 90 degree angle. The chest and upper arms form the backside of the box, while the paddle shaft forms the front of the box. The forearms form the sides of the box. Maintaining this set up, rotate.

Sprint forward stroke

ⓘ **Note:** also referred to as a *high stroke angle*.

Perform by leaning slightly forward and driving the stroke from your torso. Increase the paddle shaft angle so that the upper hand is about forehead height. Increase stroke cadence and degree of torso rotation.

Leg-drive (aka 'walk-the-boat') is when on each stroke the force from the torso rotation is transferred through the legs, to push against the boats foot pegs in a 'walking' manner. For example, during the catch phase, when the paddle is planted, the leg on the opposite side to the planted blade, allows the torso (pelvis to shoulder) to rotate forward on the catch side. During the power phase, the leg on the stroke side straightens (i.e. tensions), while the other leg bends at the knee and lifts upwards. This allows the force of the torso rotation to be maximised by being delivered through the foot rests into the kayak.

Back Strokes

Back stroke

This is not the forward stroke performed backwards. To perform, the paddle shaft is parallel with the kayak's longitudinal axis and you use the back face of the blade. The stroke starts behind the cockpit and moves along kayak's side, to exit in line with your feet. Rotate your torso so that it is parallel to the paddle shaft, which is parallel with the hull. You will be looking aft to watch your paddle placement. With the driving blades back face in the water, push downwards and forwards. As the aft driving hand lowers, the forward hand raises. The blade moves parallel and in an arc to the kayak. Rotate (unwind) to drive the stroke forward along the side of the hull, until the exit point. The full effect of the torso rotation will not occur until the shaft has moved to around 45 degrees of arc. While continuing to unwind your torso, the driving hand maintains its downward and forward motion. At the same time, the upper (non-driving) hand pulls the shaft backward, upwards and parallel to the hull and finishes in the vertical position. The blade exits the water to the side and neatly sets up for the next stroke. On every second to third rotation, look behind to where you are going.

Emergency Stop

The 'emergency stop' consists of three powerful, alternating sides (e.g. left, right, left), backstrokes in quick cadence (in succession).

Turning Strokes

Sweep Strokes

Sweep strokes are used to turn the kayak. They can be sequenced with forward and reverse strokes to provide directional stability. The effectiveness of sweep strokes is governed by leverage and power. For the greatest leverage the blade must describe a wide arc, while power must come from body twist (Australian Canoeing, n.d.).

Forward sweep stroke

Use the paddle's power face and rotating forward to start the stroke at foot area, lean out towards the stroke (i.e. 'J-lean' by raising the opposite knee to the stroke side). The raised knee is on the side of the desired direction of turn (i.e. turn to starboard (right) raise right knee). You will be leaning away from your desired direction of turn. The purpose is to decrease the waterline length on the opposite side of the boat, and allow it to turn quicker in that direction.

Push the paddle into the water adjacent to your foot area; and lean into the paddle. Keep the shaft low and parallel to your belly. Start to rotate from the torso and sweep the paddle out in a wide arc to the back of the boat. Remember to watch the paddle blade throughout the stroke. Maintain body rotation, with the blade just under the surface of the water, until you are looking at the back of your boat.

If the power phase of the stroke is considered to be in three parts: first, middle and last, then the first and last parts are the most effective for turning. The middle part tends to propel the kayak forward. During the last third of the stroke, there is a lot of power left from the unwinding torso.

Remove the blade from the water while maintaining the boat lean with the raised knee. Using the back face of the blade, skim it across the surface of the water until you are forward near your foot area. Set up on same side and repeat.

Skimming the blade over the water provides support and allows a quick brace manoeuvre to be executed if necessary to prevent capsize.

Reverse sweep stroke

Basically the same as the forward sweep stroke but in reverse. It makes the boat's bow swing towards the stroke side. Perform by using the back face of the blade and rotate the torso, so that you are looking abaft (i.e. the back of the kayak). With the shaft being parallel to the boats centre line and starting towards the back of the boat lean into the paddle and push away from the stern. Sweep forward in an arc, towards the bow.

Adjust the blade angle for support on exit and reset. Reset by skimming the blade over the water to the start position. Skimming the blade across the water provides support and allows a quick brace manoeuvre to be executed, if necessary, to prevent capsize.

To turn the kayak quickly and in a small turning circle use a combination of forward and reverse sweep strokes.

Draw Strokes

Draw strokes are used to move a kayak sideways. When performing a draw stroke, the kayak moves towards the side the strokes are performed on. Look towards where you desire to end up. Draw strokes can be described as:

Draw stroke

Sculling draw stroke

Static draw stroke

Static bow stroke.

Draw stroke

The draw stroke (aka *slalom draw stroke*) is a series of small extensions not massive reaches (Australian Canoeing, n.d.). Rotate the torso towards the side the stroke is going to be performed on for the draw. Maintain a vertical paddle shaft. With the upper hand fixed level with the forehead and with a loose grip. If you can read your watch your upper hand is in the right position (Australian Canoeing, n.d.). The lower hand is the control hand with the lower arm extending out in front of the body. Extend the blade a small distance out and plant it with the power face towards the boat. The lower hand draws the blade towards the hull. Attempt to keep both hands over the outside edge of the boat and pull the boat towards the planted blade. Keep the boat level by not leaning out towards the blade. Stop pulling before the blade reaches the hull. While the blade is still in the water, reset by turning the blade perpendicular (i.e. 90 degrees) to the boat. With the power face facing aft, push the blade out perpendicular from boat to the start point, or by pulling the blade out of the water and replanting, to the repeat manoeuvre. To minimise water piling up on the side of direction of movement, lean the boat slightly in the opposite direction to allow water to pass under the hull.

Sculling draw stroke

Unlike the 'slalom' draw stroke described above, the blade after the power phase does not exit the water. Rotate the torso towards the direction of travel. Lower the upper hand to around chin level (Australian Canoeing, n.d.). Never reach above your head. Keep the upper arm bent. Keep the control hand elbow bent and near your torso, and in front of the shoulders. Use torso rotation to drive the paddle

Use the blade's power face with the leading edge turned slightly outwards. Plant the blade out from the side and work back towards the boat, in a wave motion (e.g. back and forth, 'figure-8'). By dropping the elbow, it can quickly be a sculling brace. If the bow is swinging out, correct by moving the stroke slightly aft of the cockpit. If the stern is swings out, move the stroke slightly forward of cockpit.

Static draw stroke

The static draw stroke uses the boat's forward momentum to draw it sideways. Keep torso, hands and paddle shaft positions the same, as for the draw stroke. Keep control hand elbow near your torso. Plant the blade at an angle and perpendicular to the side of the boat, to allow forward momentum to draw boat sideways.

Static bow stroke

The static bow stroke (aka bow draw) is used to guide the bow sideways while moving forward. It allows the bow to swing quickly on the stroke side. A similar process to the static draw stroke, but the paddle is positioned forward at foot area of boat. The blade is planted at an angle to the boat into the water. Boat lean away from stroke side will allow rapid response.

Ruddering Strokes

Ruddering strokes are used to turn a kayak when the kayak is being propelled by wind and/ or waves. To be able to lean into the wave when surfing, the ruddering stroke is performed on the wave side. During this stroke do not reach backwards as this compromises the shoulder. Leaning backwards can also compromise the lower back.

Stern Rudder Strokes

Two types of stern rudder stoke are the:

Stern draw

Stern pry

Stern draw

The stern draw is a ruddering stroke whereby the paddle's blade is used as a rudder. This type of stroke is used when surfing and/or sailing a kayak. To perform place the blade's power face *towards* (i.e. facing) the hull, as it is used to *pull* against the water. The bow moves the *opposite* way from the side of stroke placement. Rotate the torso towards the side of stroke placement. Keep elbows low and close to your torso, to ensure the paddle is low and close to the hull. Pull the power face towards the hull. There will be quite a bit of resistance acting on the blade and therefore on your arms.

Stern pry

The stern pry is another ruddering stroke; like the stern draw, the power face is placed towards (i.e. facing) the hull, but the blades back-face is used to *push* against the water. The bow moves *towards* the side of the stroke placement. As with the stern draw, rotate the torso. The blade is fully submerged and the paddle shaft is parallel to the hull. Keep elbows low and close to torso; so the paddle is low and close to the hull.

Support Strokes

Braces

Braces are performed to prevent capsize. Even though the paddle is used, the righting force comes from the hips and the 'hip flick'. Remember to keep your head down on the side of the brace until the manoeuvre is completed. People talk about the 'bomb proof roll', but I think people should develop the 'bomb proof brace' to prevent capsizing. I encourage people to watch Olympic standard slalom paddlers to reinforce this point. Two terms associated with braces and bracing are the *low brace* and the *high brace*. The terms have come to refer to which of the two faces of the paddle's blade are used to brace the paddler against the water.

Practice these two braces in shallow flat water by sitting in a stable position. Next lean over to one side into an unstable position. Use the brace and hip flick to bring yourself back up to a stable position. If you have someone to practice with, go to deeper water where they can stand at the bow and attempt to roll you over, while you resist the destabilising force with a brace manoeuvre. Having someone with you is also beneficial, as they can critique you on your efforts, especially when it comes to keeping your head down until the manoeuvre is complete.

✱ **Caution:** Braces can be performed as either low or high, but you must be aware that with the high brace there is the possibility of shoulder dislocation, if performed incorrectly, or in the wrong situation.

Low brace

The low brace is a pushing down motion using the bracing blade's back face against the water for support. It is performed while holding your paddle in the correct paddling position. The shaft is brought low (near your waist) and as near to horizontal, as possible, to the water. To achieve this, the paddle shaft is brought down below the elbows, while rolling the knuckles downwards, to align the back face of the bracing blade, parallel to the water. The flatter the bracing blade is when pushing against the water, the greater will be the support developed.

High brace

The high brace is a pulling down motion using the bracing blade's power face against the water for support. While holding your paddle in the correct paddling position, the shaft is repositioned up above the elbows and inline with the top of your chest and shoulders and parallel to the oncoming water. Your elbows will need to be kept close to your torso and level with your waist. Your wrists will be facing forwards (i.e. pronated). Your knuckles will need to be rolled upwards, to bring the blade's power face parallel to the water.

The issue with the high brace is the likely possibility the elbow will move up and away from the torso and past shoulder height level. This situation can lead to a shoulder dislocation. The high brace is often used when you are broached by a high wave (e.g. surf). To prevent being pushed over and capsized by the wave, you simultaneously lean and 'hip flick' into the wave while planting the bracing blade's power face down on to the wave. Depending upon the wave size, there can be a tremendous amount of force trying to pull the arm and elbow up away from the torso and above the shoulder. Once you think that the wave has let you go and if the kayak responds, you can move into a stern ruddering stroke or the catch phase of a forward stroke. Some instructors do not teach the high brace for concern that it may lead to an injury. Many instructors do not recommend using the high brace for the same reason.

Slap brace

The slap brace (aka low support stroke, low support) is your basic and most fundamental bracing manoeuvre; and is performed as a quick, precise action. When paddling in wind and seas, or in the surf, the slap brace is used in combination with whatever main stroke (e.g. forward stroke) you are using at the time to prevent capsize. To practice, go into the shallows, so if you topple right over, you can push off with your paddle from the bottom. Topple the kayak to one side, as though you are going to capsize. Quickly slap the blade (either high or low) against the water (to prevent capsize). Ensure your head is down towards the shoulder closest to the water. Use your lower body to 'hip flick' the hull back upright, while keeping your head on your shoulder (on the side of topple) until stable on the surface.

Sculling brace

The sculling brace is a slower and different motion to the slap brace. The paddle's movement is in an elongated 'figure-8', to the side of the hull on the water's surface. To practice go into the shallows and lean the boat to one side and over-centre. Perform slow and controlled elongated 'figure-8' movements. Position the paddle just under the water's surface and perpendicular to the hull and cockpit.

Ensure the blade's leading edge is lifted up during the entire stroke (complete 'figure-8'). The blade's leading edge will alternate from edge to edge (i.e. forward, aft, forward etc.) as the paddle completes 'figure-8' motions. Cover around one metre (2-3 feet) between forward and aft movements, of the 'figure 8' sculling motion. Work the blade gradually towards the hull. Remember knee position and hip flick to right the kayak.

Low brace turns

Low brace turns are made when the boat is moving forward. It is a way to make a sharp turn and then stopping (e.g. when carving off a wave). It also uses both techniques of the low brace coupled with the reverse sweep stroke. To perform, lean into a turn via the reverse sweep stroke. Adopt the low brace position. Continue movement of reverse sweep forward from the stern to bow. The bow will swing towards the direction on which the stroke was placed (i.e. stroke placed on right side the bow moves to the right).

Rafting-up

Rafting-up is a common and frequent manoeuvre in kayaking and may be done for any number of reasons. Often to raft-up, the paddlers need to perform a draw stroke to bring the kayaks together. Once together, the paddlers can hold on to each other's kayaks or have someone hold theirs while they have their hands free.

SELF-RESCUE

The term 'rescue' here refers to the action of righting, empting and or returning a paddler into a kayak. Self-rescue is about you alone, righting a capsized kayak without wet exiting and or re-entering after a wet exit. The types of self-rescues discussed here are the:

Wet exit

Re-enter and roll

Cowboy

Paddle float rescue

Eskimo roll.

With any of the rescue techniques there are variations in technique or techniques. The end aim is to be back in the boat and underway.

Wet-exit

Wet-exit is the most fundamental self-rescue technique for a novice paddler. Points to consider are:

Remember, when fitting your skirt, ensure the release strap is outside of the cockpit and not trapped between the coaming and skirt's bungee (elastic) rand.

If the skirt release strap is trapped under the skirt, with your fingers feel forward and under the coaming for the skirts elastic. Force your fingers between the elastic and coaming and peel the skirt off.

Practice wet-exits in a controlled environment.

When wet exiting, release the skirt from the coaming and roll downwards and forward (like a half summersault under water) to extricate your legs.

Re-enter and roll

Re-enter and roll is another basic self-rescue skill, performed after a wet exit. In rough seas and windy conditions, it is the most efficient way to get back into a capsized kayak. It involves re-entering the cockpit while the kayak is upside down then performing an Eskimo roll. If you have the fitness and skills, also if the conditions and situation allow, you can refit the skirt while under water.

For stability and the conservation of energy, it can be performed with a paddle float. Ensure the paddle float has a tether on it as unfortunate people have had them blown away by the wind. You may only need to inflate one side (back face of paddle), so that once on the surface, if you are near hazards (e.g. rocks), you can manoeuvre out of the way before you empty the boat of water and reset your skirt.

Cowboy

To 'cowboy' back into your kayak, you first right the boat. Swim/haul yourself up on to the aft deck, using the deck-lines for assistance. Move forwards, parallel with the kayak's centreline, on your stomach. When your pelvis is positioned over the cockpit entrance, sit up. With your buttocks over the cockpit and your legs dangling in the water, drop your buttock into the cockpit and reinsert your legs. Obviously, it has its limitations on when it can be used, but there are paddlers who prefer this method, even in the surf zone.

Paddle-float rescue

Paddle float rescue is basically a 'cowboy' using the paddle float and paddle as an out-rigger. The paddle shaft can be: lashed to the deck, inserted in to purpose made retainers or held down on to the aft deck and cockpit combing. Note this last method in choppy conditions is difficult and can result in injury to the fingers.

Eskimo roll

① **Note:** The ESKIMO ROLL I think cannot be taught by a book, as for the majority of people it is disorientating being upside down and theory seems to just go out the window. However, it does help to sit down and think about the process and salient points (i.e. keep your head down on your shoulder, watch the blade, and hip flick). There are plenty of good books out there and DVDs that explain the different versions of the Eskimo Roll. Find an instructor and go to a pool or a quiet bit of water and practice there. 'It is better felt than telt.'

The Eskimo roll is the most efficient method of self-rescue, with its many variations in technique. It is well worth learning and developing a technique that works for you in rough water and windy conditions that you can perform on both sides (left and right).

On-side and off-side are terms associated with rolling. On-side roll refers to being able to perform a roll on your preferred side. Off-side roll refers to performing a roll on your non-preferred and or weaker side.

GROUP RESCUES

① **Note: Points to consider and remember:**

—The best rescue technique is the one that works in the situation you are in. Therefore, it is worthwhile to have a variety of techniques available to choose from.

—The purpose of the rescue is to be effective, not *pedantic*, about procedure. Use your nous.

—The first priority on capsize is the person. Ensure they are o.k. (they have wet-exited and are calm and not panicking).

—If they are in moving water (or in a surf zone) make sure they are not between the kayak and shore or hazards.

—During the rescue, communicate with each other.

—If you are the group leader and you can delegate the rescuer role; then do so. Your primary responsibility is to the welfare and control of the group. Avoid the *hero mentality*.

—Practice rescues often in windy and choppy sea conditions; and in a controlled environment (e.g. on-shore wind).

✱ **Caution:** Be aware of the effects of wind chill, cold water shock and hypothermia on a person who has been capsized.

Group rescues consist of:

Assisted re-entry methods

Assisted righting methods.

Assisted Re-entry Methods

Assistant re-entry methods discussed here consist of:

The X-rescue

The T-rescue

Flip and pump

Re-enter and pump

The wedge rescue.

The X-rescue and T-rescue

The X-rescue and T-recue are methods of empting a capsized kayak's cockpit of water, prior to the rescuee being assisted to re-enter the cockpit. The difference between the two terms X and T is the position of the capsized kayak across the deck of the rescuer's kayak, forming either an X or a T shape.

From a rescuee's perspective, the action to take after capsizing and wet exiting is to leave the capsized kayak upside down and swim to the stern and grasp the toggle. The rescuee waits for the rescuer's verbal directions. The rescuer positions their kayak at the bow and perpendicular to the capsized kayak and stows their paddle on the foredeck under the deck line or similar arrangement. If the rescuer drops their tethered paddle into the water, in certain conditions, it will get washed under their kayaks hull and may interfere with the rescue.

① **Note:** Be careful not to damage your spray skirt by dragging a kayak across it. However, if the situation dictates the rescue is the primary concern.

The rescuer grasps the toggle and the bow deck lines, and prepares to haul the up-turned kayak, up and across, their foredeck (in the majority of cases the spray skirt). Be aware that the kayak may be heavy and slippery. The rescuer verbally directs the rescuee to push down on the upturned kayaks stern. At the same time the rescuer hauls up and across their fore deck the bow of the kayak.

With the assistance of the rescuee, the kayak is seesawed up and down to empty it of water. You do not need to get rid of every last drop of water. When emptied of water, the kayak is quickly flicked around to its upright position. During the flick around to right the kayak, avoid scooping water into the cockpit. After the rescuee's kayak is off the rescuers foredeck, it is manoeuvred beside the rescue kayak (edge to edge) with its bow facing the rescue kayak's stern (bow to stern).

☀ Caution: Be careful of fingers being crunched between the two kayaks.

The rescuer leans hard over (edges their kayak) and firmly grasps the righted kayak's foredeck lines on both sides. The peak of the righted kayaks deck is near and or under the rescuer's armpit. Depending upon the conditions, the rescuee either:

Positions themselves between the two kayaks. Then grasping the deck and or deck lines of both boats, leans backwards and lifts their legs up and into their kayak's cockpit. Staying low and laying between the two kayaks, they then continue to feed themselves back into their cockpit.

Alternatively, if you are in a sea and/or swell and a rescuee tries to get between the two boats, their head can be cracked open like a coconut, with the two boats bouncing around. In this situation, the rescuee can haul themselves up over the deck from the outside. With their chest on the back deck, they insert their legs into the cockpit and twist back around to face the correct way.

After the spray skirt is refitted and when the rescuee has their paddle in their hands and is ready, the rescuer releases their kayak.

Flip and pump

The flip and pump method is very similar to the X-rescue with the exception that the capsized kayak is righted and the hands free electric bilge pump is turned on. The rescuee is assisted back into the cockpit and if required can paddle away from a hazard before refitting their spray skirt.

① Note: This is why people talk about the benefits of minimum volume cockpits; as such a cockpit can be effectively paddled some distance and even through breaking waves.

Re-enter and pump

A variation to the flip and pump method is the re-enter and pump. This involves being assisted to re-enter a flooded cockpit as described before. While the rescuer still has hold of the rescuee's kayak, the cockpit is manually emptied of water using a hand pump, bailer and or sponge. If fitted and operational, the bailing process can be complemented with the electric bilge pump.

Wedge rescue

This rescue method works with boats having minimum volume cockpits. After wet exiting, the rescuee flips their kayak upright. The rescuer paddles in at an acute angle (~45°–60°) (i.e. not perpendicular). With the assistance of the rescuee, the bow of the flooded kayak is passed to the rescuer and slid up on to their foredeck.

① Note: The kayak will be heavy and slippery.

With (or without) the assistance of the rescuee, the kayak is rolled on to its edge and drained of water. If you are in swell and sea conditions, gain assistance from the waves by timing the heaving up of the bow with the wave action. The rescuer then assists the rescuee to re-enter the kayak.

Assisted Righting Methods

These methods are useful if the capsized kayaker has the presence of mind not to wet exit and a rescuer is close by. Assisted righting methods discussed here are:

Eskimo rescue

Re-entry Eskimo rescue

Scoop rescue

Hand-of-God rescue.

Eskimo rescue

The *Eskimo rescue* is also known as the *Buddy rescue*. With the capsized kayaker still inside the cockpit, they tuck themselves forward (chest towards the deck) and raising their arms around the hull bang against it to gain attention (at least three times). They then start moving their arms backwards and forwards along the hull waiting for the bow of the rescuer's kayak to come into gentle contact with their hull.

The rescuer who is nearby and alert, paddles over to the nearest end of the upturned kayak. Grasping the end of the kayak, they swing their bow around to the waiting arms of the rescuee.

ⓘ **Note**: *there are other versions of this, but this is the preferred method, as it minimizes the possibility hitting limbs and appendages between hulls.*

If the sea conditions allow, the rescuer comes in perpendicular to the capsized kayak's cockpit. Upon feeling the bow of the rescuer's kayak, the rescuee grasps hold of it and proceeds to roll back to the surface.

Alternatively, the rescuer comes in along parallel to the upturned kayak, and leaving enough space for the rescuee to roll up, rests their paddle over their deck and the hull of the capsized kayak. The rescuer then guides the rescuee's hands to the paddle shaft. The rescuee grasps the paddle shaft and rolls up; or at least gets some air before hip-flicking backup.

Re-entry Eskimo rescue

ⓘ **Note**: *I tend to think of this method as an assisted re-enter-and-roll using the bow of the assisting kayak.*

If the rescuee wet exits while waiting to be rescued, as the rescuers bow approaches, they set their kayak on its edge and insert their legs into the cockpit. With the rescue kayak standing by, the rescuee goes under as they seat themself into their cockpit. The rescuer moves their bow within reach of the rescuee who then grabs it to assist them to roll back up. They then raft up and empty the cockpit of water and reorganise themselves to continue on paddling.

Scoop rescue

This is a variation of the re-entry Eskimo rescue. It is useful if the rescuee is incapacitated and needs to be reinserted into their kayak. With the rescuee in the water, the rescuer paddles alongside the rescuee's kayak. The rescuee's kayak is then turned on its side with the cockpit facing outwards away from the rescuer's kayak. The cockpit is flooded, allowing the kayak to sink down enough to enable the rescuee to slide back into the cockpit. Depending upon their condition, they may need to be manually assisted back into their cockpit. If there are other paddlers, one can be used as a counterweight, on the other side of the rescuer's kayak.

Once the rescuee is inside the cockpit the rescuer pulls them and their kayak around thereby 'scooping' them up. This is achieved by the rescuer grasping the rescuee's cockpit coaming with one hand and the rescuee with the other. If the rescuee is capable, they can assist in the scooping motion. If they are not capable of assisting, keep their airway open and unobstructed and their torso as close as possible to the back deck. You will need the assistance of another paddler to manage the rescuee if they are totally incapacitated.

The 'Hand-of-God' rescue

The Hand-of-God-rescue is performed when a paddler is entrapped in their cockpit; or is incapacitated upside down, but still in the cockpit. If they are conscious, they will more likely than not be panicking, so act quickly.

The first step is to get the rescuee's airway to the surface. The rescuer, paddles alongside the upturned kayak adjacent to their cockpit. They then lean and reach over the hull and grasp the cockpit coaming. They then start to rotate (it requires some force) the kayak around. You may need both hands to do this; and by keeping a downward pressure through your forearms on the hull you can stabilise yourself against their boat. Once you can get a hand on to the rescuee, keep rotating them around until their airway is clear of the water. Their kayak, at this point, is still on its side with the rescuer leaning against the hull and over the side of the boat. If the rescuee is conscious, talk to them.

The next step is to right the kayak. Manoeuvre the rescuee either forward over the foredeck or aft over the rear deck; the point being to keep their mass as close to their kayak as possible. With one hand on the rescuee and one on the cockpit coaming, push the kayak down at the same time pull it around with the rescuee. With both the kayak and rescuee on the surface, take the appropriate action for the situation you are in.

Re-entering a capsized double kayak

After wet exiting, together flip the kayak upright. With one paddler on the port side and the other on the starboard side, at their respective cockpits, decide who is going to re-enter first. The kayaker who is going to re-enter last will then hold on to the coaming of their cockpit and act as a counter-weight. The other paddler then swims up on to the aft deck behind their cockpit and then feeds their legs into the cockpit, then twists around and sits down. Once in position, the re-entered kayaker performs a sculling brace on the side the second person is going to re-enter the cockpit from. Paddle floats can also be use as an outrigger by either the first or second person.

If a person cannot swim up on to the aft deck, rig up a sling as a stirrup. The stirrup can be attached from either inside the cockpit, or from the paddle shaft of a lashed paddle, on the deck. This is where experimentation before going on a trip is necessary to work out what is required and what does and does not work for you.

TOWING

It is a distinct possibility that a fellow kayaker will become incapacitated by injury, illness or fatigue and will require assistance in the form of a tow. The Seamanship chapter talks about towlines as an item of equipment. When performing a tow, it is important all members are aware of their role. Effective group management and communication are need during this time.

The two common types of tow formations are the in-line tow and the V-tow (double-tow). The inline tow is when the kayaks are hooked up in a line, with the towee being the last boat of the chain. The V-tow is when two tow kayaks that are connected to the towee, paddle adjacent to each other, forming a 'V' shape with the towline. The tow method employed will, depend upon several factors like: the number of kayakers in the group, the health of the towee, the environmental conditions and experience in the group.

The number of kayakers in the group will generally determine what tow method is employed (in-line or V-tow). If possible, have a controller (aka 'point paddler') sit off to the side of the tow and rotate towers and keep control of the tow.

Hooking up the tow line(s) is achieved by connecting the *carbine hook(s)* to the bow deck line of the towee's kayak and the tow point of the tow kayak(s). If you have a central tow point behind the cockpit, be aware that if you are carrying a spare paddle on the aft deck, the towline can get caught on it. On a V-tow, if you have side tow points, connect up so the towline does not cross over the aft deck but passes along the side nearest to the other tow-kayak.

Depending upon the ailment afflicting the towee, they may need a supporter to hold on to them and prevent them from capsizing. While being towed, the towee and supporter, in certain conditions will become cold. Before towing, ensure they are protected from the wind and seas. Even with kags on, the towee can become quite cold. In an emergency, the plastic poncho, or large rubbish bag (with head and armholes) can be used as a windbreak over the towee and supporter. Also, ensure the towee's head is covered with a beanie or hat of some sort.

Kayaks when being towed can wander. Also be aware that a towee who is quite ill and being supported by a fellow kayaker, may be inadvertently pushing against one foot-peg and hence rudder pedal, thereby creating drag and causing the kayak to deviate.

DECK CARRIES

On odd occasions, a kayaker has come across a swimmer in need of assistance to get ashore. One method is to direct the swimmer to lie down on their stomach along the aft deck with their head facing forwards.

LAUNCHING AND LANDING TECHNIQUES

Launching and landing techniques are covered in the Real Life Paddling and Leadership chapter.

CHAPTER 5 REAL LIFE PADDLING AND LEADERSHIP

"Adapt or perish, now as ever, is nature's inexorable imperative."

H. G. Wells

① **Note:** These comments are only pointers as when paddling in wind, seas and swell you can have several conditions acting in different directions and or combining. Therefore, your paddling becomes a selection of, and adaption of, your previously learnt and practiced skills, to that situation, at that moment in time.

The majority of your paddling will be forwards (I hope!). To maintain your heading you will use a combination of forward stroke and sweep strokes. After a while, you will develop the ability to anticipate what stroke is required to control your kayak. Paddling is about developing a feel for applying the right stroke, at the right time, with the right amount of force, and at the right distance from the boat.

① **Note:** In real life paddling, think of your paddle as a tool that you can articulate and manoeuvre into a position that will assist you in getting the job done.

You can manoeuvre your hands along the paddle shaft from side to side. For example: you can be performing a forward stroke and the wind starts to turn your kayak off your desired track. By extending the paddle shaft further to one side (so that the shafts lengthwise centre is off-centre to your body) you can perform a partial sweep stroke with boat lean to bring your bow back on track.

When turning, to decrease the size of the turn circle (radius), use a combination of forward sweep stroke with body lean and reverse sweep stroke.

When paddling in swell, or in surf, you will eventually be required to reverse paddle to either slow down to minimise *pearling*, or to get out of the surf impact zone. Reverse paddling in the surf zone is quicker than trying to turn a 5.2 metre plus kayak around.

To avoid the repetitive pounding caused by choppy water, when paddling into seas approaching at or near the bow, present the bow slightly off (~10°) to the oncoming wave and let it roll under the kayak to the side of the bow. On the next wave or after the set has passed, you can correct to come back on course.

When in seas and swell, turn your kayak on the crest of a wave. When in a beam sea, lean into the wave, as it comes at and under you. Your forward stroke then becomes a brace stroke on the side of the approaching wave. You may then need to perform a sweep stoke to counteract the sterns moving off-track, caused by the movement of water.

In swells, you will find that in a trough, it feels as though you are paddling in treacle (slow hard going). Throughout, keep your paddle strokes steady to maintain your momentum, as you go up the consecutive wave face, then quickly down the back of the wave into the next trough. On occasions when going back down into the trough you may need to put in some back paddle strokes.

ON WATER NAVIGATION

① **Note:** There are a multitude of books dealing with navigation. The aim here is to use the KISS (keep it simple stupid) principle.

Planning

The message here is simple: *Fail to plan, plan to fail.* Take the time to sit down and plan your trip in the area you intend to go to and for the time of year. Never assume anything, but think through what you intend to do and about the *what ifs?*

Navigation Aids

① **Note:** Lamination and zip-loc bags tend to fail and let water in.

Kayakers carry both charts and topographical maps. To waterproof them, put the relevant charts/maps in a waterproof case, zip-lock bags or laminate them. Carrying a grease pencil to write on the plastic surface covering your chart/map is a good idea.

A *deck compass* as the name implies, is mounted on the kayak's front deck. When packing your kayak, using a deck bag or putting items inside the cockpit under the deck, be aware of ferrous items and electronic devices causing compass deviation 'error'.

① **Note**: Equipment maintenance. Periodically, check your deck compass for deviation.

It is useful to carry a hand held pocket compass as a back up to your deck compass because, in some conditions, you may not be able to see your deck compass clearly, or at all, should you lose the lighting source at night. It is also more accurate when 'fixing by cross bearings' your position.

Base plate compasses can replace the need to carry a 'Portland plotter', dividers and ruler; as you can plot a course on your chart in the same manner as you would on a map.

When paddling, your compass can fluctuate five degrees (5°) around your heading on a pleasant day, let alone when you are in chop and swell. If you were to continually look at your compass for direction you may experience vertigo and seasickness. Not notice your drift through currents and or seas and or end up 'chasing the compass', which may lead to mental fatigue.

A compass orientates you in the right direction, after that go 'map to ground'. This refers to the use of a map/chart and the identification of charted features. Features can be:

Geographical (i.e. landmarks e.g. coast line, hills, bluffs, points and or capes)

Man made (i.e. navigational marks, buildings, light sources).

① **Note**: With manmade features, they can cease to exist or can be moved.

Temporary features may be a seamark, a rock, which cover and uncover, reef breaks that only work in certain conditions and reefs. These types of features are usually shown on a chart, but may be misidentified.

① **Note**: Have your compass bearings and waypoints card readily available, as you may paddle into heavy rain and or fog and need to navigate by dead reckoning!

Three terms associated with compass use and navigation are: course, heading and bearing. Course is the actual directions steered or—intended to be steered—by a vessel through the water in reference to a meridian. Course is where your destination is, even if temporarily (i.e. a waypoint). Heading is the direction the bow of your kayak is pointing (i.e. where you are heading). Bearing is a direction to some feature. At times all three can be in agreement (i.e. all in the same direction).

When paddling in fog, you may experience vertigo and/or become disorientated. Believe your compass! Also preplanning your trip and writing down your compass headings and back bearings is important.

Hand-held GPS units have become commonplace items for many kayakers, making navigating quite easy. However, they should not be relied upon solely while navigating unfamiliar waters. GPS units are susceptible to operator error from ignorance or misunderstanding about their equipment. A common failure mode is low battery power. Reasons for battery failure can include choosing poor quality batteries, longer than expected paddling time or not knowing the battery life expectancy (time) of installed batteries. Replacing batteries whilst at sea introduces the possibility of water ingress into the battery compartment, which may lead to the unit failing.

POINTS AND OBSERVATIONS FOR TIDAL STREAMS

① **Note**: for some, paddling in turbulence is a sport and a source of fun, yet to others it may be unnerving.

If paddling against current or near tidal features with overfalls, eddies and tidal races, do so at the beginning or end of the tide cycle, when the stream is minimal.

Paddle closer to shore and on the inside of corners where flow is minimised and there are possible back eddies.

To get tidal assistance, paddle away from shore or the inside of corners. Water flows faster in deeper areas, when forced around headlands or through channels creating turbulence.

When making a small crossing of less than three kilometres (< 3 km) in an area with strong tidal streams, plan to use the slack period.

You will need to factor in variations in the slack period times like:

Slack water period (e.g. 20 to 30 minutes)

Speed of the slowest paddler

Group experience

Waiting around time to avoid collisions with shipping

Altered conditions.

References for tides and tidal streams are:

Marine weather and tides websites (e.g. BOM)

Nautical chart diamonds and corresponding tables

Sailing Directions; (Australian Pilot)

US Navy Sailing Directions.

WIND AND SEA KAYAKERS

ⓘ **Note:** The weather shore is not always protected from the wind.

Wind can either assist or hinder a sea kayaker. Some references have a table showing, the possible effect of head winds on a paddler and how much, it will reduce their speed by. All of the authors caution, that their tables are only a rough guide and or rule of thumb, since there are other factors at play, for both head and tail winds, such as: chop, swell, seas, paddler fitness and skills set. Another reference states, cross winds can reduce forward speed by two to three per cent. When this is worked out, the effect is negligible and even redundant, when factored in with the other factors at play.

When paddling into wind, keep your paddle shaft low and lean forwards maintaining good torso rotation. At winds of twenty knots and above, forward progress is hard going; at thirty knots (steady state) and above, it is very hard going and you really do not want to be out there. The wind tries to pull the paddle out of your hands and causes the exposed blade to vibrate.

In cross winds, generally a kayak will tend to turn its bow into the wind; see *weathercocking*. A kayak that is loaded too heavily, in the bow, will also tend to weathercock. If the bow tends to turn away from the wind's direction, it is called *lee cocking*. To correct for the cocking action, lean into the wind and deploy the skeg or rudder if fitted. Extend your paddle further out into the weatherside (side the wind is coming from) and perform sweep strokes or, put more force into the weatherside stroke. Do not forget body lean, as this greatly helps the kayak to turn quicker. In certain beam sea conditions, be aware and time your strokes with the passage of a wave beneath you. If your timing is out, you may find that your stroke becomes a swipe through the air, causing a momentary imbalance in stability, which may lead to capsize.

Tail winds and even aft quartering winds are generally quite useful and fun, as they assist you and you can catch rides on the wavelets. Be aware that with following seas and or quartering seas, the boat may broach (swing out at the stern and put you side onto the wave). You will need to be ready to respond quickly (instinctively) with a slap brace stroke, to prevent capsize. In these types of situations, you will find yourself using a combination of strokes as you paddle your course; hence the need to practise the different types of strokes and braces beforehand.

Topographical winds and downslope winds

When paddling along the coast near mountains, hills, valleys and cliffs, be aware that these features can cause topographical winds and downslope winds. These winds may be mesoscale or microscale in size, but the suddenness and effects of gusts coming offshore can knock a paddler over. Eddies created by cliffs can produce a flow reversal pattern, with strong gust travelling in the opposite direction to the prevailing wind.

The lee side of cliffs and islands may not provide shelter from strong winds, as large eddies of rotating turbulent wind are created by the feature's peak. Likewise, the suddenness of a cliffs edge can create a turbulent, strong downdraft gust of wind.

ESTIMATING WAVE HEIGHTS

This is the primer for great stories and where legends are born and or discredited. The problem with estimating surf height from the back is due to variables in bathymetric contours, seabed gradient, reefs, bombies, tidal effects and cross currents on shoaling, wave periods and refraction. With these other variables, some references say the face of the waves (leeward side) can range from 1.5 to 5 times the height at the rear (windward side). Add in also the human factors, then wave estimation or should I say wave height guessing is an art that is refined with practice.

Table 5-1 Estimating (guessing) wave heights	
Standing surfer	**Approximate wave height**
Waist high wave	≈ 1 m face
High as surfer	≈ 1.5 m face
Little over surfer's head	≈ 2 m face
Stacking surfers on top of each other	Two ≈ 4 m face Three ≈ 6 m face

In Australia, wave, swell and surf height is estimated from behind the wave's crest to the following trough. This is despite the stated problems associated with this method. It is helpful if you can use a gauge to estimate the wave height (i.e. surfer on a board, length of a kayak, height of a kayaker in a kayak, height of another paddlers paddle at top of its arc etc.). Table 5-1, is a table of estimates using surfer's height. Estimating wave height without a gauge to assist often results in tall tales.

One method used to determine wave height, is to measure your eye height when seated in a kayak. For example a 1.86 metre, 100 kilogram paddler's eye height is around 0.79 metre (≈ 2ft 7in) when seated in his kayak. Since wave height, is often express in feet, an approximation of 2½ foot is used. If you can look over a wave beside you, know it is less than 2½ foot. A 2½ foot wave is actually a 1ft 8in (1.67ft) or say quite small (1½ft).

SEVERE WEATHER EVENTS

Severe weather events may be macroscale weather phenomenon or microscale phenomenon. They have the potential to risk life, cause damage and pose a risk to navigation at sea and along the coast. Types of weather phenomenon classed as mesoscale and microscale are: severe weather cyclones, thunderstorms, Southerly Buster, squall lines, katabatic winds, blizzards. Severe weather cyclones can be severe tropical cyclones, tropical cyclones, and extra-tropical cyclones like the Southern Ocean cyclones and East Coast cyclones.

Characteristics of life threatening weather are possible dark dense cloud development or cumulonimbus. Large swells and seas with associated surf. Lightening, down drafts, strong winds or greater, gusts and squalls, and rain.

These phenomena can impede, cease or reverse paddling progress. In conjunction with other phenomena like tidal streams and currents, and topographical features funnelling wind, they can create hazards like wind-on-water and pose a risk to life. Surf launches and landings can be dangerous and pose a risk of injury to the paddler and anyone in the way of the boat. Lightening strikes can kill or severely injure a paddler. The risk of capsize is greater and if self-rescue techniques fail there is the risk of drowning, hypothermia or being stranded at sea and unable to get back into the kayak. The use of communication equipment is very difficult when you are in rough water, let alone if you are trying to keep hold of your boat. There is the risk of losing the boat or paddle to the wind, waves and current. Separation from your boat may result in the loss of your safety equipment (e.g. signal flares and smoke, which may be in a storage compartment). Note you are a very tiny target to find in rough water with its white caps, possible rain and poor visibility. Group rescue techniques become more difficult in these conditions and maintaining control over the group is extremely difficult. Depending upon your ratio of experience paddlers to non-experienced paddlers, you may be managing multiple capsizes and rescues. Alternatively you might *harbour up* and be left to the mercy of the elements. Heavy rain or rain and strong winds reduce visibility and make it hard to find navigational marks. The wind can also cause you to drift off track, which may be compounded by the action of waves and current.

WEATHER AND CANOEING MISADVENTURES

It would be considered gross negligence (to put it politely) to lead a group of recreational paddlers into a situation whereby it becomes *'everyman for himself'*. Sea kayaker magazine often prints articles about sea kayakers and misadventure and are well worth the reading. The following are some recent events that resulted either in death, injury or near catastrophe.[1]

On October 16, 2008 the Herald Sun printed this article about a kayaker who went out into big seas and swell and was lost at sea. The paddler was respected for his local knowledge, paddling ability, health and fitness. The article reads:

THE family of missing kayaker David Scheen has all but given up hope of finding him alive after search parties endured a frustrating third day at sea. The experienced kayaker, 39, set off from Childers Cove, near Warrnambool, about 1pm on Monday and was reported missing five hours later when he failed to arrive at his Peterborough home. His mother, Robyn Scheen, said any hope the family held was fading with each passing hour.

"(We lose hope) as every hour goes past.

"We are realistic people," she said.

"It's extremely difficult. Not knowing is the hardest part.

"For us, it's a very unscripted outcome for one of David's training sessions, as he was always very professional in his attitude, training, safety and health."

Mr Scheen's partner, Margaret Hamilton, said she began to feel uneasy when he failed to show on Monday afternoon.

"When he didn't arrive, I thought he should really have been back by now," she said.

Mr Scheen's broken kayak and life vest were found near Childers Cove on Tuesday, but search parties have been unable to find any trace of the kayaker. Two witnesses have told police they saw Mr Scheen falling out of his kayak several times on Monday afternoon, as he battled wild conditions.

A GPS tracking device fitted to Mr Scheen's kayak has yet to be located. Mrs Scheen was shocked that her son, an experienced kayaker with a good knowledge of local surf conditions, could come to grief in familiar waters.

"Knowing David, he would have been prepared and checked out the water," she said.

"Before he did anything in the water, he would always go and check it out."

Police and emergency services volunteers yesterday expanded a land and air search, scouring the coast from Warrnambool to Peterborough. Sen-Sgt Paul Heargraves said treacherous conditions had prevented jet skis from entering the waters where Mr Scheen's belongings were located on Tuesday.

"We had two jet skis here searching and they couldn't enter the water safely. We haven't been able to get them in. It's just not safe," he said.

Sen-Sgt Heargraves said rescuers were not yet resigned to searching for a body.

"We're searching for David and that's what we've got to keep in mind," he said.

"You've got to face reality—time is moving past us and we're accepting that—but we have got to keep searching."

Lightening

Thunderstorms pose a hazard to any person caught out in the open. The following extract is from the Courier Mail, February 09, 2010, which reported the story of a 14-year-old male whom, while paddling a kayak had his fishing rod struck by lightning. The article reads: *The blast blew the metal paddle from Connor's hands, as well as splitting and setting fire to a fishing rod standing in the back of his kayak. While it paralysed his arms and caused momentary blindness, he suffered only minor burns. Connor said the drama unfolded just after 4 pm when he joined family and friends at the dam to retrieve a boat that had come adrift. While there had been rumbles of thunder and light rain, no one had noticed any lightning. "I put a fishing rod in the back standing in the air and I'd only paddled about 100m . . . There was a big bang and I blacked out," he said. "My body straightened out. I was sort of conscious. I knew what was happening but I couldn't see. It threw me 10m off the kayak. "When I hit the water and woke up and opened my eyes I thought I had just fallen out of the kayak." The craft was metres away, still intact, but with the fishing rod blasted in half and on fire. Connor's father Kris jumped in and swam towards him while his mother Joanne paddled out in another kayak. "My arms were all straightened and purple and cold but my legs were OK," Connor said.*

The BOM offers the following advice for lightening:

The distance (in kilometres) to a lightning flash may be estimated by dividing the time delay (in seconds) between the flash and the thunder by three.

If you hear thunder, find shelter urgently, especially if the time delay is less than 30 seconds.

Try to remain sheltered for at least 30 minutes after the last sound of thunder.

Seek shelter in a 'hard-top' (metal-bodied) vehicle or solid building but avoid small open structures or fabric tents.

Never shelter under small groups of (or single) trees.

If far from shelter, crouch (alone, feet together), preferably in a hollow. Remove metal objects from head/body. Do not lie down flat but avoid being the highest object in the vicinity.

If your hair stands on end or you hear 'buzzing' from nearby rocks, fences, et cetera, move immediately. At night, a blue glow may show if an object is about to be struck (St Elmo's fire).

Do not fly kites or model aeroplanes with control wires.

Do not handle fishing rods, umbrellas or golf clubs etc.

Stay away from metal poles, fences, clothes lines et cetera.

Do not ride horses, bicycles or travel in open vehicles.

If driving, slow down or park away from trees, power lines et cetera. Stay inside metal-bodied (hard top) vehicles or caravans but don't touch any metal sections.

If swimming, surfing et cetera., leave the water immediately.

If boating, go ashore to shelter as soon as possible.

Be sure the mast and stays of a sailing boat are adequately 'grounded' to the water.

Offshore winds

Offshore winds are deceptive in their strength as they knock down the sea state, and may give the illusion that there is little or no wind out on the water. However, wind speeds may be 50 per cent greater than that on the land. Narrow topographical features can funnel and increase the speed of winds on to the ocean. The Geelong Advertiser on April 6, 2006 printed an article about 16 secondary school year 9 students and four instructors being swept five kilometres out to sea from Torquay, Victoria, after the Bureau of Meteorology forecasted possible 35 knot offshore winds. The article reported by Daniel Breen reads:

GALE force winds swept 20 kayakers five kilometres out to sea, sparking a dramatic rescue off Torquay yesterday. Torquay Marine Rescue crew and local surf lifesavers needed a helicopter to help find the stranded kayakers near Cosy Corner about 12.30pm yesterday.

Rescue boat driver Marc Skelton said strong gusts, driving rain and hail and rising seas added to the difficulty of trying to find and return the lost group. "You couldn't see them. They were gone and the only way we could find them was with the helicopter hovering over the top of them with the light on," Mr Skelton.

Lifesaving officials from the School Surf League State Championships, which were running close to where the kayaks set off from, also provided invaluable assistance by accompanying the rescue boat in their rubber ducks. Mr Skelton said the group, made up of 16 Lara Secondary College students on a year 9 excursion and four instructors, were lucky the extra manpower was available. He said lives could have easily been lost if the extra resources were unavailable. "There were that many kids out there that we couldn't fit them all in the craft, so they were bloody lucky that the surf club was there with extra boats to pick the rest up. If we had to go back to pick an extra lot up after our first run, I don't know what would have happened," he said.

Earlier in the day the group entered the water near Torquay Surf Lifesaving Club as part of a session with West Coast Surf School. Their entry into the water about 11.30am occurred despite a Severe Weather Warning for the region from the Bureau of Meteorology about 10am. Mr Skelton said the conditions were not only unsuitable for kayaking, but also made life extremely hard for the rescuers. "It was a situation that could have been really nasty. The wind was so strong that the jet skis could hardly get in and when the big front came in about 12.30pm you couldn't even see," he said. "Even in the boat it took about 30 minutes to get them in. We were travelling at about three knots . . . . But while the kayakers were all safe their kayaks were not so lucky. Mr Skelton said the wild weather made it almost impossible to recover the kayaks, which were last seen about 8km off the Torquay coast . . .

Peter Treby a prominent and respected sea kayaker wrote an article on this misadventure and provides some further information: *The school group paddlers were "not first-timers". They paddled Malibu 2 double sit-on-top "kayaks" made by Ocean Kayaks. They paddled near Point Danger and were blown away from shore. They were unable to get back to shore by themselves. One of the students stated "It was too strong for us to paddle back and it took us out pretty quick". People on shore summoned help . . . The kayaks were abandoned, at a loss of around $11,000, although an attempt was made to recover them with jetskis. The paddlers were said to have been picked up from as far as 5 kilometres offshore. Water temperature was 18.5C. The forecast conditions from the Bureau at 0500 on the day were for:*

"Northwesterly wind increasing to 25/30 knots, possibly reaching 35 knots offshore, then shifting west to southwesterly at 25/35 knots in the afternoon, with some stronger squalls likely. Sea rising 3/5 metres. West to southwesterly swell rising 3/5 metres."

Wind speed at Airey's Inlet (25 kms West) had increased sharply between 0900 and 0919,

when it went from a 12 knot northerly to a 31 knot north-westerly (with gusts to 41 knots) in under 20 minutes. Late in the morning, Airey's recorded:

1100: NW 25 knots, gusting to 38 knots

1127: WNW, 20 knots gusting to 28 knots

1131: NW, 19 knots gusting to 29 knots

1200: W, 18 knots gusting to 29 knots

1230: W, 18 knots, gusting to 27 knots

The conditions were described as a "freak of nature" by the surf school proprietor. But the conditions matched the forecast.

RUNNING A TRIP—ON WATER

① **Note:** The rule for group paddling speed is 'Group speed is determined by the slowest paddler.'

A rule of thumb for planning trip speed with paddlers you do not know is to use six kilometres per hour (3.2 kn), or just use three knots (5.6 km/h). Even then, novice paddlers may be slower, so allow for plenty of daylight in winter for delays. If the wind gets above Beaufort Force 4, generally novice and some mediocre paddlers will experience difficulty and will need to be closely watched, in order to be assisted, rescued and or towed. When on the water, group speed is determined by the slowest paddler.

When on the water do not overwhelm yourself with all of the tasks, but use the experience and maturity around you and delegate tasks. For example, nominate: a lead paddler, as a pace setter, a tail paddler and a navigator. Another way is to nominate a navigator/pace setter and most importantly trust them. Your aim should be to keep control of the group and achieve the events aim and goals.

In the event of capsize or other situation, use the paddlers in the group to perform the rescue or assist with the situation. Control the rescue and delegate tasks to be performed while ensuring the safety of the entire group and satisfactory completion of the task or tasks. Remain calm if the situation intensifies and keep control of the group. Ensure the individual members are performing the required tasks to remedy the situation.

Do not proportion blame or 'read the riot act' out to people on the water. If you do, it is the surest way to lose credibility as a leader. Do a proper pre-launch brief and control/lead the group on the water.

If you have a difficult paddler in the group, calmly and in an authoritative manner, speak to them about their behaviour. Assign a trusted competent paddler to buddy up with them.

Ratios for sea kayaking

Some clubs do not have ratios of instructor/guide/leader to novices or other level of paddler. This is their prerogative. Schools, TAFE, clubs, and commercial providers may choose to use the Australian Canoeing ratios. For sea kayaking Australian Canoeing state: *Acceptable ratio of leader/guide to participants for conducting group kayaking or canoeing activities at sea is 1:6 or 1:8 if using doubles.* They have higher ratios of 1:2 depending upon participants, foreseen difficult weather, sea and surf conditions. The ratios may extend out to 1:10 if all participants are adults; are competent as an individual and able to work in a group; all participants are reliable rollers; good weather, favourable streams, no spring tides, and water temperature presents little risk to paddlers. The location/route is not remote and there is access to other groups or craft. The location/route is always close to an easily accessible shoreline. The leader holds higher qualifications than required for the activity.

If there are no laid down ratios then the guide/leader needs to consider the competency, skills, knowledge and attitude of the participants and the location of the activity and foreseen weather and ocean conditions.

Night Paddling

① **Note:** On a VSKC night paddle crossing Corio Outer Harbour, it was noted by the Volunteer Coast Guard, who were escorting the pod, how difficult it was for the boat crew to see the pod they knew were there.

When paddling at night or low visibility conditions (i.e. fog), be aware of the law requirements of the country, state or territory you are in. These can be found on the respective websites. For example in Canada it is a requirement to fit a radar reflector when paddling in areas of high shipping traffic.

Kayaks can be difficult to see during the day let alone at night or low visibility conditions. A recommended practice is to tie a chemical light (glow) stick to your PFD.

For emergency purposes, attach a strobe light to your PFD. Ensure you check the battery of your strobe light before you go out on a night paddle.

① **Note:** It is advisable to replace your old batteries before you launch!

If you are leading a night paddle, ensure people have remembered to bring a torch and they can account for the serviceability of their batteries. If they have a torch, hand held or head, ensure they have it readily accessible!

Appoint an on-shore co-ordinator when running a club activity. Do not forget to lodge your float plan with a reliable contact when on a private paddle.

Ensure you have an updated float plan with current mobile phone numbers. Have the float plan readily accessible and ensure everyone has a copy.

① **Note:** See MSV and Telstra views on using mobile phones for recreational boating purposes.

Ensure all participants have communication equipment (e.g. mobile phones and their whistles).

Controlling the group

If you are leading a night paddle, refer to Risk Management topic, Pre-Launch Brief, for ideas of what to brief participants on before launching. Some points to consider are:

Lay down the protocols and accepted behaviours during the brief, because it can go horribly wrong very quickly when on the water, with limited or no visibility.

Check participant's equipment prior to launch.

Check participants have the other participant's mobile phone numbers (e.g. Float Plan or dive slate with numbers on it).

Use VHF radios to keep control of activities that involve large numbers of paddlers.

Buddy people together.

Break large numbers of paddlers into smaller groups (e.g. six or less paddlers, by using other trip leaders/sea guides).

COLLISION AVOIDANCE

Kayaks are very difficult to see by skippers of other watercraft. Refer to your local state or territory government recreational boating safety handbook and know your responsibilities between vessels and large vessels. Large vessels move faster than you sometimes expect and you may not hear one coming up behind you. Ships have a forward looking blind spot that can extend for many hundreds of metres. Large vessels cannot alter course quickly and cannot stop. Maintain a constant vigilance when approaching a shipping channel or anchorage. Take the most direct and shortest route to cross the shipping channel (i.e. perpendicular; at 90°) to the channel.

Ships are not the only collision hazard for sea kayakers. Recreational boaters (both powered and yacht) and personal water craft (aka jet ski) users pose a collision hazard. Another hazard is sea planes, of which I have had personal experience with a near miss.[2]

Collision avoidance method

ⓘ **Note:** There are other methods of determining if you are on a collision course or not. Do some research and choose and practice the method you understand.

To determine if you are on a collision course with a vessel, line up the bow with a central structure on the vessel (e.g. bridge, central masts or crane booms). Referring to Figure 5-1:

Figure A shows the bow of a vessel in the centre of the super-structure (bridge) indicating a collision course. Do not panic, but turn 90 degrees away and paddle swiftly away.

Figure B, shows a vessel with its bow to the left of its centre-line and moving away to your left. For evasive action, turn to your right.

Figure C shows a vessel with its bow to the right of its centre-line and is moving away to your right. For evasive action, turn to your left.

Points about collision avoidance

Number one try not to be a twit! Failing that:

Be vigilant all the time.

Make yourself visible by wearing hi-visibility clothing.

Paint your paddle blades a fluoro-colour.

Put reflective tape on your paddles blades.

Display a red or orange coloured flag on a metre high pole if you are stationary or fishing.

Fit a radar reflector on a pole. This is a requirement in the UK, Canada and Tasmania when in shipping lanes.

Know the meanings of the respective IALA buoyage system.

Be cautious when the sun is behind you and in the face of oncoming shipping.

Cross shipping channels at right angles.

Do not loiter in shipping channels.

Carry a VHF radio and maintain a listening watch on channels 16 and 67.

If in doubt about a vessel's movements, sit and wait in a safe area until it has passed.

Vessels approaching head on, both must alter course to starboard.

Powered vessels (i.e. power boats and jet skis) are to keep clear of yachts and rowing boats (kayaks seem to fit here). It is prudent to be vigilant and cautious around boaties and jet skiers.

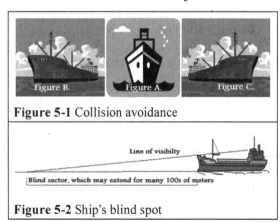

Figure 5-1 Collision avoidance

Figure 5-2 Ship's blind spot

If you or a member of the pod are about to collide with another vessel:

- As much as humanly possible, do not panic, capsize and wet-exit in front of the oncoming vessel.

- Present the kayak to the vessel and not your head or body.

- This may involve capsizing and staying in your cockpit with your body tucked up as closely as possible to the kayaks deck. It is clutching at straws, but you should have been vigilant!

If leading a pod:

- Keeping the pod close together (not ridiculously close as to cause paddle clash and collisions thereby increasing the possibility of capsize in a shipping channel).

- Do not panic any paddlers in your pod through excitable and agitated verbal communications.

- Calmly get the pod or paddler to swiftly turn at right angles to the oncoming vessel and get out of the way.

SURF ZONE

⚥ Warning: Dumpers can cause injury over shallow water or when landing on a shore. Avoid surfing over areas or landing on shores where dumpers are active.

① Note: It can be an absolute annoyance trying to launch off the beach with dumpers breaking on shore. Be careful you are not thrown back on to the shore, so wear your helmet in case.

Surfing sea kayaks

① Note: The only way to learn how to surf a kayak is to go out there and practice. If you are not getting munched then ask your-self "am I really trying?"

Some kayaks surf better than others do. Being in the surf zone is where you use a variation and multitude of strokes, braces, and sweeps in order to position yourself in the right place. In the end, handling skills in the surf comes down to practice, knowledge, attitude and not the kayak.

✒ Caution: Surfing around rocks, reefs or at low water can result in injury. It is advisable you wear a helmet when surfing.

If you take off too soon you can be *swatted* by the wave breaking on or over you. If you take off too late, the wave will go past you and you could find yourself in the break zone, after your slow or ill-timed sprint, for the next breaking wave in the set.

You need to be prepared to put on a sprint to catch a wave and it helps to thrust your torso weight forward as you feel the boat starting to surf over the crest. If you do not have enough forward speed when going over the crest, the bow can *pearl* (nose digs into the trough) and, depending upon your handling skills, you will find yourself being *munched*.

Being munched by a wave is not normally a problem but usually a good laugh. If you find yourself about to be munched and or swatted, adopt the torso forward head down, face protected by the deck position, with the paddle positioned in the set up for a roll position. The force of the wave can buffet you about a bit or if hammered by a large wave, like a rag doll; but just sit tight and enjoy the ride.

⚥ Warning: To prevent dislocating your shoulder, keep your elbows down and in, to prevent the paddle being pulled upward by the water.

When you feel the buffeting has subsided enough, attempt to roll up. If you fail, reset and try again. In the aerated white water, you may miss your first roll.

⚥ Warning: If you wet exit at any point do not get between the boat and the shore.

If you do wet exit, do not expect someone to come in and assist you. Again, it is dependent upon the situation but two boats in a surf zone is a recipe for injury.

Depending upon conditions and where you are in the surf zone, you can either follow the boat to shore or attempt any number of self-rescue techniques; you choose the appropriate one to your situation. Again, it is just practice.

Bombies (submerged and awash rocks) provide a good site for surfing as the swell passes over and or breaks over them. It is advisable to wear a helmet when surfing around bombies, reefs, and when playing in rock gardens. Always keep an eye out to seaward to ensure you are not caught out by an incoming set that breaks further out to sea than you expected.

① Note: There is the usual debate about to have a paddle leash or not to have. The choice is yours.

⚬* Caution: There is always the possibility of entanglement with paddle leases.

The use of paddle leashes is also a choice open to debate. Surf lifesavers do not normally use them, but they are paddling skis. To some, the use of a paddle lease posses the danger of entanglement. Many paddlers have found the virtue of having a paddle leash when out of their kayak. When you are separated from your boat, it is easier to swim after the kayak, or to shore, without having to carry a paddle. When separated from your boat in a surf zone, the kayak and any other kit may actually get caught in a rip or the wind may push it back out towards the sea. Normally, the incoming surf will push it to shore, but all this is relative to the conditions and your location.

① Note: The debate for kayaks with drop down rudders to have them stowed or deployed when surfing is again a topic of debate. The choice is yours.

The use of drop-down rudders in the surf zone is not encouraged by many sea kayaking instructors. However, there are others who favour their use. They cite manoeuvrability and control increases with their use. They also make the kayak easier to back paddle out of an awkward situation. However, to the 'purists' the use of a rudder is anathema at anytime, and is a sign—according to them—of poor paddling technique and skills.

Rips for sea kayakers and surfers, are very useful and provide a good breakout route from the shore. If the swell and resulting surf is big, usually in the rip channel, you may get in relatively unmolested. For getting off the beach in scary surf, or if you have surfed too far into the beach and want to get back out, hunt for the rips and use them. It needs to be pointed out that waves do break in the rips.

Surf launches

Getting off the beach in some instances can be quite tricky, if not just plain awkward. Before launching through on-coming surf, sit and observe the waves timings and look for rips or areas where the waves are not breaking as heavily. Once you have an appreciation of the waves timings, which can alter as soon as you launch, paddle hard and fast. If a wave rises up and your timing is out, back paddle and or wait till it has broken, then sprint off again.

When paddling through an on coming bore (white-water, surf), lean forward with your face and chest well down near the deck with your paddle parallel with the forward deck's side (as if you were setting up for a roll). If you present too big a surface with your torso to the wave, it will impact with quite a bit of force and can even bend you backwards over the aft deck hurting your back.

If you are leading a group:

The trip leader needs to stay on the beach to control and assist the launches and assist trashed paddlers who have been washed back up on the beach. If you have a competent lieutenant, then determine the best course of action for the situation (i.e. who stays on the beach and who goes and waits outback).

Send out an experienced paddler first who knows how to use the rips and has knowledge of swell and surf conditions. This paddler will also be the rally point behind the surf zone for the others.

When dispatching paddlers talk to them and show them the longshore currents, rips, lulls in the sets and the best way to get past the incoming breakers.

If a paddler is experiencing difficulties getting out the back and you have been working at it for quite some time be aware they will be getting tired and possibly losing confidence in their abilities.

The other paddlers already on the water may be getting quite cold or even sea sick from sitting around.

Be prepared to make the decision to bring everyone back in and try again later.

Surf landings

When coming into a surf beach exercise caution and patience. Wait out the back of the surf zone away from where any freak set will come through and clean you up. Observe the landing zone for the swell timings and direction.

Observe the resulting breakers to get an understanding of what type of breakers you and the group are going to pass through. Look for underwater hazards or indicators of their presence. Remember:

Tide height affects the type of waves breaking.

Waves with a long wave period will be wrapping in (refraction).

A 1 metre, 13 second period swell has more energy than a 2 metre, 8 second period swell.

Rips in moderate or less surf can be useful to get in through but, in large period swells and/or heavy surf conditions, be aware that if you get swatted and wet exit, you will be in a strong long-shore current and/or rip heading back out to sea.

Bringing your group in

When you are observing the landing conditions ask yourself:

Who is the lowest common denominator?

Can they safely (without physical or psychological damage) negotiate the breakers?

If the risk of damage (physical, mental or property) is present, take the group to your planned alternative landing site or make other arrangements.

Has the group been reminded about the hazards associated with surf landings?

Do they know the marshalling signals?

Have they cleared their decks?

Have they stowed any lose items inside their cockpit?

Are they wearing adequate protection for the conditions and/or location?

If you are leading a trip:

- You need to stay with the group and keep control. It is recommended you send in an experienced paddler first to act as a marshal for the remaining paddlers.

- Send in the remaining paddlers' one at a time. If they are trashed in the surf zone, wait until they are cleared from the area along with their kayak before dispatching the next paddler.

🖝 **Caution:** Be aware of paddlers who are in the water clearing boats away from the landing zone. Injuries have occurred when the process of removing a previously landed kayak has stalled and the next incoming kayak has hit the person standing in what was shallow water.

- Get the paddlers to quickly drag their kayaks up the beach away from the water's edge by the bow toggle; gel-coat is easy to repair!

Marshalling signals

Beach marshalling signals are covered in the Communications chapter.

Rules of the surf zone

Why the need for a surf zone guide? Add your body weight to that of your kayak's and factor in your surfing speed of say 18 km/h. It is plainly obvious that you are a risk to anybody in your way.

Below are some very important guidelines (unwritten rules) that kayakers need to know:

Sea kayaks when surfing are slow to manoeuvre.

Do not surf into a swimming beach.

Surfers are territorial creatures. Do not surf kayaks in their patches.

When a set is arriving, the person closest to the break has right of way. If you jump in on them you will need to take evasive action to avoid collision (e.g. capsize yourself).

When surfing with other kayaks, negotiate with the other paddlers a 'surf in paddle back out plan' (surfing circus). For example, surf in peel off to the right, paddle 50 metres along the beach then turn back out and head to the rally point.

Figure 5-3 is an illustration of a surfing session whereby kayak number one (#1) has right-of-way.

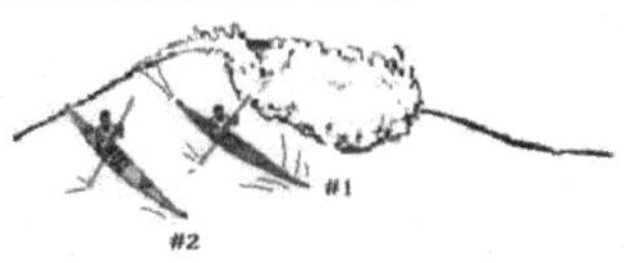

	Kayak (#1) closest to the wave bore has right of way
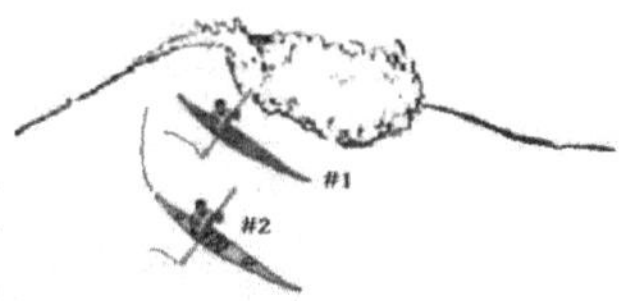	Look behind before taking-off (#2) as a kayak may have caught the wave farther out
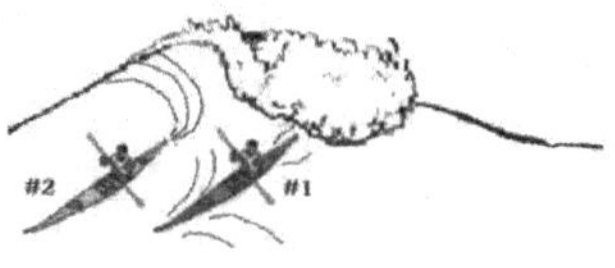	Do not drop-in on the inside, on-top of #1
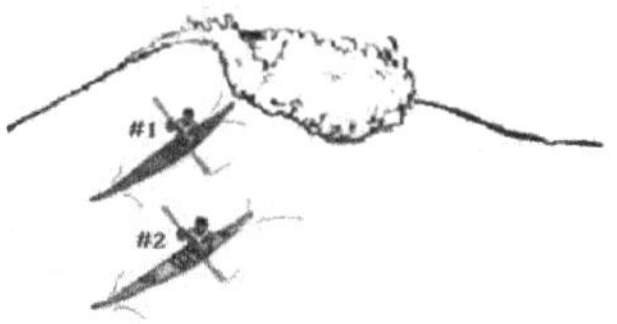	Do not drop-in on the outside of #1
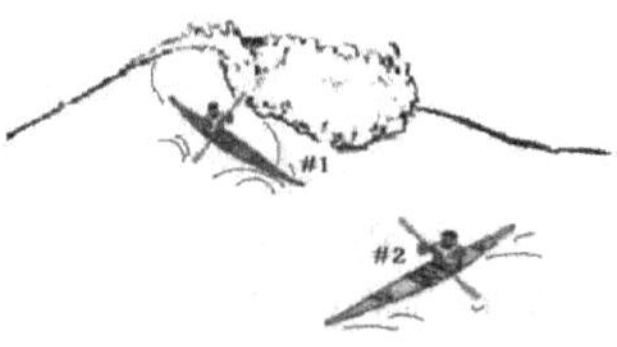	Do not hang around in and/or cut back through the surf zone!

Figure 5-3 Surfing circus guidelines

1 A good example of the informative information published by Sea Kayaker Magazine is an article by, Charles A Sutherland, The Loss of a Novice The Tragic Consequences of the Loss of a Novice, Sea Kayaker Magazine, December 2004, pp.42-45. This article analysis the death of a novice paddler, who capsized unintentionally in cold water, failed to wet exit and drowned. He had practiced a wet exit on-shore three hours before hand but the shock of the experience lead to his death. Recommendations are that novice paddlers be closely supervised during their first wet exit practice. They practice several wet exits under close supervision before going on a paddle. The first practice could also be performed without the skirt fitted.
2 A seaplane taking off in wet, windy and over cast conditions, wing passed about a metre by the bow of my kayak. This is despite my brightly coloured kayak, PFD and fluorescence painted paddle blade tips.

Chapter 6 First Aid, Health and Fitness

"I saw a woman wearing a sweatshirt with Guess on it. I said, Thyroid problem?"

Arnold Schwarzennegger

First Aid

If you have never completed a Nationally Recognised Training (NRT) course in First Aid, it is strongly recommended that you do. The first aid topics are covered both theoretically and with practicals.

A pocket size first aid book is a useful addition to a medical kit, as it can remove the conjecture of bystanders when treating an uncommon injury or poisoning. I like the publication by Dr Eric A. Weiss and Dr Michael Jacobs titled *A Comprehensive Guide to Marine Medicine* by Adventure Medical Kits.

CPR

Cardiopulmonary Resuscitation (CPR) and Expired Air Resuscitation (EAR) are taught during NRT first aid courses. If you have not learnt how to perform CPR/EAR then it is strongly recommended that you do. To be a sea guide/trip leader or instructor you need to have completed a NRT CPR/EAR training.

Exposure to the Elements

Wind Chill

① **Note:** Wind chill tables do not take into account for the wearing of wet clothing. It is fact wet clothing causes faster heat loss from the body.

There are at least two algorithms to determine wind chill. One was developed in 1946 and the other began use in some countries in 2001.

① **Note:** The Australian Chill Factor table is provided only as a guide and is subjective as the method of calculation is not known but appears to be in the old standard and not for wet clothing.

Table 6-1 Australian Chill Factor Table (dry clothes)

	Wind Speed								
k/hr	0	10	20	30	40	50	60	70	80
knots	0	5	11	16	21	27	32	37	43
20	19	16	15	14	13	13	13	13
15	13	10	8	7	6	5	5	5
10	8	4	1	-1	-2	-2	-3	-3
5	2	-3	-6	-8	-9	-10	-11	-11
0	-3	-9	-13	-15	-17	-18	-18	-19
-5	-8	-15	-20	-22	-24	-25	-26	-27
-10	-14	-22	-27	-30	-32	-33	-34	-34
-15	-19	-28	-34	-37	-39	-41	-42	-42
-20	-25	-35	-40	-44	-47	-48	-49	-50
-25	-30	-41	-47	-51	-54	-56	-57	-58
-30	-36	-47	-54	-59	-62	-64	-65	-66
-35	-41	-54	-61	-66	-69	-71	-73	-73
-40	-47	-60	-68	-73	-77	-79	-81	-81
-45	-52	-66	-75	-81	-84	-87	-88	-89
-50	-58	-73	-82	-88	-92	-94	-96	-97

(AIR TEMPERATURE (°C))

Cold Water

Cold water is a relative term. Even in temperate or moderately warm water, hypothermia will occur if a person is in the water long enough. Water conducts heat away from the body 25 times faster than air. This loss of heat can overwhelm the capacity of body metabolism to generate enough internal heat. Cold water is defined below 26 degrees Celsius (80 °F), with the greatest effects taking place from 15 degrees Celsius and the dominant concern being from 10 degrees Celsius and below.

The effects of cold water on the body can be described in four stages. The first two, in cold-water climates, cause more deaths than stages three and four. Stage one is cold shock, stage two is swimming failure, stage three is hypothermia and stage four is post-rescue collapse.

Cold shock is defined as a sudden drop in skin temperature, which causes a reflex reaction inducing hyperventilation and inducing abnormal cardiac output. After an initial involuntary gasp on entering the water, breath hold times will decrease significantly and most individuals will hyperventilate. In addition, both heart rate and cardiac output will increase significantly, imposing severe demands on the cardiovascular system with the potential for cardiac arrest in susceptible individuals (Robertson & Simpson, 1996).

It is often mistakenly assumed, an individual immersed in the sea is primarily at risk from hypothermia. Case studies have found when the body is cooled to 34 degrees Celsius, mental confusion and disorientation starts to take place. The mildly hypothermic person becomes incapacitated thereby having a *reduced ability to swim or perform self-rescue tasks*. In such a condition, the individual's ability to hold their breath is also dramatically reduced. The victim is at risk of drowning due to the inability to protect the mouth from breaking waves and spray. For these reasons, death solely attributable to hypothermia is unlikely to be the outcome from immersion (Robertson & Simpson, 1996, p. 76). Cold shock can kill in three to five minutes and in some cases instantaneously. The involuntary gasp reflex can cause the victim to inhale water and drown. If a person is not wearing a PFD they are at greater risk of drowning as the body undergoes the reaction to cold shock. The effects of cold shock normally peak within the first minute and stabilize very soon thereafter.

Swimming failure occurs after you have been in cold water for 5 to 30 minutes. Its effects include:

Loss of manual dexterity. After a few minutes, the limbs muscles are affected. Neuromuscular activity slows and body fluids literally congeal in the muscles. The victim feels the effects first in the hands and fingers. Next, the deeper tissues of the arms and legs cease to operate properly. It becomes more and more difficult to perform any tasks requiring manual dexterity, such as using flares or other survival equipment.

Inability to match breathing rate to swimming stroke.

Loss of coordination in the muscles in your arms and legs as they get cooler, increasing your swimming angle.

Increased swimming angle increases drag on the body requiring more energy to keep the head above water.

North American drowning statistics have shown that people who have been cited as good swimmers have drowned before completing 100 metres (Captain Monahan, 2009). In a web-based article titled The Chilling Truth About Cold Water Captain Monahan writes:

Table 6-2 Cold Water Survival Times
Source www.policeforum.co.uk

Water Temp (°C)	Expected Time Before Exhaustion or Unconsciousness	Expected Time of Survival without Survival Suit	Expected Time of Survival with Survival Suit
0.5	< 15 minutes	45 minutes	Up to 2 h
0.5-4.5	15-30 minutes	30-90 min.	1.5-3.5 h
4.5-10	30-60 minutes	1-3 hours	3.5-7.6 h
10-15.5	1-2 hours	1-6 hours	8-18.8 h
15.5-21	2-7 hours	2-40 hours	20-30.8 h
21-27	3-12 hours	3 hours to indefinite	Indefinite
> 27	Indefinite	Indefinite	Indefinite

"We had been more correct than we realized, several decades ago. Most victims of cold water immersion actually die of drowning, not hypothermia—and many drowning victims were very close to safety when they died. For instance, the Canadian Safe Boating Council / SmartRisk Study showed that between 1991 and 2000, 41% of those who drowned while boating were within 10 meters of shore at the time. An additional 22% were within 10 to 15 meters of shore. A British study from 1977 showed that 55% of open water drowning occurred within three meters of safety! And two thirds of drowning victims were strong swimmers."

Hypothermia occurs after 30 minutes. As a topic it will be covered further below. Hypothermia is the cooling of your body's core with the effects being:

A reduction of blood flow to the hands, feet, and surface of the body.

Intense shivering, in the early stages, as the body tries to maintain body core temperature.

Lack of shivering in the later stages.

Loss of consciousness.

Heart failure.

Post-rescue collapse can occur during and after rescue with statistics showing that up to 20 per cent of people rescued have died during or shortly after rescue (WorkSafe BC, n.d). The effects on the body after being pulled from the water can include the following:

Loss of hydrostatic pressure from the water causes a sudden drop in blood pressure. This can cause heart or brain failure.

The heart is cold and cannot pump cold blood effectively to maintain blood pressure.

The lungs are damaged from the inhaled water. This can cause a pneumonia-like illness.

Fatal bleeding from injuries may occur as your body warms up and your blood flows more freely.

Minimising the risk of cold water

Points to consider:

Dress appropriately for the conditions (i.e. dress for immersion).

Consider not paddling alone in cold water conditions.

Wear a PFD.

Try not to panic. The hyperventilation will subside, if it does not lead to unconsciousness.

Get out of the water and get protected from the wind. Wind chill will not be as dangerous as the water for heat loss, but it is dangerous.

If self-rescue attempts fail and you cannot get out of the water adopt the HELP (Heat Escape Lessening Posture). Hold the arms tight against the chest, press the thighs together, and raise the knees up to protect the groin. It is said, that it will increase survival time by nearly 50 per cent.

Groups of three or more people should adopt the huddle position. The sides of the chests and the lower torsos are pressed together, arms hugging each other around the PFD. Intertwine legs as much as possible and talk

to one another. Children succumb to cold much more quickly than adults and should be sandwiched in the middle of the group.

Consider your options before swimming to shore. If you decide to swim for shore, consider that research has shown an average person wearing a PFD and light clothing could swim about one mile (1.85 km) in water of 10 degrees Celsius and good swimmers have perished in less distance.

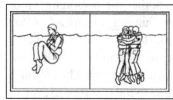

Figure 6-1 Heat Escape Lessening Postures

Plan for cold-water emergencies and develop an action plan.

Practice self-rescue and assisted rescue techniques.

Carry emergency equipment.

Hypothermia

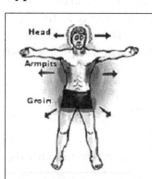

Figure 6-2 Areas of major heat loss

Hypothermia is when the body's temperature drops below 35 degrees Celsius (normal is 37 °C) (Australian Red Cross, 1995, p. 195). Different references provide a variation in survival time data. This is possibly due to the fact that there are a multitude of factors that can cause a variation in survival times. For example, age, body mass index, physical and mental health, intoxication and clothing. The main areas of body heat loss are the head, neck, sides of the chest and groin.

Symptoms

Initial immersion results in a sensation of cold. Heart, respiratory and metabolic rates are increased at first and then shivering commences becoming maximal at a body temperature of 35 degrees Celsius. As the body cools below

35 degrees Celsius (moderate hypothermia) mental confusion (irritable, irrational, difficulty of speech, confused behaviour) occurs; manual dexterity and strength are reduced to a point at which a victim might be unable to grab and hold a rescue line.

Body temperature between 33 to 30 degrees Celsius shivering is replaced by muscular rigidity. Unconsciousness occurs at about 30 degrees Celsius (profoundly hypothermic). Body temperature below 30 degrees Celsius, pupils become fixed and dilated, reflexes are lost, heart, respiratory, and metabolic rates slow and muscles become flaccid. Cardiac rhythm changes occur between body temperature 28 to 26 degrees Celsius and cardiac arrest occurs around a body temperature of 24 degrees Celsius.

First Aid

First aid for a hypothermic person consists of:

Remove from the water

Protect from wind chill (Beanies, head for shelter, put a windbreak over them)

Give warm drinks to victims who are alert

Warm body slowly (dry clothes, blanket, body heat)

Moderate hypothermia victims: Do not give warm drinks

Call for ambulance

Monitor ABC

Avoid 'After Drop' effect: no walking for at least 30 minutes, do not massage limbs or extremities

Perform CPR as required even if victim appears dead.

Burns

Gently and quickly, cool the burned skin immediately with plenty of cold water. Carefully remove any unstuck clothing around the burn. Do not burst blisters or remove anything stuck to the burnt area. Elevate burnt limbs if possible/ practical. Cover the area lightly with clean, dry, sterile burns dressing or clean cloth and keep the patient calm and quiet. Seek medical assistance as soon as possible (MSV, 2007, p. 77).

Exposure to Sun

Australia has the highest rate of skin cancer in the world, which is caused by exposure to ultraviolet radiation from the sun. Ultra violet radiation is strongest between 11 am and 3 pm Daylight Saving Time and is present all year. The kayaker is particularly susceptible, as reflected radiation from the water gives an additional radiation effect.

Preventative measures are important and clothing provides the best protection. Cover exposed areas with a hat that covers the face, ears and neck and wear a long-sleeve shirt. Apply a sunscreen to exposed areas with a maximum sun protection factor—SPF 30+ or above—water resistant, broad-spectrum sunscreen and a solar lip screen. Apply the sunscreen 20 minutes before going out and reapply every two hours.

Hyperthermia

Hyperthermia is the overexposure to heat. In hot or humid conditions people are at risk of suffering from heat illness. The two types of heat-related illness are *heat exhaustion* and *heat stroke*, which is a potentially lethal condition.

Heat exhaustion typically occurs after long periods of strenuous exercise or work in a hot environment. As a victim sweats, they lose fluid, which decreases the blood volume. Blood flows to the skin in order to dissipate body heat, thereby, reducing blood flow to the vital organs. Since the body's circulatory system is affected, the victim develops mild shock.

Signs and symptoms may include normal, or below normal skin temperature; cool, sweating; moist, pale skin progressing to red skin; nausea, headache; dizziness and weakness, exhaustion, rapid weak pulse, vomiting.

Cool the victim by getting the victim into a cool place to lay down with their legs slightly raised and rest. Loosen tight clothing and give small amounts of water to drink. Apply cool wet cloths to skin and fan the victim to increase evaporation. Monitor the victim for signs of deterioration. If the victim cannot hold down the water call for medical assistance. Keep cooling the body by any available means. If the person is unconscious place them on their side, clear the airway, tilt the head and turn the face slightly downward, then check their breathing. If breathing, leave on their side and monitor their airway, breathing and circulation. If they are not breathing, perform *expired air resuscitation* (EAR). If no pulse, perform *cardiopulmonary resuscitation* (CPR).

Heat stroke develops when the body is overheated and begins to stop functioning. Through dehydration, the body stops sweating preventing effective cooling and allowing body temperature to increase rapidly. At a point, the overheating causes the brain and other vital organs, such as the heart and kidneys, to begin to fail. If untreated, the victim will experience convulsions, unconsciousness and death.

Signs of heat stroke are: high body temperature (up to 40 °C); hot, red, dry skin; progressive deterioration of conscious state; rapid, shallow breathing. The pulse rate and strength will alter possibly from a rapid strong pulse, as the body attempts to rid the heat build up. The blood vessels dilate and blood is pumped to the skin. As consciousness deteriorates, the circulatory system starts to fail and the pulse becomes weak and irregular. If left unchecked the victim will die.

As a victim undergoes an altered conscious state, their reasoning and decision making ability, may be beyond the point of their being able to make rational decisions. Take control of the situation and cease from further activity. Get them out of the sun and rested. Start cooling them off as for heat exhaustion. Remove sweat soaked clothing. If fully conscious, give cool clear fluids. Call for medical assistance; monitor the condition carefully and minimise shock. Monitor the ABC and be prepared to perform expired air resuscitation or cardiopulmonary Resuscitation (Australian Red Cross, 2000).

Muscle cramps (aka *heat cramps*) can be associated with but are quite separate to heat related conditions. If a person starts cramping up

get them to rest in a cool place. Give them plenty of water and assist them with muscle stretches and massage of the affected area. Do not give them salt tablets or salt water to drink, as this may lead to the onset of heat-related illness, since salt increases tissue dehydration.

Bleeding

Small cuts and abrasions can be treated by cleaning the wound and applying a non-adhesive dressing. Pressure applied directly to the wound is the most effective way to stop bleeding. The injured part should be elevated and movement should be restricted as much as possible.

Occasionally, more serious injuries occur resulting in severe bleeding. These injuries may not be controllable with applied pressure. In these cases, a constrictive bandage should be used to restrict arterial blood flow. Caution should be exercised when applying this type of dressing as extended use can lead to permanent tissue damage.

The constrictive bandage should be applied to the upper arm or leg, keeping well clear of the arm joint and knee. Use a broad (7.5 cm) soft roller bandage or strip of material and encircle the limb firmly. The arterial pulse should disappear completely below the bandage. If bleeding appears to increase rather than decrease, the bandage should be released and reapplied. Once correctly applied, the time of application must be clearly recorded on the patient. The constrictive bandage must not be covered by clothing or other material. It is essential to get the patient to hospital as soon as possible (MSV, 2007, p. 77).

Bites and Stings

As you would undoubtedly know, there are a host of animals, insects and plants that can inflict irritating bites and stings through to life threatening injuries on people. Treatment for various bites and stings are taught in approved NRT First Aid courses. Queensland Health provides the following information for first aid treatment of bites and stings, unless otherwise noted.

General first aid for bites and stings

For bites or stings from these creatures refer to pressure-immobilisation first aid:

All species of Australian snakes, including sea snakes

Funnel web spiders

Blue ringed octopus

Cone shell stings.

For all other bites and stings:

Wash with soap and water and apply an antiseptic if available

Ensure that the patient's tetanus vaccination is up to date

Apply an ice-pack to reduce local pain and swelling

Pain relief may be required e.g. paracetamol or an antihistamine (to reduce swelling, redness and itch)

The patient should seek medical advice if they develop any other symptoms or signs of infection.

PRESSURE IMMOBILISATION TECHNIQUE

The pressure-immobilisation first aid technique was developed in the 1970's by Professor Struan Sutherland. Its purpose is to retard the movement of venom from the bite site into the circulation, thus 'buying time' for the patient to reach medical care. Research with snake venom has shown that very little venom reaches the blood stream if firm pressure is applied over the bitten area and the limb is immobilised. Pressure-immobilisation was initially developed to treat snakebite, but it is also applicable to bites and stings by some other venomous creatures. It is currently recommended for most life threatening venomous bites and stings in Australia.

Pressure-immobilisation is recommended for:

All species of Australian snakes, including sea snakes

Funnel web spiders

Bee, wasp and ant stings in allergic individuals

Blue ringed octopus

Cone shell stings.

Do not use pressure-immobilisation first aid for:

Spider bites other than from a funnel web spider

Jelly fish stings

Stonefish and other fish stings

Bee, wasp and ant stings in non-allergic individuals

Bites by scorpions, centipedes, beetles.

Bites to the lower limb

In Australia, call 000 for an ambulance. Overseas contact appropriate medical/rescue services.

Apply a broad pressure bandage over the bite site as soon as possible. Crepe bandages are ideal, but any flexible material may be used. Clothing, towels et cetera may be torn into strips. Panty hose have been successfully used.

Do not take clothing off as the movement of doing so will promote the movement of venom into the blood stream. Keep the patient (and the bitten or stung limb) still.

Bandage upwards from the lower portion of the bitten or stung limb. Even though a little venom may be squeezed upwards, the bandage will be more comfortable, and therefore can be left in place for longer if required.

The bandage should be as tight as you would apply to a sprained ankle.

Extend the bandage as high as possible up the limb.

Apply a splint to the leg. Any rigid object may be used as a splint (e.g. spade, piece of wood or tree branch, rolled up newspapers etc.).

Bind it firmly to as much of the leg as possible.

Keep the patient still. Lie the patient down to prevent walking or moving around. Have the patient taken immediately by ambulance to the emergency department of the nearest hospital.

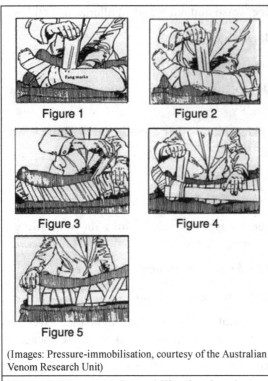

Figure 1   Figure 2

Figure 3   Figure 4

Figure 5

(Images: Pressure-immobilisation, courtesy of the Australian Venom Research Unit)

Table 6-3 Pressure immobilisation bandage

Bites to the hand or forearm

In Australia, call 000 for an ambulance. Overseas contact appropriate medical/rescue/emergency services.

Bandage as much of the arm as possible, starting at the fingers. Use a splint to the elbow and leave on. Use a sling to immobilise the arm. Keep the patient still. Lay the patient down to prevent walking or moving around. Have the patient taken immediately by ambulance to the emergency department of the nearest hospital.

Bites to the trunk

Call 000 for an ambulance. Overseas contact appropriate medical/rescue/emergency services.

If possible apply firm pressure over the bitten or stung area. Do not restrict chest movement. Keep the patient still. Have the patient taken immediately by ambulance to the emergency department of the nearest hospital.

Bites to the head or neck

In Australia, call 000 for an ambulance. Overseas contact appropriate medical/rescue/emergency services.

No first aid for bitten or stung area. Keep the patient still. Have the patient taken immediately by ambulance to the emergency department of the nearest hospital.

Additional information:

Research stresses the importance of keeping the patient still. This includes all the limbs.

Do NOT cut or excise the bitten or stung area.

Do NOT apply an arterial tourniquet. (Arterial tourniquets, which cut off the circulation to the limb, are potentially dangerous, and are no longer recommended for any type of bite or sting in Australia).

Do NOT wash the bitten or stung area. The type of snake involved may be identified by the detection of venom on the skin.

① **Note: Even if the bitten or stung person is ill when first seen, the application of pressure-immobilisation first aid may prevent further absorption of venom from the bite or sting site during transport to hospital.**

All rings or other jewellery on the bitten limb, especially on fingers, should be removed, as they may act as tourniquets if oedema develops (WHC).

Avoid peroral intake, absolutely no alcohol. No sedatives outside hospital. If there will be considerable delay before reaching medical aid, measured in several hours to days, then give clear fluids by mouth to prevent dehydration (WHC).

The snakebite victim should be transported as quickly and as passively as possible to the nearest place where they can be seen by a medically trained person (health station, dispensary, clinic or hospital). The bitten limb must not be exercised as muscular contraction will promote systemic absorption of venom. If no motor vehicle or boat is available, the patient can be carried on a stretcher or hurdle, on the pillion or crossbar of a bicycle or on someone's back (WHC).

Most traditional, and many of the more recently fashionable, first aid measures are useless and potentially dangerous. These include local cauterization, incision, excision, amputation, suction by mouth, vacuum pump or syringe, combined incision and suction ("venom-ex" apparatus), injection or instillation of compounds such as potassium permanganate, phenol (carbolic soap) and trypsin, application of electric shocks or ice (cryotherapy), use of traditional herbal, folk and other remedies including the ingestion of emetic plant products and parts of the snake, multiple incisions, tattooing and so on (WHC).

If the bandages and splint have been applied correctly, they will be comfortable and may be left on for several hours. They should not be taken off until the patient has reached medical care.

The treating doctor will decide when to remove the bandages. If a significant amount of venom has been injected, it may move into the blood stream very quickly when the bandages are removed. They should be left in position until appropriate antivenom and resuscitation equipment has been assembled.

Bandages may be quickly reapplied if clinical deterioration therapy has been effective.

Table 6-4 Standard group first aid kit contents

Roller bandages (7.5 cm x 2.3 m) x2,
Conforming bandages (5 cm x 1.5 m) x4,
Non-adherent sterile bandages (5 x 5 cm) x4,
Non-adherent sterile bandages (10 x 10 cm) x4,
Adhesive dressing strip (50 cm) x2,
Band aids x1 box,
Breathable dressing x2,
Wound closure packets (steri-strips) x2,
Gauze swabs x4,
Sports strapping tape (3.8 cm x 13 m) x1,

Space blanket x1,
Sam splint x1,
CPR pocket mask x1,
Surgical gloves x4,
Packet of cotton buds x1,

Scissors x1,
Safety pins x6,
Tweezers,
Magnifying glass,
Needle x1,
Marker pen x1,

Mylanta tablets x4,
Antihistamine tablets x1,
Paracetamol Tablets x1 packet;
Glucose tablets x6,
Oral re-hydration powder x4,

Saline solution (30 ml),
Betadine (15 ml),
Stingose x1,
Aloe vera gel x1,
Vinegar—if required x1,
Bite and burn gel x1,
Antiseptic cream x1,
Anti inflammatory cream x1,
Sunscreen x1,
Lip balm x1,
Antifungal cream x1,
Swimmers ear solution x1,
Alcohol swabs x6,
Betadine swabs x6.
Elastoplast Spray Plaster (waterproof) x1

Notes:

1. Crepe bandages are inefficient when used on the water to strap a repetitive strain injury. Use strapping tape or substitute with your repair kit's duct tape.
2. Consider a pocketknife loaded with gadgets like scissors and tweezers etc.
3. Triangular bandages are very versatile (e.g. for pads, bandages, support, securing), and can be a good substitute for crepe bandages in the individual kit.
4. An effective substitute for the sterile pad dressings are sanitary towels.

ANAPHYLAXIS

Anaphylaxis is a severe allergic reaction that can occur in sensitive individuals from exposure to any chemicals foreign to the body, including bites and stings, plants, or medications. Parts of the body, for example the face or throat, swell up so much that the patient cannot breathe. In severe cases the patient may go into shock within a few minutes and the heart can stop. For any patient who shows signs of anaphylaxis, call 000 (in Australia) for an ambulance, and have the patient taken immediately to the emergency department of the nearest hospital (Queensland Health).

FIRST AID KITS

ⓘ **Note:** First aiders are not permitted to dispense medications.

ⓘ **Note:** Within the VSKC, it is recommended you also carry a small first aid kit that is accessible at sea and can be used to treat minor ailments and injuries.

When making up first aid kits consider:

The paddling and camping environment.

The types of injuries or illness you are likely to encounter. For example:

- Soft tissue injuries: sprains, strains, cuts, splinters; broken bones, dislocated shoulder, snake bite, insect bites, rashes, sun burn, hypothermia, sea sickness, stomach upsets from suspect drinking water.

The items in Table 6-4 are an example of items carried in a group first aid kit by a medic who is also an outdoors adventure leader.

HEALTH

Medications

Some points to remember about medications and outdoors activities:

Do not forget your personal medications.

If leading a group ask if people have any medical issues or medication. Ask them where they have stowed their medication.

If it may be required on water, remind them to have it in a readily available location and not lost inside the day hatch!

Fluids Intake

Fluid intake is more important than food intake. The effects of dehydration in a day or over several days are far more severe than being hungry. A standard guide for fluid intake is 'two litres per man per day'. Depending upon fitness, body build, current effort requirements, heat, humidity et cetera, you will need to increase your fluid intake.

If you are short on potable water, ration your sweat not your water by conducting your activity in the cooler parts of the day to limit perspiration. A person sitting in an open boat in the tropics for 24 hours may lose up to 6 litres of water, mainly through perspiration. If no more than one litre is available per day, that person could die of dehydration in three days (Royal Australian Air Force Combat Survival School, 1997).

Food Intake

Having the right amount of calories for paddling is an important topic. A useful web site is *Nutrition Data*. This site provides an abundance of information, regarding personalised calorific intake requirements for many sports and what foods are the best sources for nutrition.

Chaffing

To minimise chaffing around the armpits and upper arms try using lanolin cream. Another commonly used practice to reduce chaffing is to wear the garment closest to your skin inside out so the seams are on the outside away from your skin.

Illness'

Below are some common ailments people may encounter while out on a kayaking trip with some pointers on how to manage your situation. One common effect all three ailments have is dehydration.

Seasickness

Seasickness (aka *Mal de Mer, motion sickness*) is a calamity virtually anyone can suffer from and it is suggested 90 per cent of people will suffer from it to some degree in their life (Chave, 2008).

Motion sickness relates to a person's sense of spatial orientation, whereby the brain tells the body where it is in relation to the surroundings. It is suggested that when the body, inner ear, and eyes all send different signals to the brain about your spatial orientation, it results in confusion and queasiness. It is a problem generally attributed to a disturbance in the balance system of the inner ear system. Effectively your sensory perception signals from your eyes and body gets out of synchronization with the inner ear. The inner ear nerve fibres detect the unfamiliar motion; and the central nervous system tries to make sense of all the conflicting information.

People's tolerance, or lack thereof, to seasickness varies. Some people become drowsy and need a nap while others experience an escalation to extreme nausea, vomiting, dizziness, headache, pallor and cold perspiration. It is suggested that maintaining a positive attitude helps offset the effects, but for sufferers they may just wish they were dead and become physically incapacitated.

A big trigger can be taking your eyes off the horizon, whereby your brain cannot make sense of the signals from eyes, inner ears and body sensors. Paddling in rough clapotis can also bring the onset of seasickness as your focus may be off the horizon to the situation near you. Again, like the effects, the triggers vary between individuals.

Prevention is better than the cure. There are a number of pharmaceutical products in the market place, both over the counter and prescription. If in doubt, ask the Pharmacist or a Doctor about your situation. With pharmaceutical products, there may be side affects while you are on the water (e.g. drowsiness and thirst). Non-pharmaceutical remedies include scanning the horizon and not focusing on one area. Try taking deep breaths and drink plenty of water.

Like the effects and triggers for seasickness the cure, if any for some, vary from individual to individual. However, avoid eating spicy and or rich foods, apples and drinking alcohol before launching. Herbal remedies like ginger works, and it is alleged that there is medical evidence to support this. For some, the use of pressure bands work. If it is hot weather, the symptoms may be aggravated and there is the possibility of dehydration.

Giardia lamblia

Giardia are found worldwide and are the cause of Giardiasis, a diarrheal illness caused by a one-celled, microscopic parasite, *Giardia intestinalis* (also known as *Giardia lamblia*). Once an animal or person has been infected with *Giardia intestinalis*, the parasite lives in the intestine and is passed in the stool. Because an outer shell protects the parasite, it can survive outside the host body and in the environment for long periods of time. *Giardia* is found in soil, food, water, or surfaces that have been contaminated with the faeces from infected humans or animals. Ingesting the parasite can also infect you.

Giardia infection can cause a variety of intestinal symptoms, which include: diarrhoea, flatulence, greasy stools that tend to float, stomach cramps, upset stomach or nausea. Symptoms of giardiasis normally begin one to two weeks (average seven days) after becoming infected. The symptoms may lead to weight loss and dehydration and in some people with giardiasis, they have no symptoms at all. In otherwise healthy persons, symptoms of giardiasis may last two to six weeks and occasionally, symptoms last longer.

Giardia infection can be very contagious. Follow these guidelines to avoid spreading giardiasis to others:

Wash your hands with soap and water after using the toilet and before eating or preparing food.

Do not swim in recreational water (pools, hot tubs, lakes or rivers, the ocean.) if you have Giardia and for at least two weeks after diarrhoea stops. You can pass Giardia in your stools and contaminate water for several weeks after your symptoms have ended. In the past, this has resulted in outbreaks of Giardia among recreational water users.

To prevent infection, practise good normal hygiene, and bush hygiene practices; see the chapter on minimal impact camping and toileting out bush.

Make water safe to drink by heating the water to a rolling boil for at least one minute; or use a filter that has an absolute pore size of at least one micron, or one that has been National Sanitation Foundation (NSF) rated for 'cyst removal.' If you cannot heat the water to a rolling boil or use a recommended filter, then try chemically treating the water by chlorination or iodination.

Avoid food that might be contaminated by washing it yourself in uncontaminated (safe) water. Peeling all raw vegetables and fruits before eating. Do not eat uncooked foods, when travelling in countries with minimal water treatment and sanitation systems.

Cryptosporidiosis

Cryptosporidiosis is an infection of the bowel caused by microscopic parasites, *Cryptosporidium parvum*. Once an animal or person is infected, the parasite lives in the intestine and passes in the stool. The parasite is protected by an outer shell that allows it to survive outside the body for long periods of time and makes it very resistant to chlorine-based disinfectants. Both the disease and the parasite are commonly known as *crypto*. The parasite may be found in drinking water and recreational water in every region throughout the world.

Cryptosporidium is highly contagious, and is found in soil, food, water, or surfaces that have been contaminated with infected human or animal faeces. If a person swallows the parasite they become infected, however, you cannot become infected through contact with blood. The most common symptom of cryptosporidiosis is watery diarrhoea. Other symptoms include: dehydration, weight loss, stomach cramps or pain, fever, nausea and vomiting. Some people with crypto will have no symptoms at all. While the small intestine is the site most commonly affected, Cryptosporidium infections could possibly affect other areas of the digestive or the respiratory tract. Symptoms of cryptosporidiosis generally begin one to 12 days (average seven days) after becoming infected with the parasite. In persons with healthy immune systems, symptoms usually last about one to two weeks. The symptoms may go in cycles in which you may seem to get better for a few days, then feel worse again before the illness ends. Even several weeks after the symptoms have gone a person can still be infected and be contagious.

Drinking water precautions

Cryptosporidium may be found in untreated water sources such as rivers, streams, lakes and dams because they can be contaminated by wild, domesticated or farm animals and people. To protect yourself and the environment observe the following precautions:

Avoid drinking untreated water.

If untreated water is the only water source available, boil the water before drinking or using it for food preparation. Boiling clear water for one minute on a rolling boil will kill germs including Cryptosporidiosis. If the water is very cloudy (turbid) it would be advisable for it to be kept on the boil for three minutes.

Do not rely on filters to make untreated drinking water safe to drink. Only some filters will remove Cryptosporidium from water. Use a filter that has an absolute pore size of at least one micron or one that has been NSF rated for cyst removal.

Do not rely on chemicals to disinfect water and kill Cryptosporidium. Because it has a thick outer shell, this particular parasite is highly resistant to disinfectants such as chlorine and iodine.

To prevent infection, practice good normal hygiene, and bush hygiene practices; see the chapter on minimal impact camping and toileting out bush.

If infected, for those with normal immune systems, specific treatment is not required. If there is a lot of diarrhoea, drink lots of fluids.

INJURY PREVENTION

'Prevention is better than the cure'

Some paddling injuries result from accidents; others are due to poor training practices, improper equipment, lack of conditioning, or insufficient warm-up and stretching. One issue with kayaking is the development of certain muscle groups and the under utilization of others, creating a muscle imbalance and the possibility of injury. Another common issue is the development of overuse injuries.

In paddling, stroke technique, body posture and leg placement all combine together. If you have developed a good paddling style then you reduce the chances of aggravating old injuries or developing new ones. When seated, tilt your pelvis forward to maintain the small inward curve of the lower spine. Lift your chest up and straighten your spine. Correct paddling technique generates power from the legs and lower body. This is transferred through the upper body and shoulders to the arms, hands and paddle.

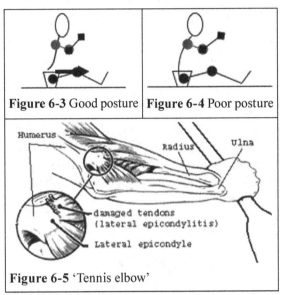

Figure 6-3 Good posture | **Figure 6-4** Poor posture

Figure 6-5 'Tennis elbow'

Any inefficiency within the bodies' kinetic chain can lead to injury. The physiological effects of poor paddling posture are excess stress on the lower spine discs, pressure on nerves in the buttocks region, overload of the thoracic and shoulder girdle muscular structure and muscle overload, stress at the base of the neck, and an inability to rotate the thoracic spine (Wilkie, 2005).

It all starts with body posture. The effects of daily bad posture positions (e.g. slouching in a chair, makes correct posture for paddling difficult to achieve). Therefore, maintaining good posture through a strong back and good core strength, overall flexibility and suppleness is important in kayaking (Eleftheriou, 2008). Good posture development is an everyday practice especially to overcome long practiced bad habits. Other than being mindful of your posture, investigate exercise regimes like Pilates and or yoga.

Some common paddler complaints are cause by over use. During exercise the muscles, tendons, bones and ligaments experience stress. When the activity ceases the tissues undergo a process of adaptation in order to be able to withstand similar stresses in the future. However, overuse

injuries occur when too little rest exceeds the adaptive capability of the tissue before the next workout and tissue injury then develops. There are a multitude of factors that come into play with overuse injuries like; the lack of flexibility, muscle imbalance, muscle weakness, the sex of a person, age, build, training regimes, lack of training and conditioning, illness and disease. So if pain persists see your doctor. Some common overuse paddling injuries are sore wrist, *Tennis elbow*, *Golfers elbow*, shoulder injuries and sore lower back.

Sore wrist, (aka *tennis wrist*) is from holding the paddle too tight and allowing a repetitive cocking motion (side to side movement) of the wrist, which over time leads to an overuse injury.

Learn, develop and practice good technique. Your wrist should not cock side to side or up and down with each stroke. Keep your wrist straight and your hand relaxed. Align the back of your hand to your forehead on the stroke as this minimises the cocking action. An option may be to consider purchasing a *crankshaft* paddle.

'Tennis elbow' (*lateral epicondylitis*) is an overuse injury leading to inflammation of the tendons and muscles of the outside (lateral) part of the elbow. Pain may also be felt in the forearm to the wrists and above the elbow. There may also be a weakening of your paddle grip.

For paddlers, it is associated with holding the paddle too tight and or having an incorrect diameter paddle shaft for your hand leading to muscle/tendon fatigue.

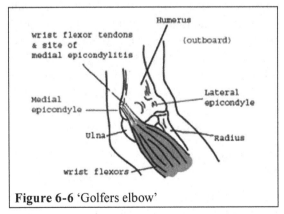

Figure 6-6 'Golfers elbow'

'Golfer's elbow' (*medial epicondylitis*) is an over use injury leading to inflammation of the tendons and muscles of the inside (medial) part of the forearm. It is characterized by pain and tenderness on the inside part of the elbow.

The muscles that control forearm, wrist and hand movement actually originate near the elbow joint. For this reason, it is worthwhile to perform strengthening exercises on the lower arms to aid in strengthening all the muscles that support the wrist and elbow.

Besides developing correct technique, a simple method employed by some people to aid in preventing a wrist overuse injury, is to apply a supportive elasticized band around the wrist. This applies compression forces on your tendons. The same remedy can be used for tennis elbow with the elasticized band being applied onto the tendons just under your elbow.

Shoulder injuries may be the result of sprains, strains, dislocations, separations, tendinitis, bursitis, torn rotator cuffs (rotor cuff), fractures, impingement and arthritis.

A common complaint amongst sea canoeists is *Bursitis* in the shoulders or elbow. Bursitis is inflammation of a bursa. Bursae are small sacs located between two adjoining structures, usually muscles, tendons and bones. Their purpose is to decrease friction and assist movement of the tendon over the bony surface. Bursae are located outside the joint itself. Since both tendons and bursae are located near joints, inflammation in these soft tissues may be mistaken as arthritis. However, arthritis involves inflammation within joints, whereas bursitis involves inflammation outside the joint (Victorian State Government, 2010). The most common sites of bursitis are the shoulder, elbow, knee and heel. If caused by injury, bursitis will resolve after a few days or weeks. However, if bursitis is caused by overuse, the inflammation will continue unless the particular activity or movement is stopped.

For kayakers, the cause of shoulder injuries may be from:

Excessive muscular force generated from the paddle blade and shaft length.

Carbon fibre paddles, because of their rigidity and strength, have also been linked to causing and/or aggravating joints and tissues of the shoulders and arms (Johnson, 2002).

Dislocations associated with performing the 'high brace' in the surf zone.

Overuse injuries including humeral head subluxation, rotator-cuff tendinitis and subacromial impingement, may result from overtraining, lack of conditioning, and poor paddling technique. Chronic tears in the rotor cuff have been associated with degeneration of the tendon through long-term over use of a previously weakened rotor cuff combined with muscular imbalance (Amtmann, 2008).

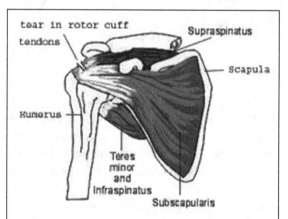

The rotor cuff is a series of four muscles whose tendons connect the humerus to the scapula.

Figure 6-7 Rotor cuff muscle group.

Prevention strategies are shoulder warm up and cool down exercises before and after paddling. The US Canoe and Kayak Federation suggests backwards paddling as an effective training technique, with warm-up and cool-down regimens including up to 10 minutes of back paddling (Eleftheriou, 2008).

Lower back discomfort while paddling may be from poor posture, incorrect ergonomics between boat and paddler, an existing injury or aggravation of an old injury, for openers. Studies report in long distance paddling, because the paddler is seated in position for a long time, the back is subjected to significant shear forces. The majority of reported back complaints were related to muscular or ligamentous strain, but spondylolysis was seen and in one series and 36 out of 42 canoeists were found to have had prolapsed discs. Spondylolysis is a specific defect in the connection between vertebrae. This defect can lead to small stress fractures (breaks) in the vertebrae that can weaken the bones so much that one slips out of place, a condition called spondylolisthesis. Spondylolysis is a very common cause of low back pain (Eleftheriou, 2008). Other causes of lower back discomfort may be from incorrectly lifting or manoeuvring a loaded kayak on land.

In some kayaks your legs form a diamond shape, with your ankles angled towards the kayak's centre line, the knees are splayed out apart to the side of the boat and raised up under the deck. If you have big feet, your feet are also splayed outward from the centre line to the sides of the hull/deck. Apparently, this position can pinch the nerve running from the knee up to the lower back, producing referred pain and or numbness in your lower back. This unnatural position has also been attributed, by some references, to cause poor circulation and leg numbness.

Other complains are numb bum, legs or feet. These conditions can be relieved by not being cramped in the cockpit and periodically moving your lower body and stretching legs and feet. To avoid or reduce numbness in the legs and feet seek out a kayak seat that has a slightly raised forward edge thereby causing your pelvis to be tilted forward. Another solution is to place a rolled up towel or inflated wine cask under your thighs to raise them up.

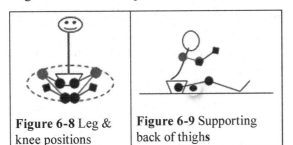

| **Figure 6-8** Leg & knee positions | **Figure 6-9** Supporting back of thighs |

Prevention strategies

The following points are some possible lower back pain prevention strategies:

Think about and improve your daily posture.

Develop a regime of stretching exercises, and strengthening exercise to support under utilised muscles. Particularly those need for kayaking.

Work on developing core strength and flexibility with yoga and Pilates exercises. If you lack the self-discipline to do the exercises on your own, join a structured exercise class.

Developing and maintaining flexible muscles and tendons is extremely important in the prevention of most soft tissue injuries. Muscle and tendon flexibility allow movement without over stretching and injury. Soft tissue injuries (sprains and strains) occur when muscles and tendons are tight and rigid, then stressed beyond their natural range of movement.

Before any exercises, perform a thorough warm up of the muscle groups you are about to stress. Omission of a proper warm up means the muscles and tendons will be tight and ridged with limited blood flow to the muscle groups you are about to stress. This results in a lack of oxygen and nutrients for the muscles to operate with and make you susceptible to soft tissue injuries injury.

Remember listen to your body and ignore your brain trying to relive the good old days when your body was more forgiving of your abuse.

Treatment

For initial soft tissue injuries, treat by compression, elevation, and rest. After the bleeding has been controlled, apply ice. If ice is unavailable, use cold compresses re-cooled every ten minutes. Cold causes the blood vessels to constrict and slows bleeding that causes swelling. It also numbs the nerve endings thereby relieving pain.

Ice applied immediately to a sprain or strain, has been found to initially inhibit blood clotting. Use ice in the second stage of treatment (Australian Red Cross, 2000).

Bill Robinson's advice for marathon paddling

Bill Robinson is a Veterinarian, VSKC member and well known 'brown water' marathon paddler. In 2005 Bill completed a 1987 kilometre solo voyage along the Murray River. In his log of the journey and at his presentation at the VSKC Annual General Meeting he makes the following points about health and comfort while undertaking such long voyages.

Blister prevention—I used Gill Pro sailing gloves and put some 5 cm Co-Plus Bandage on my thumbs each day. I did not have a mark on my hands at the end of the journey, and am very happy with this strategy. Blisters are definitely not a consequence of marathon kayaking.

Bum care—I wore Lycra shorts, padded my seat with 'Ridgerest foam', and sat on a sheepskin. I had no bum or back problems, which can often affect paddlers on long trips.

Foot care—It is important to pad your footrests and the floor of the boat where you rest your heels

Sun care—A broad brimmed hat, Polaroid sunglasses and sunscreen are essential

Tendon care—Many kayakers can develop tendonitis in the wrist of the hand they use to feather their paddle. I used a 5 cm Elastoplast bandage on the tendons above my right wrist and had no problems.

Synthetic clothing—The most wonderful synthetic clothing is available I used Lycra shorts, polypropylene thermals, Polartec fleece and a very old but trusty Gore-Tex parka. Synthetics are light, generally inexpensive and dry very easily. I believe there is no place for wool or cotton on trips such as this.

Food—Naturally, this is a personal preference, but it should be light and highly nutritious. I ate the same thing every day—Muesli, honey and milk (powdered) for breakfast. Snacks during the day of dried fruit and muesli bars. Lunch was always Vita Wheat with either peanut butter or Kraft cheese (Which does not require refrigeration). Dinner was always Basmati rice mixed with a packet of Surprise dried vegetables, a tin of sardines or salmon, and a dash of sweet chilli sauce. Tea was a great companion and I added sweetened condensed milk from a tube to it. Very special treats were Old Jamaica Chocolate (Great if you hit the wall) and Coke.

Another point made about long distance sea kayaking is to wash with freshwater as often as possible if not daily.

Stretching and warm-up exercises

Warm-up exercises are viewed by many trainers as worthwhile and even important. It is claimed that the exercises *warm-up* the muscles by increasing blood flow to them before subjecting them to strenuous activity. An observation I have made about sea kayakers is that not many of them perform warm-up and or post warm-down exercises or stretching exercises.

Benefits of warm-up and warm-down exercises are considered to be increase blood flow to the working muscles and boosted activity of neuromuscular pathways, allowing them to be fully prepared for exercise. It also enables your joints to move more freely and prepare them for any stressful impacts. All of which hopefully leads to the reduced chance of injury during activity.

Over the past decade or so, the debate to stretch prior to exercise and after, has swung in favour of the most persuasive orator. Some people think stretching prior to exercise is worthwhile while others see it as being of little benefit. Nelson and Kokkonen make the statement "*to be most effective, however, stretching should be performed both during warm-up before a workout routine and as part of a cool-down after the workout.*" Those against pre-exercise stretching quote the mantra: *'Don't stretch before you sweat.'* Post exercise stretching seems to have a larger favourable audience. The purpose of stretching is to reduce the possibility of muscle and tendon damage during exercise and reduce muscle soreness. Performed regularly as a separate exercise regime, stretching is claimed to increase flexibility. Studies have shown that less flexible people are more prone to muscular injuries. Another option to a stretching regime is to perform regular yoga and/or Pilates exercises.

Some points about stretching. Remember it is much safer to under stretch than to overstretch. Remain within a comfortable stretch zone. If you feel any pain or discomfort at any stage of the stretch then stop the stretch immediately. Be gentle on your body. Many of the stretches can be varied and performed while sitting in your kayak. When stretching, hold the stretch for 30 to 40 seconds. Apparently, any longer than 40 seconds is of little benefit.

Insect repellent

To prevent sand-flies from biting when camping, mix equal proportions of anti-septic (e.g. Dettol) with baby oil. Use the thick baby oil, as you do not want it to be absorbed to quickly into your skin. If you go paddling/camping in places like the New Zealand's Fiordlands, take this mixture with you as well as head, torso, hand and leg insect netting.

Chapter 7 Meteorology

"I cannot command winds and weather".

Horatio Nelson

Introduction

As far as weather is concerned, all activity takes place in the troposphere. The troposphere's thickness varies from about eight kilometres at the poles to 28 kilometres at the equator, and varies daily and seasonally. It contains most of the atmospheric water and more than 90 per cent of the air mass. Clouds are formed by water vapour condensation, in the lowest eight kilometres of the troposphere. The troposphere height range is from the surface, to around 15 kilometres and the stratosphere, up to 50 kilometres.

As the sun warms the earth's surface, this in-turn warms the air above. Air above a land mass is warmed more than that above water. Warm air expands and rises, creating an area of low pressure (having less weight of air). Cold air is dense and sinks, to create an area of high pressure. Winds occur because the atmospheric pressures try to 'even themselves out'. The rising warm air is replaced by the movement of cooler dense air from the sides (i.e. wind).

The rotation of the earth causes the high and low-pressure wind spirals. In the Southern Hemisphere, air from high-pressure systems spiral anticlockwise and outwards, but spirals clockwise into low-pressure systems.

Southern hemisphere latitudes

Meteorologists when talking about Southern Hemisphere weather refer to three regions of latitude as *high-latitude*, *low-latitude* and *mid-latitude*.

High-latitude refers to the region below 55 degrees of parallel and covers the Southern Ocean and Antarctica.

Mid-latitude is defined by the BOM as:

. . . areas between about 30 degrees and 55 degrees latitude. For Australia, this is the area south of a line from half-way between Geraldton and Perth (in Western Australia) to Bourke (in New South Wales). This part of Australia generally experiences a temperate climate.

Low-latitude is defined by the BOM as:

. . . areas of the earth south of the equator and north of about 30 degrees latitude. For Australia, this means the area north of a line from half-way between Perth and Geraldton (in Western Australia) to Bourke (in New South Wales). This part of Australia generally experiences a subtropical to tropical climate.

Australia's Large-scale air circulation

Australia is affected by three major air masses: cold sub-polar (Southern Ocean) maritime air, hot and dry continental air, and warm moist air from both the Pacific and Indian oceans. Australia's weather is controlled by the annual north-south migration of the Intertropical Convergence Zone (ITCZ) and the subtropical high-pressure belt (aka mid-latitude anticyclonic or high-pressure ridge).

Simplistically, depending upon the season, along northern Australia and the equator, air is heated and becomes less dense and rises. This area is called the Intertropical Convergence Zone and is also referred to as the *monsoonal trough* or *doldrums* (Australian Hydrographic Service, 2004). In summer, the ITCZ sits around 15 degrees south. A convergence line forms when north-west monsoon winds from Asia, meet south-east trade winds blowing across Australia. The result is the uplifting of moisture laden tropical air. Tropical air from the ITCZ moves southward and rises to about fifteen kilometres. Around 25 degrees to 30 degrees south, it has cooled, condensed and descends creating what is called a sub-tropical high-pressure belt. Southward of the high pressure belt, the air rises and creates an area of low pressure around 40 degrees to 60 degrees south, which is characterised by the strong westerly winds of the *Roaring Forties*. Towards and over Antarctica, the cold dry air mass descends creating relatively high pressure over the poles.

Sub-tropical high-pressure belt

A belt of subtropical high-pressure dominates Australia's weather. This belt is the main area for anticyclonic activity and consists of anticyclones, troughs, cyclones and fronts. In southern Australia, the large-scale pressure systems move from west to east. Over northern Australia, they generally move from east to west and during the wet season, they change direction to generally move from north-west to south-east.

During the year as the seasons change, the anticyclones track either northward in winter or southward in summer, as a result of the earth's axis. Therefore, with the summer heating of the Northern Hemisphere, the ITCZ moves northward to around 15 degrees to 20 degrees north. In the Southern Hemisphere, winter cooling of continental Australia, causes an increase in air density and results in the high-pressure belt moving northward to around 29 degrees south to 32 degrees south.

The extra-tropical cyclones (aka *mid-latitude depressions*, *lows*), that track west to east well below Australia, move northward closer to southern Australia. They bring with them, the effects of the strong cold (2 °C to 3 °C) westerly winds (*Roaring Forties*) and associated cold fronts. The cold fronts produce very cold southerly winds and gales. If moisture is present, it also produces rain and snow.

Southern Australia is usually the northern boarder for the westerly winds and their effect are mainly felt in winter and spring. Western Tasmania is affected by these westerlies, which result in wet and windy winters and large seas impacting on it. Australia's winter weather is usually characterised by west to east moving high-pressure systems, which typically bring three to five days of fair weather. In between the highs there is the familiar passage of low-pressure systems and their associated phenomena (i.e. cold fronts).

Semi-stationary high and low pressure systems usually develop in winter, in the Tasman Sea. They block the passage of the westerly airflow and its associated systems of highs and lows. The blocking pair is referred to individually

as *blocking high* and *cut-off low*. Both of the blocking pair pressure systems are outside their normal zones. The low or trough is positioned closer to the equator than the high. Their positions block the easterly progress of other high and low-pressure systems, which intern causes a strong north-south wind, to split the westerly wind flow around the blocking pair. A result of blocking pairs is abnormal weather patterns in south-east Australia. A cut-off low may not necessary occur with a blocking high.

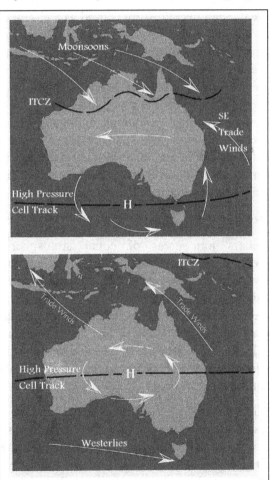

Figure 7-1 ITCZ & sub-tropical high pressure belt in January (top) and July (bottom)

AIR PRESSURE

Air pressure is the single most important weather element because it drives the winds. Air pressure is known as *barometric pressure*, and is the weight of a column of air above a location. Air pressure is affected by altitude, and meteorologists need a baseline from which to work from when forecasting weather. The standard chosen is *Mean Sea Level Pressure* (MSLP). At sea level the average pressure of air is stated to be 1.013×10^5 N/m^2 (or 14.7 lb/in^2). This value is used to define another unit of pressure, the *atmosphere* (atm). One atmosphere equals 101.3 kPa. On some weather maps overseas, a unit of barometric pressure is the *bar*. One bar equals 100 kPa; thus standard atmospheric pressure is slightly greater than one bar. In Australia, weather maps use hectopascals (hPa) as their unit of measure.

Mean Sea Level Pressure is used as a baseline, to normalise the various pressure recordings from observation stations at differing altitudes. Weather maps are therefore drawn to show air pressure at a horizontal level. This allows synoptic charts to show pressures affected by changing weather conditions, and not altitude. Mean Sea Level (MSL) air pressure can vary between 870 hPa to 1040 hPa but the norm is between 970 hPa to 1040 hPa. Refer to Appendix 1 for further information on air pressure.

Isobars

Isobars join areas of equal atmospheric pressure, and show areas of high pressure and low pressure. The various barometric pressures annotated against the isobars on a synoptic chart are normalised to the mean pressure of air at sea level, known as Mean Sea Level Pressure (MSLP). Outside of the tropics, the broad-scale wind flow is closely related to the distribution of atmospheric pressure.

Winds flow in order to distribute heat and are a result of air flowing from areas of high pressure to low pressure. Since the earth is rotating, the air does not flow directly from areas of high pressure to low pressure, but is deflected as a result of the Coriolis effect. In the Southern Hemisphere, the air is deflected to the left and to the right in the Northern Hemisphere.

Cells of high and low pressure systems are illustrated on synoptic charts using isobars, and are known as the *synoptic scale*. The central point inside a high-pressure system has a higher pressure, than the surrounding pressures. The central pressure inside of a low-pressure system is lower, than the surrounding pressures.

Difference in pressures over the earth's surface drive the winds in large swirls or eddies around the centres of highs or lows.

Winds flow roughly along the curves of high and low pressure systems as indicated by the isobars on a weather map. Wind strength is directly proportional to the distance between isobars. Additionally, frictional forces caused by the earth's surface, cause winds to flow slightly inward toward low-pressure systems (convergence) and outwards from high-pressure systems (divergence).

The pressure difference between isobars is the *pressure gradient*. The pressure gradient is a measure of the rate of change in atmospheric pressure measured over distance. The pressure gradient results in a net force, which is directed from high to low pressure. This force is called the *pressure gradient force*.

WINDS

Winds flow in order to evenly distribute heat, between the equator and polar regions. Wind direction and speed are determined by the patterns of highs, lows, fronts, and by local effects such as sea breezes and thunderstorm downdrafts.

Stronger wind speeds are associated with tropical cyclones, deep lows and cold fronts. Sudden squalls are associated with thunderstorms, heavy showers or the passage of a cold front or low-pressure troughs. These squalls can happen in clear skies (e.g. the southerly buster in NSW). The very strongest winds are caused by tropical cyclones, deep mid-latitude low-pressure systems and tornadoes/water spouts.

Geostrophic wind

Geostrophic wind is a theoretical wind that is steady, horizontal, and flowing parallel to straight isobars. The reason is, the pressure gradient force (i.e. the tendency for air to move from regions of high-pressure to low) is exactly balanced by the Coriolis force (i.e. caused by the earth rotation) and frictional forces. Frictional forces retard air masses, as they move over the earth's surface. Above the boundary layer (approximately 1000 metres), frictional forces are ignored.

Gradient wind

Gradient wind refers theoretically to a steady, horizontal wind, flowing along the curvatures of weather systems (isobars); because of this, it is a better approximation than geostrophic wind. It is a result of an imbalance between the pressure gradient and Coriolis forces. When the pressure gradient force is greater than the Coriolis force, the flow takes on a curved path around low-pressure. When the Coriolis force is greater, the curved flow is around high-pressure. The gradient level is taken from 1000 metres above the earth's surface and is chosen to be the most representative of the surface winds below. On synoptic charts the wind flowing around highs and lows are the friction free gradient winds.

Coriolis effect

The Coriolis effect affects both the atmosphere and the oceans. Coriolis effect is the apparent effect of the earth's rotation, on the motion of anything travelling across the surface of the earth. The Coriolis force is too small to notice when you walk or drive, but it affects the path of flying objects (i.e. aircraft, rockets, artillery shells). An aircraft flying in a straight line will to an observer on the ground, who is rotating with the earth, look as if it is flying a curved path. It is the appearance of this curved path that is a result of this effect. The Coriolis effect prevents the winds from the North and South poles, and equator, from travelling directly northward or southward. In the Southern Hemisphere, winds that blow towards the equator seem to move slowly and curve westwards. Winds that blow from the equator toward the poles seem to move eastward.

Wind Direction

On synoptic charts, the surface wind roughly follows the isobars. Surface wind differs from the geostrophic wind. Most change in wind direction happens between 100 to 1000 metres with little change below 100 metres at the surface.

Wind direction at the surface differs from the geostrophic winds (i.e. winds above 1000 metres)

direction, by a process called *deflection*. At the surface (under 1000 metres of height), the amount of deflection is a function of surface roughness. Wind deflects more as it passes from land to water, than it does from water to land. A variable approximation of deflection over land is 35 degrees and over water 15 degrees. Rough seas may produce a deflection of 25 degrees (Laughlin, 1997).

Decreasing from 1000 metres to the surface, the winds speed decreases and the wind changes direction. The wind deflects from the isobars of a low-pressure system to a high-pressure system. There is also an increase in turbulence and wind gusts. Increasingly rougher terrain will, increase the angle of deflection, cause a decrease in wind speed and increases gustiness (Laughlin, 1997). In short, winds do not follow isobars around coastlines or land as expected from the theory.

Backing and veering

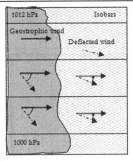 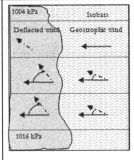

Figure 7-2 Wind backing

Figure 7-3 Wind veering

Backing and veering are terms used to describe the change of surface wind direction, from the geostrophic winds direction (deflection). The terms are independent of whether you are looking at a high or low-pressure system, or if you are facing the wind or have your back to the wind.

In the Southern Hemisphere, backing is when the surface wind, has turned counter-clockwise, from the geostrophic winds direction. Veering is when the surface wind has turned clockwise (from the observers point of view), from the geostrophic level wind direction.

Wind veers (is deflected clockwise) from the geostrophic wind direction, as it passes from water to land. Wind backs (is deflected anti-clockwise) towards the geostrophic wind direction, when it passes from land to water. The simple rule for wind deflection is; *wind will always be deflected in the direction from a high to low pressure.* The backing diagram at Figure 7-2, shows a high pressure of 1012 hPa down to a low pressure of 1000 hPa. In the veering diagram, the pressures are 1016 hPa down to 1004 hPa.

MACROSCALE CIRCULATION

Macroscale circulation (aka *synoptic scale* or *large scale*) refers to the cells of high-pressure and low-pressure systems as seen on the synoptic charts. Highs and lows range in size from hundreds to thousands of kilometres. The central point inside a high-pressure system has a higher pressure, than the surrounding pressures. The central pressure inside of a low-pressure system is lower, than the surrounding pressures. Difference in pressures over the earth's surface drive the winds in large swirls or eddies around the centres of highs or lows.

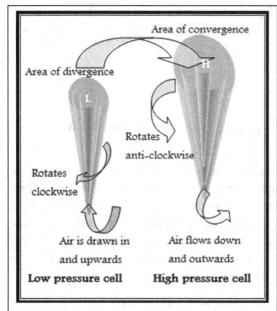

Figure 7-4 Low and high pressure air mass movement

As a general rule, inflowing air associated with low-pressure systems (aka *Lows* (L), *depression, or cyclone*) result in convergence and rising air, which often results in deep cloud formations and rainfall.

The descending out-flowing air from high-pressure systems (aka *Highs* (H), or *anti-cyclones*) results in an airflow divergence (i.e. spreading out) and is associated with more stable weather and light winds.

High-pressure system

A high-pressure system is also termed *anticyclone* or *high*. Highs consist of heavier descending air in the Southern Hemisphere. The descending air (wind) circulates anti-clockwise around the high's centre, following roughly the isobars and tends to spread outwards at the surface, refer to Figure 7-4.

During the year, anti-cyclones can cover the whole continent of Australia. The type of winds Australia experiences depends upon where the high or highs are sitting. Referring to Figure 7-5, the high to the east brought warm moist air from the Pacific Ocean, on to the East Coast from Cape York, down to East Gippsland. At the same time, Victoria received hot dry winds north-to-north-easterly winds, between 10 to 25 knots. When the cold front, came through on Sunday, the winds change to south-westerlies and on Monday were south-easterlies.

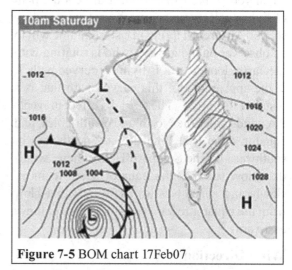

Figure 7-5 BOM chart 17Feb07

In general terms, a high-pressure centre over land usually produces fine dry weather, light winds with few clouds (because the air is descending). High-pressure gradients are weak and therefore winds are light. An *intensifying high* is one that is increasing in pressure. Air in an intensifying high near the surface spirals downwards and outwards.

Warm highs

Warm highs (that is the central air is warmer than its surroundings) are typical of sub-tropical oceans and typically pass over Southern Australia. A high-pressure centre near the coast can produce light rain, as moist sea air is directed over the land. The extreme stability of highs can cause surface air to remain near the surface, therefore causing an increase in water vapour and pollutants in the surface air. This can result in stratiform cloud, fog and smog in the outer regions of the high.

Blocking high

A *blocking high* is an intense high-pressure system that forms often in the south Tasman Sea and remains almost stationary for days to weeks. They are usually associated with cut-off lows.

Troughs

Troughs are an elongated area of relatively low pressure between two anti-cyclones. The two adjacent highs draw into the trough, polar and tropical heated air. This can result in the formation of a cold front. If the change (pressure dip), caused by the trough is small, it may not be as noticeable as a frontal change, but because of the pressure dip, it may result in gusty winds and or showers.

The pressure on each side of the trough is higher than along the axis of the troughs centreline. As a result, winds flow downward to the troughs centreline; converges and rises to form cloud and rain. Troughs can also be found in a low, depression, and even in a high-pressure ridge.

The difference between a trough and a front is that troughs have no temperature difference on either side of the centreline. A front is the interface between two air masses of different density (temperature and moisture content).

High-pressure ridge

The high-pressure ridge (aka *a ridge*, or *ridge of high-pressure*) is a high's extended (elongated) isobaric pattern. The ridge denotes higher air

pressure in relation to its surroundings, with no fully closed isobar indicating the centre.

Low-pressure systems

A low-pressure system (aka *Lows* (L), *depressions*, *cyclone*, *extra-tropical cyclone*, *mid-latitude cyclone*) is an area of lower pressure in relation to its surroundings. In the Southern Hemisphere, wind circulates clockwise around the centre of a low following roughly the isobar shapes. Lows contain lighter rising air that tends to contain more water vapour per unit volume than a high. Unsettled weather is associated with lows, if the low consists of vertically rising unstable air. Air is warmer at the low-pressure core and often moist; hence, it will rise and cool. If it cools enough, it results in condensation, cloud formation and rain. Lows generally produce clear air, because the ascending air is removing pollutants from the surface.

Cut-off low

A *cut-off low* is a low that has been completely cut off from the prevailing westerly winds. Cut-off lows may remain stationary for days or even head back east. They are usually accompanied by a blocking high. East coast lows are an example of this phenomenon.

Warm and cold core lows

The name given to a low depends on the type of core it has, either: *warm* or *cold*. *Warm core cyclones* form in the low latitudes (i.e. northern Australia) region and produce tropical cyclones, heat lows, cut-off lows and monsoon depressions. Because of the structure difference between warm and cold core lows, warm core lows generally produce greater destructive winds.

Cold core lows mainly occur in the high and mid-latitudes of Australia. These cold core lows are termed *mid-latitude depression, low temperate* or *extra-tropical cyclones*. They are a regular feature on the BOM daily weather maps. In the Southern Hemisphere, these lows, which can be greater than 1000 kilometres in diameter, pass west to east between 40 degrees to 65 degrees north and south. Cold core lows contain the coldest air at their centre throughout the troposphere. In cold core lows the coldest temperatures correspond with the lowest pressures. Winds associated with cold core lows are minimum at the surface and increase with height. The cyclonic circulation aloft is usually reflected on the surface by abnormally low daily mean temperatures, which are often accompanied by instability and showery conditions. This is the reverse to warm core lows. There are two types of fronts associated with mid-latitude lows: *cold fronts* and *warm fronts*.

Fronts

When air masses having different temperatures and moisture content meet, they generally stay separate from each other along a transition zone (boundaries) called *fronts*. Frontal boundaries always consist of areas of rising air and result in weather change. Fronts often do not occur as sharp defined boundaries between the two air masses. The frontal transition zones can be up to several hundred kilometres wide, separating the warm and cold air masses.

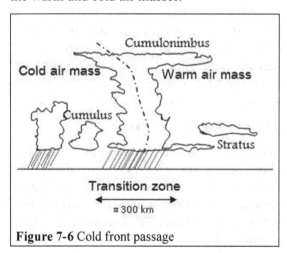

Figure 7-6 Cold front passage

Cold fronts

When Antarctic cold air moves northward and encounters warm moist air moving southward from the tropics, a cold front develops. Cold fronts are the transition zone between a colder air mass replacing a warmer air mass, by undercutting and forcing the warmer air upwards. If the moisture content is great enough in the rising air, it may rain because of the cooling effect.

Cold fronts normally produce strong gusty wind changes, which are not always accompanied by thickening cloud and rain. Altocumulus

and altostratus cloud, are often mixed in with cold front activity over much of Australia. Cumulonimbus cloud can be formed by the lifting effect of a cold front.

Warm fronts

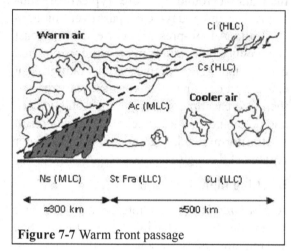

Figure 7-7 Warm front passage

Warm fronts are usually high-latitude phenomena and mainly occur over snow-covered landmasses in the Northern Hemisphere, like Russia and Siberia, northern Europe and North America. Warm fronts are infrequent over Australia, but are often seen on the weather maps, over the Southern Ocean. Particularly in winter, warm fronts have a major influence on the formation of strong winds in southern Australia.

Warm fronts are cells of warmer less dense air, in relation to the surrounding air, rising over the top of a semi-stationary but retreating mass of cold surface air. The dominating warmer air creates atmospheric instability as it replaces the cooler air.

Occluded fronts

Occluded fronts (aka *occlusions*) are belts of rain or snow. Occlude means to close, shut, shut in or out or off, or stop up (a passage etc.). They are a front formed when a generally faster moving cold front (15 to 30 knots faster), overtakes a warm front. The effect is the warm air lifts off the surface (i.e. is occluded).

There are two types of occluded fronts: *cold occlusion* and *warm occlusion*. A cold occlusion is when a colder and faster moving air mass (i.e. cold front) undercuts and lifts a warm front, and the cold air mass preceding the warm front. A warm occlusion is when the overtaking, fast and forward moving, cold air mass, is warmer than the colder air mass it is overtaking. The overtaking cold front is lifted by the colder and denser forward air mass. These various processes can intensify and expand into vast cloud systems, measuring hundreds of kilometres and lead to intensified storms.

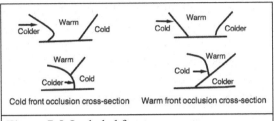

Figure 7-8 Occluded fronts

Occluded fronts are observed in the northern hemisphere, in the latitudes of Norway. For Australia, Hobart is at latitude 40 degrees south (40° S) and all of our weather occurs between 40 degrees south and the equator. As a comparison, to the northern hemisphere, Rome is around 40 degrees north (40° N). The main, general reason, why Australia is not affected by occluded fronts, is our latitude is 20 degrees closer to the equator than Norway, from where the Norwegian meteorologists in 1917 observed these phenomena and came up with the weather map symbols.

Warm and occluded fronts occur well to the south of the Australian continent. Occasionally a warm front will appear on the weather map. They are associated with complex low-pressure systems where there are successive lows south of each other.

Quasi-stationary front

A quasi-stationary front is also known as a *stationary front*, thought this is a misnomer. A front moving at five knots or less is considered to be a quasi-stationary front. A quasi-stationary front forms when a cold front or warm front slows down, or appears to stops moving, and does not appreciably replace the other air mass. The front slows or stops moving because the winds, behind and forward, of the front move parallel with, and not perpendicular too, the stationary

front. When a quasi-stationary front forms, the dense cold air stays on the ground and the warm moist air is displaced upwards often giving rise to persistent and sometimes severe amounts of rain. Since a quasi-stationary front marks the boundary between two air masses, there are often differences in temperature and wind on opposite sides of it. The weather is often cloudy and if the front is in an area of low atmospheric pressure, rain and even snow develops. A quasi-stationary front may last for several days until the atmospheric conditions allow the parallel flowing winds to change direction, allowing the front to move forward again.

The now mobile air mass may be a cold or warm front, or it may dissipate. In the tropics, quasi-stationary fronts are termed *Shear Line*.

Cool

A cool is a region between two highs and two lows that are diagonally opposed. Light variable winds occur near the centre. Fog may occur during autumn and winter periods.

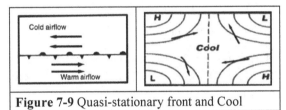

Figure 7-9 Quasi-stationary front and Cool

Temperature inversions

Temperature inversion is the reversal of cold air replacing rising warm air. During the day warm air rises and is replaced by descending colder air (relative to the warm air). At night, cold (dense) air sinks and settles to the lowest levels on the ground in thick layers of up to several hundred metres thick. Along the coast and over the land, the warm gradient air flows over and remains on top of, the colder thick blanket like layer.

Air turbulence cannot stir up the cold air, in order for it to be replaced, by the warm air above. The result is that the cold air becomes colder and the wind dies away. The inversion layer will exist until the sun begins to heat the land (which may not be until mid-afternoon), and the normal vertical temperature profile is restored.

Fog

Fog is defined as an obscurity in the surface layers of the atmosphere, which is caused by a suspension of water droplets, with or without smoke particles. Fog has been defined by international agreement, as being associated with visibility less than 1000 metres. If the visibility exceeds 1000 metres then the obscurity is a mist and or haze. There are four main types of fog formation but we are mainly concerned with *advection fog* and in particular *sea fog*.

Sea fog can occur when warm moist air moves over a surface that is cooler than the dewpoint of the warm moist air. The cooling moisture laden air, assisted with a light breeze, lowers the holding capacity to the temperature related dewpoint, to create fog.

Advection fogs can form in valleys open to the ocean, when the temperature falls in the evening combined with a sea breeze of 5 to 15 knots, to force the air upslope. Under mid-level cloud, thick advection fogs may be persistent in winter.

Weather in the tropics

The tropics can be defined as the area between the tropic of Cancer in the Northern Hemisphere and the tropic of Capricorn in the Southern Hemisphere. Both tropics lay along the 23.5 degree parallel. Different references give different positions for the northern and southern tropic boarders with 30 degrees north and south being used by Colls and Whitaker. The latitude of the tropics results in the sun always being high in the sky, which results in their being little to no seasonal variation like autumn and spring. As a result of the tropics yearly orientation towards the sun, their relationship with the oceans, and other geophysical relationships and phenomena, there are different weather pattern experienced.

Meteorologist use additional terms to explain and forecast the weather in the tropics. The following list is a synopsis of the terms and differences:

Convergence zone (CZ); is a non-frontal system (i.e. there is no temperature difference on either side). This is an area where winds of different speeds and directions meet and according to their properties produce lines of cloud (i.e. cloud bands) and rain.

Shear line; is the name for a quasi-stationary front in the tropics.

Instability line; is an isolated non-frontal band of cloud and rain in the tropics, which has no potential to develop into a tropical disturbance.

Tropical cyclone; in the Southern Hemisphere is considered (non-internationally standardised) as a clockwise rotating low-pressure system originating in the tropics, in which the ten-minute average winds exceed gale force (34 knots). (Laughlin, 1997)

Severe tropical cyclones have wind surface speeds exceed hurricane force (64 knots). Wind gusts may be up to fifty per cent stronger.

Storm surge; is a result of tropical cyclone winds and can result in coastal flooding. It is the temporary rise or fall in sea surface levels driven by surface winds and changes in atmospheric pressure. Two other factors affecting the development and extent of storm surge are *wave set up* and tides.

Tropical weather maps generally show, streamline arrows that indicate wind and the direction, without directly relating to the pressure gradient.

MESOSCALE & MICROSCALE SYSTEMS

Mesoscale systems (i.e. middle scale) typically possess short lifetimes of 24 hours or less; and are not normally evident on synoptic charts. They are however of considerable importance in determining local weather conditions and wind effects. Some of the events of interest are thunderstorms, southerly busters, squall lines, katabatic winds, sea breezes and land breezes. Some of the short-lived weather systems in the mesoscale range are also classified as microscale. Microscale phenomena last for minutes or hours, over distances of metres and or kilometres, rather than hundreds of kilometres.

Westerly gales

Westerly gales are common in late winter and early spring. They are generally associated with strong cold fronts. These strong westerly winds are modified by the topography they flow over prior to the coast. Passing off the east coast, these winds become strong offshore winds at gale force strength. Valleys like the Hunter and Shoalhaven in NSW funnel the westerly winds down to the coast, which may be stronger than the westerly winds along other parts of the coast.

Severe weather—Southerly changes

During summer, southerly changes can be cloud free but produce dangerous squalls and sudden wind shifts. Squalls and sudden wind shifts can occur with showers and thunderstorms.

Southerly buster

Southerly busters (aka *southerly burster*), occur as a result of wind changes ahead of a cold front that are trapped by the NSW coastal mountain range. Usually there is little cloud or warning of an approaching southerly buster. Cloud if present, is produced by the warm inflow air being forced to rise and produce shelf cloud (*arcus*). This may separate and produce a spectacular cloud with a tubular horizontal leading edge, known as roll cloud, which is orientated perpendicular to the coast. Wind speeds frequently reach 55 kilometres per hour (29.6 knots), with the possibility of wind speeds reaching up to 135 kilometres per hour (73 knots).

Thunderstorms

♪ **Warning**: If you see a cumulonimbus or thunderstorm clouds approaching within a few kilometres, get off the water.

♪ **Warning**: If you notice one quarter of the sky darkening with a cloud growing skyward above a darkening base, then head for shore and safe harbour.

Thunderstorms can be classified into four general types of the single-cell, isolated multi-cell cluster, multi-cell squall line and super-cell; however, super-cells are also multi-cellular. Thunderstorms are associated with cumulonimbus clouds. Cumulonimbus clouds in summer typically reach 10 kilometres plus in height and store an enormous amount of energy. Refer to Table 7-1 for pictures of cumulonimbus clouds.

As daytime heating produces hot air near the earth's surface, warm moist air rises and begins to cool; this is known as an updraft. In the updrafts, water begins to condense into tiny droplets that form the clouds. The water droplets condense in the clouds and release the latent heat from evaporation. The fast-moving updrafts start to build clouds to heights of up to six kilometres. As the rising warm moist air, is subsequently cooled, within the cloud, there are increased condensation development and the formation of ice crystals. These release further latent heat, to build clouds with heights up to 10 kilometres and sometimes higher.

① **Note**: To estimate how far away lightening is, count the number of seconds between the lightning and thunder then divide the time span by three. This is because sound travels at about 1 kilometre in 3 seconds.

At the point where the water droplets and ice crystals become too large and heavy, they can no longer be supported by the uprising air and begin to fall, producing rapid and violent downdrafts on the leading edge of the cloud. In a mature thunderstorm, updrafts and downdrafts operate side by side. The downdrafts produce high winds, heavy rain, thunder, lightening, and possibly hail.

♦ **Caution**: Despite the obvious sea conditions that would accompany downdraft phenomena, kayak paddles make a good lightening conductor.

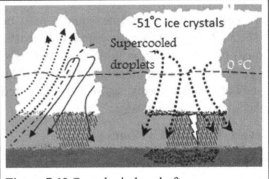

Figure 7-10 Cumulonimbus drafts

After an hour or two, the thunderstorm has released its previously stored, enormous amount, of energy. The downdrafts drag in cool dry air, which prevents further updrafts of warm moist air. The cycle is now broken and the clouds begin to dissipate.

Line Squall

● Caution: Any sharp cold front must be regarded with caution and a close weather watch maintained.

With an extremely active or severe cold front, the temperature difference between the cold and warm sectors is large. Convection (heat transfer), along the front is large, with the warm air mass being extremely unstable. Line squalls may not be forecasted, due to the fact that the front intensifies during its passage creating a thunderstorm.

① Note: Squall lines and strong winds are possible several hundred kilometres in front of a cold front.

Line squalls may be accompanied by a long low black 'rolling cloud' across the horizon in advance of the front. This is caused by the rapid advance of the cold front forcing warm saturated air to tumble over and condense out (rain). A squall line may appear as a wall of advancing cloud with spreading cirrus (Ci), but the severest effects of the squall line are near the numerous cumulonimbus (Cb) cells.

Squall lines vary in length, with the longest being those that develop in a pre-frontal trough 50 to 100 nautical miles ahead of a cold front. Squall lines can be hundreds of miles in length and between 10 to 25 nautical miles wide and travelling at 25 knots. If squall lines are formed in conjunction with strong mid-level winds, surface winds can exceed 50 knots.

In southeast Australia, line squalls may be associated with fast moving winter cold fronts. Squall lines are common in northern Australia and associated with summer heat troughs, feeder bands of tropical storms, sea breeze fronts and other convergence zones.

Severe Weather Cyclones

Tropical cyclones

Tropical cyclones form over water not land. Tropical cyclones rarely occur between 10 degrees north and south. The highest occurrence of tropical cyclones is off the coast of Mexico, in the north-east Pacific. The next highest region of occurrence is the Philippines, in the north-west Pacific. Tropical cyclones are also referred to as *hurricanes* or *typhoons*. Tropical cyclones in the south-east Pacific and south Atlantic do not occur as the water temperatures are less than 26 degrees Celsius. Tropical cyclones are unable to cross the equator, and derive their spin from the Coriolis effect. In the Southern Hemisphere they rotate clockwise and in the Northern Hemisphere, anti-clockwise. In order to cross the equator they would have to reverse their rotation. The process to do this would destroy the cyclone.

Tropical cyclones in Australia occur generally from November to April, though very few have occurred in November. The latitude spread for the formation of tropical cyclones is considerable and is dependant upon the position of the monsoonal depression, which itself may range from 5 degrees south to 20 degrees south. The two predominant regions for tropical cyclones in Australia are off the Queensland coast at around 20 degrees south and off the north-west coast of Western Australia. As a generalisation, the most affected areas of tropical cyclone activity are above 30 degrees south. The northwest Australian coastline between Broome and Exmouth is the most cyclone prone region in Australia. From 1970 to 2008, 75 per cent of severe tropical cyclones occurred in this region.

Tropical cyclones may be stationary but more often travel with a mean speed of approximately 10 knots, with individual cyclones moving much faster. Tropical cyclones in the Southern Hemisphere have a southerly component to their direction. Depending upon the latitude cyclones may change direction, which is termed *recurve*. West coast cyclones may travel south-west until 20 degrees south, then turn south-easterly or southerly. East coast cyclones do not recurve as much as west coast cyclones, but may move south-east to around 20 to 25 degrees south then turn southerly.

If a small intense low-pressure cell produces gale force winds (34 knots or greater), it is known as a tropical cyclone. Mean sea level pressures as low as 870 hPa have been recorded. Tropical cyclones form over warm (27 °C plus), waters and are powered by enormous amounts of energy.

The energy is from the release of latent heat, stored in the condensed warm water, rising into the atmosphere. Cloud bands producing heavy rainfall can extend outwards from the centre for several hundred kilometres. Over cold waters or land, the condensed warm water, loses its stored energy and the cyclone dissipates. The average duration of a tropical cyclone is five days but vary from a few hours, to a day, to more than 20 days.

Tropical cyclones announce their intended arrival with cirrus cloud development, which may appear some 300 to 600 nautical miles away. The next cloud development is continuous cirrostratus with lower altostratus then stratocumulus. As the cloud becomes denser, with the barometric pressure dropping around three hector-Pascals, light rain and showers develop. As the pressure drops winds become strong and cumulonimbus cloud moves onto the horizon, and appears to stay there for several hours. This feature is known as the *bar of the storm*. If the cyclone is to pass, the bar will drift in that direction on the horizon; if not, it will head towards you. As the bar moves closer the pressure drops rapidly, and wind speed increases. This is also accompanied by numerous and gradually increasing intensity, squall lines sweeping past with accompanying precipitation. Very dark clouds, almost continuous squalls, a precipitous drop in pressure and rapidly increasing wind speeds accompany the arrival of the bar. The cyclones centre may still be 100 to 200 nautical miles away.

As the centre approaches it is accompanied by torrential rain and gale force or greater winds. Depending upon the wind strength (at time of observation), the seas are moderately high to mountainous. As the centre arrives the pressure drops to its lowest point of 30 to 70 degrees below normal (around 980–940 hPa or lower). Winds drop to a breeze, and the skies clear enough for the sun to be seen through relatively thin cloud. The seas are confused. As the wall on the opposite side of the eye crosses, there is a reversal of the weather events experienced during the eyes approach. The next phase of the cyclone passes quicker than the approach phase, as various parts of the cyclone are narrower in the rear.

Sever tropical cyclones

Sever tropical cyclones have wind surface speeds exceed hurricane force (64 knots). Wind gusts may be up to fifty per cent stronger.

Extra-tropical cyclones

Extra-tropical cyclones are large pressure systems outside of the tropics. They are common during autumn and winter. Meteorologist, pay particular interest to the rapidly deepening systems, which can dramatically affect costal waters within hours. They can produce gale force winds, rain and rising seas and swell. They can take the form of a well-structured low with encircling isobars or as a surface low with few if any isobars around the area of low pressure. The setting up of a strong pressure gradient (isobars close together) develops strong winds or gales near or well away from the low up to many hundreds of kilometres. Two types extra-tropical low are *Southern Ocean cyclones* and *East Coast cyclones.*

Southern Ocean cyclones

Southern Ocean cyclones are enormous storms, often 200 kilometres across, generally circling the earth from west to east. Australia is on the northern edge of this cyclonic belt. In winter, this belt moves further northward, causing windy and storm conditions. The storms often bring cold fronts.

East coast cyclones

East coast cyclones have a similar intensity to a tropical cyclone. The clockwise air circulation brings gales and heavy rain to the coast, to the south of the cyclone's centre; while the weather northward often clears quickly. East coast lows are a cut-off low. East coast lows can occur any time of year and are a phenomenon occurring off the NSW coast. East coast lows is the name given to a variety of intense low-pressure systems and they can develop in a number of ways. During summer they may be the remnant of ex-tropical cyclones that have moved south along the east coast. They may have lost the characteristics of a tropical cyclone but still possess devastating power that can lash the NSW coast. They can produce gale force winds, very rough seas and heavy swells. Other causes of these intense lows can be from an easterly dip over inland NSW or the association with a cold front that moves across from South Australia. A difficult to forecast east coast low are the ones that develop off the NSW coast. These rare and occurring usually in winter events often develop at night. These small intense lows bring with them their associated phenomena and little time for warnings to be issued by the BOM. This type of mesoscale phenomena often last less than 24 hours before moving off into the Tasman Sea.

Coastal Winds

Sea breeze

Sea breezes are local winds associated with highs and warmer weather. Sea breezes are temperature driven and obtain maximum strength around mid-afternoon. As the land heats up during the day, the air becomes less dense and rises. Cooler sea air, which is heavier and therefore lower to the surface, moves into replace the less dense air over the land. In other words, higher pressure air moving towards an area of low-pressure air, at the surface. This results in a local circulation cell being established. At night and early morning, a reverse flow pattern may be established, where a light offshore breeze can be initiated. This is discussed under land breeze. Sea breezes reinforce the prevailing wind when both are heading in the same direction. Generally, light winds can be increased to moderate or fresh wind conditions.

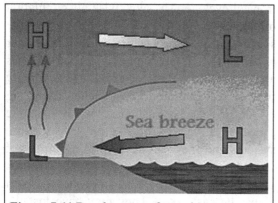

Figure 7-11 Development of a sea breeze

Sea breeze strength is influenced by the geostrophic wind strength and direction relative to the coastline, temperature gradient between the water and land; and geometry of the coastline (i.e. gulfs, bays, islands and peninsulas). If there is a very small pressure gradient, the sea breeze will generally average 15 to 18 knots. Strong sea breezes develop around October in the north and November in the south of Australia. Typical sea breezes have a speed of around 20 knots, with 30 to 35 knots having been recorded (Australian Hydrographic Service, 2004).

Land breeze

Land breezes (aka *offshore breeze*) are generally weaker than sea breezes. At night when the land cools down the sea has retained its heat. The air over the sea is warmer than the land's and therefore rises as a result of being less dense and therefore a lower pressure.

In the early morning, the cooler land air is heavier and therefore at a higher pressure than the sea's air. The cooler heavier air (i.e. wind) moves towards the warmer lighter air over the ocean. Land breezes are usually a gentle breeze of 4 to 6 knots and can extend to 5 or 10 nautical miles out to sea. On cold clear nights in winter, a land breeze situation can be more pronounced when the land temperature drops well below the sea. Important consideration needs to be paid to the early morning land breeze along the coast (NRC-RS6, 2000).

Offshore winds

Gradient winds blowing off shore (from land on to water), increase in strength (speed), by 50 per cent (0.5). This is because of the reduced frictional drag, created by the water's surface. Wind speed on the open sea, can be twice the forecasted wind speed. Wind gusts of 1.5 times the gradient wind are possible.

Offshore winds generally knock down the sea state and create a deceptive sight of calm water and light breezes against the beach. Look for white caps offshore. Determine unobstructed wind speed from mid-level cloud movement and surrounding topography. Narrow topographic features funnel offshore winds, with dramatic turbulence. Cliffs produce down drafts and reverse flow patterns. Headlands can deflect wind and gaps between landmasses can funnel the wind.

CLOUDS

Having knowledge of cloud formations is a worthwhile skill to possess for determining the approaching weather and in particular the wind. Clouds are visible evidence of the atmosphere's motions, water content, and degree of stability. They are the weather's signposts in the sky.

Clouds form by the condensation of water vapour, consisting of water droplets or ice crystals. Clouds form when the air becomes saturated by being cooled to the dew point or through the addition of moisture. Most clouds are formed through some lifting process. The excess moisture condenses on minute particles in the atmosphere, hence forming droplets. Clouds are formed through five ways of lifting: *orthographic, mechanical friction, convection, frontal activity*, and *convergence*.

Orographic lifting occurs when air is forced upward by a barrier of mountains or hills. Warm moist air moving up over mountains cools, causing the water vapour to condense and form clouds over the high ground with the possibility of rain, depending upon the amount of water vapour. The BOM states that Australia's heaviest rainfall occurs on the Queensland coast and in western Tasmania, where prevailing maritime airstreams are forced to lift over mountain ranges.

Mechanical friction is associated with strong winds and turbulence. Turbulence created by strong winds over the ground produce turbulent eddies, which causes the ground air to lift above the cooler upper air. If the properties are right in both parcels of air, the top layer cools, condenses and produces formations of stratus or other lay type cloud. Cloud produced by frictional turbulence usually does not produce rain, but may develop drizzle from the denser layers.

Convective lifting (aka *thermal lifting*) occurs when air heated at the earth's surface, rises vertically in the form of thermal currents or bubbles. Solar radiation heats the ground and the air next to it. The warm air becomes lighter and rises up (convection). If there is water vapour present, as the air becomes cooler, the water vapour condenses and forms clouds. Cumulus clouds are often the result of convection. Other forms of cloud formed by this process are Cumulonimbus, which may reach altitudes above 15 000 metres. Cumulonimbus cloud development can produce strong winds, heavy rain, hail and lightening.

Frontal activity (aka *widespread ascent*) results from the interaction of frontal air masses. When a cold frontal air mass moves into replace a warm air mass, the cooler denser air undercuts the lighter warm air, and forces it to rise ahead of it. As the warm air rises and cools it develops cloud formations along the front at all altitudes. The associated cloud and weather derived from this interaction vary enormously, according to the properties of the air masses.

Convergence lifting occurs when horizontal flowing air masses, or parts of a single air mass, converge on the earth's surface. As a result the air cannot go down but has to go up. The air rises slowly and if moist enough, condenses at the condensation level to produce extensive layers of stratus type clouds (i.e. nimbostratus, altostratus and cirrostratus) and cirrus cloud. Large-scale convergence can lift air masses hundreds of kilometres wide; however, the vertical motions of convergence lifting are typically much weaker than the vertical processes of convective lifting.

Active fast moving fronts can cause the air mass to rise faster, leading to cumulonimbus formations. The BOM sates that *convergence lifting is often associated with wave-like disturbances in tropical easterlies and may also occur with broad tropical air masses flowing to the south. Given sufficient atmospheric moisture and instability, it may cause large cloud clusters and rain.*

Cloud types

The Latin names of the clouds describe their characteristics. *Cirrus* meaning 'curl/hair', *stratus* meaning a layer, *nimbus* meaning rain bearing and *cumulus* means 'a heap'. There are two basic classifications of cloud: *cumuliform* (L. *cumulus*—heap) clouds and *stratiform* (L. *stratus*—layer) clouds.

Cumuliform (heap) cloud has a vertical growth development. Generally, buoyant lifting, rather than orographic lifting, forms these cloud types as with stratiform cloud. Cumuliform clouds produce showers rather than rain.

Stratiform (layer) cloud has an extensive horizontal development, as opposed to the more vertical development characteristic of convection or thunderstorms. Stratiform clouds cover large areas but show relatively little vertical development. Generally, they produce steady rain as opposed to showers.

Clouds are sorted into three main altitude bands of high level cloud (HLC), above 6 kilometres from the earth's surface; middle level cloud (MLC), between 2.5 up to 5 kilometres heights; low level cloud (LLC), that occur from the earth's surface up to 2.5 kilometres and one vertical development group *Cumulonimbus*, commonly known as thunderstorms. The altitude bases and heights vary and depend upon the thickness of the troposphere at nominal locations (i.e. tropics, temperate or Polar Regions). Often described as ten main cloud types, the three main altitude bands contain nine types of cloud, three in each altitude band, plus one vertical development band as shown in Table 7-1 Cloud Types.

The three main high-level cloud types are: cirrus (Ci), cirrocumulus (Cc) and cirrostratus (Cs). The three main types of mid-level cloud are: altocumulus (A), altostratus (As) and nimbostratus (Ns). The three main low-level cloud types are: stratocumulus (Sc), stratus (St) and cumulus (Cu). The one vertical development cloud is cumulonimbus (Cb).

The ten main types are further divided into 27 sub-types according to shape, height, colour, and associated weather phenomena. The common term 'mare's tails', associated with cirrus clouds, have the meteorological name of Uncinus (Ci UNC), and fall into this category.

Table 7-1 Cloud Types

High Level Cloud (HLC) 6000 to 12 000 metres
Cirroform clouds (i.e. HLC) often preclude unsettled weather even though they do not produce rain. In summer, they are often associated with windy conditions

Ci, Cirrus: (Latin meaning: *curl*) have white tufts or filaments in narrow bands. It may have dense heads, with falling streaks of ice crystals, dropping behind producing a hooked wispy hair shaped cloud, known as *mares tails*.
Usually separate from other clouds it may merge into cirrostratus or cumulonimbus. It is formed by widespread ascent but sometimes turbulence.
It is associated with cold front activity or upper level disturbances.

Cs, Cirrostratus: can be seen as *Mares tails*, or as a semi-transparent veil. It can have a smooth appearance over much of the sky, as a transparent, fibrous, whitish veil and possibly lacking definite shape,

or form (amorphous). It produces halos phenomena about the sun or moon. Cirrostratus is produced adjacent to cold fronts and is formed by widespread ascent. It may merge into cirrocumulus or possibly altostratus.

Cc, Cirrocumulus: Thin white patch, sheet or layer with small regularly arranged formations in the form of grains or ripples that may be either merged or separate. It is the true *mackerel sky*. It may merge into cirrostratus but is often associated with a front or upper level disturbance. When associated with upper level disturbances it can preclude unsettled weather.
Most unusual cloud in Australian sky, but covers large areas of the continent but does not produce rain.

Medium Level Cloud (MLC) 2500 to 6000 metres

As, Altostratus: is a greyish/bluish sheet, often having a appearance, as waves or ripples, across the sky. It is thin enough to reveal a vague sun without any halo, but possibly a corona. Altostratus often merges into nimbostratus. It is caused by widespread ascent and when presented as a thick deck, it is usually associated with cold fronts or upper level disturbance. Translucidus gives the appearance of the sun as viewed through an opaque glass veil. (*Altostratus translucidus* shown)

Ac, Altocumulus: has a white/grey patch, bands or sheet of regularly arranged flattened globules of cloud, in waves or rows. Sometimes called *mackerel sky*, in reference to its scale like appearance however, the term actually refers to cirrocumulus. A corona may be visible around the sun. Usually caused by turbulence and not associated with a change in the weather. Types include: *Undulatus (Un):* parallel undulations (corrugations in either patches, sheets, or layers). (Altocumulus *undulates* shown)

Altocumulus Castellanus (Cas): name refers to the turret or crenellated shape cloud formation. Usually it is associated with altostratus, but it can turn into altocumulus. When associated with altocumulus, it means atmospheric instability, with possible thunderstorms and or other severe weather, like tropical cyclones. (Altocumulus *castellanus* shown)

Ns, Nimbostratus: (Latin: nimbus meaning: cloud, halo) is a medium level cloud, with a dense grey/dark thick layer. Often with ragged or diffused base and associated with continuous rain. It usually extends up to the high-level ceiling and merges with altostratus. It may also extend to low levels and cover hills. Cloud bases around 150 metres result in continuous rain and or drizzle. Scud cloud (Pannus) may form beneath it and may be observed rapidly moving across the sky, being pushed by the wind. (Nimbostratus 150 to 2500 m shown).

① Note: Nimbostratus in some references is classed as low-level cloud

Low Level Cloud (LLC) Surface to 2500 metres

Sc, Strato-cumulus: form can be a grey/whitish patch, sheet or layer of separate or partly merged globular masses, or rolls with dark shading and generally irregular appearance. Possibly, the most frequently seen cloud in Australia. It is most frequent with winter highs, creating what is termed *anticyclonic gloom*, when moist air is trapped under an inversion layer. It produces no shower activity and is particularly noticeable in Melbourne. (Strato-cumulus opacus 600 to 1500 metres, shown).

Cu, Cumulus: (Latin meaning: *heap*). Exists as individual cells (puffs of cloud) or as massive columns (vertical rolls or towers). When sunlit, appear white heaped puffs to massive columns; usually sharp outline but may be ragged. Tops may freeze and produce localised showers. Generally observed with grey flat bases, that starts from 700 metres to 2000 metres; and even reaching the mid-level altitudes. Similar to stratocumulus, except cumulus is taller and has no organised structure. Cumulus may turn into stratocumulus at night, or over the ocean.

Cumulus humilis (Latin *humilis*, meaning: lowly) is a fair weather cumulus, which appears as individual cells, with bases possibly at 500 metres over the ocean, to 1000 to 2000 metres over land. During considerable instability and thermals, they continue to grow taller to form cumulonimbus. Cumulus humilis, (shown) ranging from 600 to 1500 metres. Heights are from the base, as tops may reach into MLC altitudes

St, Stratus: (Latin meaning: spread, laid down). Grey 20 to 200 metre thick layers with fairly uniform even base from which drizzle or light rain may descend. If ragged in appearance, called 'fractostratus'. Obscures hills and tall buildings; produces poor visibility, like fog and is referred to as 'ground fog'. (Clouds are one form of condensation the others being fog, mist, rain and dew; stratus cloud is fog.). *Stratus*, (shown), heights from 150 to 600 metres.

Vertical Development Cloud Classed as low-level cloud, in reference to the height from which the bases start.

Cb, Cumulonimbus: is commonly known as thunderstorm clouds. Cumulonimbus is a heavy dense cloud with a large vertical development. The bases are at the low or medium levels, with the tops possibly reaching the tropopause. Cloud development can produce strong winds, heavy rain, hail and lightening.

Cumulonimbus Calvus (Latin *Calvus*, meaning: bald) clouds with the large cauliflower head prior to further growth and the anvil shaped head; which indicates a storm is still developing.

The familiar **Cumulonimbus incus** (Latin *incus*, meaning: anvil) has anvil shaped heads. Refer to the thunderstorm notes for further information.

Cumulonimbus (Note: darkened base)

Cumulonimbus calvus (Note: large cauliflower shaped towers)

Cumulonimbus incus

THE WEATHER MAP

☀* BOM Caution: *Getting the latest Chart. Refresh your browser to ensure you get the latest chart. This also applies to forecasts, warnings and satellite pictures available on this service.*

Weather maps are actually synoptic surface weather charts (aka *synoptic chart*). The term synoptic is derived from *synopsis* meaning a short statement, summary and or outline. The Macquarie dictionary defines a synoptic chart as: *a chart showing the distribution of meteorological conditions over a region at a given time.*

The weather map shows the familiar highs and lows, troughs and ridges, as well as frontal activity associated with Australian weather. Shaded areas on weather map show where there has been rain, in the previous 24 hours. Wind information is derived from the isobars however, in the tropics, wind direction is shown with arrows that have a series of barbs on their tails, to indicate speed. Weather maps are issued with a written forecast message for both land area forecasts and marine and ocean forecasts. This information is useful in interpreting the synoptic chart and is commonly relied upon.

Types of synoptic charts

There are two types of synoptic chart (aka *synoptic map*), the *analysis* and *prognosis*. The analysis chart is a snapshot of the weather situation at the base observation time (valid time). Prognosis charts are a forecast of the weather situation for the specified time. This type of chart indicates how the weather patterns are expected to develop (i.e. the four-day MSLP Prognosis chart).

Three BOM charts, which are useful to recreational mariners, are:

Australian Region MSLP analyses

Australian Region MSLP prognoses

Indian Ocean Region MSLP.

Chart levels

Surface charts are labelled 'MSL' for Mean Sea Level. Upper air charts are labelled with the pressure level in hectopascals (hPa) (e.g. 500 hPa). Note that pressure decreases upwards in the atmosphere (e.g. the 250 hPa level, is higher than the 500 hPa level).

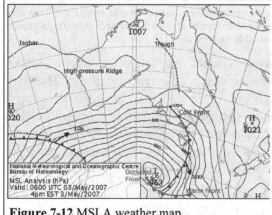

Figure 7-12 MSLA weather map

BOM charts are updated every three hours, some every six hours, some every 12 hours, and others every 24 hours. 'Valid time' is the time when, the chart is valid. The 'issue time' is the time when, the chart is issued. The analysis chart is a snapshot of the weather situation at the

valid time. Prognosis charts are a forecast of the weather situation for the valid time.

Chart symbols

When interpreting a weather map, an understanding of some systematic weather patterns is needed, as well as knowledge of how to interpret the drawn information. The weather map is issued with a legend that shows the names of the different symbols used and the units of measure.

Isobars

On a weather map, isobars join areas of equal atmospheric pressure, and show areas of high pressure and low pressure. The various barometric pressures annotated against the isobars are normalised to the mean pressure of air at sea level, known as Mean Sea Level Pressure (MSLP). The weather map's legend will state the unit of measure applied to the barometric pressures (e.g. hectopascals). Isobars are drawn at 4 hectopascal intervals. The pressure difference between isobars is the pressure gradient.

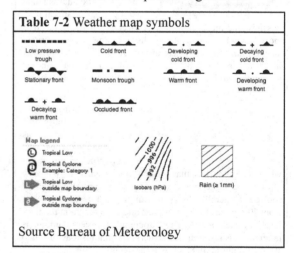

Table 7-2 Weather map symbols

Source Bureau of Meteorology

Cells of high and low pressure systems are illustrated on synoptic charts using isobars, and are known as the synoptic scale. Winds flow roughly along the curves of high and low pressure systems as indicated by the isobars on a weather map. Additionally, frictional forces caused by the earth's surface, cause winds to flow slightly inward toward low-pressure systems (convergence) and outwards from high-pressure systems (divergence). The average speed of low-pressure systems and their associated cold fronts over southern Australia can be estimated as approximately 25 knots. High-pressure systems move at an average speed of approximately 15 knots.

Outside of the tropics, the broad-scale wind flow is closely related to the distribution of atmospheric pressure. That is it is related to the pressure gradient and latitude. In the tropics, the Coriolis effect is not as strong. Tropical weather maps generally show, streamline arrows that indicate wind and the direction, without directly relating to the pressure gradient.

Wind strength is directly proportional to the distance between isobars. On a weather map, when isobars are drawn spaced close together, compared to other isobars with a larger space between them, it indicates a high-pressure gradient and therefore higher wind speeds. This phenomena and strong winds are associated with low-pressure systems, near cold fronts, and in the westerly airstream south of Australia. A larger space between adjoining isobars indicates a low-pressure gradient, and lighter wind. This phenomenon is associated with high-pressure systems. Low latitudes (i.e. closer to the equator) produce higher wind speeds than higher latitudes for the same isobar spacing.

When you estimate from the synoptic chart the theoretical direction of the winds, by following along parallel to the isobars, remember the closer you get to the surface (land or water), the more the wind deflects towards the pressure gradient (from high to low pressure) (Laughlin, 1997). In short winds do not follow isobars around coastlines or land as expected from the theory. The isobars on a synoptic chart show gradient wind or friction free wind that is above 900 metres. Gradient wind follows the curves of the isobars. Friction affected winds are winds measured at a height of 10 metres above the surface. To determine the surface wind direction from the synoptic chart the rule of thumb is to veer the gradient wind by 10 degrees over water and 30 degrees over land. For example a WNW wind is 230 degrees true, travelling over land the surface winds direction would be 260 degrees true.

Other observations about isobars are: within in five degrees of the equator winds can blow perpendicular to the isobars. Isobars dipping towards the pole then turning back towards the equator is referred to as *Polar dip*. It is an area of cyclonic shear and indicates the possibility of a low forming.

Ridges and troughs

The method of illustrating and identifying a high-pressure ridge and a low-pressure trough are shown at Figure 7-12 and Table 7-2.

Fronts

The methods of illustrating different frontal activity are shown at Figure 7-12 and Table 7-2. The symbols used to illustrate fronts were made during World War One by Norwegian meteorologist. These meteorologists put forward a theory about frontal activity known as the *Norwegian Cyclone Model*. They likened the boundary line separating two air masses to the military term 'front' for opposing armies. The barbs associated with the cold front symbol are alleged to represent the spike helmets of the German army. The round dome symbol used for warm fronts is alleged to be derived from the dome shaped helmets of the British.

Cold fronts replace warm air with cooler air, which may cause significant cloud and weather development according to the properties of both air masses. They are more frequent and vigorous over southern Australia. Warm fronts replace cold air with warmer air. They occur mainly over the Southern Ocean as Australia's latitude restricts their occurrence over land. Occluded fronts are phenomena mainly in high-latitudes, where a fast moving cold front moves in and undercuts a warm front and overtakes it, causing unsettled weather and winds. Quasi-stationary fronts (aka stationary fronts) develop when a cold front or warm front slow or stops moving. This is due to winds blowing parallel to the stationary front, instead of perpendicular. In this situation, the isobars are nearly parallel with the front, which make it an easy characteristic to identify on a synoptic chart. This type of fronts causes heavy rain and even snow falls in the right atmospheric conditions.

Time stamping

Some weather charts are time-stamped in Coordinated Universal Time (UTC) (aka 'Zulu' Time (Z)). This is equivalent to Greenwich Mean Time (GMT). To convert the weather maps UTC to Australian local time perform the following: Australian Eastern Standard Time (EST) is UTC + 10 hours. Central Standard Time (CST) is UTC + 9.5 hours Western Standard Time (WST) is UTC + 8 hours.

The period of *daylight savings time* (DST) is determined by State or Territory Governments. At the start, local clocks are advanced one hour and at the end of the period, clocks are turned back by one hour. Across Australia's three time zones, the BOM denotes the three DST zones as: EDT—Australian Eastern Daylight Time, CDT—Australian Central Daylight Time, and WDT—Australian Western Daylight Time. The weather maps are time-stamped for example as EDT (i.e. UTC + 11 h).

Wind roses

Wind roses are found printed in the Australian Pilot. Wind roses are used to show wind speed and wind direction. The BOM uses long-term averages data, collected over 15 years or more, for the compilation of their wind roses. The data is generally collected from 9 a.m. and 3 p.m. observations. Wind roses are used to summarize the occurrence of winds, over a set period of time (e.g. for a month, at a set time and location, showing their frequency, direction and strength).

The size of the centre circle represents the percentage (frequency) of calm conditions. A larger circle would represent a higher frequency of calm conditions. Wind direction, is represented by 'telescope' branches. The branches are orientated to the eight points of the compass (N, NE, E, SE, S, SW, W, NW), with the rose being orientated to North.

To represent the wind speed ranges (strength), each individual 'telescope' is divided into segments of different thickness and colour. Each segment length is proportional to the frequency of winds blowing from the indicated direction. In other words, a longer 'telescope' segment; show a greater frequency of wind blowing from the indicated direction. The thicker the 'telescopes' segment the greater the wind speed.

Wind barbs

Wind barbs are a common way to show wind direction and strength on weather maps in tropical areas. The wind barb's shaft is orientated along the wind's direction (*The feather end points into the wind*). The wind barb's *tail* feather indicates the forecasted wind strength. A full-length feather on the shaft of a wind barb represents 10 knots. A half-length shows 5 knots. A 15 knot wind, is represented by, one-half and a full-length feather. A 30 knot wind, is represented by, two full-length barbs. A thick black feather and or a triangle feather represent 50 knots plus winds.

WEATHER FORECASTING

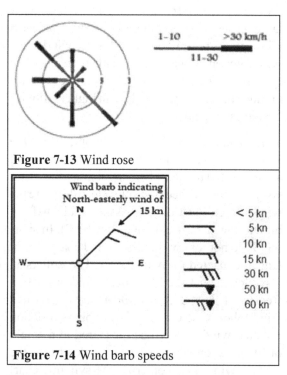

Figure 7-13 Wind rose

Figure 7-14 Wind barb speeds

Sources of information

For planning, the most common source of information about marine weather is the Internet. Appendix 2 lists useful websites that can be accessed to plan a trip and find out information about marine weather. However, there are times when there is no Internet access and the old-school ways of getting information is reverted to. Depending upon the situation you are in, they all have their limitations for availability, practicality, accessibility, currency and timeliness of information, range—communications equipment, the requirement for electricity—batteries, power supply etc.—and personal knowledge and skill to implement one or more of the options. One or more of the following methods are able to provide weather information:

Newspapers

Public radio (i.e. AM/FM transistor radio receivers)

TV broadcasts

27MHz broadcasts by Limited Coast Stations

VHF voice radio (Operators certificate required)

Telephone Weather Services (TWS)

RSS feeds

Satellite communications (i.e. satellite phones)

HF radio (Operators certificate required)

HF/MF SSB radio receivers

Observation and recording of marine and weather signs

Asking yacht and or fishing boat crews.

THE BUREAU OF METEOROLOGY

The Bureau of Meteorology (BOM) is a primary source of Internet weather information for mariners. Many of the other weather websites reference information from the BOM. The BOM marine forecast service is designed for small craft engaged in commercial activities and recreational users such as offshore ocean yacht racers. The Australian coastline is broken up into coastal areas with the relevant forecast being accessible by a map or drop-down menu for the area of interest.

Types of marine forecasts

The three types of marine forecast currently available are *coastal waters forecast*, *local waters forecast* and *high seas forecast*. The coastal

waters forecast extends 60 nautical miles offshore from the coast. It provides a précis of the current weather situation, a forecast of winds, seas, and swell (both primary and secondary if applicable). If applicable, *coastal waters wind warnings* are also flagged for the affected State's/Territories coastal area. If there is no warnings the forecast will say so. Local waters forecasts are designed for bays, harbours and inland waterways on which large numbers of recreational and commercial vessels operate. In Victoria, Port Phillip, Westernport Bay and the Gippsland Lakes are covered under local waters forecasts. The high seas forecast is designed to meet the International Convention of Safety of Life at Sea (SOLAS) agreement. These forecasts are also broadcasted by radio and satellite for ships on the high seas.

Forecast and warnings issue times

Coastal waters and local water forecasts are issued by Regional Forecasting Centres, in the respective State's capital city. Coastal waters forecasts are for areas within 60 nautical miles off the coast. Generally issued twice daily but monitored for any changes, with updates being issued as required.

Marine weather warnings are issued as coastal waters wind warnings, ocean wind warnings, and warnings for storm tide and dangerous surf/large waves. Warnings for coastal waters are issued whenever strong winds, gales, storm force or hurricane force winds are expected. The initial warning attempts to provide around 24 hours lead-time (sometimes out to 32 hours) and warnings are renewed every 6 hours (BOM, 2011).

Warnings wind speed categories

The following wind speed categories are based on 10 minute averages, and are used by the BOM for coastal and high seas wind warnings:

Strong wind warnings are issued for winds of 26 to 33 knots

Gale warnings are issued for 34 to 47 knot winds

Storm force wind warnings are issued for 48 to 63 knot wind range

Hurricane force wind warnings are issued for winds of 64 knots or more.

In the tropics, hurricane force winds are associated with severe tropical cyclones of Category 3 and above.

Forecast and warnings delivery systems

Bureau of Meteorology weather forecasts and warnings are delivered by Internet, recorded telephone services, public radio/TV broadcasts, VHF voice radio and HF voice radio. Other sources include HF radiofax, telephone-weather fax and satellite communications. Current and updated information about the delivery systems can be found on the BOM website.

Other aids to forecasting marine weather

In addition to weather maps, forecasts and warnings a person can also access radar imagery and satellite images. The BOM provides information on weather, wind, waves, tides, tidal streams, sea levels, sea temperatures, currents and historical data like averages and trends. Currently the BOM is introducing a very useful forecasting tool called *Forecast Explorer*. It is designed for both the marine and land environments. Marine Forecast Explorer shows detailed graphic information on weather (temperature and rainfall), wind and waves.

BOM wind definitions and terminology

For this manual, the Australian Bureau of Meteorology (BOM) is the primary source of marine weather information. The following definitions are used by the BOM to define winds.

Wind speed

Observed wind speed is the average speed of the wind, over a 10 minute period, at a height of 10 metres above the surface.

Gusts

Gusts are increases in wind speed lasting for just a few seconds. The speeds are typically 30 to 40 per cent higher than the average wind speed, but stronger gusts are likely in the vicinity of showers, thunderstorms and frontal systems.

Squall

A squall is an abrupt and large increase in wind speed, with duration in the order of minutes, and which diminishes rather suddenly. Approaching gusts and squalls can be identified on the water by what are termed 'cat's paws'. These are small but numerous ripples streaking across the surface.

Beaufort number and descriptors

For marine weather, the BOM references the Beaufort wind scale. The Beaufort wind scale uses observations of the effects of wind on trees and or the state of the sea to estimate wind speed. The *Description at sea* is for a vessel *far from land* (i.e. in deep water and for a fully developed sea). Strictly speaking, the scale and descriptors are for a fully developed sea; meaning the wind has travelled over its maximum distance and has imparted energy into the water, to produce waves of maximum height. If you refer to nautical wind, time and fetch tables, you will see the correlation. The following warning used to be attached to the copies of the Beaufort scale issued to mariners: *A guide to show roughly what may be expected on the open sea, remote from land.* A complete Beaufort scale of winds table, as used by the BOM, is at Table 7-4.

Wind direction reporting

N	0°	E	90°	S	180°	W	270°
NNE	22.5°	ESE	112.5°	SSW	202.5°	WNW	292.5°
NE	45°	SE	135°	SW	225°	NW	315°
ENE	67.5°	SSE	157.5°	WSW	247.5°	NNW	337.5°

Table 7-3 Compass points & bearings

Wind direction is reported from the direction the wind is coming from. Forecasts use eight compass points to report the expected direction the wind, and sixteen compass points for observation recordings. The compass point and bearing at Table 7-3 has the eight forecasting compass points in bold text.

BOM Forecasts of winds

Wind speed forecasts over land, are reported in kilometres per hour (km/h). Over water, it is reported in knots (kn). Some countries report wind speed in metres per second (m/s).

Table 7-4 Beaufort scale of wind forces

PLEASE NOTE: "Beaufort scale numbers and descriptive terms such as 'near gale', 'strong gale' and 'violent storm' are not normally used in Bureau of Meteorology communications or forecasts".

Beaufort scale number	Descriptive term	Units in km/h	Units in knots	Description on Land	Description at Sea
0	Calm	0	0	Smoke rises vertically	Sea like a mirror.
1-3	Light winds	≤19	≤10	Wind felt on face; leaves rustle; ordinary vanes moved by wind.	Small wavelets, ripples formed but do not break: A glassy appearance maintained.
4	Moderate winds	20-29	11-16	Raises dust and loose paper; small branches are moved.	Small waves—becoming longer; fairly frequent white horses.
5	Fresh winds	30-39	17-21	Small trees in leaf begin to sway; crested wavelets form on inland waters	Moderate waves, taking a more pronounced long form; many white horses are formed—a chance of some spray
6	Strong winds	40-50	22-27	Large branches in motion; whistling heard in telephone wires; umbrellas used with difficulty.	Large waves begin to form; the white foam crests are more extensive with probably some spray
7	Near gale	51-62	28-33	Whole trees in motion; inconvenience felt when walking against wind.	Sea heaps up and white foam from breaking waves begins to be blown in streaks along direction of wind.
8	Gale	63-75	34-40	Twigs break off trees; progress generally impeded.	Moderately high waves of greater length; edges of crests begin to break into spindrift; foam is blown in well-marked streaks along the direction of the wind.
9	Strong gale	76–87	41-47	Slight structural damage occurs—roofing dislodged; larger branches break off.	High waves; dense streaks of foam; crests of waves begin to topple, tumble and roll over; spray may affect visibility.
10	Storm	88-102	48-55	Seldom experienced inland; trees uprooted; considerable structural damage.	Very high waves with long overhanging crests; the resulting foam in great patches is blown in dense white streaks; the surface of the sea takes on a white appearance; the tumbling of the sea becomes heavy with visibility affected.
11	Violent storm	103-117	56-63	Very rarely experienced—widespread damage	Exceptionally high waves; small and medium sized ships occasionally lost from view behind waves; the sea is completely covered with long white patches of foam; the edges of wave crests are blown into froth.
12+	Hurricane	≥118	≥64		The air is filled with foam and spray. Sea completely white with driving spray; visibility very seriously affected

Accessed from www.bom.gov.au/lam/glossary/beaufort.shtml 19Dec07 Note: The "Description at sea" above does not mention the formerly printed "far out to sea", where the waves are in deep water and unaffected by the sea floor.

The Bureau of Meteorology's, forecasts of wind speed and direction, are average (or mean) values, over a 10 minute period, taken at a height of 10 metres. Wind speeds usually increase with height above the sea-surface. When there are expected variations along a coastal area, a range may be given (i.e. 15 to 25 knots).

Forecasts of gusts are not included as routine broadcasts, however statistically it is estimated that gusts, typically exceed the average wind speed by about one third. For example, if the forecast (average) wind speed is 15 knots, you can expect gusts of around 20 knots (e.g. 15 x 1/3 = 5, 5 + 15 = 20). Gusts are generally associated with showers, thunderstorms and fronts.

BOM forecasting of waves

Refer to the chapter on oceanography and the topic Wave forecasting.

BOM land area forecasts

The BOM issues twice daily land area forecasts and updates as required. The forecasts also flag current weather warnings for the State/Territory. Of interest is the State forecast, which is designed for users to quickly ascertain expected conditions across the State. It provides information on the current weather situation, temperatures, wind speed in kilometres per hour, and rainfall across the state. District forecasts provide a general forecast for the designated districts. Additionally they include UV warnings and UV index information.

Graphical views of the States/Territories weather are also available. Forecast Explorer—land view, short-term forecast map (aka MSLP Prognosis chart), the forecast map for the next four days and the Australian weather region MSLP Analysis map are all available tools to compliment the land and marine area forecasts. Two other useful graphical representations weather maps are the Asia MSLP Analysis map and the Indian Ocean MSLP Analyses map.

READING THE SIGNS OUTSIDE

Observation and recording of marine and weather signs

It is worthwhile teaching yourself how to interpret the weather signs out side. Keeping a notebook on the subject can do this. Collect the weather maps and the BOM observations for the maps as well as the BOM Notes on the Weather, satellite images and radar images. Also note down your observations for the period of time of the forecast. Purchase a pocket/wrist-watch barometer and practice with it and note down the pressure readings in your observations. You can also make an aide-memoire (a note book to help you remember) and write in the other natural signs of changing weather, like the behaviour of birds, animals and insects and take it with you when you are outdoors. With good information and practice your knowledge and skills will develop.

Weather signs in the field

① **Note:** the following signs are a possible indication. The only way to really forecast the weather from the signs is to get outside and do it on a regular basis.

A red sky in the morning, heralds possible bad weather approaching.

A grey morning is the result of dry air above the haze, formed by the collection of dew on dust particles in the lower atmosphere.

Early morning mist rising from a valley means fair weather.

With fog or mist, there is a possibility of condensation but not rain unless the wind picks up and blows the fog/mist away.

On a fine day, a noticeable increase in wind strength heralds a weather change.

If a wind is constant and dry, the weather will remain constant, until the wind drops or changes. There will then be the possibly of rain.

If clouds start descending, bad weather is approaching.

If low level clouds heading in one direction and upper level clouds heading in another, forecasts a surface wind change in the of direction of the upper level clouds direction.

A rainbow in the afternoon heralds fair weather.

A red sun or sky at sunset means there is little moisture in the atmosphere and it is unlikely to rain the next day.

If the sun is pale and watery looking when setting, it heralds windy and or rainy days.

A grey overcast evening sky, heralds' rain, since dust particles are laden with moisture.

A corona around sun or moon. A large ring indicates good weather (but there could be a moderate breeze). It is associated with Cirrus and Cirrostratus cloud. Moisture in atmosphere is evaporating and the weather will be fine. After fine weather, a corona heralds wind. A shrinking corona heralds rain. A ring around moon at night means Cirrus or Altostratus cloud, which heralds the approach of a warm front and possible rain.

A clear night sky means settled weather. There is a possibility of a cold night and even frost, since there is no insulating cloud cover.

When there is a multitude of stars clearly visible one night and the next night only a few stars are visible, it heralds a change in weather.

Campfire smoke rising steadily heralds settled weather. If smoke swirls or moves back down, it heralds approaching wet weather.

Refer to Table 7-5 for a description of possible cold front cloud patterns.

Hours prior	Cloud	Weather
48	Clear sky or small Cu	Fine; north-east wind
24	Medium Cu; Ci approaching from west	Fine; gusting northerly winds
12	Overcast Ci or Cs; large Cu	Possibility of showers; strong north-westerly winds
6	Overcast Ci or Cs; some Ac, large Cu and some Cb	Some showers; possibility of lightening to west and south-west; strong north-westerly winds
Front	Ci, Ac, As, large Cu and Cb	Showers, squalls and storms; wind backing to south-west
After	Cu, Sc & As clearing	Showers and clearing rain; cooler southerly or south-easterly winds

Table 7-5 Possible Cold Front Clouds Patterns

Refer to Table 7-1 for cloud types and abbreviations.
Source Keith Colls and Richard Whitaker, AWH, 2nd Ed.

AIR PRESSURE & INSTRUMENTS

By combining information from the barometer, weather maps and forecasts from the media, and personal experience from sky watching, you can make the most of the Bureau's weather service. Refer to Appendix 1 for further information on air pressure.

Absolute Pressure

Absolute pressure is also referred to as *actual*, *local*, and/or *ambient* pressure. In aviation, it is referred to as *QFE*. It is the actual pressure in any location, at any given time. Mean sea level pressure (MSLP or QFF in aviation), is the pressure at sea level. Mean sea level pressure is the pressure normally given in weather reports by the media.

When barometers are set (normalised), to match the local weather reports, they measure pressure reduced to sea level and not the actual local air pressure. For example, the absolute air pressure reported from Mt Hotham is lower, than that reported from Aireys Inlet. This is because Mt. Hotham is at a higher altitude than Aireys Inlet, which is on the coast. However, base lining the reported local air pressure to sea level normalises for everyone in the state, the daily normal range of atmospheric pressure fluctuations. Normalising the reported pressures from different locations, allows the isobars drawn on a weather map to be meaningful.

Typical Mean Sea Level pressure is around 1013 hPa. It can drop to 990 hPa for a deep low, and rise to around 1040 hPa for an intense high. Depending upon weather conditions air pressure at sea level can fluctuate between 950 hPa to 1050 hPa. For a tropical cyclone, MSLP may fall to around 900 hPa. On a stable day, air pressure can fluctuate plus or minus one hectopascal (±1 hPa).

Relative Pressure

Relative pressure (aka *QNH* in aviation) is used to perform air pressure measurements and calculate elevation—sea level is assumed to be zero pressure. In aviation, setting the altimeter to read QNH tells the pilot the airfield's elevation. Effectively the altimeter will read the local elevation and display the barometric pressure. Setting the altimeter to QFE the elevation of the airfield is set to zero. QNH is the air pressure transmitted in weather reports.

Barometer Display

Barometric air pressure is corrected to sea level, regardless of the physical location (in the mountains or on the coast), of the barometer. The air pressure at sea level is assumed to be zero. This zero pressure is called QNH. Dependant on weather conditions, the air pressure at sea level fluctuates, between 950 and 1050 hectopascals. Even on a stable day, there can be fluctuations in air pressure of plus or minus one millibar (±1 mbar), due to the temperature. This corresponds to a deviation in altitude of plus or minus eight meters (±8 m). Fast changing weather, like cold fronts, can cause a change by up to five hectopascals in one day and the deviation in altitude can amount to up to 40 meters.

Reading bar charts

When using measuring instruments, consult the manufacture's documentation for the type of instrument you are using. The following is only a guide to reading bar charts:

One hectopascal equals one millibar.

Typically, isobars on weather maps are of 4 hectopascal scale.

Air pressure can rise and fall by 2 hectopascals during the day as a norm.

A change (especially a fall) of 5 hectopascals in 24 hours indicates approaching front or Low.

A change (especially a fall) of 3 hectopascals in 3 hours indicates stronger winds (possibly up to gale force) in the next 6 to 12 hours.

A change (especially a fall) of 9 hectopascals in 3 hours indicates stronger winds (possibly up to storm force) in the next 3 hours.

If travelling towards the on-coming expected weather you may need to add 1 to 3 hectopascals of pressure rise or fall during the 3 hour period. If travelling away from the expected weather the reverse is true.

Table 7-6 Short term barometric wind indicators

Wind	Barometer: Falling weakly	Wind	Barometer: Rising weakly
NW	Weak front, generally moderate winds	NW	Light winds. Coastal sea breezes
NE	Scattered thunderstorms & possible local gusts, light to moderate winds	NE	Light winds. Coastal sea breezes
SW	Weak southerly change, Winds may freshen with change	SW	Moderate to locally fresh SW winds
SE	Freshening winds, particularly in the east	SE	Light winds. Coastal sea-breezes
Wind	**Barometer: Falling strongly**	**Wind**	**Barometer: Rising strongly**
NW	Strong front approaching, Gales possible	NW & NE	—
NE	Strong winds likely	SW	Strong winds moderating quickly
SW	Cold front approaching. Strong winds likely	SE	Winds moderating quickly
SE	Rare in summer but, can lead to strong winds particularly in the east	Source BOM, Boating Weather Series, Wind Waves Weather, Victorian Waters	

CHAPTER 8 OCEAN ENVIRONMENT

"A man who is not afraid of the sea will soon be drowned, for he'll be going out on a day he shouldn't. But we do be afraid of the sea, and we do only be drowned now and again."

From The Arran Islands by J. M. Synge

CURRENTS

For mariners moving water is one of two reasons for the discrepancy between dead reckoned and actual boat position (aka *drift*). Water in motion is termed *current*, its direction is termed *set* and its speed is termed *rate*.

Ocean currents are the horizontal movement of water not caused by tides and usually follow a seasonal pattern. Ocean currents are referred to by their force mechanism either *wind driven* or *thermohaline*.

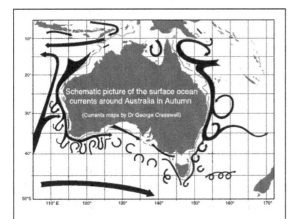

Figure 8-1 Ocean surface currents around Australia
Credit: George Cresswell, CSIRO Marine and Atmospheric Research

Wind driven currents drive the majority of the world's surface currents and makes up ten per cent of the oceans currents force mechanism. The wind affects the upper 100 to 200 meters of water depth but the flow of the wind driven currents can extend beyond 1000 meters in depth. Thermohaline currents are driven by differences in heat and salt and are typically sub-surface and make up 90 per cent of the world oceans.

The horizontal circular closed loop movement of the wind driven currents are called *gyres*. The Antarctic Circumpolar Current, also called the West Wind Drift is the only ocean current to circulate the earth. Ocean eddies are spawned by strong ocean currents and are typically 100 to 200 kilometres in diameter and circulate both clockwise (cold) and anti-clockwise (warm). Ocean eddies are found in the East Australian Current.

Other factors influence the oceans currents rate and set like the Coriolis effect, land masses the depth and shape of the ocean's floor, gravity, solar heating and factors like El Niño.

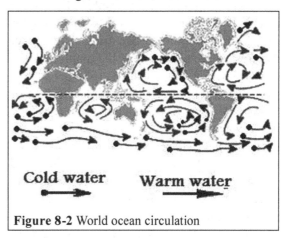

Cold water   **Warm water**

Figure 8-2 World ocean circulation

Other types of currents

In addition to wind driven and thermohaline ocean currents there are several other types of currents:

Seasonal current is a current that changes speed and or direction due to seasonal winds. The mean circulation of ocean currents is semi-permanent and experience little periodic or seasonal change.

A **periodic current** is current that changes its speed and direction cyclically, at regular intervals (i.e. tidal currents aka tidal streams).

A **coastal current** is one, which flows outside the surf zone, roughly along the coast.

Longshore currents (aka *littoral current*) are generated by waves hitting the beach at an angle and which flow parallel and inside the surf zone.[1]

Rip currents (aka *rips*) are the result of the incoming wave's water returning back out to sea from a beach or other land mass. They are discussed further under Rip Currents.

GENERAL WAVE THEORY

Wave terminology

All waves have certain properties in common. For water waves, the following terminology is applied. The peak is the crest; the bottom is the trough. The horizontal distance between crests is the wavelength (L). When describing water wave characteristics, the centre line is referred to as the mean or equilibrium level and is a little lower than halfway between the crests and troughs. The distance between the centre line and either the crest or trough is called the amplitude and is a measure of how much a wave rises or falls from its usual position (i.e. height). The number of waves that pass a certain point in one second is the wave's frequency. For water waves, the time interval between successive crests is the wave period (P) in seconds (sec) and the speed of a wave is in knots (kn). The speed of a wave does not depend upon its amplitude or frequency but the flexibility and density of the medium.[2] When you increase frequency, you decrease wavelength.

When two opposing waves with the same amplitude meet, they pass straight through each other. However, in the region of overlap they can interfere with each other. When the crests align with crests and troughs align with troughs, the wave is said to be *in-phase*. The crests of the two opposing waves, and troughs, can combine to produce a peak and trough, with greater amplitude than that of the two individual waves (i.e. at the point of intersection the crest becomes higher and the trough becomes deeper. This is known as *constructive interference*. When an opposing crest meets a trough (*out-of-phase*), they oppose each other. This is known as *destructive interference*. When opposing waves with phases somewhere between the two extremes of in-phase and out-of-phase meet, it results in a *partially destructive* interference wave. The combining peaks and troughs, reach a value somewhere between the maximum possible displacements.

Wind waves

Wind waves are also known as *sea waves, local seas* and *seas*. Ocean waves are primarily caused by wind. Friction between the wind and water imparts energy into the water to form waves.[3] Wave height, length and period depend upon fetch (straight unobstructed distance the wind moves over), duration time of the prevailing wind, wind speed and water depth.[4]

A two knot breeze will cause the water to ripple and when the wind ceases, surface tension restores the surface of the water. Wind above two knots forms more stable gravity waves as gravity takes over from surface tension and waveform progresses to produce pointed crests and rounded troughs. The wind reinforces the waveform by producing a downward force on the windward side and eddying over the crest to decrease pressure on the leeward side. As the wind increases to around seven knots, the crest of the waves steepen until they become unstable and break possibly producing observable scattered white caps. At around 12 to 15 knots wind speed, frequent white caps are observed producing ocean chop (i.e. choppy conditions). Far out to sea in deep water, which cannot affect the wave's motion, the height of these wind waves created by Force 4 winds may be 0.5 to 1.25 metres high.[5] These small deep-sea waves have a short period wavelength and the imparted wind energy is near or at the surface. As the wind changes direction or stops, the wind waves in that area dissipate their energy quickly and cease because they are outside the wind generation area. When the wind is blowing, sea waves travel in the direction of the prevailing wind. These sea waves generally move slower than the wind, due to slippage between the wind and the waves it is generating. As the wind's speed, duration and fetch increase, the sea waves build up. During gale conditions over 800 nautical miles for 59 hours, waves can be expected to reach a height of around eight metres. During storm conditions, with Force 10 winds for 59 hours over a thousand nautical miles, wind waves of around 15 metres high can be expected. It is these larger waves which become swell.

Swell waves

Swell waves (aka *swell*, *wave train*, *groups* and or *sets*) are groups of waves that have moved away from their area of generation. For example, swells arriving along the western Victoria coastline are more likely than not, wave trains generated from a storm or storms, down in the Southern Ocean, in the region of the *Roaring Forties*. When the wind, generated by the storm, changes direction, stops, and or the wave speed exceeds the wind speed (as a result of decreasing wind speed), the waves keep travelling on in the direction they were generated as swell, regardless of local winds.[6]

At the time of generation, individual wind waves merge and combine and increase in size and speed. If the storm can escalate in intensity (wind velocity of Force 10 or greater), in duration (time), and unobstructed area (fetch of 600–1000 nautical miles) then more energy can be imparted into the growing wind waves, which become bigger (50–60 feet) and faster moving. The storm creates waves of different energies (measured as wave periods) that eventually group together regardless of wave heights as a wave train (swell) and leave the area of generation. The sea waves with their short wave length lose their small amount of energy and dissipate. Since waves of the same wave period have the same speed, the faster groups move off ahead of the slower groups. As a result, you could see the larger period swells one day then followed by the successive smaller period swells days later as the swell 'drops off'. The swell waves become more rounded and regular in height (clean swell) as they travel, providing no other winds are influencing the swell and creating chop. As the wave train (swell) moves from its area of deep-water generation, with periods of 14 second or more, it can theoretically travel around the world if unobstructed.

If you increase any or all of the wind variables of velocity, fetch and duration you will get larger swells. Larger swells have more energy and are called long-period swells, with a wave period of 14 seconds or greater.[7] Long period swells move faster and even through the smaller, less energetic, slower moving groups of short-period swells, which have a wave period of less than 14 seconds.[8] The swells of different energies do not combine therefore swells of different speeds do not combine, because wave (swell) period is directly proportional to speed.

Wave characteristics in deep water

As a wave travels in deep water (where the wave cannot touch the seabed and be modified), only it's shape moves forward as the water particles (matter) are not taken with it. In this condition a boat will bob up and down and not go forward appreciably with the wave.

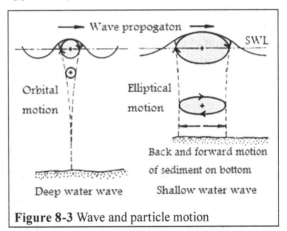

Figure 8-3 Wave and particle motion

The theory is, if you imagine a wave passing from left to right, as the wave passes, a water particle at the surface (e.g. 12 o'clock position), is causes to move and roughly follow a circular orbit, see Figure 8-3. As the wave crest passes, the particle is lifted and moves forward (in a clockwise direction), giving the illusion of the water's movement forward. As the crest passes, the particle is orbiting in a clockwise direction, travelling around past the three o'clock position. As the trough approaches, the particle at the three o'clock position then starts to travel in the opposite direction of the wave (pulse of energy). As the trough passes the six o'clock position, the particles orbital motion is in the opposite direction to that of the wave. The particle continues in its clockwise orbit to eventually return to the surface and begin another orbit.

Wave characteristics in shallow water

Shallow waters tend to produce short seas, which are waves that are steep sided. Be aware that a two metre ground swell can turn into a three to four metre breaker in shallow water.[9]

As the waves approach the shallow coastline, they begin to feel the sea floor (*feel bottom*). Water drags against the sea floor, slowing its forward speed and distorting the circular orbits to elliptical, creating the horizontal back and forth motion under water. The shallower the water, the slower the waves speed, since wave velocity is proportional to the square root of the depth. In shallow water (d ≤ 0.8H) the waves speed becomes a function of depth but the wave's period (amount of energy), remains the same, while the wavelength becomes shorter. With the same amount of energy but shorter wavelength, the wave height increases and the wave is said to shoal.[10] When a swell shoals, it is termed *ground swell*.[11]

The effect of a shorter wavelength and increased wave height can be dramatic depending upon the steepness of the sea floor and height of the tide, which can amplify the effects. A *rage sea* occurs when the ground swell breaks over a shoal, even in calm conditions. Approaching this area from seaward is considered dangerous, depending upon conditions, as a paddler or even a recreational and or commercial vessel can be 'swatted' by large breakers.

As the wave slows at the bottom, water piles up (*shoaling*), until eventually the wave reaches a critical point (depth of water is around 1.3 times the wave's height) when the steep faster moving crest falls forward and collapses (*breakers*).[12] A series of breaking waves (*surf*) disintegrate into turbulent sheets of water, called *bores*, that dissipates the wave's energy and carries sand and 'trashed' kayakers up onto the beach in the *swash*.

Reflection, Refraction and Diffraction

Reflection (aka *clapotis*) occurs when a wave encounters a vertical or near vertical feature like a cliff or groyne and rebounds. That is to say reflected back on itself with little loss of

energy.[13] *Standing waves* are caused in a situation whereby the rebounding waves interact with the incoming waves to produce a stationary up and down motion and steep sided lumpy waves (i.e. *confused seas*).

Figure 8-4
Wave reflection

Figure 8-5
Wave refraction

Refraction is wave bending and can be caused by current action around headlands. If a wave contacts the bottom at an angle to the beach each part is slowed in succession as depth decreases and the wave aligns itself to the bathymetric contours, which causes a change in direction (refraction) as the wave *wraps in*. Wrapping also occurs around headlands with long period swells. This affects your planned rest stop plans, as the beach is no longer protected and you have to surf in. Then depending upon the wave height and period, you then need to figure out, how you are going to get back off the beach.

Diffraction is the bending of waves around an object towards the *shadow region* behind the object. Picture an island rising steeply out of deep water with a swell impacting on one side. As the wave contacts the steeply rising island, the wave energy bends around it somewhat and passes slightly into the shadow region behind the island. With an island rising up in shallow water, the waves would refract and wrap around the island.

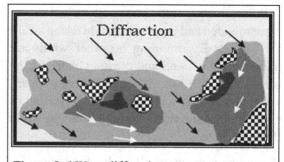

Figure 8-6 Wave diffraction

With diffraction there is a rule of thumb: only if the wavelength is smaller than the size of the object will there be a significant shadow region. The seaward side of our deep-water island (obstacle) would receive the larger waves but the island being larger than the wave's length would, through diffraction, cause the wave's energy to be propagated sideways around the island. This creates a shadow region on the leeward shore and therefore calm water.

Types of breaking waves

There are three basic types of breaking waves, whose shape is determined by the steepness of the beach the wave is arriving at. They are *plunging*, *spilling* and *surging waves*.

♀ Warning: Dumpers can cause injury over shallow water or when landing on a shore. Avoid surfing over areas or landing on shores where dumpers are active.

① Note: It can be an absolute annoyance trying to launch off the beach with dumpers breaking on shore. Be careful you are not thrown back on to the shore, so wear your helmet just in case.

Plunging wave (aka *dumpers*) and tubing waves are when the wave shoals quickly over a few metres. An example is when a wave contacts a reef or steep sand bar. The forward trough stalls but the following crest continues at speed until it runs into the stalled trough. The forward momentum of the impacting crest causes the wave to jack upwards and rapidly forward, forming a tube.

Spilling waves break gradually over a considerable distance, as a result, of a gentle sloping seabed. As the wave slows and steepens, on contact with the gentle sloping seabed, only the crest breaks and spills down the face. Spilling waves can peak on an outer bar, then spill across the next bar, to go on and reform in an inner longshore trough before spilling over an inner bar.

Surging waves occur when there is a steep seafloor leading up to the beach. The wave peaks up and transforms into swash on the beach without actually appearing to break. They occur on steep sloping seafloor beaches when the waves are low. They can also be observed when large waves have broken offshore to later reform in the surf zone to then surge on to the beach as low waves.

Wave bore (aka *wave of translation*), is the mass of white water produced after the breaker (any one of the three types of breaking wave) has collapsed.[14] It is different to a wave because it actually moves water towards the shore. Kayakers can surf the steep portion of breakers assisted by gravity and once the wave has collapsed may broach and ride in sideways on the leading edge of the wave bore or just get 'munched'.

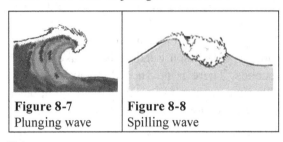

Figure 8-7 Plunging wave	**Figure 8-8** Spilling wave

Rips

Rip currents (aka *rips*) are formed from the water that has arrived as surf and then starts returning out to sea (backwash). Rip currents exist on all beaches where there is surf. In Victoria, spacing ranges from 50 metres on Port Phillip beaches, to 500 metres on high wave west coast beaches. Headlands and reefs produce additional rips called topographically controlled rips and mega-rips, can be formed during big seas. Rip channel are often between 0.5 to 1.0 metre deeper than the adjacent bar, reaching a maximum depth of 3 metres.

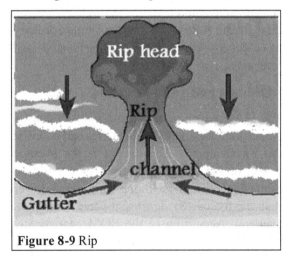

Figure 8-9 Rip

Usually two returning currents travelling parallel to the shore in deep longshore feeder troughs (aka *gutters*) will meet and turn seaward via a deeper rip channel through the surf zone. As the rip current exits behind the breakers it widens and dissipates or in some cases meanders as a larger rip head.

Table 8-1 Swell Description Table					
Length (m)		Height (m)		Period	
Short	0-100	Low	0-2	5 sec	
Average	100-200	Moderate	2-4	10 sec	
Long	> 200	Heavy	> 4	15 sec+	

Rip current speed usually dissipates within two to three times the width of the surf zone. An average rip current in a 50 metre wide surf zone can carry a person outside the breakers in 30 seconds. There is no such thing as undertow with rip currents; it is breaking waves that push people down for around two to three seconds.

① **Note:** The velocities of rip currents differ dramatically, but can reach three knots.

Headland, reefs and rocks may develop dangerous surfaces and stronger rips in certain conditions. If the surf is against the rocks, there may be a rip channel next to the rocks.

WAVE FORECASTING

① **Note:** Wave heights quoted in forecasts are for 'significant wave height' in deep water.

① **Note:** Waves to twice the forecast height could be expected during a typical day trip.

The Bureau of Meteorology (BOM) provides marine forecasts and warnings for local waters, coastal waters and high seas as well as tide and tidal stream times. The chapter on meteorology has a description of the BOM marine and land forecasts.

BOM Sea and swell forecasts

The BOM forecasts of sea and swell in coastal waters forecasts are given in metres and describe the waves height. This height is the average height of the highest one-third of the waves. Some waves will be higher and some lower than the forecasted significant wave height (i.e. average). According to the BOM, statistically it is estimated that about one in every 2000 to 3000 waves (three to four times a day) will be approximately twice the height of the significant wave (i.e. average wave height). Forecasts for high seas describe sea and swell using terms such as slight, moderate, rough et cetera in place of wave heights in metres.

Terms

Deep water is defined as water at least deeper than one-half the wavelength between crests of the existing waves, which is considered to be about 60 meters for ocean swell. Other references describe it as water deep enough not to affect the motion of the surface waves by contacting the bathymetry of the ocean floor. In terms of figures, generally, water deeper than 1000 feet. However, refer to the information on shoaling and surf.

Waves

Combined sea and swell (aka *total wave height* or *sea state*). It refers to the combined seas and swells encountered on open waters.

Confused sea state is the result of several sets of swell waves interacting from different directions causing a *confused sea*.

Sea waves (aka *wind waves*) are generated by local prevailing winds. Their height, length and period varies according to fetch (unobstructed distance the wind blows over), length of time the wind has been blowing for, and water depth. When the wind dies away the waves dissipate. They are distinguishable by their *white-caps* around 15 knots plus of wind.

Swell waves (aka *swell*) are the regular long period waves that have been generated by distant weather patterns and have continued on from their area of generation. The swell description, at Table 8-1, has been modified to incorporate the period column from Greg Laughlin's, *The User's Guide to the Australian Coast*, 1997. Having a wave period makes it easier to understand the energy of the swell. However, other sources report 2 metre swells having a 13 to 15 second period. Swell direction is given from the region the swell is coming from using the eight points of the compass. For example, a south-west (SW) swell comes from the south-west (SW) and is heading north-east (NE).

Primary swell is now a term featured in BOM marine and ocean forecasts. Primary swell may also be called a *dominant* swell. It is given in comparison to a forecasted *secondary swell*. It is a forecast of the height and direction of a swell with the highest energy component in the forecasted area.

Secondary swell is a forecast of the height and direction of a swell with the second highest energy component in the forecasted area. It is a swell that has been developed by a separate distant weather system that will at some point intersect with a primary swell in the area of forecast. Secondary swell is only reported if it is considered by the BOM to be relevant.

Rouge waves (aka *king wave*, *freak wave*) are the common names to describe the less frequent highest waves in a wave group. When wind waves and/or a combination of swell waves join, they can produce a very high wave. These can be typically greater than twice the significant wave height. Rouge waves are known to occur in areas where ocean currents run opposite to the prevailing sea and swell and where waves overrun each other, generating steep and dangerous seas (BOM, 2011). Other factors, which can also influence wave height, are tides, distant weather systems and shape and depth of the seabed.

Table 8-2 Theoretical wave times		
Times higher than the significant height	Re-occurrence wave interval	Re-occurrence time interval
1.86	1 in 1000	Less than 6 hours
1.95 (~twice)	1 in 2000	Every six hours
2.25	1 in 25 000	Every 2 days
2.5	1 in 300 000	Every 24 days

Sea state describes the combination of sea waves and swell. See total wave height. A calm sea state describes an undisturbed sea surface. A confused sea state describes a disturbed sea surface.

Wave measurement

Maximum wave height refers to the most frequently encountered maximum wave height, which can be up to twice that of the significant wave height.

Peak Wave Period (aka *swell period*) refers to the period in seconds between the swells of the primary swell component. The larger the time difference, the greater the amount of energy associated with the swells.

Significant wave height is the average of the highest one-third of waves in deep water. It serves as an indicator of the characteristic size of the highest waves. Some waves will be higher and some lower. Estimates of maximum wave height and re-occurrence interval are set out in Table 8-2.

Total wave height (aka *sea state,* or *combined sea and swell*) is the combination of wind waves and swells, as they tend to merge. The BOM forecast gives a sea prediction and a swell prediction. To determine the predicted sea state use:

$$\text{Total Wave Height} = \sqrt{(Sea^2 + Swell^2)}$$

For example, a 1 metre sea and a 2 metre swell forecast would be a 2.2 metre sea state.

$$\text{Sea state} = \sqrt{(1^2 + 2^2)} = \sqrt{(1 + 4)} = \sqrt{5} = 2.2 \text{ m}$$

Wave height is measured from trough to crest. In Australia the measurement is taken from the back of the wave.

Wave length refers to the mean horizontal distance between successive crests (or troughs) of a wave pattern.

Wave period refers to the average time interval between passages of successive crests (or troughs) of waves.

TIDES

① **Note:** Refer to the Navigation Topic, Chart Data and Terms, for terms, abbreviations and acronyms associated with tides.

The actual tide is a wave, correctly called a *tidal wave*, not to be confused with storm surges and tsunamis. Tides are the periodic vertical rise and fall of water in the oceans, seas and bays, caused by the interaction of the gravitational forces between the earth, moon and to a lesser extent, the sun. The rise and fall of tides is not uniform. Tidal streams are also known as *tidal currents*, and are the periodic horizontal movement of water, which occur because of tides.

Tides in the deep ocean are zero at the amprodromic point and average less than 20 centimetres over much of the ocean. However, as the tidal waves moves toward the coast and cross the relatively shallow continental shelves (less than 150 metre deep), they are amplified due to the wave shoaling processes and increase in height from up to one to three metres. In addition, large embayments can amplify the tide by a process of tidal wave resonance, which causes the tide to reach heights of several metres.

Tides are classified as being *micro-tidal* when less than two metre range, *meso-tidal* when between two to four metre range and *macro-tidal* when greater than four metres. Macro-tidal areas in Australia can be found from Port Hedland to Darwin.

Tides are distinguished by their cyclic patterns. The three commonly defined patterns are *diurnal*, *semi-diurnal* and *mixed tides*. One tidal cycle is defined as the sequence of vertical water movement from one high water, through a low water, to the next high water. Tides are defined by a *tidal day* also known as a *lunar day*. A lunar day is approximately 24 hours, 50 minutes of a mean solar day.

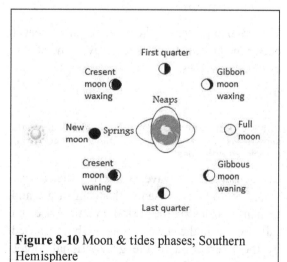

Figure 8-10 Moon & tides phases; Southern Hemisphere

Qualitatively, diurnal tides go through one cycle in a tidal day. Semi-diurnal tides go through two cycles, of relatively equal heights, in a tidal day.

Semi-diurnal tides complete one cycle about every 12 hours (i.e. two high waters and two low waters in a tidal day). The next category of tides is mixed tides. In fact, all tides are mixed, but the name usually refers to tides that are not predominantly diurnal or semi-diurnal. Mixed tide cycles are a combination of diurnal and semi-diurnal tides. Mixed tides can occur at six-hour intervals, producing four high waters and four low water events during a tidal day. They may also be characterised by a large inequality in either the high and/or low waters heights. Examples of the different types of tides can be found along the Western Australian coastline. In the northern part of Western Australia (i.e. Carnarvon northwards) the tidal cycle is known as being semi-diurnal. In the southern part of the state, the tidal pattern is considered as mixed tides, consisting of both semi-diurnal and diurnal tide cycles.

Table 8-3 Summary of moon & tides			
Moon Phases			
New Moon	First Quarter	Full Moon	Last Quarter
Drawn as			
Full Black	½ White towards sun	White	½ black towards sun
Abbreviation			
NM	FQ	FM	LQ
Moon Rises			
Dawn	Noon	Dusk	Midnight
Moon Sets			
Dusk	Midnight	Dawn	Noon
Tides			
Springs	Neaps	Springs	Neaps
High Water Level			
Highest	Lowest	Highest	Lowest
Low Water Level			
Lowest	Highest	Lowest	Highest

Several points need to be made about tides:

The rise and fall of the tide, does not closely follow the movement of the moon around the earth, due to the shape of the earth, landmasses and depth of the oceans.

Physical features can affect tides. Shallow bays and inlets have greater tidal ranges than the ocean. For example, the 2.3 metre spring tide range inside Westernport Bay, compared to the approximate 1.1 metre spring tide range, experienced along the ocean front of Phillip Island.

- Narrow inlets delay tides. An example of this can be found in Port Phillip, which experiences an approximate three hour delay between high water at the northern end (Williamstown), compared to the Heads at the southern end.

- Weather can affect tides. Higher temperatures result in lower tides. High-pressure systems depress the ocean, while low-pressure systems allow the ocean to rise. Onshore winds and big swell produce higher tides. Offshore winds and small swells delay tide times.

Lunar effect on tides

Spring tides (aka *springs*) occur during the periods of new moon and full moon producing the highest high water and lowest low water of the lunar month. The term spring tides, has no relationship with the seasons. Spring tides are caused during the period of full moon when the sun, earth and moon are in-line (phase) and during the period of new moon when the sun, moon and earth are in line (phase).

Neap tides (aka *neaps*) occur during the periods of first quarter, last quarter moon phases and produce the lowest high water and highest low water of the lunar month. There are about seven days between spring and neap tides. Neap tides are caused during the period of first quarter and last quarter when the sun, earth and moon are at right angles to each other and the pull of the sun is at right angles to the pull of the moon.

Perigee occurs once a month when the moon is closest to the earth (i.e. 357 248 km on June 3, 2004). The lunar influence exerts a greater gravitational force on the tides. When perigee occurs during the same time as springs (possibly three times a year) you can have significantly greater tide ranges.

Apogee occurs once a month and is when the moon is farthest away from the earth (i.e.

406 574 km on June 17, 2004). It exerts the least gravitational force on the tides.

Tidal Range

Tidal range (aka *range of tide*) is the difference in height between consecutive high and low waters. For example a high water may be 2.2 metres and the consecutive low water 0.6 metres; the tidal range would be 1.6 metres.

In Victoria and South Australia, tidal ranges are less than three metres. In northern Australia (the *Top End*) certain areas experience eight metre tidal ranges, for example Darwin Harbour.

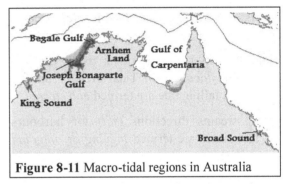

Figure 8-11 Macro-tidal regions in Australia

In other parts of the Top End, for example the Gulf of Carpentaria, they experience semi-diurnal tides, with places like Melville Bay, in Arnhem Land, experiencing a possible tidal range between 3.1 to 0.36 metres. Down in the south-east corner, between Mornington Island and the town of Karumba, they only experience diurnal tides that can reach 4.8 metres.

At Broad Sound, Queensland, (between Rockhampton and Mackay) on the southern Great Barrier Reef, the area experiences a range of 8.2 metres between the months of December to February and June to August (Thomas, 2002).

The tide range along the West Australian coastline varies from approximately 12 metres at Collier Bay in the Kimberley, to about 0.7 metres in Fremantle. King Sound, near the town of Derby, in north-west Western Australia can experience the second largest tides in the world at the end of March and April each year. During this time King Sound can experience 8.2 metre high waters and 1.5 metre low waters (Thomas, 2002).

The highest recorded tidal range in the world reaches 15–17 metres in Canada's Bay of Fundy in Nova Scotia. The smallest tides occur in the Mediterranean, peaking at just 2–3 centimetres.

TIDAL STREAMS

The tidal wave does not carry water along with it, but its passage along the coast does produce periodic horizontal movements of water, called *tidal streams*, which flow in and out of harbours and along the coast. They are related to the rise and fall, of the local tide and are influenced by past and existing weather.

① **Note:** North American writers and a few Australian call tidal streams, tidal currents, and rip tides.

Terms and data associated with tidal streams are:

Tidal streams running with a rising tide are termed *flood stream*. Tidal streams running with a falling tide are termed *ebb stream*.

Tidal streams directions (*set*) for harbours and rivers are termed *ingoing* or *outgoing* stream.

Offshore tidal streams are referred to by their direction of travel (i.e. *south going* or *stream setting 180°*). Stream setting 180° means the stream of water is heading south.

Tidal streams in charts and publications are for average spring or neap tide.

Maximum rates shown on charts are normally for springs but can be obtained any time. Above the flood or ebb arrow may be found the spring rate of the tidal streams.

Two types of geographical features affect the behaviour of a tidal wave in different ways:

A small tidal basin (bay, estuary or harbour) that is open to the ocean by a large entrance. The stream's rate at the opening is at maximum, when tide height in the basin is changing most rapidly (i.e. about mid way between high water and low water). The water level in the basin remains about the same as the ocean's level.

A large tidal basin opened to the ocean by a small entrance. The stream's rate at the opening is at maximum, when it is high water or low water, outside of the basin. Slack water at the entrance occurs about midway between the ocean's high water and low water times.

An example of a large tidal basin opened to the ocean by a small entrance can be found at the entrance to Port Phillip (aka *Port Phillip Bay*) in Victoria. The Tidal stream flow behaviour, created by this type of geographical feature, is described below. The explanation is for a semi-diurnal, 12 hour tide cycle, which would take place somewhat in this manner.

Starting at high water and zero hours, on the ocean side of an embayment, the tide will *turn* and become an *ebb tide* (i.e. the water level will go from high water down to low water). After three hours, the *out-going tide* is halfway between high water and low water, at what is termed *mid-tide*. At mid-tide, the tidal stream is in a state known as *slack water*. This is where, at and/or near the embayment's orifice, the flow of water (i.e. stream) is slowing down, stopping, and then reversing its set (aka direction). After mid-tide on an ebbing tide, the tidal stream becomes an *ebbing stream* (aka *out-going stream*). It will continue to be an ebbing stream throughout the next tidal change, three hours later, when the tide reaches low water and begins to change to a *flood tide* (aka *in-coming tide*). Six hours later, at the change of tide from low water to high water, the tide becomes a *flood tide*. The out-going tidal stream is now at, or near to, its maximum rate (i.e. speed). The tidal stream continues on in its set, regardless of the changing tide conditions. Nine hours later, around the time of the flood mid-tide, the tidal stream once again enters a phase of slack water, whereby it once again reverses its set. At flood mid-tide, the tidal stream now follows the flood tide and becomes a *flood stream* (aka *in-going stream*). Three hours later, the in-going stream will reach its maximum rate around the next high water. As this tide changes from high water to low water, twelve hours later, the tide becomes an ebbing tide. The tidal stream will continue to be a flood stream, for a further three hours, until the time of the ebb tides mid-tide, when the tidal stream will repeat its phases of slack water and set change.

Tidal streams are influenced by past and present weather and are related to rise and fall of the tides. There is a general in-flow into a bay, bights or harbour, although the direction of the stream may cross the entrance (e.g. French Pass, New Zealand (KASK, 2003, p. 73)).

---

1 Some references state the littoral current extends to behind the breakers.

2 Ice crystals forming in seawater increase the internal friction, this produces a smooth sea surface even in a gale or when seas are beating against the outer edge of an ice pack. Hail or torrential rain can also flatten the sea even in high winds.

3 Conservation of energy: Energy cannot be created or destroyed but changes form (i.e. potential energy to kinetic energy and vice versa). The other causes of water waves can be tides or seismic activity in the form of submarine earthquakes and volcanic eruptions, which can cause tsunamis. Wind waves have been recorded over 100 feet high with tsunamis heights recorded even higher.

4 There is a theoretical relationship between wave height, length and period to fetch, wind duration and speed which can be found in tables. Also, refer to the Beaufort Scale for probable wave heights.

5 Bureau of Meteorology, Dept. of Administrative Services, Boating Weather Series: Wind Waves Weather Victorian Waters, 1989. Pp.22-23. How far is "far out to sea"? Possibly refers to deep water, where the ocean floor cannot affect the wave.

6 Unlike wind and current, waves are not deflected appreciable by the earth's rotation but travel in the direction of the generating wind.

7 Some references quote greater than 15 seconds for long period swells and less than 15 seconds for short period swells.

8 A swell train travels at half (½) the speed of its individual waves in deep water and they are bound to the group by their shared energy (period). $S_{swell} = ½S_{free-wave}$. Therefore, a 10 second period swell train has half the free waves 30 knot speed (i.e. around 15 knots). When the swell 'feels the bottom' the individual wave speed (30 kn) reduces to the groups speed (15 kn). This means that both the individual waves and the groups speed will now be 15 knots for a 10-second period swell in shallow water.

9 A 1 metre high wave with an 8 second period travels around 12 knots. A 1 metre high wave with a 12 second period travels around 18 knots or 30 per cent faster and has more energy (wave energy is directly proportional to the square of the amplitude). To determine the depth when a swell will 'feel the bottom' using wave period (P), square the period number and multiply the result by 2.56. $L_{swell} = 2.56P^2$

10 Wave period is as important as wave height when describing waves because it translate to energy. A 1 metre high wave with an 8 second period, travels around 12 knots. A 1 metre high wave with a 12 second period, travels around 18 knots; or 30 per cent faster and contains more energy (wave energy is directly proportional to the square of the amplitude). Longer period swells move faster and are deeper.

11 Some surf forecasters refer to ground swell as the 'clean' wave trains, which have travelled thousands of nautical miles from their area of generation.

12 A shoaling wave of 1 metre will break in about 1.3 metre of water. A 2 metre wave will break in 2.6 metres of water.

13 Clapotis is from the French meaning 'leaping of water'.

14 Wave of translation (aka wave bore) is not the same as the wave of translation associated with displacement hull wave making resistance.

CHAPTER 9 NAVIGATION—RULES AND REGULATIONS

Ninety per cent of fatal accidents involve the Skipper not having enough boating knowledge and experience. Every boat, whether it is a ship, a yacht, a dinghy, a sailboard or a personal water craft (PWC) such as a 'jetski', must have a person in charge—a Skipper. It is the Skipper's responsibility to ensure safety, which includes knowing and understanding the rules that apply before heading out on the water.

Maritime Safety New Zealand

References for navigation rules

For all of the navigation rules and regulations, refer to the relative government marine safety website to obtain the latest information about marine navigation rules.

Sea kayakers encounter vessels under sail and or power. The vessels may be under command of a commercial or recreational licence holder even though the sea kayaker does not require a boating licence. To operate safely around sail and power vessels it is prudent to know 'steering and sailing rules' thereby knowing your responsibilities and the responsibilities of other skippers. This information has been included in Appendix 4.

BUOYAGE SYSTEM

Australia, New Zealand, Europe, United Kingdom, Africa, the Gulf and some Asian countries use the *International Association of Lighthouse Authorities System 'A'* (IALA System 'A') of buoyage. Other countries, notably North, Central and South America, Japan, Republic of Korea and Philippines use IALA System 'B'. The IALA Systems 'A' and 'B' are also referred to as The IALA Maritime Buoyage System (MBS) Regions 'A' and 'B' respectively.

The difference between the two Regions is the use of the colours red and green to mark channels with its lateral buoys. On approach from seaward, Region 'A' has its lateral port-hand buoyage colour coded red and the starboard-hand as green. Region 'B' has the opposite; port-hand buoyage is green and starboard-hand is red. If the lateral marks are numbered, Region 'A' uses even numbers for the port-hand and odd numbers for the starboard-hand. The opposite numbering system is used in Region 'B'; port-hand buoys are odd numbers and starboard-hand buoys are even numbered. All other rules and aspects of the IALA Maritime Buoyage System are the same in both Regions 'A' and 'B'.

① **Note:** Be aware, that large commercial vessels may pass close by these marks.

IALA Region 'A' MBS types

Under the IALA System A, there are five types of marks: *Lateral, Cardinal, Isolated Danger, Special* and *Safe Water.*

Lateral marks

Lateral marks are used to indicate the port (left) and starboard (right) sides of the channels when travelling in the direction of buoyage, that is, into port.

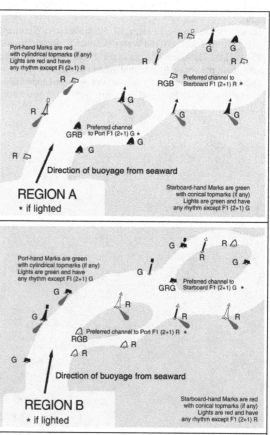

Figure 9-1 IALA Regions 'A' & 'B' Lateral buoys

Port-hand marks in IALA Region 'A' are coloured red and the basic shape for a buoy is cylindrical (aka 'can'); it may or may not be fitted with a topmark. Starboard-hand marks are coloured green and in exceptional circumstances black. The basic buoy shape is conical (with or without a topmark). Region 'B' also uses cylindrical buoys for port and conical buoys for starboard.

Lateral marks may or may not be lighted. If lit, they may display any rhythm other than composite group-flashing (2 + 1) used on modified lateral marks indicating a preferred channel.

When numbered, even numbers will lie on the port (left) marks and odd numbers on the starboard (right) marks when travelling in the direction of the buoyage, that is, from seaward.

Cardinal marks

Cardinal marks are used to indicate: the location of the most suitable navigable water, the safe side on which to pass hazards and danger (e.g. rocks, wrecks, shoals), and to draw attention to a feature in a channel.

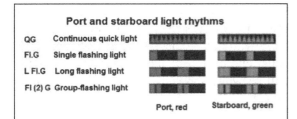

For regions using the IALA Region 'A' MBS port lateral marks are red and starboard are green.

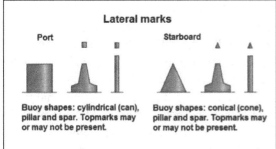

For regions using the IALA Region 'A' MBS port lateral marks are red and starboard are green.

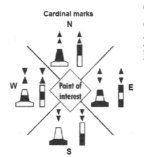

Cardinal marks are coloured coded with yellow and black horizontal stripes.

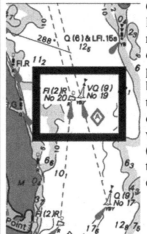

Combination of lateral and cardinal markers used to define a channel. A port lateral marker buoy (No. 20) is used to define the left side of the channel and a west cardinal marker (No. 19) is defining the right side of the channel.

Special marks

Topmark if fitted

Special marks are coloured yellow and may or may not be fitted with a topmark.

Special marks

 Topmark (if fitted)

Port-hand   Starboard-hand

If can and or cone shapes are used they indicate the side on which the buoy should be passed.

Figure 9-2 IALA MBS markers

To understand the meaning of a cardinal mark, the kayaker needs to be aware of their geographical position and compass directions; therefore a compass is required to indicate where the best navigable water lies. The mark is placed on one of four quadrants that relate to one of the four compass cardinal points of north, east, south and west.

Cardinal marks are colour coded with black and yellow bands. The shape of a cardinal mark is not significant but in the case of a buoy, it will be a pillar or a spar. The most important feature of a cardinal mark in the daytime is the black double cone (double triangles) topmark and the four different arrangements that indicate the relevant direction of safe passage from the mark.

The colour code arrangement, for direction indication, can be remembered by the fact that the tops of the triangles point towards the black band(s). To differentiate between the west and east cardinal marks, notice how the west cardinal mark resembles (loosely) a 'W' on its side. North has two triangles pointing upwards and south has two triangles pointing downwards.

If lit, the mark will show a white light of a continuous Quick Flashing (around one per second) or Very Quick Flashing (around two per second) characteristic. The light rhythm will indicate the particular quadrant (north, south, east and west) of the mark. The light sequence starts from the north mark having a *continuous* Quick or Very Quick flash sequence. Moving clockwise to the east mark, at the three o'clock position, it is recognised by *three* Quick or Very Quick flashes. The south mark at the six o'clock position is recognised by six Quick or Very Quick flashes. The west mark at the nine o'clock position is recognised by *nine* Quick or Very Quick flashes.

Combination of lateral and cardinal marks

A combination of both a lateral mark and cardinal mark are used to define channels is some areas. Referring to Figure 9-2 notice on the chart section, above the *tidal diamond 'A'*, the channel is defined by a combination of: lighted port lateral mark (No. 20), and a lighted west cardinal marker (No. 19). On entry to the channel, the port lateral marker (drawn as a 'can shape with smaller square on top' and an 'R' [for Red] below) needs to be on a vessels port side (left). This conforms to the IALA 'A'

buoyage direction. The west cardinal marker signifies safe water to its west. Thereby defining the channel.

Special marks

Special marks are used to indicate a special area or feature, the nature of which can be found by consulting a chart or sailing directions. These marks are used to indicate for example: spoil grounds (an area where dredging material is dumped), pipelines and recreational areas.

In Victorian waterways, Special marks are often used to indicate no boating zones. Special marks are always yellow in colour with the topmark, if fitted, being a single yellow X. If a light is fitted it is coloured yellow and may have any rhythm not used for white light (i.e. FlY, FL (4) Y).

Isolated danger marks

Isolated danger marks are located on or moored above an isolated danger of limited area that has navigable water all around it. Isolated danger marks may not always be centrally positioned over a danger and it is advised not to pass to close by. The mark is coloured with red and black horizontal stripes, when practicable, and fitted with double black spheres (two big black balls) one on top of the other. If lit, the light will be white showing a group of two flashes, FL (2).

Safe water marks

Safe water marks are used to show that there is navigable water all around the mark. These marks can be used as a centre line, mid-channel or landfall buoy. The shape of the buoy is spherical, pillar or spar and it is coloured with red and white vertical strips. The buoy shape is optional, but should not conflict, with that used for Lateral or Special marks. The topmark is fitted if practicable, and is a red sphere (big red ball). If lit, an isophase occulting or single long flashing white light is exhibited.

New Dangers

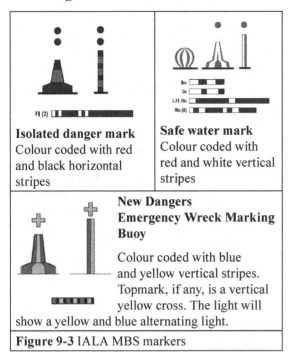

Isolated danger mark
Colour coded with red and black horizontal stripes

Safe water mark
Colour coded with red and white vertical stripes

New Dangers Emergency Wreck Marking Buoy

Colour coded with blue and yellow vertical stripes. Topmark, if any, is a vertical yellow cross. The light will show a yellow and blue alternating light.

Figure 9-3 IALA MBS markers

The term *New Dangers* is used to describe newly discovered hazards not yet shown in nautical documents. New Dangers include naturally occurring obstructions such as sandbanks or rocks or man-made dangers such as wrecks. New Dangers may be marked using Lateral, Cardinal, Isolated Danger marks or by using the Emergency Wreck Marking Buoy. The marking of the new danger may be removed when the New Danger has been sufficiently promulgated or the danger otherwise resolved. The shape of the Emergency Wreck Marking Buoy is pillar or spar and is coloured with blue and yellow vertical stripes. The topmark, if any, is a vertical yellow cross. The light will show a yellow and blue alternating light (VRBSH, 2011).

SHIPPING LIGHTS AT NIGHT

ⓘ **Note**: Refer to your local state or territory government recreational boating safety handbook for further information on shipping navigation lights.

Paddling around harbours at night, ships are hard to detect with all the harbour, city and bridge lighting around; even though they are sounding the five short blasts signal—unsure of your intentions. Some ships even have a powerful white spotlight on the bow, which can

be hard to distinguish from the wharf working lights when viewed from only a few feet above the water.

Of interest, is the strong propulsion turbulence created by the tugboats. When berthing a ship, their propulsion turbulence has been known to capsize kayakers. On one instance, a paddler crossed the propulsion wash on the other side of the river and well away from the operation, (so he thought). His boat got caught by the turbulence, capsized and then was washed under the wharf!

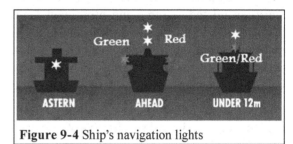

Figure 9-4 Ship's navigation lights

DREDGING OF CHANNELS

Be familiar with the day-shapes for vessels. Know which side to pass on when dredging is taking place. Also beware that the dredge can be reversing and going forward and there are strong eddies being produced by the propellers.

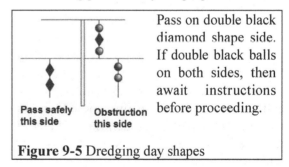

Pass on double black diamond shape side. If double black balls on both sides, then await instructions before proceeding.

Figure 9-5 Dredging day shapes

CHAPTER 10 NAVIGATION— CHARTS AND PUBLICATIONS

"A perfection of means, and confusion of aims, seems to be our main problem."

Albert Einstein

NAVIGATION CHARTS

Mariners use charts not maps for marine navigation. Sea Kayakers use both charts and topographical maps because charts show maritime related features and prominent land features of interest to commercial or military mariners, where as topographical map show better detail of the land features such as hills, gullies and camping areas.

Charts contain information on soundings (spot and contours), drying heights, heights of features, hazards (rocks, shoals, reefs, wrecks), foreshore, navigational aids (lights, buoys, leads), prominent land features, facilities, latitude and longitudes, compass roses and magnetic variation. Charts are orientated northwards to the top of the chart. The compass rose printed on the chart provides information on magnetic variation from north.

CHART CATEGORIES

Charts are classified by scale ranging from about 1:2 500 to 1:14 000 000. A chart, which represents a small area, is called a *large-scale chart* and one, which covers a large area, is called a *small scale chart*. Since these terms are relative, there is no sharp delineation between them. Therefore, a 1:25 000 scale chart is large when compared to a 1:75 000 but small scale when compared to one of 1:7 500.

As scale decreases so too does the amount of detail provided. In all navigation, the largest scale chart available should be used since they contain more detail. Small-scale charts covering large areas are used for route planning and offshore navigation. Larger scale charts, called plans, are used on approaching land. Several methods of classifying charts by scale exist. For example, the National Ocean Service has a

category called *Sailing charts* and is typically smaller than 1:600 000.

The Defence Mapping Agency, Hydrographer Topographic Centre, categorise sailing charts in with general charts. As an example of chart classification the following has been provided:

World charts are the smallest scale and are used to show information such as ocean routes, ocean currents and magnetic variation.

Ocean charts are the next scale and are typically of 1:10 000 000 scale, but are generally smaller than 1:600 000. They cover large areas like the North Pacific Ocean and Indian Ocean. The shoreline and topography is not shown in much detail but they are used for planning and position fixing on long ocean voyages.

General charts are used for coastwise navigation where courses lie inside outlying reefs and shoals. The scales typically range from around 1:150 000 to 1:600 000.

Coastal charts are used for inshore navigation, typically 1: 50 000 to 1:150 000 scale. They are intended for inshore coastwise navigation.

Plan charts (aka *harbour charts*) provide great detail and are used for harbour and river navigation. The scale is generally larger than 1:50 000.

Scale

The scale is simply the ratio expressed in comparative measurements of one size to another. Scale can be represented in two forms: a *representative fraction* (RF) and or a *linear scale*.

Representative fractions, express the distance on a chart as a fraction of the corresponding distance on the surface. Representative fractions are used to express the distance on a chart/map/ drawing as a fraction of the corresponding distance of the surface and or object.

If the scale is 1:25 000, every distance on the chart/ map is 1/25 000th of the distance on the ground. Using a scale of 1:25 000 and metric units of 1 centimetre to 1 kilometre, 1 kilometre (1000 m) has been divided into 25 000 parts (1000 m / 25 000 = 0.04 m, which is 4 cm). Therefore on a 1:25 000 scale chart/map, 4 centimetres equal 1 kilometre. On a map, each 1 centimetre equals 250 metres (1000/4 = 250). The maps 1 cm x 1 cm grid square (formed by the *eastings* and *northings*) equals 250 m x 250 m on the ground. Using a scale of 1:50 000, 1 centimetre equals 500 metres. 1:100 000 scale represents 1 centimetre to 1000 metres (1 km) on the ground.

Using the imperial system 1 inch to 1 foot, the RF is 1/12 since there are 12 inches to 1 foot. One inch to 1 yard the RF is 1/36 since there are 36 inches to 1 yard. One inch to 1 mile the RF is 1:63,360 since there are 63,360 inches to the mile (statute).

Using a nautical mile which is ~72,913 inches, the RF is 1:72 913 inches to a nautical mile. Using a 1:300,000 chart, 1 inch represents 300,000 inches on the earth, which is greater than a nautical mile. To find the amount of nautical mile(s) to an inch, divide the scale by the number of inches in a nautical mile (e.g. 300,000/72,913 = 4.114). Thus the scale of 300,000 (inches over the earth) is the same as a scale of 4.114 (approximated to 4.1) nautical miles to an inch on a chart.

To find the number and or fraction of an inch in a nautical mile, divide the number of inches in a nautical mile by the chart scale (e.g. 72,913/300,000 = 0.243). Thus, there are approximately 0.2 inches to a nautical mile on the chart.

If the chart has a scale of 60 nautical miles to 1 inch the RF is 1:4,374,780. This is worked out by:

$$1:(60 \times 72,913) = 4,374,780$$

Linear scale is drawn to assist in the measurement of distance. On a chart, distance is usually worked out by using the latitude increments found along the side of the chart. The linear scale consists of two sets of divisions. To the right of the zero, the scale is graduated in primary divisions. To the left of the zero, it is divided into secondary divisions.

On a map, the linear scale can be measured with the side of a base-plate compass, ruler, a piece of string or the edge of a piece of paper. Using a piece of paper as an example, the paper is placed between two points (e.g. A & B) and marked off. The marked paper is then laid against the map's linear scale. Working from right to left point B is lined up against the nearest primary graduation that allows point A to lie inside the secondary graduations. Point A will correspond somewhere along the secondary graduations where the distance can be determined by the level of detail of the secondary graduations (e.g. 100 m, 50 m, 25 m etc.).

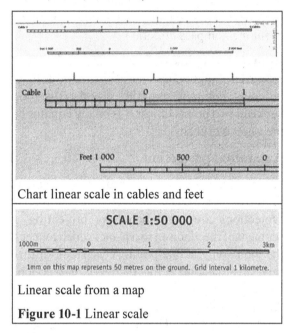

Chart linear scale in cables and feet

Linear scale from a map

Figure 10-1 Linear scale

PROJECTION

Projection is the term used when converting parallels and meridians (aka *graticule*) from a globe to a flat sheet. Charts and maps are made up of combinations of projections and hence the different types of projections. The three classes of projection are planar (aka azimuthal), cylindrical and conic. The common two projections for marine charts are Mercator and azimuthal.

Mercator projection

Mercator projection belongs to a family of projections known as cylindrical projections. Nearly all charts for coastal and inshore navigation use the Mercator projection. Mercator projection is a method whereby the curved surface of the earth is drawn on a flat piece of paper. It is created by visualizing the earth's surface being put inside a cylinder of paper and contacting the sides (e.g. at the equator). If you open out the cylinder, the chart has one or two lines that are free from distortion (i.e. the equator), because this is where the cylinder contacted the globe. As the meridians are shown parallel to the chart they do not converge towards the poles.

This creates an error towards the poles and where by Greenland is shown to be wider than it actually is. However, this conformal projection is useful to navigators because a line drawn between any two points on a chart can be followed without changing compass direction.

Rhumb lines (lines of constant bearing) are shown as straight lines on a Mercator projection but may not represent the shortest distance between two points unless it is on the equator or the same meridian.

Azimuthal projection

Another type of projection used is the azimuthal projection (aka planar projections). Azimuthal projections are constructed by projecting a segment of the globe on to a plane, which touches the globe only at one point. A variation of this type of projection is the Lambert's projection, which is useful for areas like continental Australia that have similar east-west, north-south dimensions. The azimuthal equidistant projection is useful to show travel points from a central position, since the points on the map are in constant relative position and distance from the centre.

Gnomonic projection

Gnomonic projections belong to a family of azimuthal projections (aka planar projections). Cylindrical projection is not suitable for long distance navigation or navigation particularly at higher latitudes. This is where the gnomonic projection is useful. For ocean navigation, gnomonic projections are generally preferred for long distance planning to show *great circle* routes.

Great circle routes show the shortest distance between two positions over a large area. This is a type of azimuthal projection used where directional relationships are important.

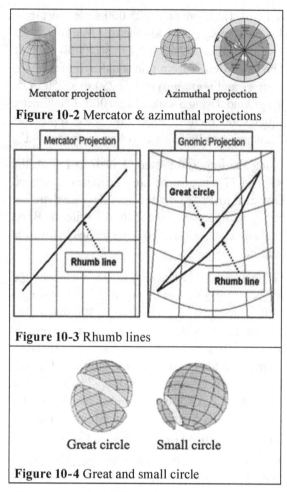

Mercator projection   Azimuthal projection

Figure 10-2 Mercator & azimuthal projections

Mercator Projection   Gnomic Projection

Great circle

Rhumb line

Rhumb line

Figure 10-3 Rhumb lines

Great circle   Small circle

Figure 10-4 Great and small circle

Great circle and Small circle

A great circle is a section of a sphere, which contains a diameter of the sphere. If you divide a sphere along any plane that results in two equal hemispheres having the same diameter as the sphere, you have a great circle. The earth's shape closely resembles a flattened spheroid and not a sphere. The earth has extreme values for the radius of curvature at the equator of 6336 kilometres, and at the poles 6399 kilometres. Therefore only the meridians and the equator are great circles. A great circle becomes a straight line in a gnomonic projection. Great circle distance is the shortest distance, between any two points on the surface of a sphere, as measured along a path on the surface of the sphere. That is, not going through the interior of the sphere. A great circle on the surface of a sphere is the path with the smallest curvature. This means that an arc, called an *orthodrome*, is the shortest path between two points on the surface. On the earth, the meridians are on great circles, which mean the equator is a great circle.

The circumference of the small circle is therefore less than the circumference of the sphere circle, when it is equally divided in two. The other parallels are not great circles, since their diameters would be less than the equator's but they do lie in planes parallel to the equator. Sections of the sphere, which do not contain a diameter, are called small circles.

As an example of a large and small circle, refer to Figure 10-4. The two spheres both have a diameter of say 0.3 metres. On one, cut the two hemispheres in half and you have equal diameters, and therefore circumference (i.e. great circle). However, if you dissected a small piece from the other sphere, the resulting small circle's diameter would be say 0.1 metre and less than the original sphere's of 0.3 metre.

Geographic Grids

Geographic grids are lines forming a reference network of grids on a map, which are used to find a location, with reference to the network of lines. The most common geographic grid uses east-west lines called *parallels* and north-south lines called *meridians*. The network of parallels and meridians is called the *graticule*.

Latitude

Latitude is a horizontal reference position on the earth's surface in parallel to the plane of the equator. Horizontal lines circle the earth from due east to west and are called parallels. The latitude scale defines latitude as north (N) or south (S) of the equator. The equator is referenced as zero degrees (0°). The North Pole is referenced as ninety degrees north (90° N or +90°) and the South Pole is referenced as ninety degrees south (90° S, −90°).

Parallels

The horizontal latitude lines circle the earth from due east and west. Depending upon the text, they are known as *parallel of latitude, parallels of latitude* and or parallels.

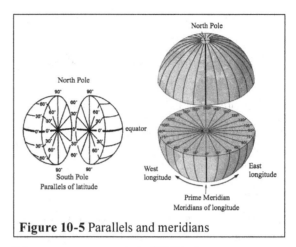

Figure 10-5 Parallels and meridians

Linear measurement of latitude

The distance between each degree of latitude on a sphere is exactly the same regardless of where it is measured. For example, the distance between 20° and 40° South, is exactly the same as between 20° and 40° North. However, because the earth is not a perfect sphere but an oblate ellipsoidone, there are inaccuracies in distances for one degree of latitude between the equator (1843 m) and the poles (1862 m). In other words, one degree (1°) of latitude can vary from 59.7 nautical miles near the equator, to 60.3 nautical miles near the poles. In terms of minutes, one minute (1') of latitude covers 1843 metres at the equator and 1862 metres at the poles. To overcome this discrepancy, a nautical mile has been fixed at 1852 metres (6076.12 ft) and is known as the *international nautical mile*. The nautical mile approximates closely to one minute (1') of arc at latitude 48°.

With the equator being zero degrees latitude and the poles being 90 degrees north or south, one degree of latitude equals 60 nautical miles (nm). One degree of arc is further subdivided into 60 minutes (of arc not time). One minute (') equals one nautical mile (e.g. 60° ÷ 60' = 1 nm). Therefore on the sides of a small scale chart (e.g. Mercator projection chart) the scale of latitude figures represent one nautical mile for each minute (of arc).

Degrees, minutes and seconds of arc

Degrees (°) of latitude are divided into 60 minutes (') and minutes are divided into

60 seconds ("). For the purposes of calculation and navigation:

One degree (1°) of latitude equals 60 nautical miles (nm)

One minute (1') of latitude equals 1 nautical mile

Seconds can be expressed as a tenth (1/10) of a minute of latitude (i.e. 1/10th of a nautical mile).

Longitude

Longitude refers to the vertical converging north-south geographic grid lines that run from pole to pole around the earth. The widest point of the meridians is at the equator where they are 111 kilometres (69 miles) apart.

Meridians

These vertical lines are called meridians. The meridian of longitude (zero) passing through the Greenwich observatory, in England, is referred to as either the *Greenwich meridian* or *prime meridian*. Cartographers divide the earth up into 360 slices using meridians. Meridians measure longitude as the angular distance from the centre of the earth in the plane of the equator west from the prime meridian 0° to 180° and east from the prime meridian 0° to 180°. At 180 degrees east or west is the meridian known as the *International Date Line*.

Linear measurement of longitude

The distance between any two meridians is greatest at the equator and nothing at the poles where they converge. Therefore, the linear distance of a degree of longitude varies depending upon its latitude. For example, at latitude 0° (equator), longitude 30° is approximately 1800 nautical miles but at latitude 60° longitude 30° is approximately 900 nautical miles.

Longitude and time

Time measurement uses the following notation: Hour (hr, h), minutes (min, m) and seconds (sec, s). Rotation of fifteen degrees of longitude equals one hour of time (i.e. the earth rotates fifteen degrees (15°) in one hour). One degree (1°) of rotation equals four minutes of time. The angle between an out stretched arms opened

thumb to index finger is estimated to be fifteen degrees (15°). If you forget your watch and you can see the sun then you can determine the time.

Nautical twilight

Beginning of morning nautical twilight

The beginning of morning nautical twilight is defined as '*the instant in the morning, when the centre of the sun is at a depression angle of twelve degrees (12°) below an ideal horizon. At this time in the absence of moonlight, artificial lighting or adverse atmospheric conditions, it is dark for normal practical purposes. For navigation purposes at sea, the sea horizon is not normally visible*' (Geoscience Australia, 2007).

Ending of evening nautical twilight

The ending of nautical twilight, is defined as '*the instant in the evening, when the centre of the sun is at a depression angle of twelve degrees (12°) below an ideal horizon. At this time in the absence of moonlight, artificial lighting or adverse atmospheric conditions, it is dark for normal practical purposes. For navigation purposes at sea, the sea horizon is not normally visible*' (Geoscience Australia, 2007).

Co-ordinates

Latitude and Longitude

The position of a place or object (e.g. boat) can be described in terms of latitude north or south of the equator and longitude east or west of the prime meridian. This two-dimensional positional information giving geographic coordinates is known as *latitude* and *longitude*. Latitude and longitude measurements are termed *lat./long.* For example, on the chart AUS 788 Cape Otway is lat. 38° 51' S Long. 143° 30' E.

Because latitude 38° 51' and longitude 143° 30' exist in both the Southern Hemisphere and the Northern Hemisphere and west of the prime meridian, the coordinates must have the appropriate suffix applied to them of: S for south, N for north, E for east and W for west.

Positional information can be broken further down into degrees, minutes and seconds. Seconds of arc are expressed as one-tenth (1/10) of a minute of latitude or longitude. Therefore, on a chart there are ten (10), one-tenth (1/10) of a second, increments. Each one-tenth (1/10) of a second increment is six (6) seconds of latitude and or longitude (i.e. 10 x 6 sec = 60 seconds).

When latitude is expressed as seconds, the distance is one tenth (1/10) of a nautical mile (e.g. 1852 m ÷ 10 = 185.2 m).

Two-dimensional positional information can be given in either geographic (latitude and longitude) coordinates or grid coordinates. When giving co-ordinates the latitude (*x coordinate*) is given first then longitude (*y coordinate*).

Maps and grid references

Maps have grid lines superimposed over their surface. These grid lines are equally spaced vertical and horizontal lines intersecting at right angles forming a grid square. Grid coordinates (aka references) are determined from vertical lines called *easting* and horizontal lines called *northings*.

To give a map coordinate start at the left (easting) corner of a grid square then select the bottom (northing) corner of a grid square that intersects the easting. A grid square on a 1:100 000 scale map represents an area of 1000 metres by 1000 metres (i.e. one square kilometre. A 1:25 000 represents an area of 250 metres by 250 metres).

CHART INFORMATION

Chart number

The chart catalogue number of the issuing authority is shown in the lower right and upper left margins of the chart. The following is an example of issuing authority prefix letters:

AUS—Australian

NZ—New Zealand

B.A.—British Admiralty

INT—International

The Australian Hydrographic Service produces Australian area charts. An identifier in the following format identifies Australian produced charts: AUS 788. Two index charts are used to find the required charts:

AUS 65000—Australia—Index of Nautical Chart Publications Northern Portion.

AUS 65001—Index of Nautical Chart Publications Southern Portion. The 1:150 000 medium scale charts are produced for coastal navigation.

Chart 5011 (INT 1)

The meaning of chart symbols, marks, abbreviations et cetera found on Admiralty Charts are defined in the publication '*Chart 5011 (INT 1)—Symbols and Abbreviations used on Admiralty Charts*'. The publication covers all the colours, symbols and lay out of Admiralty charts.

When working with charts refer to Chart 5011 (INT 1)—which is a book—and the primary key to symbols and abbreviations used on Admiralty and International Charts compiled by the UKHO (United Kingdom Hydrographic Office).

The following information is contained in Chart 5011 (INT 1) and is broken down into sections with a capital alpha character designator:

General

- A Chart Number, Title, Marginal Notes

- B Positions, Distances, Directions, Compass

Topography

- C Natural Features

- D Cultural Features

- E Landmarks

- F Ports

- G Topographic Terms

Hydrography

- H Tides, Currents

- I Depths

- J Nature of the Seabed

- K Rocks, Wrecks, Obstructions
- L Offshore Installations
- M Tracks, Routes
- N Areas, Limits
- O Hydrographic Terms

Navigation Aids and Services

- P Lights
- Q Buoys, Beacons
- R Fog Signals
- S Radar, Radio, Satellite navigation Systems
- T Services
- U Small Craft (Leisure) Facilities

Alphabetical Indexes

- V Abbreviations of Principle Non-English Terms
- V Abbreviations of Principle English Terms
- W International Abbreviations
- X Index

Chart Title Block

The chart title block contains important information and should be consulted before using the chart. Information includes:

Chart title

Survey and date of survey

Units of sounding (metres or feet/fathoms)

Datums for soundings, drying heights and heights

Projection

Scale of chart, on Mercator projections, at stated latitude

Explanatory notes on chart content

Cautionary notes about hazards, scale issues, anomalies

Corrections to be applied to GPS positions.

Chart boarder information

Other useful information is contained around the boarders of the chart. In particular:

The chart number in the Admiralty series is located at the top left corner and bottom right corner

Next to the Admiralty series number is the International (INT) chart series number

On post May 2000 charts, the bottom right corner contains Customer Information including:

- Edition number
- Edition date
- Pre May 2000 charts have the customer information located at the bottom right of chart.

Next to the customer information is Notices to Mariners, which contain:

- The year dates and number of Notices to Mariners
- The dates (usually bracketed) of minor corrections included in reprints but not formally promulgated (abandoned as a method of correction in 1986)
- Charts revised prior to May 2000 have the legend 'Small corrections'.

Publication note (imprint) showing date of publication as a New Chart

Reproduction and copyright acknowledgement and note

When applicable the legend 'WGS 84 POSITIONS can be plotted directly on this chart' is printed

Reference to adjoining chart

Linear boarder scales (latitude and longitude). On smaller scale charts, the latitude (vertical) boarder should be used to measure Sea miles (aka nautical miles) and Cables

Conversion scales to allow approximate conversions between metric and fathoms and feet units. On older charts, conversion tables are provided instead.

Linear boarder scales (Latitude and Longitude)

The latitude and longitude scales are used to fix the position of a place or object (e.g. boat). Two-dimensional positional information is derived from the latitude and longitude scales.

Latitude scale

The latitude scale is located on the sides of the chart and is used for distance measurements. The latitude scale defines latitude as north (N) or south (S) of the equator. The equator is referenced as zero degrees of latitude. One degree of latitude equals 60 nautical miles. One minute of latitude equals 1 nautical mile. One second is one tenth of a nautical mile.

Longitude scale

ⓘ **Note**: The longitude scale is not used for distance measurement.

The longitude scale is located across the top and bottom of the chart and defines the position as either east (E) or west (W) of the prime meridian. Charts are orientated northwards along the lines of meridian. Distance varies with latitude and therefore the longitude scale is not used for distance measurement.

Compass rose

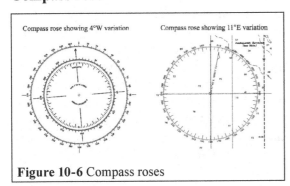

Figure 10-6 Compass roses

On Mercator charts, compass roses are provided at convenient locations for the purpose of plotting bearings and courses. The north position is *True North*. All bearings on a chart are true bearings unless converted to magnetic bearings and annotated as such. The roses show the magnetic variation at the time of printing and the annual change. To determine a position by the *position and bearing* method, the compass rose and latitude scale are used.

CHARTED DATA

ⓘ **Note**: inconsistencies of terminology can be found among charts of different countries and between charts issued at different times by the same country.

Admiralty charts illustrate two types of features, those that are hazardous to shipping, and those that are of interested to mariners.

Chart colours

There are two common methods for illustrating charts using colours, as shown at Figure 10-7. One method uses three colours: tan, green and blue. Tan shows ground that is always dry. Green represents intertidal areas. Blue shows areas that are always under water (in reference to the charts datum).

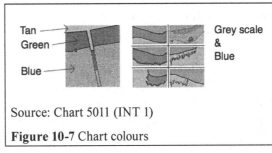

Source: Chart 5011 (INT 1)

Figure 10-7 Chart colours

The other method of colouring uses two colours: blue and grey. Various shades of blue indicate depth while grey shows features and hazards. This type of colouring is often found on the *Fishing Maps* available from camping/sporting stores.

Chart datum

The level of the ocean is continuously changing as a result of the rise and fall of the tides. The heights of places where there is no tide and have been illustrated on a map and or chart, are for heights above *mean sea level*.

The depths indicated on a chart, are related to an arbitrary level called the *chart datum*. The chart datum may have been determined by either: mean low water springs (MLWS), lowest astronomical tide (LAT), or other method. The chart datum shows the low water level, below which the tide will seldom fall, in the area of the chart. The depths shown on a chart are therefore the minimum depths experienced. The predicted heights of the tides need to be added to the charted depth to determine the sounding.

Previously the Australian chart datum was mean low water springs, however tidal heights fall below MLWS. The lowest tide level can be predicted to occur under average meteorological conditions (e.g. no storms) and under any combination of astronomical conditions. LAT is increasingly being used as the chart datum, for all new Australian charts. Be aware some chart's datum use MLWS and others use LAT. Furthermore, in other countries charts may still be found that use other methods of determining a chart datum (e.g. Indian springs low water (ISLW), lowest normal low water etc.).

Shoreline

Dry land is illustrated on charts by the colour tan. A surveyed shoreline is drawn as a solid line. A broken line (i.e. series of dashes) indicates an unsurveyed shoreline, whereby the charted shoreline position is an approximate only. A dotted line represents the low water line, if the variation between high water and low water differs considerably.

Natural foreshore features may also be illustrated such as hills, cliffs, sand dunes, flat coast, stony or sandy shores, marshes, swamps, rivers and lakes. For example, sandy shores are represented by a series of dots following parallel to the solid line indicating a shoreline. Vegetation such as trees, mangroves and palms may also be marked on a chart. Natural features are covered under Chart 5011 (INT 1) section C.

Man made features are also indicated on charts and are covered by Chart 5011 (INT 1) under sections D (Cultural features), and E (Landmarks), F (Ports).

Contour lines

Contour lines are drawn lines connecting places of equal depth. On metric charts and recent fathom charts, colours are used to distinguish different levels. Colours make it easier for a mariner to quickly identify areas of shoaling water. Green is used to show a *drying contour* that represents features, which expose at low water, as they are higher than the chart datum.

Blue tint in one or more shades and tint ribbons are used to illustrate different limits according to the charts scale, purpose and the nature of the bathymetry. Generally, depths of five metres or less (< 5 m) have a distinguishing darker shade of blue. As the depth increases to 10 metres the shade of blue lightens, or the area may be white with the 10 metres contour having a blue ribbon. Depths below 10 metres are illustrated as white. Further information can be found in Chart 5011 (INT 1) section I (Depths).

Nature of the seabed

The nature of the seabed—including intertidal areas—may also be illustrated and or annotated with an abbreviation (e.g. S is sand, R is rock, Co is coral etc.). Information about the nature of the seabed is of use by mariners for the purpose of anchoring their ships. For kayakers and small boat operators, it can provide useful information about where to land (e.g. the letter M printed on a green area informs the user the intertidal zone consists of mud). Further information can be found in Chart 5011 (INT 1) section J.

Rock hazards

The four illustrations at Figure 10-8 show the various method of illustrating rock hazards. The first is a rock awash, at level of chart datum. The second is an underwater rock over which the depth is not known, but is considered to be a danger to surface navigation (shipping). The third is a rock that does not cover. The fourth is a rock that covers and uncovers. With this last type of feature, when it is exposed above the water, it is said to have a *drying height*. Further chart information can be found in Chart 5011 (INT 1) section K.

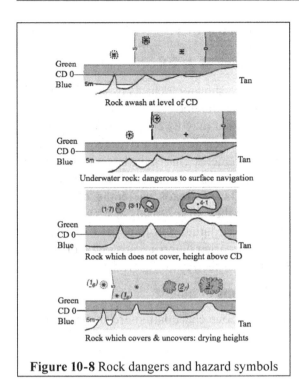

Figure 10-8 Rock dangers and hazard symbols

Beach zone hazards

The method of illustrating a hidden danger or an area of multiple dangers is through the use of a danger line as shown in Figure 10-9. A danger line is a series of dots around or along a feature that is considered dangerous to navigation (e.g. a rock that covers or uncovers, a series of bombies forming a reef, a coral reef).

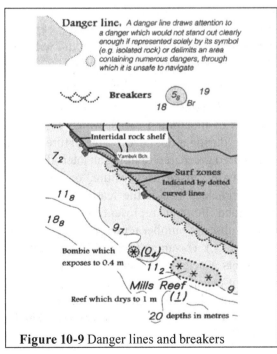

Figure 10-9 Danger lines and breakers

Surf zones may be illustrated by rows of dots forming semi-circles. In certain cases, the row may only be one deep and not two deep, as illustrated. The abbreviation 'Br' may also indicate breakers. In other cases, the chart may have a note along the lines saying 'breaks heavily in SE weather' to warn mariners of the danger. Further information can be found in Chart 5011 (INT 1) section K.

TIDAL TERMS

① Note: inconsistencies of terminology can be found among charts of different countries and between charts issued at different times by the same country.

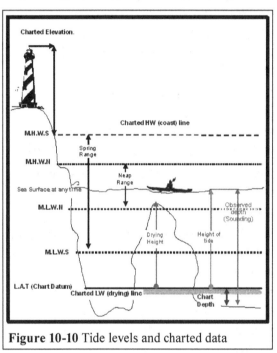

Figure 10-10 Tide levels and charted data

Referring to Figure 10-10, the following terms are applied to charts.

Chart datum (CD) is an arbitrary reference point level below which depths are given on a chart. Chart datum may also be referred to as Low Water (LW) line. Chart datum is determined on the initial area survey and will vary from place to place, depending upon the areas tidal range. The datum may be taken as a height below, which the tide at that place seldom falls under normal weather conditions.

Half-tide is when the height of the MSL is added to the charted depths. The result will be the average depth of water, which may be expected at half tide.

Highest Astronomical Tide (HAT) is the highest level of water, which can be predicted to occur under any combination of astronomical conditions.

High Water (HW) is the highest level reached by the sea during one tidal oscillation.

Lowest Astronomical Tide (LAT) is the lowest level to which sea level can be predicted to fall under normal meteorological conditions.

Low Water (LW) is the lowest level reached by the sea during one tidal oscillation.

Mean High Water Neaps (MHWN) is the average heights of water at neaps recorded over an average year.

Mean High Water Springs (MHWS) is the average heights of water at springs recorded over an average year. Heights of land features on mariner's charts are given above MHWS.

Mean Low Water (MLW) is the average height of all low waters at a given place. About half of the low waters fall below it and half above.

Mean Low Water Neaps (MLWN) is the average heights of water at neaps recorded over an average year.

Mean Low Water Springs (MLWS) is the average heights of water at springs recorded over an average year. Usually shortened to low water springs.

Mean Sea Level (MSL) is the average level of the surface of the sea calculated from observations taken over a long period of time. In areas where there is little or no tide (e.g. the Baltic Sea), mean sea level is used as the chart datum.

Tidal height is the vertical measurement of the surface of the water and the tidal datum (vertical datum).

Tidal range is the vertical difference between successive high water and low water.

CHARTED DEPTHS AND SOUNDINGS

Indications of depth

Depths are shown on charts by small numerals spread over the body of the chart. The units of measurement may be either fathoms or meters. These numbers (e.g. 7_3) are related to the chart datum. On metric charts, the larger print number (i.e. 7) reads as 7 metres and the smaller print number (i.e. 3) reads as tenths of a metre. Therefore the figure 7_3 reads as 7.3 metres depth below chart datum. On imperial measurement charts, the larger number reads as 7 fathoms and 3 feet (or 45 feet) below chart datum.

Indications of height

Heights above chart datum are shown by three methods, depending upon whether the feature is man-made or a natural feature on dry land, or if it is a natural feature that covers and uncovers through the action of tidal movements.

Significant to navigation man-made features have the features height above mean high water springs inside brackets (e.g. (134) meaning 134 metres above MHWS).

Features that are always dry (i.e. they are higher than the charted MHWS) are marked with a *spot height dot*, with accompanying positive figure(s) written on the feature. If the feature is to small to write on, the features 'always dry' exposed height is marked with a spot height dot with the height written inside enclosed brackets beside the feature as shown in Figure 10-8.

The last illustration at Figure 10-8 shows the methods of illustrating rocks, which cover and uncover, during a tidal cycle. The feature would be coloured green, representing an intertidal area. Additionally, inside the feature, or annotated within brackets beside the feature, will be an underlined number representing unit metres with a subscript number representing tenths of a metre (i.e. $\underline{3}_7$). The underlining of the unit number represents a negative value. In this case, the $\underline{3}_7$ represent negative 3.7 metres (−3.7 m), from the chart datum. That is, this feature raises 3.7 metres above the chart datum but will be below the height datum (i.e. MHWS).

Tide levels and soundings

The depth of water between a vessels hull—and or keel—to allow safe navigation, is of concern to skippers. Predicted tide heights, called *soundings*, are added to the charted depths printed on a chart. The charted depths are taken from the chart datum and are positive values. Features extending above the chart datum are negative values, because they diminish or entirely displace the amount of water, and therefore clearance, between the vessel and the hazardous (to shipping) feature.

For example, in Figure 10-11 the man made feature called 'The Annulus' shows a depth of 1.5 metres (15). The tide at low water (for this particular time and day) is 0.2 metres. At high water the tide is predicted to be 1.2 metres. Therefore, at low water, the water depth at the charted area would be 1.7 metres.

Tidal Levels referred to Datum of Soundings							
Place	Lat S	Long E	Heights in metres above datum				
			MHHW	MLHW	MSL	MHLW	MLLW
Port Welshpool	38° 15'	146° 27'	2.6	1.7	1.4	1.1	0.2
Rabbit Island	33 55	146 31	1.8	1.6	0.9	0.2	0.0

Table 10-1 Chart tide levels table

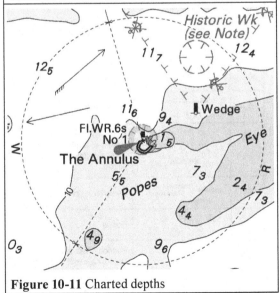

Figure 10-11 Charted depths

At high water, the depth would increase to 2.7 metres. At any period between low water and high water, the depth can be determined by using the Rule of Twelfths.

In the absence of tide tables or the Internet, the chart provides, if applicable to shipping, a Tidal Levels table. Charts show tide levels referenced to the *Datum of Sounding tables* as shown at Table 10-1, which in this example, refers to chart AUS 181 Corner Inlet.

Also, note that the printed data on the chart was incorrect and a pen amendment was carried out to update the chart. Mariners are advised of chart amendments through the *Australian Notices to Mariners Correction List*, produced by the Australian Hydrographic Service.

Methods for determining water level depth and tidal stream movements include the Rule of Thirds, Rule of Twelves and the 50/90 Rule. These will be discussed later in Practical Navigation

ⓘ **Note:** For sea kayakers paddling around Corner Inlet, French Island, Mud Island, Swan Bay and between Rhyll and Newhaven, you need to be aware of the tides if you do not want a long portage through mud or a long slow 'hull dragging' experience.

Currents

Ocean currents are the horizontal movement of water not caused by the gravitational interactions between the sun, moon, and earth (i.e. tides), and usually follow a seasonal pattern. Ocean currents are referred to by their force mechanism either wind driven or thermohaline.

Tidal streams (aka tidal currents) are the periodic horizontal movements of water caused by gravitational interactions between the sun, moon, and earth (i.e. tides), which flow in and out of harbours and along the coast. They are related to the rise and fall, of the local tide and are influenced by past and existing weather.

Currents are sometimes shown on charts with arrows giving the set (direction) and possibly figures showing the rate (speed). The information refers to average conditions that may differ considerably at any given time, according to weather and tide conditions.

Tidal Diamonds

Tidal streams are usually indicated on large-scale charts of harbours and coasts by a diamond enclosing a capital letter as shown in

Figure 10-12. The diamond corresponds to the tidal stream table located in a convenient position on the chart. The tidal stream table shows the periods of slack water, the geographical position of the diamond on the chart (using latitude/longitude coordinates), the set (direction) of the stream in true degrees, and the rate in knots at different periods for spring and neap tides.

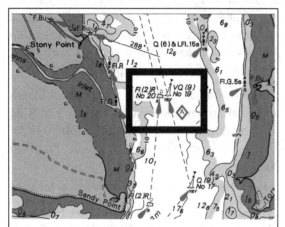

Figure 10-12 Tidal diamond on a chart

Tidal Levels Referred to Datum of Soundings

Place	Lat S	Long E	Height in Metres above Datum				
			MHWS	MHWN	MSL	MLWN	MLWS
Stony Point	38°22'	145°13'	2.9	2.4	1.7	1.1	0.6

Tidal Streams referred to H.W. at DEVONPORT

Hours	Geographical Position ◇	A 38°23'.4S 145°15'.0E			B 38°26'.4S 145°15'.5E			C 38°27'.0S 145°10'.2E		
		Directions of streams (degrees)	Rates at spring tides (knots)	Rates at neap tides (knots)	Directions of streams (degrees)	Rates at spring tides (knots)	Rates at neap tides (knots)	Directions of streams (degrees)	Rates at spring tides (knots)	Rates at neap tides (knots)
Before High Water -6		171	0.8	0.3	269	0.9	0.4	247	2.0	0.8
-5		016	0.2	0.1	086	0.4	0.2	282	0.3	0.1
-4		354	1.2	0.5	089	2.0	0.8	064	1.5	0.6
-3		356	2.0	0.8	087	2.5	1.0	064	3.2	1.3
-2		354	2.1	0.8	088	2.5	1.0	063	3.7	1.5
-1		356	1.9	0.8	090	1.9	0.8	083	3.4	1.4
High Water 0		357	1.3	0.5	089	1.1	0.4	063	2.6	1.1
After High Water +1		005	0.3	0.1	068	0.2	0.1	062	1.2	0.5
+2		182	1.0	0.4	284	0.7	0.3	252	0.6	0.3
+3		173	2.1	0.9	267	2.1	0.8	240	2.9	1.2
+4		174	2.1	0.9	267	2.7	1.1	240	3.1	1.2
+5		176	1.9	0.8	268	2.3	0.9	241	3.2	1.3
+6		173	1.1	0.4	267	1.4	0.5	242	2.6	1.0

Table 10-2 Chart tide levels and Tidal Stream data

The tidal diamond A, at Figure 10-12 corresponds to the table for 'Tidal Streams referred to H.W. at Devonport', shown at Table 10-2.

Tidal stream and hazard symbols

Figure 10-13 illustrates several chart symbols, which it is considered prudent for a sea kayaker to know the meaning of. To remember the difference between the flood stream arrow and the ebb stream arrow remember that the 'f' for the **f**lood stream arrow has **f**eathers drawn on its shaft. Further information can be found in Chart 5011 (INT 1) section H.

NAVIGATION MARK SYMBOLS

Australia uses the IALA System A of buoyage markers. These *marks* are comprised of a combination of lateral and cardinal systems. Marks may be buoys, piles, or beacons. Charts use a wide variety of symbols and notations to define objects, features, dangers and other information for the safe operation of shipping.

Buoys and Beacons

Buoys and beacons may also display a letter indicating a colour. The letters indicate the following colours: B, Black; G, green; R, red; W, white; and Y, yellow. A combination of colours designators may also be used such as RBR, RW, BY, BYB, YB, and YBY et cetera.

40	3kn →	Flood tide stream (with mean spring rate)
41	3kn →	Ebb tide stream (with mean spring rate)
42	#)))) ~~→	Current in restricted waters
43	~~~→ (see note)	Ocean current. Details of current strength and seasonal variations may be shown
44	(wavy lines)	Overall tide rips, races
45	(spiral symbols)	Eddies
46	◇ D	Position of tabulated tidal stream data with designation

Source: Chart 5011 (INT 1) section H
Figure 10-13 Current, tidal stream and hazard symbols

Marks may also be identified on a chart by a combination of different characteristics, such as showing colour code designators (e.g. BRB) but not showing a top mark. A common selection has been included at Figure 10-14 Navigation mark symbols. Further information can be found in Chart 5011 (INT 1) section Q.

During daylight buoys are identified by their shape and colour code. The colour code is printed underneath the symbol using a letter or letters (e.g. R, G, Y, YB, RB). If a buoy is lighted, then the chart shows this fact by using a symbol that resembles a plump escalation mark on its side emanating from the buoy symbol's base. It will also have a notation informing the navigator of its lighting sequence. Further information can be found in Chart 5011 (INT 1) section P.

Buoyage lighting sequences

When the light exhibited is not white, the colour is indicated in the chart abbreviation by Y, R or G for yellow, red or green. Group flash is a group of two or more flashes and is abbreviated as Fl(number of flashes in group) (e.g. Fl(2) i.e. group of two flashes, or VQ(9) i.e. group of nine flashes).

Light flashes may be combined in groups; each including the same number of flashes and in which the groups are repeated at regular intervals. The eclipses (periods of darkness) separating the flashes within each group are usually of equal duration; and this duration is clearly shorter than the duration of eclipse between two successive groups.

In Figure 10-12 the port lateral mark No. 20, (near the tidal diamond 'A') has the notation Fl(2)R. This represents a group flashing light, regularly repeating a group of two red flashes, with the duration of light being shorter than the period of darkness.

The abbreviation GpFl(?) for group flashing is obsolescent and the international Fl(?) is the current abbreviation. Refer to Symbols and Abbreviations used on Admiralty Charts, Chart 5011 (INT 1).

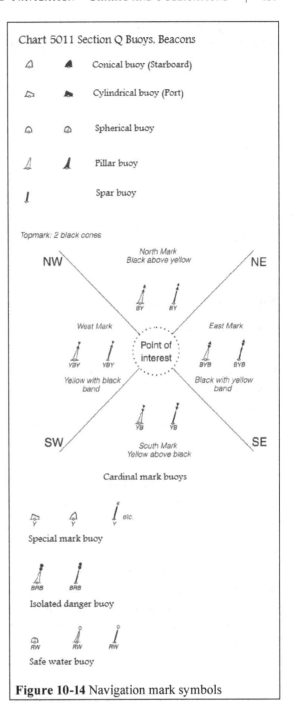

Figure 10-14 Navigation mark symbols

Period

The period of a light (time between the start of successive sequences) is indicated in seconds with the lower case letter 's' following the numeral in the notation. A notation of FlR5s means single red flash every five seconds. The interval, known as the period of light, is the time between the beginning of one flash and the beginning of the succeeding flash. For occulting, alternating, group flashing, or group occulting lights the time shown indicates the interval of time occupied by one complete cycle.

Fl(3)WR. 18s73m 19/15M

Label	Description	Label	Description
F	Fixed	UQ	Ultra quick
Occ	Single occulting[1]	FFl	Fixed and flashing
Gp Occ	Group occulting	Alt Wr	Alternating white/red
Iso	Isophase (equal flashes)	B	Black (for markers not lights)
Fl	Single flashing	W	White
Gp Fl	Group flashing	R	Red
LFl	Long flashing	G	Green
QkFl	Quick flashing	Bu	Blue

Table 10-3 Navigational light descriptors

Chart indications for lights

The distance light can be seen depends upon its brilliance and the meteorological visibility at the time. The distance at which a light can be seen in clear weather is shown against most lights but not against buoys. Most coastal lights are exhibited from sunset to sunrise and in restricted visibility.

The height of a light given on charts and or in the Admiralty List of Lights is taken from the centre of the lantern above Mean High Water Springs. The charted or listed geographical range that a light may be seen in clear weather is expressed in nautical miles for an observer's eye height of 4.5 metres; and when the sea level is that of Mean High Water Springs. A geographical range table is provided at the beginning of each volume of the Admiralty List of Lights (NRC-RS 6, 2000).

Cape Otway lighthouse has the following lighting sequence notation on a metric chart. Broken down into its parts, the notation means:

Group flashes (Fl(3))

Colours of light (WR)

Period, time taken to display one full sequence of flashes and eclipses (18s)

Elevation of light above MHWS or if no tide above MSL (73m)

Luminous range in nautical miles in clear visibility (19/15M).

Interpreted the notation conveys the following information about Cape Otway lighthouse: group of three White/Red flashes, at 18 second intervals, displayed 73 metres above MHWS, with a luminous range of 19 to 15 nautical miles. The white light is visible at 19 nm, and the red at 15 nm.

Admiralty publication on lights

Details of all lights except those of buoys with an elevation of less than eight metres are contained in the *Admiralty List of Lights*, which is published every twelve months. Each volume refers to a particular part of the world and is republished at intervals of about seventeen months. Complete instructions for interpreting these lists are contained in the forward to each volume. Details of other buoys are provided on the largest scale chart of the area. The Americans have a similar Coast Guard publication titled the *Light List*.

Lighthouses

Lighthouses are used to indicate harbor entrances, isolated dangers off the coast, or a promontory, cape or headland. They may appear as a tower or as a solar powered unmanned light structure. Some lighthouses have distinctive colours or colour bands that can be used to identify them and are described in Light List publications. On charts and at sea, lighthouses can be distinguished by the light's characteristics both color combination and length of flash.

NAVIGATION PUBLICATIONS

Along with charts, supporting publications are necessary to supplement the charted information. The following materials are part of the supporting publications:

Pilots (aka *Sailing Directions*) are intended to be read in conjunction with the navigation chart. Pilots are produced by several agencies such as the United Kingdom Hydrography Office (British Hydrographer of the Navy), Australian Hydrographic Service and Australian State Government maritime agencies. Pilots are designed for use by the merchant mariner on all classes of ocean-going vessels and contain essential information on all aspects of navigation. Sailing Directions are complementary to Standard Nautical Charts. An example of a Pilot is the Australia Pilot, Volume II, 6th edition, 1982. Chapter 1 contains information about navigation and regulations, country and port information and natural conditions. Natural conditions provide information about currents, tides and tidal streams, sea and swell, climate and weather, winds et cetera. Chapter 2 provides information on Bass Straight. Positional information is given for features and navigational markers, as well as other pertinent information required for safe passage.

Admiralty List of Lights gives full details of all official navigational lights and fog signals throughout the world. The publication is available from the UKHO (British Hydrographer of Navy). Volume K of the Admiralty List of Lights covers Australian waters.

Chart 5011 (INT 1) is a required booklet for all navigators. (Maritime Safety Queensland, 2004). It contains guidance on all the symbols and abbreviations used on Admiralty and International charts. It also contains useful information when using charts produced by other chart producers (e.g. maritime Safety Queensland boating safety chart series). Chart 5011 (INT1) is based upon the 'Chart Specifications of the IHO' (International Hydrographic Organisation) adopted in 1982 with later adoptions and corrections. The layout and numbering accords with the official IHO version of Chart INT1.

Notices to Mariners (NtMs) contain the amendments to navigational charts and publications (Pilots, List of Lights, and Admiralty List of Radio Signals). They are issued by the Australian Hydrographic Service (AHS)—formerly the RAN Hydrographic Office. Contained within the Notices to Mariners are Navigation Warnings.

Tide tables, are produced by both the Australian Hydrographic Service (AHS) and State Governments. The Australian tide tables produced annually by the RAN cover all Australian Ports, Papua New Guinea and the Solomon Islands. The Bureau of Meteorology website provides links to tide and tidal stream information.

UPDATING AUSTRALIAN ADMIRALTY CHARTS

Charts are 'living' documents. Information affecting the safety of navigation for mariners is constantly being received by the Australian Hydrographic Service (AHS). The information may be in the form of an individual report of a newly discovered danger, or it may be a buoy or beacon that has been moved or removed. At other times the change can be as large as an entire new survey. In all cases, the AHS has the obligation to publish details of new and altered information affecting the potential safety of mariners. Equally, the AHS states *that many mariners have a legal obligation to apply these updates to their charts—and there are several tales of woe to show why having an up to date chart is a good idea for all vessels, ranging from large cargo ships to racing yachts.*

The AHS issues corrections and changes to charts through the 'Notices to Mariners' (NtMs), as an annual and in 26 fortnightly editions. Permanent relevant corrections should be made on a chart using a magenta coloured pen. Do not use red ink as in red light conditions the information becomes invisible. Temporary corrections should be made in pencil. The correction year and Notices to Mariners number should be annotated outside the left bottom chart margin. The AHS states *this is a requirement for all SOLAS vessels, most other commercial vessels and even some offshore racing yachts.* However it is considered prudent and good practice for recreational mariners to follow the same updating procedures. For detailed information about correcting Admiralty charts refer to AHS website.

NON-ADMIRALTY AND OVERSEAS CHARTS

Australia

Maritime Safety Queensland (MSQ) produces inshore boating safety charts aimed at recreational and commercial mariners, with charts tailored specifically to Queensland waters. A legend of symbols and abbreviations is shown on each chart and may not correspond to Admiralty Chart 5011 symbols and abbreviations. Over time these charts may be updated and replaced by MSQ. Information about these charts can be found on the MSQ website.

Parks Victoria is the local authority responsible for recreational boaters on Port Phillip and Westernport Bay and produces a chart, termed a 'guide', for both locations. Refer to the Parks Victoria website to ensure you have the latest version of the 'Boating on the Bay A guide to recreational boating on Port Phillip Bay' and Boating on Western Port A guide to recreational boating on Western Port'. Both guides show navigational information and the boundaries of marine parks.

There are a series of 'Fishing Maps' produced by the Australian Fishing Network and available through outdoor, fishing and boating outlets. The maps come with a warning 'Although this map is drawn to scale, it is not intended to be used for navigational purposes'.

Other sources of 'charts' may be found (e.g. the New South Wales Boating Guide to Port Stephens and the Myall Lakes). However these documents are intended as a guide and may not be accurate or up to date.

Overseas

United Kingdom

In the United Kingdom the United Kingdom Hydrographic Office (UKHO) produces nautical charts, Notices to Mariners and Pilots (aka Sailing Directions) for worldwide coverage in 74 volumes. Other publications available are Admiralty Tide Tables (4 volumes), Admiralty List of Lights and Fog Signals (10 volumes),

List of Radio Signals (6 volumes) and 'The Astronomical Almanac'. The UKHO also provide a free download of 'Extracts from The Mariner's handbook NP100'. The NP100 contains useful information about Admiralty charts and publications, the IALA buoyage system, basic meteorology, tides, currents and the characteristics of the sea.

Of use to sea kayakers researching an area in which to go paddling, are the Admiralty Leisure Chart Folios. These folios, though not fully covering the coastline of the United Kingdom, contain on average 17 charts per folio. The folios provide a wide range of useful information to a wide spectrum of users from professional mariners, and ocean racing yachtsmen, through to recreational dingy and motor boater users.

The information contained in the folios ranges from coastal areas, slipways, harbours, marinas and pubs. Each folio contains information on tides, radio services, chart symbols and abbreviations and IMO Life Saving Signals. The folios are updated via the online Leisure Notices to Mariners. Leisure Notices to Mariners, are updated weekly.

United States of America

In the U.S.A. the National Ocean and Atmospheric Administration (NOAA) produces nautical charts for most of the United States, with a library of over 1000 charts encompassing the coasts of the U.S., the Great Lakes, and the U.S. territories. The National Geospatial-Intelligence Agency (formerly the National Imagery and Mapping Agency (NIMA)) is responsible for producing ocean charts, charts of some Pacific Islands and foreign waters charts. The U.S. Army Corps of Engineers is responsible for producing charts on the Mississippi River and other inland waterways.

The NOAA produces charts, Coastal Pilots and U.S. Chart No. 1,—which is the equivalent publication to the Admiralty Chart 5011. They update their nautical charts with corrections published in U.S. Coast Guard Local Notices to Mariners (LNMs), National Geospatial-Intelligence Agency Notices to Mariners (NMs), and the Canadian Coast Guards Notices to Mariners (CNMs). The NOAA website provides links to Notices to Mariners, which provides updated information about changes to maritime navigation. The NOAA website also provides abundant free resources and links to pertinent websites for use by both professional and recreational mariners.

The Current Light Lists, and Light Lists Corrections can be found on the USCG Navigation Centre website. Information can also be found in the relevant Pilot.

The U.S. Coast Guard has a website called the Boating Safety Resource Center. This website provides a host of information useful to American recreational boaters. The website has links to other maritime websites (e.g. American Canoe Association, marine weather and tides) and provides access to free resources. Of interest are the sections on Navigation Rules, State and Federal Boating Laws, and Federal Regulations. Two useful downloads are the U.S. Coast Guard's Aids to Navigation and U.S. Coast Guard's Navigation Rules.

The USCG Aids to Navigation provides the recreational boater/water user with the basic knowledge required to safely navigate U.S. waterways using the U.S. Aids to Navigation System (USATONS). The publication provides navigation rules (i.e. 'Rules of the Road') and information about how to navigate safely using the IALA Region B system of buoyage. This includes information on how to react to on-coming traffic, over-tacking and crossing another's course (i.e. path). Information is also provided on basic chart reading, night lighting requirements and tips on night navigation. The publication is comparable to the Australian recreational boat user publications produced by the various states and territories.

Information on the requirement for lighting requirements of vessels less than seven metres or boats under oars is found in the USCG Navigation Rules International-Inland.

The USCG Navigation Center is geared towards electronic navigation. Some of their primary areas are GPS, DGPS, electronic navigation and charting and maritime communications.

They also provide Local Notices to Mariners, Lights List and corrections. Some of the other documentation that may be of interest to sea kayakers researching paddling in the U.S. includes Navigation Rules, Navigation Regulations, MF and HF Channels, Marine Safety Information Broadcasts, VHF Channels and Frequencies.

Canada

In Canada, there are three government bodies that hold information relevant to sea kayaking navigation and planning: Transport Canada, Canadian Coast Guard and Canadian Hydrographic Service. Transport Canada's website Marine section has two useful publications: Boating Safety Guide TP—511 and Sea Kayaking Safety Guide—TP14726. The Canadian Coast Guard's website provides a pdf of The Canadian Aids to Navigation Systems. This document describes the IALA Region B system of buoyage used in Canada. The Canadian Hydrographic Service's website provides a list of available Canadian charts, Sailing Directions, and Tide and Current Tables as well as where to obtain them. The department also provides Notices to Mariners, and a pdf of Chart No. 1 Symbols, Abbreviations and Terms used on [CHS] Charts.

New Zealand

Land Information New Zealand (LINZ) produces the official nautical charts for New Zealand, certain waters of Antarctica and the South West Pacific. For symbols, terms and abbreviations used on nautical charts, LINZ recommends that you refer to the following two publications: the latest edition of Chart 5011 (INT 1) Symbols and Abbreviations used on Admiralty Charts, or Karte 1 (INT 1) Symbols, Abbreviations, Terms used on Charts, published by the German Federal Maritime and Hydrographic Agency. Charts are updated through LINZ produced Notices to Mariners. LINZ also produces an annual edition of the New Zealand nautical almanac. This document contains a navigation lights list, maritime safety information, astronomical information and tide tables.

GUIDE TO USING CHARTS

Maritime Safety Queensland offers the following advice to commercial boat operators, when using charts:

Always us the largest scale chart because:

- Any errors are reduced to a minimum
- If the chart is distorted, these errors will have the least effect
- More detail is shown
- The printing plate from which it is made is corrected before the plates of small-scale charts.

Transfer positions from one chart to another by bearing and distance from a point common to both charts and check by latitude and longitude. This is most necessary because the graduations on the two charts may differ

Always check the vessel's position as soon as possible after its position has been transferred from one chart to another. (Not practical for sea kayakers while on-water)

Always us the nearest compass rose because there will be less effective distortion and the correct variation will be used

Remember the change of variation printed on each compass rose

Use only recent and up-to-date chart editions.

① **Note:** For sea kayakers and recreational boat operators the following information is only reference information as to what is on the government websites and what is required of professional mariners.

Important Information For Chart Users

The Australian Hydrographical Service on its website issues the following important information for chart users.

The following Australian and Admiralty publications should be referred to when using Australian Nautical Charts, Seafarer Raster Navigational Chart (RNCs) and Australian ENCs. Note: you should ensure that charts and publications are kept corrected. (In Australia, this can be done by referring to the AHS website).

The following navigation related documents are publish for use with Australian produced charts:

Symbols, Abbreviations & Terms Used on Australian Charts

Notices to Mariners #17—Symbology Used on Australian Navigational Charts. This document contains symbology, which has not been adopted in the International Hydrographic Organisation INT 1 (symbols & abbreviations) publications for use in Australian Navigational Charts.

The following publications satisfy Chapter V of the SOLAS Convention as amended in 2002 and promulgated for Australia under AMSA Marine Orders Part 21, Order 6 of 2003, which details carriage requirements for nautical charts and publications necessary for the intended voyage by commercial vessels. It is included here as a guide to the range of publications available for voyage planning. The required documents are:

Australian Notices to Mariners—Updated fortnightly

Annual Australian Notices to Mariners

Australian National Tide Tables

Seafarer Tides

Australian Seafarers Handbook.

These publications satisfy Chapter V of the SOLAS Convention as amended in 2002 and promulgated for Australia under AMSA Marine Orders Part 21, Order 6 of 2003, which details carriage requirements for nautical charts and publications necessary for the intended voyage.

Chart handling and storage

Use soft lead (2B) pencils when plotting on a chart and erase out dated plots. Do not obscure chart information when writing on a chart. Draw lines and make labels no larger than necessary.

You may decide to use a thin sheet of acetate (clear plastic) graduated with grids corresponding to the scale of the chart. The acetate is placed over the chart and written on during the plotting process, thereby protecting the chart and extending is life.

Store charts by rolling them up and not folding them, as this prolongs the life of the chart and prevents navigational information from being erased in the fold lines.

ELECTRONIC NAVIGATIONAL CHART

Electronic navigational charts (ENC) for use with chart plotters, GPS devices and other electronic devices (i.e. computers) are available and often-used in-lieu of paper charts. There are several products on the market and the user needs to research the product for their intended use; and be aware of the need to update the product with the latest corrections and versions.

GLOBAL POSITIONING SYSTEM (GPS)

The Global Positioning System (GPS) is one of a number of satellite based Global Navigation Satellite Systems (GNSS). The GPS was put in place by the United States Department of Defence and is also known as NAVSTAR. In the 1980s civilians were given access. In May 2000, full GPS operation was given to civilians with the removal of Selective Availability. Turning off Selective Availability greatly improved accuracy for civilian users.

GPS is a network of 24 orbiting satellites positioned around 20 000 kilometres (~12,000 miles) above the earth. The solar powered satellites orbit the Earth twice within 24 hours. The satellites transmit a series of radio signals (50 watts or less) to ground stations on Earth, which accurately track and determine their position. A GPS satellite transmits two low power radio signals, designated L1 and L2. Civilian GPS receivers use the L1 frequency of 1575.42 MHz in the UHF band. Being in the UHF band the signals are line-of-sight, meaning that they travel in a straight line. They can pass through clouds, glass and plastic but will not penetrate solid objects. They can also be reflected off solid objects like buildings and mountains. Thick foliage can also block the signals from a receiver.

GPS position depends on very accurate time references. The 907.1 kilogram (2000 pound)

5.18 metre (17 foot wide, with solar panels extended) satellites have atomic clocks from the United States Naval Observatory fitted on board to provide the required accurate time references. When a GPS receiver picks up a GPS satellite's radio signal it compares the time of its transmission to the time it was received. The difference tells the GPS receiver how far away the satellite is.

To determine a latitude and longitude position (i.e. two-dimensional position) the GPS receiver needs signals from three GPS satellites. Using four or more satellites in view, the receiver can calculate latitude, longitude and elevation (i.e. three-dimensional position). When a receiver has determined the users position it can then calculate other information like speed, track, bearing, distance to destination and more.

GPS accuracy depends upon the type of receiver the user has. Hand held units have an accuracy of 10 to 20 metres. Units operating Differential Global Positioning System (DGPS) have accuracy less than ten metres with specialised units and equipment having accuracy to 10 to 15 centimetres.

Differential Global Positioning System (DGPS) uses an additional receiver fix from a stationary known position nearby, known as a beacon. The additional receiver fix refines the fixes received from the satellites. In Australia, corrections either come from an Australian Maritime Safety Authority (AMSA) marine beacon (useful up to 300 km inland) or an OmniSTAR satellite service, which covers the entire country.

The latest technology for GPS accuracy is the Wide Area Augmentation System (WAAS). Instead of using a fixed ground station signal being transmitted to a receiver, it uses a signal from a geo-stationary satellite. The signal from one of the two geo-stationary satellites over the equator, receive correction data from 25 ground reference stations in the USA. This correction signal is broadcasted to the satellites from one of two stations on either coast of the USA. The geo-stationary satellites transmitted signal is received and decoded by one of the regular channels already present in a GPS receiver. Garmin state that a WAAS capable receiver can give accuracy greater than three metres 95 per cent of the time. WAAS is the common name for the generic name SBAS (Space Based Augmentation System) or WADGPS (Wide Area Differential GPS). Currently WAAS is only available in the USA.

There are many sources of GPS signal error, for example:

Atmospheric conditions in the ionosphere and troposphere can slow the satellites signal down as it pass through the atmosphere.

Receiver clock errors occur, since the receivers clock is not as accurate as the atomic clocks onboard the satellites. Timing differences may exist between the satellites and the receiver, thereby causing errors.

Signal multipath is a term used to describe what happens when a GPS signal is reflected off an object, such as a tall building or rock face, before being reaching the receiver. The signal reflection increases the time the signal takes to reach the receiver.

Orbital errors (aka ephemeris errors) occur when the satellites location is incorrectly reported.

Satellite geometry/shading refers to the relative position of the satellites at any given time. Ideal satellite geometry occurs when the satellites are wide apart. If they are inline or a tight group poor geometry results causing errors.

Number of visible satellites picked-up and used by the receiver determines accuracy. Three or more satellites are need for a two-dimensional or three-dimensional fix respectively. The more satellites a GPS receiver can "see" the better the accuracy.

Electronic interference also causes errors.

OTHER GLOBAL NAVIGATIONAL SATELLITE SYSTEMS

Apart from GPS there are other Global Navigational Satellite Systems (GNSS). The Russian Federation has the GLObal Navigation Satellite System (GLONASS). Like GPS it was developed during the cold war and is controlled by the military. It is also designed to have 24 satellites in its constellation and transmit two navigation signals. Its usefulness is limited due to lack of funding the project receives. China has the regional COMPAS/BeiDou (Big Dipper) navigation system. It is used for Navigation in China and surrounding regions. The European Community through the European Commission and in conjunction with the European Space Agency plans to put in place the European Satellite Navigation System (Galileo). The driving force behind this project is to reach full autonomy in satellite navigation away from the US. Currently the US has control of the only fully operational global satellite system. Japan is proposing and developing a GNSS called Quasi-Zenith Satellite System (QZSS). QZSS is intended to address the problems inherent when using GNSS in dense urban areas.

DATUMS

With the increased use of GPS hand-held receivers an understanding of the difference between a datum and a projection is require to reduce operator errors. A datum is a *framework* that enables Geodesist to define coordinate systems. The framework includes the use of an ellipsoid/spheroid in conjunction with a reference frame and in conjunction with parameters like plate tectonic movement. A projection is one of many mathematical methods (e.g. Mercator, Transverse Mercator, and Universal Transverse Mercator etc.). These mathematical methods use the geographic coordinates (i.e. latitude and longitude), which have been determined through the use of a datum on a curved surface (i.e. the earth), and transfer them onto a flat surface (i.e. a map or chart).

A datum is any numerical or geometrical quantity(s) that act as a reference point to measure other quantities. In Geodesy, cartography and navigation there are two types of datum used: the vertical datum and the horizontal datum. The vertical datum is used to measure height. The horizontal datum is used for the determination of horizontal position.

As previously mentioned in this chapter, the earth is not a sphere but an irregular shaped object, being wider at the equator than at the poles. The earth's irregular shape with its irregular topographical features is too complex and difficult to accurately describe mathematically, so it is the practise of Geodesist to reference the earth to a more uniform shape. The geometric shape used is the ellipsoid. In the Geodetic community, they use the term ellipsoid and spheroid interchangeably when talking about the earth's shape. A spheroid is described as being an ellipsoid that is evenly rounded and close to the shape of a sphere.

A horizontal datum may be defined at an origin point on the ellipsoid so that the ellipsoids centre aligns with the earth's centre of mass. From here the earth can have latitude and longitude determined over its surface, known as *geographic coordinates*. Each country or region developed their own horizontal datum or datums based on two-dimensional coordinates. Example of these types of datums are the Australian Geodetic Datum 1966 (AGD66), Australia Geodetic Datum 1984 (AGD84), New Zealand Geodetic Datum 1949 (NZGD49), North American Datum 1927 (NAD27), European Datum, Ordnance Survey of Great Britain 1936 Datum, Tokyo Datum and Indian Datum. However, because the ellipsoids were positioned over the area of best fit for each country or region, the derived geographic coordinates were mismatched between countries and even between states within countries. In Australia for example, AGD84 was a revision of AGD66, but was not accepted by all states and departments, even though there was a 200 metre difference in the same positions between the two. One reason for the mismatch in geographic coordinates was the misalignment of the referenced spheroids centre, from the Earth's centre of mass.

With the advent of the 'space-age' greater accuracy could be obtained in determining the position of the earth's centre of mass and the type of ellipsoid to be used. This was achieved through the use of satellite constellations and known fixed stations around the earth, which were used to establish a *reference frame*. With this knowledge the ellipsoid was positioned to coincide with the earth's centre of mass. This refinement, to position the spheroid over the earth's centre of mass, is termed *geocentric*. Using a reference frame and an ellipsoid/spheroid, it is possible to workout the geographic coordinates (latitude and longitude) and heights around the earth. In general terms these two sources of information constitute a datum. For greater accuracy continental drift is factored in.

Today there are two commonly used ellipsoids used to describe the earth's shape. One is the *Geocentric Reference System 1980* (GRS80) determined by the International Association Geodesy (IAG). The second is the *World Geodetic System 1984* (WGS84) determined by the US Department of Defence (DOD). The two commonly used reference frames are the *International Terrestrial Reference Frame* (ITRF) as determined by the IAS and the US DOD WGS84. The main difference between ITRF and WGS84 reference frames is the choice of fix stations used in their adjustment. The difference between ITRF2000 and WGS84 is generally less than 10 millimetres.

Since the earth is dynamic and through improved measuring techniques there has been revisions to the datums used. These changes are known as *realisations*. Since its implementation WGS84 has had several realisations. Realisations are annotated after the initialism by brackets containing an alpha character and/or numerals. The numerals relate to the date of the observation (e.g. WGS84 (G1150)); G refers to the method of observation being GPS. The number is the epoch based on the GPS week number starting at UTC 29 September 1996. Without a realisation or epoch, a datum is of no use to Geodesists. Through the enhancements (realisations), WGS84 is at the point where it closely aligns with the ITRF derived datum. For sea kayakers and general users of GPS, the differences are of little significance.

WGS84 is of significance because it is what the GPS uses. GPS receivers compute and store coordinates in terms of WGS84, then transform them to other datums when the information is displayed. WGS84 is also the default datum for many geographic information systems (GIS) packages. In Australia the Australian Hydrographic Office is issuing charts referenced to WGS84. Older charts are progressively being updated from AGD66 to WGS84. The charts provide clear advice on which datum is being used.

The Geocentric Datum of Australia (GDA) is the latest Australian three-dimensional coordinate system, replacing the Australian Geodetic Datum (AGD). The old AGD related to the two-dimensional Cartesian coordinate system known as Australia Map Grid (AMG). The two versions of AMG were: Australian Map Grid 1966 (AMG66) and Australian Map Grid 1984 (AMG84). Under this system heights were related to a separate vertical datum called the Australian Height Datum (AHD), which measured heights using mean sea level approximations as the datum.

The Geocentric Datum of Australia 1994 (AGD94) is the national geodetic datum of Australia. It references the GRS80 ellipsoid and the International Terrestrial Reference Frame 1992 (ITRF92), Epoch 1994. The projection chosen for defining grid coordinates is the Universal Transverse Mercator using the GRS80 ellipsoid. This system of coordinates is known as Map Grid of Australia 1994 (MGA94). The ITRF is computed annually and is sufficiently refined that changes between successive ITRF epochs, is in the order of a couple of millimetres only. At present, except for a small difference the application of mathematics, the WGS84 reference ellipsoid is essentially the same the GRS80 ellipsoid used with the ITRF and hence GDA94.

New Zealand previously used the New Zealand Geodetic Datum 1949 (NZGD1949). Since its definition, points have moved up to 2.5 metres. As with the AGD66/84 datums the NZGD1949 was not geocentric and therefore did not readily relate to other global Earth models. In 1998 New Zealand introduced the geocentric datum New Zealand Geodetic Datum 2000 (NZGD2000). The NZGD2000 is based on the GRS80 ellipsoid and the ITRF reference frame, ITRF96 at a reference date of 1 January 2000, epoch 2000.0. Given that

NZGD2000 and WGS84 reference frames are very closely aligned, for most practical purposes (for use by laymen), the coordinates between the two systems can be considered the same.

The official height datum is the New Zealand Vertical Datum 2009 (NZVD2009). It gives heights as compared against sea level to within 0.5 metres. NZGD2000 as measure against the GRS80 ellipsoid produces differences in heights of up to 35 metres from sea level. From the determination of geographic coordinates that are related to a curve surface, with a global reference frame and ellipsoid/spheroid, the coordinates need to be 'projected' on to a two-dimensional flat surface to make a map/chart. The process of converting coordinates between datums and projections is call *coordinate transformation*. In New Zealand the majority of maps are produced using the Transverse Mercator projection, which is base on a north-south orientated cylinder. The official projection for topographic mapping is the New Zealand Transverse Mercator 2000 (NZTM2000). Prior to NZTM2000 New Zealand used a projection titled New Zealand Map Grid (NZMG), which was based on the geodetic datum NZGD1949. NZTM2000 is used by Land Information New Zealand (LINZ) for 1:50 000 and smaller scale maps projection. The Transverse Mercator projection was chosen because it is an internationally recognized projection type that exhibits a low level of distortion at its east-west extents. The LINZ website states that the Transverse Mercator projection is the same as the Universal Transverse Mercator (UTM) projection but with a different origin latitude and different false easting and northing.

The United States previously used the North American Datum of 1927 (NAD27) based on the Clark ellipsoid of 1866. With satellite technology the North American Datum of 1983 (NAD83) was introduced based on the ITRF GRS80. NAD83 was defined to remain constant with the movement of the American continental plate. WGS84 though closely related to GRS80 was defined with respect to the average of stations positioned around the globe. The United States National Spatial Reference System of 2007

(NSRS2007), also referred to as NAD83 (2007), is a refinement of the NAD83 datum using data from a network of very accurate GPS receivers at Continuously Operating Reference Station (CORS).

Different nations within Africa have recognized the use of the Global Navigational Satellite System (GNSS), particularly the US GPS based on WGS84. Work is now underway to develop an African Geodetic Reference Frame (AFREF), with a focus of possibly using GPS technology. Priority has been given to developing transformational data for the already existing local and national mapping products to GNSS reference systems.

Certain European nations have adopted the European Terrestrial Reference System 1989 (ETRS89). ETRS89 is the GPS coordinate system standard used for high-quality GPS surveys throughout Europe. The system is based on the GRS80 ellipsoid but is tied to a stable part of the European plate to prevent the previous 2.5 centimetres per year drift in coordinates from European stations. ETRS89 is the Economic Unions recommended reference frame and has been adopted by civil aviation.

In Britain ETRS89 is the national coordinate system for 3D GPS positioning. It is a much more exacting definition of the GPS coordinate system than the WGS84 standard. Consequently, ETRS89 coordinates are also WGS84 coordinates, but general WGS84 coordinates do not necessarily meet the ETRS89 standard. For topographical mapping and all other Ordnance Survey mapping at all scales, the *national coordinate* system is used. The national coordinate system (aka National Grid) uses a geodetic datum based on the Airy ellipsoid, a terrestrial reference frame (TRF) titled Ordnance Survey Great Britain 1936 (OSGB36). For a projection it uses Transverse Mercator, which allows the use of easting and northing coordinates.

CHAPTER 11 PRACTICAL NAVIGATION

"I have never been lost, but I will admit to being confused for several weeks".

Daniel Boon

Navigation is the art of taking a vessel safely from one place to another. If a vessel is insight of land she can establish her position by taking bearings of recognised features on the land or seamarks; or by using electronic devices such as GPS.

Pilotage is the part of navigation, which concerns the safe conduct of a vessel in the vicinity of coasts, in narrow waters, and in the vicinity of dangers and hazards.

Due to the space limitations on a sea kayaks foredeck and exposure to the elements, performing chart work while on-water is not practical; and therefore all planning chart work needs to be performed on land. However this does not mean you cannot perform alterations on-water as required for the current situation. The use of electronic devices by a competent user (i.e. GPS with updated charts and correct chart datum) makes navigating on-water an easier task when performing fixes and corrections to course, heading and bearings.

COMPASSES

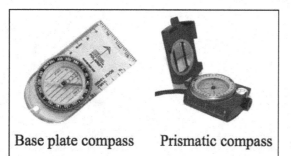

Base plate compass   Prismatic compass

Figure 11-1 Pocket compasses

The Chinese knew about compasses about 3000 years before the Europeans and it is thought that Marco Polo brought one back to Venice circa 1260 AD. Prior to this, the sun and stars were used to orientate the navigator in conjunction with and or without land features. The magnetic

compass is a very basic piece of equipment, made from a magnetised piece of metal used as a needle, to point to the earth's magnetic north and a graduated ring with either numbers or cardinal points on. Compasses come in a variety of forms with different features. On a kayak, either a fixed or removable deck compass (aka *steering compass*) can be fitted. Some kayakers when on a trip in an unknown area choose to carry a pocket compass in their PFD as a backup to the deck compass and as a means to reduce parallax error when taking a fix.

Pocket compasses generally can be base plate, base plate with sighting mirror, hand-held bearing compass and or a prismatic compass. A suggested pocket compass to carry is one of the base plate types. Furthermore, the advantage of a base plate compass with sighting hairs or sighting mirror is, if you are required to perform a resection (aka *back bearings*) to find your position, the sighting types decrease the possibility of parallax error between the observer, compass and feature being sighted; and thus, give greater accuracy of recorded bearing. Prismatic compasses also have a rear hairline sight allowing for greater accuracy of sighting and bearing recording, but are bulkier than base plate compasses and required protractors to be carried for map/chart work; whereas, a base plate compass can also be used as a protractor.

Base plate Compass

The base plate compass was invented in the 1920s in Sweden for the sport of orienteering. This type of compass is also known as an orienteering compass or protractor compass. For the uninitiated, a simple explanation on how to use a base plate compass is at Appendix 5.

Compass points

Depending upon the type of compass, the compass points will be made up of graduations with numbers, cardinal points or combination of both. These points will possibly be stamped on the fixed outer ring, or printed on a compass card, which rotates inside the housing and is common on prismatic type compasses.

Cardinal points and bearings

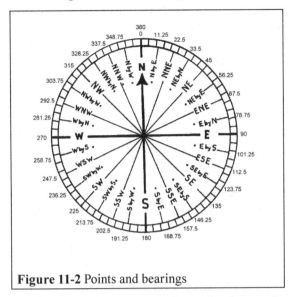

Figure 11-2 Points and bearings

The term cardinal points refer to the four main divisions of a compass being: north, east, south and west. Halfway between the cardinal points, are the four half-cardinal points of: north-east, south-east, south-west, and north-west. In between the half-cardinal points are the eight intermediate points of: north-north-east, east-north-east, east-south-east, south-south-east, south-south-west, west-south-west, west-north-west and north-north-west. In between the intermediate points are the sixteen *by-points* of: north by east, north-east by north, north-east by east, east by north, east by south, south-east by east, south-east by south, south by east, south by west, south-west by south, south-west by west, west by south, west by north, north-west by west, north-west by north and north by west. Notice with by-points how the first letter is either a cardinal or half cardinal point and the last letter is always a cardinal.

The other method of referring to compass directions is through bearings in either mils or degrees of arc. Many military forces have adopted the French *millieme* system, which is based on the approximation of a milli-radian (6283 per circle). There are several variations used but the *mil system* as used by Australia, utilizes a compass circle that is divided into 6400 units. The mil unit of angular measurement is defined as: 1 mil equals 1 meter separation at 1000 meters distance. One mil also corresponds

to 1 yard separation at 1000 yards. Note the units (metric or imperial) do not matter. If two features are ten kilometres (10 000 metres) away and are measured with your compass as being 100 *mils* apart in azimuth, then you know the two features are 1000 metres apart. This makes calculating azimuth easier than if using degrees. Modern military compasses use scales in both degrees and mils.

In degrees of arc, the compass is divided into 360 degrees with north being 000°. Note that compass bearings are written down and communicated as three figure numbers; east is 090°, south is 180° and west is 270°. When referring to a feature using a compass, the bearing is read from an azimuth of north (000°) to the feature. Azimuth refers to the direction of a feature or object as measured from north, clockwise around the navigator's horizon.

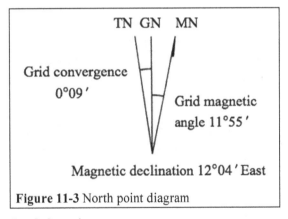

Figure 11-3 North point diagram

Back bearings

Back bearings, are used in many situations while navigating. Knowing how to perform a back bearing is particularly useful when you have paddled into a poor visibility situation and need to turn back. They are also used to determine your position on a map and may also be referred to as a *resection*.

Magnetic North & True North

① **Note:** Meridians of longitude are aligned with true north on a Mercator projection chart.

The magnetic pole is situated northward of the upper Hudson Bay area. This is where the magnetic needle points to on a compass and is referred to as *magnetic north* (MN). Magnetic north varies (variation) slightly from place to place and year to year. Geographical north called *true north* (TN), is the fixed northern end of the earth's axis of rotation.

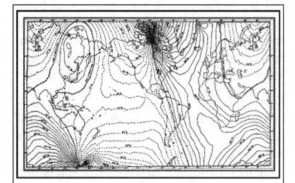

Figure 11-4 Isogonic chart of earth's magnetic field

MN and TN on charts

① **Note:** Do not confuse the terms magnetic variation with compass deviation.

On nautical charts, the difference between true north and magnetic north is called *magnetic variation*. On Mercator projection charts, the top of the chart points to true north as there is no grid north overlaid on charts.

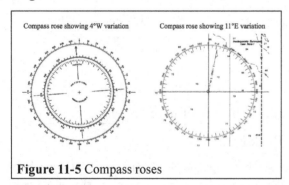

Figure 11-5 Compass roses

The compass rose

The chart's compass rose outer ring shows bearings in relation to true north, the inner ring in relation to magnetic north. The compass rose printed on the relevant chart shows the magnetic variation for the area in which a vessel is operating together with the variation's rate of change (e.g. AUS 357 compass rose shows 13°10'E 1994 (2'E)).

TN, MN and GN on Maps

Maps have a *grid north* (GN) overlaid on them. Grid north lines, called *eastings*, on a map do not line up exactly with the meridians of true north

except, if a cartographer has aligned one of the eastings with a standard meridian (true north-south line). On the rest of the map, there is an angular difference between grid north eastings and meridians of true north. The angular difference between GN and TN (eastings and meridians) is called *grid convergence* and is usually around one or two degrees. For map reading purposes, all plotted bearings are referred to as grid bearings.

The purpose of eastings is to allow the map to be orientated northward using a base-plate compass. This simplifies the process of plotting and reading compass bearings on a map. The *north point diagram* in a map's margin shows the difference in degrees and minutes between true north, grid north and magnetic north. This difference between grid north and magnetic north is called magnetic declination.

Magnetic variation

Magnetic variation is also known as *magnetic declination* by landlubbers. Magnetic variation is the angular difference in bearings, between true north on a chart and magnetic north, as shown by a compass needle. Where true north and magnetic north appear to be in agreement it is termed *zero line*.

Correcting for easterly variation

① **Remember:** for easterly variation 'chart to compass, variation east, magnetic least' and/or 'remove compass off map/chart remove variation'

If magnetic north lies to the east of true north the variation is said to be easterly and the bearing has a suffix 'E'. To convert an easterly chart bearing to a magnetic bearing, subtract the variation. To convert a magnetic bearing to a chart bearing, add the variation.

Correcting for westerly variation

If magnetic north lies to the west of true north, the variation is said to be westerly and the bearing has a suffix 'W'. To convert a westerly chart bearing to a magnetic bearing, add the variation. To convert a magnetic bearing to a westerly chart bearing, subtract the variation.

Compass deviation

Compass deviation is the effect of magnetic influences (iron, steel, nickel; electromagnetic fields) on the compass needle. This is irrelevant to paddlers providing they do not pack a source of magnetic interference near the compass or miss-treat their compass.

Bearings and chart-work

Compass bearings on charts are *True*. For example, Port Phillip Bay Heads flood tidal stream is 38° (i.e. 38°T). The 'T' suffix is not required and therefore not used but some American books use it.

ⓘ **Note**: the use of 'M' is the official abbreviation for nautical mile but the unofficial 'nm' is very common and understood.

Magnetic bearings are written as 38°M. The 'M' suffix is required. The official abbreviation is 'Mag', however it is commonly expressed as 'M' and found used in naval documentation.

PLANNING

When planning a navigation route on a paper chart, the following pieces of equipment are required:

Pencil (2B soft lead)

Soft rubber

Pencil sharpener

Parallel ruler

A means to determine compass bearings, being either a:

- Magnetic compass (base-plate compass), or
- Portland square (aka Portland plotter, Douglas plotter), or
- Protractor (aka compass protractor).

A means to determine and measure distance, being either a:

- Parallel ruler, or
- Dividers.

When planning an on-water navigation route, electronic devices and software is also used.

Such devices are Global Positioning Systems (GPS) and computers (e.g. iPads, laptops, chart plotters etc.). The user needs to know how to use and be competent with the electronic device (e.g. GPS) before setting out on to the water. The device should have fresh batteries installed, be waterproof or in a waterproof pouch/container. Changing batteries on-water may result in water entering the device and device failure.

ⓘ **Note**: For sea kayakers and recreational boat operators the following information has been added to show the range of information available for navigational planning.

Reference to some or all of the following documentation is required for navigational planning:

Navigational charts of the appropriate area

Topographical map

Speciality maps

Chart 5011 (INT 1) Symbols and Abbreviations used on Admiralty Charts

Tide and tidal stream tables (aka tide tables)

Maritime regulations (E.g. Victorian Recreational Boating Safety Handbook or other state or country's recreational boating safety handbook)

Pilots (aka Sailing Directions)

Cruising guides (aka coastal guides)

Notice to mariners (Navigational Warnings are contained within the Notice to Mariners)

Admiralty List of Lights

Deviation cards (not necessary for sea kayakers)

Operational orders (if guiding for a company).

When navigating on-water without an electronic device, the navigator also requires a:

Watch

Waterproofed chart of the area (e.g. plastic laminated, or a waterproof map pouch)

Means to write on the waterproofed chart (e.g. a grease pencil, over-head projector pen)

Means to clean off old chart work from chart or pouch

Route card detailing distances from and to, timings, bearings and back-bearings, features used as waypoints along the way

Means to secure all deck items to one another and the deck or person.

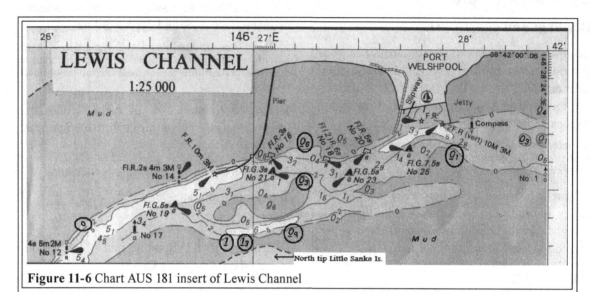

Figure 11-6 Chart AUS 181 insert of Lewis Channel

Table 11-1 Lewis channel low water table
① **Note:** *A negative value answer means exposed and a positive value answer means depth.*
Tide height: 0.27 metres at low water, on 5Feb05.

Chart Sounding	Predicted Tide Height	Chart Sounding	Result		Comment
1_3	0.27	−1.3	−1.03	Exposed 1.03 m	Re North tip Little Snake Island
1_2	0.27	−1.2	−0.93		
1_1	0.27	−1.1	−0.83		
1	0.27	−1.0	−0.73	Exposed 0.73 m	Re North tip Little Snake Island
0_9	0.27	−0.9	−0.63		
0_8	0.27	−0.8	−0.53	Exposed 0.53 m	Re between #16 & #18 buoys
0_5	0.27	−0.5	−0.23	Exposed 0.23 m	Re #16 buoy
0_4	0.27	−0.4	−0.13		
0_3	0.27	−0.3	0.03	Exposed	30 mm of exposed mud
0_2	0.27	−0.2	0.07	Under water	70 mm of covering water

DETERMINING HEIGHTS ON A CHART

Drying Heights

"All the difference between a long haul and an easy paddle in"

When working with charts, check the charts information to ensure you are working in metric and not imperial measurements. Also be aware that for may people they are accustomed to maps where a negative value for height would be below the chart datum (i.e. zero metres); but on charts, a negative value is above the chart datum.

Drying heights refers to a feature (i.e. bombie, reef, mud flats etc.) that is exposed during low water, but is covered during high water, particularly MHWS. To determine a sounding, for the purpose of safe navigation, add the predicted tide height to the charts indicated depths.

With reference to Figure 11-6 and Table 11-1 that were used to determine the soundings for a 0.27 metre low water on February 5, 2005 at Port Welshpool. At the end of the pier, is a charted depth 5_1 indicating a water depth of 5.1 metres, below chart datum. To determine a sounding, add the predicted 0.27 metre low water tide. The resulting sounding is a water depth of 5.37 metres, at that point during the low water.

Drying heights are negative values. For example, the 1_3 charted drying height, just above the northern tip of Little Snake Island, is indicating negative 1.3 metres (–1.3 m) from the chart datum. This informs the mariner that the feature, a mud bank, exposes 1.3 metres above the chart datum.

① **Note:** When you add the charted drying height to the predicted tide level, you actually perform a subtraction.

Therefore to determine the drying height sounding for this 1.3 metre exposed mud bank, add the –1.3 metre charted drying height figure to the predicted low water tide height of 0.27 metre (–1.3 m + 0.27 m = –1.03 m). At low water the banks are still exposed.

The 0_2 chart sounding is negative 0.2 metres (–0.2 m, –200 mm) above the chart datum; adding the 0.27 metre (270 mm) low water height (–200 mm + 270 mm = 70 mm). This sounding would produce a theoretical 0.07 metre (70 mm) of water over the mud bank.

ESTIMATING TIDE HEIGHT

Rule of Twelfths

The Rule of Twelfths is used to work out tide height. However, it can be used to understand the strength of a tide cycle change. It works on the assumption tides are fairly normal.

Referring to Figure 11-7 and going from high water (HW) to low water (LW). During the first period, the tide is assumed to have fallen one twelfth (1/12th) of its tidal range (TR), between the high water and the low water. During the second period, the receding tide's height, falls by two twelfths (2/12th) of the tidal range. During the third period, the receding tide's height falls by three twelfths (3/12th) of the tidal range. During the fourth period the receding tide's height, again falls, by another three twelfths (3/12th) of the tidal range.

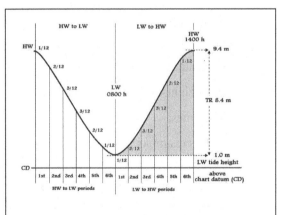

Figure 11-7 Tidal range divided into fractions of twelve over six periods

During the fifth period, the receding tide's height again falls by two twelfths (2/12th) of the tidal range. During the sixth period, the receding tide's height falls by one twelfth (1/12th) of the tidal range. When the tide floods it rises by the same ratios.

It is because of the assumption, tides rise and fall in a fairly normal manner, you can estimate the timings of the maximum tidal stream that would occur during the third and fourth periods. This is when the rate of tidal decay is at its greatest and therefore the volume of moving water increases.

As an example, to determine tide height using the Rule of Twelfths you need to know and perform the following:

1. Draw up a table as shown in Table 11-2.

① **Note:** The key to working the Rule of Twelfths is determining the tide range.

Table 11-2 Example uses of the Rule of Twelfths for determining tide heights and times

Time	0800	0800 0900	0900 1000	1000 1100	1100 1200	1200 1300	1300 1400	1400
Hour (Period)		1st	2nd	3rd	4th	5th	6th	
Fraction of Tidal Range	LW	1/12	2/12	3/12	3/12	2/12	1/12	HW
Tide Range (m)	0.0	0.7	1.4	2.1	2.1	1.4	0.7	0.0
Tide Height (m)	1.0	1.7	3.1	5.2	7.3	8.7	9.4	

2. Determine the tide range (TR) between high water and low water.

2.1 HW – LW = TR

9.4 m – 1.0 m = 8.4 m

3. In the low water (LW) and high water (HW) columns enter the predicted:

3.1 Tide heights, and

3.2 Tide times.

3.2.1 For this example: LW is 1.0 m at 0800 h, HW is 9.4 m at 1400 h.

3.2.2 To determine the times for the six time periods, divide the time range by six.

① **Note:** You can perform the sums for the period's fractional tide range all together filling in the 'tide range' row, or individually as you work your way across the table's columns. The method shown is for the first option.

3.3 Determine all of the period's fractional tidal rise values by dividing the 8.4 m tidal range by the three fractional values of 1/12, 2/12 and 3/12:

8.4 m ÷ 1/12 = 0.7 m

8.4 m ÷ 2/12 = 1.4 m

8.4 m ÷ 3/12 = 2.1 m

① **Note:** After determining the first periods, and incidentally the sixth period's, fractional (1/12) tidal rise (e.g. 0.7 m) you need only double the result (2 x 0.7 m = 1.4 m) for the second and fifth period tidal range of 2/12. For the third and fourth periods, 3/12 of the tidal range, you need only to triple the first periods tidal rise result (3 x 0.7 m = 2.1 m).

3.3.1 Enter the fractional tidal ranges values in their respective 'Tide Range' cells for each of the six periods.

① **Note:** Determine each period's fractional tide range and add it to the previous tide height.

4. Determine the first period's tide height (TH) by the sum:

LW + 1/12 TR = TH[#1]

1.0 m + 0.7 m = 1.7 m

4.1 At the end of the first period (0800-0900 h) the water level is 1.7 metres above chart datum.

5. Determine the second period tide height by:

(LW + 1/12 TR) + 2/12 TR = TH[#2]

(1.7 m) + 1.4 m = 3.1 m

5.1 At the end of the second period (0900-1000 h) the water level is 3.1 metres above chart datum.

6. Determine the third period tide height by:

(LW + 1/12 TR + 2/12 TR) + 3/12 TR = TH[#3]

(3.1 m) + 2.1 m = 5.2 m

6.1 At the end of the third period (1000-1100 h) the water level is 5.2 metres above chart datum.

① **Note:** During the third and fourth periods the tidal stream, if relevant, will be flowing at its maximum rate.

7. Continue adding the next periods tidal range fractional value to the previous periods tide height for the remaining fourth, fifth and sixth periods:

(LW + 1/12 +2/12 + 3/12) + 3/12 = TH[#4]

(5.2 m) + 2.1 m = 7.3 m

(LW + 1/12 +2/12 + 3/12 + 3/12) + 2/12 = TH[#5]

(7.3 m) + 1.4 m = 8.7 m

(LW + 1/12 + 2/12 + 3/12 + 3/12 + 2/12) + 1/12 = TH[#6]

(8.7 m) + 0.7 m = 9.4 m

ESTIMATING TIDAL STREAM RATE

The following two methods, *Rule of Thirds* and the *50/90 Rule*, are used to estimate the time and rate of tidal streams (tidal currents).

To highlight the differences between the two methods the following data will be used for both method examples. The tidal stream information at Table 11-3 came from the BOM website for the September 3rd, 2005 and relates to Port Phillip Bay (PPB) Heads (aka *The Rip*).

Table 11-3 Tidal Stream Predictions for PPB Heads on September 3, 2005

Tide		Tidal Stream		
Time	Ht (m)	Slack	Maximum	
		Time	Time	Rate
0457	0.40	Time	Time	Rate
1205	1.21	0034	0417	−3.1
1746	0.70	0757	1149	4.5
2340	1.09	1456	1757	−2.3
		2100	2348	2.0

Notes for Table 11-3 Tidal Stream Predictions for PPB Heads on September 3, 2005. The tidal stream rates are in knots. The in going tidal stream is setting 38° and shown on the BOM website as positive (+) figures. Outgoing stream is setting 200° and shown on the BOM website as negative (−) figures.

① **Note:** the phase difference on the day between the tides for Port Phillip Bay Heads and the tidal streams for 'The Rip' (e.g. high water at 1205 hours and maximum stream rate at 1149 hours).

Rule of Thirds

The Rule of Thirds is a simple method used to estimate when and at what time, a tidal stream will be running. You will need to know the maximum rate and the time of slack water. You can also use the time of high water or low water but be aware of tides that are out of phase with the maximum tidal rate (e.g. 'The Rip').

In Table 11-4 the reference point for completing the table was:

1. The maximum (Max) rate of 4.5 knots (kn); and

2. Time of slack water, 0757 hours rounded up to 0800 hours (h), has been tabulated.

Table 11-4 Rule of Thirds

Periods	Slack water	1st	2nd	3rd	4th	5th	6th
				Max Rate			
Time	0800*	0900	1000	1100	1200	1300	1400
* 0757 h rounded up to 0800 h		Thirds of max. rate					
		1/3	2/3	3/3	3/3	2/3	1/3
1/3 MR value		1.5	3.0	4.5	4.5	3.0	1.5

Notice how the maximum rate goes over two time periods from 1100 and 1200 hours.

3. Next, simply divide the predicted maximum rate by three (i.e. 1/3), and tabulate the result in the first and sixth periods.

4.5 kn / 3 = 1.5 kn

4. The second and fifth periods are 2/3 of the maximum rate. Simply double the 1/3 maximum rate result.

1.5 kn x 2 = 3.0 kn

50/90 Rule

① **Remember:** tidal streams may not run uniformly each side of the maximum rate.

The 50/90 Rule is an easy method to estimate the tidal stream's rate, using the predicted maximum rate and six periods of time, from slack water to slack water. Effectively the rule assumes a predicable increase in the stream's rate to maximum rate, followed by a predicable decrease in rate to the next slack water.

To determine the stream's flow pattern for one movement (in going or outgoing), the total time the stream is setting is divided up into six periods. Each of the periods, represent the time of an estimated percentage of the tidal stream's maximum rate.

Table 11-5 The 50/90 Rule for Tidal Streams

Tidal stream setting: 038°, in-going

	Slack water	Periods						(slack water)
		1st	2nd	3rd	4th	5th	6th	
% Max Rate	0%	50%	90%	Max Rate	90%	50%	0%	
Time (h)	0757	0914	1031	1149	1251	1353	1456	
Rate (kn)	0	2.2	4.05	4.5	4.05	2.2	0	

The 50/90 refers to percentages of the maximum flow rate (i.e. fifty and ninety per cent of estimated maximum rate). For this rule, the reference point is the stream's maximum rate and time it occurs; plus slack water times.

In this method several conditions are assumed:

1. The maximum rate and time will occur in the third period.

2. The rate is considered to be ninety per cent (90%) of the maximum rate in the periods prior to and after the stream reaches predicted maximum rate (i.e. second and fourth periods).

3. During the first and fifth periods, the stream's rate is considered to be fifty per cent (50%) of its maximum rate.

By using Table 11-3, Table 11-5 has been completed for a tidal stream movement between 0757 to 1456 hours. To estimate the times and rate of the tidal stream using the 50/90 Rule, it is a simple matter of:

1. In the third period column called *Maximum (Max) Rate*, tabulate the time and maximum rate (i.e. 1149 hours and 4.5 knots).

2. Enter the two slack water periods, on each side of the maximum rate, in the time row *slack water* columns (i.e. 0757 and 1456 hour).

3. Denote on the table, the stream's direction (i.e. in going).

4. Determine the interval times.

4.1   Determine the time in minutes from slack water at 0757 h to maximum rate 1149 h.

3 h 52 min = 232 min

232 min / 3 = 77.3 min

4.2   Repeat for 1149 to 1456 hours.

3h 07 min = 187min

187 min / 3 = 62.3 min

Notice it takes 3 hours 52 minutes, from slack water to the maximum stream rate (i.e. 0 to 4.5 knots). After reaching maximum rate, it takes the in going stream 3 hours 07 minutes to slow down ready for the next slack water.

5. Populate the time interval cells by adding the respective time intervals for:

5.1 Slack water to maximum rate of 77 minutes per period (e.g. 0750 h + 77 min = 0914 h).

5.2 Maximum rate to slack water of 62 minutes per period (e.g. 1149 h + 62 min = 1251 h).

6. Determine the stream rates for 50% and 90% of the maximum rate of 4.5 knots. 90% of 4.5 kn = 4.05 kn

① **Note:** This is fast for a weekend sea kayaker when combined with seas and weather.

The reason for six periods of time, and not six hours, is because the stream's rate may be slower for the first periods to maximum than the remaining periods to slack water, as shown in the example.

There may be occasions when you have 60 minute periods. For time periods of other than 60 minutes of stream running in a certain direction (i.e. west going 5 hours and east going for 7 hours), correct by:

5 h x 60 min = 300 min / 6 periods = 50 min W

7 h x 60 min = 420 min / 6 periods = 70 min E.

CHART PLOTTING

Navigation and plotting terms

The following terms are used in chart work and during navigation:

Bearing is the horizontal direction to some feature. Expressed in angular units (i.e. degrees) from a reference direction, usually from 000° (north) at the reference direction clockwise through 360°. Bearing is often designated as true, magnetic, or grid.

Course is the actual directions steered, or intended to be steered, by a vessel through the water in reference to a meridian. Expressed as an angular distance (i.e. degrees) from north, (i.e. from 000° clockwise through 360°). Course is where your destination is, even if temporarily (i.e. a waypoint). Course is often designated as true, magnetic, or grid. Course is not track. 'Course made good', and 'course over ground' are misnomers. 'Track made good' and 'track' respectively are the preferred terms to the above misnomers.

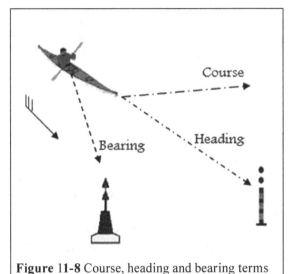

Figure 11-8 Course, heading and bearing terms

Current is the large-scale, persistent circulation of water unrelated to tidal movements (MSQ, 2004). In American literature currents may be classified as tidal and non-tidal (Bowditch n.d.). Tidal currents are what we (UK, Australia New Zealand et. al.) refer to as tidal streams.

Dead reckoning (DR) refers to the navigational process of deriving a position on the basis of courses steered and distances travelled since the last known position fix (MSQ, 2004).

Drift is the distance the current has moved a vessel during the time it has been in its influence, expressed in nautical miles (nm).

Estimated position (EP) is a dead reckoning (DR) position corrected for the effects of leeway, steering error, tidal streams and current.

It is the most probable position of a vessel determined from incomplete data or data of questionable accuracy. The distinction between an estimated position and a fix or running fix is a matter of judgment (Bowditch n.d.).

Fix refers to the position determined without reference to any former position. Also the common intersection of two or more lines of position obtained from simultaneous observations (Bowditch n.d.).

Heading is the direction the bow (nose) of your kayak is pointing (i.e. where you are heading). Expressed in angular units (i.e. degrees) from a reference direction, usually from 000° (north) at the reference direction clockwise through 360°. Heading is often designated as true, magnetic, or grid. At a specific instant the heading and course may or may not coincide.

Leeway is the effect of wind on a ship and causes its track across the ground to lie at an angle from the course steered (MSQ, 2004).

Rate is the speed of the current expressed in knots (kn).

Set is the direction towards which the current is flowing, expressed in true bearings (°T).

Tidal stream is the horizontal movement of the water caused by gravitational interactions between the sun, moon, and earth. In American usage it is referred to as tidal current.

Track is the intended and or desired horizontal direction with respect to the earth. Expressed as an angular distance (i.e. degrees) from north, (i.e. from 000° clockwise through 360°). Track is often designated as true, magnetic, or grid. The actual path followed by a vessel over the ground, such as may be determined by tracking. In chart work, the path of intended travel with respect to the earth as drawn on the chart. When underway track may be different to course due to factors such as making allowance for currents, seas and wind or steering to resume 'track' (Bowditch n.d.).

'Track made good' refers to the single resultant direction from a point of departure to a point of arrival at any given time. This is the preferred term to the misnomer 'course made good' (Bowditch, n.d.).

Vector is any quantity, such as a force, velocity, or acceleration, which has both magnitude and direction, as opposed to a 'scalar', which has magnitude only. Such a quantity may be represented geometrically by an arrow of length proportional to its magnitude, pointing in the given direction (Bowditch, n.d.).

Plotting considerations

Before plotting the track the navigator needs to consider the effects of currents, tidal streams and wind. This is done through sourcing the relevant data from media (e.g. websites) and navigational publications. This data can then be used in one or more of the methods previously described, in determining the times of water levels, rates and settings.

Chart plotting involves choosing the correct chart and 'plotting' (marking in) the planned track in pencil. The track can consist of several straight lines joining selected points of a desired route. The track is plotted to avoid (lead clear) any dangers and or to make account for currents and tidal streams.

Table 11-6 Chart plotting symbols

Symbol	Terms and Alternative Terms
	There are various alternative terms found in different publications describing plotting a track. The following have been included to assist the reader in deciphering the various explanations of authors from different countries.
⟶	**Course** vector (aka Course to Steer, Course & speed, Course over ground, Course to be made good, track to steer)
⟶⟶	**Track** vector (aka Track Over Ground, Water Track, *Course & speed made good*) NB, 'Course & speed made good' is a misnomer (Bowditch, n.d.)
⟶⟶⟶	**Set & Drift** vector (aka Tidal Stream, Tidal Drift, Set & Drift vector)
⭕ 1130	**Fix**, shown on a chart as a circle with time of observation

	Estimated position (EP), shown on a chart as a triangle with time
▲ 1000	

When the track is pencilled onto the chart the true and magnetic courses are written alongside the lines and annotated accordingly. This data should then be transferred to a route card for use during the voyage.

Effect of wind

The effect of wind on a boat is leeway. Leeway can only be estimated by experience of the boats behaviour to either lee-cock or weathercock. It can be estimated by observing your progress towards a feature. This allows you to judge the amount the boat has been moved left or right off its course. Mariners can factor leeway to the true course when plotting but sea kayakers need to compensate for its effect while paddling through judgement.

Effect of current

There are three dimensions to current for the navigator: set, rate, and drift. In navigation, tidal streams may be handled similarly to currents provided due allowances are made for the constant changing direction and speed of such streams (MSQ, 2004). See 'Determining a Ferry Glide Passage' and 'Ferry Gliding Using the Half-tide Method'.

Measuring distance

ⓘ **Note:** The longitude scale is not used for distance measurement.

Distance varies with latitude and therefore the longitude scale is not used for distance measurement.

ⓘ **Note:** Use the latitude scale along the sides of the chart for distance measurement.

Since distance on a chart alters with latitude, distance on charts should be measured from the latitude scale across from the position being recorded.

Determining direction

ⓘ **Note:** Use the compass rose nearest your plot.

When determining direction on a chart use the compass rose closest to your plot.

Plotting symbols

Table 11-6 Chart plotting symbols, contains the basic navigation plotting symbols used when plotting vectors.

Plotting latitude and longitude

Using a parallel ruler and a set of dividers, or just a parallel ruler, you can plot latitude and longitude. The point to observe is, keep your ruler square with the latitude and longitude scales.

① **Note**: When plotting latitude and longitude on a chart, the point to consider is to keep the ruler parallel with the meridian and parallel lines as you move it to the lat./long. position.

Using a ruler and dividers, lay the ruler parallel with a parallel of latitude on the chart. Move the ruler's edge to the desired position, parallel to the side of the chart. The ruler, if of sufficient length, would have also crossed a meridian of longitude drawn on the chart. Next open a set of dividers, and measure off the distance along the meridian between the rulers edge to the longitude scale (at the top or bottom of the chart, which ever is appropriate to the position). From the meridian move the dividers along the transferred parallel of latitude, as shown by the ruler's edge, and check at the latitude scale that the ruler is square. Read off the latitude and longitude coordinates. Alternatively you can draw in the latitude and longitude with a ruler.

Plotting bearing and distance

① **Note**: Bearings here are true and distances are in nautical miles.

Using a parallel ruler and dividers, a position can be described by its bearing and distance from a known position. Positional information in the form of 90 C. Otway 2 refers to a position that lies in the direction of 090° from Cape Otway lighthouse and 2 nautical miles distance. To plot this information first measure off 2 nautical miles from the latitude scale nearest the known feature. Second place a rule over the nearest compass rose with the ruler's edge being on a bearing of 090°. Next, move the rule until the edge passes through Cape Otway lighthouse. Now with the dividers, measure off (lay off) 2

nautical miles at 090° from the lighthouse along the edge of the ruler.

DETERMINING A FERRY GLIDE PASSAGE

① **Note**: Do not confuse currents (i.e. ocean currents) with tidal streams.

Ferry glide is a term used by river canoeists to describe a method of crossing a river or manoeuvring around obstacles, by using the current and not wasting your energy on paddling against the current. As a sea kayaker, you may at some point use tidal streams and ocean currents to arrive at your destination.

Plotting a course using vectors

There are several methods for determining a ferry glide angle. In a vector plot, the line has both magnitude and direction, which means the length of a line, is proportional to the velocity it represents.

The following method is suited for crossings over waters influenced by tidal streams, if the distances are short (e.g. Queenscliff to Point Nepean at the southern end of Port Phillip). In areas prone to strong tidal streams and where there is shipping (e.g. 'The Rip') you are best to cross just before or at slack water. This will allow you greater control of the situation.

Considerations when plotting

This is a 'best guess' exercise. On the day you will need to adapt your plot to the current situation. The following points need to be considered when performing a vector plot:

The table 'Speed Conversions' at Appendix 1 has been provided to assist in your calculations. To allow for wind and other variables in your planning, it comes down to experience and observing different level paddlers.

Tidal streams do not always follow an even time between ebbing and flooding. For example, the flood may run longer than the ebb stream. The corresponding stream's set may not be on the reciprocal bearing.

Use of the 50/90 Rule will assist you in understanding the tidal streams rate, times and set without the effect of wind and seas.

Speed of the crossing is dependant upon such factors as level of skills, knowledge, attitude and fitness of the participants. As a guide and for ease of mental calculations, try 3 knots (5.6 km/h) for novice and weekend paddlers. Novice paddler may even be slower than 2.5 knots (4.6 km/h). Obviously more experienced and fitter paddlers will be faster.

Perform the plot using knots and nautical miles, then convert to metric kilometres per hour (km/h) and kilometres (km).

Use 1 centimetre (10 mm) to represent 1 nautical mile per hour (i.e. 1 knot) or 1 nautical mile (nm).

When performing the plot use True bearings and correct for variation by converting to magnetic (M) when you have finished the plot.

Mark magnetic bearings on a chart with a capital 'M'. The capital M is also used to indicate a sea mile, (i.e. nautical mile).

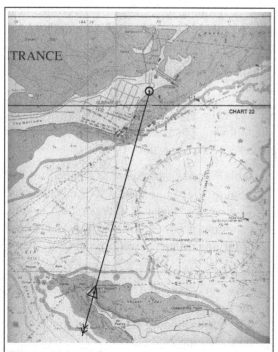

Figure 11-9 Track vector

Mark the vectors with the respective arrow symbols to differentiate between vector lines.

Ideally, use the Fix and Estimated Position (EP) symbols.

The lengths of AC and CB are not important as long as they are proportional to the speed they represent. CB above can extend past the intersection point (B) on the track vector.

Ferry glide plot using vectors

Plotting a ferry glide using vectors involves six steps consisting of drawing the three vectors: track, set and drift, and course; followed by determining: speed made good, time, and magnetic bearing.

1. First step is to determine the **track vector** (track over ground). This consists of three sub-steps.

1.1 Referring to Figure 11-9. Draw a line between your start point (fix) and your desired end point or waypoint (estimated position [EP]). Mark this line with two arrowheads.

1.2 Measure the track bearing. *Here the track vector bearing is 197°.*

1.3 Measure the distance. *Here the distance is 2.2 nautical miles.*

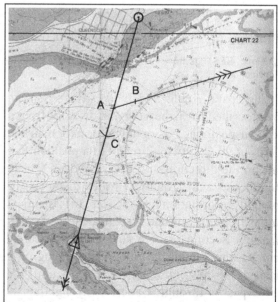

Figure 11-10 Set and drift vector

2. Second step is to determine the **set and drift vector**. This consists of two sub-steps.

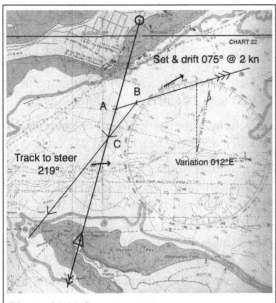

Figure 11-11 Course vector

2.1 Determine the tidal stream's set by one of the following methods. Using the charts 'Tidal Streams referred to' table, if present, the appropriate pilot, website or by measuring the angle of the appropriate direction flood or ebb arrow on the chart. *Here the set is estimated to be 075°.*

2.2. Referring to Figure 11-10, mark along the track vector, at any convenient location, a point. *Here identified as 'A'.*

2.2.1 Starting at point 'A' on the track vector, draw a set & drift vector line: in the direction (set) of the tidal stream and longer than required. Mark the vector with three arrowheads.

3. Third step is to determine the **course vector**. This consists of four sub-steps.

3.1 Determine the stream's rate you expect to encounter. *Here the flood stream is 1.5 knots.*

3.1.1 Referring to Figure 11-10, using a scale of 1 cm to equal 1 nautical mile (nm); from point 'A', mark off at 1.5 cm, along the set and drift vector, a dash. *This is point 'B'.*

3.2 Determine an estimated paddling speed (e.g. 3.0 knots). Ensuring you use the same scale of 1 cm to equal 1 knot as before:

3.2.1 Set a pair of dividers to 3.0 cm.

3.2.2 Pivoting from point 'B' on the set & drift vector, scribe an arc across the track vector.

3.2.3 The scribed arc intersecting across the track vector is point 'C'.

3.3 Draw a course to steer vector using a ruler, from point 'B' to 'C' as shown in Figure 11-11. Mark with one arrowhead.

3.4 Determine the course to steer bearing by measuring the angle of the vector. *Here the bearing is 219°.*

4. Fourth step is to determine the **speed made good**.

4.1 From point A measure the length to point 'C'. *Here (AC) is 2.0 cm and represents 2.0 knots.*

4.1.1 With an estimated paddling speed of 3.0 knots, crossing a 1.5 knot tidal stream will decrease your paddling speed down to 2.0 knots.

ⓘ **Note:** Paddling speeds conversions table are at Appendix 1—Tables.

5. Fifth step is to determine **time**.

5.1 Determine the time to cross the tidal stream by dividing the track distance by speed made good. *Here, 2.2 nm / 2.0 kn = 1.1 hours.*

5.1.1 If there were no tidal stream influence, the 2.2 nautical miles crossing at 3.0 knots paddling speed would take 0.7 hour (i.e. 42 minutes). Therefore, a 2.2 nautical mile crossing on 219° against a 1.5 knot tidal stream setting 75°, would reduce our paddling speed by 1 knot and increase paddling time by 0.4 hours (i.e. 24 minutes).

① **Note:** Always check the magnetic variation against the chart or map being used. For Victoria, the magnetic variation is between 12°-13° east.

6. Sixth step is to convert True to Magnetic bearings.

6.1 Convert the true bearings determined on the chart to magnetic bearings, for use on the water. On this chart there is an easterly variation of 12 degrees. *Here 219° True is 207°M (magnetic).*

6.1.1 However, the track (aka course) to steer on your deck compass is 205°M, because when paddling and steering off the deck compass, it is impractical to use bearings other than increments of 005° (i.e. 200°, 205°, 210° etc.) because of the boats motion.

Ferry Gliding using the Half Tide Method

① **Note:** This method (like all the other methods) is based on the assumption that the tidal streams are uniform for the entire crossing and there are no other environmental factors affecting the crossing.

The half tide method (aka *slack water, mid-straight method*) is best suited for use on longer distance crossings. The theory is to paddle on one compass bearing and utilise the tidal stream; and by slack water be midway through the crossing. Then allow the corresponding tidal stream to bring you back to the track.

Example one using ferry glide half tide method

Refer to the example at Figure 11-12.

1. Determine the track distance from point A to B (e.g. 20 nm).

2. Determine the bearing (e.g. 295°) and convert it to a magnetic bearing (e.g. 283°M).

3. Determine timings for the crossing by using your estimated paddling speed (e.g. 3.5 kn); calculate estimated paddling time (i.e. 20 nm / 3.5 kn = 5.7 h).

① **Note:** Utilize the Australian Pilot, appropriate charts and tide tables.

4. Determine the currents set (direction) and times of ebb and flood (B & C). In this example, the flood stream used is: tidal stream setting NE (045°) from 0800 h to 1400 h.

5. Plot the tidal stream information and times into a 50/90 Rule table, like that shown in Table 11-7.

Refer to Table 11-7, which tabulates the above data into one tidal cycle with its corresponding flood and ebb streams.

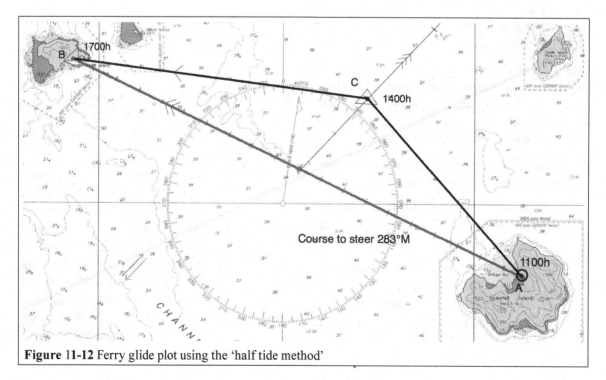

Figure 11-12 Ferry glide plot using the 'half tide method'

① **Note**: It is not a case of 'mind in neutral', even though only one compass course is needed, you still need to use transits and check your position.

After plotting your half tide ferry glide, the purpose is to paddle on one magnetic compass bearing (i.e. 283°M); and let the tidal stream (tidal current) move you off of your track vector (AB) until the stream reverses its set and returns you back to the track vector. Refer to Figure 11-12.

20nm / 3.5kn = 5.7hr	Slack water	Tidal stream setting: Flood (045°)						Tidal stream setting: Ebb (225°)					
		One Tidal Cycle Periods											
		1st	2nd	3rd	4th	5th	6th	1st	2nd	3rd	4th	5th	6th
% of Max. Rate	0%	50%	90%	Max Rate	90%	50%	0%	50%	90%	Max Rate	50%	90%	0%
Time (hour)	0800	0900	1000	1100	1200	1300	1400	1500	1600	1700	1800	1900	2000
Paddle distance (nautical mile)				0	3.3	6.7	Mid Crossing 10nm	13.3	16.7	20			
Paddle time (hour)				0 ETD	1	2	3	4	5	6 ETA			
Rate (knots)													

Table 11-7 The 50/90 Rule and the half-tide method

Example two using ferry glide half tide method

Alternatively, if you were to paddle a 10.5 nautical miles crossing at 3.5 knots paddling speed, it would take a theoretical three hours to perform.

Using Table 11-7 and with the same tidal information from Figure 11-12:

1. At 1400 hours you want to be midway through the crossing when it coincides with slack water (turn of the tide).

2. Estimating it will take three hours to perform the crossing, you need to divide the time in half (i.e. 1.5 hours).

3. Subtract the 1.5 hours from the midway time of 1400 hours to get an estimated time of departure (ETD) of 1230 hours.

4. Your estimated time of arrival (ETA) will be 1530 hours (1400 h + 1.5 h = 1530 h).

① **Note**: Use favourable conditions (e.g. neap tides, wind strength and direction, weather systems etc.).

① **Note**: If you find the conditions or some other situation will not allow you to safely complete a crossing, do not adopt the 'death or glory option. Do not go or if already underway turn back, if needs be.

ON WATER CORRECTIONS

Fixing by Position Lines

A fix is the term given when two or more position lines lying in different directions are referenced simultaneously with the position of the vessel will be found at the intersection. Fixing is a term used to describe the process of determining a vessels position. A position line is obtained from a compass bearing to a landmark or seamark. A position line is any type of line, either straight or curved, drawn on a chart, along which a vessels position is known to lie.

Fixing by cross bearings

Fixing by cross bearings is also known as performing a resection. This is where carrying a hand held sighting base plate or prismatic compass is very useful, since a deck compass is less accurate, being situated several feet away from the observer, combined with the normal fluctuation caused by the motion of the kayak.

① **Note**: On land with a base plate compass, the accuracy of a measurement is unlikely to be less than two degrees of arc. A two-degree error gives roughly thirty metres of error for every kilometre.

A fix by cross bearings is performed with a compass and two or more position lines, as shown in Figure 11-13. Unlike boating, kayaking requires you to stop and perform your measurements.

1. Choose three features that are between 60 and 90 degrees apart.

2. To reduce error:

2.1   If only two features are obtainable, try to get their bearings to intersect as close as possible to ninety degrees (right angles).

2.2   The third bearing is called a *check bearing* and its function is to reduce the error.

2.3   Select features near you rather than distant ones.

2.4   Take the bearings as quickly as possible.

2.5   If using temporary features like buoys, note they are an unreliable source and should not be relied upon.

3.   Record the bearings to the three features and:

3.1   Correct for magnetic variation to get the 'true bearing' (T). For example, for an easterly variation: magnetic to chart, add variation.

3.2   Convert the three true bearings to back bearings by subtracting 180 degrees.

4.   From each of the three features, plot each respective true back bearing. Hopefully, you will end up with the three lines intersecting each other. This will be your position.

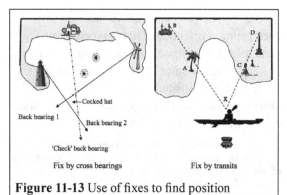

Figure 11-13 Use of fixes to find position

5.   Because there is always, a degree of error, you may end up with a small triangle being formed by the three intersecting lines. This small triangular area is called a *cocked hat*. This expression came from the eighteenth century Royal Navy triangular shaped hats the officers wore. If the cocked hat is small, then you are most likely in the centre of the triangle. If the cocked hat is large and you have recalculated

and have the same result, assume your position to be at the corner of the cocked hat nearest any possible danger (e.g. reef).

Running Fix

Running fixes are used to establish a vessel's position, when there is only a single feature in sight at any time. The deck of a kayak does not lend itself to being user friendly, when it comes to plotting a running fix. Since a chart table and drawing implements are required, refer to one of the references if you desire to know how to perform this type of fix.

Transits

Transits are a navigational method to determine your position and to keep your course. When ships enter Port Phillip through the heads, they use transits in the form of *leading marks* and *clearing marks* to stay in the channel. Refer to chart AUS158 Port Phillip Entrance for an example. Other forms of transits include *leading line* and *clearing line* and *beam marks*. American authors refer to transits as *ranges*.

Referring to Figure 11-13, objects are said to be *in transit* when two objects (e.g. AB) are observed to be in line with each other. It follows, the observer must be somewhere on the joining line. If a kayak had a chart table, both objects would be marked with a position line through them and a true bearing found from the chart compass rose.

Transits can also be two features in line astern or one in front of the bow and the other directly behind; you are somewhere along this line of position.

Using transits to find your position

Taking a fix by transits can be accomplished by using two sets of transits as shown in Figure 11-13. To determine a position the observer choses four marks shown here as AB and CD. When they are in transit, the observer can determine his position at X).

Using transits to steer a straight course

Transits are also used to: steer a straight course, and determine amount of drift. Beam and quartering winds as well as tidal streams move you off your course (i.e. drift). To keep yourself on course by steering a straight course, use transits, as they give you immediate feedback when you are moving off your line of position.

To use transits, pick two stationary features/objects that are in the distance and along your course. Gradually, turn the bow and align it with the two features/objects.

During your voyage, you may use many transits to counteract the environmental factors that move you off course. When one transit is no longer of use, discard it and choose another.

Drift

It is the apparent movement of the furthest feature/object, which indicates your direction of drift. If the furthest feature/object moves to the left, your drift is to the left and you are said to be *left of course*. To compensate for being left of course, turn the bow to the right until you can maintain your course.

If the furthest feature/object moves to the right, your drift is to the right and you are said to be *right of course*. To compensate for being right of course, turn the bow to the left until you can maintain your course.

Aiming off

To prevent yourself from being moved past your aim point, you may need to overcompensate for the effect of drift. To do this, aim up-wind or up-stream, using your transits. It is better to drift down-wind or down-stream than have to paddle back up to where you want to be.

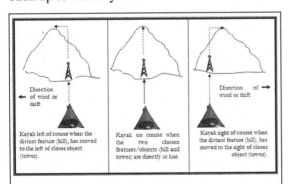

Figure 11-14 Correction of drift using transits

The amount you compensate will depend entirely upon the situation you find yourself in. Use the wind and streams to your benefit and not your detriment.

Estimating your drift rate

A method of determining your drift rate is at Appendix 1. Today most people just use a GPS.

Dead Reckoning

Dead reckoning (DR) is used when you have no features to navigate off. It is simply a process of recording from your last known position the time you have spent travelling on your bearing.

For dead reckoning, you need to know your paddling speed for the conditions and situation you are in and time taken. Then it is a simple case of arithmetic using the following formula:

Distance = speed x time

Time = distance / speed

Speed = distance / time

With distance, speed and time conversions, time is in hours and decimals of an hour, not minutes (i.e. 0.1 hour = 6 minutes).

Since sea kayakers do not have a chart table, refer to one of the references for an explanation on how maritime navigators perform a dead reckoning plot. Refer to Appendix 1—Tables for decimal hours to minutes.

Planning a Landfall

When planning a landfall plan to approach your destination upwind or up current. This may avoid you having to paddle back up into the wind or current.

In areas of boating traffic use the IALA system of buoyage markers and light to assist you in low light conditions. Knowing these rules will assist you in avoiding a collision with another vessel.

Chapter 12 Communications

"There was a time when nails were high-tech. There was a time when people had to be told how to use a telephone. Technology is just a tool. People use tools to improve their lives."

Tom Clancy

Electronic Communications

Mobile Phones

The Australian Maritime Safety Authority (AMSA) lists what it considers to be the three most important things you should do to ensure your safety while boating/sea kayaking:

Check the weather before you go

Always let someone know your plans

Carry a marine radio not just a mobile phone.

Their reasoning for not relying on a mobile phone is:

A mobile phone can only reach one person, and can easily get water damaged, run out of battery life, or the reception can drop out. If this happens, your one link to the world is gone. A radio Mayday can be heard by many people at the same time and is a lot more reliable (AMSA, n.d.).

At time of writing Telstra's CDMA network was shut down in 2008 and replaced by the GSM network system; known as the Next G network.[1] For remote areas, Telstra provides the best coverage network and options. Options include applicable mobile phones and antennas. The Telstra web site has a map of Australia, Bass Straight and Tasmania showing the Next G reception areas. For New Zealand the Telecom website has a map showing mobile phone coverage. Telecom New Zealand has the following safety warning about mobile phone coverage:

If you're heading into the bush or high country, then we recommend you don't rely on your mobile phone, but take alternatives like mountain radios or a satellite phone, just in case.

If you're going out on the water, there are even more factors that can affect your mobile signal, so please be safe and follow the Maritime New Zealand standards by carrying marine VHF as your primary means of communication.

Satellite Phones

Satellite phones (aka *sat-phones*) can be hired for expedition sea kayaking. For their size and weight, they are the best option to get reliable communication with the outside world. However, you still have the same safety issues as with mobile phones, that is, you can only talk to one person in an emergency. There are also the familiar issues with battery charge and recharging over extended periods.

SPOT Satellite Systems

SPOT Personal Tracker (aka *SPOT 1*), SPOT Satellite GPS Messenger (aka *SPOT 2*) and SPOT Connect are text based messaging systems using satellites. These systems are becoming a popular means of keeping in contact with the outside world when on a trip. SPOT 1 and SPOT 2 enable the user to send an emergency assistance required message to the GEOS International 9-1-1 Rescue Centre; a help required message to family and friends, OK pre-written message to family and friends; and a live track of the journey to family and friends. The messages are sent to recipient's mobile phones via SMS text or to an email address. The SPOT Connect enables a 'smart phone' to become a satellite text communicator.

The units send an emergency SOS (life threatening) message and GPS location to the GEOS International 9-1-1 Emergency Response Centre in the USA. This organisation can then contact Emergency Services in the appropriate country.

The help function enables the user to send a help message with GPS location to predetermined SMS and e-mail addresses. The email message has a link to Google Maps™ that can show your location. This function is designed for non-life threatening situations where the user can contact family and friends.

The check-in/OK function enables the user to send a pre-written message, with GPS location, to family and friends through SMS or email.

SPOT 2 has the added function of sending a custom pre-written message to family and friends. It works exactly in the same manner as the check-in/OK function.

The track progress function allows the user to send a 10 minute plot of the journey over 24 hours with the ability to continue the track for another 24 hours.

The SPOT Connect provides the user who has an appropriate 'smart phone', with the ability to use the smart phone's texting capabilities to send 'live' text. The smart phone becomes a text capable satellite communicator with the same and similar functions mentioned above of the two earlier versions.

As technology improves, other devices will become available providing greater communicating ability with the outside world. The SPOT units are a user pay item with an annual subscription fee. Additional services can be purchase through the SPOT organisation.

Radios

Marine radios are the best method for calling assistance if in distress and monitoring and/or updating rescue operations. They inform a wider spectrum of listeners about the situation. This enables close by vessels to render assistance more readily than the Emergency Services. It also enables capable craft to fix your position by use of radio direction finding methods.

27 MHz marine band radios

You do not require a Marine Radio Operators Certificate of Proficiency, to use a 27 MHz marine band radio (aka *27 Meg*). This type of radio under favourable conditions has a range between 5.4 to 27 nautical miles (10–50 km). For sea kayaking a 27 Meg marine radio has several disadvantages that make it impracticable to carry on board. Some of disadvantages are: its size and weight; the need for it to be dry and at the same time, be readily available; battery size and weight, including their maintenance

requirements, are amongst the issues that restrict and even preclude their use.

VHF radios

The term VHF stands for *Very High Frequency*. There is a wide range of waterproof, hand held VHF Radios. The common standard used to qualify a radio as being waterproof is, JIS Grade 7. This standard means the radio is waterproof to a submersion depth of one metre for thirty seconds. These radios are suitable for operation near the coast and provide contact with limited coastal stations and other vessels that are within range.

VHF radios can receive the scheduled weather forecasts and warnings on channel 67. They allow the operator to contact more than one person if assistance or help is needed through channel 16, or one of the bands reserved for recreational boaters.

The disadvantage with the radio is its antenna height. VHF is effectually line of sight. Yachts get around the issue of a short transmitting distance, by fitting the antenna on top of the mast. In a sea kayak, the 15 centimetre antenna would only be about 75 centimetres from the water. VHF marine radios also suffer from blind spots behind hills and thick vegetation. Repeater stations if in range can provide an increased area of coverage.

MF/HF radios

Ideally, a MF/HF radio is the best option, as the communications range is in thousands of kilometres around the world. It is the only radio recommended by the Australian Maritime College (AMC) for vessels undertaking lengthy coastal voyages. However, for sea kayakers on the water there are some major issues: size and weight; the need for a power supply to recharge the battery; battery size; aerial mounting; and the need for it to be dry just for openers.

On investigating several MF/HF options the best was an Australian radio 'mini-pack' but its mode of operation was, stop and deploy; that is land and put the antenna up. Cost for this compact radio ranged between $3600 to $4300. In the end, you cannot use it in your kayak on the water.

Marine Radio Operators Certificate of Proficiency

To operate VHF and MF/HF radios you need to hold a Marine Radio Operators Certificate of Proficiency (MROCP). The Australian Maritime College (AMC) issues the MROCP to eligible candidates who have passed the written examination. The course material is in the Marine Radio Operators Handbook, which can be ordered from the AMC. The best method of obtaining a MROCP, is by enrolling in one of the many classes run by the various yachting clubs.

Single Side Band Short Wave Radio Receivers

A common method of receiving the BOM scheduled weather forecasts is with a single side band (SSB) short wave radio receiver. The term receiver means you cannot transmit but you can receive short wave radio broadcasts (e.g. weather, news, music). Depending upon your budget there are several suitable radio receivers. VSKC kayakers have purchased the SW7600GRS from Sony Australia and the slightly larger but cheaper Sangean ATS-505.

MARINE RADIO COMMUNICATIONS

Basic Radio Theory

Radio waves make up part of the electromagnetic spectrum and are identified by either their frequency (f) or their wavelength (λ). Frequency is the number of oscillations the wave makes in one second and measured in hertz (Hz) (i.e. cycles per second). Wavelength is the distance between wave crests, measured in metres and is simply the distance that the wave travels as it goes through exactly one cycle.

The act of a radio wave travelling from one point to another is called propagation. When radiated from an antenna, a radio wave may start its journey in a variety of directions. However, normally only one path is used to reach the station with which we want to communicate. Transmission paths can be short or long, may travel along the ground, or be reflected from the upper parts of the atmosphere.

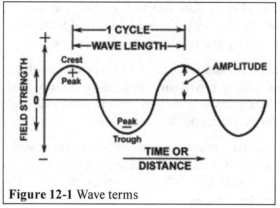

Figure 12-1 Wave terms

The primary transmission path of a radio wave is determined by the propagating characteristics of its frequency and the direction and manner in which it is radiated by the antenna. With radio waves, the basic transmission paths are ground wave and sky wave.

Ground wave transmission

Ground waves are radio waves that travel close to the earth's surface. When these are transmitted over the earth, they take three separate paths to the receiver: a direct path (direct wave), a ground reflected path (ground reflected wave) and a surface path (surface wave). All ground waves fall into one of these three wave types.

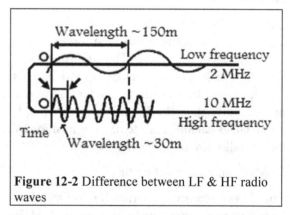

Figure 12-2 Difference between LF & HF radio waves

The first type is called *direct wave*. Direct waves travel along a line-of-sight (LOS) path from the transmitting antenna to the receiving antenna.

Typical communications using this transmission path are the *Very High Frequency* (VHF) sets like the marine 156 MHz band. For transmission/reception success there must be a clear path between two stations (ship to ship, ship to shore) since direct waves continue to travel in a straight line until an object interrupts them or weaken over a great distance. Under normal conditions, atmospheric conditions have minimal effect, as there is no reflection of VHF radio energy from the ionosphere.

The second type is called a *ground reflected wave*, which also travels in straight lines and like all radio waves can reflect, to some degree, off certain surfaces, mountains and trees. With high frequency waves, the wavelength is shorter, which increases the chance that the wave can be deflected or reflected. The difference between the direct wave and the ground reflected wave is at some point between the sending and receiving stations, the wave is reflected off the ground. A phase change occurs when a wave is reflected from the earth's surface. It arrives at the receive antenna 180 degrees out of phase to the direct wave. This causes some fading of the received signal. If two waves with the same amplitude arrive at the receiver 180 degrees out of phase, they can cancel each other out. However, if the direct wave and reflected wave arrive in phase, the received signal is increased. These effects are known as *multipath effects* or *wave interference*.

The third type of ground wave is the *surface wave*. At certain lower frequency ranges, the waves are affected by the earth's electromagnetic properties and will bend around the curvature of the earth. Depending on the conductivity of the surface the wave is travelling over, the surface wave path may be more applicable for communications between ground stations where lower frequencies are used.

Conductivity is a measure of the ability of a medium to conduct electric current or the efficiency with which a current is passed. The type of soil and water along the propagation path determines the earth's conductivity. Land areas with poor conductivity, quickly attenuate (weaken) radio signals. *Attenuation* is the process whereby a radio wave weakens over distance. If ground waves are transmitted over seawater the direct wave travels the short line-of-sight distance but the surface wave may travel up to 700 miles. You can communicate with stations out of your line-of-sight by using systems that take advantage of these lower

frequencies. Lower frequencies result in greater wave penetration and at *very low frequencies* (VLF), usable radio waves can be received some distance below the ocean's surface.

Sky wave transmission

The other type of transmission path is called the *sky wave*. Sky waves are waves that have been transmitted upward at many different angles and are reflected back to the earth by the ionosphere. During daylight hours, the ionosphere is a series of four layers of ion concentration in the earth's atmosphere termed D, E, Fl and F2 regions.

Region D of the ionosphere serves only to attenuate the strength of radio waves and does not provide any useful reflection of the waves. This region fades out at night. Region E also fades at night but provides some reflection of radio waves during the day. Sky waves that bounce off region E can provide communications up to about 2400 kilometres (around 1300 nm). F1 and F2 Regions of the ionosphere do not fade out at night, but combine to form a single region. You can communicate using F region sky waves over distances greater than 2400 kilometres. Region F is especially useful at night, when the two lower (intervening) regions D and E have faded.

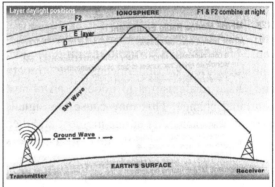

Figure 12-3 Simplified sky-wave and ground wave propagation

Sky waves undergo attenuation loss on encounter with the ionosphere. The amount depends upon the height and composition of the ionosphere as well as the frequency of the radio wave with maximum ionospheric absorption occurring around 1400 kHz. In general, atmospheric absorption increases with frequency and is only a problem in the SHF and EHF frequency range.

The ionosphere is in a state of constant flux (variation) and is classified as being either *regular* or *irregular*. Therefore, sky-wave communications are not completely predictable. Regular ionosphere variations occur as a result of the earth's rotation around the sun and the sun's own regular variations.

Basic variation types are: daily variations caused by the rotation of the earth; seasonal variations caused by the seasonal tilt of the earth on its axis; 27 day variations caused by the rotation of the sun on its axis; and 11 year variations caused by the sunspot activity cycle of the sun.

The F region can be particularly erratic because of the regions rapidly fluctuating conditions in the layer. A sky wave reaching a receiver may have travelled any variation of sky way paths. A single reflection off the ionosphere is called a *one-hop* signal. A sky wave that has been reflected back down to the earth's surface, then back up to the ionosphere, then to the receiver, is called a *two-hop* signal. A sky-wave path with multiple reflections is called a *mutlihop* signal. The layer from which the sky wave is reflected is also used to describe the type of signal; for example a one-hop F signal can be received around 4000 kilometres (≈2200 nm) away.

Sky waves undergo *polarization* due to the sky wave path (i.e. one-hop or two-hop etc.), which cause phase changes to occur at each reflection. The fluctuating ionosphere causes the strength and phase relationships to undergo an almost continual change. This may cause the signals to reinforce each other at one moment and then cancel each other out the next, in a process called *fading*. *Polarization error* occurs when the reflected sky wave undergoes polarization in the ionosphere along with a change in direction of travel. *Night effect* occurs at sunrise and sunset, as the ionosphere restructures, causing maximum polarization error and erratic receiver reception.

Radio frequency spectrum

The radio frequency (RF) spectrum is part of the electromagnetic spectrum; and is further divided into eight bands as shown in Table 12-1. The frequency band standard as described below is derived from the International Telecommunications Union (ITU) radio regulations. The ITU is the leading United Nations agency for information and communication technology issues. It is also the global focal point for governments and the private sector, in developing networks and services. For marine communications, the frequency bands of concern are VHF, MF/HF and HF 27 MHz.

Each of the radio frequency bands has different transmission characteristics. The frequency range of a band determines how the waves propagate and how far they travel. The lower frequency bands of VLF and LF travel as both surface waves and as sky-waves. UHF and higher frequency ranges propagate only as direct waves (i.e. LOS). An important point to remember is wave energy is proportional to the wave frequency. Lower frequency transmitters must use higher transmission power to get usable signal strength as shown above.

27 MHz and VHF 156 MHz frequencies

For marine communications over short distances, two types of radio sets are used: the 27 MHz (aka *27 Meg*), and VHF. These two bands have their frequencies divided into channels (i.e. VHF channel 16, uses a frequency of 156.800 MHz and in 27 Meg, channel 88 uses a frequency of 27.88 MHz).

Predominately, frequencies of 27 MHz and above do not reflect from the ionosphere and radio wave propagation is via ground waves, thus reducing the communications to line-of-sight. The 27 MHz is in the HF band and radio wave propagation under certain atmospheric conditions reflect off the ionosphere and permit communications over hundreds or thousands of nautical miles, in a process called *skip*.

Band & Abbreviation	Range of frequency	Range of wavelength	* As a guide only for the understanding of concepts. Ranges are approximate and not accounting for any variables (e.g. ionospheric variations, time of day or night, seasons, useable antenna orientation and height).		
Audio frequency (AF)	20 Hz to 20 kHz	15 x 10⁶ to 15 x m			
Radio frequency (RF)	10 kHz to 300 000 MHz	30 x 10³ to 0.001 m			
The Eight Sub-divisions of the Radio Frequency Spectrum			**Note:** Types of radio sets, transmission/reception distances and power figures vary between different sources.		
Extremely high frequency (EHF)	30 to 300 GHz	0.01 cm to 0.001 m			
Super high frequency (SHF)	3 to 30 GHz	0.1 to 0.01 m	*Ground wave**	*Sky-wave**	*Tx power**
Ultra high frequency (UHF)	300 to 3000 MHz	1 m to 0.1 m	*0-83 km*	*NA*	*≤ 0.5 kW*
Very high frequency (VHF)	30 to 300 MHz	10 to 1 m	*0-48 km*	*80.5-241 km*	*≤ 0.5 kW*
High frequency (HF)	3 to 30 MHz	100 to 10 m	*0-83 km*	*161-12 872 km*	*0.5-5 kW*
Medium frequency (MF)	300 to 3000 kHz	1000 to 100 m	*0-161 km*	*161-2415 km*	*0.5-50 kW*
Low frequency (LF)	30 to 300 kHz	10 x 10³m to 1 x 10³ m	*0-83 km*	*805-12872 km*	*> 50kW*
Very low frequency (VLF)	10 to 30 kHz	30 x 10³ to 10 x 10³ m			

Table 12-1 The Radio Frequency Spectrum

The 27 MHz sets have all their channels within the 27 MHz band and have a range between six to thirty nautical miles. This can be reduced by bad atmospheric conditions or if one station is blocked by a feature, such as an island.[2] Channel 88 (frequency 27.88 MHz) is used to monitor distress signals and to receive incoming calls. Channel 86 (frequency 27.86 MHz) is a supplementary distress and calling channel and is also used to transmit safety messages.

The 27 MHz sets require low power for operation and as a result, the quality of antenna is important. A set experiencing poor performance may be the result of sub-standard quality or incorrectly adjusted radio antenna.

The average distance of direct wave communications is limited by the height of the transmitter and or receiver's antenna. At frequencies greater than 30 MHz (VHF and above) with antennas at ground level a direct wave is normally limited to around the 37 kilometres (20 miles) due to the curvature of the earth.[3] If you increase the height of either antenna, you will be able to increase the distance between ship-to-ship communication by around 20 kilometres (11 nm) and ship to shore to around 50 kilometres (27 nm).

However, for kayakers using VHF hand held sets the distances are immensely reduced. As a guide, VHF communications between two stations, over an all-water path, are possible to a maximum range approximately the combined line of sight distance of each station. Under certain atmospheric conditions, often in summer, a phenomenon called *ducting* occurs. This phenomenon allows VHF communications over hundreds even thousands of nautical miles. Do not rely on these phenomena for communications.

MF/HF Frequencies

Medium Frequency (MF) ground waves provide reliable service, but the range for a given power is reduced greatly as discussed. MF range varies from about 400 miles (~643 km) at the lower spectrum of the band to around 15 miles (~24 km) at the upper end for a transmitted signal of one kilowatt. However, these values are influenced by the power of the transmitter, the orientation and efficiency of the antenna, and the type of terrain over which the signals travels. Elevating the antenna to obtain direct waves, possibly may improve the transmission.

At lower MF frequencies, sky waves are available both day and night. The ionosphere absorbs lower MF frequencies until a maximum frequency of around 1400 kHz. At higher frequencies the absorption decreases allowing the increased use of sky waves. Since the ionosphere changes with the hour, season, and sunspot cycle, the reliability of sky-wave signals is variable. By careful frequency selection, transmission ranges up to 8000 miles (~12 874 km) with one kilowatt of transmitted power are possible via multi-hop signals. MF/HF radios transmit the greatest power of up to 400 watts. Note however, the frequency selection is critical. If it is too high, the signals penetrate the ionosphere and are lost in space. If too low, the signals are too weak. In general, sky-wave reception is equally good by day or night, but lower frequencies are needed at night.

High Frequency (HF), like the higher medium frequencies, has a limited ground wave range of a few miles. Elevating the antenna may increase the direct wave distance of transmission. In

addition, the height of the antenna does have an important effect upon sky wave transmission. Maximum usable communication frequencies fall generally within the HF band. The Table 12-2 summarises maritime allocated MF/HF bandwidths up to the VHF channels.

Frequency Band	Bands	Rough usage guide	Examples of frequencies within bandwidth	
MF: 300-3000 kHz	1 MHz 1000 kHz	Usable ground waves & sky-waves propagation	≈1400 kHz	Ionosphere allows reflection of sky-waves
			1715 kHz	Inshore boating service frequencies call & working
			1725 kHz	
	2 MHz 2000 kHz	Tx day or night to a station up to around 54 nm (100 km)	2182 kHz	Distress, urgency, safety and calling
			2201 kHz	VMC Australian Weather & Navigation Warnings East
			2284 kHz	Yachts and pleasure vessel, calling and working
HF: 3-30 MHz	4 MHz 4000 kHz	Tx daytime for > 54 nm No response to 2 MHz Night if 2 MHz unsatisfactory	4125 kHz	Distress, urgency & safety only
			4426 kHz	VMC Australian Weather & Navigation Warnings East
	6 MHz 6000 kHz	Tx daytime if 4 MHz are unsatisfactory Tx night if 2 MHz & 4 MHz are unsatisfactory	6215 kHz	Distress, urgency & safety only
			6230 kHz	VMC Australian Weather & Navigation Warnings East
	8 MHz 8000 kHz	8, 12, 16 & 22 MHz Provide progressively greater communication distances. Used when lower frequency bands are unsatisfactory.	8176 kHz	VMC Australian Weather & **Navigation Warnings**
			8291 kHz	**Distress, urgency & safety only**
	12 MHz 12 000 kHz		12 290 kHz	Distress, urgency & safety only
			12 365 kHz	VMC Australian Weather & Navigation Warnings East
			12 359 kHz	Alternative call carrier frequency; simplex basis; Tx < 1 kW
	16 MHz 16 000 kHz		16 420 kHz	Distress, urgency & safety only
			16 546 kHz	VMC Australian Weather & Navigation Warnings East
			16 537 kHz	Alternative call carrier frequency; simplex basis; Tx < 1 kW
	27 MHz 27 000 kHz	Usable ground wave propagation Sky-waves usually not reflected by ionosphere but penetrate ionosphere and are lost to space	27.88 MHz	Channel 88; distress, urgency, safety & calling
VHF: 30-300 MHz	156 MHz 156 000 kHz	Usable ground wave propagation	156.800 MHz	Channel 16; distress, urgency, safety & calling 55 VHF channels

Table 12-2 Example of MF/HF frequency bands

Selection of MF/HF Frequencies

A guide for frequency selection is to select lower frequencies when close to the required station, and higher frequencies when further away. At night, selection of a frequency lower than the necessary one used during the day is more likely to be effective. The saying is: '*The higher the sun, the higher the frequency.*' The correct frequency selection is the lowest one that provides satisfactory communications.

Forms of Frequencies

When a series of waves are transmitted at a constant frequency and amplitude it is termed a *continuous wave* (CW). Continuous waves are only heard at the very lowest radio frequencies as an audible hum of high pitch in the receiver. Radio direction finding uses the continuous wave directly but it is usually modified in some manner through a process called *modulation*. Through modulation, a sound *signal* is encoded on the continuous wave, which then serves as a *carrier* wave for the audio information.

The frequency range of normal speech is about 50 Hz to 500 Hz and could be easily converted into electromagnetic energy and transmitted. However, the antenna would need to be nearly eight kilometres long. Transmission of speech over radio waves is via the use of a carrier wave and a lower frequency modulator wave. This is achieved by converting speech sound waves, via a microphone, into an electromagnetic energy audio signal. The signal is then used to modulate (regulate or adjust to a certain measure) the carrier signal. By doing this, low frequency speech signals can be transmitted with the characteristics of higher frequency radio waves. Three types of modulation are: *Pulse modulation* (PM), *Frequency modulation* (FM) and *Amplitude modulation* (AM). We are only concerned with FM and AM radio waves.

Frequency modulation

Frequency modulation (FM) is when the modulating signal is used to adjust the frequency (the amount of oscillations per second) of the carrier wave. Therefore, as shown in Figure 12-4, an FM transmission consists of a constant amplitude wave with frequency varying about a central rest frequency.

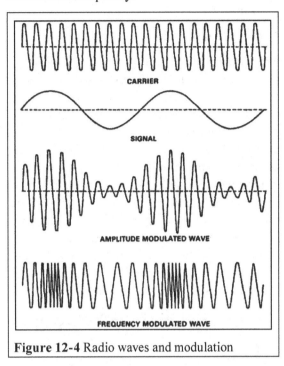

Figure 12-4 Radio waves and modulation

FM broadcasts use the higher RF spectrum frequencies. FM commonly uses VHF radio frequencies for high-fidelity sound broadcasts and for analogue TV sounds. FM is virtually immune to any type of external interference; has a greater dynamic range; and handles sounds of higher and lower frequencies. Because FM broadcasts utilises the higher RF, the sky waves are limited to virtually line-of-sight and do not refract (reflect) like the lower RF. Instead, because of the curvature of the earth, around 80 kilometres (50 miles), the waves travel straight off the earth, penetrate the ionosphere and are lost to space.[4] While FM stations do not interfere with each other, they require tall antennas that are best situated on high features like mountains. The further away from the receiver, the higher the antenna needs to be, until it is impracticable. The geographical coverage area for a high powered FM transmitter can be up to 100 kilometres. Less powerful FM transmitters have a mush less coverage area. Another issue is, since FM and TV signals are line-of-sight. They can be stopped or reflected, by features like mountains and or buildings. On encountering solid objects, like buildings, reflections create ghost images in

TV pictures and a 'swishing sound' when you listen to FM radio, while driving around tall buildings.

Amplitude modulation

Amplitude modulation (AM) is the process of varying the amplitude and thus the energy output of the carrier wave, by superimposing the audio signal wave on it. Audio transmitted using AM, affects the carrier wave, by changing the amplitude (height) of the carrier wave, as shown in Figure 12-4. Unfortunately, this type of modulation is subject to static interference from such things as engines, electrical systems and environmental phenomena, especially lightening storms. Amplitude modulation also limits the loud-to-soft range of sounds that can be reproduced (called *dynamic range*), and the high-to-low sound frequency range.

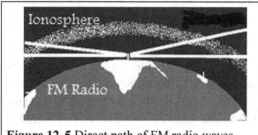

Figure 12-5 Direct path of FM radio waves

In addition to the amplitude variations of the carrier, the superposition of the audio signal produces new RF signals, with frequencies close to that of the carrier frequency. For example, using a 600 kHz carrier, it is modulated by a 1 kHz audio signal. The two new RF frequencies developed will be 600 kHz ±1 kHz (i.e. 599 kHz and 601 kHz). These two new frequencies are called *side bands*. The lower frequency (e.g. 599 kHz) is the *lower sideband* (LSB) and the higher frequency (e.g. 601 kHz) is the *upper sideband* (USB). Therefore, for a range of audio frequencies the frequency range of the sidebands would be the carrier frequency plus or minus the highest and lowest audio frequencies. The total space occupied by both sidebands and the carrier frequency of an AM signal is called a *channel*. The range of frequencies is the *channel bandwidth*.

AM transmissions are inefficient in terms of power (kW) and much is wasted. Around two

thirds of the power is concentrated in the carrier wave, which carries no useful information, other than a hum in the receiver's set. The remaining power is split between two mirror image side bands, that contain identical information, and therefore, only one side band is needed.

To increase transmitter efficiency, the carrier is suppressed and one of the side bands is filtered out. With only the carrier suppressed, amplitude modulation becomes three times more power efficient. In Figure 12-6, the carrier has been suppressed and the USB has been filtered out, allowing all available power to transmit on the LSB.

When the AM SSB receiver receives a signal, the suppressed carrier frequency (600 kHz) is re-inserted at the RF stages. For weak signals, the receivers have an RF amplifier attached to the antenna. The amplifier takes the incoming signal and amplifies it to a level that can be processed by the receiver's other components.

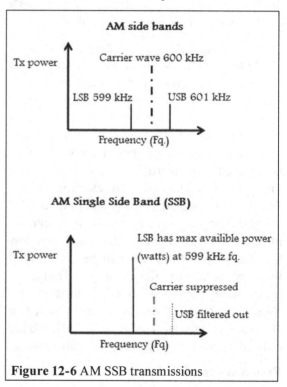

Figure 12-6 AM SSB transmissions

For marine use, SSB transmission and reception is mandatory on all MF/HF marine frequencies, except 2182 kHz. For transceiver operations, select LSB, unless told otherwise to go to USB. If a transceiver is operating in AM mode, it will receive SSB signals as an unintelligible garble, but if operating in SSB mode, it will receive the signals intelligibly and possibly with a slight whistle. SSB is an option on some 27 MHz sets, but when transmitting or receiving distress signals, AM mode should be selected on channel 88 (27.88 MHz).

Types of Transmissions Channels

There are two types of transmission channels used in all marine communications, *simplex* and *duplex*.

Simplex channels are ones on which transmission and reception take place on the same frequency. In Australia, all radiotelephony distress and calling frequencies or channels, are operated in this mode. This enables stations on the same frequency and in range, to monitor a single frequency and allow listeners to hear both conversations. The 27 MHz sets use simplex channels. The VHF channel 16 is a simplex channel. To transmit a signal, the press to talk (PTT) switch is activated (*pressed*) and has to be de-activated (*released*) in order for the recipient to respond to the call. This is one of the reasons operating protocol is required (i.e. 'over' or if finished 'out').

Duplex channels use two different, but paired frequencies, one for transmission and another for reception. This allows stations fitted with the appropriate equipment to transmit and receive simultaneously. Pairing of frequencies into one channel enables radiotelephone calls to be conducted in the same manner as landline telephone calls, with each party being able to speak and hear at the same time.

VHF REPEATERS

Technical: Marine Repeaters; How They Work

The following article was written by Marcus Grinblat, the Communications manager for Coast Guard Victoria and is used with permission.

Now that the Coast Guard has established Repeaters along most of Victoria's coast, it is timely that we reiterate what a repeater is

and its benefits to us. The repeaters that are currently in the trial phase are what are known as 'Talk-Through' repeaters. Irrespective of how this is technically achieved, it simply takes our transmission on one frequency and re-broadcasts it on another. This happens at the same time (i.e. whilst you have the PTT (Press to Talk) button down) the repeater is receiving your transmission on the input frequency of the assigned repeater channel and transmitting it on the output frequency of the repeater.

In order to do this, the channel assigned for a repeater has to have one frequency for receive and another for transmit. These channels are known as DUPLEX channels as opposed to SIMPLEX channels, which receive and transmit on the same frequency (e.g. CH16 and CH 67). This is why SIMPLEX channels cannot be used for Talk-Through repeaters. If it tried to transmit on the same frequency as it was receiving a station on (at the same time) then the repeater would lock out and receive nothing. There are only a handful of duplex International Marine channels that are assigned for repeater use. Once a repeater is out of its theoretical range, the channel can be allocated again—not less than three repeaters apart.

Some further points to consider:

Since the repeaters are usually situated high up, often a remote hill top or sometimes a high tower or other structure, the range is considerably more than if you were talking on a simplex channel boat to boat. Remember VHF is line-of-sight. The repeater may have a 40 nautical miles radius of usable range which means that if two vessels are in opposite direction to the repeater in the above example, the effective boat to boat range will be 100 nautical miles.

Any marine station has access to the repeater as long as they have the appropriate duplex channel. Most, if not all, marine radios have the full 55 international channels fitted.

Remember—a duplex channel receives on one frequency and transmits on another. This switching is done internally in the radio when you press the PTT switch and let it go.

As such, unless you and the station you are talking to are within range of the repeater you will not hear each other—even if you are only half a mile apart! Each radio is listening for the repeater and not listening to the input to the repeater.

The other thing that most repeaters have built in is a small delay between when you stop transmitting on the input to the repeater and when the repeater stops transmitting on its output. This delay can typically be between 1 second and 4 seconds and is known as the repeater TAIL.

This can be used to see if we can access a repeater, or not, by selecting the appropriate repeater channel for the area we are operating in and momentarily pressing the PTT button on that channel (only after we are sure it is not in use) and listening for the repeater TAIL.

This also gives an indication of how strong the repeater is back to you. No tail—means you are not 'getting into' or 'triggering' the repeater. A noisy tail—means you are probably noisy into the repeater as well.

A noise-free tail—usually means you are getting into the repeater fairly well.

Most repeaters, when you are on the fringe of their range, will transmit better than they will receive your signal due to the equipment used and power levels at either end.

A word of caution: Make sure your radio has 'International' channels selected and not 'USA' or 'Canadian'.

Incorrect selection will not be able to trigger a repeater with anything other than International even though you may be easily within range.

International has duplex operation on the repeater channels assigned in Australia and New Zealand.

As operators of Coast Guard Base Stations, your signal into your 'local' repeater will not normally vary.

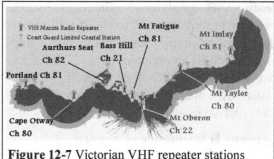

Figure 12-7 Victorian VHF repeater stations

Repeater location	Channel	Area of Coverage
Mt. Imlay	81	Eden, Mallacoota—Marlo
Mt. Taylor	80	Marlo—Seaspray
Mt. Fatigue	81	Corner Inlet, south to Deal Island
Mt. Oberon	22	Port Albert, Wilsons Promontory Sth.
Bass Hill	21	Westernport to Cape Liptrap
Arthurs Seat	82	Westernport, Port Phillip, Immediate Coastal areas
Cape Otway	80	Cape Otway—Port Fairy
Portland	81	Port Fairy—SA border.

Table 12-3 Victorian Coast Guard Repeater Network

As Coast Guard base operators, we will normally work through the repeater, which covers our normal area of operations—even though we may be able to get into a repeater further away we would not normally broadcast weather on a repeater that is 'out of area' (e.g. weather for Port Phillip being broadcast on Wilson's Promontory repeater taking up air time).

Also, remember if someone calls up on CH16, it may be best to change to the local repeater channel as a working channel. An exception to this rule is when you know that you have good transmission to a station on simplex. Therefore there is no need to tie up repeater channel unnecessarily.

Base stations should constantly monitor their local repeater.

As time goes on and boat operators become aware of, and comfortable with, the repeaters you will find boats will call direct on the repeater channel rather than going through CH16.

Experience in New Zealand has found this to be the case. Remember though that all vessels should still be encouraged to monitor CH16 whilst at sea. Most will probably opt to dual watch CH16 and their local repeater.

ⓘ **Note:** Always update technology, organisational and bureaucratic information before launching.

ⓘ **Note:** For updated and current information on Victorian Coastal Radio Stations and VHF repeaters go to the Marine Safety Victoria website, and then go to the publications page.

VHF Repeaters in Tasmania

Repeater stations are a stand-alone receiver and transmitter used as a VHF range extender. The nominal range of each repeater is 80 kilometres, but this will vary from repeater to repeater and in some areas along the coastline, it might be in a shadow zone. The repeaters were originally intended for vessel-to-vessel communications, but it soon became apparent that all repeaters could be monitored from shore stations, when several link radio stations were fitted. This effectively increased VHF monitoring range and consequently enhanced VHF safety monitoring around Tasmania. The repeaters are monitored by Volunteer Radio Stations around the coast.

Location	Channel Number	Monitored by: (limited hours)
Maatsuyker Island	82	Coast Radio Hobart
Cape Sorell	80	Strahan Radio
Bluff Hill Point	81	Smithton Sea Rescue
Dazzler Range	80	Tamar Sea Rescue
Mount Horror	82	Tamar Sea Rescue, St Helens Marine Rescue
Cape Tourville	80	Coastguard Freycinet
Mt Raoul (owned by RYCT)	81	Tascoast Radio
Three Hummock Island	21	Smithton Sea Rescue, Burnie Radio

Table 12-4 Tasmanian VHF repeater stations
Source MAST

To access a repeater, you need to be in range of the closest repeater (remembering that VHF is line-of-sight) and then transmit on the repeaters frequency in your location. It is essential you check that your unit is set to *international*, as this ensures the duplex frequencies. You then use the radio to call another vessel or coastal station as normal. To prevent people over using the repeater channel, the repeaters have a 30 second time out facility. This means that after 30 seconds of continual transmission, they

automatically switch off for a couple of seconds. They can be re-activated by momentarily *keying* (releasing and repress) the press to talk switch (transmit key) on the radio and then continue transmitting.

ⓘ **Note:** Technology, organisations and bureaucracy changes, so always update your information before launching.

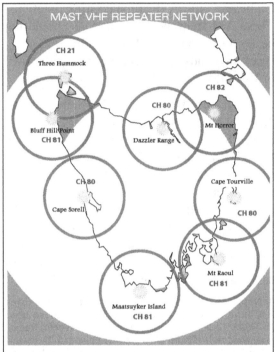

Figure 12-8 Tasmanian MAST repeater network
Source MAST

According to Marine and Safety Tasmania (MAST), in Tasmania, most repeaters are monitored from shore by volunteer coastal radio stations. Hours of monitoring do vary from season to season but, as a general rule, they are monitored from 8 am to 5 pm daily. The shore stations broadcast weather forecasts over the repeater frequencies. They are also able to offer vessel position reporting whilst at sea. They can also be used for passing distress and urgency messages such as *Mayday* and *Pan Pan* calls, although these calls should also be made on the recognized distress frequency of Channel 16 to notify other vessels in the vicinity.

ⓘ **Note:** Refer to the MAST website to get the most recent and updated index of marine radios.

In Tasmania, the coastal radio stations are manned and run by volunteers and donations can be made to these people. See the Marine and Safety Tasmania (MAST) website for details.

Short Wave Radio

The term *short wave* (SW) came about in the early days of radio when the norm had been the use of long waves. Today short wave, medium wave and long wave are frequency designations applicable to AM broadcasting stations. These AM frequency designations should not be confused with the ITU's radio frequency spectrum bands as discussed earlier and shown in Table 12-5

You will observe in Table 12-5 how the two different classifications of radio waves overlap. SW is SW and has its own frequency range. HF is HF and has its own frequency range. SW is not HF but it does cross both the MF and HF frequency ranges. As a result, SW receivers can pick up MF/HF broadcasts within the SW frequency range. This is why a SW radio with SSB capability can pick up marine weather forecasts and navigation warnings for Australia's east coast from VMC at Charleville, QLD.

ⓘ **Note:** LW, MW and SW bands in different countries may have different frequency ranges to those used in Table 12-5. The ITU through the World Radio-communication Conference (WRC) periodically review and allocate SW broadcasting frequencies. However, this does not mean there is conformity between different countries. For example, in the Sangean ATS-909 literature the following bands are divided into the corresponding frequencies: LW 153 to 519 kHz, MW 520 to 1710 kHz and SW 1.711 to 29.999 MHz.

To get VMC Charleville all you need to do is enter the frequencies into your SW SSB receiver (radio). Use the Marine Safety Victoria website to get the frequencies.

Some points about using a SW SSB receiver:

Familiarise yourself with the radio before you need it on a trip and even take the literature about the type of radio you have if you are not sure of radio operations. People have not done this!

Pre-enter desired frequencies and SSB mode before you go on a trip and familiarize yourself with the equipment.

If a transceiver is operating in AM mode it will receive SSB signals as an unintelligible garble but if operating in SSB mode it will receive the signals intelligibly and possibly with a slight whistle.

In AM radio wave propagation, the radio waves behave in the same manner as MF/HF radio waves. Therefore when it comes to tuning in for reception the same guidelines apply (i.e. *the higher the sun the higher the frequency selection*).

Gain is a term used with antennas. Gain is measured in decibels (dB) and is not the creation of power, but rather a simple refocusing of energy from all directions to a specific direction. On transceivers (only on 27 Meg and MF/HF sets) and SW SSB radio receivers, the gain control is used to vary the strength of received signals and has a similar effect as the volume control. Keep the gain control close to or at maximum, unless the signals are unusually strong, and use the volume control to adjust signals to a comfortable level.

AM Broadcasting Frequency	ITU radio bands	
	LF	30 kHz
Long wave 153 – 279 kHz		to
		300 kHz
	MF	300 kHz
Medium wave 531 – 1602 kHz		to
Short wave 2310 – 25 820 kHz ~2 – 26 MHz		3000 kHz
	HF	3000 kHz
		to
		30 000 kHz

Table 12-5 Difference between AM broadcasting bands and ITU frequency bands

When using an SW SSB radio, be patient. Use the signal strength indicator when you are hunting for a signal. The signal strength indicator will register only when there is a SSB transmission and not when there is a pause or no voice transmission.

If you are operating a transceiver with a manual clarifier control (found on some 27 MHz and MF/HF sets operating SSB) it is a means of fine-tuning the incoming SSB signals that sound distorted. The distortion is often described as a voice signal sounding like Donald Duck. Clarification is achieved by adjusting the frequency of the re-inserted carrier, which may be slightly out. If there is, no clarifier control the set will have another means of fine-tuning incoming signals.

On SW SSB radios when you have SSB reception, that is unintelligible alternate between USB and LSB mode selections. As a guide for tuning-in for SSB transmissions, for frequencies below 10 MHz first try LSB; and for frequencies above 10 MHz first try USB.

Tune for maximum intelligibility by ensuring the *step control* is selected to *slow* and utilise the *manual tuning control* (aka rotary knob). Depending upon the set, 'slow' allows 40 Hz adjustments to be made instead of 1 kHz increments.

In Australia, the primary coverage area for Radio Australia broadcasts is outside continental Australia and although reception within Australia is possible, the quality may vary significantly. However, listeners in North Queensland and north-west Western Australia should be able to obtain reliable reception of Radio Australia in the 13, 15, 17 and 21 MHz bands which are broadcast from Shepparton and Brandon. The ABC also uses short wave to broadcast ABC Regional Radio to Alice Springs, Katherine and Tennant Creek. Listeners in the Northern Territory will need a radio receiver capable of tuning into frequencies between 2 MHz and 26 MHz (ABC Radio, n.d.).

Stereo and Mono radio broadcast are either *monophonic* (mono) or *stereophonic* (stereo) sound. Stereo radio provides greater realism because it contains two channels of sound signals:

left and right; Mono contains one channel. To receive stereo broadcasts, the listener must use a stereo receiver. A mono receiver can still receive stereo broadcasts. However, the sound will be monophonic. If radio signal strength is low, stereo sound reception can be distorted but can often be improved by switching the receiver to mono mode.

Radio Antennas

Just as important as the transceiver, transmitter, receiver or radio set is the antenna. The transmitter radiates RF energy into space when transmitting. On reception, it gathers the RF energy from space and passes it on to the receiver. On MF/HF sets, the antenna may be a long wire or a vertical whip type. 27 MHz and VHF radio sets are normally of the whip-type construction. Antennas for the three types of marine radio sets cannot be interchanged. It is important to check the antenna's insulators for cracking and or deterioration and replace the faulty components. Salt build up on the insulators will reduce antenna efficiency.

Any antenna is better than no antenna and vertical antennas are in fact, quite directional except in the horizontal or azimuth plane. A dipole antenna is the name given to the simplest type of antenna. For short wave reception, a portable dipole antenna can be made from copper wire. It does not matter if the wire is thick or thin, insulated or bare, stranded or solid, as they will all perform adequately. Higher antennas generally outperform lower antennas so if you are trying to receive the marine weather forecast on your SW radio use a long wire antenna erected as high as possible. To get the required antenna height for the terrain you are in, throw a line (fishing line with a sinker or cordage) over a high tree branch and hoist up your wire antenna. If you are using a MF/HF set out bush, you will need to have an insulator between the erection line and antenna wire to avoid *flashover*. You can improvise an insulator with a button, plastic utensil or use nylon cordage. The best insulators are plastic and glass with wood being classed as good and cloth or rope being fair. If you are going to use a rock face to support your antenna, use a counterpoise to hold the wire away from the face.

PHYSICAL COMMUNICATION SIGNALS

① **Note:** If you are warning of a danger, use a whistle in conjunction with the hand or paddle signal.

Paddle Signals

Depending upon the conditions and or distance apart you may need to resort to paddle signals. Be aware that paddle signals can also be hard to see in certain circumstances (e.g. sun light, large waves). A common selection of paddle signals is at Table 12-6. To make your paddle more obvious paint the blades a fluoro colour.

Hand signals

Because of environmental factors and separation distances, hand signals are a common means of communicating with fellow participants in an activity. A common selection of hand signals is at Table 12-7.

Whistles

Oddly enough, a whistle is not listed in the VRBS handbook minimum safety equipment requirements. However, it is a requirement of the VSKC that every paddler carries on the PFD a pea-less whistle. The *Fox 40* is a commonly carried whistle.

A criticism that is often voiced, is in certain conditions and most likely, the conditions when you want to raise attention, the whistle is drowned out by the environmental conditions. Despite this complaint more often than not, you will hear a whistle blast.

Whistle signals are given to gain people's attention. If required, combine whistle signals with hand and paddle signals. Ensure all participants in an activity upon hearing a whistle blast, know to '*STOP and look around*'. Allow people time to respond to your whistle signal.

The following whistle signals are used to gain attention to yourself or warn of imminent danger. To distinguish between different whistle signals, the following whistle blast definitions apply: 'short blast' is of 1 to 2 seconds duration; a 'long blast' is of 4 to 6 seconds duration. When signalling, wait 10 seconds between

sequences. Whistle signals and their meaning are at Table 12-8.

Stop—hold position and look around
Hold paddle horizontally above head

Form up on me;
Come in here
Extend paddle vertically up in line with centre of body

Move left or **right;**
Go straight ahead
Extend paddle horizontally and point paddle in required direction

Action/warning	Signal
Accelerate; Imminent danger	Extend paddle vertically with one arm and wave from side to side. • Use a whistle
Back paddle (i.e. Reverse)	Paddle held horizontally above head and rock up and down. (Back and forward (horizontal) motions are very difficult to see from a distance)

Danger/hazard; Urgent stop and look around	Hold paddle horizontally overhead with both hands and move up and down. • Use a whistle

Table 12-6 Paddle signals

Table 12-7 Hand signals

Signal	Meaning
	Thumb and index finger forming a circle: • Are you ok? • Mimic signal back if reply is 'yes'
	Thumb up: • Affirmative, yes
	Hand on head is used from a distance instead of thumb signal: • Are you ok? • Mimic signal back to reply if 'yes'.
	Hand performing a slashing motion across throat is used from a distance instead of thumb signal: • Negative, no
	Thumb down: • Negative, no
	Wave arm or arms in an up and down (flapping) manner: • Help • Use whistle signal also
	• Smoke & flares

• V-sheet Coloured orange with either a black V or with a black square and circle

Table 12-8 Whistle signals

Sequence	Meaning(s)
One to two short blasts	Stop and look around
Three short blasts	I need assistance (help)
Two long blasts	Look around; Imminent danger (Gain attention to **surfing** visual signals)

1 The USA primarily uses the CDMA network system. In 2012 there are around 190 countries that primarily use GSM system networks including Australia, New Zealand, UK, Europe.

2 Note different references state different figures for transmission ranges. There are a multitude of reasons for the variations in transmission distances as discussed in the text. Use the information only as a guide to gain an understanding of the principles of radio communications.

3 Other references state 50 km (80 km).

4 The figures for departure of radio waves from the earth's surface due to curvature vary in different references. This is most likely because of the reference point used for describing the wave's path (i.e. height and

orientation of antenna, type of transmission etc.).

CHAPTER 13 EMERGENCY PROCEDURES

"For the execution of the voyage to the Indies, I did not make use of intelligence, mathematics or maps."

Christopher Columbus

SEARCH AND RESCUE IN AUSTRALIA

Maritime and aviation search and rescue (SAR) services are the responsibility of Australian Search and Rescue (AusSAR) who are a division of the Australian Maritime Safety Authority (AMSA).

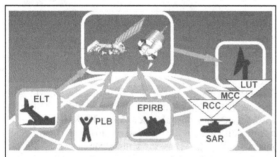

Figure 13-1 SAR contact overview

AMSA is the operating authority of the Rescue Coordination Centre (RCC Australia) in Canberra. RCC Australia has the responsibility for coordination of SAR operations. For SAR of small vessels (pleasure and fishing) a National Plan relegates responsibility for SAR operations to State and Territory police forces. State and Territory police forces involve the resources of their own Water Police, and the various marine rescue organizations like the Australian Volunteer Coast Guard, Royal Volunteer Coastal Patrol and Volunteer Marine Rescue.

The RCC in Victoria, for both land and sea incidents, is the Victoria Police, Water Police and Search and Rescue Squad. The RCC is located in Melbourne at Williamstown and is staffed 24 hours a day. Refer to Appendix 1 for contact numbers. In Victoria, upon reporting a lost or overdue person to a police station or by calling 000, the information is passed on to the RCC. The initial location is confirmed and local assets

dispatched to search the area. The local assets, who may be government, volunteer, or civilian, search the area using the most appropriate and available means. This may involve using fixed wing or rotary wing aircraft, or boats. Depending upon the reports from the initial responders, further assets are deployed (Bate, 2008).

EPIRBS

Emergency Position—Indicating Radio Beacons (EPIRBS) are the maritime equivalent to aviation's Emergency Location Transmitter (ELT) and land use Personal Locator Beacons (PLB). Some points:

ELT and PLB are not suitable for, nor recommended for shipboard use (Australian Maritime College, 2002).

EPIRBS are used in life threatening situations.

EPIRBS should not be carried as an alternative to an approved marine radio transceiver and should be considered a supplement rather than a replacement (Australian Maritime College, 2002).

It is law in Victoria to carry an approved EPIRB if more than two nautical miles offshore.

406 MHz EPIRBS

Since February 1, 2009 the digitalised 406 MHz frequency is the only frequency picked up and processed by the Cospas-Sarsat satellite system. The satellites will not pick up the 121.5 MHz frequency. The 406 MHz EPIRB will still transmit to civil aircraft and SAR on 121.5 MHz. The satellite component of the 406 MHz has an effective locating radius of less than 2.7 nautical miles (< 5 km).[1] The SAR vessel 'homing in' will perform final location.

Some of the advantages of the 406 MHz EPIRB over the older style (121.5/243 MHz) are:

Its signal can be detected and located at any place on the earth's surface.

It does not have a 'black spot' when the satellite is not in range of the analogue signal, since the digitalise frequency is memorised by the satellite and downloaded to a local user terminal (LUT). The LUT sends the information onto RCC Australia.

Owner/operator identification.

On obtaining a 406 MHz EPIRB, it is registered with RCC Australia. If activated RCC Australia have the required details to contact the owner/operator, an on-shore contact and the information about the vessel used by the owner/operator.

The latest generation of beacons have the ability to be picked up by geostationary satellites that cover 85 per cent of the earth and thus making near instantaneous detection.

Some models have the ability of transmitting position data memorized from an interface with satellite navigation receivers (GPS function).[2]

There are two categories of 406 MHz beacons:

- Category 1, are activated either manually or automatically and are stored in a special bracket equipped with a hydrostatic release.

- Category 2, are manual activation only units and are the sort used by sea kayakers.

Care and maintenance

An EPIRB must not be tested except strictly in accordance with the manufacturer's instructions for self-testing. Refer to the manufacture's Owner's manual concerning recommended servicing and battery replacement.

✿* **Caution:** Technical and procedural information can change rapidly. Do not rely on this article, as it is a guide and not authoritative information. Always check the information source or other authoritative source to ensure you get the most accurate and up to date information. Go to the AMSA website to access the latest information.

406 MHz Personal Locator Beacons

Personal locator beacons (PLB) are generally carried by sea kayakers because of their size and weight. There are two types of 406 MHz PLB on the market. The first type does not incorporate Global Positioning System (GPS) circuitry and the second type has GPS functionality. The GPS

functionality has improved location accuracy from kilometres down to metres. To ensure you purchase a PLB that will meet Australian Standards and Class Licence requirements, go to the Australian Maritime Safety Authority website.

COSPAS-SARSAT system

COSPAS-SARSAT is a global distress warning system operating 406.0–406.1 MHz frequency band. The 406 MHz frequency is coded with each beacon's unique identity (ID), which is used to determine the position of the beacon and to alert the nearest Search and Rescue services (SAR).

The COSPAS-SARSAT system consists of:

Distress beacons (PLB or EPIRB).

Satellites on polar orbits (LEOSAR) and geostationary satellites (GEOSAR).

Local User Terminals (LUTs).

Mission and Rescue Control Centres (MRCC's).

Rescue Coordination Centres (RCCs) or Search and Rescue (S.A.R.) Points of Contacts.

COSPAS-SARSAT is an international system utilising Russian Federation and United States low-altitude earth orbit (LEO), near-polar orbiting satellites (LEOSAR) and satellites in geostationary earth orbit (GEO), which form the GEOSAR System. Both are used in detecting and locating activated 406 MHz Satellite beacons.

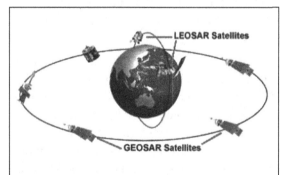

Source: International Satellite System For Search and Rescue
Figure 13-2 LEOSAR and GEOSAR satellites

When activated, the PLB transmits to the satellite portion of the COSPAS-SARSAT System (i.e. LEOSAR and GEOSAR networks). GEOSAR includes GPS latitude and longitude coordinates when GPS data is present. This message is picked up by the COSPAS-SARSAT satellite system, which in turn stores and continuously retransmits the information to the earth stations called Local User Terminals (LUT).

The message transmitted is unique for each PLB, which provides identification of the transmitter through computer access of registration files maintained by RCC Australia or other National Authority in other countries.

Remember, if your PLB is not registered, Search and Rescue (SAR) authorities do not know who you are, or how to contact anyone who might know anything about your situation.

If a PLB does not have GPS functionality the beacon is picked up by LEOSAR. The position of the distress is calculated typically within one nautical mile anywhere in the world, using Doppler techniques. The typical waiting time for calculating a position in average latitudes is estimated to be less than one hour. The beacon distress message is transmitted in real time to the nearest LUT within view of the satellite. The satellite also stores the information for later transmission to other LUTs.[3]

The LUT processes the Doppler-shifted signal from the LEOSAR and determines the location of the beacon. Then the LUT relays the position of the distress to RCC Australia, where the distress alert and location information is immediately forwarded to an appropriate Rescue Coordination Centre (RCC) (e.g. RCC Victoria). The RCC dispatches Search and Rescue (SAR) services.

Geostationary satellites orbit the earth at an altitude of 36 000 kilometres, with an orbit period of 24 hours, thereby appearing fixed relative to the earth at approximately zero degrees latitude (i.e. over the equator). A single geostationary satellite provides GEOSAR uplink coverage of about one third of the globe, except for polar regions. Therefore, three geostationary satellites equally spaced in longitude can provide continuous coverage of all areas of the globe between approximately 70 degrees North and 70 degrees South latitude (International Cospas-Sarsat Programme).

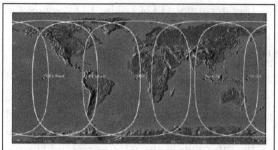

Source: International Satellite System For Search and Rescue
Figure 13-3 GEOSAR satellite orbits

Geostationary satellites (GEOSAR) bring with them the benefit of detecting, within minutes, distress signals transmitted anywhere in the world. This is because GEOSAR satellites are stationary and the system has no Doppler capabilities at 406 MHz range, but will instantly relay the distress alert to any of the LUT stations.

When there is GPS data included in the distress message, SAR authorities instantly know your location to within 100.6 metres.[4] Such accuracy speeds up the SAR reaction time by eliminating the need for one of the LEOSAR satellites to pass overhead.

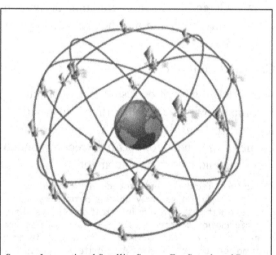

Source: International Satellite System For Search and Rescue
Figure 13-4 GPS Satellite system

The GPS system is a satellite group that enables a GPS receiver to determine its exact position to within 30 metres anywhere on earth. With a minimum of 24 GPS satellites orbiting the earth at an altitude of approximately 17 703 kilometres they provide users with accurate information on position, velocity, and time anywhere in the world and in all weather conditions. Because most SAR organisations presently are not equipped to home in on the 406 MHz Satellite PLB signal they home-in utilising 121.5 MHz signal.

and purchase a unit with built in GPS. This ensures the best response." Note: James is a member of the Victoria Police SAR squad.

3 The respective satellite systems have an associated LUTs. For LEOSAR system the LUT is referred to as LEOLUTs and GEOLUTs for the GEOSAR system.

4 Figures vary in different literature from 30 m, 45 m, 50 m, to 110 yards.

1 The 121.5/243 MHz EPIRB had an effective location radius of 11 nm (20 km).

2 Refer to VSKC Seatrek magazine, Autumn 2008, Issue 60, pp.16-17 Emergency Position Indicating Radio Beacon (EPIRB), by James Bate. "There is a local manufacturer KTI, whose units are worth a look. It is worthwhile spending the extra money

CHAPTER 14 CONSERVATION

"Man has lost the capacity to foresee and to forestall. He will end by destroying the earth."

Albert Schweltzer

MINIMAL IMPACT CAMPING

Minimal impact camping refers to practices and procedures aimed at protecting, maintaining, restoring and enhancing the environment. The aim of conducting minimal impact camping practices is the conservation of the environment. This is achieved by awareness and a conscious effort through implementing minimal impact practices.

Rubbish

Reduce the amount of rubbish you make by using reusable containers, and taking excess packaging off products before you leave home. Carry rubbish bags with you.

If you have carried it in, carry it out. Carry out all your rubbish, including those easy-to-forget items like silver paper, plastic wrappers and orange peel, which do not easily decompose. If you come across other people's rubbish, carry it out as well.

Do not burn or bury rubbish. Rubbish is likely to be dug up and scattered by possums and other animals and may injure them. Repeated digging by campers disturbs soil and encourages weeds and erosion.

Disease control

The DSE is concerned with the increasing cases of gastroenteritis (diarrhoea and vomiting) in some high-use areas, which is caused by exposure to human faecal waste. *Giardia*, a human bacterial parasite is also of concern. Giardia lives in mountain streams contaminated by faecal waste, and causes chronic diarrhoea and an array of other nasties. It has been found in the USA and New Zealand, and is in some alpine areas of Australia. Avoid *gastro* and help ensure that Giardia does not spread to new areas by observing these guidelines. More information on Giardia is in the section on first Aid, Health and Fitness.

Where there is a toilet, please use it. In areas without toilets, bury your faecal waste. Choose a spot at least 100 metres away from campsites and watercourses. Dig a hole 15 centimetres (6 inches) deep (take a hand trowel for this purpose). Bury all faecal waste and paper, mixing it with soil to help decomposition and discourage animals from digging it back up. If you are staying in one area for a few days, dig a communal latrine. Sources and advice vary on the measurements but generally a trench 15 to 20 centimetres (6–8 inches) wide and 46 to 90 centimetres (18–36 inches) long and 46 centimetres (18 inches) deep. One source has it as 4 feet deep and 18 inches wide. Mark the area with a chemical stick or a reflector so no one is unpleasantly surprised during the night. Other methods of going to the toilet are to dig a pit below the high water mark or taking the aqua-dump, which is self-explanatory. Make sure you do it far enough away that nothing comes back to haunt you or other paddlers.

Carry out sanitary pads, tampons and condoms. Zip-loc bags are useful for this. In high-use areas, river valleys without toilets and snow areas, you should consider carrying out human waste to a suitable sewage system. Flies and small animals love faecal waste and food. Cover all food. Avoid putting it on hut tables, furniture and other places frequented by flies and animals. Boil water for at least five and preferably ten minutes before drinking in high-use areas or areas with low water flow.

Do not wash in streams and lakes. Detergents, toothpaste and soap (even biodegradable types) harm fish and water-life. Wash 50 metres away from streams and lakes, and scatter the wash-water here so that it filters through the soil before returning to the stream. Use gritty sand and scourers instead of soap to clean dishes. Do not throw food scraps into streams or lakes.

Campsites

When choosing a campsite, be aware of and respect cultural, historical and sacred sites. Look for low impact campsites. Sandy or hard surfaces are better than boggy or grassed areas. Camp at an existing campsite rather than a new one, and keep at least 20 metres away from watercourses and the track. Spend only two or three nights at each campsite.

Use modern camping equipment. Use waterproof tents (with floors and tent poles) and foam sleeping-mats to minimise damage to camping areas. Digging trenches around tents is damaging, and unnecessary if the tents are erected on a well-drained or raised site. Other considerations are:

Do not dump an entire flotilla of boats on fragile coastal plants

Do not muscle in on other groups

Do not spread out over the campsite and use up more area than reasonable

Are permits/permission required?

How many people can camp in the area?

How many hikers/kayakers visit the area?

Are there composting toilets?

Is there a good source of fresh water?

Leave campsites better than you found them, by removing rubbish and dismantling unnecessary or unsafe fireplaces.

Access

Be aware of what you are walking on, both flora and fauna. Avoid crashing about in the bush and stick to a single track to access frequently visited places within the camp. Use constructed walkways and tracks where applicable. Be aware of bird nesting areas (e.g. South Channel Fort) where the birds nest on the ground.

Be aware of ecologically vulnerable areas like mangroves. Do not trample on the pneumatophores.

Campfires

Wood fires may be lit in fireplaces for cooking and warmth in most parks, forests and public land, but a number of restrictions apply to ensure that fires do not escape and fireplaces are safely constructed. On days of Total Fire Ban the following are prohibited:

All fires in the open air (including campfires and portable gas or liquid fuelled stoves).

All gas or liquid fuelled appliances in tents, tent type trailers and vehicles.

There are five fire ban districts in Victoria and it is your responsibility to know if a total fire ban is declared. Refer to the Bureau of Meteorology website or contact local DSE or CFA offices. If in any doubt about the safety of lighting a fire, please do not light it.

Use only dead fell wood. Standing trees, even dead ones are a home for wildlife and a part of the scenery. Do not cut down or damage standing trees or vegetation. Firewood is in short supply in many areas. Fallen branches house and feed many small mammals, invertebrate and other species. These habitat branches if damaged or destroyed, may only regenerate or be replaced (if at all) over extended periods of time, particularly in alpine and coastal areas. Gather firewood well away from your camp and use it sparingly, or better still, bring your own.

Observe the relevant fire lighting regulations:

In National and State Parks and most other Reserves, fires must be in a properly constructed fireplace.

Elsewhere, a built-up fireplace of stone, metal or concrete, or a trench at least 30 centimetres deep is satisfactory. Previously used sites are preferred.

The fire must be no bigger than one square metre.

Three metres around the fire must be cleared of material that may easily catch fire. Generators and gas or liquid fuelled appliances used in the open must be sited in a 1.5 metre cleared area.

The fire must not be left unattended.

Be absolutely sure the fire is out. Before you leave, feel the ground underneath the coals. If it is still warm the fire is not out. Put it out with water, not soil.

Always try to use a fuel stove when camping. Compared with campfires, fuel stoves are cleaner, a lot easier to use in wet weather, cook food faster and do not scar the landscape. Ensure that every member of your family or friends camping with you has warm clothing and good tents, so fires will not be needed for warmth.

Wild life

① **Note:** there are some places in Australia, particularly up North where you will not have to worry about animals eating your scraps, you have to worry about them eating you. Washing dishes at the water's edge is definitely not a good idea in such circumstances.

Do not feed animals, especially around huts and campsites. Feeding causes unnaturally high and unbalanced animal populations dependent on human food. Some animals become a nuisance, while others become susceptible to diseases such as 'lumpy jaw' from eating refined foods.

If paddling or hiking in countries with bear populations know and follow the recommended camping and travelling practices. These can be found on the relevant Park websites. For example the campsite should have three separate areas separated by 100 metres apart (e.g. a triangle arrangement) for sleeping, preparing and eating food, and toileting. Store food and cooking equipment at least 10 feet off the ground and 4 feet outwards, from the tree's trunk along the branch.

Rats and other pesky mammals are often found around huts and campsites. These animals have been known to eat through backpacks and dry bags. When camping store your food, rubbish and dry bags back in the kayak.

Be aware of risk management strategies for animals like crocodiles, sharks and snakes. Do not corner, threaten, torment or try to catch wildlife. Do not threaten a mother (an adult) and her young. If you come across introduced and feral animals (e.g. foxes, feral pigs, cats, dogs, rats, stoats) report the sightings to Parks management.

When fishing, know the legal fish size and limits. Booklets are available from the relevant State or Territory Government offices. In Australia, report illegal fishing via the illegal fishing hot line (13-FISH). Do not discard tangled or unwanted fishing line but carry it out as rubbish.

Fungus

A destructive micro-organism to flora is the pathogen *Phytophtora*. The Phytophtora is generally unobservable to the human eye but its destructive effect on susceptible flora is not. The name derives from two Greek words, *phyto* meaning 'plant' and *phthora* meaning 'destruction'. The first species to be identified *Phytophtora infestans* was responsible for the potato famine in Ireland during the mid-nineteenth century.

There are some 200 identified species to the genus Phytophtora worldwide. Strictly speaking the genus is not a fungi but a water mould, but is still referred to in literature as a fungi. Another name for Phytophtora is *root rot*. Other variations to the names may involve the use of the species name or its affect; for example Phytophthora cinnamon, which is found in Tasmania, is also known as *cinnamon fungus, jarrah dieback* and *wild flower dieback*.

There is little that can be done to prevent the natural spread of the micro-organism other than controls put in place by horticultural organisations and government services. To control one mechanism of movement, campers are asked to be aware of the micro-organism and areas where it has infected the flora, in order to prevent its spread by human contact into uncontaminated areas. Before setting out on a trip and before returning home wash down and clean equipment and footwear. When out in the wilderness, follow basic hygiene protocols.

Freshwater Pathogens and Pests

In Australia and New Zealand, native freshwater habitat is under threat from freshwater pests and pathogens including *Batrachochytrium dendrobatidis* (Chytrid frog disease), *Mucor amphibiorum* (platypus Mucor disease) and the freshwater algal pest *Didymosphenia geminata* (Didymo).

Mucor disease is caused by a native mainland fungus (*Mucor amphibiorum*). Since its introduction into Tasmania, circa 1982, it affects the platypus population there with a deadly ulcerative infection.

Didymo (aka *rock snot*) is a freshwater algae. It has not yet been found in Australia (which includes Tasmania) but there is a high risk that it may be introduced from overseas in fishing and other freshwater recreational equipment. The algae is now found in New Zealand's South Island waters. Didymo does not grow in waterways where the mean winter air temperature is above 5 degrees Celsius, but in susceptible areas, it takes only one cell in a single drop of water for the algae to spread between waterways. The algae attaches to rocks and submerged plants where it rapidly multiplies and spreads. It forms thick brown blooms that completely smother waterways and destroys habitat. Once established it is impossible to eradicate. To prevent spreading these and other pathogens and pests, follow hygiene and disease control measures for the areas you are visiting and returning from.

WILD LIFE

Croc wise strategies

The Estuarine crocodile (*Crocodylus porosus*) is found in Sri Lanka, India, Burma, South-East Asia, Indonesia, New Guinea, the Solomon Islands, Vanuatu, Australia and the Caroline Islands. Ocean going crocodiles have landed in Fiji (RR, 1987). Along the Australian coast, they are found from Port Headland in Western Australia upwards across the Top End and down the Queensland coast to Gladstone. In Australia they are a protected animal and cannot be hunted.

Crocodylus porosus is the largest living reptile in the world. Its common names are estuarine crocodile, saltwater c., 'Saltie', Indo-Pacific c. The common names are misleading, since estuarine crocodiles are not restricted to salty or brackish water of tidal rivers but are also found far inland in freshwater billabongs, rivers and swamps. *C. porous* can tolerate salinities ranging from 0 per cent (freshwater) to 35 per cent in full strength sea water, and have even been recorded in water twice as saline (70%) as sea water (Beatson, 2010).

Estuarine Crocodiles are active throughout the year. They are highly territorial, and intolerant of other members of their species. Large crocodiles (i.e. 2 m or bigger) are considered dangerous to people. During the breeding season large males will travel vast distances in search of a mate and are a threat to people.

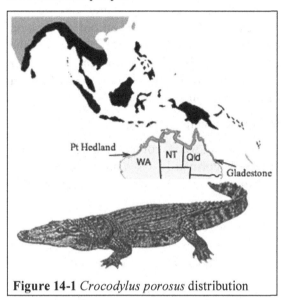

Figure 14-1 *Crocodylus porosus* distribution

Crocodylus porosus will travel great distances over land between waterways and or water sources and to feed on carrion. Though it travels slowly over land, at around 3 to 4 kilometres per hour, it is capable of fast bursts of speed (up to 17 km/h), but quickly becomes exhausted.

Crocodiles are an opportunistic ambush hunter, preferring to hunt at night. They will eat anything that they can overpower and kill. Crocodiles have excellent above water and under water vision and a keen sense of smell. Sensory pits along the outside of their jaw and on the inside of their mouth, can detect minute changes in water pressure. When attacking, it can launch half of its body length up an embankment or out of the water at speeds up to 60 km/h.

Animals over 2 metres eat just about anything that comes into range e.g. lizards, fruit bats, wallabies, kangaroos, domestic animals, sharks, fish, feral pigs and cats, water buffalo and other crocodiles. Crocodiles over 3 metres (~10 ft) will not hesitate to take people (Billabong Santuary, n.d.).

It is a myth that the animal prefers to eat rotting flesh. When it has eaten it's full of a prey, it abandons the carcass, which drifts off and possibly becomes lodged in river debris and or mangroves. It does not deliberately stuff the carcass somewhere to rot before eating. If it does return to the carcass, researchers think that the animal is after the fish and other vertebrates feeding there. After killing its prey the crocodile will eat its fill and then in an orderly fashion other crocodiles will feed on the remains. If the crocodile has a lair under an embankment it may return with it there but will only eat its fill then discard the remains.

Risk management strategies

The following is a compilation from several sources but primarily based on the advice given by Animal Health Australia. If in doubt consult state and territory regulatory bodies.

All estuarine crocodiles are potentially dangerous. Obtain knowledge about the environment and of risk situations contained in it.

Never take unnecessary risks in crocodile habitat. You are responsible for your own safety.

It must be assumed that any body of water in northern Australia may contain large and potentially dangerous estuarine crocodiles.

Estuarine crocodiles live mainly in tidal reaches of rivers, as well as in fresh water sections of lagoons, swamps and waterways up to hundreds of kilometers from the sea, but most often within 100 kilometres of the coast. They can even occur along some beaches and around offshore islands.

Estuarine crocodiles are ambush hunters. Do not assume that a shallow pool, drainage canal or even a ditch is safe, especially if the water is muddy.

Do not allow pet dogs to roam near the water. Supervise children at all times and explain the dangers.

Estuarine crocodiles camouflage themselves well in lagoons, swamps and waterways. Every care must be taken when travelling in these areas, especially when walking in tall grass. If crunching sounds in the undergrowth are heard, leave the area immediately.

Estuarine crocodiles are most active at night. Do not walk around at night without a torch if fishing or camping near water.

Estuarine crocodiles can be more aggressive during the breeding season, from September to April.

Female crocodiles can be particularly aggressive when defending their nests and young hatchlings. Nesting generally occurs during the wet season.

Obey crocodile warning signs, if present. Never provoke, harass or interfere with crocodiles, even small ones. Never knowingly approach a crocodile.

Minimum safety distance is at least 25 metres, noting that a large crocodile can launch itself from water at speeds up to 60 kilometres per hour. On land they can perform a quick start sprint up to 17 km/h for a short distance.

If camping on a beach, be aware that Estuarine Crocodiles sometimes come ashore at night.

Boats and vehicles must never knowingly be brought within 10 metres of a crocodile.

Never swim or wade through any water in the area where crocodiles may live.

When fishing stand at least 3 metres back from the water's edge, and cut the line if it becomes entangled rather than wade in.

Only cross over rivers at shallow water sites or rocky areas in the narrowest section. Do not cross the river if the water is more than knee deep (30 cm).

Swimming or standing in water above knee-height near a crocodile warning sign or where estuarine crocodiles are frequently seen, is illegal in protected areas (you can still enter the water if you have a reasonable excuse, e.g. launching a boat).

Never dangle your arms or legs over the side of a boat. If you fall out of a boat, get out of the water as quickly as possible.

Never feed crocodiles—it is illegal and dangerous

Avoid sites where carcasses are concentrated, as crocodiles may have congregated in that area.

Camp at least 2 metres above the high water mark and at least 50 metres from the water's edge. Avoid places where native animals and domestic stock drink.

Do not leave or discard rubbish or food scraps, including fish, around your campsite. Be careful other campers have not previously left rubbish or scraps behind.

Do not prepare food, wash dishes or pursue any other activities near the water's edge or adjacent sloping banks.

Do not collect water from the same location every day. Always obtain water from shallow flowing water sites.

If visible or the eyes are shining at night, stand at least a few metres back from the water's edge and do not stand on logs, branches or rocks that overhang deep pools.

Never ride an all terrain vehicle through flood water greater than 0.3 metre. Where ever possible park vehicles at least 5 metres from the water's edge and in a clear area to avoid surprises. Always check for the presence of crocodiles before alighting.

Stay well back from any crocodile slide marks. Slide marks are distinctive bare smooth spots on banks of rivers, lagoons and wetlands where crocodiles habitually haul themselves on shore or slide back into the water. Crocodiles may still be close by and may approach people, boats or vehicles.

Action to take if confronted by aggressive crocodile:

- Safety to self: maintain sight of crocodile while retreating as rapidly as possible, climb a tree or get into a safe place (vehicle).

- Safety to group: raise the alarm and identify location of crocodile to others. Ensure all team members are accounted for and uninjured.

- Safety to others in vicinity—use communications to inform others. Ensure you have the necessary equipment, know where it is and know how to use it (e.g. radios, first aid kit).

Most attacks have occurred on swimmers or on people canoeing or bending down at the water's edge. This low profile seems to elicit a greater predatory response than from a person standing upright, even if in shallow water.

A person seized in the water by an Estuarine Crocodile has little chance of escaping without serious injury, if at all. Resulting wounds are usually horrific and likely to become infected.

For further information refer to the references.

Selected Estuarine Crocodile Attacks

In 1998, a group of NSWSKC members were paddling the Cape York Peninsular, when one of the crew, was attacked by a saltwater crocodile. The attack took place at a beach on Macarthur Island where the crew had stopped and were standing in the clear water of the foreshore. According to Mike Snoad, who was there, the crocodile grabbed Arunus Pilka by the leg and was trying to drag him into deep water. Dave Winkworth, who was naked nearby, ran and jumped on to the crocodile, scaring the reptile away. Arunus had to be medivac out by helicopter.

Bathurst Bay, north Queensland, October 2004 a 4.2 metre, 300 kilogram estuarine crocodile attacked and dragged Andrew Kerr out of his tent after he was woken up. The crocodile grabbed him by the legs while his wife Diane grabbed him and their baby's cot. Alicia Sorohan, a 60-year-old grandmother came to Andrew's rescue and sustained injuries also. It was not until her son Jason, arrived with a firearm, that the predator's attack was stopped.

Cape York Peninsula, April 2005, Jason Lewis who was travelling the world using human powered transport. Paddling from Lizard Island to the mainland, he planned to camp on a sand bar but there were two crocodiles there. Upon seeing him they entered the water and started to follow him and close the distance. To escape the reptiles he landed and ran off up the beach leaving his packed sea kayak behind. He later tried to scare off a crocodile that had remained at his kayak but this only resulted in a damaged paddle. The next day he was able to get to his kayak and get the satellite phone out and call for assistance.

East Alligator River, Northern Territory, April 2005. Geoff Bolitho was fishing in his boat when suddenly a 4 metre saltwater crocodile leaped into his boat and bit him on the head. He survived the attack and resulting injuries.

Pentecost River, in the Kimberley WA, 2005 a couple were woken up in their tent when a crocodile came up and grabbed it. They were able to escape to the roof of their car where they spent the remainder of the night.

Sandy Robinson during her attempted circumnavigation of Australia by sea kayak was attacked by a large estuarine crocodile. The attack took place on June 5, 2007 at Villis Point near Cape Direction far north Queensland. While landing, the crocodile grabbed the kayak's stern, despite the black and yellow diagonal striped painted 'shark proof rudder' said to warn off sharks! Sandy rapidly exited the boat and ran off up the beach to safety. Obviously another colour scheme is needed to warn off estuarine crocodiles.

Shark wise strategies

Sharks seem to capture the imagination of many people. Of the 482 species of shark in the world, 182 are found in Australian waters (ASAF, 2009) and only a few have been known to be involved in unprovoked attacks against people. World wide it is estimated that there are 70 to100 shark attacks resulting in 5 to 15 deaths annually (Burgess). In Australian waters, over the last two centuries, there have been 217 recorded fatal shark attacks (ASAF, 2012).

Shark species known to be dangerous to people from unprovoked attacks include the White Pointer (*Carcharodon carcharias*), Tiger Shark (*Galeocerdo cuvier)* and Bull Shark (*Carcharhinus leucas*). Sharks categorised as potentially dangerous to people, due to their size, are the Wobbegong (*Orectolobus sp.*), Hammerhead (*Sphyrna sp.*), Blue Shark (*Prionace glauca.*), Mako (*Isurus sp.*), and Grey Nurse Shark (*Carcharias taurus)*.

Many of the attacks on people occur near shore with numerous mauling's occurring on swimmers, spear fishermen, divers and surfers. There have also been several reported occasions where a shark has nudged a kayaker into the water, or bitten the stern or hull of a kayak.

There are several theories why these wild animals attack people. What is disputed is that these creatures deliberately target people as a food source. Considering the amount of attacks, both fatal and non-fatal, over the last two hundred years in Australian waters, and the increased numbers of people entering the shark's environment, the yearly statistical average for fatality by shark attack is one per cent (1.06%) (ASAF, 2009).

The mechanism for why people get attacked is not clearly understood. However, it is the animal's size and ability to inflict massive wounds on people that make it a potential dangerous animal. For example, when sharks feed off a dead whale, they often excise enormous chunks of flesh. Often, on people, the animal only bites the victim once. Unfortunately the power of the jaws, size of teeth and force of impact, result in lacerations, incisions, avulsions and amputations, leading to massive blood loss and shock.

Several theories abound as to why these wild creatures perform unprovoked attacks on humans and may involve one or more of the following thoughts. It is thought that the animal is being inquisitive and testing the object for edibility. It is responding to territorial invasion, or it may be related to the invasion of the shark's personal space. The shark may have been disrupted during its breeding behaviour. Some attacks may be directly associated with feeding behaviours. Some authors have suggested that only rogue sharks or injured sharks attack humans, however, there is no scientific evidence to support this theory (ASAF, 2009).

With the depletion of marine creatures through poor fishing practices, both commercial and recreational, many countries have moved to protect certain orders and species. Concerning the white shark, South Africa created legislation to protect the animal in 1992 followed by Namibia, the Maldives, Malta, and the United States (California and Florida). In 1996 the International Union for the Conservation of Nature (IUCN) listed the white shark as vulnerable. In New Zealand the white shark is protected under the Fisheries Act 1996 and Wildlife Act 1953. In 1997, the Australian white shark was place under protection by the Commonwealth Endangered Species Protection Act. Currently, the white shark is listed as a threatened species under the Environmental Protection and Biodiversity Conservation Act 1999.

White shark (Carcharodon carcharias)

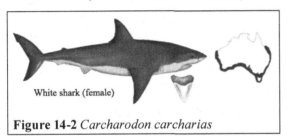

White shark (female)

Figure 14-2 *Carcharodon carcharias*

The white shark (*Carcharodon carcharias*; family Lamnidae i.e. Mackerel sharks) is found throughout the world in temperate and subtropical oceans, all major basins and the Mediterranean Sea.[1] White sharks appear to prefer waters with a temperature of 15 to 22 degrees Celsius but the temperature range can be between 4 to 27 degrees Celsius (CCSA, n.d.). They have been recorded in tropical waters including the Coral Sea, New Caledonia, central Pacific, northern Brazil and the south-west Indian Ocean. White sharks are uncommon in Australian waters but there are areas where encounters appear to be more frequent (MCBEA, 2002). Around Australia, the species has been reported in the coastal waters of all states. However, predominantly their range extends from southern Queensland (Rockhampton), around the southern coastline of New South Wales, Victoria, Tasmania, Bass Straight Islands, South Australia (SA) through to the North West Cape in Western Australia

(WA).[2] Individual white sharks have been tracked travelling from South Africa to Western Australia and from South Australia to New Zealand.

Great white sharks have a torpedo-shaped body with a pointed snout and large non-nictitating black eyes. The nostrils are located on the underside and forward of the mouth and open outwards. It is claimed, that they can smell a drop of blood in 100 litres (25 gallons) of water and detect the source up to 5 kilometres (3 miles) away (Nation Geographic, n.d.). Their mouth contains 5 to 7 rows of large (up to 76.2 mm or 3 inches), serrated triangular teeth. The teeth are arranged on what can be described as a conveyor belt that replaces lost teeth. The upper jaw has tooth positions for 24 to 26 teeth and the lower jaw 22 to 24 teeth. A 6 metre animal is reported to have a bite force of 18 kilonewtons (kN). It has five gill slits per side. White sharks possess large pectoral and first dorsal fins, then very small second dorsal and anal fins. Their body has a distinct caudal keel before the broad crescent shaped vertical tail. The top lobe of the tail is slightly larger than the lower. The dorsal colouring can vary from grey, grey-brown to bronze with some specimens possessing rare colouring of almost black to bluish. Their lower ventral surface displays a sudden change to white.

Females reach larger sizes than males, growing to a possible 6 metres, attaining a weight of 3000 kilograms and may reach an age of 50 to 60 years. Individual sharks of about 5 metres in length are estimated to be 15 to 25 years old. The average size is reported to be 3.7 to 4.9 metres. The biggest white shark accurately measured was a 6.1 metre female, caught in 1988 at Prince Edward Island in the North Atlantic off Canada (RFSE, n.d.).

Females do not reproduce until they are at least 4.5 to 5 metres in length and at an estimated age of between 12 to 17 years. In contrast to most fish, which spawn millions of eggs each year, fertilization is internal with a gestation period estimated to be 12 months (but possibly 18 months), leading to the birth of relatively few pups (between 2 and 17) each time.[3] It is thought that they do not breed every year but only once every 2 to 3 years. The CSIRO warns that with low reproduction rates the white shark populations are vulnerable to human interference and would recover very slowly if reduced in abundance.

The white shark's diet is varied and ranges from pelagic and demersal finfish, sea turtles, marine mammals (seals, sea lions, dolphins, dead whales and sea otters) and some invertebrates such as squid and crustaceans.[4] Juvenile white sharks (less than 3 metres) feed primarily on squid, fish, stingrays and other sharks. When the sharks reach 3 to 4 metres in length, marine mammals, where available, appear to become included in the diet. Although in some areas, large white sharks will continue to prey on fish such as snapper, salmon, mackerel, tuna and other sharks. It is suggested that the migration of fish stocks are what cause the white shark to follow a set migration path. The eating of sea mammals such as seals at the various colonies is more akin to a "Maccas stop", while the shark makes its way to its hunting grounds for fish stocks (Stranard, 2010). In Westernport, the main driver for the seasonal appearance of white sharks is due to seasonal fish stocks despite there being an Australian fur-seal breeding colony at Seal Rocks off Phillip Island. In South Australian waters the Australian sea-lion and New Zealand fur-seals are the main pray (CCSA, n.d.). Due to the size and rich nutritious content of sea mammal blubber, the white shark needs only to feed infrequently. However, being endothermic it requires 10 times more food than its cold blooded counterpart (RFSE, n.d.).

Carcharodon carcharias, though uncommon, is credited with most attacks on people. The animal is found in coastal and shelf waters but is most likely to be encountered around coastal waters inhabited by pinnipeds and around offshore reefs. For kayakers, Kent Stranard of White Tag, "strongly recommends" they avoid places like Lady Percy Julia Island and Seal Rocks as this is a known "Maccas stop" for white sharks. As a danger to people, in Australia, it is credited with the most unprovoked attacks.

White sharks are close relatives to the mako and porbeagle sharks They are occasionally mistaken for the mako shark, but the short fin mako's upper body is metallic blue with a snow white underside. The long fin mako is a blue-black with a white underside. Makos possess long slender pointed teeth, as opposed to the white sharks triangular teeth.

Tiger shark (Galeocerdo cuvier)

Tiger sharks (*Galeocerdo cuvier*) are found worldwide in warm tropical and subtropical seas, where they inhabit both shorelines and open waters well off the continental shelf.[5] They have been found at depths of 150 metres.[6] In Australia, they are found in the waters off southern NSW (mainly in summer), upwards and across northern Australia and down the west Australian coast to Perth. The species is most active at night, when it comes closer inshore or nearer the surface. Individual tiger sharks have proven to undertake long migrations. One specimen in a three month period, travelled from the Australian coral reef to Papua New Guinea, then to the Gulf of Carpentaria where it was caught (NSW DPI, 2007).

The tiger shark's head has a broad snout with the body possessing tiger-like, striped markings on a dark, grey-brown dorsal with off-white underbelly. Other colourings range from pale to dark grey or blue-grey. Juveniles display dark vertical bar markings, which fade in larger specimens. It is distinguished by a long tapered tail. The teeth are heavily saw-edged, cockscomb shaped and the same in both upper and lower jaws. The razor sharp teeth possess coarse serrations, which have fine secondary serrations.

Tiger shark

Figure 14-3 Galeocerdo cuvier

Both male and female tiger sharks grow at similar rates and may reach 6 meters in length.

Most encountered individuals range between 3.4 to 4.3 metres in length. Male maturity range is from around 3 metres (2.26–2.9 m and may reach 3.7 m). Females are larger than males, maturing between 2.87 to 3.3 metres. In 1957 a female was caught and measured as being 7.4 metres (24 ft.) and weighing 1414 kilograms (3,110 lbs.) (Shark Research Institute, Inc, 2005).

Tiger sharks are lecithotrophic viviparous, whereby the young develop from internal eggs after internal fertilisation. Litter sizes vary from 10 to 80 pups with an average litter size of 35. Breeding usually occurs in summer every two years. Pups when born, range in size from 50 to 75 centimetre. Pups born off Townsville, in Queensland, are born as large as 80 to 90 centimetres.

This animal is a true opportunistic scavenger, taking a wide range of prey. Primarily fish and reptiles, including both sea snakes and turtles. Other commonly found prey, are mammals (primarily cetacea i.e. dolphins and porpoises) and dugongs. Other reported food items include clams, jellyfish, sea birds, other sharks, various livestock such as cattle, horses, dogs, chickens and people. It would appear that just about anything they can catch alive or find dead, as well as a variety of inanimate flotsam items can be eaten. Flotsam and jetsam found to have been eaten include a coil of copper wire, nuts, bolts, lumps of coal, boat cushions, clothing, a Senegalese native drum, an unopened can of salmon, driftwood, cans of paint and cigarette packets.

Its occurrence in shallow water, where recreational water users are found, along with its indiscriminate diet and large size, make it one of the most dangerous sharks. However, divers have found them to be inquisitive and circle the divers. Others have swum with the animals and not been attacked. In the book *Sharks Silent hunters of the deep*, Ron and Valerie Taylor share their thoughts and experiences with these creatures, in the chapter titled *Not All Sharks Are Killers*. Valerie writes:

"*. . . his* (a 3.5 m tiger shark) *behaviour confirmed what we have known for years: that sharks, even dangerous ones, are far more intelligent than is generally believed. If handled in the right way, they will perform in a manner that shows that they have at least as much ability to comprehend a situation as many land animals do"* (Reader's Digest, 1990, p. 128).

Bull shark (Carcharhinus leucas)

Bull sharks *(Carcharhinus leucas)*, are also known in Australia as: river whaler, freshwater whaler, estuary whaler, Swan River whaler.[7] The term whaler was given to a variety of species from their habit of despoiling whale catches, in the early days of Australian and New Zealand whaling (Reader's Digest, 1990, p. 176). In other parts of the world the common names for this widely dispersed animal are: cub s, Ganges s, river s, Zambezi s, shovelnose, slipway grey s, square-nose s, Van Rooyen's s (Reader's Digest, 1990, p. 176).

This widely distributed shark is found along coastlines in tropical and subtropical oceans. In Australia it is found from the NSW central coast upwards and across the Top End and down to Perth. Their distribution extends south to Sydney during the warmer summer months and to at least Wollongong (NSW DPI, 2008). It is the only widely distributed shark that has been found to penetrate far into fresh water, for extended periods, where it sometimes breeds. In South America it has been found thousands of kilometres up the Amazon River. In Nicaragua it has been reported to leap out of the water to navigate rapids (like salmon), to reach Lake Nicaragua (National Geographic, 2010).

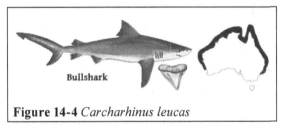

Figure 14-4 *Carcharhinus leucas*

The Bull Shark can be recognised through a combination of characteristics including a stout body, small eyes and a short snout that is broader than it is long, lending to its name. The teeth are triangular, with sharp serrated edges. Their top surface is grey with a usually off-white belly colouring, sometimes with a pale stripe on the flank. The adults do not possess fin markings. The species has a second dorsal fin about one third the height of the first, and no skin ridge between the two dorsal fins. (McGrouther, 2010).

Adults can range from 2 to 3.5 metres in length and weigh from 90 to 230 kilograms. Females normally give birth in estuaries and river mouths to young that range in size from 55 to 80 centimetres. The juveniles can remain in the river for up to 5 years. It is a dangerous shark due to its aggressive nature, powerful jaws, broad diet, abundance, and its habitat preference for shallow, murky inshore waters. (NSW DPI, 2005). Bull sharks have an omnivorous diet, which includes fish, other sharks and rays, turtles, birds, molluscs, crustaceans, dolphins and terrestrial animals.

Risk management strategies

Some risk management strategies, as identified by Australian Shark Attack File, are:

Do not swim, dive or surf where dangerous sharks are known to congregate.

Always swim, dive or surf with other people.

Do not swim in dirty or turbid water; waters with known effluents or sewage.

Avoid swimming well offshore, near deep channels, canals; swimming or surfing in or at river/harbour mouths; or along drop-offs to deeper water; be aware that sharks may be present between sandbars or near steep drop offs.

Do not rely on sightings of dolphins to indicate the absence of sharks; both often feed together on the same food.

Avoid areas with signs of baitfish or fish feeding activity; diving seabirds are a good indicator of fish activity; if schooling fish start to behave erratically or congregate in large numbers, leave the water.

Do not swim with pets and domestic animals.

Look carefully before jumping into the water from a boat or wharf.

If possible do not swim a dusk or at night.

Do not swim near people fishing (commercial and recreational) or spear fishing.

If a shark is sighted in the area leave the water as quickly and calmly as possible.

Snake wise strategies

There are between 2500 to 3000 species of snake world wide; divided into 47 families.[8] Snakes are found on every continent of the earth, except Antarctica. They range in latitude northwards of the Artic Circle in Scandinavia down to Tasmania in Australia. Countries that do not have terrestrial snake populations include New Zealand, Greenland, Iceland, and Ireland. Venomous snakes are not found in Chile, Madagascar, Polynesia, New Caledonia, Cuba, Haiti, Jamaica and Puerto Rico (FM 21-17).

Within the 47 families, there are around 600 species of snake considered to be venomous.[9] These species are found only in the following five families *Atractaspidae*, *Colubridae*, *Elapidae*, *Hydrophiidae* and *Viperidae*.

In Australia, through the destruction of natural habitat, introduced pests, both flora and fauna, and ignorance, several species of snake are at risk, with some even being listed through the Environment Protection and Biodiversity Conservation Act 1999 (EPBC Act) as Critically Endangered. In Australia all species of snake are a protected animal, which means you cannot kill them. In the USA 10 species are listed as threatened and seven species listed as endangered under the Endangered Species Act.

Snakes are generally shy creatures and avoid confrontation unless provoked. However there are a few venomous snakes (mainly Asian vipers) that are described as irritable and aggressive. When reviewing the multitude of literature available about snakes, the majority of bites in the West were on intoxicated males trying to capture or kill the creature. Access to medical facilities and treatment also reduces the possibility of mortality from a potentially lethal bite. This can be seen in the death rates from snake bite in Asia compared to the West.

The World Health Organisation (WHO) estimates that venomous snakes bite around 2.5

million people worldwide each year, resulting in 125 000 deaths. Asia has the highest incidents of fatal envenomation with around 100 000 cases, followed by Africa with around 20 000 cases annually. However the true incidence is unclear, under reported and misunderstood (Cruz et al).

Terrestrial snakes

In Australia there are around 140 identified species of land snake and 32 species of sea snake. It is thought that out of all of the Australian species, 12 can inflict a potentially lethal bite. Each year in Australia, it is estimated that between 500 to 3000 people are bitten by snakes in Australia (Isbister, G.K.). However the true incidence is unclear. Of the reported incidents perhaps 300 require treatment with antivenom. Surveys suggest that around 3 to 4 people die each year from snake bite (ARVU). Statistically the majority of defensive snake bites are 'dry bites' whereby the snake does not envenomate its protagonist. Figures show that there is a 20 to 60 per cent possibility of envenomation except for the taipan (ARVU). Taipans envenomate nearly every time they bite defensively.

All of Australia's venomous snakes are from the family *Elapidae*. The Australian land snake species of major medical interest are *Pseudonaja texilis* (eastern brown snake), *Pseudonaja nuchalis* (gwardar aka western brown snake), *Pseudonaja affinis* (dugite), *Notechis scutatus* (common or mainland tiger snake), *Notechis ater* (black or island tiger snake), *Oxyuranus scutellatus* (coastal taipan), *Pseudechis guttatus* (blue-bellied black snake aka spotted black snake), *Pseudechis australis* (mulga snake aka king brown snake), *Pseudechis porphyriacus* (red-bellied black snake), *Acanthophis sp.* (e.g. common death adder *Acanthophis antarticus*), *Austrelaps sp.* (i.e. Australian copperheads: lowlands copperhead (*Austrelaps superbus*), highlands copperhead (*A. ramsayi*), pygmy copperhead (*A. labialis*)), *Tropidechis carinatus* (Clarence River snake).

Snakes of medical interest to the north of Australia and the islands are *Acanthopis sp.* (death adders), *Oxyuranus sp.* (taipan), *Pseudnaja sp.* (black snakes). In the Indonesian archipelago and South-East Asia, snakes of interest include *Bungarus sp.* (kraits), *Vipera sp.* (vipers) and in Asia the *Naja sp.* (cobras). Snakes of interest in Africa in addition to some Asian distributed vipers are *Bitis arietans* (puff adder). From the family *Elapidae*, *Dendroaspis sp.* (mamba snakes) and from the family *Colubridae*, *Dispholidus typus* (boomslang snake). In the Americas the majority of potentially lethal snakes belong to the family *Viperidae*. Of note are *Agkistrodon contortix* (American copperhead), *Lachesis mutus* (Bushmaster), *Bothrops atrox* (Fer-de-lance), and the *Crotalus species* (rattlesnakes). In North America the majority (75 per cent) of snake bites are from the *Crotalus* species.

A common species of snake that you may come across in Australian rain forest are pythons, from the family *Boidae*. These inoffensive animals can often be seen sunning themselves in the available light on the forest floor or just nonchalantly moving along the forest floor or foliage. Non-venomous snake bites may lead to localised severe infection, due to the bacteria from the reptiles mouth.

Aquatic Snakes

Decades ago when I was working up in Far North Queensland, I was told that all sea snakes, though highly venomous and inquisitive have small fangs at the rear of their mouths and can only bite your fingers, if provoked. This statement is not entirely true.

True sea snakes live and reproduce primarily in tropical seas. These aquatic reptiles belong to the family *Hydrophiidae*.[10] Of the 54 currently identified species, 32 species live and breed in Australian tropical waters. Species in this family are thought to have derived from terrestrial snakes belonging to the family *Elapidae*. Like other *elapidae* they are referred to as *proteroglypha*, that is, snakes having paired permanently erect (i.e. fixed) fangs that precede the other teeth of the upper jaw.

These creatures are generally found around reefs and are described as very curious and attracted to light. They are also fascinated by elongated objects like high-pressure air hoses on SCUBA air tanks (Campbell). They are described as aggressive only during the mating season, which for the Australian species is in winter. Provoked sea snakes become very aggressive and persistent requiring repeated 'kick-offs' with dive fins (Campbell).

A genus of *Hydrophiidae* is *Laticauda (sea kraits)*.[11] Unlike their terrestrial namesakes, sea kraits are regarded as docile and non-aggressive, as indeed are the majority of *Hydrophiidae* species. Sea Kraits are also terrestrial and come ashore to digest their food, shed their skin, mate and lay their eggs.

The majority of recorded bites on humans are fishermen, who while clearing their fishing nets of entangled sea snakes, get bitten on rare occasions. Like venomous snakes from the family *elapidae*, sea snakes have the ability to control envenomation. Though sea snake venom is highly toxic, a defensive bite may be a 'dry bite' whereby the victim is not envenomated.

Risk management strategies

Some risk management strategies are:

Do not threaten or make a snake feel threatened.

- Do not corner or trap a snake.

- Do not try to catch a snake.

Be vigilant when walking through the bush or along a track.

Be vigilant around water sources.

Wear appropriate clothing in areas where snakes are usually found (e.g. enclosed footwear, gaiters)

Do not step over a fallen tree or log before looking to see if the obscured side is clear.

Be vigilant when picking up firewood.

When moving a log or an item like a piece of sheet corrugated iron, pick the item up by rolling or lifting it towards your body. Endeavour to keep the base of the item in contact with the ground at your feet. The gap will be facing away from your legs. The lifted item will act as a barrier between you and any startled snake.

When camping, during the day roll up your sleeping bag. Keep your tent zipped up.

Pinnipeds

There are thirty-five species of seal that inhabit the world's oceans, from polar waters to tropical waters. In Australian waters, there are ten recorded pinniped species. The first five species are classed in the family *Otariidae* (eared seals) with only one species being endemic, the Australian sea-lion. The remaining five are classed in the family *Phocidae* (earless or true seals).[12]

Three species, the Australian sea-lion (*Neophoca cinerea*), New Zealand fur-seal (*Arctocephalus forsteri*) and Australian fur-seal (*Arctocephalus pusillus doriferus*), breed on the coast of the Australian mainland, Bass Straight islands, Tasmania and its near shore islands. A further three species, the Antarctic fur-seal (*Arctocephalus Gazelle*), Subantarctic fur-seal (*Arctocephalus tropicalis*) and southern elephant seal (*Mirounga leonine*) breed on the Australian Subantarctic islands of Macquarie Island, Heard Island and the McDonald Islands. The last four species: leopard seal (*Hydrurga leptonyx*), crabeater seal (*Lobodon carcinophagus*), Ross seal (*Ommatophoca rossii*) and Weddell seal (*Leptonychotes weddellii*) breed in Antarctic waters. The Ross seal (*Ommatophoca rossii*) is found on pack ice and the Weddell seal (*Leptonychotes weddellii*) is found on fast ice adjacent to the Antarctic mainland. Leopard seals (*Hydrurga leptonyx*) and Elephant seals (*Mirounga leonine*) are frequent visitors to Tasmania.

Seals are grouped as either otariid (aka eared seals) or phocids (aka true seals). Otariid seals have obvious ears, large fore-flippers and hind flippers, which bend forward. These mammals use their flippers to walk on land. Included in this family are fur seals and sea lions. Phocids have less distinguishable ears, relatively small fore-flippers and cannot turn their hind flippers forward. To move on land, these mammals 'hump' their way along the ground on their bellies.

This article will deal with the three species of pinniped most likely to be encountered by sea kayakers. The New Zealand fur-seal (*A, forsteri*), Australian fur-seal (*A. p. doriferus*) and the Australian sea-lion (*Neophoca cinerea*). If paddling in Tasmania you may also encounter transient southern elephant seals (*Mirounga leonine*) and or leopard seals (Hydrurga leptonyx).

New Zealand fur-seal

New Zealand fur-seal
(*Arctocephalus forsteri*)
Population: ~57 400 (1999)
Conservation status: Lower risk, conservation dependant
Diet: Feed primarily on fish and cephalopods, also seabirds (incl. little penguins)
Longevity: Male: 15 years; female: 26 years
Adult weight: Males 120–180 kg; females 35–50 kg
Adult size: Males 150–250 cm; females 100–150 cm
Mating season: Mid-November-mid-January
Gestation: 8–9 months
Sexual maturity: Females: 6 years;
Males hold territories at about 9 years of age
Pupping season: Late November to mid-January
Pupping interval: 1 year
Birth weight and size: 4–6 kg, 60–70 cm
Weaning: 8–12 months

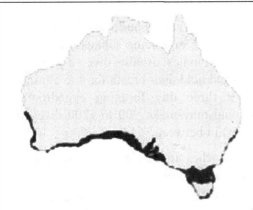

Table 14-1 New Zealand fur-seals

The New Zealand fur-seal (*Arctocephalus forsteri*) is also known as the 'South Australian fur-seal' and 'long-nosed fur-seal'. Most of the Australian population (77%) is located in central South Australian waters from Kangaroo Island to the southern Eyre Peninsula. A. Forsteri breed in New Zealand, along the south coasts of Western Australia and South Australia, and at Maatsuyker Island, off south-west Tasmania. Recently, it has been reported that A. Forsteri have established small breeding populations on several islands in Bass Strait. Non-breeding A. Forsteri have been reported in the Perth metropolitan area of WA, along the east Australian coast particularly

at Montague Island in NSW, Queensland south of Fraser Island and even in New Caledonia. It is suspected that A. Forsteri travelled to the east coast sites from either South Australia or New Zealand. However, there is only one authenticated case of a trans-Tasman crossing in 1994. Tagging evidence would suggest migration from South Australian waters to the east coast sites. The preferred habitats of New Zealand fur seals are rocky parts of islands with jumbled terrain and boulders.

The New Zealand fur-seal (A. forsteri) can be distinguished from the Australian fur seal (A. pusillus doriferus) by its uniformly darker coat colour, high pitched call as opposed the Australian fur seal's deep bark and relatively long pointed nose and smaller body size. Additionally, both species move differently on land, with the New Zealand fur seal using an observed "hopping" motion, with fore-flippers moving simultaneously. The Australian fur seal moves with an observed "waddling/rocking" from side to side motion, as it moves one fore-flipper independently of the other.

Australian fur-seal

The Australian fur-seal (*Arctocephalus pusillus doriferus*) is also known as the 'Tasmanian fur-seal' and 'giant fur seal'. *A. p. doriferus* is found from the coast of NSW, down around Tasmania to Victoria and South Australia. Breeding colonies of Australian fur seals are restricted to Bass Strait with four colonies on islands off the Victorian coast and five on islands off the Tasmanian coastline. The largest breeding colonies are at Lady Julia Percy Island and Seal Rocks at Phillip Island in Victoria, and at Judgement Rocks and Reid Rocks in Tasmania. It is the most common seal in Tasmanian waters and breeds on small isolated rocks in Bass Strait between October and January. Haul-out sites extend from southern Tasmania through the Bass Straight islands into southern NSW (Montague Island and Steamers Head, Jervis Bay) and Kangaroo Island in South Australia. In Victoria the animals can be found at Cape Bridgewater, Apollo Bay, Port Phillip Bay, the islands around Wilsons Promontory and the Skerries. Australian fur seals typically inhabit rocky parts of islands with flat, open terrain. They occupy flatter areas than New Zealand fur seals at sites where they both occur.

Australian fur-seal
(*Arctocephalus pusillus doriferus*)
Population: ~92 000 (1999)
Conservation status: Lower risk, conservation dependant
Diet: Feed primarily on fish and cephalopods, also seabirds
Longevity: Males > 19 years; females > 21 years
Adult weight: Males 218–360 kg, Av. 279 kg; females 41–113 kg, Av. 78 kg
Adult size: Males 201–227 cm, Av. 216 cm; females 136–171 cm, Av. 157 cm
Sexual maturity: Females: 3–6 years; males hold territories at 8–13 years of age
Mating season: November-January
Gestation: 8–9 months
Pupping season: late October to late December
Pupping interval: 1 year
Birth: Live young
Birth weight and size: 5–12 kg, 60–80 cm
Weaning: 10–12 months

Table 14-2 Australian fur-seals

Australian sea-lion

The Australian sea-lion (*Neophoca cinerea*) is also known as the 'hair seal'. *Neophoca cinerea* inhabit breeding areas from Houtman Abrolhos (near Geraldton), WA, through the Australian Bight, Ayre Peninsular to The Pages east of Kangaroo Island, SA. About 30 per cent of the population is in WA and the remainder in SA. Unlike the two species of fur-seal discussed, they have a wide spread distribution of small colonies. Unlike *A. forsteri* they prefer sheltered sides of islands, bays and sandy beaches.

Both sexes of *Neophoca cinerea* have stocky bodies, a large head and short narrow flippers.

Apart from their size, the sexes are easily identified by coat colour. The male has dark brown fur with mane-like yellow areas on the neck and top of the head. The females have a silver grey to fawn coloured fur on the back and creamy coloured underneath. Pups are born with a chocolate brown fur, which is lost after the first moulting phase. They have a second layer of fur under the top fur layer, which helps them to keep warm in the cold water, together with a thick layer of fat. They are described as being a very social animal and gather in groups of 10 to 15 and can be observed spending time sunbaking on sandy beaches and rocks.

Sea-lions are hosts to a number of internal and external parasites. Internal parasites consist of tape worms, fluke worms, round worms and mites. External parasites consist of lice. The presence of lice in the coats of the animals is the reason for the scratching commonly observed.

When hunting, a male bull was recorded diving to 270 metres and being submerged for seven minutes. Females usually dive to around 80 metres and hold their breath for 4 to 5 minutes. Over a three day foraging expedition an individual may make 900 to 1200 dives with little rest in between.

Sandy beaches are the preferred places for the Australian sea-lion to come ashore. However, it is in the rocky areas where breeding occurs. Pups are born in gullies or crevices in the rocky sections of the beach.

Neophoca cinerea unlike other mammals, do not have an annual breeding cycle. They breed over a 5 to 7 month period every 17½ months, with some reports of a two to three year break between births. In one year they may breed in summer and the following breeding period will be winter. Breeding cycles and periods also vary greatly between different colonies, as the various colonies are breeding at different times of the year. During breeding males do not form harems but do aggressively guard the area where the breeding female is. Bulls may stay ashore for four weeks during this time. Females jealously guard their pups however males are responsible for pup mortality. Mothers (aka cows) can be away at sea for around three days foraging for food before returning to their pups.

Australian sea-lion
(*Neophoca cinerea*)
Population: ~ 10 000–12 000
Conservation status: Lower risk, near threatened as male numbers < 10 000 (1999)
Diet: Feed primarily on fish, sharks, rock lobsters, cephalopods and seabirds
Longevity: 17–25 years
Adult weight: Males to 300 kg; females 61–104 kg, Av. 77 kg
Adult size: Males 200–250 cm; females 132–181 cm
Sexual maturity: Females: 4–6 years; males 8–9 years of age
Mating season: Over 5 months
Gestation: 12 months
Pupping season: 5–7 months; anywhere from January to June
Pupping interval: 17–18 months up to 36 months
Birth: Live young
Birth weight and size: 6.4–7.9 kg, 62–68 cm
Weaning: 15–18 months

Table 14-3 Australian sea-lions

Risk management strategies

The biggest threat to the above aforementioned adult otariid is death caused either accidentally or deliberately (and therefore illegally) by commercial fisherman and their equipment.

As a threat to kayakers, be aware that they will attack and have trashed kayaks. When viewing these animals Parks and Wildlife Tasmania set the following guidelines:

Do lower sails when closer than 200 metres to haulouts.

Do not approach within 100 metres if circumnavigating, 200 metres between mid-October and mid-January.

Do anchor more than 50 metres away from the haulout, 100 metres away between mid-October and mid-January.

Do not swim near the shoreline as bulls hold territories during the breeding season.

Do anchor downwind and refrain from making loud noises.

Do not get on the haulout. Panicking seals can easily attack or run over visitors and haulouts are very slippery to walk on.

---

1 Kingdom: Animalia, Phylum: Chordata, Subphylum: Vertebrata (fishes, amphibians, reptiles, birds, mammals), Class: Chondrichthyes (Gk: chondro = cartilage; ichthys = fish; cartilaginous fishes: rays, sharks and relatives), Subclass: Elasmobranchs (sharks and rays), Superorder: Euselachii (Gk: eu - true and selachos - shark), Order: Lamniformes (mackerel sharks), Family: Lamnidae (mackerel sharks, porbeagles and white sharks), Genus: Carcharodon (from the Greek karcharos—sharpend and odious—teeth), Species: Carcharodon carcharias.
2 MCBEA, 2002, A white shark has been reported as far as Mackay, QLD.
3 Note the maximum number of 17 is at variance with all articles reviewed, with 10 being the most consistent maximum number cited.
4 Pelagic fish live in the water column of coastal, ocean and lake waters, but not on the bottom. Demersal fish live on or near the bottom of the sea or lakes.
5 Order: Carcharhiniformes; Family: Carcharhinidae (Requiem sharks); Genus: Galeocerdo, Species: cuvier
6 Shark Research Institute cites depths of 305 metres.
7 Order: Carcharhiniformes; Family: Carcharhinidae (Requiem sharks); Genus: Carcharhinus; Species: leucas. In this family, there are 12 Genera of which 8 are monotypic (i.e. one species per genus). Of the 48 species in this family, 29 belong to the genus *Carcharhinus*.
8 These figures depend upon the classification method used, as there is no universal agreement between biologists. Many sources quote 18 families but after much research and time I elected to use the classification method chosen by the University of Michigan Museum of Zoology.
9 Some references cite 375 venomous species.
10 The taxonomy of sea snakes is in dispute by members of the scientific community. At best the scientific classification of sea snakes can be described as unclear. After much research in this murky matter, I have elected to use the taxonomy of the University of Michigan Museum of Zoology. I have endeavoured to use and or transpose the correct suffix to define order, family, sub-family, or genus. However it needs to be noted that depending

upon the classification method chosen by the primary authors, the number of species in an order, family or genus varies between sources. In these cases I used the information that appeared to be consistent across authors.

11 The taxonomy followed is Kingdom: Animalia, Phylum: Chordata, Sub-phylum: Vertebrata, Class: Reptilia (reptiles), Order: Squamata (lizards, snakes, amphisbaenids), Family: there are 47 families identified. Of interest here are family Boidae (e.g. pythons and boas), family Elapidae (e.g. brown snakes, taipan, black snakes, cobras, kraits etc.), family Hydrophiidae, (e.g. sea snakes and sea kraits), family Acrochordidae (file snakes). Family Colubridae, which are distinguished by their teeth. Most have fixed teeth but some species have enlarged and or grooved posterior maxillary teeth, which enable the animal to envenomate its prey primarily through biting—and holding on to the prey— and chewing. There are 304 genus in this family, which makes up around 75 per cent of the world's snake species. Of interest here are the genus Homalopsis (water snakes), and Natriciteresi (marsh snakes). Family Viperidae (snakes having retractable upper jaw fangs in front of the back teeth); common name: vipers.

Within a family there is the genus followed by the species (sp.) and possibly sub species (spp.). In the naming of a species, the genus is written first and is spelt with a capital first letter. The species follows but is spelt in lower case letters (e.g. Pelamis platurus (yellow-bellied sea snake), Aipysurus laevis (olive sea snake).

12 Scientific Classification; Kingdom: Animalia, Phylum: Chordata, Class: Mammalia, Order: Carnivora, Suborder: Caniformia, Superfamily: Pinnipedia.

CHAPTER 15 SEAMANSHIP

The sea finds out everything you did wrong.

Old Norwegian Adage

CORDAGE & KNOTS

Fibre Characteristics

Nylon is the most elastic of all cordage fibres. It has high stretch and strength characteristics and minimal strength loss when exposed to sunlight. It is ideal for use where stretch and energy absorption are important.

Polyester is a low stretch fibre having a high strength-to-weight ratio, very good abrasion resistance either wet or dry; and excellent weathering characteristics. Spun Polyester is fuzzy. Filament Polyester is smooth. It is a good choice for running rigging requiring moderate to low stretch and good durability. Often referred to by its DuPont trade name of: Dacron, instead of polyester.

Polypropylene is a lightweight fibre, possessing minimal stretch and moderate creep (it gets longer under sustained load) characteristics. It has low water absorption characteristics and floats; but is very susceptible to UV degradation. Four millimetre diameter braided polypropylene clothesline cordage comes in 15 metre lengths and can be used as a towline.

Spectra, possesses very high strength with very low stretch characteristics. It is lightweight and will not absorb water. Its low melting point makes it susceptible to friction. It becomes very slippery when wet and creeps under load. Spectra, is the Allied name for High Modulus Polyethylene (HMPE) fibre.

Towlines

☀* **Caution:** Obviously, you do not tow a kayak through a surf zone!

Different sources (clubs and organisations) vary about the length of towline cordage required. Required towline lengths varying from 10 to 20 metres. For example, Transport Canada in their publication Sea Kayaking Safety Guide, TP 14726 has the regulation that kayakers carry

a 15 metre heave line. The KASK manual for New Zealand sea kayaking, has the requirement for a minimum 10 metre towline of 6 millimetre diameter cordage.

The VSKC, NSWSKC and AC have a standard towline length of 15 metres. This ensures uniformity within the club(s) and makes communications easier between towers.

Many different reasons are given to justify a particular length. For the 15 metre length tow line, the common reason cited in Australia, for this 49.21 foot length is: 'so a towee does not run into the back of the tower when in a swell'. However, I have never seen or heard of any valid data or evidence to support this statement. Despite the multitude of comments from paddlers asking "why so long?"

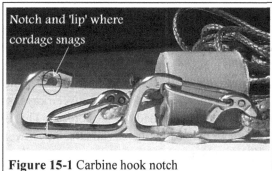

Figure 15-1 Carbine hook notch

The majority of VSKC members use four to six millimetre *Venetian blind* (drapery) cordage. The advantage is, it can be easily rolled up and stored. I have not heard of a towline snapping. However, do not use the Zenith® Venetian Blind Cord, which has a *natural cotton* solid braided jacket over a longitudinal core. Instead, use the Zenith® Starter Cord, which has a *synthetic nylon* hard braided jacket. The Starter Cord has high strength and durability, high resistance to oil, petrol, rot, mildew, sunlight and weathering, making it suitable for external use.

Making your tow-line

When making up a towline, do not forget to put a float on the end of the line, so when it is unhooked from the towed kayak, the carbine hook does not sink and foul.

With small diameter cordage (3–4 mm), select a carbine hook (e.g. a wire gate snap hook), which does not have an interlocking gate with a notch in it, as the notch's lips catch on the cordage.

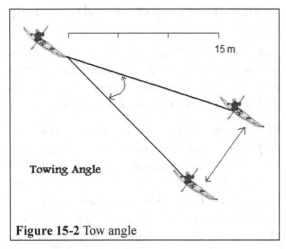

Figure 15-2 Tow angle

Towing angle

In a V-line tow, you need to maintain an acute angle between the two lines, to ensure the load on the towrope is evenly distributed, and the workload shared. The line will be experiencing dynamic loading, and exceeding an acute angle will more than likely result in a failure. The greater the angle, hence distance between kayaks, amplifies the tensile loads on the cordage. This is where a 15 metre towline has an advantage over a 10 metre line.

Knots & Hitches

Knots and hitches are the *same but different*! Knots secure other lines, cordage, tapes, and ropes together. Hitches are formed around an item and are generally made taught on the same line, cordage or rope. Ropes, cordage and lines of different materials, weaves and diameters have different strengths and characteristics. As a generalisation, knots on average will reduce the strength of a rope by 50 per cent. A splice reduces rope strength by around 10 per cent.

Terms for the parts of a rope are the *standing end*, which is the part of a rope secured to an object. The *running end*, which is the end of the rope; and the *standing part*, which is the bit in between. If you double a rope and hold the middle or make a flat loop, it is termed a *bight*. Useful knots and hitches to know are the reef knot, sheet bend, fisherman's knot, bowline, alpine butterfly, truckies hitch, taut-line hitch and clove hitch.

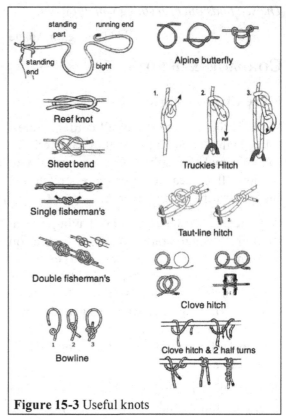

Figure 15-3 Useful knots

The reef knot is used to joint two pieces of cordage of equal diameter. Note: the two running ends are both on the same side of the knot. If they are diagonally opposed the knot will slip undone; this type of knot is called a *Thief knot*. The cordage retains 43 to 57 per cent of its tensile strength. Small size nylon ropes are liable to slip without breaking.

The sheet bend is used to secure two ropes of different diameters together. The cordage retains 48 to 58 per cent of its tensile strength. Small size nylon ropes are liable to slip without breaking.

The fisherman's knot (aka *prussic knot*) is use to tie two pieces of cordage together of the same diameter. When pulled together it binds on itself and can be quite awkward to undo. The cordage retains 50 to 58 per cent of its tensile strength.

With the bowline knot you can create a secure loop that will not slip and easily unties. The cordage retains 67 to 75 per cent of tensile strength.

The alpine butterfly (aka *gunners loop*) is used to make a non-slip loop along the standing part of the rope. To make a loop at the standing end, make a figure eight knot.

The truckies hitch is a very useful hitch for tying down loads, as the running end can be used to apply tension. The advantage is with the slippery half hitch. An overhand knot forming the loop would cinch down when the hitch has tension applied. The slippery hitch allows easily undoing of the overall truckies hitch.

The taut-line hitch is often used on tent or fly ropes. It is useful because you can reapply tension to the cordage. Place the running end around a pole, make a turn below this, then bring the rope up across the standing part around the pole and tuck through.

A clove hitch (aka *round turn and two half* hitches) is used to make fast a rope on a spar/rail. It needs both ends to be tied off with two half hitches, or it can work its way loose.

REPAIR KIT

The type of construction materials used on your boat, will determine what is the best way to make a temporary repair. The universal repair material is tape, either 'gaffer tape', 'duct tape', or 'cloth tape'. Basically anything that will stick to the kayak and keep water out. Before going on a trip, test your chosen tape for its adhesion qualities on your boat. With plastic boats, many adhesives will not adhere. Experiment with silicone adhesives and find one that adheres to your kayak, but back up with tape. Fibreglass boats are easy to repair, by making a scab patch using resin and cloth. Remember the repair does not need to be pretty, just functional. A professional repair and replacement of gel-coat can be done when you get home.

Repair and replacement items carried depends upon what you are using and how your boat is fitted out. For a fibreglass kayak, I carry one of the Selleys *Fibreglass Repair kits*, which contain resin, catalyst, glass mat and a small brush. If you do not carry acetone to clean up your brush and to prep the surface, it may be worthwhile carrying another small brush. Also

carried is a small selection of sand paper from 320 to 600 grit. In terms of tools, I carry a small multi tool with pliers, scissors, and a pair of rubber gloves.

For the boat's electric pump, prior to replacing the SPST switch with a magnetic switch, I carried a spare switch, already with the wires pre-crimped with a socket and plug. This allowed for a straight change over in the field. For the footrests and rudder, I carried spare wing nuts, shackles and pre-measured spectra rudder cable. For general repairs of camping equipment I carry seam seal (polyurethane glue), duct tape, needles and dental floss. A spare rubber seal for the Trangia® fuel burner transport lid and a spectacles repair kit.

REPAIRS

Polyethylene Repairs

Polyethylene (PE) boats can be deformed and dented, usually around the cockpit bilge, if left in the sun or on roof racks. To fix the damage, pour hot water into the cockpit over the dent. If the dent is resistant to just the hot water, a bottle or screw jack can be rigged up to 'pop' the dent out. Scratches and the fine 'fuzz' of plastic slithers can be cleaned up with a shaving razor. Deep gouges can be filled in by using a soldering iron to smooth over the damaged area and filling in the deepest part of the gouge. If you have lost material, cut a slither of plastic from either the cockpit or hatch edge and melt it into the gouge. The repair can be tidied up with a smooth file. Damage outside of your repair capability, can be repaired by the plastic welding process. Check your phone directory to fine a person who can weld plastic. Even though the boats are manufactured with UV stabilisers in their construction, UV rays are the enemy of these boats and they should be stored out of the sun.

In the field, PE can be temporarily repaired with duct tape. PE resists the adhesion properties of many sealants. The Selleys All Clear® co-polymer multipurpose sealant has had the most success when bonding items onto PE boats. With sealants, adhesives and putties, you need to experiment at home first to ensure they will adhere to the PE. With the advances in technology and materials science, hopefully soon, there will be an effective and permanent repair product on the market for use on PE.

Composite Repairs

On composite materials, you have two choices; pay someone or do-it-yourself (DIY). There are many articles on the web by boat manufacturers and in magazines about DIY repairs. When performing a repair there are some basic steps, which need to be followed.

Safety precautions need to be adhered to with Material Safety Data Sheets (MSDS) being available from the manufacturer's website for the materials you are using. Wear: skin, eyes and respiratory protection when working with polymers, chemicals and products.

Be aware that the different resins and solvents if inappropriately stored can have a chemical reaction and cause a fire. Rags contaminated with catalysts should not be disposed in the same rubbish bin as those contaminated with accelerators. Use a metal rubbish bin with a firm fitting lid and have an appropriate fire extinguisher in your work space.

Surface preparation involves removing damaged material and preparing the area for the application of a repair material. For resins, there are two forms of adhesion: *mechanical* and *chemical*. For the resins to be effective and be as strong as possible on the repair, you need to expose laminate reinforcement material. If you were to just apply a resin over an old resin (gelcoat) you can achieve a chemical bond but it will be weak and will easily succumb to failure modes. For gelcoat repairs, you need to remove the shiny surface of the surrounding gelcoat with emery/wet and dry paper.

Cleanliness is an important part of site preparation. The resins will not adhere to surfaces that are contaminated with salts, dust, wax et cetera. Moisture needs to be excluded, so you may need to remove more material than you first thought. Remove any delamination that is present, as it may have trapped moisture. Areas or items that have salt water trapped inside need

to be drained and flushed with fresh water, then flushed with methylated spirits and left to dry. The methylated spirits displaces the moisture and assists in drying.

When purchasing masking tapes do not go for the cheap versions, but look for good quality tapes and ones that can be used with chemicals.

Gelcoat repairs are straight forward depending upon what type of damage you are repairing. Light scratches can be polished out with an extra cut car polish using a car polisher or by hand. Deeper scratches can be polished out with 1200 to 1000 grit emery paper and water. When carrying out gelcoat repairs, have a wide selection of sandpapers and wet and dry papers for sanding purposes. Work in a taped off area and wash off the residue regularly and inspect your work. Apply masking tape about 6 millimetres from the edge of the damage. This is to protect the rest of the good gelcoat from damage caused by your sanding, and prevents you removing good material than you need to. You may need to start with a coarser sand paper, like 800 grit or even coarser, depending on the depth and extent of damage. However, the coarser the sand paper the more work is required to polish out the marks left by the paper. It is best to be patient and work with the finer papers. After the sanding phase, use extra cut polish, then cream polish to finish up the surface and bring it to a shine. If you are going to use a mechanical polisher, be aware of heat building up in the gelcoat resulting in a gelcoat burn. Another issue to consider when sanding is to keep an even pressure applied to the surface. If you apply too much pressure in different areas, you will end up with scalloping (small depressed areas) in your gelcoat.

Fine star cracks (stress fractures) need to be opened up by gouging out material along the length of the crack and then have flowcoat applied. Areas where the gelcoat has been chipped completely away exposing the reinforcement material will also need to have any damaged removed and the site prepared for re-gelcoating using flowcoat.

Mask-off around the damage site, with two inch masking tape. Place the tape about 25 millimetres away from the damage edge. Next apply one inch masking tape around the damage site, but exposing about 6 millimetres (~¼ inch) of gelcoat from the damage edge. Then stack on top of the first one inch tape, 4 to 6 layers of one inch tape to act as a sacrificial surface during the sanding process. The one-inch masking tape layers will be worn away by sanding action and will need to be replaced, in order to protect the good gelcoat underneath.

Using medium grade (80 grit) sandpaper, sand out the damaged gelcoat area and any delamination; being careful not to damage any reinforcement material underneath. If you have damaged reinforcement material, you will need to apply a cloth and resin repair. After preparing the damaged area for repair, wipe it down with acetone and let it dry.

If you are repairing a coloured surface other than white, you will need to colour match the flowcoat using pigment paste. Ensure you do this before adding the catalyst! Mix up the flowcoat and apply to the repair area. When you have finished applying the flowcoat the material will be slightly raised above the surface of the existing gelcoat surface of the hull. Try to feather the edges as much as possible.

When the flowcoat has cured, it can be sanded down, using for example 240 grit sandpaper, down to the finer wet and dry papers (400 grit). Depending upon the size of the repair you may need to start sanding with coarser sandpaper. Be aware of the pressure you are applying as you can cut too much repair material away and put new deep scratches back into the repair. To protect the good gelcoat underneath the previously tape off area, you will need to reapply 25 millimetre masking tape around the repair. Sand down the repair using finer (400–800 grit) grades of wet and dry paper, using water, and fair in the repair to the existing gelcoat. Finish off by polishing the repair area the same as if for removing small scratches.

Structural damage is best repaired by someone who knows what he or she is doing. When repairing composites, you need to know what resins were used in the manufacture (i.e. polyester,

vinylester or epoxy). There are formulas for determining the size of repair area for certain types and size of damage, but a rule of thumb is 'the repair area is twice the diameter of the damage area' (e.g. a 10 mm diameter hole, after clean up, would have a 20 mm diameter repair placed over it). The surface needs to be cleaned and prepared, damaged materials removed and edges cleaned up. Mask-off the repair area about 6 millimetres wider than the required repair.

Depending upon access, you may need to apply a patch from the outside or inside. If you do not have access (like at the bow or stern) you can inflate a balloon and force it in place under the damage. Then you can insert cardboard between the balloon and hole to create a surface from which to work from. Alternatively, you can apply wetted-out glass fibre tape to the cardboard then insert the cardboard through the hatch on a telescoping pole and position over the hole. Then insert a piece of wire through the cardboard and reinforcement material and pull into place. Once in place, insert the balloon up behind the repair to hold it in place under pressure. It is a lot easier if someone is around to help you! Once the reinforcement material has cured in place, you can apply flowcoat and restore the gelcoat exterior of the boat.

Other useful repair products

Sikaflex®-291 is a very useful sealant for adhering items like thigh braces, and cockpit coaming to a composite kayak. Once set the item is held firmly in place. It is useful because you do not have to use any polyester or epoxy resins and reinforcement material to complete the job. If you have used methylated spirits to remove moisture from a faying surface (a gap between two surfaces), make sure there is no methylated spirits residue left in the gap. If there is any residue, the Sikaflex® will not set.

Araldite® is useful as a substitute for resin. It can be used with glass fibre reinforcement mat to make fixtures like cargo loops. If the modification is in the wrong place or not needed, then it is simply removed by lifting (pulling/prying) off.

Bote-Cote epoxy resin is a low viscosity, high solids epoxy resin developed for modern wooden boat building. It is the base material for all coatings, glues, and lamination with synthetic fibers. It can also be used on composite materials. The company also makes fillers that are used to fill in gaps in the job.

Divicell® foam is a useful product for manufacturing stiffeners and formers for kayaks that have an area that flexes and needs strengthening. It can also be used with glass reinforcement material to strengthen attachment areas for sail masts and tow points.

Leaking spray skirt

If you suspect that your spray skirt is leaking, hold it up into the light and stretch it out to see if you can find any pinholes of light shining through. Other reasons for your skirt letting water into the cockpit are that the neoprene (depending upon quality) has become saturated with water. Check also any areas where the spray deck has been stitched and ensure the seam seal backing tape is still in place and serviceable. Also check to see if the elastic that secures the spray skirt to the cockpit coaming is tight enough to form a reliable seal; sometimes the elastic cord's joining stitching (at the back of the skirt) has come undone allowing the bungee to separate and loosen off.

If you have eliminated the skirt as the major culprit, check the boat's cockpit coaming seam (where the coaming joins to the deck) has not cracked. This can be done by pushing up and down the coaming to see if it is moving up and down; as it should be solid with the deck.

Fairleads

Under certain circumstances, deck line fittings that have been secured to the deck by fasteners, have been pulled out of the deck through the inappropriate use of the deck lines and force. To prevent these types of fairleads from being ripped out, replace the smaller washers with larger 'penny washers' if you think this will be a concern.

Chapter 16 Kayak Ancillary Systems

"Invention is the most important product of man's creative brain. The ultimate purpose is the complete mastery of mind over the material world, the harnessing of human nature to human needs."

Nikola Tesla

Bilge Pumps

There are four options available that people employ when it comes to bilge pumps in kayaks. First is the hand-pump and it is recommend you carry one as a backup, to any one of the following three. The second is the fixed-hand-operated bilge pump, located on the deck, behind and to the side of the cockpit. The third is a foot-operated-pump, fixed to the cockpit forward bulkhead. The fourth is the electric bilge pump.

The foot operated and electric bilge pumps are the preferred methods of pumping out a flooded cockpit. Both methods allow the paddler to return to paddling and when suitable, refit the spray skirt, while the cockpit is being emptied of water. Chill-Cheater (aka Reed) make a spray skirt with a 'bale-hole' in order for the paddler to use a hand-pump with the skirt fitted in place.

Advantages of the foot operated (manual) bilge pumps are their simplicity of construction and weight. The manual bilge pumps are usually a hand operated pump, modified and fitted to the cockpit forward bulkhead. Depending upon price, a manual bilge pump has a capacity of 55 l/min when hand operated. The capacity during foot operation would depend on how fast you can pump your foot. These pumps have also been known to fail, with several paddlers going back to electric bilge pumps.

The other preferred hands free option is the electric bilge pump. It has the advantage of being relatively quick in empting a flooded cockpit. Its disadvantages can be weight from over engineering or poor selection of components. The other disadvantage is the possibility of electrical failure due to poor engineering and particularly, poor maintenance.

Electric Bilge Pump Circuit

The preferred electrical bilge pump for a single kayak is the 12 volt, 500 gallon per hour (GPH) type.[1] For a double kayak utilizing only one electric bilge pump the 1100 GPH pump is often used. Pumps are fitted either on the aft or forward cockpit bulkhead depending upon the seat configuration. Podded seats and foam seats, which are adhered to the cockpit deck, require the pump to be fitted on the forward cockpit bulkhead.

When you purchase your bilge pump, it often comes with a set of instructions. The instructions tell you what diameter piping and outlet fittings you are also required to get. All up, it can cost around $100 to fit a pump, without a battery box and using a single pole single throw (SPST) switch.

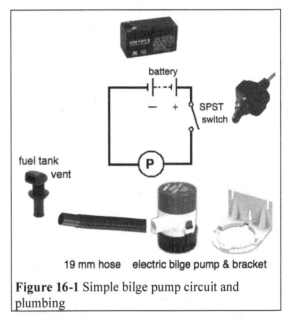

Figure 16-1 Simple bilge pump circuit and plumbing

Electrical wires used in the marine environment should be *tinned*. This means that the exposed wire has solder applied to it. This is done to reduce corrosion caused by the marine environment, which is accelerated when current passes through the wires.

Connections can be the weak link in the pump electrical circuit. Options include using self-sealing quick connectors as used on motorbikes/

boats or standard quick connectors (aka electrical crimps), as used in cars. Use tin-plated copper connectors instead of the aluminium types in the marine environment.

When crimping connectors to a wire, remove only enough insulation for the wire to reach the end of the barrel of the terminal. With the crimping tool, grip the terminal in the correct die, fully insert the wire into the terminal, and squeeze. If the crimp barrel has a seam, the crimping tool's indent should be opposite. On many connectors, first crimp the tinned wire to the connector then reposition to crimp the connector to the wires insulation. After crimping the connector to the wire, use the *pull-test* to test the security of the crimp. This simply means pulling on the connector to se if it comes lose or off.

① **Note:** when using sealants to waterproof your electrical connections ensure you use one that is non-corrosive and is suitable for electrical connections.

Depending upon the insulation around the electrical crimp connector terminal (ECCT) you may or may not need to seal the ends with a sealant. If you do need to use a sealant people have used silicone and or urethane sealants or hot glue. If using silicon sealants, ensure that they are rated to be used on electrical components. If they are not, the sealants constituents will corrode and destroy the electrics.

The most common switch used for the circuit is the waterproof toggle switch. This is a simple 'single pole single throw' (SPST) switch. The unit is sealed but water can enter the switch if the boot is damaged or incorrectly fitted. To reduce the risk of water entering the switch internals, use Vaseline or silicone grease inside the boot and around the opening of the toggle, as this may assist in keeping water out, if the boot fails.

The waterproof toggle switch comes with two wires attached. As a suggestion, attach a plug (male) ECCT to one wire and a socket ECCT (female) to the other, with the corresponding wires and ECCT going to the battery. This configuration is useful if you need to change a switch in the field. On your spare switch, in your repair kit, have the same connector configuration. Usually the switch is located on

the opposite side to the day hatch and you need to work *blind* to change the switch over, with your hands inside the day hatch. This method allows easy connection of the switch to the battery and minimal excess wiring.

① **Note:** whatever ever you chose remember the weight factor of your modification.

Other switch options around are, the momentary press switch, in either electrical or pneumatic form. Some have also wired in a float switch, to automatically start the pump when required. To prevent inadvertent selection of the toggle switch, which can and does happen, some have even fitted a buzzer into the circuit!

Magnetic Switches

An alternative option to the SPST toggle switch is to use a magnetic switch (aka magnetic slide switch). This type of switch uses a 'reed switch' and magnet.

This type of switch mechanism removes the possibility of the SPST rubber boot failing—as there is none—and water entering inside the switch. Neil Brenton makes a product called the *MagnetX*, which is an aftermarket option. Neil's idea is now being used by Nadgee kayaks to operate their boats bilge pumps.

Another DIY options for making a magnetic switch, is to buy three bulb reed switches (aka NC Reed Switch) and mount them inside a tube (e.g. a pen casing, aluminium tubing etc.). Three reed switches are used inside the casing to provide redundancy for the fragile mechanisms. A strong magnet affixed to the pre-existing bungee cord across the deck in front of the cockpit, activates the normally open reed switches.

I prefer to use a good quality magnet. I use 'rare earth' magnets, which are very strong. However, cheaper magnets can be used. A disc magnet measuring 25 x 5 millimetres can be resined into a soft drink bottle top or any protective cap. The top/cap can be drilled to receive the bungee cord that passes over the cockpit deck. Chalky Thomas makes up and supplies aluminium cases, purposed built to house the magnets.

The use of reed switches requires a relay. An automotive horn relay is ideal. The relay can be fitted in the battery box. If you use a relay with an internal diode (unlike the horn type) ensure you wire it up the correct way! Once wired to the bilge pump, the reed switches (in their casing) are mounted inside the cockpit underneath the bungee with the magnet.

The wiring can be neatly mounted using 'adhesive cable tie mounts' and zip-ties. If using the adhesive cable tie mounts, remove the adhesive tape from the underside of the mount and fix the mount to the kayaks surface using urethane sealant or equivalent. The other end of the wiring is connected to the relay and battery inside the battery box. To make watertight any access hole through the bulkheads, use the wiring waterproof cable glands. The cable glands come in various sizes. When correctly wired up, sliding the magnet along the bungee cord, over the reed switches, activates the pump.

Chalky Thomas builds the above fore mentioned magnetic switches as a kit. This kit comes with the adapter to recharge your battery without taking it out of your kayak, with either a solar panel or battery recharger. His kit is modular and can be connected to a solar panel that is recharging your battery while you are on the water. There is also the option to piggyback a portable battery for use in recharging your electronic devices at the campsite. These kits are available through East Coast Kayaking.

Bilge Pump Battery Housing

The battery is usually fitted to a bracket or in a battery box in the day-hatch or aft-hatch, if no day-hatch. Depending upon how water tight the hatches are or just as a precaution some fit a battery box to protect the battery from moisture and the possibility of items inside the hatch detaching a terminal connection. Containers chosen to be battery boxes are plastic sealable containers (e.g. Tupperware or Pelican boxes), and polycarbonate terminal boxes that have a polyurethane gasket. Terminal boxes are available from electrical hardware retailers.

To help protect the battery terminal from corrosion try Vaseline. If the battery is not inside a battery box, some have had success with 'Blue-Tac'® encapsulating the terminals.

BILGE PUMP BATTERY

A common battery used for the electrical system is the *Century PS Series PS1220 12 V 2 Ah* sealed lead acid battery.[2] This battery weighs 1.0 kilogram and measures 178 x 35 x 60 millimetres; plus the height of the 4.7 millimetres spade type terminals. You may elect to go for a lighter and smaller battery like the 12 V 1.2 Ah Ps1212 that weighs 0.6 kilograms and measures 97 x 43 x 52 millimetres (58 mm including terminals). Batteries are advertised with an amp hour (Ah) printed on the side. Below is an explanation of the meaning of 1.2 Ah.

Ampere hours

Ampere hours (Ah) (aka *Amp hours*), refers to battery capacity and is the number of amps a battery will deliver over a specified period of time. It can also be described as a measure of the energy the battery can store and deliver to a load (e.g. bilge pump motor). The batteries capacity is the maximum sustained amperage (current) drawn from a fully charged battery over a specified time (industry standard: 20 hours at 26.7 °C), to a point (10.5 volts for a 12 V battery), where the battery is at 100 per cent depth of discharge (DOD) (i.e. the battery will not power your 12 volt system).

Table 16-1 State of Battery charge	
Voltage @ 21°C	State of Charge
12.6+	100%
12.5	90%
12.42	80%
12.32	70%
12.20	60%
12.06	**50%**
11.9	40%
11.75	30%
11.58	20%
11.31	10%
10.5	0% DOD

Therefore, theoretically, a 2 Ah battery will deliver 0.1 A, every hour over 20 hours, at 26.7 °C, before reaching DOD of 10.5 V during continuous operation.

To properly operate a specific electrical device, the battery's operating voltage must be matched to that of the device. The correct battery capacity must be selected, in order to provide the necessary operating time. The battery must be able to deliver the power required. The smaller the batteries' inner resistance, the higher its power output (i.e. its internal resistance must be smaller than that of the device it is going to power).

The data sheet for the bilge pump will tell you the motors amperage draw (e.g. for one brands 500 GPM pump its amperage (Amp) draw is 1.9 A). A serviceable and fully charged 2 Ah battery, theoretically, will power a 1.9 amp motor for 63 minutes: (2 Ah / 1.9 A = 1.05 x 60 = 63). A 1.2 Ah battery, theoretically, will power a 1.9 amp motor for 37.8 minutes. It is theoretical because the depletion rate is exponential and not linear. Therefore your continuous operating time would be less than determined above. Depending upon the volume of your kayak's cockpit and the extent to which it is flooded, you will only operate your pump for several minutes per evacuation.

Battery Maintenance

Battery usage requires care. The life expectancy of the lead-acid battery is primarily dependent upon how heavily the battery is routinely discharged before being recharged. A battery, which is regularly discharged, until only 10 per cent of the rated capacity remains, (i.e. 90 per cent of its capacity has been used), will have a much shorter life expectancy than an identical battery which is rarely discharged below 50 per cent.

ⓘ **Note:** Use the Original Equipment Manufacture's data for charging.

Battery maintenance requires care. Overcharging and undercharging will seriously affect their life and performance. There are many types and therefore quality of battery chargers on the market. Contemporary charges usually have a microprocessor, which takes information from the battery about its charge state and regulates the recharge, to maintain a fully charged state without overcharging.

When looking for a charger, read the marketing information on the box to ensure it is suitable to charge a small amp hour battery (e.g. 2 Ah). If the charger is for larger capacity batteries, you will destroy your battery.

The charging of wet cell (flooded) and Absorbed Glass Mat (AGM) batteries usually have the same charge profile and therefore are mutually conducive. If you have a Gel constructed battery, ensure the charger data informs you it is suitable for Gel batteries.

All lead acid batteries when stored for prolonged periods or are irregularly cycled, become prone to a lead sulphide build-up on the plates. If the battery is regularly recharged this is not an issue, as the sulphate turns back to sulphuric acid. If left unchecked, the sulphate can precipitate to the bottom of the battery and harden, making the reversing process more difficult. A lead-acid desulphator (aka zapper) can be use in an attempt to reverse the damage and restore the capacity of the battery. However, it will not resurrect a badly damaged battery.

Testing a battery

Obviously, you cannot test the specific gravity of a sealed lead acid battery. The method employed is the load test, which removes amps from the battery. A load test can only be performed if the battery is at or near a full charge.

In the absence of original equipment manufacturer (OEM) data for load testing, as a guide, the on-load voltage should not drop below 11.4 volts. If it does, you have an indication of a faulty battery. To measure voltage, use a digital voltmeter (multimeter) in the DC voltage setting.

For kayaks with an electrical bilge pump, test your 12 volt battery with the pump running (under-load). If you put a multimeter across the terminals, (positive [+] and negative [−]), with no load, you will not get a correct reading of the batteries voltage but, pick up the surface residual voltage.

After charging the battery, refit it to the kayak and test it by turning the pump on. Wait around six hours, before putting a multimeter across the terminals to get an accurate check of the charge.[3] Alternatively purchase and use an electronic load tester. Instructions on its use will come with it.

Keep the battery charged if not in use. If you are not paddling for several months you will need to periodically (every few months) check the battery's capacity. Batteries are subject to an internal discharge (aka self-discharge). The rate is determined by the battery type (Absorbed Glass Mat or Gel construction), and the metallurgy of the lead used in its construction.

Electrics Maintenance

Perform regular inspections of electrical terminals and fittings. The switch rubber boot is prone to damage and deterioration. If your pump is intermittent on start or during operation, check the switch and boot. Another option is to change the switch 'on spec' every 12 to 18 months.

Silicon spray is useful to help prevent corrosion of electrical fittings. If you have the battery inside a battery-box, ensure the seal is not damaged. Lubricate the seal with a silicon spray. Check inside the box as part of your maintenance plan, to ensure the absence of water ingress and or moisture build up, thereby ensuring the fittings are not corroding.

RECHARGEABLE BATTERIES

Batteries are defined as either primary or secondary. Primary batteries are designed for one discharge of electricity. Secondary batteries are designed to be rechargeable.

Common primary batteries are the Mercury-oxide 1.35 V button cell, Alkaline-manganese 1.5 V button cell, Silver-oxide 1.55 V button cell, 3 V Lithium-manganese button cell, Alkaline-manganese 1.5 V round cell batteries and Zinc-carbon 1.5 V round cell. All these types are used in watches, calculators, toys, flashlights, radios, cameras, hearing aids and electronic devices.

An example of the variety and types of common secondary batteries are the 1.2 V Nickel-cadmium cells, used in some power tools, camcorders, mobile telephones and cordless telephones or the 1.2 V Nickel-metal-hydride cell. There is also the 1.4 V per cell, Lithium-ion cell used in some mobile phones, laptop computers and camcorders.

One advantage primary batteries have over secondary batteries is the unavoidable rate of self-discharge. Primary batteries over a 12 month period can experience less than one per cent

and up to four per cent rate of self-discharge, depending upon construction. Secondary batteries can lose between 10 to 25 per cent charge per month.

Recharging mobile phone batteries

Mobile phones have become a major form of trip communication, in preference to radios, for both ship to shore and weather forecasts. There are several options available to recharge your mobile phone batteries out bush. There are commercially available chargers that are powered by AA batteries or the like. The use of solar panels and rechargers. The use of the mobile phones vehicle/car charger and a 12 volt battery.

① **Note**: continuously leaving the phone on a rapid charger can shorten the battery lifespan.

Vehicle chargers are typically rapid chargers that allow for a faster charge of the phone's battery. To prevent battery overcharging and damage many of the vehicle chargers now have intelligent integrated circuitry (IC).

Figure 16-2 VPA and mobile phone VPA adapter

VSKC member Julian Smith carries a VPA that can be connected to any 12 volt battery power sources. You can then utilise your mobile phone's car charger (12 volt adapter). This is achieved by obtaining a car cigarette lighter socket (VPA) and making up some wires with connectors and alligator clips so that it can be to connect to a battery. Car cigarette lighter sockets are readily available from hobby and car shops.

Simply make up some wires using the appropriate sockets on one end to fit onto the lighter socket and alligator clips on the other end for the battery terminals. With a 12 Vdc battery and the lighter socket, you now have a power source to recharge your battery using your mobile phone's car recharger.

Another method as used by marathon paddler Bill Robinson is to connect the VPA to an eight pack of AA batteries. You can get the battery pack cradles from hobby/electrical shops. Bill seems to think that eight batteries last around ten days with heavy use. However, before you set off on a trip do your own checking and testing of your equipment at home.

SOLAR PANELS

Carrying solar panels is becoming quite popular with kayakers for recharging camera and mobile phone batteries. One kayaker wired up a 5 watt, Uni-solar® Flexible (USF) panel, on to the aft deck of his kayak. He described the panel as being waterproof and very robust. Another panel being used with success is the *Brunton, Solaris* foldable solar panel array. This panel provides 12 watts and 800 mA at 15.6 Vdc. By wiring up a vehicle power adapter (aka cigarette lighter socket), you can use a battery car charger kit, to charge your batteries. Products like the *Silva Solar II* foldable, all terrain solar cell, recharges mobile phones, GPS, radios or iPads et cetera via a 12 volt adapter. If you visit the websites of the above business, you can access further information.

Cheaper options involve using ridged 10 watt solar panels that can be attached with bungee, to the aft deck and wired up to a battery. The battery may be either the bilge pump battery or an auxiliary battery. During the day, the solar panel recharges the auxiliary 12 Vdc SLA or lithium battery. The auxiliary battery can be kept in a battery box with a VPA and rechargeable battery charger. This can be used to recharge mobile phones, radios, camera batteries et cetera, as well as recharge AA batteries.

When the kayak is being stored, the bilge pump battery can be left connected to the solar panel. This ensures that the battery is always fully charged. This is useful if you are not in the habit of regularly checking and maintaining the battery's condition and voltage.

Depending upon the manufacturer, the smaller useful ridged solar panels measure 295 x 255 x 23 millimetres and are capable of developing 5 watts of power (depending upon sunlight conditions). This is enough power to trickle charge a 12 Vdc SLA battery during the day. The cost of the panel is around $60. You will also need a solar panel regulator, which costs around $27. If you want to recharge more than your bilge pump battery or mobile phone use a 10 watt or greater solar panel.

RECHARGING iPADS

To recharge an iPad you need 10 watts of power. The iPad requires 5 volts at 2 amps (2000 mA) for it to recharge. When looking for a battery to recharge your iPad ensure that it can supply 5 volts at a minimum of 2 amps. I have a Brunton Sustain battery that is recharged during the day by a solar panel. This battery supplies 5 volts at 600 milliamps, which can recharge a mobile (cell) phone but not an iPad. The Sustain can supply 12 volts at 3800 milliamps but the voltage needs to be regulated down to 5 volts. This is achieved by making a 5 volt 2 amp regulator. Chalky Thomas makes battery packs and regulators for iPads and other electronics. Contact East Coast Kayaking for further information.

LIGHT SOURCES

Deck compass illumination

Some people have wired their deck compass up to a battery source (e.g. bilge pump battery, for illumination at night). Another method used has been the inserting a chemical light stick inside the compass housing, but this has been met with limited success for some. I prefer to just use my head torch.

Chalky Thomas manufactures a battery operated bilge pump kit that has the option of also supplying power to a LED to illuminate a deck compass. Contact East Coast Kayaking for further information on how to acquire the kit.

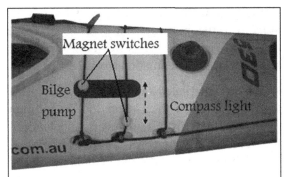

Figure 16-3 Magnetic switches retro fitted to deck bungee to operate a bilge pump and navigation light

Kayak illumination

ⓘ **Note:** Check your State/Territory and or countries boating laws to ensure you are displaying the correct navigation lighting.

Countries who are signatories to the International Maritime Organisation have adopted a set International Regulations for the Preventing Collisions at Sea. As a result kayak illumination between sunset and sunrise is covered by the regulations. In Australia, New Zealand, USA and Canada for example a vessel under seven metres in length if not displaying side and stern lights, shall have ready at hand an electric torch or lighted lantern showing a white light which shall be exhibited in sufficient time to prevent collision.

Well meaning people have chosen to display a blue light while paddling between sunset and sunrise, which may help them identify each other but it has caused confusion and the ire of Port Authorities. In New Zealand it is stated that it is against the law to use a blue light.

You can purchase a suction mounted side and stern light device but it affects night vision, if mounted forward and is obscured by the paddler if mounted aft as viewed from the front. A solution has been to mount a 360 degree white light on a metre high removable pole behind the paddler. In Victoria, Neil Brenton makes up light poles, which have been used with success on the Bay where there is traffic and on 55 nautical mile crossings of Bass Straight.

---

1 Output open flow of 1890lph, (31.5lpm) depending upon the condition of the battery.
2 There are charging differences between the two types of sealed lead acid batteries Absorbed Glass Mat (AGM) and Gel construction. "The smaller batteries you find in house alarm systems, computer UPS (uninterruptible power supply) boxes, etc., that say "sealed lead acid", "spill proof", or "maintenance free", are almost always AGM type batteries. If it doesn't say "gel" on it, or have a "G" in the part number, it's not a gel." www.chargingchargers.com/tutorials/batteries.html accessed 11Jun09. N.B.: Use the Original Equipment Manufacture's (OEM) data.
3 Some sources say wait up to 12 hours before testing.

Chapter 17 Leadership

"Show me a poorly uniformed troop and I'll show you a poorly uniformed leader."

Sir Baden-Powell

Trip Leader

What is a trip leader?

Short answer: **'a cat herder'**.

Leadership is the art of influencing and directing others in a task by gaining their confidence, respect and co-operation. To lead people you need to understand and respect them. People have different physical, emotional and mental capabilities. Inherent qualities and surroundings shape character; attitudes being influenced particularly from past experiences but also ignorance.[1]

Needs motivate behaviour. All people are subject to the external pressures of their surroundings (social and physical) as well as their own individual needs, yet people's behaviour in response to their needs, varies considerably. Some of the low (basic) level of needs a person has is the need for protection (i.e. shelter and warmth, water, rest, and food). When these basic needs are satisfied an individual will seek to satisfy the next level of needs like the need for social interaction, status, personal satisfaction and security.[2] If a need is not being met, people respond through their individual behaviour.

Many of the activities an individual pursues relate to status; that of achieving some form of standing within a group; personal recognition.[3] Gaining status in the eyes of peers involves recognition of factors like their achievements, abilities, moral qualities and behaviour. Complementary to gaining status is losing it, or "losing face".

Everyone desires personal recognition for what they do and achieve. The desire for recognition and approval can show itself when the going gets tough and a person sticks it out with the group even at the risk of loss. Other possible motivators for behaviour in tough circumstances may come from moral qualities, mateship and fear of losing self-respect with self or of blame from others. Whatever the motivator, it is unusual for a person to risk their status by acting in a way, which brings condemnation from their peers.

A person's continued support and co-operation can depend upon their receiving recognition of their efforts from their peers and leaders. Recognition of a person's efforts is important in satisfying parts of their emotional needs and gaining their future support. A desire for status is often expressed by the behaviour of a person to attract attention to them-selves through annoying, peculiar or negative behaviour and or talking him or herself up.

Personal satisfaction is important to an individual through doing something worthwhile. Sometimes the approval and or support of others is not needed for them to peruse their activities for the personal satisfaction they draw from their own efforts may be the only reward needed. People require the opportunity to express their individualism and make full use of their abilities. Self-respect suffers when an individual does not have the opportunity to make useful contributions.

Emotional and physical security needs are powerful influences in a person's psyche and determine a person's behaviour. Emotional security implies the need for companionship, a sense of belonging and identity.[4] The knowledge that an individual is a part of a group and that someone is interested in all aspects of the individual's well being is a major influence in that individual's emotional security and response to a group and a leader.

The desire to be free from pain, suffering, ill health and avoid death is a natural feeling. There are also higher-level needs for adventure and excitement that can risk the desire to be healthy and alive. When a person is willing to expose him or herself to risk or even danger, through sport or work, it is for the satisfaction of other higher needs like excitement, adventure, status or duty.

Club (team)

A club can be looked at as a group of teams with the same interest.[5] Individuals bring to a club their own distinct abilities, attitudes, needs and personality. Standards accepted by the club, to achieve a common goal, provide a basis for common attitudes and understanding. A member does not lose their individuality because of accepted standards but has a baseline from where mutual understanding and direction can be established.

Within a club that is not based around competition with other clubs, teams develop naturally through shared values, personalities and goals. A meeting point for people is when the club has an activity. People get to learn the abilities and personality of others in the club, and personal relationships and loyalties develop. As trust and mutual dependence grow, small groups develop within the club as people bond.

Members of a small group identify themselves closely with the group's achievements. As group, success increases, the achievements foster solidarity and high morale. It is the attitude of the small group's towards other club members and groups that determine if it is a clique with in a club.

TYPES OF LEADERSHIP

Within a club, you are only a leader when you turn around and people are following you. Teams work when the leader recognises the need for the individuals to have security and self-confidence. Members of a team work better when their views and opinions are recognised as being important to the successful accomplishment of an activity or club's goals. A leader needs to realise the benefit when forming a plan, of seeking the views and opinions of the group. The degree to which a leader allows the group to influence the plan can be described as 'leadership style'.

Leadership Style

Variance in leadership style

There are three main types of style. People tend to adopt one style but need to learn to be flexible, and know how to adopt the appropriate style for the environment and situation. The styles are:

Authoritative (autocratic), the person controls the activity or situation. It is suitable when there is: stress or danger; a large group of people; and or time is short. If adopted in the wrong situation goals will not be achieved, people will demonstrate discontent through apathy or aggression.

Participative (democratic), the person encourages suggestions from the group in order for them to identify with the plan. Plan future activities, by discussing them with the group. Let people buddy up with whom they desire and lets them share skills or knowledge. When advice is needed, they suggest a number of alternatives from which the group can select one, which seems best. It is suitable for problem solving, instructing or when under personal hardship. When adopted correctly it is observable through goals being achieved, hostility and aggression will be minimal and friendliness will predominate among the group with a willingness to cooperate.

Free Rein (Laissez faire), the person stands back and lets the group do its own thing. It is useful when the group knows what it is doing but can result in confusion, inactivity and discontent when adopted with large groups or when people need support and guidance.

By taking a functional approach to leadership, a leader can break down the activity into its component parts of goals, the group and the individual. The leader is then in a position to decide what to do and how to go about it by selecting a leadership style that is appropriate to the situation and course of action.

Eight Principles of Leadership

Acknowledge your own leadership strengths and weaknesses, and pursue self-improvement.

Seek and accept responsibility:

- Be accountable.

Lead by example:

- Be fit, alert, cheerful and interested.
- Control your emotions with difficult people.

- Be calm, confident and optimistic in all situations.

- Exercise initiative and encourage other to do the same.

- Share the dangers and hardships experienced by the group.

Make sound and timely decisions:

- Be prepared.

- Think and plan ahead of the needs and 'what ifs?'

- Develop solutions to these needs and ideally practice the solutions before a situation arises.

Keep people informed of the overall and current situation and up to date with changes in the plan:

- Be flexible and adaptable.

- Make sure the activity or task is understood and achievable for the group.

- Communicate and do not assume.[6]

- Ask questions of people, so you have an understanding of their situation.

Know the people you are dealing with and consider their welfare.[7]

Develop other people's leadership potential.

Use peoples abilities and potential to develop a team.

FUNCTIONAL LEADERSHIP

This approach was developed to help people attempting leadership roles, to be more effective in their daily interaction with others. The emphasis is on the behaviour of the leader in relation to the participants (followers) he is leading.[8] Participants in any situation will individually accept or reject the leader and within the group, they will actually determine whatever personal power the leader may have.[9]

According to the functional leadership model, there is no best way to influence people. The style of leadership the leader adopts with a group or individual, depends upon the readiness level of the people, the leader is trying to influence.

Table 17-1 Four Leader Behaviours (Styles)

Task behaviour (guidance, influence) and relationship are separate and distinct dimensions, which can be graphed to identify four basic leadership styles; refer Table 17-1.

Situational leadership is based on the interplay among: task behaviour—the amount of guidance and direction a leader gives; relationship behaviour—the amount of team support a leader provides; and the readiness levels the participant's exhibit in response.

The four leadership styles that can be adopted depending upon the situation are shown in:

The first quadrant (S1-style 1) is characterised by giving above average amounts of guidance and direction (task behaviour) but provides below average amounts of support to participants (relationship behaviour): autocratic.

The second quadrant (S2-style 2) is characterised by giving above average amounts of both task behaviour and relationship behaviour.

The third quadrant (S3-style 3) is characterised by giving above average amounts of relationship behaviour and below average amounts of task behaviour.

The fourth quadrant (S4-style 4) is characterised by giving below average amounts of both task behaviour and relationship behaviour: laissez faire.

Leaders need to be flexible in their attempts to influence people. The more a leader adapts his behaviours to the situation the more effective their attempts to influence become.

The relationship between leaders and followers is the crucial variable in a leadership situation. If people decide not to follow, then they will not concern themselves with what people of influence think, the group, or what the implication of their actions may be.

Referring to Table 17-2 under *Follower Readiness*, in situational leadership, 'readiness' is defined as the extent to which a follower has the ability and willingness to accomplish a specific activity.

Ability ('able' and 'unable') is the knowledge, skills and experience a person or group brings together for a particular activity.

Willingness ('willing' and 'unwilling') is the extent to which a person or group has the confidence, commitment, respect and motivation to work together.

Sometimes people are not really unwilling but unsure or insecure about a situation. The extent to which people bring willingness into a situation affects their present ability and the amount of knowledge, experience and skills brought to a specific activity will affect competence, commitment and motivation.

Readiness levels are combinations of ability and willingness. Referring to Table 17-2 and the lower table labelled *Follower Readiness*.

Readiness level 1 (R1) is low level of readiness to follow. Unable & unwilling: participant is unable and lacks motivation and commitment. Unable and insecure: participant is unable and lacks confidence.[10]

Readiness level 2 (R2) is moderate level of readiness to follow. Unable but willing: participant lacks ability but is motivated and makes an effort. Unable but confident: participant

lacks the ability but is confident as long as the leader is there to supply support (guidance).

Readiness Level 3 (R3) is moderate level of readiness to follow. Able but unwilling: participant has the ability to work within the requirements or perform a task but is unwilling to use that ability. Able but insecure: participant has the ability to perform a task but is insecure or apprehensive about doing it.

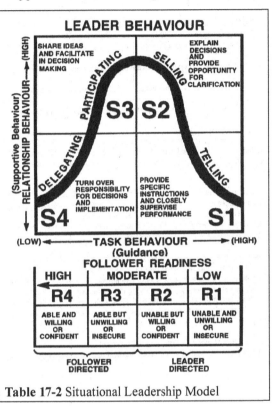

Table 17-2 Situational Leadership Model

Readiness level (R4) is high level of readiness to follow. Able and willing: participant has the ability to perform and is committed. Able and confident: the participant has the ability to perform and is confident about doing it.

Referring to Table 17-2 and the upper table titled *Leadership Behaviour*; the curved line represents the high probability of the combination of task behaviour (the amount of guidance required from the leader) with relationship behaviour (amount of supportive behaviour required from the leader). To use, find a point along the arrow of the follower readiness table. Move vertically up, until you intersect the curved line representing leader behaviour. This will tell you the appropriate leadership style for that type of follower. Table 17-3 is a summation of the combinations in the Situational Leadership model.

Readiness Level	Appropriate Style
R1-Low Readiness Unable or unwilling or insecure behaviour	S1-Telling High Task, Low Relationship
R2-Low to Moderate Readiness Unable but willing or confident	S2-Selling High Task, High Relationship behaviour
R3-Moderate to High readiness Able or unwilling or insecure	S3-Participating High Relationship, Low task behaviour
R4-High Readiness Able/competent and willing/confident	S4-Delegating Low Relationship, Low task behaviour

Table 17-3 Summation of the combinations of the Situational Leadership Model

In situational leadership, the follower has the problem! The leader can get any behaviour desired depending upon the followers behaviour. The follower's behaviour determines the leader's behaviour. Situational leadership is not a prescription with hard and fast rules, for in behavioural sciences, there are no rules.

Leadership and Motivation

Some individuals apply more effort in achieving goals than others. The amount of effort, a person applies to tasks, is a reflection of their own level of motivation. Motivation in co-habitation activities (club, work, sport, etc.) can be thought of as, a willingness to exert effort towards achieving a team or organisational goal in order to satisfy some other individual need. The individual's expended effort, is proportional to their requirement to satisfy that need. Therefore, in order to achieve a group task, it is a requirement that the individual's need is compatible to and consistent with, the team's goal or task.

A key motivational theory is Maslow's *Hierarchy of Needs*. Developed in 1968 by an American psychologist; Abraham Maslow, the Hierarchy of Needs, is a theory that attempts to explain the motivation needs of individuals.[11]

A key principle to the theory is; an individual is motivated by unsatisfied needs. Once a need is met and the desire satisfied, it is no longer a motivating factor. The theory describes needs, as a series of levels arranged in a hierarchy of importance. Since lower-order needs of shelter, food and water, are largely met, the higher order needs emerge and require satisfaction. Only when the lower order needs have been satisfied, will the individual feel motivated to achieve goals that satisfy their higher order needs.

Referring to the pictorial representation of Maslow's Hierarchy of Needs at Table 17-4, the lower order physiological (physical) needs are the basic needs of life—air, clothing, shelter, water, sleep, food, sex. With the majority of physiological needs being satisfied, an individual seeks to satisfy the next order of needs.

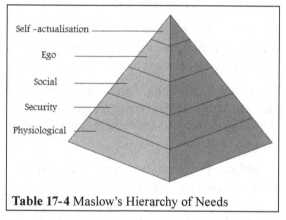

Table 17-4 Maslow's Hierarchy of Needs

Security (safety) needs arise out of an individual desire to predict, plan for and control the outside influences of life. Safety needs may be defined as needs pertaining to personal security, financial security, job security, health and well-being and the setting up of safety nets like insurance policies and bank accounts.

Social needs include the need for friendship, affection and a need to feel part of a team or society. People have a basic desire to belong and to be accepted by those in their environment. Their environment could be made up of small family groups through to large social groups; clubs, professional organisations, religious groups and sporting clubs. The need to belong and the desire to love and be loved, if ignored, can lead to loneliness, social anxiety and clinical depression. In some cases the desire to belong, can over-ride an individual's physiological and security needs. This can be demonstrated in the case whereby a person suffering from anorexia has ignored the physiological desire to eat and the security of health for social acceptance and belonging.

Ego (esteem) needs are the need for recognition of achievement, from individuals, peers, subordinates or co-habitation group. Everyone has the need to be respected, to have self-esteem and self-respect. Also known as the *belonging need,* esteem presents itself as the normal desire of all individuals to be accepted and valued by others. People need to engage themselves in an activity or activities, through such mediums as a profession, sport or a hobby, which provides a sense of contribution, to feel accepted and self-valued. Imbalances at this level can result in low self-esteem and inferiority complexes. People with low self-esteem seek respect from others and their need will lead them into behaviour that will try and satisfy the need. Maslow identified and categorised two types of esteem need and classed them into low and high. The low esteem need version, contained the needs for the respect of others, status, recognition, fame, prestige, and attention. The higher version contained the needs based more on inner competence as achieved through experience for self-esteem, strength, competence, mastery, self-confidence, independence and freedom.

Self-actualisation need is the final level in Maslow's hierarchy of needs and manifests when lower level needs have been satisfied. The motivation to realize one's own maximum potential and possibilities is considered to be the primary motive or the only real motive, with all other motives being the master motive's various forms.[12]

Maslow's Hierarchy of Needs is a good tool for examining individual levels of motivation while conducting an outdoors adventure activity. When individuals are wet, cold, hungry, tired and nervous, they will be less inclined to work towards achieving group goals and tasks (social needs and ego needs). A leader needs to be cognisant of this fact that individuals are motivated by needs. During an activity, the leader must remain vigilant, to ensure that the individual and group needs are met, that the goals of the activity are met and that safety is not compromised.

GROUP BEHAVIOUR

A group may be defined as a number of people whom either have come or have been put together, for a purpose and are broadly classified as:

Formal groups, which are created by an organisation for a specific purpose. Grouping provides a means of organising work into segments, which then enables the organisation to achieve its overall goals. Formal groups are usually structured in to hierarchical order, with individuals being appointed to head the various sub-groups within the organisation.

Informal groups result from individuals having areas of shared interest like that of sports, hobbies and religious beliefs. These types of groups can form inside formal groups and often have leaders who are appointed by group consensus, rather than appointment by a higher authority.

Group Development

The aim of group development is to achieve a cohesive team. Group cohesion is achieved when members are invested in the group's purpose, its task, and to other members of the group. Importantly, highly cohesive groups perform better than non-cohesive groups, especially if the groups are small. Groups are especially important when undertaking dangerous tasks, such as high-risk jobs and outdoors activities, where the cooperation of all members is necessary to achieve the task effectively and safely. When tasks are interdependent of each other, the collaborative actions of cohesive individuals and groups will greatly assist in the successful achievement of a task or tasks. Cohesive groups are self-policing and contribute significantly to the control of the member's behaviour. The cohesive group is a valuable mechanism that has more of an immediate effect on a member's behaviour than the control exerted by the leader.

Since groups are made up of individuals, the group develops and grows through a series of stages. Each stage of group development has different implications on the individual behaviour and for group's performance. These group growth stages are not discrete, but appear as levels in the group evolution from beginning to end. The different stages of group development from beginning to end are:

Forming: this is the initial stage, when group members, first meet and learn about the task or tasks to be completed. It is characterised by a sense of uncertainty and awkwardness and perhaps for some, anxiety. The group's norms and standards have yet to be defined and members are eagerly looking to discover what is the acceptable behaviour standard within the group. Most members are polite, resulting in a superficial level of harmony and cooperation. The group begins to explore and try to understand the nature of its members; their interests, abilities and values.

Storming: refers to the second stage, which is characterised by individual assertive behaviour. This behaviour may result in some group instability and conflict. Informal leaders begin to appear, power struggles may erupt and conflict may arise about how the task should be accomplished. The members of the group have each begun to feel comfortable enough with their new environment to take some risks in revealing more of their personalities. Each person wants to feel a sense of individual importance and to influence the group (by finding a niche).

Norming: refers to the stage in which the group becomes more cohesive, as the individuals are normalised and settle into their group. By this stage, the group will have defined its roles and the various relationships among roles. Appropriate behaviour will also have been established and an identifiable group culture will have started to emerge. Close

bonds and relationships are formed between members of the group. Members of the group will take responsibility for resolving conflicts and strengthening friendships.

Performing: is the desired stage and is achieved when the group is working well as a team. As a team, the group works toward achieving goals or tasks set before it. It is reasonable to expect the group to be working smoothly and productively together. Decision making and problem solving is shared within the group. At this stage, the group is mature enough to attend to its own needs, both in terms of task and relationship matters. Group members are able to remove the focus on themselves and their position, to see how other people in the group are feeling, in order to make sure all are supported.

Mourning: (adjourning stage), is the final stage and occurs when the group has achieved its task, or when the group is disbanded. Feelings of sorrow and loss, accompany this stage, as members find themselves in a situation that does not satisfy their individual needs in the same way as before.

A leader needs to recognise all stages of group development while leading an adventure based activity. While personality issues and individual values can affect the achievement of the overall goal, it is the failure to achieve the enabling goals, which is the most common cause of group disintegration. At any stage, a group may begin to doubt its capability, values, or even leadership. Leadership of the group at this point is critical as the group may plateau or even revert to a previous formative stage.

LEADERSHIP COMMUNICATION

When leading a group remember that the majority of people have initiative and creativity, so use your communication skills to tap into it. Allowing people to contribute promotes high levels of self-esteem, establishes trust and openness that is essential for a team to operate effectively and efficiently.

During a verbal conversation, it has been found that people use the following sensors in greatly differing percentages: sight 75 per cent, hearing 13 per cent, touch 5 per cent, taste 3.5 per cent and smell 3.5 per cent. To be effective in communicating, you need to select the most appropriate sensors. It is not what you say it is how you say it. Facial, body posture and hand gestures as well as tone, are as important as the words you choose to use.

Communication breakdown frequently occurs. Everyone has been in a conversation where the meaning (purpose and or intention) was unclear. Three broad ways in which communication can break down are: if it is blocked entirely, nothing gets through to the receiver; distorted, the message is interpreted differently than intended; or filtered, when only part of the message gets through.

Assertiveness

Overcoming communication breakdown can be achieved through assertiveness.[13] Assertiveness is a learnt skill of self-expression appropriate to the situation, by which one stands up for one's basic rights without violating the basic rights of others. Assertiveness in conversation is simple, honest direct communication, which involves knowing what you want and making it clear to others. Being assertive, results in you having greater confidence and control over your life. This is because you take responsibility for satisfying your needs. Assertiveness develops self-esteem and it is more likely to develop closer and more satisfying relationships with others. Assertion involves respect of the other party's rights. It is not bullying, harassing or demeaning another. It does not imply unquestioning approval or agreement. It does imply you respect their basic rights (e.g. that to be heard).

Assertion involves letting people know your rights. If you are not direct about your feelings, of what you need, then you leave yourself open to misinterpretation or you may even be ignored. In cases where a person or group has been ignoring you, they may be surprised and taken aback by your assertiveness; but do not let this dissuade you, be assertive.

Do not expect people to read your mind, for when they get it wrong, an insecure leader's behaviour's may be to divert the blame; be aggressive or irritated; ridicule (bag) the person; or a combination of poor behaviours. In any case, it makes the recipient feel stupid and as a leader, you will lose credibility within sections of the group.

Types of assertion

Basic assertion is a simple expression of standing up for personal rights, beliefs, feelings or opinions.

Empathic assertion is used when you chose to do more than simply express yourself. It involves making statements that show you take responsibility for your own feelings and do not lay blame on other persons by using 'you' statements. Instead of 'you' try: 'I feel . . .' (Emotional), 'When . . .' (Situational), 'Because . . .' (Effect).

Escalating assertion is used when you need to:

Analyse conflict

Determine your needs

Propose a resolution to a conflict

Negotiate change.

Conflict

Conflict is normal. The way we react to it can be either appropriate or inappropriate. There are basically three types of conflict: conflict of emotions, value conflicts and conflict of needs. Conflict can result from situations involving: a crisis, tension, misunderstanding, incidents and discomfort. Conflict resolution strategies used by people may be avoidance, diffusion or confrontation.

Avoidance: some people are not confrontational. These people suppress their emotional response, ignore or withdraw entirely from the situation.

Diffusion: is a delaying tactic. Attempts are made to tone down or defuse a situation; keep the issues so unclear that attempts of confrontation are stalled even if only temporarily.

Confrontation: can be achieved in two ways through dominance or negotiation. Dominance through power strategies may involve physical force, punishments, insults, making fun of (bagging), demeaning, embarrassing, the use of bribery or inducements, ostracising, or the formation of cliques. Usually there is only one 'winner' at first but the behaviour, creates ongoing and possibly escalating conflicts.

Negotiation strategies involve being assertive and both parties negotiate a compromise solution that is mutually satisfying to all parties involved in the conflict. The desired outcome is a win—win situation for both parties, where both walk away with respect for the others needs. The following strategies are required:

Diagnosis of what type of conflict: emotional, values, needs or a combination.

Initiation of confrontation is required whereby, it is assertively stated, what effects, the conflict is having on you. This does not mean attacking, embarrassing or demeaning the other party in private and particularly in public.

Listen and focus on the emotions first by treating with respect the other person's attitude, which will be conveyed by their behaviours.

Listening is achieved through both voice and body language—the way you look at them, tone of voice, gestures and the selection of words. For many an act of will power (self-control) is needed to prevent disrespect. The goal of listening is to understand the content of their idea's or proposals; and the meaning it has for them and how they feel about it. You need to be able to step back and see their point of view from where they see it.

Listen and restate the issues back, to the other's satisfaction to prevent misunderstanding. When feelings are strong, misunderstanding for whatever reason is prone to happen. When you have heard the other persons feeling on the matter, you have earned the right to speak your point of view and express your feelings.

Briefly state your point of view. Say what you mean and mean what you say. Disclose your feelings.

Values conflicts rarely have any solution because nothing concrete or tangible is involved. Dealing with this type of conflict at the emotional level may help people with opposing beliefs to better understand one another; develop tolerance for each other's position; and occasionally influence their attitudes and actions.

---

1 Just because someone has good skills as a kayaker does not mean that they have been developed as a leader. Many an expedition or voyage has fallen apart because the leader or most dominant person has not been taught to lead. A dominant personality will only go so far.
2 Social interaction varies greatly with individuals but consider the use of solitary confinement as a punishment by the correctional services to modify behaviour.
3 Consider why some people choose professions, institutions, possessions, associations and social circles.
4 Consider why people join clubs.
5 Consider a rugby or cricket club comprised of different levels of teams (i.e. 'A' grade, 'B' grade etc).
6 Assumption is the mother of all stuff-ups and the resulting discontent.
7 Consider what type of person is drawn to sea kayaking; what are their attributes and character?
8 This is to prevent the leader adopting only one style of leadership for all situations.
9 Functional leadership is a model and not a theory. A theory attempts to explain why things behave as they do. A model is a pattern of already existing behaviours that are known and can be learned and therefore repeated.
10 Participant (i.e. a follower). (Leader is not a dirty word! Follower is not a demeaning word it is an action)
11 In 1943, he put forward a paper A Theory of Human Motivation.
12 Towards the end of Maslow's life, he identified another level after self-actualisation and called it Self-transcendence, which is helping others achieve self-actualisation.
13 Assertiveness not aggression.

CHAPTER 18 RISK MANAGEMENT

"Prior preparation prevents poor performance"

Variation of British Army 7-Ps

Table 18-1 Example of a RAMS form

		Risk Analysis and Manage System (RAMS)		
Risk Identification	**Risks**	1. Potential risks (Accident, injury, other forms of loss)		
		People	**Equipment**	**Environment**
	Causal Factors	(Hazards, Perils, Dangers)		
Risk Management strategies	**Normal Operation**	Strategies to manage potential risks & 'Action-on' routine occurrences		
	Emergency Plan			

Risk management has been around for a long time and there are a multitude of ways to perform Risk Analysis and Management. The one thing they all have in common is the goal of identifying and managing risk. Risk is often divided into three sub-categories of:

Absolute risk

- There are no safety controls in the environment you are in.

Real risk

- Is absolute risk adjusted by safety controls and is the amount of risk that actually exists.

Perceived risk

- Is dependent upon the individual and varies from person to person and may not even be related to either absolute or real risk.

We are concerned with real risk and perceived risk. In sea kayaking there is the absolute risk of a head injury if a paddler unsuccessfully surfs over a bombie. So we modify the absolute risk to real risk, by wearing safety equipment (e.g. helmet), or avoid the situation in the first place. Only one of the solutions is capable of avoiding risk while the other reduces the risk so the consequence is less severe.

Following on, to one sea kayaker, surfing over bombies is perceived as dangerous and fool hardy, while to another, it is perceived as a skill and a source of exhilaration.

TERMS

To provide commonality between risk management terms and definitions, the following terms and definitions have been set out below:

Risk management—Is the process of reducing potential loss to an acceptable level.

Risk—Is the potential for injury or loss. It is the potential for an incident or accident to occur. It is a combination of consequence, exposure and likelihood of a specific incident. The loss may be physical, psychological, emotional, social or financial.

The loss may be physical, psychological, emotional, social or financial.

Danger—Gives rise to risk. Danger is divided into two forms: perils and hazards.

Perils—are the source of the loss (e.g. shallow reef, lightning bolt, stone fish).

Hazards—are the conditions, which increase the likelihood of the loss (e.g. big swell, thunder storm, portaging a kayak through shallow water in far north Queensland).

Accident—Is an undesired event, which results in harm to people, damage to property or loss to process (an interruption or disruption to routine or the programme).

Incident—Is an undesired event, which under slightly different circumstances, could have resulted in an accident.

Risk Analysis and Management System

Risk management is not new or unique and is defined as all the procedures and practices used to prevent or reduce accidents (loss). As part of its risk management the Victorian Sea Kayak Club (VSKC) runs a Sea Proficiency course. There are many Risk Management strategies, used to identify risks and eliminate or create strategies to deal with them; so choose one you know. If Risk Management is new to you, there are many good books you can get from the library on the subject.

Here are the basic concepts for performing a Risk Analysis and Management System (RAMS).

Key areas to focus on are:

People

Equipment

Environment.

Within each of these three areas are topics to investigate:

Risk identification—what are the potential risks and causal factors?

Casual factors—are in fact dangers.

Risk management—what strategies can be put in place to manage them?

Actions on—what backup is necessary should a risk be realise (eventuate)?

Risk Identification

Identify and prioritise accidents or incidents (risks) you are trying to avoid.

Identify and number the causal factors (dangers) of each identified risk under the each of the three main areas of people, equipment and environment.[1]

Risk Management

For each causal factor determine a strategy to reduce the risk to an acceptable level by adopting one of the following management techniques:

Avoidance—Avoid totally the risk since frequency or severity is unacceptable despite best efforts to manage them.

Reduction—Reduce risk by using determined risk management strategies.

Transference—Transfer risk to a skilled person or give the participants the information to make their own choice and take the responsibility themselves.

Retain—Your assessment of the risk has determined the frequency and severity are low.

The previous steps are for the development of a 'normal operations plan'. The normal operations plan can also develop the content of your pre-launch brief and for informing participants on 'Action-on' (i.e. what to do if?) For example, action-on group spread, capsize and separation.

Emergency Plan

The last stage involves pre-planning emergency strategies. Determine an emergency plan of action for coping with each of the initially identified potential risks, should they be realised (eventuate).

Conclusion

Outcomes of the RAMS process will determine how you conduct your activity. Depending upon your audience, you can tailor to suit what information is disseminated; formulate your float plan and pre-launch brief, and ensure everyone knows what is going on.

Table 18-3 is an actual RAMS form developed for a winter paddle in cold water (< 12 °C), with a group of novice paddlers. Table 18-3 is an example of a float plan, which needs to be suited towards the type of activity being run. Following on from risk management it is important to communicate with the participants what they need to have and bring. Also, communicate your plan for the weekend. Below is an example of an instruction to novice sea kayakers about paddling to Portarlington in winter. As a leader, you need to think of the information that may not be common knowledge to new paddlers.

Aim:

State the aim of the activity.

Overview

Breakdown the activity into time slots and or events depending upon the activity.

Day one: date

Rendezvous, map reference

Travel from and to; distances

Timings: estimated time of departure (ETD) and estimated time of arrival (ETA)

Breaks and meals as applicable.

Ancillary information

Inform people of conditions and situations that could affect the paddle. This information also helps people to self assess their abilities and fitness to attend the paddle and helps them to pack and wear the right kit and clothing.

Weather conditions that could cause cancellation or delay.

Water temperatures; particularly in winter and autumn.

Time on water paddling (travelling).

Reminder to carry potable water and food in the case you cannot land at planned rest stops.

Administration

Tasks that need to be completed in order for the event to be successful.

Logistics

Transportation, parking, drop off and pickup, car shuffles and resupply.

Equipment

Put an equipment list in as an annex.

Remind people of what safety equipment is legally required to be carried depending upon location and to check serviceability of clothing, safety gear and equipment before the event.

Table 18-2 Example of a previously used RAMS form		
Dangers: perils & hazards	**Normal operation**	**Emergency plan**
Port Phillip Bay water temperature < 12°C	Dress for immersion No cotton garments Wear quick drying garments Carry spare AOW[2] beanie	Perform assisted rescue Monitor/Assign a buddy
Wind chill	Carry wind protection (e.g. cag) Wear thermal under clothing Carry a warm drink Carry snacks	Carry an emergency wind break (e.g. plastic rubbish bag or poncho) Monitor
	On-land: Ground sheet Wet weather over pants and jacket Warm jacket Brew kit or warm thermos Dry thermal top	Find or make shelter Dress in dry clothing Rewarm with warm drink
Hypothermia	Protect from wind and monitor/assist Get to shore and rewarm	Use an emergency signalling device Sever hypothermia call 000
Novice sea kayakers	Send an information sheet Thorough on-shore brief Monitor on paddle Adhere to group spread prevention measures Demonstrate hand & paddle signals	Buddy up

Inappropriate equipment (sea kayak, safety, clothing etc)	Check equipment and clothing for appropriateness Correct deficiencies Deny ability to participate on trip	
Wind and sea state greater than force 4 on either day (e.g. forecasted wind greater than 15 knots)	**CANCEL PADDLE** Options Relocate to sheltered waters	
Not reaching destination	Contact on-shore co-ordinator when at destination	No contact by group after 1600h attempt to call: Group Home contact (to see if anyone has checked in) No contact with group by 1630h call 000
Car accident driving home	Warn participants of driver fatigue Encourage them to take a nap before departing or while travelling but not driving.	Buddy up if possible

Float plan

A float plan is part of the risk management process. Below is an example of a float plan that you will need to draw up and adapt to suit your trips.

Table 18-3 Example of a Float Plan

Adapt to Suit Event					
Note: Do not forget to leave a copy with an on-shore contact					
Note: Ensure other paddlers in the group have a copy of the contact phone numbers					
Date From:			Date To		
Trip Location:					
Overview of "On-Water" Trip Plan:					
Number of Paddlers:		Number of Sea Kayaks:			
Day One:	From:		To:		Distance:
Day Two:	From:		To:		Distance:
Day Three:	From:		To:		Distance:
Communications					
Primary Mobile Phone:			Switched on between:		
Marine Radio:	Fq. type:		Switched on between:		
Emergency equipment carried: smoke & flares, V-sheet, signal mirror, sea marker dye					
Overdue Procedures					
Consider the trip overdue if you are not contacted by:			Day & Time:		
			Day & Time:		
			Day & Time:		
Action on failed contacts:					
1.	Try several of the paddling group's mobile phones. (See Paddler's List Below.)				
2.	Try the Home contact phone numbers to see if one of the group have contacted home.				
3.	Ring 000 and give details of this trip plan.				
Participants					
Paddlers Name:	Boat colour, deck/hull	Trip contact phone number	Car registration and description	Home contact	Home Phone & contacts Mobile number
Note: Repeat above participants rows for as many as required					
Control					
Organizer:			On-water leader:		
Logistics					

Day Departing Home:			Group Meeting at & time:		
Caravan Park or Camping at: (Refer Annexes for lists)					
Car Shuffle: Car & Rego# left for pick up at:					
Weather Forecast at Annex:					
Day 1 Launch Location & time:			Off-water at & time:		
Escape Route Options:					
Camping at:					
NOTE: repeat above daily travel information for as many days required					
Finish Location:			**Finish time:**		

Emergency Signalling Devices Carried

Individual Signalling Devices:	Signal mirror Whistle Handheld flares & Smoke	Y/N	EPIRB (406MHz) SPOT Mobile Phone (Telstra Next G) Mobile Phone (Optus/other)	Y/N	Strobe light Flashlights Chemical light sticks	Y/N
Group Signalling Devices:	Marine Radio: VHF, 27 MHz, HF Satellite phone	Y/N	Camera flash Marker dye Aerial flares Vee Sheet	Y/N		

PRE-LAUNCH BRIEF

When on the beach you need to communicate to everyone about the event, what is expected and what to do if an unplanned situation arises. Even though you sent a written instruction to participants do not be disappointed if someone has not read it or if someone has forgotten something.

When dealing with new kayakers introduce yourself and ask subtle questions about their sea kayaking experience. You may need to make a decision about their suitability to go on the trip. When dealing with club members, remember that you are herding cats. That is, you have a group of individuals that are attending a social function.

Give yourself time to observe the participants get ready to launch so that you can detect and correct errors or replace missing kit. This will reduce the possibility of wasting time when it is time to launch.

Before launching, you will need to give a brief to the participants about the days activity. The best method for ensuring you give a through and appropriate briefing is to use a briefing memory aide (aka aide memoire). The purpose is so you do not forget what to say or take with you. You do not have to say everything from the suggestions below, but what is relevant to the situation on the day. The format: Activity, Environment, Administration, Control and Signals are an easy way to structure what needs to be said when briefing a group. Make up a laminated card as an aid memoire, as shown in Figure 18-1, to assist you during the brief.

When giving a brief, ask for questions to be held until you are finished, however be polite when someone does interject, even if the answer is the next point!

① **Note:** The information below is written so you can sit down and think about all of the information that may be relevant to you particular trip. Below is an example of an aid-memoire used by David Golightly.

- DAVID GOLIGHTLY—PRE-DEPARTURE BRIEFING NOTES:
- WELCOME & INTRODUCTIONS
- SIGNING OF TRIP WAIVER PROFORMA
- DESTINATION, DISTANCES, TIMETABLE & PROPOSED REST STOPS
- WEATHER FORECAST, TIDES, STREAM FLOWS, TIME OF SUNSET
- AWARENESS OF PADDLING ENVIRONMENT, NAVIGATION
- FOOD, WATER, GEAR, CLOTHING
- GROUP BEHAVIOR, SIGNALS, NUMBERS
- FRONT & REAR LEADERS
- EXISTING INJURIES
- WARM-UP EXERCISES

Figure 18-1 Example of a simple aide memoire

Activity

Introduce yourself and the group to each other.

Describe what you have planned for the level of the group.

Orientate and show on a chart where you are planning to go and heading.

Point out features that will assist people in identifying the course to steer.

Environment

Weather forecast

Sea state

Tides and Tidal Streams.

Administration

Timings (e.g. launch, rests, meals, stops, return, length of time on water).

Location of first aid kit, emergency clothing, shelter and communications.

Reminder to take their personal medication (e.g. asthmatics, and have it on them or in the cockpit in a dry bag or in the day hatch).

Reminder what to take (e.g. lunch, snacks, water, sunscreen).

Ask if everyone has signed the VSKC Trip Waiver Form.

Control

Tell group that speed of group is dependent upon the slowest paddler

Tell required group spread: depends upon conditions

Buddy novices with capable paddlers

Nominate a lead and trailing boat

Actions on: capsize, separation,

Medical situation (e.g. hypothermia).

Signals

Mobile phones

Emergency contact numbers

VHF radios

Emergency contact channel

Smoke and flares

Whistles

Signal mirrors.

Any Questions

Open the brief to questions. If you have forgotten something in the brief, it may get brought up here by a question from the group.

Pre-launch Observations

When people are getting ready, pay attention to their behaviour and equipment. Look to see if they have any problems or deficiencies that you can discreetly assist with.

Missing Kit

People often turn up to a paddle without pieces of kit (e.g. cag, whistle, hat). If you are running a paddle and or assisting and have any spare kit, it may come in use down on the beach.

PARTICIPANT ACKNOWLEDGEMENT OF RISK

Trip waiver form

A final part of risk management is the legal protection of the participant, club volunteer trip leaders and the club. To protect the trip leaders and the club, the Victorian Sea Kayak Club's lawyers produced this *Release and Waiver of Liability, Indemnity Agreement and Assumption of Risk* form, which participants on a VSKC trip are request to read and sign.

VICTORIAN SEA KAYAK CLUB Inc. Registered No. A17985B

THE VICTORIAN SEA KAYAK CLUB is a group of people who enjoy paddling in open waters. There is no such thing as a completely safe trip, as even the most sheltered and protected waters can become dangerous in adverse conditions. Weather is not always predictable, adverse changes can, and will, occur suddenly. Even with the best information at the time, available conditions can be misjudged. Please read carefully Release and Waiver of Liability, Indemnity Agreement and Assumption of Risk. The trip coordinator on club organized trips acts as a focal point to bring together the ideas, energies and resources of the group but are not formal leaders. They are not paid.

RELEASE AND WAIVER OF LIABILITY

INDEMNITY AGREEMENT AND ASSUMPTION OF RISK

Read carefully before signing

I am aware that my participation in VSKC activities are dangerous, physically demanding and hazardous, involving risk of injury, death, or personal property loss or damage. The risks include, but are not limited to, injury or fatality due to immersion underwater, impact with submerged or exposed objects, slipping and falling, accident or injuries in remote places without medical facilities, sprains, strains, dislocations, or other injuries, exposure to temperature extremes or inclement weather, accidents while travelling to and from activity sites and other risks that may not be known. I am also aware that weather and sea conditions are unpredictable and are dangerous.

In consideration for being permitted to participate in these activities I AGREE.

AGREEMENT

The Club agrees to allow the participant (a current financial member of the Club) to be involved in activities sponsored or run by the Club or by any member of the Club ("the activities") on the following conditions set out below

Any person who is involved in any such activities associated with sea kayaking does so at their own risk and hereby attests that they can swim and are medically and physically fit to participate.

It is a condition of participating in the activities that its members, officers and agents are absolved from all liability arising from injury or damage howsoever caused (whether fatal or otherwise, and whether caused by negligence or other breach of duty) arising out of the activities.

For myself, my dependents, my heirs, executors or administrators, I waive, release and discharge the Club, and any of their respective officials, servants, volunteers

and agents from and against all and any claims or actions which I (or persons claiming through or under me) may have against them or any of them with respect to death, injury or loss of any kind whatsoever suffered or incurred by me even if such death, injury or loss was caused by or contributed to by the act, default or omission (amounting to negligence or otherwise) of the Club, and any of its respective officials servants or agents.

It is also a condition that the participant is solely responsible for the seaworthiness of any equipment used by the participant

The Club is entering in to this Agreement as trustee and agent for its members, officers and agents.

To be signed by members and guests participating on this trip Location:

Trip Date:

---

1 Some risk identification methods categorise risk by Likelihood (probability of each identified event happening), Exposure (how often and how long exposed to each identified risk), Consequence (the magnitude of the potential consequence of an incident needs to be assessed. The potential consequence may require assumptions and judgements to be made on insufficient information.)
2 AOW, Accessible On Water

Chapter 19 Victorian Coast

"It is always in season for old men to learn"

Aeschylus

Kayaking the Coast

ⓘ **Note:** For information on other paddling destinations refer to Appendix 2—Contact Numbers & Websites, Interesting Sites. Many of the club websites have useful articles and trip reports and contacts.

ⓘ **Note:** Another source of local knowledge for an area are the commercial operators.

People have asked me to put in information about kayaking the Victorian coast, but there are too many variables. You need to be able to access and read the nautical chart and topographical maps for the area you would like to kayak. You can also use Pilots and access websites for Parks Victoria, Parks and Wildlife Tasmania, NSW National Parks and Wildlife Service, Queensland Parks and Wildlife Service and or the Great Barrier Reef Marine Park Authority. By getting training from a recognised training provider or joining a club is a beneficial way to gain knowledge and experience. Above all you need good judgement and self-awareness to know when and not to launch.

However, within this chapter, under the topic of the Victorian Capes, I have included an article I wrote for the VSKC magazine Sea Trek, about paddling Victoria's west coast (Southern Ocean).

Direction of buoyage

In Victoria the direction of buoyage runs from east to west and into ports from seaward. When entering port, the port-hand (red) mark should be passed on the kayaks port (left) side. When heading out to sea the port-hand mark (red) should be passed on the kayaks starboard (right) side.

Victorian Coast

Victoria's coast is 1230 kilometres long, with rocky coast accounting for 419 kilometres. The coast is impacted by both the Pacific Ocean and Southern Ocean. More specifically, it is boarded by the Southern Ocean to the west of Cape Otway, Bass Straight between Cape Otway and Wilsons Promontory, and the southern Tasman Sea (South Pacific Ocean) in the east.

Types of Victorian Beaches

The Victorian coast extends between 37.5° S to 39° S and has typically temperate middle latitude beaches, which are composed of quartz sand grains mixed with shell fragments. There are seven process that impact Victorian beaches: Ocean and sea waves, tides, ocean currents, local wind driven currents, upwelling and downwelling, sea surface temperature and biological processes (ocean biota). The westerly wind stream produces an easterly water flow through Bass Straight combined with wind and wave energy that produces energetic surf and a large coastal dune system.

Most of Australia's beaches are classified as being in the micro tidal range (tidal range less than two metre) with the exceptions being in the west around Exmouth Peninsula and in the north, where the tidal range is from three to ten metres. In parts of South Australia and Western Port Bay, the tidal range can be above two metres but the wave height is low.

Victorian Water Temperature

Water temperature along the Victorian coast is the result of two main factors. First, is the overhead position of the sun, which is determined by the latitude of the coast between 37° 30' S and 39° S. Second, is the source of Victorian coastal water from two opposing directions. From the east comes the warmer East Australian Current and from the west the cooler Southern Ocean. Included in the mix is the Bass Straight Water current that flows into and mixes with the different temperature waters in Bass Straight.

As a generalised explanation, during the warmer months, particularly around March, the coastal water temperature in southern NSW varies around 21 to 22 degrees Celsius. In eastern Victoria, it varies around 21 to 19 degrees Celsius and western Victoria it is around 18 degrees Celsius. During the cooler months particularly around September, coastal water temperatures in southern NSW vary around 17 to 15 degrees Celsius; in eastern Victoria, it varies from 14 to 13 degrees Celsius and along the central and western Victorian coast, it is around 13 degrees Celsius.

Victorian Waves

For western Victoria and west Bass Straight, waves primarily result from the mid-latitude cyclones (lows), moving over the Southern Ocean. In summer, the lows are well into the Southern Ocean and it can take up to two days for the waves to reach the coast as long moderate to high swells. In winter, the lows can pass closer to and even over the coast creating large seas and swell. These waves on average originate from the south-west (SW) and range from two to three metres in height, with a 12 to 14 second period.

Data from Cape Northumberland (SA), shows SW swells ranging from zero to two metres, occur during 30 per cent of the year. Two to four metre swells, occur 60 to 70 per cent of the year, with peak increases in winter.

Eastern Victoria's waves are mostly westerly wind waves (seas), high easterly swell and effects of East Coast Cyclones. The westerly winds create calm shore wave conditions and seas offshore depending upon strength. As the coast aligns more north southeast from Cape Conran, the westerly waves increase in size and dominate. Around Gabo Island, southerly and easterly waves dominate over south-westerly waves. Refer to Table 19-1, for a comparison between western and eastern Victoria's waves.

Table 19-1 Victorian Coast Typical Wave Data		
Source: Andrew Short, Beaches of the Victorian Coast, 1997		
	Western Victoria	Eastern Victoria
Average wave height	1.5–2 m	1.5 m
Maximum wave height	5 m	3 m
Average wave period	12–14 sec	8–10 sec
Predominant Direction	SW	SW, NE

As far as the Victorian coast is concerned, the seas and swells generated by East Coast Lows generate the biggest waves, which impact the Gippsland coast, from the east and north-east. On average, the waves range from 2 to 3 metres at 10 to 12 seconds.

VICTORIAN TIDES

Tidal waves arrive on the Victorian coast twice a day and are referred to as semi-diurnal (or half-daily) tides. The tide in Victoria has no impact on the oceans wave height. The arrival of the tidal wave will impact on the breaking wave height, as the tide modifies the depth of water immediately seaward of the beach.

The tides in Bass Strait originate from the tidal wave travelling southwards down the Australian east coast, at around 600 kilometres per hour in the deep water. For Victoria, the tidal wave first reaches Gabo Island near Mallacoota and the Gippsland coast. As the northern part of the wave passes the eastern entrance of Bass Strait, some of it is deflected into the shallower Bass Straight.

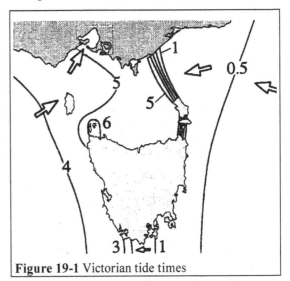

Figure 19-1 Victorian tide times

Bass Straight is a shallow continental shelf channel or sea, with an average depth of 50 to 70 metres. This causes the tidal wave to slow down to around 80 kilometres per hour. The remaining southern part of the tidal wave continues travelling at high speed, in the deep waters around the southern and western sides of Tasmania. This wave reaches the western Victorian coast entrance some three hours later, after encountering the eastern Victoria coast. The wave front entering from the west meets the wave front entering from the east, causing large tides along a north-south line in the middle of Bass Strait. Tides enter the eastern and western entrances of Bass Straight three hours apart because, a tidal wave moves faster in deep water than in shallow water.

As a result, of the tidal wave entering Bass Straight, from both the east then the west, three hours apart, the resulting inflows meet in the middle of Bass Strait. The wave is defected south toward the north coast of Tasmania, resulting in northern Tasmania having a large tidal range. The ebb tide appears to be the reverse of this situation.

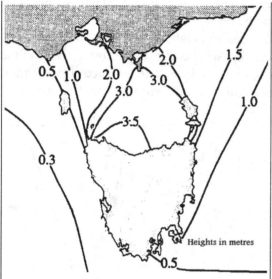

Figure 19-2 Victorian and Tasmanian tide ranges

The dissipation of tidal energy is large within Bass Strait, compared to the adjacent ocean. The turbulence in the water column is usually associated with velocity shear (where the lines converge) around the islands and through the constrictions at either end.

As mentioned above, the shallow waters of Bass Strait amplify the tidal waves that meet in the middle of Bass Strait and deflect it downwards toward northern Tasmania. The convergence of the two inflows causes a large tidal range. Bass Strait and Western Port Bay, amplify the tidal wave, where in eastern and western Victoria, as well as Port Phillip Bay, the range comparatively remains low.

The tidal wave entering Westernport is further amplified by the shallow bay and tidal wave resonance. This produces a spring tidal range that varies around 2.3 metres. The narrow 3.5

kilometre entrance to Port Phillip Bay called *The Rip*, restricts and slows down the tidal wave so that it takes a further three hours to reach Port Melbourne. Port Phillip has a spring tidal range that varies around 0.6 metres, whereby along the coast, at and near Port Phillip Heads, the spring range, is around 1.1 metres. Tide height to the west of Cape Otway decreases.

Table 19-2 Victorian ocean tide (approximate) times		
Location	**Time (hours)**	**(- i.e. earlier) (+ i.e. later)**
Gabo Island	−5.5	Vic/NSW boarder
Mallacoota Inlet	−2.6	
Snowy River Entrance (Marlo), Lakes Entrance	−2.8	
Port Albert Pier, Welshpool Pier	+1.5	
Port Welshpool (Rabbit Island)	+10	See Rabbit Island (Port Welshpool) tables
Wilsons Promontory		**Flinders Is.** East boarder Bass Straight
Waratah Bay	+0.05	
Venus Bay	0.0	
Inverloch Pier	+0.25	15 min
Phillip Island, Ocean	0.0	Seal Rocks to C. Woolamai
Western Port	−0.6	See Western Port tables
Mornington Peninsula, Ocean	0.0	Mornington Ocean Beaches, C. Schanck, Flinders
Port Phillip Bay Heads	0.0	See PPB Tables
Queenscliff Pier	+0.5	~5.2 km inside PPB
Rip Bank	−0.25	~800 m outside the PPB Heads
Barwon Heads (Bridge)	+0.25	15 min
Lorne	−0.33	20 min
Apollo Bay	−0.41	25 min
Cape Otway		**King Is.** West boarder Bass Straight
Port Campbell	−0.72	-0.72 ≈ 43 min +13 min Portland
Warrnambool	−0.5	
Portland	−0.5	
Nelson		Vic/SA boarder

① **Note:** Web sites for Victorian tides can be found on the Bureau of Meteorology website

Gippsland tides

The Gippsland Authority looks after 720 kilometres of coastline from Andersons Inlet (Venus Bay) through to Mallacoota (Victoria / NSW boarder). The Authorities' web site has the tide tables for this section of coast and provides the following information about the nature of the tides in this region:

Based on analysis of observed tides at Lakes Entrance an average time variation from the Port Welshpool (Rabbit Island) predictions has been found of 2 hrs 36 mins, which has been adopted for 2004.

The variations for Point Hicks, Marlo, Mallacoota and Gabo Island have been deduced from the Australian National Tide Tables variations for Eden.

Analysis also shows a great variance with the time of tide being regularly 25 mins both earlier and later with some variations to 40 mins. Therefore, caution must be taken when using the Rabbit Island predictions for East Gippsland.

VICTORIA'S WIND DRIVEN COASTAL CURRENTS

Westerly winds reinforce Bass Straight water currents and generate westerly coastal currents along the Gippsland coast. Westerly winds push surface water eastward and toward the coast, creating a slightly higher water level at the coast. This causes coastal surface water down-welling (warming), whereby water moves down-slope across the inner continental shelf.

Occurring most commonly along the western Victorian coast and Gippsland coast, during strong summer northerly and easterly winds, is a process of upwelling (cooling). The strong winds move the coastal surface water seaward, creating a depression along the affected coastline. Cold bottom water, from below the inner continental shelf up-wells (moves up) to refill the depression. Other factors such as tides, winds, (onshore, offshore and longshore currents), and ocean waves have an effect on local currents.

FACTS AND FEATURES ABOUT PORT PHILLIP

Port Phillip is also known as Port Phillip Bay. Port Phillip took its present shape 8000 years ago. During the last glacial period about 18000 years ago, the sea level was about 130 metres lower than today. The Yarra, Werribee and Little Rivers formed a delta reaching the sea between Cape Otway and King Island.

Port Phillip coastline is 264 kilometres, with a length of 58 kilometres, a width of 41 kilometres and a total area of 1950 square kilometres. The deepest point is 24 metres but nearly half the bay is less than 8 metres deep. It has a volume of 25 cubic kilometres. There are 146 beaches that occupy 177 kilometres or 68 per cent of this coastline.

Water temperature is influenced by Bass Straight Water temperature and the thermal effect of heating and cooling caused by the shallow depth of the bay that can create a 12 degrees Celsius difference between summer and winter water temperatures. In winter Port Phillip Bay, has an average mid bay temperature of 10 degrees Celsius and in summer of 21 degrees Celsius.

There is very little mixing between Bass Strait ocean water and Port Phillip Bay water, resulting in a flushing time for Port Phillip Bay, of around 12 months. Ocean tides enter the bay but are reduced in speed and size. Ocean swell only affects a few beaches near the entrance. Most, movement of Port Phillip Bay waters is due to wind rather than tides.

Water level within Port Phillip is also affected by prolonged winds blowing in one direction. Southerly gales (winds of 34–40 kn) can cause the water level to remain above the mean level continuously for some time after. Northerly gales can have the opposite effect on water's mean level.

Port Phillip beaches can be wave dominated in periods of strong and gale force winds that produce waves of limited height and length and a wave period of about 5 seconds. Waves are determined by the Bays irregular shape, fetch, varying depths and different wind strengths.

For information about sea breezes in Port Phillip, refer to the BOM booklet: Boating Weather Series, *Wind Waves Weather Victorian Waters*, for a fuller explanation. For information about wave heights in Port Phillip Bay, refer to the diagram in the Victorian Recreational Boating Safety Handbook.

The Rip

'The Rip' is the entrance to Port Phillip, between Point Lonsdale and Point Nepean. It is 3.5 kilometres wide, but the reefs projecting from these points reduce the navigable width to about one kilometre.

For about 800 metres outside the 'Heads', there is a shallow rocky flat known as the 'Rip Bank'. The water deepens outside this flat to 30 metres and inside the Heads to as much as 90 metres.

This inequality of depth (94 metres to 13.6 metres in the middle) combined with tidal streams running between 5 to 8 knots at their strongest, causes the world-renowned The Rip. Freshets and wind affect the velocity of the tidal streams and the times of predicted slack water.

Port Phillip Sea Pilots have this to say:

The Rip is still a very dangerous area for all craft because of the strong tidal flow and the uneven nature of the seabed and is at its worst when a full ebb tide of up to 10 knots meets a southerly gale. This and the fact that slack water is three hours after high and low water explains why so many ships were wrecked there in the early days. The ship's captain timing his arrival for low water and expecting to get the first of the flood tide through the entrance found that he was caught in the strongest part of the ebb tide, and in trying to enter could be swept on to Point Nepean.

The Point Lonsdale Pier was built in the late 1890s to assist in the retrieval of people from ships wrecked, coming in through The Rip. Lifeboats were stationed at Queenscliff near The Rip for 120 years from 1856.

EXTRACT FROM AUS CHART 143—NON-TIDAL CHANGES IN SEAL LEVEL & TIDAL STREAMS.

Water level within Port Phillip is much affected by winds blowing for a long period in one direction and may remain above mean sea level continuously for some time after Southerly gales, or below mean sea level continuously for some time after Northerly gales.

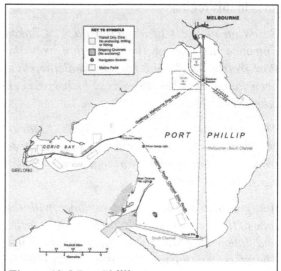

Figure 19-3 Port Phillip

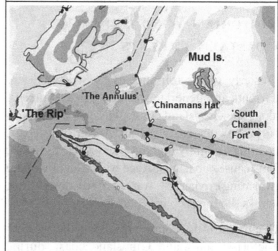

Figure 19-4 Entrance to Port Phillip

At about the time of high and low water in the entrance the stream runs at its strongest, 5 < 8 knots; slack water occurs at about three hours before and after high water in the entrance, and the stream runs in from about three hours before till three hours after high water, out at other times; the time of slack water and the velocity of the *streams are affected by wind & freshets (rush of flood in fresh water flowing into sea (salt water).*

Caisson M and Chinaman's Hat

There was at one stage two structures called 'Chinaman's Hat', one built in 1942 and the latest in 2001. The original Chinaman's Hat (aka *Caisson M*) is located near the South Channel and Mud Island. GPS marking: S38° 17.25', E144° 43.55'. The old World War II Chinaman's Hat is marked as 'Caisson M' on chart Aus 158. Caisson M was built as part of the defence system during World War II the building was octagonal in shape and resembled a Chinaman's hat. A photo-electric beam was mounted on the structure to detect incoming ships by a break in the beam. It was employed particularly at night, when enemy ships might try to slip undetected through Port Phillip Heads and attack Melbourne. Prior to its removal, the original Chinaman's Hat (Caisson M) fell into a state of disrepair and became little more than an outcrop resembling a dilapidated gigantic 44 gallon drum with a post out of the top. It became home to a group of Australian fur seals, which were regularly seen in the warmer months lounging on its rocky surface. However, the predominantly young male seals, which have been evicted from the larger breeding colonies at Phillip Island, can also be seen at the new artificial habitat.

In September 2001 after eleven months and $210,000 work was completed on the new Chinaman's Hat as a habitat for fur seals. The pitched roofed pylon structure has a deck for the seals and was built by Parks Victoria and funded by the Central Coast Board. It is located near: S38° 17.34', E144° 43.52' not far from the site of the removed Caisson M.

South Channel Fort

This artificial island of 0.7 hectares was constructed in the 1880s between 1879 and 1888, as a strategic defence post. Additionally, the fort was to act as a sea-lane channel marker, to illuminate the South Channel at night and electronically explode mines under attacking ships that had breached the defences at the Heads. It was part of a triangle of defence that included Point Nepean and Queenscliff. 'The Annulus', which is also referred to as 'Popes

Eye', off Queenscliff, was also planned to be part of the Heads defence strategy.

South Channel Fort, is located 5.95 kilometres north-east of Sorrento. South Channel Fort was constructed from 14 000 tonnes of bluestone boulders and cement with a sand overburden. It is 121.9 metres long, 76.4 metres wide and 6.4 metres above sea level. Today the fort is part of Mornington Peninsula National Park and includes antiquated rusting and crumbling gun emplacements and underground passages. Visitors are allowed, but are asked to keep to the formed walking tracks to avoid trampling nests of White-faced Storm Petrels and their camouflaged eggs.

The Annulus

The Annulus (aka *Pope's Eye*) was first planned as a fort to protect Port Phillip's West Channel. Construction began in the 1880s, but was never completed. Located 5 kilometres northeast of Portsea and constructed in a semi-circle of blue stone, it is 2.5 metres above the surface at low water. Also known as the 'Annulus Fisheries Reserve' and sometimes referred to as 'Popes Eye'. Part of the Harold Holt Marine Reserve, Pope's Eye is home to a vast array of other aquatic life, including seals, rare fish and corals. Its boundaries extend from a 100 metres radius at the centre of the Annulus. It is a protected rookery for Australasian Gannets and is the first known gannet colony in the world on an artificial structure.

Located at S38 16.6970°, E144 41.8328°. On the mariner chart Aus 158 (scale 1:37 500) the south cardinal marker (VQ(6) + LFl. 10s 9m 8M) is titled Popes Eye. This has caused some confusion for people who associate the name with the Annulus. The Annulus structure is about 1.6 kilometres north of the south cardinal marker and on this chart is identified by the No.1 West Channel marker (Fl. WR.6s 7m 7/5M). The Annulus can be clearly identified using the mariners chart Aus 143.

South Channel Pile Light

The South Channel Pile Light was built between 1872 and 1874 at a cost of 1550 pounds, which is the equivalent to $3000 today. The 'cottage style' lighthouse was completed in 1874 and was occupied by lighthouse keepers until the early 1900s. The light was finally switched off in 1985, having operated as a navigational beacon for some 111 years. In 1998, it was removed from its original location and restored. After restoration it was situated in its present position 3 kilometres off Rye pier. The original pillars were left at the original location for the purpose of a seal haul out. Public access to the Pile Light is by boat and is limited to viewing of the outside of the structure. The South Channel Pile Light is located in Port Phillip Bay: navigational coordinates S38° 20.399', E144° 49.022' (AGD 66), or 3 kilometres off the Rye pier. Melway ref: 168 F2.

Mud Islands

Mud Islands are the surface expression of the Great Sand, the largest shoal in Port Phillip. They consist of three shrubby sand islands enclosing a shallow tidal lagoon, which is fringed by salt marsh. The island group is 1200 x 900 metres in size; has a total area of 86 hectares with a land area of 60 hectares and reaches a height of 4 metres. Despite the name, the islands, including their outer beaches, are mainly composed of shell sand. Resembling an atoll, Mud Islands form a unique feature in the southern Australian landscape.

Formed by wind and wave action, Mud Islands are 'anchored' by outcrops of phosphate rock. This rare rock type forms below guano deposits as phosphate from guano (accumulations of bird droppings), which leaches down and combines with shell sand to form hard calcium phosphate. Phosphate rock is resistant to marine erosion and keeps the entire system in place.

Mud Islands support nine native vegetation communities, sea-grass meadows, sand dunes, mud flats, salt marshes and a diversity of life ranging from marine invertebrates to fish and birds. Seventy species of birds have been recorded on the islands, which provide essential breeding, feeding and roosting areas for many migratory sea birds and waders. Eighty-seven species are recorded and fifteen of these have been recorded nesting. The entire area above high water mark is used for nesting, with some

species forming extensive colonies. The major species are Silver Gull, Straw-necked Ibis, Australian White Ibis and White-faced Storm-Petrel. Other colony forming birds are Australian Pelican, Crested Tern and Caspian Tern.

The central lagoon is visited by thousands of intercontinental waders in the warmer months. Access is by boat only, private or charter. As shallow waters surround the islands, visitors are warned to be cautious when attempting a landing. Small boats may anchor onshore but larger boats must remain in deeper waters.

Port Phillip

Paddling in Port Phillip Bay is a source of relaxation and enjoyment for many kayakers. The north and east areas of Port Phillip are built up with commercial and residential property along the shoreline. Access to the bay can be made at any of the sandy public beaches.

✦ **Caution:** Port of Melbourne is a busy port. The Yarra River and Maribyrnong River in this area hold shipping lanes and docking facilities.

① **Note:** launching from a boat ramp, you may upset 'boaters', especially if there is a group of kayakers.

If you would like to paddle up the Yarra River, you can launch from Sandridge beach in Port Melbourne or Williamstown beach. The boat ramp at 'The Warmies' in Newport is on the Yarra River and provides a good access point.

The western side of Port Phillip includes Altona Bay to Point Cook. The coastline down to Geelong has very little residential development. After Werribee South (Werribee River mouth), there is an exit point at Kirk Point but after that, the next exit point on the west bank, is at Avalon. From the Werribee River mouth there are six kilometres of navigable river until you reach the Werribee golf course. Here the river is very shallow for about 200 metres before deepening again. There is a further two kilometres of river before obstructions prevent you from entering the Werribee zoo precinct. The entire length of the Werribee River is a bird watchers delight. Heading south from Werribee South is land belonging to Melbourne Water and the Western Treatment Plant. This section of shoreline down to the Sand Hummock, at Point Wilson, is host to many migratory birds and is managed by Melbourne Water. For access to the land, go to their website for information on how to get permits.

In 1983, the western shores of Port Phillip Bay, including the Bellarine Peninsula, were designated a Wetland of International Importance under the Ramsar Convention. This classification included the Western Treatment Plant's Lake Borrie and its surrounding lagoons and coastal mudflats. Under the Convention, sites must meet criteria based on the characteristics of the wetland or its value in supporting plants, animals or waterfowl. The area can house an estimated 65 000 birds at any one time. The plant is considered to be one of the top 10 bird watching areas in Australia, with over one third of the country's species being recorded there (about 270 species). This is second only to Kakadu National Park. Twelve species of flora and fauna found at the Western Treatment Plant are listed under the Flora and Fauna Guarantee Act.

To get to Avalon, you pass Point Wilson. Point Wilson has a BOM automatic weather station, and you can access observation data about the area on the website. Point Wilson also has a long pier managed by the Department of Defence, which is used to unload ships carrying dangerous/ hazardous cargo. There is a 300 metre exclusion zone around the jetty. After Point Wilson, you are in the 'Outer Harbour'. After Point Lillias, you are in Corio Bay and the city of Geelong. Corio bay makes for pleasant paddling around the foreshore. Around the suburb of Corio is Hovells Creek. This area makes for easy launching access or a place for lunch. On the south-eastern shoreline of Corio Bay, is Point Henry and then the Outer Harbour. Heading eastwards along the shoreline is the Bellarine Peninsula and the town of Clifton Springs. This area has cliffs and rocky stretches of shoreline making exit difficult in an emergency. The Bellarine Peninsula juts into Port Phillip with the town of Portarlington located at the north-western end. From Portarlington, it is a 17 kilometre paddle back to Werribee South. Paddling around Portarlington, is very pleasant

with its turquoise coloured waters and white sand beaches. After St. Leonards on the eastern shore of the peninsula, there is no car access until you reach Queenscliff. As you approach Queenscliff, you will encounter tidal streams. Swan Bay is a very shallow bay with poorly marked channels through the intertidal mud flats. Swan Island is Government land and you cannot land on it.

✦ **Caution:** when paddling in southern Port Phillip, be aware, there are tidal streams running. Also, be aware of wind on water.

✦ **Caution:** watch out for shipping and the ferry service between Queenscliff and Sorrento.

The southern end of Port Phillip has many historical and natural features of interest. At the Sea-Pilot station, in Queenscliff, is 'Caffyn Cove' from where Paul Caffyn in 1981–82 set out and completed his circumnavigation of continental Australia. On top of the bluff is a plaque commemorating his achievement, organised by David Golightly of the VSKC. It is also the place from where Freya Hoffmeister and Stu Trueman set off on their successful Australian continent circumnavigations. Crossing from Queenscliff, over Port Phillip, to Portsea, you pass the Annulus. There are many features to see in this area with the old forts, Quarantine station, Mud Island, 'Chinaman's Hat' and South Channel Pile Light off Rye. Launching from Sorrento near the ferry terminal, you can complete a 25 kilometre circuit of the South Channel fort, Mud Island, Chinaman's Hat.

ⓘ **Note:** The Queenscliff Coast Guard performs many rescues of people on sit-on-top kayaks, who underestimate the nature and effect of tidal streams and winds in the area.

Paddling northwards along the coast back to Melbourne, you pass many delightful beaches. North of Frankston is Seaford and the Patterson River. Here near the boat ramps is plenty of area to access the water and parking. Edithvale-Seaford Wetlands is another Ramsar site, having recorded over 190 bird species, including 25 international migratory birds.

Heading further north along the shore is Mordialloc then Black Rock and Half Moon Bay. Both places have parking. At the Sandringham yacht club in front of East Coast Kayaking, is parking and access to the water in the marina.

PORT PHILLIP AND WESTERN PORT SHIPPING LANES

Both Port Phillip and Western Port have large vessels (cargo ships, oil tankers, cruise ships and military vessels) transiting the waters. Refer to the appropriate charts, shipping websites and the VRBS handbook for information about shipping, and transit lanes and anchorages.

In Port Philip, know where and pay attention to the inner anchorage and outer anchorage zones. Trying to figure out if a ship is going to one of the transit lanes or is going to anchor in the anchorage area can be a bit tricky. Note, if you are crossing Port Phillip Bay from Point Cook to Black Rock, ships alter course quite quickly and manoeuvre in and

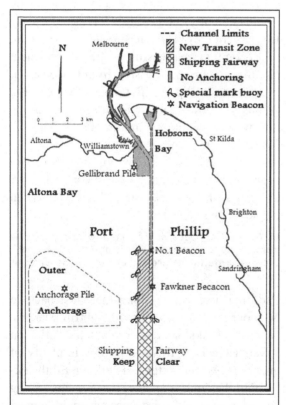

Figure 19-5 Port Phillip Shipping lanes and anchorage

around the anchorage area. Be mindful of yachts and the racing circuits in the bays.

When paddling around the Port of Melbourne at night and/or in the Yarra River around the shipping, be familiar with the sound and light signals in the VRBS handbook, chapter 2.

WESTERN PORT BAY

Prior to 1970, Western Port bay had several names. In 1798, George Bass named it Westernport. The Victorian Sailing Directions prior to 1927, referred to the entire bay as Port Western and the Port of Western Port when referring to the actual port boundaries.

Western Port is the traditional home of the Bunurong (Boonerwrung) people. George Bass on the 5 January 1798 was the first recorded European to discover Western Port. Bass had set out from Sydney with six volunteers in a 29 foot whaleboat on 3 December 1797, to explore the coast of Victoria and Tasmania. Part of the exploration, was devoted to discovering if Tasmania was connected to the mainland or not.

Passing Gabo Island and rounding Wilsons Promontory, they continued along the coast to reach the eastern entrance to Western Port. Bass named the port *Western Port* because it was the most westerly harbour known to Europeans on the east coast at that time. During their two week stay inside the harbour, a partial examination of the harbour and coasts ware made. During this time, the western entrance was discovered but was not navigated. On their return to Sydney on 25 February 1798, Bass reported to Governor Hunter the existence of a fine body of water, sheltered from the storms and rough seas. He also recommended that it should be marked on the charts for future reference.

In 1801, Governor King despatched Lieutenant James Grant in the Lady Nelson, to make a detailed survey of Bass' discovery three years before. Grant sailed south and entered Western Port through the western entrance on 21 March 1801. He then set up camp on a small island inside the eastern entrance, which he named Churchill Island after English farmer, John Churchill of Dawlish. Churchill had given Grant some seed, which he was to plant on the island.

After the Lady Nelson returned to Sydney, it was given to the command of John Murray, who on 5 January 1802 discovered Port Phillip Bay. During that same year, a French ship *Le Naturalist* under the command of Captain Hamelin, entered Western Port via the western entrance. The French sailors were the first to make a thorough survey of the port and surroundings, during which time; they circumnavigated French Island, and named it *Ille des Francois*.

In the early nineteenth century, Western Port bay played a role in the struggle between Britain and France over sovereignty of the land. Soldiers and convicts were dispatched from Sydney, to form an outpost at Western Port to deter possible occupation by the French.

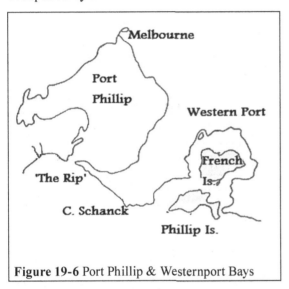

Figure 19-6 Port Phillip & Westernport Bays

During the 1800s, sealing became a major industry in the area. It is estimated that within the first few years of sealing in Bass Straight waters 100 000 seals were killed for their fur and oil. The log of Capt. James Kelly records during January 1813, 924 sealskins were harvested, over a four-day period, at Seal Rocks. The skins fetched 4 shillings 6 pence in Sydney and 25 shillings in London. Seal oil fetched 4 shillings a gallon.

Following the establishment of the Port Phillip Settlement in 1835, sheep farming was started on Phillip Island in 1839. Development in the area continued to grow with many small schooners and ketches carrying cargo and passengers between Melbourne and several places on the foreshore of Western Port. During the ports European history, many of natural resources were harvested and became sources of industry for the area. The industries included fishing, crayfishing, oystering and the harvesting of seaweed, salt and sea-grass; which continued up to the 1960s. Mangroves were harvested and used for making potash and soap. Timber and particularly wattle bark (bark from Mimosa trees) was harvested for use in the tanning industry. Black swans were hunted and their skins used for millinery. Agricultural industries that have taken place over the years have been the farming of cattle, sheep, and pigs; and the growing of chicory and onions.

In 1868, a regular ferry service commenced between Phillip Island and Stony Point. In 1911, the Royal Australian Navy showed interest in the area and in 1921, the naval base *Cerberus* was opened.

French Island

Kayaking around French Island can be achieved in a day. The island has about 60 kilometre of coastline. If you include your launch and return ports, then the trip turns out to be a 70 kilometre or so paddle. You need to plan the circumnavigation in conjunction with the tidal stream around the island. If you mismanage the tidal streams, you may become literally 'stuck in the mud' at the northern and particularly northeast end of the island. For many people, French Island is a destination for their first over-night camping experience from a kayak. The southern regions of French Island offer great paddling opportunities along with the area across East Arm on the coastline of north and northwest Phillip Island. Middle Bank to the northwest of Phillip Island also gets some challenging surfing conditions.

☀ **Caution:** when paddling in Western Port be aware, there are tidal streams running. Also, be aware of wind on water.

Phillip Island

Phillip Island offers both 'blue water paddling' and bay paddling. The 60 kilometre island can be circumnavigated in a day (~8.5 hours). You are best to catch the out-going stream from New

Haven and head down the Eastern Entrance for Cape Woolamai. You will encounter waves across the bar but you can also pick your way around the breaks. Entering back into Western Port, you pass Seal Rocks and the wild life observatory at Point Grant. You can encounter large swells if the tidal stream is out-going and will make slow progress, until the stream turns and runs back in. The paddle from Rhyll to Newhaven, past Churchill Island, is across the intertidal area. It is best to sit out in the deeper water than battle through the shallows.

There are some good surfing opportunities in the East Entrance near Cleenland Bight on the Middle Sand. In addition, the ocean beaches from Cape Woolamai to around the Smiths Beach area get nice surfing waves. On the western side of Phillip Island, Cat Bay can get some good waves breaking off the south point.

VICTORIA'S CAPES

Victoria has had during its European history, 22 features termed as capes. Though the term cape, in some cases, is ambiguous and one wonders how some of the features ever got the title. The following information is part of the Victorian Sea Kayak club's 'Cape Contour Challenge' devised and researched by David Golightly. The point of the challenge is for club trip leaders, to take members out on adventurous trips along the Victorian coast. Even though there is an inconsistency in the naming of capes, the position was taken to include any feature that at some point, in recent history, was called a cape. This means a feature like *Sutton Rocks*, which was formerly named Cape Montesquieu, is included. The Australian continent's most southern feature is called *South Point* and is located at Wilson Promontory, in Gippsland.[1] The promontory itself is a cape when compared to Cape Otway in the west, but the southern point does not receive the title of Cape and is not included in the official club list. However, it is included by the participants as a 'cape to bag'.

Table 19-3 Victoria's Capes according to the VSKC Cape Contour Challenge

West Victoria	
CAPE MONTESQUIEU, NKA Sutton Rocks	
Location:	38° 08' S, 141° 10' E
Discovered by:	Nicolas Baudin
Nationality:	French
Year of discovery:	1802
Origin:	Charles Motesquieu, French political philosopher
Notes:	Sutton Rocks, Discovery Bay. Between Nelson and C. Duquesne (A numpty of a cape but a pain to get to!)
CAPE DUQUESNE	
Location:	38° 22' S, 141° 22' E
Discovered by:	Nicolas Baudin
Nationality:	French
Year of discovery:	1802
Origin:	Abraham Duquesne, French naval officer
Notes:	W of Cape Bridgewater, Part of the greater feature C. Bridgewater
CAPE BRIDGEWATER	
Location:	38° 23' S, 141° 23' E
Discovered by:	James Grant
Nationality:	British
Year of discovery:	1800
Origin:	Duke of Bridgewater
Notes:	W of Portland
CAPE NELSON	
Location:	38° 26' S, 141° 32' E
Discovered by:	James grant
Nationality:	British
Year of discovery:	1800
Origin:	HM brig Lady Nelson
Notes:	W of Portland, C. Nelson Lighthouse
CAPE SIR WILLIAM GRANT, AKA C. Solicitor	
Location:	38° 24' S, 141° 37' E
Discovered by:	James Grant
Nationality:	British
Year of discovery:	1800
Origin:	Probably a relative of James Grant
Notes:	Portland (airstrip), between Grant Bay and Nelson Bay
WEST CAPE, on Lady Percy Julia I.	
Location:	38° 25' S, 141° 59' E
Discovered by:	Most likely by James Grant who also named Lady Julia Percy Island.
Nationality:	British
Year of discovery:	TBC
Origin:	TBC
Notes:	S or SSW Pt NKA Pinnacle Point S Pt—38°25.538'S 141°59.925'E SSW Pt—38°25.422'S 141°59.748'E Un-named point SW of island at 38°25.030'S 141°59.606'E

CAPE FREDERICK on Lady Percy Julia I.	
Location:	38° 24' S , 142° 00' E
Discovered by:	TBC
Nationality:	TBC
Year of discovery:	TBC
Origin:	TBC
Notes:	NE point of Lady Julia Percy Island, ~21 km W of Port Fairey and ~8 km off the coast from Yambuk hamlet

CAPE REAMUR, NKA Boulder Pt	
Location:	38° 23' S , 142° 08' E
Discovered by:	Nicolas Baudin
Nationality:	French
Year of discovery:	1802
Origin:	Rene Reumur, French scientist (inventor of the thermometer)
Notes:	AKA c. Reaumur Between Port Fairey and Portland

CAPE VOLNEY	
Location:	38° 46' S , 143° 16' E
Discovered by:	Nicolas Baudin
Nationality:	French
Year of discovery:	1802
Origin:	Constantin Volney, French historian
Notes:	Near Pt Reginald and Johanna Bch

CAPE OTWAY, AKA C. Albany Otway	
Location:	38° 51' S , 143° 30' E
Discovered by:	James Grant
Nationality:	British
Year of discovery:	1800
Origin:	Commissioner of British transport board
Notes:	Cape Otway lighthouse

CAPE MARENGO	
Location:	38° 47' S , 143° 39' E
Discovered by:	Nicolas Baudin
Nationality:	French
Year of discovery:	1802
Origin:	Napoleons victory over Italy at Marengo
Notes:	Hamlet of Marengo, south of Apollo Bay. (A numpty of a cape!)

CAPE PATTON, aka c. Patten	
Location:	38° 41' S , 143° 50' E
Discovered by:	James Grant
Nationality:	British
Year of discovery:	1800
Origin:	TBC
Notes:	Grey River a hamlet south the village of Kennett River, north of Apollo Bay. Next lighthouse is ~34 km east at Aireys Inlet

Port Phillip Bay Heads	
East Victoria	
CAPE SCHANCK, aka C. Shank	
Location:	38° 27' S , 144° 54' E
Discovered by:	James Grant
Nationality:	British

Year of discovery:	1800
Origin:	Named after Capt John Schank R.N. The designer of the innovative sliding keel on the Lady Nelson
Notes:	C. Schanck lighthouse

CAPE WOOLAMAI	
Location:	38° 31' S , 145° 19' E
Discovered by:	George Bass
Nationality:	British
Year of discovery:	1798
Origin:	Australian aboriginal name, imported from NSW, for snapper (fish)
Notes:	Phillip Island SE point

CAPE PATERSON, AKA C. Patterson	
Location:	38° 40' S , 145° 36' E
Discovered by:	James Grant
Nationality:	British
Year of discovery:	1800
Origin:	Col Paterson of New South Wales Corps
Notes:	

CAPE LIPTRAP	
Location:	38° 54' S , 145° 55' E
Discovered by:	James Grant
Nationality:	British
Year of discovery:	1800
Origin:	John Liptrap Esq. of London (sponsor)
Notes:	C. Liptrap lighthouse

Wilsons Promontory, South Point	
Location:	39° 08' S , 146° 22' E
Discovered by:	
Nationality:	
Year of discovery:	
Origin:	
Notes:	**Australia's Southern most point.** ~4.4 km from South East Point to east and the lighthouse ~13 km from Cape Wellington to east.

CAPE WELLINGTON	
Location:	39° 04' S , 146° 28' E
Discovered by:	Captain John Lort Stokes
Nationality:	British
Year of discovery:	1846
Origin:	Named at the anniversary of the battle of Waterloo
Notes:	East side of Wilsons Promontory Lighthouse is SW ~8.5 km to west at SE Pt.

CAPE CONRAN	
Location:	37° 48' S , 148° 43' E
Discovered by:	TBC
Nationality:	TBC
Year of discovery:	TBC
Origin:	Captain Lewis Conran, member of Smythe's survey expedition of 1849-52
Notes:	Gippsland. Lighthouse

EAST CAPE	
Location:	37° 48' S , 148° 44' E

Discovered by:	TBC
Nationality:	TBC
Year of discovery:	TBC
Origin:	TBC
Notes:	Cape Conran. Part of C. Conran!
CAPE EVERARD, nka Point Hicks (FROM 1970)	
Location:	37° 46' S , 149° 16' E
Discovered by:	Capt James Cook (Point Hicks), C. Everard by Capt John Lort Stokes
Nationality:	British
Year of discovery:	1770
Origin:	Zachary Hicks, Capt James Cook's 2IC: Everard likely named after Mr John Everard.
Notes:	Gippsland. NKA Point Hicks since 1970, Lighthouse
CAPE HORN	
Location:	37° 29' S , 149° 40' E
Discovered by:	TBC
Nationality:	TBC
Year of discovery:	TBC
Origin:	TBC
Notes:	On the Mallacoota river, (a numpty!)
CAPE HOWE	
Location:	37° 30' S , 149° 58' E
Discovered by:	James cook
Nationality:	British
Year of discovery:	1770
Origin:	Admiral Richard Howe
Notes:	**Victoria—NSW boarder**. Lighthouse located on Gabo Island

Victoria's Southern Ocean Capes

The following is an article I wrote for the VSKC magazine Sea Trek about paddling Victoria's Southern Ocean capes. If you desire to get in close and see the cliff features and wild life then you need to plan and have time set aside to drop everything and travel to Portland. In this area of western Victoria, you have Cape Duquesene, Cape Bridgewater, Cape Nelson, Capes Sir William Grant and Lawrence Rocks. To the west of Cape Duquesene, you have Discovery Bay and kilometres of sand and dunes to the town of Nelson and the South Australian boarder. Along this monotonous stretch of sand are Sutton Rocks (aka Cape Montesquieu). To the east of Portland and closer to Port Fairy, the coastline consists of low hills with the water being reef dominated. This area includes named features like Boulder Point (aka Cape Reamur), 'The Crags' and McKechnie Crags. Eight and a half kilometres out from the hamlet of Yambuk,

is Lady Julia Percy Island, with Cape Frederick and West Cape.

The coastline west of Cape Otway receives the swells from the Southern Ocean. Even in relatively 'flat' conditions big green hills of water ('yamas'), roll into the bays and thunder on to the exposed section of beaches, or hammer the cliffs creating an explosive plume of green and white water up the faces. The resulting shockwaves rebound and radiate outwards from the area of impact and are easily visible from the cliff tops, rebounding for 300 to 400 metres plus. As you approach the cliffs from a kilometre away, the big green water 'yamas' roll in from one direction and cross paths with the rebounding waves. This wave action creates box like depressions, which isolates you from the surroundings and other paddlers. Closer to the cliffs, the water's surface ripples and vibrates erratically up and down, as if a giant loudspeaker was underneath and cranked up too loud. On November 1st, 2009 when Greg Murray, Roger Bellchamber, John Evertze and myself were paddling from Cape Bridgewater SLSC to Portland past Cape Nelson, John made the observation "You would not want to paddle around here with a sea."

Cape Nelson is 50 metres high and is the site of a lighthouse built in 1884, which stands at 75 metres above sea level. Nearby basalt headlands are capped with dune calcarenite, which rise to 100 metres and have been eroded by waves to reveal patches of basalt rock. Nelson Bay is ringed by cliffs whose western faces are pock-marked with sea caves. After Cape Sir William Grant, it is a short paddle to Lawrence Rocks and the Gannet colony. The estimated 6000 gannets have covered the Rocks with guano, creating a white layered covering like that of white marzipan icing on a cake. The rock is divided in two by a 10 metre or so wide gauntlet. On this particular day whilst visiting the Rocks, John decided to 'run the gauntlet'. In fact, he had been thinking about it from the previous evening's indulgences at Johno and Di's place. The swell on this particular day was not Southern Ocean 'big' but it easily hid paddlers in its troughs on occasions. As John set off thru the gauntlet we all watched a set roll in and explode green and white water up into the air then ram its way through the gauntlet creating a five metre wall of water. Timing and luck is everything. When John set off, he was soon lost in the trough and would momentarily appear as a black speck in the tumultuous cascade of white water. The remaining three of us, paddled to the north side of the Rocks eagerly awaiting John's safe arrival. It was at the north side of the rocks that he was surprised by a swell coming from the west between the Rocks and Point Danger.

The water in this area is deceptive and there are a few chart features worth mentioning. The first is 'Big Reef' in Grant Bay. This 3.9 metre feature is like a 'snake in the grass' minding its own business but ready to strike out. The swells gently roll into the bay, but all of a sudden, there is a massive wall of turbulent white water extending in line for a considerable distance, striking anything within its range. The day we observed this reef 'working', we were all surprised by two points of interest. The first point was that the swell sizes did not appreciably change prior to and after the event. The second was the length of time the reef worked before there was nothing but turquoise water again. For the next hour or so, to our surprise, the reef did not work again. Apparently, some local commercial fishermen lost their fishing boat there, on one of the occasions when the reef worked. The other area to keep a watchful eye on is Little Reef, off Point Danger. Here the water between the Rocks and Point Danger moves quite strongly as it is lifted upward by Little Reef and funnelled between the two features. Little Reef decreases in height but extends out to Lawrence Rocks and creates some terrific surfing waves if you are in the right spot. If you are not then you are in for a 'heart stopper' of a moment.

The paddle to Portland is very pleasant with its cliffs and two sandy beaches. The harbour is extensive and provides sheltered paddling. Fishermen, returning from their days fishing, clean their catch at the boat ramp where seals and birds congregate to feed; while out in the harbour, the odd 'Noah' swims in and chews on the stern of a 'plastic fantastic kayak'. To the west of Portland, harbour is Cape Bridgewater.

Here you find seal colonies perched along the rocky coastline below the 130 metre high, basalt cliffs. Bridgewater Bay is a 13 kilometre wide flat beach and host to a wide (~300 m) surf zone. The bay receives waves with an average height of 1 to 1.5 metre. From the SLSC,— which was established in 1947—it is a short three kilometre paddle out to the base of Cape Bridgewater and the first seal colony. Here there is a large sea cave that smells like a chook shed in summer. Another five kilometres to the west is Cape Duquesne and then Descartes Bay and Discovery Bay.

Near the village of Port Fairy is the hamlet of Yambuk with Lady Julia Percy Island situated 8.5 kilometres to the south of the beach. The sand beach has a large surf zone with three to four places that regularly reform the incoming breakers. Even in low swell conditions the surf is powerful, with irregular breakers rising up behind the regular breaker lines. Lady Julia Percy Island was known as 'Deen Maar' or 'Dhinmar' by the local aboriginal people. The almost 40 metre high, flat, tree denuded, basalt rock is the remnant of a volcano and covers about 130 hectares. As Australia's only off-shore volcano it is listed as a geological monument of national significance by the Geological Society of Australia. In 1800, Lieutenant James Grant named the island 'Lady Julian's Island' but over time it has been transcribed to its current name. During the period of white colonisation, the island was exploited for seals and bird guano. The island has a population of around 23 000 Australian Fur seals and is one of four breeding colonies in Australia. The seals venture approximately 30 kilometres out to the continental shelf to feed on squid for a week at a time, before returning to the island. The island itself is ringed by cliffs and has one decent landing site. The island itself has restricted landing status by the Department of Conservation and Natural Resources. Two of the cape contours challenge capes are located on the island: Cape Frederick and West Cape. The east facing cliffs have multiple sea caves and at the south-east end of the island there is the 'Blow Hole'.

Twelve kilometres to the north-east and on the coast is Cape Reamur, which is now known as Boulder Point. This is an unremarkable, low, rocky feature extending into the ocean. The coastline is shallow and holds a multitude of reefs and bombies. The land features are low hummocks and grazing land. To paddle to Lady Julia Percy Island via Port Fairy takes you past Boulder Point and is almost a 50 kilometre return journey. Departing from Yambuk beach and circumnavigating the island the returning to Yambuk via Boulder Point is almost a 36 kilometre paddle.

The next cape is 106 kilometres away—as the crow flies—on a bearing of east-south-east and is known as Cape Volney. It is located next to Reginald Point in the Otway National Park and forms part of the cliff line that raises 190 metres from the ocean. Access points to the Cape are Port Campbell, the Gellibrand River at Princeton or Melanesia and Johanna beaches. Johanna is a 3.6 kilometre long beach, which faces south-west and receives waves averaging 1.5 metres. The 250 metre wide bar is capable of holding one to three metre plus waves. Melanesia beach located between Lion Head and Bowker Point and faces south-south-east. It is guarded by a patch reef network with land access being via vehicle and walking track. The launch from Port Campbell is a preferred option and provides a magnificent vista of bays, stacks ('The Twelve Apostles') and cliffs. Once on the water there are limited landing opportunities and those that are available in other than benign conditions may be considered tricky to dangerous. In calm conditions with low swell, you feel the currents around the various reefs, like Cat Reef, working against you. [2]

Twenty-five kilometres away—via the coast— is Cape Otway and the north-west boundary of Bass Straight. This area also receives high-energy waves—regularly 1.5 metres—and contains several beaches and features. Beaches and features along this section include Point Flinders, Station Beach, Glenaire Beach and the Aire River mouth, Sentinel Rocks, Eagle Nest Rock, Dinosaur Cove and Johanna Beach. Cape Otway is flanked by Point Flinders to the west

and Point Franklin to the east. The coastline has cliffs rising up from the reefs. The charted depth is less than four metres with the heavily breaking reef in front of Cape Otway lighthouse being 2.6 metres. Strong currents move around Point Franklin. Landing places are Parker River or Blanket Bay. Blanket Bay has numerous reefs around it. The nearest settlement is Marengo and the first 'cape' on the Westside of Bass Straight- Cape Marengo. The hamlet has a camping ground with close access to the water. To the east is the town of Apollo Bay.

WILSONS PROMONTORY

Corner Inlet

⬥ **Caution:** this area has tidal streams and is intertidal.

⬥ **Caution:** watch out for shipping accessing Toora Channel and the docks at Barry Beach.

Corner Inlet is classed as coastal waters. It is however, another location that provides many people with their first experience of camping out of a kayak. In this area, you are in the northern end of Wilsons Promontory, (aka 'The Prom'). To camp in this area you need to contact Parks Victoria and arrange permits. People often launch from either Port Welshpool or Duck Point.

① **Note:** since the devastating Victorian bushfires in 2009, the northern Prom was burnt out. Since then Johnny Souey has been closed to camping. However, there is a campsite at the northern end of Five Mile Beach.

Tin Mine and Johnny Souey (aka Johnnie Sussie) Cove, are pleasant camp areas. As you go further south along the Proms east coastline, you have the options of camping at Five Mile Beach, Sealers Cove, Refuge Cove or Waterloo Bay.

① **Note:** after Waterloo bay, there are no landing beaches until you reach Oberon Bay on the Westside of the Prom.

⬥ **Caution:** the Prom is exposed to the weather and ocean. It can receive severe weather conditions, cold fronts, big seas and rebounding waves, making extremely difficult kayaking conditions.

South of Waterloo Bay is Southeast Point and the lighthouse perched on the granite cliffs. Rounding the point and passing Fenwick Bight is South Point, the most southerly point of Continental Australia. After passing the granite cliffs in this area, you enter Oberon Bay, which has a campsite. The next bay is Norman Bay and the hamlet of Tidal River. This hamlet houses a camping ground, Park Victoria Offices and a kiosk/general store.

The west coast of the Prom has the Glennie Group and Anser Group of islands. Heading northwards is Waratah Bay and Cape Liptrap. Walkerville has a campground in Waratah Bay on the beach.

BASS STRAIT

According to the Australia Pilot, 6 ed., 1982, Vol.2, Chap. 2, p.46: Bass Straight's northern boundary lies between: Cape Otway (38° 51' S & 143° 31' E) and Wilson's Promontory (39° 31' S, 146° 23' E). The southern boundary lies between Cape Grim (40° 41' S, 144° 41 E) and the NW point of Tasmania, Eddystone Point (41°00' S, 148°21' E).

Bass Strait is a shallow continental shelf channel or sea with an average depth of 50 to 70 metres. Its shallowness affects both the tides and ocean swells, causing very confusing seas, which give the Strait a reputation for being one of the roughest stretches of water in the world. Bass Strait connects the Great Australian Bight (Southern Ocean) to the Tasman Sea (South Pacific Ocean) and is affected by water masses from both regions, which are different in temperature and salinity.

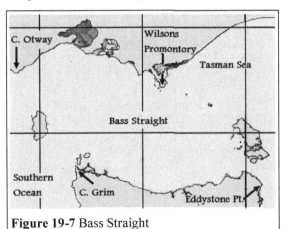

Figure 19-7 Bass Straight

Bass Straight currents generally set east in line with the Southern Ocean current but directional change can occur in any season. Rates around two to three knots have been recorded some

of them onshore around the coasts of South Australia, Tasmania and King Island.[3]

Tidal streams are generally west setting on the tidal wave rise and east on its setting. In the channels and around headlands, rates of up to three knots are obtained but elsewhere, the rates seldom exceed one knot. Offshore tidal streams are overshadowed by either, the Southern Ocean and or the East Australian Current. Strong tidal streams are found around headlands and port entrances like Port Phillip Bay and Western Port.

In the confines of Bass Strait, the water masses are mixed through tide and wind action. The saltier, cold (1 °C to 3 °C cooler than the Tasman Sea), surface waters sink, in a process called downwelling. In winter, the sinking waters flow steeply down the continental shelf slope, like a waterfall. Beginning midway between Flinders Island and the Victorian coast, the downwelling extends north almost to Jervis Bay, off the New South Wales coast. From there the continental shelf edge changes from north south to east west. This downwelling feature is called the *Bass Strait Cascade*. Water leaves the eastern end of Bass Straight at a depth of 70 to 80 metres, plunging underneath the East Australian Current, to a depth of around 400 metres; at which point the densities of the two waters match. From here, it spreads north along the east Australian shelf edge; and has been identified up to 1200 kilometres away. While the Bass Strait Cascade is pouring eastwards, the predominantly westerly winds are driving currents from west to east.

1 Governor Hunter named Wilsons Promontory after Thomas Wilson, a London merchant trading with Australia (Macquarie Dictionary).
2 Paddling west from Port Campbell to 'The Arch', 'London Bridge' (what remains of it), past the town of Peterborough and 'Wild Dog Cove' you come into the 'Bay of Martyrs'. In this bay, you have 'Massacre Bay', 'Crofts Bay' and the 'Bay of Islands'. When consulting the chart you will notice the many reefs and bombies. Even in low swell to calm conditions, these bombies work and produce large breakers, which scare the heck out of you as they rush and crash in.
3 Australia Pilot, 6 ed., 1982, Vol.2, Chap. 2, pp. 14 & 46.

Acronyms Abbreviations & Symbols

Abbreviations & Acronyms

A	1. SI for Ampere, electrical current, (amp), (I)
	2. Amplitude
ABC	1. Airway, breathing, circulation 2. Australian Broadcasting
ABS	1. Acrylonitrile butadiene styrene
	2. Polyacrylonitrile-co-butadiene-co-styrene
AC	1. Alternating current (electrical)
	2. Australian Canoeing
Ac	Altocumulus (cloud), (AC)
AF	Audio frequency
AFN	Australian Fiducial Network
AFREF	African Geodetic Reference Frame
AGD	Australian Geodetic Datum of YYYY
AGM	Absorbed Glass Matt
Ah	Amp hour
AHD	Australian Height Datum
AHS	Australian Hydrographic Service
Aka, a.k.a.	Also known as
Al	Alternating (light), (Alt.)
AM	Amplitude modulation
A_M	Midship section area
AMC	Australian Maritime College
AMG	Australian Map Grid
AMSA	Australian Maritime Safety Authority
Anch.	Anchorage
ANS	Australian National Spheroid
ANSI	American National Standard Institute
AOW	Accessible on water
AP	Assumed position
App.	Appendix
Appr.	Approach.
AR	Aspect ratio
AS	Australian Standard (prefix)
As	Altostratus cloud
ATU	Antenna tuning unit
AUF	Australian Ultralight Federation (now RAA)
AUS, Aus,	Australia, (Aust.)
AUSREP	Australian ship reporting system
AusSAR	Australian Search and Rescue

A_W	Waterplane area
A_x	Area of maximum transverse area
B	1. Centre of buoyancy (CB)
	2. Beam
B.	Bay
Bch, bch	Beach
Bk.	Bank (e.g. sand bank)
bkw	Breakwater
B/L	Length/beam ratio, beam/length ratio
B_M	Midship beam
Bn	Beacon
B_{OA}	Beam overall
BOM	Bureau of Meteorology
Br, br	Breakers
BSW	British Standard Whitworth
Bu	Blue
B_{WL}	Waterline beam
B_x	Beam maximum section
C.	Cape
c	Wave velocity
c.	Circa (about, approximately)
CB	Centre of buoyancy, (B)
C_B	Block coefficient,
Cb	1. Cobbles
	2. Cumulonimbus cloud
Cc	Cirrocumulus cloud
CCG	Canadian Coastguard
CD	Chart Datum, Datum for sounding reduction
CDT	Central Daylight-saving Time
CDMA	Code Division Multiple Access
CE	Centre of effort
cf.	Compare (L: *confer*)
CFA	Country Fire Authority
CG	Centre of gravity, (C, G)
CH	Compass heading
Ch, Ch.	1. Channel (Radio)
	2. Chapter
	3. Chain (length)
CHS	Canadian Hydrographic Service
Ci	Cirrus cloud
CL	Centreline
CLA	1. Centre of lateral area
	2. Cigarette lighter adapter
CLP	Centre of lateral pressure

CLR	Centre of lateral resistance
cm	Centimetre
CNav	Circumnavigation
CNM	Canadian Coast Guard's Notices to Mariners
Co	Coral
col., cols	Column(s)
C_M	Midship section coefficient
CORS	Continuously Operating Reference Station
COSPAS-SARSAT	USA & Russian SAR satellite system used to detect EPIRBs
CP	Centre of pressure
C_P	Prismatic coefficient
CPR	Cardiopulmonary Resuscitation
crs	Course
Cs	Cirrostratus cloud
CSIRO	Commonwealth Scientific and Industrial Research Organisation
CST	Central Standard Time
CTS	Course to Steer
Cu	Cumulus cloud
C_V	Volumetric coefficient
C_{VP}	Vertical prismatic coefficient
CW	Continuous wave
cwt	Hundredweight
C_X	Maximum transverse section coefficient, (sectional area coefficient)
Cy	Clay

D	Aerodynamic drag
d	1. Day (SI)
	2. Draft, (T)
DC	Direct Current
deg.	Degrees
DGPS	Differential Global Positioning System
DIN	Deutsches Institut for Normung
DIY	Do-it-yourself
D/L	Displacement/length ratio
DOD	Depth of discharge (Battery)
DR	Dead reckoning, Ded reckoning
dr., dr	Dram (Imperial weight measure)
Dr	Drag on hull
DSC	Digital selective calling (Radio)
DSE	Department of Sustainability & Environment (Vic.)
D_{WL}	Design waterline
DZ	Danger zone

E	East
EAC	East Australian Current
EAR	Expired Air Resuscitation
EC	Electronic chart
ECCT	Electrical crimp connector terminal
Ed., Eds	Editor(s)
ED	Existence doubtful
ED50	European Datum 1950
EDD	Estimated date of departure
edn	Edition
EDT	Eastern Daylight—saving Time
EGC	Enhanced group calling (Radio)
EHF	Extremely High Frequency (30-300 GHz)
ELF	Extremely Low Frequency (3-30 Hz)
ELT	Emergency Location Transmitter (SAR)
e.g.	for example (L: *exempli gratia*)
ENC	Electronic navigation chart
Ent.	Entrance
EP	Estimated position
EPIRB	Emergency Position Indicating Radio-beacon
EST	Eastern Standard Time
Est.	Estuary
et al.	and others (Latin: *et alii*)
ETA	Estimated time of arrival
etc.	*et cetera* (L), and so forth, and so on
ETD	Estimated time of departure
ETRS89	European Terrestrial Reference System 1989

F	1. Fahrenheit (temperature)
	2. Fixed light
	3. Force (aerodynamics)
FB	Freeboard
ff.	Following
FFl	Fixed and flashing (light), (F.Fl.)
Fj.	Fjord
fig., figs	Figure(s)
Fl	Single Flashing light, (total duration of light shorter than total duration of darkness), (Fl.)
Fl(2)	Group flashing (light), {Fl. (2)}
Fl(2+1)	Composite group flashing
FM	Frequency modulation
fm., fms	Fathom (6 feet)
F_n	Froude number

Fn., fnn.	Footnote(s)
FRP	Fibreglass reinforced plastic
F_s	Side force of water
F_T	Total aerodynamic force
ft	Foot, feet
fur., fur	Furlong (Length)

G	1. Green
	2. Gravel
	3. Centre of gravity, (CG)
G.	Gulf
g	1. gram(s)
	2. acceleration due to gravity
gal., gal	Gallon
GB	Grid bearing
GDA94	Geocentric Datum Australia of 1994
GEOSAR	Geostationary earth orbit satellite for SAR
GRPF	Glass Fibre Reinforced Plastic
GRS80	Geodetic Reference System 1980
GH	Grid heading
GHz	Gigahertz (1 000 000 000 hertz)
GIS	Geographic Information System
Gk	Greek
GNSS	Global Navigation Satellite System
GM	Metacentric height
GMA82	Geodetic Model of Australia 1982
GMDSS	Global Marine Distress and Safety System
GMT	Greenwich mean time
GNSS	Global Navigation Satellite System
GPH	Gallons per hour
GPS	Global Positioning System
gr., gr	Grain (Imperial weight measure)
GRP	Glass reinforced plastics
GSM	Global System for Mobiles
GZ	Righting arm

H	High (pressure system)
h	1. Hour (SI)
	2. hr, hour(s)
HAT	Highest Astronomical Tide
Harb.	Harbour
Hbk, hbk	Handbook
Hdg.	Heading
HDPE	High Density polyethylene
HF	High Frequency (3 to 30 MHz)

HLC	High level cloud
HM	High modulus
hPa	hectopascal
HS	High strength
HTP	High Performance Thermoplastic, HTP PE
HW	High water
Hz	Hertz (SI, frequency)
H3E	'AM', (AM, SSB & full carrier)

I.	Island
IALA	International Association of Lighthouse Authorities
Ibid.	In the same place (i.e. book, chapter, page, etc. (L: Ibidem))
IC	Integrated circuit
i.e.	that is (L: *id est*)
ill., ills	Illustrator(s)
in, ins.	Inch, Inches (Imperial measure, 12 in to 1 foot)
inHg	inches of mercury
INM	International nautical mile
INMARSAT	International Marine Satellite Organisation
IQ	Interrupted quick flashing light
Is.	Islands
Iso	Isophase light, (duration of light and darkness equal)
ISLW	Indian spring low water
ISO	International Organisation for Standards
ITRS	International Terrestrial Reference System
ITU	International Telecommunications Union
ITCZ	Intertropical Convergence Zone (Meteorology)
IVQ	Interrupted very quick flashing light

J	Joule (SI) for energy, work, quantity of heat, expressed form N m
J3E	'SSB', (AM, SSB, suppressed carrier)
JIS	Japanese Industrial Standard

KASK	Kiwi Association of Sea Kayakers
KE	Kinetic energy
kg	Kilogram (SI, 1000 g)
kHz	Kilohertz (1000 Hz)
km	Kilometre (1000 m), (0.54 of a nm)
km/h	Kilometres per hour (SI)

kn	Knot, nautical mile per hour
Kt	Knot, nautical mile per hour
kW	Kilowatts

L	1. Low (pressure system)
	2. Latin
	3. Aerodynamic lift (aerodynamics)
	4. Cross wind force
	5. Effective length (speed/power calculations)
L.	Lake
L or l	Litre (SI)
l., ll.	Line(s)
LAT	Lowest Astronomical Tide
L/B	Length/beam ratio, (B/L)
lb.	Pound weight
LCB	Longitudinal centre of buoyancy
LCF	Longitudinal centre of floatation
LCG	Longitudinal centre of gravity
LCS	Limited coastal station (Radio)
LDPE	Low Density polyethylene
Le.	Ledge (e.g. underwater ledge)
LED	Light emitting diode
LEO LEOSAR	Low-altitude earth orbit satellite for SAR
LES	Land earth station (Radio)
LF	Low frequency
LFI, L Fl	Long-flashing (flash 2s or longer)
L/H	Length/draft ratio
LINZ	Land Information New Zealand
lk	Link (Imperial measure of length)
LLC	Low level cloud
LLDPE	Linear Low Density polyethylene
l/min	Litres per minute
LNM	Local Notices to Mariners
L_{OA}	Length overall
LOP	Line of position
LOS	Line of sight
LSB	Lower side band (radio)
LUT	Local User Terminal (SAR)
LW	Low water
L_{WL}	Load waterline, Waterline length

M	1. Magnetic (compass bearing)
	2. Official abbreviation for nautical mile
	3. Mud
	4. Metacentre
m	1. metre (100 cm, 1000 mm)

	2. minutes (SI)
	3. mass
mA	Milliamps (electric current)
Mag.	1. Magnetic
	2. Magnitude
MAST	Marine and Safety Tasmania
MB	Magnetic bearing
mb, mbar	Millibar (non-SI Australian legal units)
MBS	Maritime Buoyage System
MCA	Maritime & Coastguard Agency (UK)
MDPE	Medium Density polyethylene
MEK	Methyl ethyl ketone
MEKP	Methyl ethyl ketone peroxide
MF	Medium frequency (300 to 3000 kHz)
MHHW	Mean Higher High Water
MHLW	Mean Higher Low Water
MHW	Mean High Water
MHWN	Mean High Water Neaps
MHWS	Mean High Water Springs
MHz	Megahertz (1000 000 hertz)
mi	Mile
min	Minute (time interval)
MLC	Medium level cloud
MLHW	Mean Lower High Water
MLLW	Mean Lower Low Water
MLW	Mean Low Water
MLWN	Mean Low Water Neaps
MLWS	Mean Low Water Springs
mm	millimetre (0.001 m)
mmHg	millimetres of mercury
MMSI	Maritime mobile Service Identity
MN	Magnetic north
Mo	Mores flashing light. Mo (A), Morse code signal A
MPa	Mega pascals
MRCC	1. Maritime rescue control centre
	2. Mission and rescue control centres (SAR)
MROCP	Marine Radio Operators Certificate of Proficiency
m/s	metres per second (SI)
MSDS	Material Safety Data Sheets
MSI	Maritime safety information
MSL	Mean Sea Level
MSLP	Mean Sea Level Pressure
MSQ	Maritime Safety Queensland
MSV	Marine Safety Victoria (2011, see TSV)
Mt	Mount
Mtn	Mountain
MTL	Mean Tide Level

N	1. North
	2. Newton, (SI, force)
NA	Not Applicable
NAD	North American Datum of YYYY
NB	Take careful note, (L: *nota bene*)
NE	Northeast
NDK	Nigel Dennis Kayaks
NGA	National Geospatial – Intelligence Agency
NIMA	National Imagery and Mapping Agency
NKA	Now known as
nm	Nautical mile (aka sea mile), not official but is used and understood internationally.
n mile	Nautical mile, largely accepted in Australia but not internationally.
Nm	1. Nautical mile (International nautical mile; equivalent to 1852 m or 1.85 km)
	2. Newton metres (torque)
	1. Nautical mile
NM	2. Notices to Mariners
NMT	Not more than (Used with danger bearings)
NOAA	National Ocean and Atmospheric Administration (U.S.)
Np	Neap tide
Ns	Nimbostratus
NSF	National Sanitation Foundation
NSRS2007	US National Spatial Reference System
NT	Northern Territory
NtMs	Notices to Mariners
NSW	New South Wales
NSWSKC	New South Wales Sea Kayak Club
NW	Northwest
NZ	New Zealand
NZGD	New Zealand Geodetic Datum
NZMG	New Zealand Map Grid
NZTM	New Zealand Transverse Mercator
NZVD	New Zealand Vertical Datum

OAL	Over All Length
Oc	Single occulting light, (total duration of light longer than total duration of darkness)
Oc(2)	Group occulting
OD	Ordnance Datum
OEM	Original Equipment Manufacture
op. cit.	In the work cited or mentioned (L: *opera citātō*)
OSGB36	Ordnance Survey Great Britain 1936
oz	ounce (imperial measure, 16 oz to 1 pound weight)

P	Pebbles
p., pp.	Page(s)
Pa	Pascal (SI for pressure, stress. Express in N/m^2)
PAN	1. French: *panne*, breakdown
	2. Polyacrylonitrile
para., paras	Paragraph(s)
Pass.	Passage
PE	Polyethylene
PET, PETE	Polyethylene terephthalate
PFD	Personal flotation device
PIC	Plug-in charger
pl.	Plate
PLB	Personal locator beacon
PM	Pulse modulation
PP	Polypropylene
PPB	Port Phillip Bay
PPBE	Port Phillip Bay Entrance (The Rip)
PPBH	Port Phillip Bay Heads (The Rip)
PPS	Second postscript, (L: *post postscriptum*)
PS	Postscript, (L: *postscriptum*)
Pt, Pt.	Point
pt., pts	Pint
pt	Part(s)
PTT	Press to talk (radio)
PVC	Polyvinyl Chloride aka Vinyl
PWC	Personal watercraft

Q	1. Continuous quick flash, (repetition rate of 50 to 79 – usually either 50 or 60-flashes per minute), (QkF)
	2. Torque
Q(2)	Group quick, e.g. Q(x)
QFE	Absolute air pressure, 'actual', 'local', 'ambient'
QFF	Mean Sea Level (air) Pressure
QLD	Queensland
QNH	Relative air pressure
qr	Quarter (Avoirdupois weight)
qt	Quart (Imperial capacity measure)
QZSS	Quazi-Zenith Satellite System

R	1. Red
	2. Rocks
R.	River
RAA	Recreational Aviation Australia
RAAF	Royal Australian Air Force
Rad	Radian (SI, plane angle)
RAN	Royal Australian Navy
RCC	Rescue Coordination Centre (SAR)

Rep	Reported, but not confirmed
Rep (1960)	Reported in the year 1960, but not confirmed
	Radio frequency
RF	Reef
R_F	Frictional resistance
R_R	Residual resistance
rr.	Regulations
RSI	Repetitive strain injury
R_T	Total resistance
RTM	Resin transfer moulding
R_n	Reynolds number
R_w	Wave making resistance
Rx	1. Receiver (Radio)
	2. Received frequency (Radio)

S	1. South
	2. Sand
s	1. Second (SI, time interval)
	2. Shark
SAR	Search and Rescue
SART	Search and Rescue Transponder, Survival craft radar transponder
SB	Side band (radio)
SBAS	Space Based Augmentation System
SSB	Single side band (radio)
Sc	Stratocumulus cloud
SD	Sounding of doubtful depth
SE	Southeast
ser.	Series
SES	1. State Emergency Service
	2. Ship earth station (Radio)
Sh, Sh.	1.Shells
	2. Shoal
SHF	Super High Frequency (3–30 GHz)
SI	Système International
Si	Silt
SKM	Sea Kayaker magazine
SLA	Sealed lead acid (battery)
SLF	Super Low Frequency (30–300 Hz)
S/L	Speed/Length ratio
SOLAS	Safety of life at sea, SOLAS convention
Sp	1. Spring tide, (Spr.)
	2. Specie
Spp	Species
SPDT	Single pole double throw
SPF	Sun protection factor
SPST	Single pole single throw
ss.	Sections

St	1. Stones
	2. Stratus cloud
suppl.	Supplement
SW	1. Southwest
	2. Short wave (radio)
S_w	Wetted surface area

T	1. True (compass bearing)
	2. Draft, (d)
	3. Period (e.g. frequency f = 1/T)
	4. Thrust
t	Tonne (Metric weight measure)
Tas.	Tasmania
TM	Transverse Mercator
ton	Ton (imperial weight measure)
Tx	1. Transmitter (Radio)
	2. Transmitted frequency (Radio)
T_x	Draft section (Re: C_x sectional coefficient)
TR	Track (navigation)
TRF	Terrestrial Reference Frame
TSV	Transport Safety Victoria (formally MSV)
TV	Television

UHF	Ultra high frequency (300–3000 MHz)
UKHO	United Kingdom Hydrographic Office
ULF	Ultra low frequency (300 Hz–3000 Hz)
UNC	Unified National Course
UNF	Unified National Fine
UPR	Unsaturated polyester resins
UQ	Ultra quick flashing light, (Ultra quick repetition rate of 160 or more – usually 240 to 300 – flashes per minute)
USATONS	U.S. Aids to Navigation System
USB	Upper side band (radio)
USCG	United States Coast Guard
USF	Uni-solar® Flexible solar panel
UTC	Coordinated Universal Time
UTM	Universal Transverse Mercator
UTS	Ultimate tensile strength
UV	Ultra-violet

V	1. Volt (SI: electrical potential difference, electromotive force. Expressed as W/A)
	2. Volume
v., vs	*Versus* (L), against
v	Velocity
v^2	Acceleration, velocity squared
var.	Variation

Vac	Volts alternating current
Vdc	Volts direct curent
VHF	Very High Frequency (30–300 MHz)
Vi	Violet
Vic.	Victoria
viz.	namely, (L: *videlicet*)
VLF	Very Low Frequency (3–30 kHz)
vol., vols	Volume(s)
VPA	Vehicle power adapter
VQ	Continuous very quick, (Very quick repetition rate of 80 to 159 – usually either 100 or 120 – flashes per minute)
VRBS, VRBSH	Victorian Recreational Boating Safety Handbook
VSKC	Victorian Sea Kayak Club

W	1. Watts (SI: power, e.g. measure of rate of change of electricity into light of light bulb. Expressed in J/s))
	2. West (compass direction)
	3. White
WA	Western Australia
WAAS	Wide Area Augmentation System
Wd	Weed (including Kelp)
WDT	Western Daylight-saving Time
WGS84	World Geodetic System 1984
WHO	World Health Organisation
Wk	Wreck
WL	Waterline
WRC	World Radio-communication Conference
WST	Western standard time

Y	Yellow
yd, yds	yard(s)

Z	Zulu time

Symbols	Meaning
<	less than
>	greater than
≤	less than or equal to
≥	greater than or equal to
√	square root
≈ or ~	almost equal to (e.g. about, around, close to)
°	degrees (of arc)
‘	minutes (of arc)
“	seconds (of arc)

°C	degrees Celsius
°F	degrees Fahrenheit
®	Registered trademark
™	Trademark
&	And
@	At
%	Per cent, percentage

Greek Letters		
α	1.	Angle of attack, Gk: small letter alpha, (aerodynamics)
	2.	Angles
	3.	Angular acceleration
λ	Wavelength Gk small letter *lambda*	
ρ	Density, Gk small letter *rho*	
Δ	Displacement, Gk capital letter *delta*	
τ	Shear stress, Gk small letter *tau*	

APPENDIX 1 PLANNING TABLES

Conversion Factors

Convert units in rows at left by multiplying the factor in the intersecting units columns

LENGTH	cm	in	ft	m	km	nm	
centimetre	1.0	0.3937	0.0328	0.01	0.0	0.000005	
inch	2.54	1.0	0.0833	0.0254	0.0	0.000014	
foot	30.48	12.0	1.0	0.3048	0.0003	0.000164	
metre	100	39.4	3.28	1.0	0.001	0.00054	1.09 yd
kilometre	100 000	39 370	3280	1000	1.0	0.5397	
Sea Mile	185 300	73 000	6080	1853	1.853	1.0	

SPEED	kn	m/s	km/h	mph	Knot (kn)
knots	1.0	0.515	1.853	1.152	Nautical mile: (n mile, M, ') Unofficial but often used (nm)
m/s	1.943	1.0	3.600	2.237	US nautical mile, International mile and Sea mile are all the same i.e. 1.852 km
km/h	0.540	0.278	1.0	0.621	Sea mile is the length of one minute of latitude and is the principle means of expressing distance on Admiralty charts.
mph	0.868	0.447	1.609	1.0	

Imperial & General Measures

Imperial Linear	in.	ft	yd		mm	m	km
1 Admiralty nm		6080					1.853
1 International nm	72,913	6076					1.852
1 statute mile	63,360	5280	1,760				1.609
60 nautical miles (nm)				1 degree of latitude			
1 cable		607.6		1/10 of a sea mile		≈ 185	
10 cables				1 Admiralty nm			
1 fathom (fm)		6		15 fathoms = 1 shackle		≈ 1.828	
1 millinch "thou"	0.001			1/1000" (one thousandth of an inch)	(25.4 μm)	25.4e⁻6	
1 inch (in.)	1	12	36		25.4		
12 inches	12	1		1 foot	304	0.304	
1 yard (yd)	36	3	1		914	0.914	
3 ft 3 ¼ in	39.371		1.094	1 metre			
5 ½ feet				1 pole, rod, or perch			
1 link (lk)	9.92	0.66			201	0.201	
100 links				1 chain			
4 poles		66	22	1 chain		20.116	
1 chain (ch)							
10 chains		660	220	1 furlong		201.168	
10 square chains				1 acre			
1 furlong (fur)							
8 furlongs				1 mile			
80 chains				1 mile			

Avoirdupois weight		Angular Measure	
Used for all general merchandise			
1 grain (gr)		60 seconds (sec., ")	1 minute (min., ')
1 dram (dr)	27.344 gr	60 minutes	1 degree (deg., °)
16 drams	1 oz	45 degrees	1 oxtant
16 ounces (oz)	1 pound	60 degrees	1 sextant
14 pounds (lb)	1 stone	90 degrees	1 quadrant or right angle
28 pounds	1 quarter (qr)	360 degrees	1 circle or circumference (cir.)
4 quarters (qr)	1 hundredweight		
8 stones	1 hundredweight		
1 hundredweight	112 lbs		
20 hundredweight (cwt)	1 ton		
1 ton	2240 lbs		
1 metric ton (tonne)	2204 lbs		

Capacity				
4 gills	1 pint (pt)	1 pint	0.125 gal.	0.02 cubic feet (ft³)
2 pints	1 quart (qt)	8 pints	1.0 gal.	0.1604 ft³
4 quarts	1 gallon (gal., gall.)	16 pints	2.0 gal.	0.3208 ft³
1 gallon	277.42 cubic inches (in³)			
2 gallons	1 peck	1 US gallons	0.83 gal.	3.785 l
4 pecks	1 bushel	6 US gallons	5 gal.	
8 bushels	1 quarter (qr)			
4 quarters	1 load	1728 cubic inches (in³)		1 cubic foot (ft³)
36 bushels	1 chaldron	27 cubic feet		1 cubic yard (yd³)

Système International d'Unitès (SI Units)

SI Prefixes				SI Base Units
exa	E	10^{18}	1 000 000 000 000 000 000	The strength of the SI system is its *coherence*. There
peta	P	10^{15}	1 000 000 000 000 000	are seven base SI Units. SI base units are from which,
terra	T	10^{12}	1 000 000 000 000	all other quantities are derived. The base units are:
giga	G	10^{9}	1 000 000 000	Length—metre (m)
mega	M	10^{6}	1 000 000	Mass—kilogram (kg)
kilo	k	10^{3}	1 000	Time—second (s)
hector	h	10^{2}	100	Temperature—Kelvin (K)
deca	da	10^{1}	10	Current—Ampere (A)
deci	d	10^{-1}	0.1	Luminous intensity—candela (cd)
centi	c	10^{-2}	0.01	Amount of substance—mole (mol)
milli	m	10^{-3}	0.001	
micro	μ	10^{-6}	0.000 001	Other units are derived from these, for example:
nano	n	10^{-9}	0.000 000 001	The unit for force is the Newton (N). The Newton (N)
pico	p	10^{-12}	0.000 000 000 001	is defined as N = kg m/s²
femto	f	10^{-15}	0.000 000 000 000 001	
atto	a	10^{-18}	0.000 000 000 000 000 001	

SI Derived Units		
Quantity	**Unit**	**Equivalent SI base unit**
Area	Length squared	m^2
Volume	Length cubed	m^3
Density	Mass per cubic volume	kg/m^3
Speed	Distance travelled per unit time	m/s
Acceleration	Speed changed per unit time	m/s^2
Force—Newton	Mass times acceleration of object	$kg\ m/s^2$
Pressure, stress—Pascal (Pa)	Force per unit area	$kg/(m\ s^2)$
Energy, work, heat—Joule (J)	Force times distance travelled	$kg\ m^2/s^2$
Electric potential, Voltage—Volt (V)		$kg\ m^2/A\ s^3$
Electrical resistance—Ohm (Ω)		$kg\ m^2/A^2\ s^3$
Power, radian flux—Watt (W)		$kg\text{-}m^2/s^3$
Frequency—Hertz (Hz)		1/s

Imperial and Metric Equivalences

Length

in.	in.*
0.1	3/32
0.2	3/16
0.25	1/4
0.3	9/32
0.4	3/8
0.5	1/2
0.6	9/16
0.7	11/16
0.75	3/4
0.8	25/32
0.9	7/8

in.	mm
1/16	1.587
1/8	3.175
3/16	4.762
1/4	6.35
5/16	7.937
3/8	9.525
7/16	11.112
1/2	12.7
9/16	14.287
5/8	15.875
11/16	17.462
3/4	19.05
13/16	20.637
7/8	22.225
15/16	23.812
1	25.4

in.	m
1	0.025
2	0.051
3	0.076
4	0.102
5	0.127
6	0.152
7	0.178
8	0.203
9	0.229
10	0.254
11	0.279
12	0.305
13	0.33
14	0.356
15	0.381
16	0.406
17	0.432
18	0.457
19	0.483
20	0.508
21	0.533
22	0.559
23	0.584
24	0.61
25	0.635
26	0.66
27	0.686
28	0.711
29	0.737
30	0.762
31	0.787
32	0.813
33	0.838
34	0.864
35	0.889
36	0.914

ft	m
½	0.152
1	0.305
1 ½	0.457
2	0.61
2 ½	0.762
3	0.914
3 ½	1.067
4	1.219
4 ½	1.372
5	1.524
5 ½	1.676
6	1.829
6 ½	1.981
7	2.134
8	2.438
9	2.743
10	3.048
11	3.353
12	3.658
13	3.962
14	4.267
15	4.572
16	4.877
17	5.182
18	5.486
19	5.791
20	6.096
21	6.401
22	6.706
23	7.01
24	7.315
25	7.62
26	7.925
27	8.23
28	8.534
29	8.839
30	9.144
35	10.668
40	12.192
45	13.716
50	15.265

Weight

oz	g	kg
0.003	0.1	0.0001
0.017	0.5	0.0005
0.035	1.0	0.001
0.070	2.0	0.002
0.176	5.0	0.005
0.352	10	0.01
0.500	14.1	0.014
0.705	20.0	0.02
0.881	25.0	0.025
1.000	28.3	0.028
2.000	56.6	0.056
3.000	85.0	0.085
3.527	100.0	0.1
4.000	113.3	0.113
5.000	141.7	0.141
5.291	150.0	0.15
6.000	170.0	0.17
7.000	198.4	0.198
7.055	200.0	0.2
8.000	226.7	0.226
9.000	255.1	0.225
10.000	283.4	0.283
10.582	300.0	0.3
11.000	311.8	0.311
12.000	340.1	0.34
13.000	368.5	0.368
14.000	396.8	0.396
14.109	400.0	0.4
15.000	425.2	0.425
16.000	453.5	0.453
17.637	500.0	0.5
21.164	600.0	0.6
24.691	700.0	0.7
28.219	800.0	0.8
31.746	900.0	0.9

lb	oz	kg
1		0.45
2		0.9
2	3	1.0
2.2		1.0
3		1.3
4		1.8
4	7	2.0
5		2.2
6		2.7
6	10	3.0
7		3.1
8		3.6
8	13	4.0
9		4.082
10		4.5
11		4.99
11	0	5.0
12		5.4
13		5.8
13	4	6.0
14		6.3
15		6.8
15	7	7.0
16		7.2
17		7.7
17	10	8.0
18		8.1
19		8.6
19	3	9.0
20		9.072
21		9.5
22		9.9
22	1	10.0
23		10.4
24		10.8
24	4	11.0
25		11.3
26		11.7
26	7	12.0
27		12.2
28		12.7
28	11	13.0
29		13.1
30		13.6
30	14	14.0
31		14.061
32		14.5
33		14.9
33	1	15.0
34		15.4
35		15.8
35	4	16.0
36		16.3
37		16.7
37	8	17.0
38		17.2
39		17.6
39	11	18.0
40		18.1

lb	oz	kg
41		18.5
41	14	19.0
42		19.051
43		19.5
44	1	19.9
44		20.0
45		20.4
46		20.8
46	5	21.0
47		21.3
48		21.7
48	8	22.0
49		22.2
50		22.6
50	11	23.0
51		23.1
52		23.5
52	15	24.0
53		24.4
54		24.9
55	2	25.0
56		25.4
57		25.8
57	5	26.0
58		26.3
59		26.7
59	8	27.0
60		27.2
61		27.6
61	12	28.0
62		28.1
63		28.5
63	15	29.0
64		29.030
65		29.4
66		29.9
66	2	30.0
67		30.3
68		30.8
68	5	31.0
69		31.2
70		31.7
70	9	32.0
71		32.2
72		32.6
72	12	33.0
73		33.1
74		33.5
74	15	34.0
75		34.019
76		34.4
77		34.9
77	3	35.0
78		35.3
79		35.8
79	6	36.0
80		36.2

lb	oz	kg
81		
81	9	
82		
83		
83	12	
84		
85		
86	0	
86		
87		
88		
88	3	
89		
90		
90	6	
91		
92		
92	10	
93		
94		
94	13	
95		
96		
97		
97	0	
98		
99		
99	3	
100		
101		
101	7	
102		
103		
103	10	
104		
105		
105	13	
106		
107		
108		
108	0	
109		
110		
110	4	
111		
112		
112	7	
132.28		60
143.3		65
154.32		70
165.3		75
176.37		80
187.4		85
198.42		90
209.4		95
220.46		100
231.5		105
242.5		110

Notes:
1. * approximate
2. To convert decimal fractions to fractions:
a) For decimal feet, take the decimal fraction of feet and divide (/) by 0.08333 (i.e. 1/12) to get inches and decimals of an inch, e.g. using 5.19 ft, take the decimal 0.19 and divide 0.08333. Result 2.28 inches.
b) From the result 2.28 in. take the decimal 0.28. To get fractions of an inch divide by 0.125 for eights, (1/8), 0.0625 for sixteenths (1/16), 0.03125 for thirty-seconds (1/32) and 0.015625 for sixty-fourths (1/64). E.g. converting decimal 0.28 in. to a sixty-fourth fraction divide 0.28 by 0.015625 to get 17.92 (0.28 / 0.01562 = 17.62). The answer 17.92 is 0.92 larger than 17/64.

c) Therefore 5.19 ft approximates to 5 ft 2-17/64 in.

Time to Paddle Distance at Speed Table

km	nm	5.0 km/h (2.6 kn) h:m:s	5.6 km/h (3.0 kn) h:m:s	6 km/h (3.2 kn) h:m:s	6.6 km/h (3.5 kn) h:m:s	7 km/h (3.7 kn) h:m:s	7.5 km/h (4.0 kn) h:m:s	8 km/h (4.3 kn) h:m:s
1	0.54	0:12:00	0:10:42	0:10:00	0:09:00	0:08:30	0:08:00	0:07:30
2	1.08	0:24:00	0:21:24	0:20:00	0:18:00	0:17:00	0:16:00	0:15:00
3	1.62	0:36:00	0:32:06	0:30:00	0:27:00	0:25:30	0:24:00	0:22:30
4	2.16	0:48:00	0:42:48	0:40:00	0:36:00	0:34:00	0:32:00	0:30:00
5	2.70	1:00:00	0:53:30	0:50:00	0:45:00	0:42:30	0:40:00	0:37:30
6	3.24	1:12:00	1:04:12	1:00:00	0:54:00	0:51:00	0:48:00	0:45:00
7	3.78	1:24:00	1:14:54	1:10:00	1:03:00	0:59:30	0:56:00	0:52:30
8	4.32	1:36:00	1:25:36	1:20:00	1:12:00	1:08:00	1:04:00	1:00:00
9	4.86	1:48:00	1:36:18	1:30:00	1:21:00	1:16:30	1:12:00	1:07:30
10	5.40	2:00:00	1:47:00	1:40:00	1:30:00	1:25:00	1:20:00	1:15:00
11	5.94	2:12:00	1:57:42	1:50:00	1:39:00	1:33:30	1:28:00	1:22:30
12	6.48	2:24:00	2:08:24	2:00:00	1:48:00	1:42:00	1:36:00	1:30:00
13	7.02	2:36:00	2:19:06	2:10:00	1:57:00	1:50:30	1:44:00	1:37:30
14	7.56	2:48:00	2:29:48	2:20:00	2:06:00	1:59:00	1:52:00	1:45:00
15	8.10	3:00:00	2:40:30	2:30:00	2:15:00	2:07:30	2:00:00	1:52:30
16	8.64	3:12:00	2:51:12	2:40:00	2:24:00	2:16:00	2:08:00	2:00:00
17	9.18	3:24:00	3:01:54	2:50:00	2:33:00	2:24:30	2:16:00	2:07:30
18	9.72	3:36:00	3:12:36	3:00:00	2:42:00	2:33:00	2:24:00	2:15:00
19	10.26	3:48:00	3:23:18	3:10:00	2:51:00	2:41:30	2:32:00	2:22:30
20	10.80	4:00:00	3:34:00	3:20:00	3:00:00	2:50:00	2:40:00	2:30:00
21	11.34	4:12:00	3:44:42	3:30:00	3:09:00	2:58:30	2:48:00	2:37:30
22	11.88	4:24:00	3:55:24	3:40:00	3:18:00	3:07:00	2:56:00	2:45:00
23	12.42	4:36:00	4:06:06	3:50:00	3:27:00	3:15:30	3:04:00	2:52:30
24	12.96	4:48:00	4:16:48	4:00:00	3:36:00	3:24:00	3:12:00	3:00:00
25	13.50	5:00:00	4:27:30	4:10:00	3:45:00	3:32:30	3:20:00	3:07:30
26	14.04	5:12:00	4:38:12	4:20:00	3:54:00	3:41:00	3:28:00	3:15:00
27	14.58	5:24:00	4:48:54	4:30:00	4:03:00	3:49:30	3:36:00	3:22:30
28	15.12	5:36:00	4:59:36	4:40:00	4:12:00	3:58:00	3:44:00	3:30:00
29	15.66	5:48:00	5:10:18	4:50:00	4:21:00	4:06:30	3:52:00	3:37:30
30	16.20	6:00:00	5:21:00	5:00:00	4:30:00	4:15:00	4:00:00	3:45:00
31	16.74	6:12:00	5:31:42	5:10:00	4:39:00	4:23:30	4:08:00	3:52:30
32	17.28	6:24:00	5:42:24	5:20:00	4:48:00	4:32:00	4:16:00	4:00:00
33	17.82	6:36:00	5:53:06	5:30:00	4:57:00	4:40:30	4:24:00	4:07:30
34	18.36	6:48:00	6:03:48	5:40:00	5:06:00	4:49:00	4:32:00	4:15:00
35	18.90	7:00:00	6:14:30	5:50:00	5:15:00	4:57:30	4:40:00	4:22:30
36	19.44	7:12:00	6:25:12	6:00:00	5:24:00	5:06:00	4:48:00	4:30:00
37	19.98	7:24:00	6:35:54	6:10:00	5:33:00	5:14:30	4:56:00	4:37:30
38	20.52	7:36:00	6:46:36	6:20:00	5:42:00	5:23:00	5:04:00	4:45:00
39	21.06	7:48:00	6:57:18	6:30:00	5:51:00	5:31:30	5:12:00	4:52:30
40	21.60	8:00:00	7:08:00	6:40:00	6:00:00	5:40:00	5:20:00	5:00:00
41	22.14	8:12:00	7:18:42	6:50:00	6:09:00	5:48:30	5:28:00	5:07:30
42	22.68	8:24:00	7:29:24	7:00:00	6:18:00	5:57:00	5:36:00	5:15:00
43	23.22	8:36:00	7:40:06	7:10:00	6:27:00	6:05:30	5:44:00	5:22:30
44	23.76	8:48:00	7:50:48	7:20:00	6:36:00	6:14:00	5:52:00	5:30:00
45	24.30	9:00:00	8:01:30	7:30:00	6:45:00	6:22:30	6:00:00	5:37:30
46	24.84	9:12:00	8:12:12	7:40:00	6:54:00	6:31:00	6:08:00	5:45:00
47	25.38	9:24:00	8:22:54	7:50:00	7:03:00	6:39:30	6:16:00	5:52:30
48	25.92	9:36:00	8:33:36	8:00:00	7:12:00	6:48:00	6:24:00	6:00:00
49	26.46	9:48:00	8:44:18	8:10:00	7:21:00	6:56:30	6:32:00	6:07:30
50	27.00	10:00:00	8:55:00	8:20:00	7:30:00	7:05:00	6:40:00	6:15:00

Speed, distance and time

Distance = speed x time

Time = distance ÷ speed

Speed = = distance ÷ time

Bilge Pump Flow Rates

Gallons per hour (US GPH)	Litres per minute (l/min)	Litres per hour (l/hr)	Gallons per hour (US GPH)	Litres per minute (l/min)	Litres per hour (l/hr)
1	0.0631	3.785	750	47.325	2838.75
360	22.716	1362.6	800	50.48	3028
400	25.4	1514	1100	69.41	4163.5
500	31.5	1892.5	1250	78.875	4731.25

Kilometre to Nautical Mile Conversions

km	nm	km	nm	km	nm	km	nm
1	0.54	11	5.9	25	13.5	75	40.5
2	1.08	12	6.5	30	16.2	80	43.2
3	1.62	13	7.	35	18.9	85	45.9
4	2.16	14	7.6	40	21.6	90	48.6
5	2.70	15	8.1	45	24.3	95	51.2
6	3.24	16	8.6	50	26.9	100	53.9
7	3.78	17	9.2	55	29.7		
8	4.32	18	9.7	60	32.4		
9	4.86	19	10.3	65	35.1		
10	5.40	20	10.8	70	37.8		

Nautical Mile Conversions

nm	in.	ft	yd	mile	m	km
0.1	7 291.34	607.612	202.537	0.115078	185.20	0.1852
0.2	14 582.7	1 215.22	405.074	0.230156	370.40	0.3704
0.3	21 874.0	1 822.83	607.612	0.345234	555.60	0.5556
0.4	29 165.4	2 430.45	810.149	0.460312	740.80	0.7408
0.5	36 456.7	3 038.06	1 012.69	0.575390	926.00	0.9260
0.6	43 748.0	3 645.67	1 215.22	0.690468	1 111.2	1.1112
0.7	51 039.4	4 253.28	1 417.76	0.805546	1 296.4	1.2964
0.8	58 330.7	4 860.89	1 620.3	0.920624	1 481.6	1.4816
0.9	65 622.0	5 468.50	1 822.83	1.03570	1 666.8	1.6668
1.0	72 913	6 076.12	2 025.37	1.15078	1 852.0	1.8520

Cardinal, intercardinal & intercardinal subdivisions to degrees

N	000°	E	090°	S	180°	W	270°
N by E	011.25°	E by S	101.25°	S by W	191.25°	W by N	281.25°
NNE	022.5°	ESE	112.5°	SSW	202.5°	WNW	292.5°
NE by N	033.75°	SE by E	123.75°	SW by S	213.75°	NW by W	303.75°
NE	045°	SE	135°	SW	225°	NW	315°

Compass card uses the three figure method. North is 000°, East is 090°

Chart, Map and Drawing Scales

Chart/Map					
Scale	On map	Over ground	Scale	On map	Over ground
1:10 560	6 in.	1 mile	1:62 500 1:63 360	1 in.	1 mile
1:24 000 1:25 000	1 in. 2-½ in. 4 cm	2000 ft. 1 mile 1 km	1:126 720	½ in.	1 mile
1:31 680	2 in.		1:250 000	~ ¼ in. 4 mm	1 mile 1 km
1:50 000	~1-¼ in. 2 cm	1 mile 1 km	1:253 440	¼ in.	1 mile

Drawings		
	Imperial	Metric
1/16 in. to 1 foot (i.e. 1/16 in. of drawing is equal to 12 in. of actual object being drawn)	1:192	1:200
1/8 in. to 1 foot (i.e. in 1 ft there are 12 in. In 12 in. there are 96 parts of 1/8 in.)	1:96	1:100
¼ in. to 1 foot (i.e. there are 48 parts of ¼ in. in 12 in. That is four quarters[parts] in one inch {4 x ¼ = 1} & 4 x 12 = 48)	1:48	1:50
½ in. to 1 foot	1:24	1:20

Degrees of Arc and Distance

Degrees	Minutes	Seconds	nm	ft	m
1°	60'		60		111
	1'	60"	1	6076	1852
	0.25'	15"	0.25	1519	463
	0.10'	6"	0.1	607	185.2
		5"	0.08	486	148
		1"	0.02	121	37

Manually determining drift rate

To manually estimate your drift rate:

1. You need to know the length of your kayak and have a watch.

2. Pick a stationary feature/object parallel to you (e.g. a moored boat, buoy).

3. Paddle until your stern is level with the object.

4. While timing yourself, let the current/wind push you back until your bow passes the object at which point you record your time.

Knowing the length of your boat, (i.e. 5.8 metres (19 ft)) and the recorded drift time (i.e. 3 seconds), you can estimate the stream's rate or the effect the wind is having on your forward speed.

19ft / 3sec x (1nm / 6076ft) x (3600 sec / 1 hour) = 3.8 nm/h (i.e. 3.8 kn).

Or make it easy:

Boat length 19 ft / drift time 3 sec x 0.6 = 6.333 x 0.6 = 3.8 kn

Recording latitude and longitude

The alpha character letter, 'H' represents latitude south (S) or north (N) of the equator and longitude east (E) or west (W) of the prime meridian.

Note on GPS units like Garmin, the alpha character 'h' is put at the front of the degrees numeric characters.

There are several formats for giving latitude and longitude with the following being examples of the different formats:

Degrees and decimal tenths degree

- ddd.ddddd°H
- GPS format: hddd.ddddd°

Degrees, minutes and decimal tenths minute

- ddd°mm.mmm'H
- GPS format: hddd°mm.mmm'

Degrees, minutes and seconds.

- Known as the sexagesimal system
- ddd°mm'ss.s"H
- GPS format: hddd°mm'ss.s"

For marine weather systems, Australian and International practice is to use degrees and tenths of a degree (decimal degrees).

For example, a latitude coordinate of 25.4°S is read: twenty-five decimal four-tenths degrees south; and not: twenty-five degrees four minutes south.

To convert sexagesimal (base sixty) bearings

To convert the degree and decimal tenth 121.135° into degrees, minutes and seconds:

First keep the 121°

To get minutes, multiply the decimal part of the sexagesimal by 60. (.135) x 60 = 8.1

- The whole number of this answer remains to become 8 minutes (i.e. 8')

To get seconds, multiply the decimal part of the minutes answer by 60. (.1) x 60 = 6

- The answer becomes 6 seconds (i.e. 6")

Therefore the degrees, minutes and seconds of the sexagesimal 121.135° is 121° 8' 6"

To convert decimal minutes to minutes and seconds

To convert a decimal minutes into minutes and seconds, it is the same process as converting a sexagesimal.

A bearing of 38°18.330'S is handled in the following manner.

The degrees remain unchanged (i.e. 38°)

The whole minutes remain unchanged (i.e. 18)

The decimal minutes are multiplied by 60

- Therefore .330 x 60 = 19.8
- Rounded up the answer is 20 seconds

Therefore a bearing of 38°18.330'S is

38° 18' 20"S

Remember on a small-scale chart, latitude and longitude seconds are expressed as one-tenth (1/10) of a minute. Therefore, there are ten one-tenth (1/10) increments. Each one-tenth increment is equal to six (6) seconds.

Mental maths

For speed conversions

As a guide to perform quick mental conversions:

m/s to knot (kn).

- Multiply m/s by 2 (i.e. double m/s) therefore,

- 3 m/s x 2 ≈ 6 kn

Knot (kn) to km/h.

- Multiply km/h by 2 (double knots) and subtract 10% therefore,

- 6 kn x 2 = 12

- then subtract 10% of the answer (12)

- 12-1.2 ≈ 10.8 km/h

To determine a percentage of a knot

To determine 90% of a 3 knot tidal stream:

Convert the percentage to a decimal
   90% is 0.9

Remove the decimal point from the answer and
   multiply the numbers together
   9 x 3 = 27

Return the decimal point in the answer
   2.7 knots

Therefore, 90% of 3 knots is 2.7 kn

To convert the decimals to minutes

To convert the decimals to minutes multiply by 60
0.4 x 60 = 24'

By quick mental arithmetic
4 x 6 = 24

To calculate a back bearing

To easily calculate a back bearing mentally, perform the following; for bearings between:

000° to 180°, add 200, and subtract 20

180° to 360°, subtract 200, and add 20

Air Pressure

Average sea-level pressure is:

1.013×10^5 N/m²

101.325 kPa

1 atmosphere (atm)

1013.25 mbar

760 millimetres of mercury (mmHg, torr)

29.921 inches of mercury (inHg)

14.7 pounds per square inch (lb/in²)

At sea level the average pressure of air is stated to be 1.013×10^5 N/m² (or 14.7 lb/in²). This value is used to define another unit of pressure, the *atmosphere* (atm). One atmosphere equals 101.3 kPa. On some overseas weather maps, a unit of barometric pressure is the *bar*. A bar is a CGS unit of measurement. One bar equals 100 kPa; thus standard atmospheric pressure is slightly greater than one bar. In Australia, weather maps use the SI unit for pressure the hectopascal (hPa) as their unit of measure.

Mean Sea Level (MSL) air pressure can vary between 870 hPa to 1040 hPa but the norm is between 970 hPa to 1040 hPa. The highest recorded was in Siberia in 1968 at 1084 hPa. The lowest was in conjunction with a 1979 typhoon that recorded at the tip 870 hPa.

Millibar and hectopascal

A bar is a centimetre-gram-second system (abbreviated CGS or c.g.s) unit of pressure. A millibar (mb or mbar) is a meteorological unit of pressure equal to one-thousandth of a bar.

SI units have replaced the use of CGS, metre-kilogram-second system (MKS), and imperial measurement systems for scientific study. The pascal (Pa) and hence hectopascal (hPa) are SI units. For the purpose of measuring purely mechanical systems involving units of length, force, pressure, mass et cetera there is a straightforward conversion between the two units of CGS and SI.

A dyne is a CGS unit of force. Dyne per centimetre squared (dyne/cm²) is the CGS unit of pressure. A pascal is equivalent to one newton

(1 N) of force applied over an area of one meter squared (1 m^2) and is expressed as:

1 Pa = 1 N $\cdot$ m^{-2} (or 1 Pa = 1 N/m^2).

The unit-conversion factors are all powers of 10, thus 1 bar equals 1 000 000 dyne/cm^2, or 10 N/cm^2, or 100 000 N/m^2, or 100 000 Pa, or 1000 hPa, or 100 kPa.

One hectopascal equals one millibar (1 hPa = 1 mbar). This is shown by 1 mbar being one-thousandth of a bar (1 mbar = 0.001 bar). Therefore 1 mbar equals 1000 hPa/1000 = 1 hPa.

APPENDIX 2 CONTACT NUMBERS AND WEBSITES

AUSTRALIA	
Distress & Call—Radio	Refer to the VRBSH, ch.1, Marine Radio 27 MHz ch.88 & ch.86 VHF ch.16 & ch.67
Emergency—phone (Australia)	**000**
EPIRB accidental set off (24 h)	1800 641 792
Crime Stoppers	1800 333 000
Customs Watch	1800 06 1800
Illegal fishing	13 FISH (133 474)
Lost credit card	1800 224 004, (02) 0059 7480
Weather and Ocean Information (Australia)	
BOM Telephone Weather Services (TWS)	www.bom.gov.au/other/tws/twsdir.shtml
Marine Weather, Swell and Tides by internet	www.bom.gov.au www.surf-forecast.com/breaks/ . . . www.baywx.com www.seabreeze.com.au www.eldersweather.com.au http://magicseaweed.com www.weatherchannel.com.au www.buoyweather.com (User pay)
BOM Marine & Ocean (VHF & HF Radio) Communication Services	www.bom.gov.au/marine/radio-sat/marine-radio-sat.shtml
Marine Safety (Australian Government Departments)	
-Australian Maritime Safety Authority -Marine Safety Victoria (now Transport Safety Victoria (TSV)) -NSW Maritime -SA Dept Transport, Energy & Infrastructure -Maritime Safety Queensland -WA Dept Planning & Infrastructure -Marine & Safety Tasmania (MAST) -NT Transport Group, Marine Safety	www.amsa.gov.au www.transportsafety.vic.gov.au www.maritime.nsw.gov.au www.transport.sa.gov.au/safety/marine/index.asp www.msq.qld.gov.au www.dpi.wa.gov.au/imarine/19100.asp www.mast.tas.gov.au www.marinesafety.nt.gov.au
AMSA Distress Beacons -Approved models -Essential information	http://beacons.amsa.gov.au/index.asp http://beacons.amsa.gov.au/approved_models.asp http://beacons.amsa.gov.au/essential_info.asp
Victorian Useful Contacts and Information	
Victoria Police RCC (SAR)	(03) 9399 7500 1800 135 729 (toll free)
Port Albert Coastal Patrol	5183 2347
Port Welshpool Coastal Patrol	5688 1537
Parks Victoria— Wilsons Promontory	1800 350 552 (03) 5680 9555
Port of Melbourne -Wave Data -Shipping Movements in Port Phillip Bay	www.portofmelbourne.com/ www.portofmelbourne.com.au/waves.asp
Victorian Regional Channels Authority Gippsland Ports (Tides & Weather) Port of Hastings	www.regionalchannels.vic.gov.au www.gippslandports.vic.gov.au www.portofhastings.vic.gov.au
Weather by Coast Radio Melbourne for Port Phillip Bay and Westernport	VHF channel 16 SECURITE, switch to channel 67 Broadcast times refer to the VRBSH, ch.1, Marine weather information

Limited Coast Stations (i.e. volunteer organisations and fishing clubs)	27 MHz channel 88, supplementary channel 86 VHF Ch.16, supplementary Ch. 67
VHF marine radio repeaters	www.transportsafety.vic.gov.au www.coastguard.com.au/location/victoria.html
NEW ZEALAND	
Kiwi Association of Sea Kayakers (**KASK**) -Provides useful links to other websites when planning	www.kask.org.nz
Maritime New Zealand -Provides information for recreational boaters and a PDF document SAFE BOATING: An Essential Guide.	www.maritimenz.govt.nz
Water Safety New Zealand -Provides information for recreational boaters	www.watersafety.org.nz
New Zealand Coast Guard -Tides and tide times -Marine weather VHF radio channels around New Zealand Maritime safety: Rules of the sea Marine education: buoys, beacons and markers	www.coastguard.co.nz
Land Information New Zealand (*Whatungarongaro te tangata toitū te whenua*) -Provides a calculator to convert various datums -Provides a free on-line book on map reading and compass use	www.linz.govt.nz
Department of Conservation (*Te Papa Atawhai*) -Provides information for camping	www.doc.govt.nz
New Zealand Weather (metservice.com) -Provides marine weather forecasts	www.metservice.com
CANADA Canadian Coast Guard Transport Canada (Safe Boating Guide TP 511E (2011)) Transport Canada (Sea Kayaking Safety Guide TP 14726)	http://www.ccg-gcc.gc.ca/eng/CCG/Home www.tc.gc.ca/eng/menu.htm www.tc.gc.ca/eng/marinesafety/tp-tp14726-menu-1098.htm

UNITED STATES OF AMERICA
United States Coast Guard Navigation Centre
United States Coast Guard Boating Safety Resource Center
National Ocean and Atmospheric Administration, nautical Charts and publications
National Geospatial-Intelligence Agency
This is one of the greatest marine resource sites on the World Wide Web. Refer to the web site of the National Geospatial-Intelligence Agency, Marine Safety Information for free downloads of:
Chart No.1This publication contains a description of the symbols, abbreviations and terms that appear on nautical charts produced by the National Geospatial-Intelligence Agency, the National Ocean Service and the International Hydrographic Organization.
Sailing Directions, both Planning guides and Enroute, e.g.:
    ■ Pub 120 Sailing Directions (Planning Guide), Pacific Ocean and South-East Asia
    ■ Pub 127 Sailing Directions (Enroute), East Coast of Australia and New Zealand
    ■ Pub 175 North, West and South Australia
The 'American Practical Navigator'.
	www.navcen.uscg.gov/index.php
	www.uscgboating.org/default.aspx

UNITED KINGDOM	
United Kingdom Maritime and Coast Guard Agency -Admiralty Easy Tide Service -Met Office Shipping Forecasts and Gale Warnings -Leisure and the Seaside -Weather	www.dft.gov.uk/mca/
UK Government Directory Service -Boating and travelling by water	www.direct.gov.uk

INTERESTING WEBSITES	
Education -Australian Canoeing -Outsdoor Victoria	http://www.canoe.org.au http://outdoorsvictoria.org.au
Food -Nutritional data -Food-to-go, the book	www.nutritiondata.com/tools/calories-burned http://ourhikingblog.com.au/food-to-go
First Aid -Marine first aid -Marine medical kits -Cancer Council Victoria	www.marine-medic.com.au www.islandcruising.co.nz www.cancervic.org.au
Clubs -Kiwi Association of Sea Kayakers (KASK) -Maatsuyker Canoe Club, Tasmania. Jeff Jennings -NSW Sea Kayak club (NSWSKC) -Queensland Sea Kayak Club Inc. -Tasmanian Sea Canoeing Club Inc. -Victorian Sea Kayak Club (VSKC)	www.kask.org.nz/ www.vision.net.au/~jennings/ www.nswseakayaker.asn.au/ www.qldseakayak.canoe.org.au www.kingston.org.au www.vskc.org.au/
People Peter Bray, UK Peter Carter, SA Nigel Dennis Laurie Ford, Tas. Harvey Golden Freya Hoffmeister Nick Shade Vaclav Stejskal Virtual Kayak Museum Matt Watton, Tas. John Winters David Zimmerly	www.peterbrayadventurer.com www.users.on.net/~pcarter/index.html www.seakayakinguk.com www.tassie.net.au/~lford/index.htm#links www.traditionalkayaks.com http://freyahoffmeister.com www.guillemot-kayaks.com/guillemot http://oneoceankayaks.com www.vikamus.de www.netspace.net.au/~mwatton/index.html www.greenval.com www.arctickayaks.com

APPENDIX 3 A STUDY OF PAST VICTORIAN WEATHER FORECASTS

Difference between forecasted and actual weather

The following information has been included to show the difference between forecasted weather and actual. The BOM synoptic chart and forecast were both issued July 13, 2005 and were used as part of a weather-watch, prior to a planned trip in 2005. The trip was cancelled on the Thursday evening but what was interesting with the forecasted weather for the weekend, was how much faster the front was travelling and how much higher the wind speeds became. The area of interest is the Victorian central coast between Cape Otway in the West and Wilsons Promontory in the East.

Of note is the weather forecasted for Saturday July 16, 2005. The steady state winds were considerably higher than the forecasted as attested by the issuing of a Gale Warning that morning. The winds for the morning were forecasted as strong winds (22–25 knots) and gusting to possibly 35 knots. The afternoon winds were forecasted as increasing to 30 knots (near gale, 28–33 knots) and gusts possibly reaching 42 knots.

The forecast data and observations data collected on Saturday 16th, have been tabulated in table A3-1 for easier comparison. By Sunday July 17, 2005 the winds were dropping to 25 knots south-westerlies and the swell running at 11–16 feet (3.3–4.8 m) dropping by one foot at 4 pm.

State Forecast
Issued at 2300 on Wednesday the 13th of July 2005
Warnings: Nil.
Weather Pattern: A broad trough of low pressure will persist over Victoria on Thursday. A cold front will cross the Bight on Friday then move through Victoria on Saturday. An associated low-pressure system will move south of Tasmania on Sunday.
Friday: Variable winds 5 to 10 knots tending southerly at 10 to 15 knots then easing to 5 to 10 knots at night and tending northerly.

Table A3-1 Tabulated Events of Saturday 16 July 2005								
Synopsis for Saturday July 16, 2005 Cold front crossing Victoria **Gale Warning Current**		Time	Temp (°C)	Wind (knots)		Gusts (knots) 40% >	Pressure (hPa)	Rain (mm)
				Direction	Speed			
Forecast	Victoria State Forecast	Morning		N-NW	20-25	~35		
		Later		W-SW	20-30	~42		
BOM Observations	Location							
	Cape Otway	1100 h		N	38		1002.4	
		2100 h		WSW	44		1007.6	5
	Fawkner Beacon (Northern Port Phillip Bay)	1300 h		N	40			
		1957 h		W	42			
	South Channel Fort (South Port Phillip Bay)	2150 h				49		
	Wilsons Promontory	2304 h	7.9°	W	31	W 56	1004.2	8.4

Saturday: North to north-westerly winds strengthening to 20 to 25 knots during the morning then shifting west to south-westerly at 20 to 30 knots.

On Saturday July 16, 2005, the BOM issued the following at 2150 h:

Explanatory Notes

A cold front will cross the remainder of Victoria tonight (Saturday). A high pressure system will develop over South Australia on Sunday before slowly moving into western Victoria late Monday and Tuesday then reaching the east of the State on Wednesday.

Strong northerly wind developed in the west this morning then spread eastwards. Strongest gusts were 49 knots [91 km/h] at South Channel Island, 47 knots [87 km/h] at Mt Gellibrand, 46 knots [85 km/h] at Cape Nelson and Dunns Hill and 45 knots [83 km/h] at Rhyll. There were morning fog patches in the north and east then a mainly cloudy day with just brief sunny breaks in southern areas.

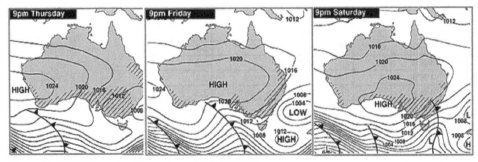

Figure A3-1 BOM four-day forecast issued July 13, 2005

Difference between estimated wind speed factor and actual

The aim here in this example is to show how much stronger wind gust can be above the estimated 40 per cent (a factor of 0.4) of the steady state wind. The BOM forecast for the central waters region and observation data taken at Wilsons Promontory on the August 1, 2007 have been tabulated in Table A3-2.

The following BOM forecast was issued for Cape Otway to Wilsons Promontory with a coast wind warning:

Coastal Waters Wind Warning
For Cape Otway to Wilsons Promontory
Issued at 9:50 am EST on Wednesday 1 August 2007
Synoptic situation
A deep low-pressure system well south of the Bight is directing a vigorous north-westerly airstream over Bass Strait with embedded cold fronts. The next cold front in the series will brush western Bass Strait tonight.
Warnings: Gale Warning
Cape Otway to Wilsons Promontory
North/north-westerly wind 20/30 knots increasing to 25/35 knots tonight and locally reaching 40 knots offshore. Seas rising 4 to 6 metres. Westerly swell rising 2 to 4 metres.
The next warning will be issued by 4 pm EST Wednesday.
Please be aware: Wind gusts can be a further 40 per cent stronger than the averages given here (**a factor of 0.4**), and maximum waves may be up to twice the height.

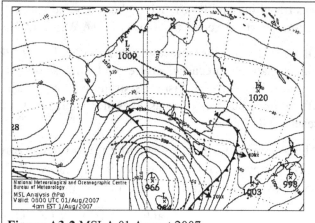

Figure A3-2 MSLA 01 August 2007

From the BOM Observations recorded at Wilsons Promontory, note how:

The steady state wind is at the lower end of the Beaufort wind scale for a strong breeze.

How over a 5.5 hour period, the steady state wind went from a gentle breeze (7 kn) to the lower end of a strong breeze (23 kn).

Table A3-2 shows the differential between steady state wind as forecasted and the accompanying gusts. If you are on the water, you need to be aware of the possible wind gusts strengths. This table is here to show just how much greater the wind strengths can be, compared to the warning of 40 per cent (factor 0.4). Note the increase factor between steady state and gusts, averaged a factor of 2.3.

Table A3-2 Tabulated BOM observations for Wilsons Promontory							
Wilsons Promontory		Selected Recordings from 0430 h to 1000 h					
1Aug07	°C	Direction	Steady State kn	Gusts kn	hPa	Differential Increase Steady to Gusts (kn)	Increase Factor
01/10:00am	12.6	W	**23**	**43**	1002.7	**20**	**1.9**
01/09:30am	12.3	W	23	40	1003.1	17	1.7
01/08:39am	12.1	WNW	22	51	1003.2	29	2.3
01/08:00am	11.7	WNW	**16**	**38**	1003.3	**22**	**2.4**
01/07:31am	11.5	WNW	17	36	1003.1	19	2.1
01/07:27am	11.5	WNW	16	43	1003	27	2.7
01/06:31am	11.8	WNW	**17**	**56**	1002.2	**39**	**3.3**
01/05:00am	12.2	WNW	19	37	1001.7	18	1.9
01/04:30am	12.1	N	7	16	1001.8	9	2.3

APPENDIX 4 BOATING RULES AND REGULATIONS

A child of five would understand this. Send someone to fetch a child of five.

Groucho Marx

In the interest of boating safety, the following information has been included from the Victorian Recreational Boating Safety handbook.

Steering and sailing rules

Sea kayakers encounter vessels under sail and or power. The vessels may be under command of a commercial or recreational licence holder even though the sea kayaker does not require a boating licence. To operate safely around sail and power vessels it is prudent to know 'steering and sailing rules' thereby knowing your responsibilities and being able anticipating the other vessels action. The reason for knowing these rules can be likened to a push-bike rider needing to know the rules of the road.

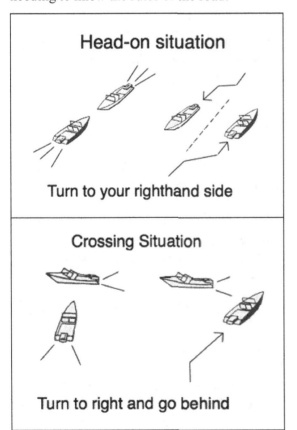

Head-on situation

Turn to your righthand side

Crossing Situation

Turn to right and go behind

Power and sail vessels

Power-driven vessels shall keep out of the way of sailing vessels and rowing boats.

Sailing vessels approaching one another and each has the wind on a different side, the vessel, which has the wind on the port side shall keep out of the way of the other.

When each sailing vessel has the wind on the same side, the vessel, which is to windward, shall keep out of the way of the vessel that is leeward.

When a sailing vessel with the wind on its port side sees another sailing vessel to windward and cannot determine with certainty whether that sailing vessel has the wind on its port or its starboard, it shall keep out of the way of that other sailing vessel.

Power-driven vessels meeting head-on or nearly head-on <u>shall alter course to starboard</u> so that each may pass on the port side of each other.

When two power-driven vessels are crossing, the vessel with the other on its starboard side shall keep out of the way and avoid crossing ahead of the other vessel. The other vessel must maintain its course and speed until it is apparent that the vessel required to give way is not taking appropriate action.

In **narrow channels** or channel approaches <u>all vessels in narrow channels</u> shall keep as far as practicable, to the starboard side of the channel.

A vessel engaged in fishing shall not impede the passage of any other vessel navigating within a narrow channel or fairway

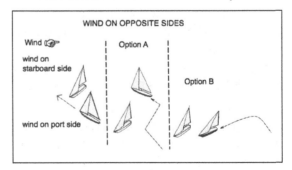

WIND ON OPPOSITE SIDES

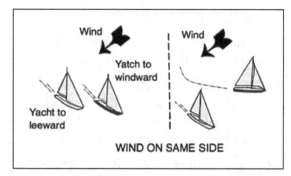

A vessel shall not cross a narrow channel or fairway if such crossing impedes the passage of a vessel that can safely navigate only within such channel or fairway

Any vessel shall, if the circumstances of the case permit, avoid anchoring in a narrow channel

A sailing vessel and a vessel under 20 m in length shall not impede the passage of any vessel, which can safely navigate only within a narrow channel or fairway.

All vessels, whether sail or power, overtaking another vessel when the boats are in sight of one another shall keep out of the way of the vessel being overtaken. That is, if a vessel is coming up with another from any direction, which is more than 22.5 degrees abaft her beam, it shall be deemed to be the overtaking vessel until finally past and clear.

If in doubt, assume that you are the overtaking vessel and keep clear. Alteration of course by either vessel does not relieve the overtaking vessel of the responsibility of keeping clear

If overtaking or approaching a vessel engaged in waterskiing always keep at least 50 m from the skier and vessel combination

Joint emergency action

The giving-way vessel shall take early and positive avoiding action: make course/speed alterations obvious to the other vessel; avoid crossing ahead of the vessel with right of way; if necessary stop or reverse.

A series of five or more short and rapid blasts on a whistle or horn should be used to indicate that insufficient action is being taken to avoid collision.

The vessel with the right of way shall keep its course and speed.

It should take avoiding action only if that taken by the giving-way vessel is insufficient. If necessary it should take whatever action is available to keep clear and avoid a collision.

If a power-driven vessel is taking action to avoid a collision with another power-driven vessel, it shall, if possible, avoid altering course to port. This action does not relieve the vessel operator of handling obligations.

Steering and sailing rules—restricted visibility

In restricted visibility, reduce to minimum speed. When hearing the fog signal of another vessel ahead, proceed with caution until danger of collision is over or stop until you have ascertained the danger.

Responsibilities between vessels

A vessel under power gives way to:

A vessel not under command

A vessel unable to manoeuvre easily (including large vessels navigating in or near a channel or fairway)

A vessel engaged in fishing (with apparatus such as trawling gear restricting its ability to manoeuvre)

A sailing vessel (but see below).

A sailing vessel must keep clear of:

A vessel not under command

A vessel unable to manoeuvre easily (including large vessels navigating in or near a channel or fairway)

A vessel engaged in fishing (with apparatus such as trawling gear restricting its ability to manoeuvre).

Large vessels

Recreational vessels have a responsibility to stay well clear of large vessels. Small craft are prohibited from impeding the passage of big ships. All boat operators should take note of the following:

Big ships operate at all times of the day and night

The speed of a ship can be deceptive and may travel at speeds in excess of 20 knots

Ships can weigh up to 100 000 tonnes and do not have brakes. They cannot stop or change course suddenly and will travel a long distance before stopping

A ship's blind spot can extend for many hundreds of metres ahead

Bow waves caused by a ship can swamp a small boat hundreds of metres away

Sailing vessels do not have right of way over big ships

A ship may sound five short blasts on its whistle if it believes you are at risk of a collision. Small vessels must take evasive action immediately.

Harbourmaster's directions

In port waters the relevant harbourmaster may make special directions concerning the navigation and operation of recreational vessels.

For instance in port waters for Port of Geelong, Port of Melbourne and Port of Portland the following directions apply:

The master of a vessel less than 25 m in length shall ensure that the vessel keeps out of the way of:

Vessels more than 25 m in length

A tug or launch assisting the movement, berthing or unberthing of another vessel

The master of another vessel less than 25 m in length shall ensure the vessel does not approach within 30 m of a ship berthed at a tanker terminal.

A copy of the Harbourmaster's Directions for the Port of Melbourne, Geelong, Hastings, Portland and Gippsland Ports is included in the Port Operating Handbook, which can be purchased from the relevant authority.

NAVIGATIONAL RESPONSIBILITIES (LEGAL)

Most collisions between vessels result from carelessness: everyone on the water has a legal, as well as moral, duty to maintain a proper lookout and travel at a safe speed at all times.

This duty includes the handling of a vessel and observing the rules, knowing the limitations of your vessel, being aware of potential hazards and allowing for the actions of others, both reasonable and unreasonable.

It pays to take care (negligence)

An operator can be deemed to be negligent if proper care was not taken subject to circumstances. When someone handles his or her vessel in such a way as to cause an obvious and serious risk of physical injury to another using the same waters, or to property, that is reckless navigation.

The authorities and the courts regard both recklessness and negligence most seriously.

Dangerous navigation—propelling a vessel at speed or in a manner causing real or potential danger to any person or property—is also a punishable offence. So is any use of a vessel resulting in nuisance or causing obvious annoyance to any other person, deliberately or accidentally.

Navigation Considerations

Getting there and back

Conditions can change quickly. It is not uncommon on Victorian waters for there to be sudden onsets of fog, dust and rough weather that can severely restrict visibility. This is where a compass, nautical chart, depth sounder and basic navigation aids come in handy. A GPS system can also be a valuable piece of equipment to have on board.

Operating at night

Navigating at night can be hazardous. It is more difficult to judge speeds and distances at night or in restricted visibility, than during the day. You must take every precaution. Vessels under way must show the proper lights from sunset to sunrise and in restricted visibility. You must also be able to tell from the lights of other vessels what they are, what they are doing and their direction of travel, so you can take the right timely action to avoid collision.

You must familiarise yourself with navigation hazards, fixed or otherwise, lit and unlit, and whose position may occasionally change. Know where they are, from unlit buoys to rocks and shoals, and keep their position in relation to your vessel constantly in mind. Spotlights and torches may be used, but take care not to dazzle other people on the water, or yourself.

Always travel at a reduced speed to increase your safety margin. Keep a careful lookout around you for hazards and other vessels and, for extra reassurance, travel in company with another vessel or vessels where possible.

Only specified navigation lights can be shown at night. Any other lights on-board must not interfere with the range and arc of visibility of navigation lights.

A sharp lookout is important when the background of bright lights on shore tends to obscure the lights of other vessels, buoys and marks. This is especially true in waters close to populated areas, such as the shore of Port Phillip Bay where even larger ships can be hard to see.

Operating Rules

The operation of a vessel can often be affected by physical conditions such as the direction of the wind, the depth of the water and visibility. When operating any type of vessel, always allow plenty of time and space in which to carry out any manoeuvre.

Operators of small vessels should appreciate the difficulties of large ships manoeuvring in congested or restricted sea areas or ports and, as a general rule, keep well clear of shipping.

The Steering and Safety Rules and the lights and shapes, which must be displayed are set out in the International Regulations for Preventing Collisions at Sea (1972).

A good lookout must be kept by sight and hearing. The operator must be fully aware of the boating environment, especially in bad weather, restricted visibility or darkness. Don't forget to look all around you—even behind you. The operator is responsible at all times for keeping a proper lookout.

The specific operating rules for each Victorian waterway are set out in the "Vessel Operating and Zoning Rules". An up to date copy of the rules can be accessed on TSV's website.

Speed restrictions

Speeding, together with alcohol, is one of the principle causes of boating accidents on Victoria's waterways. The Victorian Water Police are empowered to use speed measuring devices to detect speeding vessels.

Speeds are limited by law, for specific boating areas, to meet local operation and safety conditions and usage. All speeds are measured in knots for the purpose of the Marine Act 1988 and the Marine Regulations 2009.

General safety/operating rules

'Access lanes' provide access to the shore by waterskiers at speeds greater than 5 knots when otherwise it might not be possible. Bathers are not permitted within an 'access lane'

Bathers must remain more than 50m from a boat ramp when it is in use or about to be in use

'No wash zones' are where a vessel must proceed at a speed that creates minimal wash

Areas may be set aside where specific activities are prohibited (for example, no waterskiing, no bathing)

Areas may be set aside for exclusive use or for special purposes (for example, sailing vessels only)

On inland waters, vessels are required to travel in an anticlockwise direction in relation to the approximate centre of the waterway, except in a speed restriction zone or where local rules provide for travel in a clockwise direction.

Details of speed restrictions and local operating and usage rules are generally displayed on signage on the shore or marked by buoys or beacons in the water.

All vessels must travel at a safe speed at all times. A safe speed cannot be expressed as a maximum or minimum number of knots because it varies with circumstances and conditions. The operator must always assess the safety of the vessel's speed. A safe speed is one at which the vessel can be stopped in time to avoid any danger which arises suddenly.

Further information can be obtained from the relevant waterway manager (municipal council, water authority).

Alcohol and drugs

'Drink driving' laws are strictly enforced with the objective of safety for all.

The Victoria Police are empowered to use breathalysers to help detect operators exceeding alcohol limits. Heavy penalties apply to offenders

Alcohol increases body-heat loss, reducing your survival time if you fall overboard. It also increases the pulse rate, leading to rapid exhaustion in survival situations

Prescribed medications and other drugs can also pose problems. Many preparations for seasickness, hay fever and other allergies can make you feel drowsy or easily confused. Check with your doctor or chemist on the possible side effects of any drugs you are obliged to take before you go boating.

APPENDIX 5 BASIC COMPASS USE

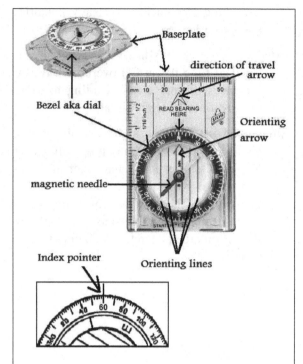

In this figure, the bezel showing north (N) as indicated by the index mark, below the wording 'Read Bearing Here'

Figure A4-1 Compass parts

The base plate compass consists of the following basic sub-assemblies as shown in Figure A4-1. There are many and varied shapes of a base plate compass. However, the straight edge of the base plate is used to lie along the line of intended direction of travel. The outer rotating bezel (aka dial) has cardinal points and degrees of arc around the circumference. The graduation increments will depend upon the compass but may be two or five degree increments.

Inside the compass housing are three items of significance: the orienting arrow, orienting lines and magnetic compass needle. The orienting arrow and orienting lines are used to align with a chart's meridian or a map's easting (north-south running line on map). This is achieved by rotating the bezel until the orienting arrow points to north (grid north on a map). The magnetic compass needle, points north-south, with the north half of the needle being coloured and or marked with a letter N, for north. Depending upon the make and or model of the base plate compass there is a index pointer either as part of the top rim of the compass housing and or as part of the tail of the direction of travel arrow, located in the centre forward section of the base plate. The index marker may also be identified by the wording 'Read Bearing Here'. If the index pointer is on the rim of the compass housing, the bezel will be of transparent plastic. As the bezel is rotated around the housing, the cardinal points and or degrees of arc (bearings), on the bezel, will pass over the top of the index mark. When the orienting lines are parallel with the meridian, the bearing will be identified by the index marker underneath.

The base plate compass is both a **protractor** and a **magnetic compass**. When setting a course, with a base plate compass ignore the magnetic compass needle when you are performing your chart work.[1] At this stage of your chart work, you only need the protractor function of the compass.

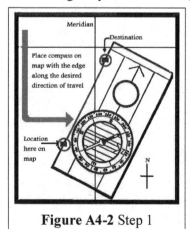

Figure A4-2 Step 1

Protractor function

Using the protractor function to find a bearing from point A to point B:

Step 1, lay the base plate along the intended course (path), while ensuring the direction of travel arrow is point in the direction of desired travel (e.g. from point A to point B).

Step 2, rotate the bezel to align the:

• Orienting arrow with the chart's north. If the orientating arrow is pointing south, your bearings will be 180° out!

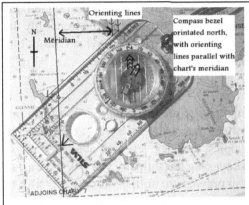

Figure A4-3 Step 2, using a chart

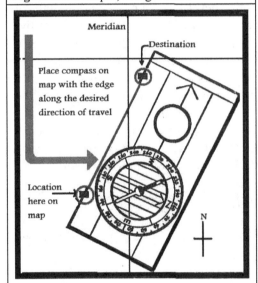

Figure A4-4 Step 2, using a map

Figure A4-5 Travelling to the bearing

- Orienting lines parallel with the meridian (easting, aka north-south line, on a map). On a chart, the meridian may not be near by the compass, but the process is still the same.

At the index pointer, read off the bearing. This will be a true bearing on a chart and a grid bearing on a map.

Compass function

Remove the protractor from the chart. Now using the compass feature of the base plate compass. Convert the true bearing of the protractor to a magnetic bearing for use with the compass.

To correct for the variation between the chart and the compass. If using a map corrected for the declination, which is the same as variation. If the variation is east remember 'grid to magnetic subtract'. If the variation is west then add the chart's variation to the true bearing of the compass.

After converting the true bearing to a magnetic bearing, orientate the compass until the magnetic needle rests inside the orienting arrow. Both tips of the arrow and the north portion of the needle will be inline.

To orientate the needle into the orienting arrow, hold the compass in front of you at about stomach height. Moving your feet, rotate your body until the needle aligns itself with the orienting needle.

Using the travel arrow as your reference, look up and out at the direction indicated by the travel arrow. This will show you the feature on the chart (point B) that you desire to go to.[2] Once you have orientated yourself and can see the feature, in many instances you will not need the compass as you can travel by using just the chart/map to ground.

For a free book on map reading and compass use go to the Land Information New Zealand website.

---

1 To avoid confusion at this basic level of explanation, I will ignore any short cuts or tips in order to keep the terms to a minimum.
2 That is if it is not hidden by another feature.

Appendix 6 Fishing

"Right place, right time, right bait, right gear"

☙ Warning: When trawling around bombies pay attention to the swell or perceived lack thereof.

The above saying sums up fishing quite succinctly, but here are a few other pointers to assist you in catching fish. Small hooks catch both small fish and big fish. Sinkers are for holding the bait down, not for clubbing and knocking the fish out with; try split shot.

Some fish are top feeders and others bottom feeders. You will need a variety of rigs to suit. If you are after bottom feeders, put the hook 500–700 mm below the sinker. If they are top feeders put the hook above the sinker so that the bait is off the bottom. You can use 'dropper loops' above the sinker to attach the leaders with hooks.

Trawling

When trawling from your kayak with lures, it is worthwhile removing the centre treble hook. This aids in preventing the lure from having multiple catching points to hook-up on your spray skirt or clothing.

For lure line, avoid using a nylon fishing line and trace, as it can become unmanageable as you are paddling. Use two to four millimetre blind cordage or brickie line and then a five-kilogram nylon fishing line trace, of a metre or so in length.

2-4mm cordage   Swivel   1-2m trace

When trawling, run the cordage over your shoulder. You can feel if you have caught something and the line is out of the way while you paddle.

Most fishing gear in shops is designed to catch hopeful fishermen. Homemade lures can be made from clear plastic tubing. Use 15 mm diameter plastic tubing, around 70 mm long, fitted with a #1 or #1/0 hook.

Fishing knots

Attached is a diagram showing several methods for tying fishing knots. The knot is generally the weakest part of your rig. Wet nylon fishing line before clenching the knot closed.

Bait

Fresh bait is the preferred bait. For sea fish use shellfish found in the area you are fishing in (e.g. pippies, muscles, left over abalone, bread). When kayaking it is unlikely you will have a bait pump so prawns are unlikely to be accessible to you. Crab meat falls off the hook.

A bait that never fails for me is cunjie (cunjevoi). It is a sea squirt (*Pyura stolonifera*) that lives attached to rocks along the coast. It can be identified by the clumps of brown tough skinned polyps and its ability to squirt water out of its orifice. It can be harvested at low water when it is exposed. If you are in Sydney, check to see if the area you are harvesting it from is not protected. It is found from around Perth to South-East Queensland and Tasmania.

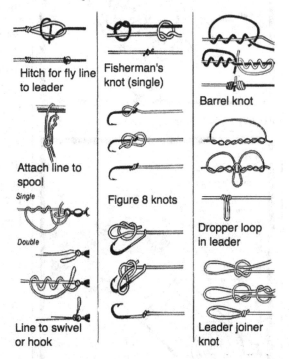

Dragging fish carcasses alone the shoreline before and after low water can bring sand worms towards the surface of the wet sand. It takes a bit of practice to catch and pull out the worms from the wet sand, but they are a good bait to use.

If you improvise a net you can catch small baitfish in rock pool or in the shallows. Bait for freshwater fish include small crayfish, worms, insects, and bread. Eels will take raw meat.

Times to go fishing

Some GPS units have a fishing algorithm that predicts the best times to go fishing. Here are some broad tips to assist you in fishing times. The saying "Moon by day, fish by day; moon by night, fish by night", generally holds true. Four to three days before and after the Full Moon and New Moon phases. Inland (freshwater) the four days after Full Moon. One hour before and after sunrise and sunset, moon rise and set. Low light overcast and wet days. One hour before and after high water and low water. Before unsettled weather. If they are not biting, make a hand spear with a multi-prong head and go after them in the water.

APPENDIX 7 CANOES: A BRIEF HISTORY

Canoe definition

Canoe as a word, is a superordinate and therefore used by the author to represents human powered boats that are paddled as opposed to rowed. It includes but not limited to the hyponyms coracles, skis, open-canoes, out-rigger canoes, kayaks and sit-on-top kayaks. In addition, canoes may be rigged for sailing. They may also be fitted with side boards, drop down keels or rudders to aid directional stability. They may also be fitted with out-riggers to aid lateral stability. The form of the canoe is a result of its function (e.g. hunting, fishing, transport on rivers, lakes, or ocean, recreation, touring, or racing), available resources and the ingenuity of the builder.

The word *canoe* is a French word (circa 1545–1455) taken from the Spanish word *canoa*. The word canoa was introduced into the Spanish language by Christopher Columbus (circa 1493) from his use of the Caribbean Islands Arawakan Indians word for their dug-out canoes *canaoua*. (Harper, 2010).

Several sources cite Garcilaso de la Vega (1539–1616) the Spanish poet, as the person who defined the word as an open boat.[1] However the British used the word to describe all forms of paddled boats as opposed to boats rowed with oars.

Reed boats

From petroglyphs it is thought that the use of reeds as a building material to make boats dates back 12 000 years. An archaeological find in Kuwait revealed a 7000-year-old reed sea-going boat that was sealed with bitumen. As the function of the reed boat grew, so to did its form (shape and size). These boats ranged in size from small paddle craft to large sail and oar propelled vessels. Evidence of their use by ancient man has been found in Egypt, Mesopotamia, Bolivia and Peru. Today these boats can still be found in use in Peru, Bolivia and Ethiopia.

Coracles

A *coracle* (Welsh) or *currach* (Irish) is a light-weight bowl shaped boat. Some authors suggest that its history goes back some 9000 years. Made from available materials such as wicker (woven reeds), supple tree branches (e.g. willow), bamboo, clay, skins and bark and later in history canvas. In northern India coracles were fashioned from earthenware, while in Iraq they were known as *quffa*, with the woven baskets being sealed with bitumen. Early Britons made their coracles from a willow frame over which animal skins were stretched. Versions of these boats have also been found in use by the American Plains Indians, Mongolians, Tibetans and various peoples in South-East Asia. Other versions of the coracle are the Irish currach, which is larger and holds more than one passenger. This boat was also used in western Scotland and Wales.

During the 1960s, coracles were still used by Welsh salmon fishermen. Today in Vietnam and other places in South-East Asia, coracles are still in use by some fishermen.

Dugout canoes (Pirogues)

Dugout canoes have possibly been used by man since the Stone Age and have been found in use throughout the world. Archaeological evidence includes a 10 000-year-old specimen found in Africa and a 900-year-old specimen found in Ireland. Dugout canoes are fashioned out of a single log but may also be fitted with an outrigger for additional stability.

The term *pirogue* (also *piragua*) comes from the French (probably from *Galibi*) and refers to a canoe or open boat hollowed from the trunk of a tree.[2] An example of the word being used to describe a dugout canoe can be found in the French naming of outrigger canoes in Polynesia.

The type of tree used to make a dugout canoe depends upon the region where the canoe is fashioned. In Peru, dugout canoes of between 3.5 to 9 metres are fashioned from *marupa* or the prized *canela moena* trees. In New Hampshire, USA, Native Americans used chestnut and pine trees. In New Zealand (*Aotearoa*) the *tōtara*, *kauri*, *mangeao*, *rimu*, *kahikatea*, and *matai* were native trees used to fashion dugout canoes by the Maori. The most popular was the tōtara; while on the North Island the abundance of kauri made it a popular material.

Dugout canoes have been fashioned for use on rivers, estuaries, bays and the ocean. As an example of Polynesian canoes, the Maori war canoes (*waka taua*) ranged in size from 9 to 30 metres long with the larger vessels being able to carry around 100 warriors. The larger waka taua were constructed in sections (e.g. three sections) and held in place with mortise and tenon joints and lashed together. Double hulled vessels (*waka hourua*) were also constructed and rigged with crab-claw sails (made from materials like flax, raupō leaf and supplejacks) and used on ocean voyages across the Pacific Ocean. In Fiji, the *ndura*, sighted by Captain Cook, measured 36 metres.[3] There are reports of these canoes carrying up to 250 people. Maori canoes fitted with an outrigger were known as a *waka ama* but this apparently disappeared by the nineteenth century. However, the Micronesians are credited with the most sophisticated outrigger dugout canoes called the *baurua* and *proa*. The hulls had an asymmetrical shape and were always sailed with the outrigger facing the wind. In New Zealand the smaller *waka tētē* and or *waka pakoko* (depending upon the bow piece) were fashioned usually from one log but could also have been constructed out of two logs. These vessels were used on inland and coastal waterways for ferrying people and goods. The general purpose *waka kōpapa* was smaller than the waka tētē and waka pakoko and fashioned from one log. Unlike the lager waka they did not have carvings, stern or bow pieces, thwarts or gunwales. They were used on rivers, estuaries and bays for fishing, and ferrying people and goods. My great grandfather and other early nineteenth century settlers in New Zealand used canoes and dugouts to travel from Tokirima to Taumarunui for supplies along the Ohura and Whanganui rivers.

Waka paddles were single bladed and made from a variety of native Aotearoa woods such as *kahikatea, matai, mānuka, maire*, the heart of *pukatea*, and *tawa*. Long paddles are known as *hoe whakatere, hoe whakahaere* or *urungi*. Short paddles are called *hoe*, or *hīrau*. To manoeuvre a waka upstream a pole (*toko*) was a viable option.

In the South Island the indigenous people made two types of raft the *mōkihi* and *mōkī* from bulrush (raupō) and flax (harakeke). The mōkihi was made by bundling bulrushes and or flax flower storks. The paddler would straddle the bundled material and paddle using their hands or a wooden paddle. The mōkī was larger than the mōkihi and build from bundles of bulrushes and or flax plants lashed together to resemble a boat. These were used for ferrying people and goods along the South Island's waterways. On the Chatham Islands (*Wharekauri*)—which lies 800 kilometres east of New Zealand—the Moriori people had limited suitable wood for building waka. The four types of waka built by the Moriori were the: *waka pūhara, waka rimu, waka pahī* and *waka rā*. The waka rā was constructed with similar materials and in a similar manner to the South Island mōkihi. Waka pūhara and waka rimu had carved sternposts and flat hulls with twin keels constructed out of poles or small beams. The bottom and sides were constructed from dried flower stalks of flax. Bull-kelp (*rimurapa*) was inflated and used as flotation in the bottom of the hull. The waka rimu though similar to the Waka pūhara had the sides and bottom of the hull covered only with bull-kelp. The waka pahī was an ocean going boat used between the islands and also had bull-kelp as a flotation material. It was constructed with twin keels of matipou wood, up to nine metres in length with the stern post made from akeake.

In the northern interior of Alaska/British Colombia, Canada and along the south-eastern coast of Alaska, dugout canoes were used by the indigenous peoples. The canoes were used to ferry people and goods as well as war parties along the inland water ways and between islands. The seaworthy canoes were constructed from a single log and could travel hundreds of miles over the sea. Before the arrival of Europeans, dugout canoes travelled between southeast Alaska and Kodiak Island.

Bark canoes

Examples of bark canoes are found in Australia. The movie Ten Canoes (Ralf de Heer and Peter Djigirr, 2006), bring this little known Aboriginal boat on to the mainstream public domain and a revival of the traditional ways amongst the local people. The aboriginal peoples (Ganalbingu language group, e.g. Yolngu clan and Djinba clan) of the Arafura Swamp in Arnhem Land, Northern Territory, built a unique style of bark canoe (Ganalbingu: derrka, Djinba: nardan) as a means of getting themselves into the swamp to hunt and gather food (i.e. magpie geese eggs). By selecting appropriate trees (eucalyptus tetradonta, stringy bark) an approximate 4 m x 0.9–1 m x 0.01 m cylindrical strip of bark was removed and then left submerged in the water over night. The next day the soaked section of bark was heated over a fire allowing the heat and steam to make the bark pliable. The material was put into a 'jig', consisting of solid sticks inserted in to the ground, which forced and formed the ends together so that they could be sewn with fibre. The bow section of the canoes were shaped to a fine cut back prow and sewn together along the top edge to enable the boat to part the tall swamp grass. Variations of the canoes included up to four thwarts (cross-beams), tensioned laterally with fibre twine, to keep the sides apart. Others were observed having branches lashed to the upper sides in the manner of a gunwale. The Gamedi Indigenous Bark Canoe held by the Australian Maritime Museum (ARHV Number: HV000272) measures length over all (LOA): 4.14 metres (13.58 ft), breadth overall (BOA): 0.87 metres (2.85 ft). The method of propulsion was a long pole when moving through the swamp but when paddled on a river system the occupant was seated and used their hands.

Another version of an Australian aboriginal canoe is held by the South Australia Museum. The Mungo, Avoca Station, Darling River Indigenous Bark Canoe (HV000161) from New South Wales, is an early twentieth century example of a bark canoe fashioned from the bark of the River Red Gum (*Eucalyptus camaldulensis*). The exhibit measures 6 m x 1 m (19.69 ft x 3.28 ft) and is typical of the canoe

used on such inland rivers as the Darling and Murray rivers. It was made from a single sheet of bark with branches acting as thwarts at the ends to prevent the canoe collapsing inwards. The canoe was formed with a wide almost flat hull, formed with rounded up ends (bow and stern), with sharply raised sides creating a low freeboard (area between the water's surface and the top of the canoe's sides). The canoe could carry one or two people and their possessions/goods and was propelled with a paddle.

The Australian aboriginals from the Whitsunday area in North Queensland built and used a canoe for use on open water between the islands and mainland. The Australian Museum holds an example of the Whitsunday Island Indigenous Bark Canoe (ARHV Number: HV000038). This specimen is typical of the canoe built in this area and measures 2.58 metres (8.46 ft) long by 0.53 metres (1.74 ft) wide. It was constructed from three panel sections of melaleuca tree bark. The edges of each bark panel have branches sewn/lashed to them. All the panels taper to a point at the bow and stern, with the bottom panel curving upwards. The side panels' top edge, both forward and aft, curve downwards to meet the upwards curving bottom panel. When the panels were stitched together, another branch was fitted and chalked (waterproofing) along the seam and lashed into place. Another branch was fitted as a transverse former to keep the sides apart. This arrangement formed a flat bottomed canoe with a chined hull, possessing a high freeboard (as compared to other Australian Aboriginal canoes).

Native Americans of the 'Woodland Nations', also built bark canoes; the shape of which can be identified in the form of modern day open canoes like the 'Canadian canoe'. Of the two distinct language family groups (Nations) of the East Woodland Peoples the Algonquian tribes relied more upon hunting and fishing than horticulture for survival. As a result of their nomadic hunter gather life style they came to rely upon their skills to build birch bark canoes to traverse the waterways of the Canadian Shield. Birchbark comes from the birch tree (genus: *Betula*) that is found extensively throughout Canada. It is described as being smooth, hard, light, resilient and waterproof; ideal qualities for a boat's skin. Paper birch (aka white birch) was the sought after material for use as a canoe skin with an estimated eight to twelve trees, being required to skin one canoe. If there were insufficient supplies of paper birch, then spruce bark was utilised. The use of spruce bark was common, particularly in the western Subarctic. Frames were usually made from strips of cedar (white cedar) that had been soaked and manipulated into the required shape. Where cedar was unobtainable, heavier pine was used. For thread/ lashings, the women would dig up white pine roots, and or spruce roots (*watap*), debarked, and split them in half to make them more supple. Another reference stated that they were also boiled. Stakes were driven in to the ground to form a canoe bed jig in the shape of the canoe. The top gunwale was lashed to the stakes at the desired height. The bark (aka *rind*) was laid inside the jig and lashed to the gunwales with the outer white surface of the rind facing inside the canoe. After the rind was sewn together, forming two sides and a flat bottom, the thwarts (lateral cross members) were fitted. The jig stakes were removed and the ribs were fitted creating the shape of the canoe. Waterproofing of the seams was achieved through a mixture of spruce gum (resin), tallow (fat, suet) and charcoal. The resin alone was brittle when dried, but when mixed with tallow and pulverised charcoal, it becomes a tacky conglomerate that was worked into the seams and joints. However, it is reported that the mixture when flexed (through the action of moving on the water) would break off in chunks, making the task of re-resining a common and even daily maintenance task. In areas where birch-bark was absent, canoes were constructed from hickory and elm bark. If trees were unavailable for the canoe's skin, moose hide and buffalo skin was used. In addition to the soft-skin canoe, wooden dugouts (aka [Fr.] pirogues) were commonly used in areas with no suitable bark.

So successful was the construction and design of the bark canoe, the French in 1750, set up a factory at Trois-Rivières, Quebec, Canada. This was in response to demand out stripping supply by fur traders and explorers (Voyageurs). Based on the Algonkian birch bark canoe 'The North West Company' (NWC) utilised three types of canoe. The *canot de maître*, which measured 12 m x 2 m x 0.75 m, was used between Montreal and Lake Superior. It was crewed by eight to twelve men, including their equipment. It could also carry passengers and 90 pièces of 40 kilogram (90 pounds [lbs.]) cargo bundles. A reconstructed 10.9 metre (36 foot) long Montreal canoe could carry in addition to crew, 2721 kilogram (6000 lbs.) of cargo, but only required four men to portage the empty vessel. A 7.6 metre (25 ft) bark canoe could carry 1360 kilograms (3000 lbs.) of cargo and only required two people to portage an empty vessel. The *canot du Nord* measured 7 m x 1 m x 0.2 m and was used for travel in the interior. The crew consisted between six to four men and could carry a cargo of 1700 kilogram (~4000 lbs.). A canoe would not usually last longer than two seasons and the NWC would purchase 70 units each year to replace its aging fleet. The third type of canoe was the five metre long *canot léger* or *canot batard*. This is described as an 'express' canoe used to carry important people, reports, and news to and from different posts in the Northwest. Paddles were carved from cedar and or spruce, with cedar possessing the qualities of strength, suppleness and lightness. Three sizes of paddle were utilised. The first type measured from the ground to under the chin. The second type used by the steersman (gouvernail) measured around 1.8 metres (~6 ft) long and around 101 to 127 millimetres (4–5 inches) wide. The third type was used by the bowmen (avant) and foremen when negotiating rapids and or leaping small falls; and was around eight feet long.

A distinct version of the Algonkian birch bark canoe was the Kootenay-Salish canoe, built for the swift flowing rivers of southern British Columbia, Canada (west coast of North America). Built using similar techniques, its form varied through the use of an extended keel and a cutback bow and stern up to the gunwales.

In central Alaska, the Athabascan speaking people of the interior, made a birch bark hunting canoe that measured around 12½ feet (3.8 m) long and weighed 25 to 35 pounds (11.3–15.8 kg). Alaska's interior forests are termed 'boreal forests' and contain birch, aspen, alder, willow, and cottonwood trees. A wooden frame was made from timbers and then skinned with three sections of birch bark forming the two sides and bottom. The bark was sewn to the frame using spruce roots. The spruce root seam line was sealed with pitch. Grass and or moss were used for cushions.

Soft-skin/Animal hide boats

Open boats

Before European contact, skin-covered kayaks (*qayaq*) and open *angyapiks* and *umiaks* (*umiaq*) were used in Alaska by all of the northern groups: the Aleuts [Unangax] of the Aleutian Chain; the Alutiiqs [Sugpiat] of Kodiak Island archipelago, Prince William Sound and outer Kenai Peninsula; the Inupiat; Central Yup'ik; Siberian Yupik and Cup'ik.

In the Bearing Sea the Yupik peoples of St Lawrence Island built an open skin boat called an *angypik*. On mainland Alaska the Inupiaq version was called an umiaq. The angypik frame was constructed from driftwood and when covered with walrus hide weighted less than 500 pounds (226.8 kg).

These flat bottomed boats ranged in size from 17 to 60 feet and could carry up to 20 people. These boats were used for travel and hunting and could carry greater than three tons of meat. When the arctic peoples moved camp, the women rowed the umiak using oars and a person sat at the back using an oar as a tiller. When used to hunt whales, the men used single blade paddles for propulsion.

To the Russian fur traders in the Aleutians, the umiak was known as a *Baidara* and/or *Bidara*; to describe the large skin covered boat. The umiak has been called 'the women's boat', but historically, paddling kayaks was not unequivocally the domain of Inuit men. MacRitchie in his paper titled *The Kayak in North-Western Europe*, (1912), p.510, cites several references to Inuit women paddling kayaks, taken from records as far back as 1612.

Unlike the Inupiaq who paddled their umiaq, the Yupik also rigged their boats to carry sail while hunting whales and walrus'. Laurel A. Neme Ph. D, reports about the reskinning of an *Angyapiget* (traditional walrus hide hunting boat in the Siberian Yupik language), which is performed every three to four years. Neme, describes the angyapiget as like a round bottomed canoe measuring 20 to 25 feet (6.1–7.6 m) in length, 5 to 6 feet (1.5–1.8 m) wide and weighing around 500 pounds (226.8 kg). The boat could carry up to 25 people and carry up to five tons of cargo. The ancestor used driftwood for the frames but now milled timber such as hickory and oak is utilised as well as marine grade sealants and paints. The angyapiget's skin covering was obtained from the hides of female walruses. The female hides were preferred by the boat's captain over bull hides for their smoothness, flexibility and ease to work with. After soaking two hides for nine days in a pool, it took the effort of five men to manoeuvre the two sections alongside each other under the frame. The captain's wife and other skin-sewers then proceeded to sew the two over lapping halves together using braided whale tendon greased with blubber. Once joined, the skin was then positioned up over the upturned frame by the men and pulled taught. It was then loosely lashed in to place with sealskin cordage. A hole was then marked out in the centre of the boat for an engine and cut out and the edges lashed to the frame. After letting the hides sit and dry on the frame for a few days, it is checked for tautness then painted.

Kayaks

Interestingly, there were a multitude of designs, shapes, lengths and volumes in the kayaks built by the arctic people. Their form was developed in response to functionality through hunting for survival. In 1983, David Zimmerly wrote in an article titled *Form Followed Function—And The Function Was Hunting* that 40 different native kayak designs had been catalogued. The Inuit of Siberia, Alaska, Canada and Greenland built kayaks of different designs to meet the particular requirements of material availability, and the need for stealth, load carrying capacity and seaworthiness. Sea mammal hunting required stealth and the conditions of the arctic region saw four basic types of sea-going kayak developed.

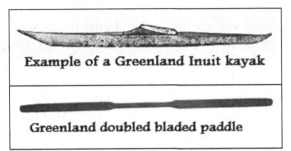

Example of a Greenland Inuit kayak

Greenland doubled bladed paddle

As the Alaskan and Siberian aboriginal kayaks (*qayaq* and *iqyax*) differed from region to region so too did the Greenland kayak (*qajaq*) vary in form around the country. Harvey Golden in his book titled *Kayaks of Greenland The History and Development of the Greenlandic Hunting Kayak, 1600–2000* categorised the many different types into thirteen distinct types. As a generalisation, the Greenland Inuit developed long low profile, low volume sea kayaks of 5.2 to 5.5 metres (17–18 feet) in length with pointed upswept ends and a beam around 0.48 metres (19 inches). Due to the construction method of skin-on-frame they had hard chines and a V-shaped hull.

As a general outline, the Inuit men of Greenland constructed the frame mainly out of wood but also used baleen, bone and antler. Wood was either sourced from driftwood, trade lumber or locally grown timbers. In more recent times metal and plastic from flotsam or crash debris has been used to build kayaks. After the frame was completed the next step was the fitting of the skin covering (*amiq*). The skin coverings were sourced from both sea and land mammals, with the type of skin utilised varying by region, availability and tradition. The common sea mammals used for the amiq were the walrus, sea lion and seal. Greenland has four types of seal and depending upon the size of seal utilised, it may be expected, to take from two to six skins, to cover a kayak. The men hunted the mammals but it was the women who prepared the skins. Depending upon the preparation method employed the colour of the skin would vary from black to white and include reddish

browns, yellows, buff et cetera. The men would initially stretch the skin over the bow and stern but it was then the women's task to sew the skins together using their various types of stitching methods. These methods varied by region but the method required that the needle not pass through the skin but captured the material between the inner and outer surfaces. One type of thread used was seal tendon but by the 1970s nylon fishing line was used. After the women had sewed the skins, the seams were then ready to be waterproofed with oil from blubber and blood. By the early twentieth century paint was used. The need for re-skinning depended upon many factors but the time frame ranged from twice a year to biennially.

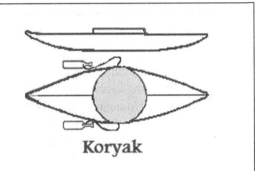

Koryak

Length—2585mm, Beam—72mm, Depth to Sheer—255mm, Weight 15kg. C_p 0.56, Loaded kayak stable to 45 degrees. Theoretical speed 3.5 kn.

The Inuit here developed over 25 self-rescue techniques to compensate for the precarious nature of the hull. Those who could not self-rescue or be rescued perished. Those who could not master kayaking did not kayak. Because the kayaks were so narrow the hunters would tow their prey home. An issue the hunter faced when spearing a seal was if and when the wounded creature would turn and dive under the kayak. The spear would be attached to a lanyard and if the animal dove down and passed under the kayak's hull, the hunter could be capsized. From the Danish statistics compiled in 1888 for deaths of Inuit men in southern Greenland during that year, out of 90 deaths, 24 (27 per cent) were from drowning in kayaks.

The Inuit of Baffin Island build flat-bottomed highly stable kayaks and did not have any recorded self-rescue techniques for capsize. One version had flared sides and a high coaming around the cockpit almost eliminating the need for a spray-deck. On top of their broad flat decks they could carry up to 453 kilograms (1000 pounds) of quarry.

The Koryak peoples from Kamchatka developed very short wide beam kayaks, measuring around 2.7 to 3.0 metres (9–10 feet) with a beam of around 0.71 metres (28 inches). These craft were used for hunting near shore and were propelled with small table-tennis-bat size paddles that were attached to the kayak with a lanyard. The kayak's width compensated for the deep V-shaped bottom to keep it reasonably stable. For additional stability, rocks were used as ballast. Due to the small size of the vessel any quarry was most likely towed ashore otherwise the kayak's deck would have been awash. In adverse conditions the Koryak did not go to sea in these craft.

Across the Bering Sea, a kayak in all four Alaskan Eskimo languages is spelt as *qayaq*, and or *iqyax*.[4] In Unangax (Unalaska in the Aleutian Island chain), the iqyax is also known as a *baidarka* and/or *bidarka*. The word was used by Russian fur traders, to describe the regions kayaks. Baidarka means "small boat" and is the diminutive form of the Russian word *baidar*, which referred to the larger open bilge, animal skin hull boats of the Ukraine.

The Kodiak (Pacific Yupik) kayak is a close cousin of the Aleut iqyax, but shorter, wider and with a pointed stern. Both have a bifurcated bow. The ridged deck is common to all kayaks from Norton Sound (an inlet of the Bering Sea on the western coast of Alaska) southwards. This kayak was built for hunting small sea mammals and Dr David Zimmerly recommends it as "a good recreational kayak for varied sea conditions." It is unusual in that it was normally paddled in a kneeling position, using a single bladed paddle.

Jan Steinbright describes a recently made qayaq using traditional methods by Frank Andrew's family members. The Caninermiut style Yup'ik qayaq was the type used in the Kwigillingok and Kipnuk regions. The qayaq had an average length of 15 feet (4.5 m) and weighted less than 70 pounds (31.7 kg) but they were built to suit the individual paddler and could support 1000 pounds (~450 kg) of weight. The builders collected driftwood for the frame then formed the frame by carving the curve-grained white spruce driftwood stumps in to the desired shapes and members. The frame pieces were held together by lashings and wooden pegs. The frame was covered using five bearded seal skins. To sew the skins effectively, the Yup'ik peoples devised two special types of thread made from caribou sinew. Caribou is not native to the Kwigillingok area so it was obtained through trade with other indigenous groups who dwelt further inland in Alaska. A group of women would sew the seal hides around the frame using a special type of stitch that required the sewer not to pull it to tight. Then a slither of grass was inserted to form a whipstitch and soak up any moisture, thereby creating a watertight seam. Once the sewing started the women would keep sewing, even through the night, as the task had to be completed in one session and not left to stand. The final step was to coat the skin and seams with a waterproofing agent like blubber or seal oil. Grass mats were weaved and used for insulation and seating comfort in the cockpit. They also served the purpose of absorbing moisture and helped prevent the qayaq from being water logged.

Qayaqs built in the same region differed in form with hunters from differing groups being able to identify other groups of hunters by their qayaqs silhouette. Qayaqs built by the central Yup'ik had a circular hole in the bow, which was used as a handhold to pull the qayaq up onto an icefloe or sledge. On the southern peninsula leading out to the Aleutian Island chain, the iqyax (baidarka) bows of the Sugpiaq (Alutiiq, Pacific Yupik) had a distinguished upswept and split forward bow. According to Nick Tanape, the Sugpiaq split bow allowed the lower portion to serve as a cutwater and the upper portion, described as a floatation piece, allowed the boat greater manoeuvrability in rough seas. Within the region, the split bows of the Unangax people's uluxtax's, had a more accentuated upsweep than the Sugpiaq split bow. The Unangax people's uluxtax and iqyax bows though split and having the same function–to act as a cutwater and offering stability–were also different in form to each other.

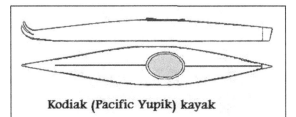

Kodiak (Pacific Yupik) kayak

Length 4340mm, Width 656mm, Weight ~20kg. C_p 0.65, Theoretical hull speed 4.6kn. Note the hogging along the deck-line profile.

The Aleut referred to their kayaks as *Iqax* for a single (one man kayak) and *Ulluxtadaq* for a double.[5] Prior to European contact, only the Aleut and Pacific Eskimo had craft with more than one cockpit. Through contact with Russian settlers, the Aleut build baidarka with three cockpits, in order to take a passenger or hunter. It is suggested, that it was through the influence of the Russian fur traders, that the baidarkas were fitted with sails and rudders.

The Aleut (people from the Aleutian archipelago) had a vastly different looking version of the sea kayak to the Siberian Koryak, yet they were known to put rocks in their kayak for ballast. The use of ballast would appear to have been a successful attempt to improve stability since both groups did not rely on recovery techniques.

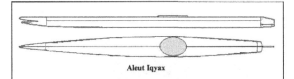

Aleut Iqyax

Length 5814mm, Beam 434mm, Weight 20kg. C_p 0.62, Theoretical speed 5.3kn. The hull skin was gathered together at the stern and tied with a thong and acted as a drain plug. This type of kayak was described by Capt. James Cook (1778) and other early explorers.

The Aleuts were known to venture ten miles out to sea in search of a quarry and often spend longer than 12 hours paddling. For drinking water they carried bladders that also doubled as floatation bags. Usually travelling in pairs they would make catamarans of their kayaks in heavy weather. The sleek fast kayaks were around 5.2 to 5.8 metres (17–19 feet) long with a beam around 0.43 to 0.48 metres (17–19 inches). Due to their skin-on-frame construction they were multi-chined with a moderate V-shaped hull and wave shedding decks.

Westerners and Canoeing

During the 16th and 17th centuries, whalers brought back to England and Holland from Greenland, Inuit kayaks. In another account, Greenland kayaks were on display in Norway circa 1430, Denmark circa 1647 and three in Scotland and one in Orkney circa 1700 (MacRitchie, 1912). These curiosities were displayed to the public in churches and town halls; and in one case, complete with a preserved Inuit kayaker. It has been suggested by some authors, that the Greenland kayak, possibly through its availability to public viewing, has become the most recognised form of kayak; the Eskimo kayak stereotype.

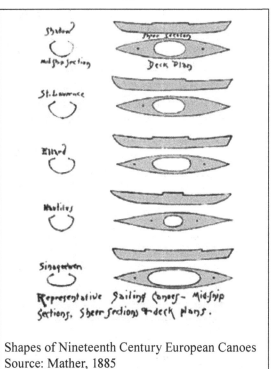

Shapes of Nineteenth Century European Canoes
Source: Mather, 1885

In the nineteenth century canoeing became a popular past time in both the USA and Europe. Previously, canoes and kayaks were used by French, British, Colonial and Russian fur traders in their respective areas of operation. However, it would appear that through the adventures of John MacGregor in his Rob Roy canoe and his written accounts, published in magazines and books, people were inspired to go paddling for enjoyment, adventure and competition.

Rob-Roy canoe

The following extract and canoe diagrams (above) are by Frederic G. Mather, in his article: The Evolution of Canoeing published in 1885, and shows the variety of boats that were around (Mather, 2010).

The Rob Roy has a keel of an inch or so, which is to its disadvantage in shooting rapids. But in the use of the single bladed paddle the keel helps to keep the canoe straight to its course without such a decisive twist in the hand of the paddler. The original Rob Roy of MacGregor's was fifteen feet long, twenty-eight inches beam, and nine inches deep at the cockpit, which was located amidships, and was fifty-four inches long and twenty inches wide. The owner, after the experience of one season, confessed that a length of thirteen feet and a breadth of twenty-six inches would be more satisfactory to him and we must believe him, because he distributed tracts to the natives in all parts of Europe. In a general article, written after a trial of several summers, Mr. MacGregor states that the length may vary from twelve to fifteen feet; that the beam may vary from twenty-six to thirty inches; depth from ten to sixteen inches.

The American Rob Roy has usually had a length of fourteen feet; a beam of twenty-six inches; and a depth of eight and a half inches. The length, in all of these cases, is, of course the point of the stem to the point of the stern; although the proposition to measure at the waterline has been seriously put forth. The weight of an average-sized Rob Roy ought not to be over sixty-five pounds, as a weight much in excess of that makes the canoe more troublesome at portages. As a paddling canoe the Rob Roy served well enough in the bladed of a pioneer. A seven-foot double blades being six inches broad was an effective propelling instrument. The single mast, rigged with a lug and sprit, was as much as the egg-shaped bottom could carry, for the Rob Roy was a poor sea-boat by the side of the later forms of canoes. The India-rubber apron might keep the captain dry, but there was no need of having his apron and his deck constantly wet.

Plate from the book 1000 Miles in the Rob Roy Canoe

The adventures of MacGregor inspired many people to undergo adventures in canoes. One person in particular was the Reverend Fred C. B. Fairey. This man started canoeing on Port Phillip in Victoria (1876). In 1877 he canoed from north Tasmania along the east coast down to Hobart alone. He is generally accepted as the 'father of Australian sea kayaking'.

Arctic exploration

Plate from the book *Farthest North*

During the Voyage of the *Fram* (Nansen's Arctic research ship of 1893–96) he had the crew build six double kayaks measuring about 12 feet long, 3 feet wide and 18 inches deep (3.658 m x 0.914 m x 0.457 m). Their purpose was to be the escape vehicles in case the Fram was destroyed by the pack-ice. The crew would then make their way back to civilisation across the Arctic Ocean in the kayaks.

In 1895, Fridtjof Nansen and Hjalmar Johansen kayaked and dog-sledged back to Terra Firma from a failed attempt to reach the North Pole. Departing the Fram, the two men set out with two special built single kayaks attached to sledges drawn by dog teams. The pack-ice became impenetrable and the two men had to make their own way back to civilisation. This meant they used the sledges to get them to the open Arctic Ocean before paddling for civilization. The islands that were inhabited were the Norwegian Svalbard group. During their trek south, they landed on an island in the Franz Josef Land archipelago. After wintering there, they set off in their kayaks and stumbled upon a British Arctic expedition that assisted them in returning to civilisation. The illustration is from Nansen's book Farthest North. Note the skis on fore deck and sledges on aft deck. The kayak's frames were made from bamboo, which was carefully lashed together. The dimensions of one single were 3.7 m x 0.7 m x 0.3 m and the other was deeper by 0.08 metre. The frames weighed 7.3 kilograms (16 lb). The kayaks total weight after covering with sailcloth and waterproofed with a mixture of tallow and paraffin was 16.3 kilograms (36 lbs.).

Modern day canoeing

Today canoeing in Western countries is primarily used for recreation, leisure, competition, or adventure. In the recreation category, fishing and general paddling on sit-on-top kayaks has become very popular. However, hunting from kayaks, appears to be a rare pursuit for the arctic people, with the tinnie and outboard motor now taking over the role. In Africa and South-East Asia canoes of various forms are still used to transport goods and for hunting/fishing activities.

Brief Overview about Competitive Canoeing

In Australia one canoeing body Australian Canoeing (AC), divides canoeing into the

following disciplines based around competition: Slalom, Freestyle, Wildwater, Canoe Sailing, Canoe Polo, Canoe Marathon, and Canoe Sprint. The eigth discipline is classed as Recreational and includes sea kayaking. The International Canoe Federation (ICF) also include as a competition discipline Dragon Boat racing and is at time of writing attempting to define the discipline of Ocean Racing into the relevant categories based on boat designs and the varied ocean and environmental conditions experienced. Other 'paddle sports' on their website include Rafting, Wave ski and Life Saving.

The seven ICF disiplines

Canoe slalom

Canoe Slalom's first competition was in Switzerland in 1922. It made its debut as an Olympic discipline at the 1972 Munich games in Augsburg, Germany but it was not until the 1992 Barcelona games at La Seu d''Urgell, Spain that it was reinstated to the Olympic programme. The discipline involves paddlers negotiating a 300 metres natural or man-made whitewater course in single kayaks for the K1 events and single or double canoes in the C1 and C2 events as well as team events. According to the Australian Canoeing website only men compete in double kayak and canoe classes. The white water course contains currents, rapids, waves and eddies of which the paddler navigates their kayak or canoe between 18 to 24 pairs of suspended poles known as 'gates' that are situated above sections of the course. The paddlers make two timed runs of the course and if they touch one of the poles, or miss a gate completly, penalty times are added to the time achieved on that run by the judges. After the second run the sum of the two times is used to determine competition placing. Slalom boats are required to meet minimum length and weight requirements with kayaks being restricted to a minimum 3.5 m x 0.6 m and a minimum weight of 9 kilograms. Todays designs are lighter, sleeker and faster through the use of modern materials like carbon, kevlar and epoxy resin; enabling the boats to be made lighter and more ridgid than the polyethylene (plastic) but are comparitively fragile.

Canoe Freestyle

Canoe Freestyle (aka Rodeo), is a new sport whereby paddlers perform as many aerobatic tricks and manouvers on a natural or artificial river feature (hole or wave) in 45 seconds. Compeditors are awarded points for the type and difficulty of tricks performed. At the elite level the sport is conducted on a national and international level while at a non-competitive level it is enjoyed as a recreational sport. The type of kayaks used in this white water sport have a flatter hull and different volume displacement from the river runner kayaks allowing the participants more control and creativity in their 'gymnastic' routines. Types of manoeuvres performed and scored are: cartwheels, pirouette, loops, airwheel, endos et cetera.

Wild-water Canoeing

Elio K1 sprint kayak

Salom kayak

Perception Wavehopper wild-water kayak

Water polo kayak

Advantage Kayaks Super Tourer TK1 kayak

Fluid white-water kayak

Wild-water Canoeing (aka Wild-water racing, Down-river racing); utilizes a 4.5 m x 0.6 m distinctive 'diamond' shape, unstable rudderless kayak and is described on the AC website as "*the ultimate combat, human versus river . . . one of the most physiologically and psychologically demanding of all the canoe/kayak disciplines*".[6] Competition events may involve 400 metre sprints to 133 kilometre races with classic races being held approximately over six to ten kilometres courses. The grade of water encountered is from flatwater to grade 4 rapids. Paddlers compete in single kayaks (K1) events as well as in single canoe (C1) and double canoe (C2) events. The kayaks have a distinctive 'diamond' shape deck, which is created by wings behind the cockpit that are a result of design requirements to meet the minimum beam racing rules. The hull is narrow and rounded making the kayak an unstable platform. The solo canoes are

4.3 m x 0.7 m; the two-person whitewater canoes are 5.0 m x 0.8 m. At the elite level the ICF board programs a World Championships every two years with Tasmania being the location of all six Wildwater World Cup races in October/ November 2009.

Canoe Sailing

Canoe Sailing by Europeans is dated back to Ferdinand de Magellan in the year 1520 with recent competition history being traced back to the late nineteenth century. In 1866, the Canoe Club on the Thames was formed through the endeavours of a Scottish lawyer John MacGregor. MacGregor had beome renowned for his adventures in boats he designed and named 'Rob Roy' after the famed Scottish outlaw of whom he was related. His adventures took him paddling and sailing his Rob Roy canoes on the rivers and canals of Europe, the Baltic and Middle East. He wrote about his adventures in a book titled *1000 Miles in the Rob Roy Canoe* which helped popularise canoeing as a middle class sport in Europe and the United States.

The Canoe Club, is located on the River Thames at Trowlock Island Teddington, near central London. It recieved royal patronage with the Prince of Wales, Prince Edward, becoming the Commodore. He held this position for 30 years. In 1873 by command of Queen Victoria, the club became the Royal Canoe Club (RCC). Today the RCC is the oldest canoe club in the world, promoting both canoeing and kayaking, with focus on Canoe Sprint and Canoe Marathon disiplines. Its members compete in both World Championships and Olympic Game canoe disiplines.

On the otherside of the Atlantic, canoeing was also popular with middle class businessmen and professionals. As a result of this interest, the New York Canoe Club (NYCC) was formed in 1871. In 1880 the American Canoe Association (ACA) was formed. In 1883 a retired sea captain and ACA Secretary Charles "Barnacle" Kendall paddled and sailed over three thousand miles from Lake George, New York, to Pensacola, Florida. With the growth of the sport on both sides of the Atlantic the NYCC and ACA held the first international competition in 1886 titled the International Challenge Cup. Today the NYCC International Canoe (IC) Challenge Cup is the second oldest sailing trophy after the America's Cup. In 2008 Hayden Virtue became the first Australian sailor to win the prestegious cup and become the IC World Champion.

The current class of canoe with a 10 metre square sail and sliding seat was adopted by the International Canoe Federation (ICF) in 1946. The object of ICF rules is to ensure the hull shape and sail area are as uniform as possible. The boats principle diamensions are 5.18 m x 1.01 m with a sail area of 10 metres square. Today design features such as full length battens, high aspect ratio sails, carbon fibre masts, light weight foam sandwich construction along with materials like glass, keylar, mylar have all contributed to the development and continued longevity of this sport.

Canoe Polo

Canoe Polo involves two teams of eight players paddling polo canoes on a thirty-five metre by twenty-three metre body of water attempting to score as many goals as possible against the other team with a round ball. During play, only five members per team are on the water during the two ten minute periods. The types of paddles used are double bladed and are to be less than 600 mm x 250 mm. The kayaks have strict regulations set upon them to ensure paddler safety with the boats being restricted to a maximum of 3 m x 0.6 m.

Canoe Marathon

Canoe Marathon is conducted over distances greater than 15 kilometres with National Championship races being conducted around the 38 to 42 kilometre distance. The ICF define Canoe Marathon as:

"In Canoe Marathon the competitor races over a designated long distance course on water not subject to prescribed standards. The competitor must take the water as it is found and be prepared, if it is necessary, to carry his or her canoe around an impassable obstacle, or between two waterways."[7]

Australian Classes of kayak used are the TK-1 single Touring Kayak, TK-2 double Touring Kayak, TC-1 single Touring Canadian and TC-2 double Touring Canadian. International classes of kayaks used are the K-1, K-2, K-4, C-1, C-2, C-4 (men). All kinds of building materials are permitted in the construction of the boats. TK-1 and TK-2 kayaks are permitted to have a trailing rudder. Measurements of the TK-1 are maximum length 4.572 metres and a minimum waterline beam of 0.508 metres; TK-2 maximum length 5.487 metres, minimum waterline beam 0.533 metre; TC-1 and TC-2 maximum length 5.03 metres, minimum waterline beam 0.712 metres. Kayaks are propelled with double bladed paddles; Canadian canoes are propelled by single bladed paddles. Other types of classes in canoe marathon are multi-sport kayak, ocean skis, racing skis and sea kayak.[8]

In Australia one canoe marathon event of note is the Red Cross Murray Marathon.[9] The event first started in 1969 with eight canoeists paddling a 250 mile course. Each year from 27–31 December the five day 404 kilometre Red Cross-Hearald Sun Murray Marathon takes place from Yarrawonga through to Swan Hill in Victoria. With just over 1000 paddlers and 3000 plus crew and officials. All of the funds raised are channeled back into community service programs and emergency services.

Canoe Sprint

Canoe Sprint formerly known as Flatwater Racing has been an Olympic sport since the 1936 Berlin Games in Germany. Australia's first gold medal was won by Clint Robinson at the 1992 Barcelona Olympic Games in the K1 1000 metres final. The ICF define Canoe Sprint as:

The aim of a Canoe Sprint competition is for people to race each other in kayaks and canoes over a clearly defined unobstructed course in the shortest possible time according to the rules.[10]

The types of boats raced are the K1, K2, and K4 class kayaks and in the canoe classes C1, C2, and C4. The ICF recognises 'International Boats' as K1 kayaks measuring a maximum of 5.20 metres and weighting a minimum of 12 kilograms; K2 (max. length 6.5 m, min. Weight 18 kg); and C1 (max. 5.2 m, min. weight 16 kg). The kayaks are required to be *"a sit-in (Kayak type) not a sit-on (Surf Ski type)"*.[11] For directional control the kayaks are permitted to have a rudder fitted to the underside of the hull; canoes are not permitted to have rudders fitted. In kayaks the paddler is seated facing forward using a double bladed paddle; while canoeists paddle kneeling and use a single bladed paddle. Distances raced are 200 metres, 500 metres and 1000 metres. However, depending upon the type of event: Olympic, World Championship or Australian Championship, will determine the race distances being contested (e.g. in the Olympics only 500 m and 1000 m events are contested).

Modern Materials

Canvas is a material that replaced mammal skins for Alaskan aboriginals, since it was cheaper than seal skins. Canvas has drawbacks when compared to skins as it is not as elastic, has less abrasion resistance, and was prone to split and break. It was also noisy and removed the element of surprise for the hunter in his kayak. As an example for using canvas, Dr. David Zimmerly built a reconstructed Hooper Bay, Alaskan kayak and advises using 6.4 metres of heavy canvas (10, 12, or 14 oz.) and waxed nylon sail-makers heavy thread. The canvas was waterproofed with two layers of dope, as used in aviation. Harvey Golden built a replica Greenland kayak in 2009 measuring 19 feet 3-3/8 inches (~5876.7 mm) by 19-1/8 inches (486.1 mm) wide. The kayak was covered with 8 ounce canvas. A frequently asked question Harvey receives, is what type of material does he use to 'skin' his boats? Answer, a polyester cloth.

Fridtjof Nansen, a Norwegian zoologist and oceanographer, during his 1893–1896 Arctic Expedition on board the 'Fram', had several kayaks made aboard ship. The two single kayaks measured 3.7 m x 0.7 m x 0.3–0.38 m. The 7.3 kilograms (16 lbs.) frames were constructed from bamboo and they were covered with sailcloth and waterproofed with a mixture of tallow and paraffin. The overall weight when completed was 16.3 kilograms (36 lbs.). After a failed attempt to reach the geographic North Pole the men extricated themselves to Franz Josef Land. They then planned to kayak to either Spitzbergen or Novaya Zemlya. However, they encountered a British expedition in the archipelago that assisted their return to Norway.

Other modern materials used to cover 'soft skin' boats include but not limited to Nylon (~26 oz.), Polyester (~13 oz.), and Ceconite, which, is a polyester-dacron blend used for ultra-light aircraft skins.

Metal and in particular aluminium has been used as the skin of canoes. In certain instances, discarded aircraft fuel tanks (aka drop tanks) have been used because of their rounded tear drop form and ease of modifying the tank into a canoe.

Wood is still used to manufacture canoes. Wooden canoes are light and beautiful to look at. Two methods of building wooden canoes are the 'stitch and glue' and 'strip built'. Strip built kayaks are built from timbers like red and or white cedar and redwood. Other woods employed are Spanish cedar, clear white pine, mahogany, walnut, cherry, paduk, bubinga et cetera. Stitch and glue canoes can be built out of marine plywood ranging from 3 millimetres to 6.3 millimetres (⅛—¼ inch) thick and bound with epoxy adhesives. Both construction methods utilise composite materials, epoxy glues, fillers, and varnishes.

Polymers are substances ranging from proteins to aramid fibres (e.g. Kevlar®). In this discussion on canoe materials, polymers can be grouped in to two distinct categories: thermoplastics and thermosets. Thermoplastics can be reheated and remoulded and include plastics like polyethylene (PE) which are widely used in the manufacture of canoes through process like rotational moulding (aka rotomolding). The general characteristics of canoes manufactured from PE (aka Tupperware boats) are their robustness, durability and impact absorption; however, they are not indestructible and are prone to damage from ultra-violet (UV) rays. Through the advances in technology PE plastics come in varied forms (e.g. High Density PE, HDPE) and in laminated structures, which provide strength with comparative weight savings. Thermosetting plastics are polymers that are irreversibly cured (cannot be remoulded) and include epoxy resins and polyester resins. Thermosetting plastics are used in glass reinforced plastics (GRP) whereby composite materials like: glass fibre, carbon fibre (aka graphite fibre), aramid fibre and polyester fibre are used to reinforce the thermosetting plastic. Without the reinforcement material, the brittle thermosetting plastic does not have the mechanical properties of impact resistance and flexibility, required for the manufacture a canoe. In the past decade canoes were being manufactured using polycarbonates. Canoes made from this material fall in between PE boats and GRP boats for weight, while possessing good scratch resistance and resistance to UV degradation. Other materials coming in to use include polyacrylonitrile-co-butadiene-styrene (ABS). Used by the automotive industry, this vinyl polymer is strong, lightweight and possesses good shock absorption qualities.

1 Garcilaso de la Vega aka "El Inca" (1539-1616). 1605, Garcilaso wrote a romanticised novel from eyewitnesses accounts of the Spanish Hernando de Soto's exploration (1539-1543) in the lower Mississippi Valley, (Florida, USA), titled La Florida de l'Inca (1722), 'The Florida of the Inca'.

2 The Macquarie Dictionary Online © 2009 Macquarie Dictionary Publishers Pty Ltd. Galibi: noun 1. a Caribi people of French Guiana.

3 Fiji is classified as part of Melanesia.

4 The term Eskimo (a pejorative roughly meaning: 'eaters of raw meat') refers to a number of groups inhabiting the coastline from the Bering Sea to Greenland and the Chukchi Peninsula in NE Siberia. Until the 1970s the term Eskimo was a collective name given to the inhabitants of northern Alaska, northern Canada and Greenland (the Inuit) and or the indigenous people of western Alaska including the Aleutian Islands and eastern Siberia (the Yupik). Today the natives of Arctic Canada collectively call themselves "Inuit" simply meaning 'people'. In Alaska native Alaskans refer to themselves as 'Inupiat' and 'Yupik'. and may further defined themselves by their spoken language or tribe (e.g. Aleut), others of whom prefer their native terms, Unangan and Alutiiq. In Siberia, these people may be known as the 'Yuit'.

5 Uluxtax, or double-hatch Unangax boat (Steinbright).

6 http://www.canoe.org.au/ . . . ,Wildwater/83/2268/ accessed 24Apr09

7 International Canoe Federation Canoe Marathon Competition Rules 2009

8 www.marathon.canoe.org.au, Class Distances accessed 26Apr09

9 As of 2009, the YMCA has taken over running of the event.

10 International Canoe Federation Canoe Sprint Competition Rules 2009

11 Ibid. P.13, para 8.5.1

APPENDIX 8 SEA CANOEING STORIES

To the unknown Arctic kayaker; to whom kayaking was a means of survival and their personal stories are lost to history.

Westerners and sea canoeing

William Dampier, (1621–1715) English Buccaneer, Explorer and Naturalist. In May 1688 Dampier elected, as was his right as a Buccaneer, to be put off the Privateer "Cygnet". Captain Read marooned Dampier, two other Englishmen, four Achin sailors and a Portuguese sailor on the largest of the Nicobar Islands north of Sumatra; being what Dampier assumed was a place least likely to be visited by ships. The marooned sailors traded an axe for a sea-going canoe but their attempted escape failed when the canoe capsized while trying a surf launch. Several days later the Achin sailors had fitted outriggers and a mast with the sails being made from palm mats. Their plan was to contour the island then perform a 120 nautical mile plus crossing to Achin on Sumatra's north coast. Dampier was aware of the approaching western monsoon weather but hoped to make use of the winds. By the third day of their crossing a strong current had kept them insight of the Nicobar Islands. By the afternoon of day four, the clouds had become black and the wind and sea was rising. Dampier recalled *'our little ark in danger to be swallowed by every wave.'*[1] Dampier, a man accustomed 'to hardships and hazards', who had walked across the isthmus of Panama to raid the Spanish on the Pacific coast, fought in raids and skirmishes, sailed around Cape Horn and across the Pacific, 'confessed that for once his courage failed.'[2] By the morning of the fifth day, they spotted land but the wind and seas were still up, leaving the mariners cold, exhausted and hungry but alive. By the evening with the wind dropping away, Dampier realised the land they were making for was Golden Mountain on Sumatra. After another thirty hours of paddling they entered the Passanjan River but were too weak, from the ordeal of their voyage, to paddle up the river to the fishing village that the Archin sailors knew existed. After 12 days of being nursed to health by the villagers the crew set off on a three day, 100 nautical mile trip, to Achin and the English Factory belonging to the East India Company. After reaching the settlement the Portuguese sailor died soon afterwards and it took a further six weeks of recuperation for the gravely ill sailors to recover.

John MacGregor (1825–1892) has become renowned for his adventures and touring in canoes he designed and named 'Rob Roy', after the famed Scottish outlaw, of whom he was related. His adventures took him paddling and sailing his Rob Roy canoes on the rivers and canals of Europe, the Baltic and Middle East. He wrote about his adventures in a book titled *1000 Miles in the Rob Roy Canoe on Rivers and Lakes of Europe* and also was a contributor to magazines such as *Boys Own*. His writings between 1865 and 1892 have been credited as the herald, which helped popularise canoeing as a middle class sport in Europe, Britain, the United States and Australia. Other books by MacGregor are: *The Rob Roy on the Baltic: a canoe cruise through Norway, Sweden, Denmark, Sleswig, Holstein, The North Sea, and the Baltic (1867), The voyage alone in the yawl Rob Roy, from London to Paris and back by Havre, the Isle of Wight, South Coast, &c., &c (1868)* and *The Rob Roy on the Jordan, Nile, Red Sea, & Gennesareth, &c.: a canoe cruise in Palestine and Egypt, and the waters of Damascus (1870).* There is anecdotal commentary that John MacGregor spent part of his youth in Halifax, Nova Scotia and may have learnt how to paddle there.

Fridtjof Nansen, (October 10, 1861–May 13, 1930), Norwegian zoologist, oceanographer, explorer, humanitarian, laureate of the Nobel Peace Prize. Norway's first ambassador to Great Britain and Chairman of the Norwegian League of Nations Association. The League of Nations High Commissioner for the repatriation of World War One Prisoners of War.

As a young man he was an outstanding skater and skier. He won the national cross-country skiing championship twelve times in succession. At eighteen, he broke the world record for one-mile skating. As a zoologist he predicted the existence of the 20 millionths of a millimetre wide synaptic cleft—a gap between the processes of two nerve cells—which through the advent of the electron microscope, we now know exists, and is the point of nerve signal transmission. In 1888 he became the first man to lead an expedition to successfully cross the Greenland ice-cap. Prior to returning to Norway, he lived with the Inuit of west Greenland and recorded their culture in his 1893 book *Eskimo Life*. While living with the Inuit, he learnt to kayak and how to build kayaks. Nansen said of the kayak: "The kayak is beyond comparison the best boat for a single oarsman ever invented."[3]

Nansen's appreciation of the kayaks ocean going value was to be used by him on his 1893–1896 Arctic Expedition on board the *Fram*.[4] The primary reason for the voyage was to research the Arctic Oceans currents by freezing the *Fram* deliberately into the pack-ice. The pack-ice drifts from east to west and Nansen hoped it would drift the *Fram* near to the geographic North Pole. In 1895 he and **Fredrick Hjalmar Johansen**, from a latitude of 84°4' N, made an unsuccessful bid for the North Pole. Taking thirty days' rations for twenty-eight dogs, three sledges, two kayaks, and a hundred days' rations for themselves, the men toiled for 140 miles to reached the highest latitude ever attained of 86°13.6' N, "when the ice became impassable."[5]

On setting out for the North Pole Nansen built two special purpose kayaks that were towed across the ice on sledges drawn by dog teams. The kayaks were primarily designed to carry the cargo required to reach the North Pole. Knowing that they would not be able to return to the *Fram* the plan was then to trek and kayak back to the ocean, after negotiating the pack-ice and lanes, at Franz Josef Land and then kayak to either Spitzbergen or Novaya Zemlya. The kayak's frames were made from bamboo, which was carefully lashed together. The dimensions of one single were 3.7 m x 0.7 m x 0.3 m and the other was deeper by 0.08 metres. The frames weighed 7.3 kilograms (16 lbs.). The kayaks total weight after covering with sailcloth and waterproofed with a mixture of tallow and paraffin was 16.3 kilograms (36 lbs.).

During their kayak retreat across the pack-ice, they endured extreme cold, the occasional dunking into the polar sea and an attack by a polar bear. Using incorrectly drawn maps and accidentally letting their watch wind down, they became "geographically embarrassed". Reaching Franz Josef Land they were force to winter there over the next ten months. Continuing on in May 1896, through the Franz Josef Land archipelago, before the ocean crossing to Spitzbergen, the kayaks at one stage drifted from their moorings. With no other option available, Nansen jumped into the icy water and proceeded to swim, a considerable distance, after the drifting kayaks. During his swim he could feel the effects of hypothermia and narrowly avoided succumbing to it. The next day while paddling, Nansen's kayak was attacked and holed by a walrus.

On June 17th the men had the unbelievable good fortune to cross paths with Frederick Jackson, leader of a British scientific and exploratory expedition working in Franz Josef Land. Two months later, on August 13th 1896 Jackson's expedition vessel deposited Nansen and Johansen at the port of Vardø, in northern Norway. Coincidentally, it was the same day the *Fram* reached open water.

Franz Romer, German adventurer, crossed the Atlantic Ocean solo in a kayak in 1928. Departing Lisbon, in March 1927, in a canoe equipped with oar-locks, sails and a motor, he set out to 'row' across the Atlantic to New York. His canoe was named the *Deutsche Sport*.[6] He crossed from the Canary Islands to Saint Thomas in the Virgin Island before arriving in August 1928 in Puerto Rico. The initial crossing of the Atlantic took 58 days. Two weeks later he departed for Florida but he was lost at sea in a hurricane.

Oskar Speck (1907–1995), German (job seeker) and adventurer. From 1932 to 1939 Oskar Speck travelled 50 000 kilometres in his kayak from Germany to Australia. Speck lost his job as a Hamburg electrical contractor in 1931 when the Weimar Republic (1919–1933) economy was crippled by the Great Depression (1929–early 1940s depending upon country) despite overcoming the discriminatory regulations of the Treaty of Versailles and World War One reparations, obscene inflation and political extremism. Speck described the times saying "The times in Germany were catastrophic . . . all I wanted was to get out for a while." For the 25-year-old speck "Leaving Germany and seeing the world seemed like a better option." His initial plan was to go and find work in the Cypriot copper mines.

Taking a train to the Danube River in Ulm, he paddled his converted double, collapsible kayak *Sunnschien* down the Danube and Varda rivers to Bulgaria and Yugoslavia. Reaching the Mediterranean at Thessalonika in Greece, he sailed and island-hopped along the Aegean then hugged the coast of Turkey and crossed over to Cyprus. Enroute to Cyprus, Speck decided not to pursue his job seeking endeavours but "see the world", describing his kayak as a "first class ticket to everywhere."

Speck's boat was a modified five-and-a-half metre, two person folding kayak from Pionier Faltboot Werft fitted with a rudder, small gaff sail and water tanks capable of holding five gallons. Vitals consisted of condensed milk, tinned meat, sardines, cheese and chocolate. Also stowed aboard were a pistol, camera and clothes.

Departing Cyprus, he headed for Syria and made his way to the Euphrates River where he was shot at after refusing hospitality from local tribesmen. Unperturbed, he voyaged on to Iran and the Persian Gulf, where he had to order a replacement kayak. From there he made his way along the coast of Pakistan and by 1935, three years after leaving Germany, dressed like a nineteenth century European explorer in a white pith helmet and khaki shorts, he skirted the west coast of India and reached Ceylon (Sri Lanka). After receiving a new kayak from Pionier Faltboot Werft, who became his main sponsor and supplier of four kayaks for the seven year voyage, Speck paddled along the east coast of India and reached Burma in 1936. By now, he was a media curiosity and was pursued by local newspaper journalists as he travelled along the west coast of Siam (Thailand), Malaya (Malaysia) through to his arrival in the Dutch East Indies (Indonesia) in 1937.

On the island of Java, he acquired a 16 mm cine-camera, as an addition to his still-camera, and using black and white cine film documented the rest of his voyage with the vigour of a passionate anthropologist recording the cultural diversity of the people he encountered. He recorded Balinese children hunting fish in shallows using a bow and arrow; Timorese villagers performing a dance with swords; and New Guinean tribesman killing and eating a turtle.[7]

On the island of Lakor, northeast of Timor, Speck was attacked by local tribesmen. He was woken one night by 20 people armed with spears, swords and machetes who dragged him from his kayak and tied him up while his supplies were looted. Speck was hit and kicked in the head, resulting in a burst eardrum. After several hours he was able to loosen his bindings, retrieve some of his property including his clothing, films and camera and slip back into his kayak.[8] After reporting the attack to officials, he had to wait for a year before setting off again. During this time while waiting for the arrest and trial of the ring leaders, he had an ear operation. After the trail and when he was fit to travel, he set off from the provincial capital of the Tanimbar Islands, Saumlaki on the island of Jamdena. He voyaged to the Kei Islands, with a new boat on the longest leg of his island hopping, to reach Dutch New Guinea (aka Netherlands New Guinea; now Western New Guinea and or West Papua). Sailing along the northern coastline of New Guinea via Hollandia (today Jayapura in the Papua Province of Western New Guinea) to Madang (then the Territory of New Guinea; now Papua New Guinea) and down around to Port Moresby. After traversing the Gulf of Papua he arrived at the south-western town of Daru in 1939. He discovered here that Australia was at war with Germany but was allowed to make the four kilometre crossing from mainland Papua New Guinea to the island of Saibai in the Torres Straight Islands group, which was and is recognised as part of Australia.

On the 20th of September 1939, to greet him at the beach in Saibai were three Australian policemen. Their comments to Speck were "Well done, feller!" they said, shaking his hand warmly. "You've made it—Germany to Australia in that. But now we've got a piece of bad news for you. You are an enemy alien. We are going to intern you."[9] After being transferred to Thursday Island (around 73 nautical miles away) for interrogation, (cameras and the Nazi swastika flag he had on the bow of his boat would not have helped matters even though he had been away from Germany for the rise of the Nazi government in 1933). As an enemy alien, he was transferred to the Tatura Internment Camp in the Goulburn Valley of Victoria for the duration of the war. After the war, Speck got a job as an opal cutter.

Dr Hannes Lindemann, German physician and adventurer, made two solo transatlantic crossings by canoe. In 1955, he paddled a 23 foot African dugout canoe made from a mahogany log and measuring two and a half feet wide and twenty-five feet long, from Liberia to Haiti. The deck was covered with plywood leaving a small cockpit in the stern and a hatch before the mast. The bow and stern where blocked off with bulkheads and filled with sealed empty containers. The mast was made of ironwood and the boom from a rare red camwood. After a first failed attempt, he departed Oporto (Porto) Portugal for the Canary Island. The Canary Islands lie about 210 kilometres (~130 miles) off of the north-western African continent. After three weeks at sea experimenting with drinking sea water for survival and two weeks of voyaging after losing his rudder he was picked up by the mail steamer *Gomera* and taken to Gran Canaria. After repairs and a refit, on the 25 October 1955 he departed the harbour of Las Palmas de Gran Canaria on the "Big Jump" across the Atlantic. After 65 days at sea he landed at the harbour of Christiansted on the island of St. Crouix in the U.S. Virgin Island.

In 1956 he paddled/sailed a seventeen-foot production model Klepper Aerius II double folding kayak, named *Liberia III*, from Las Palmas in the Canary Islands around 3,000 miles to the Caribbean island of St. Martin/St. Maarten and the port of Phillipsburg in 74 days. His voyages were motivated by his intellectual desire to understand the effect of the human body and mind to stress through what can be described as experiments using himself. On his 1956 voyage he encountered hurricanes, monstrous seas then becalmed, encounters with sharks, whales, capsize on two occasions and battling thirst, hunger, mental disorientation, hallucinations and lack of sleep. He documented his two voyages in the book *Alone at Sea A Doctor's Survival Experiments During Two Atlantic Crossings in a Dugout Canoe and a Folding Kayak*, (Germany, Pollner Verlag, 1998).

Verlen Kruger (USA) passed away at 82 years of age on August 2, 2004. He is credited with 11 world records involving canoeing. In the early seventies (April 17, 1971 to October 10, 1971), he and a friend Clint Waddell paddled over 7,000 miles from Montreal to the Bearing Sea. The expedition was called the Cross Continent Canoe Safari (CCCS). Their trip was filmed under the title, *"Never Before—Never Again"* however, this was just the beginning. During his lifetime he paddled over 100,000 miles, which according to the Guinness Book of Records is 30,000 miles farther than anyone else. He holds the all time longest journey ever made by canoe, at 28,043 miles during his expedition titled *"The Ultimate Canoe Challenge*. He also holds the record for the second longest, at 18,232 miles during his *Two Continent Canoe Expedition*.

The Ultimate Canoe Challenge (29 April 1980 to 15 December 1983) saw Verlen paddle from Red Rock Lake, Montana to Quebec City then over to the Atlantic Ocean and down to the Florida keys and back up the Gulf of Mexico to the Mississippi. He then paddled northward until he came to Arctic Ocean and Tuktoyaktuk, in the Canadian North West Territories. Turning south he paddled through Alaska to Skagway where he went back on to salt water. Heading down the coast he went on the east side of Vancouver Island, and then followed the Pacific Ocean coastline south to the Baja Peninsula. From there he paddled northward to the Colorado River. After following the Colorado River he zigzagged and ported the waterways of the countryside and ended back up in Canada and the Great Lakes. From there he navigated his way to Lansing, Michigan.

The Two Continent Canoe Expedition was from Inuvik, North West Territories (NWT), and Canada on June 1986 to Cape Horn, South America on March 1, 1989. On this expedition Vern was accompanied by **Valerie Fons**. Starting at Inuvik, when the ice breaks, they paddle 1,800 miles up the Mackenzie River. Following a part of the historic fur trade route through the NWT and Saskatchewan they navigated the "Voyageur's Highway" to Grand Portage, Minnesota on Lake Superior. Racing to beat the winter freeze, they paddled four of the Great Lakes (L. Superior, L. Michigan, L. Huron and L. Erie). After paddling past Detroit to Toledo, they headed for the state of Indiana then Ohio. From here they made their way south to Mobile, Alabama. From Mobile, they headed east around the Gulf of Mexico to Miami, Florida.

At Miami, the nature of the route changes completely as the team heads across 2,300 miles of the Caribbean Sea. In two *Sea Wind* canoes designed by Verlen they island-hop the entire Caribbean Chain. They completed over 100 open crossings, with up to 12 of the crossings requiring them to paddle through the night.

After leaving the island of Trinidad, they entered Venezuela, South America and headed up the Orinoco River.[10] The Orinoco connects to the Negro River through an unusual natural canal. The Negro River is a major tributary of the Amazon River, which meets at the city of Manaus, Brazil. Paddling east, down the Amazon River they joined another tributary, the Madeira River.[11] At the source of the Madeira River, they faced one of the biggest challenges of the expedition, a portage overland to a small tributary of the Paraguay River, in a remote wilderness region called the Mato Grosso in far west Brazil.[12] They then connected with the Paraguay River.[13] The Paraguay flows southwards through Brazil, Bolivia, Paraguay and Argentina and connects to the Parana River. From the confluence with the Paraguay River, the Parana River flows some 820 miles (1320 km) through Argentina passing the city of Buenos Aires and emptying into the South Atlantic Ocean. Once back on the ocean they followed the Argentinean coastline, into the Straits of Magellan and over to the city of Punta Arenas, Chile. From here, they navigated the archipelago of Tierra del Fuego, around Cape Horn and back to Punta Arenas. A new book about his feats has recently been published by his widow under the title: *All Things Are Possible*.[14]

Derek Hutchinson, a British kayaker who passed away October 10, 2012. Derek is described by some as 'the father of modern sea kayaking'. In 1975 he had a failed attempt to cross the North Sea in a 16 foot baidarka, and was rescued by a passenger ferry after 34 hours at sea. In June 1976, with **Tom Catsky** and **Dave Hellywell** he completed the crossing from Felixstowe (UK) to Ostend (Belgium) in 31 hours, setting a world record for *a known* distance travelled in a kayak. Another adventure to his credit was the crossing of the *Corryvreckan whirlpool* (aka *The Hag*). This treacherous section of water is located between the Isle Jura and the Isle of Scarba, off Scotland's west coast. During this crossing he and his companions encountered 30 foot waves and 8 to 9 knot currents. In 1978 he led a kayak expedition around the Aleutian Islands in the North Pacific Ocean. By 1980 he had circumnavigated Prince Edward Island and had set out to paddle Alaska's inland passage. After becoming interested in sea kayaking in the 1960s, after a pool rolling session by **Alan Byde,** he went on to become a world renowned paddler, Instructor, boat designer and builder. Two of his kayak designs in use today are the Gulfstream and Sirocco.

As an author, he wrote and illustrated *Sea Canoeing* 1975–76. Later the book was renamed *The Complete Book of Sea Kayaking*. Today it is in its fifth printing and has been translated into several languages. As an Instructor he was a senior coach in the British Canoe Union and helped develop the standards for the various sea kayaking awards.

Nigel Foster and **Geoff Hunter** credited as the first duo to circumnavigate Iceland in 1977.

Frank Goodman credited as the first to circumnavigate Cape Horn, South America in 1977.

Jon Turk, an adventurer who after completing his Ph.D. in chemistry in 1971 realised he, was not suited to a life indoors. His adventures include an attempted to round Cape Horn, Chile, solo in a kayak (1979). Row the Northwest Passage; dogsled the east coast of Baffin Island. Kayak from Ellesmere Island to Greenland. Ride a mountain bike through the Gobi desert. Make the first climbing ascents of big walls on Baffin Island. Make the first ski descents in the Tien Shan Mountains in central Asia; and spent two years paddling the North Pacific Rim.[15]

After paddling a canoe along the inside Passage from Vancouver, Canada to Glacier Bay, Alaska, Jon decided to paddle 500 miles through the Magallanes De La Antartica Chilena region's archipelago to Isla Hornos and around Cabo de Hornos (Cape Horn). On January 9, 1979, he departed Puerto Natales in a Folbot and spent the next few days learning how to balance comfortably and develop an effective forward stroke! By day 32 after leaving Puerto Toro on the eastern side of Navarino Island he was in position to see Isla Wollaston on the horizon. On day 33, he observed the unsettled conditions as cloud formations rushing over head after the surface wind had abated; *"I told myself to wait, but refused to listen."* Launching to get as far as possible along Punta Guanaco, Jon had convinced himself that he was able to out run the approaching southwest storm coming in from the Pacific Ocean and the northeast storm coming in from the Atlantic Ocean. Captured by the weather, he was trashed on the southeast corner of Punta Guanaco. During his trashing, he was capsized and wet-exited. He tried to hang onto his boat but the force of the breakers hitting the boat, resulted in his right shoulder being dislocated. After being tumbled about, he ended up between the kayak and the rocky shore. After being hit by the boat and pinned against the rocks, he managed to free himself and while still in the water, reset his dislocated shoulder He then proceeded to retrieve his equipment and damaged kayak, which had smashed on to the rocks and broke in two. In deteriorating weather conditions, he set about setting up shelter and getting warmth back into his body. The next day he set off on a four-day trek overland for Puerto

Toro.[16] An account of his solo navigation to Cape Horn is described in his book *"Cold Oceans: Adventures in Kayak, Rowboat and Dogsled"*, (1999).

Jon Turk in 1999 set off on a 3,000 mile voyage around the North Pacific Rim, from Japan to St. Lawrence Island, Alaska. Departing northern Japan on June 14, 1999 with **Franz Helfenstein**, the men encountered 50 to 100 mile crossings. Along the central Kurils (the archipelago between Japan and Kamchatka) they encountered 20 foot standing sheer waves and were trapped in a whirlpool for two days. Of this Jon remarked *The central Kurils made Cape Horn seem like a picnic cruise on Lake Powell.* After 69 days (August 1999) they reached Petropavlovsk, Kamchatka; covering the 1,000 miles at an average speed of 14.5 miles per day.

Returning to Kamchatka the following May with wife **Chris Seashore** they picked up their Russian "Guide" **Misha**, who had never paddled before! On May 20, 2000 the pod, paddling 'Prijon Kodiak' kayaks, set out on the 2,000 mile journey hoping to achieve their goal of reaching Alaska in 100 days. Encountering frequent storms, sea ice, sub-freezing temperatures and perilous situations by June 19th they had voyaged some 500 miles at a pace of 13.2 miles per day. Trapped by sea ice the pod ventured on a five day portage up one river and down another to reach the sea again. At Ossora, Chris pulled out of the expedition. Voyaging northwards the men set a relentless pace and by mid August encountered the start of the winter storms blowing south from the Arctic. Jon reports: *"the swells in the North Bearing Sea are puny compared to the huge waves off Cape Horn, but the currents here are confused: the wind blows from every direction, fog lies over the land for days at a time and the waves are bunched together and agitated with erratic deep water breaks."* After reaching the city of Providenya, the expedition was thwarted by bureaucracy and denied permission to cross the Bearing Straight. Undeterred Jon and Misha paddled for 13 hours, to cover the 38 mile crossing of the Anadyr Straight to St. Lawrence Island, Alaska.[17] An account of this expedition can be found in Jon Turk's book *In the Wake of* *the Jomon: Stone Age Mariners and a Voyage Across the Pacific.*[18]

Paul Caffyn, Australian adventurer living in New Zealand. First to circumnavigate New Zealand's South Island; as described in his book *Obscured by Waves*. The next summer (1979), he kayaked 1,700 miles to be the first solo paddler to circumnavigate the north island in his kayak *Isadora*; named after Isadora Duncan, a free spirit of the dance.[19] After he crossed the Cook Strait, he published his second book *Cresting the Restless Waves*. In August 1979, he and Max Reynolds crossed Foveaux Strait and circumnavigated Stewart Island. He then published his third book *Dark Side of the Wave*. In 1980, Paul teamed up with Nigel Dennis to complete the first kayak 2,200 mile circumnavigation of Great Britain in 85 days.

Round Australia Kayak Expedition (RAKE), took place from December 28, 1981 to December 23, 1982, 360 days. During this time, Paul paddled 9,420 nautical miles (17 446 km). The account of this voyage can be found in the book *The Dreamtime Voyage—Around Australia Kayak Odyssey* by Paul Caffyn. Twenty-five years later, on the December 2, 2007, a brass plaque was unveiled above the launch/landing site for Paul's adventure at Queenscliff Victoria. Paul's modified HM Nordkapp kayak *Lalaguli* (Australian Aboriginal for 'water nymph'), to the sounds of a Scottish Piper, was carried down to the Queenscliff Museum where it has been put on display.

In 1985, Paul completed a solo 4,400 mile circumnavigation of the four main islands of Japan in 112 days. In August 1991 after three arctic summers of paddling 4,700 miles, he completed the circumnavigation of the Alaskan coastline from Prince Rupert in British Columbia to Inuvik, in the North-West Territories of Canada. In August 1997, Paul and **Conrad Edwards** circumnavigated 550 miles around New Caledonia. Over two summers in 1998 and 1999 both men kayaked from Narsarssuaq, Greenland, 1,400 miles along the west coast to Upernarvik. In January 2002, the duo kayaked 610 miles from Kuala Lumpur, Malaysia north to and around the island of Phuket in Thailand.

David Taylor and **James Moore** credited as the first duo to circumnavigate The Faroe Islands located mid way between Shetland and Iceland, in 1985.[20]

Ed Gillet, American adventurer, single headedly paddled a stock standard Tofino double kayak, by Necky Kayaks, 2,200 miles from California to Hawaii in 1987. He carried 25 gallons of fresh water and was victualled for 60 days. It took him 63 days to paddle and kite sail from Monterey Bay to Maui.

Howard Rice, American adventurer who in 1991, solo voyaged around Cape Horn, Chile, in a sailing canoe. The Armada de Chile recognised his achievement and awarded Rice the Certificate of Merit and inducted him into the Cape Horners Society.[21]

Hayley Shephard, is a New Zealand kayaker living in Canada. In 1999, she was the first woman to solo circumnavigate by sea kayak the 1200 kilometre coastline of Vancouver Island. In 2005, she was the first woman to sea kayak alone around the rugged and exposed coast of the sacred Haida Gwaii (Queen Charlotte Islands).[22]

Pablo Basombrío, team leader; **Martín Grondona** and **Emilio Caira** from Buenos Aires, Argentina. In 1999, the trio set off from a location west of the town of Ushuaia in Argentina's Tierra del Fuega for Horn Island and the famous Cape Horn. The group paddled plastic kayaks. They carried a 26 day supply of vitals that were designed to provide each man with 6,000 calories per day. After waiting out storms and 70 knot winds, they circumnavigated Horn Island in a counter clockwise direction and ended up staying on the island for three days while a storm abated. Horn Island is a 1,500 foot high black basalt rock that since the 1978 war between Chile and Argentina is covered with landmines. Breaking their risk management strategies of not being on the water after 1530 hours they attempted a 10 mile crossing to Herschell Island. During the crossing, the storm they 'wished' instead of reasoned had passed almost claimed their lives as it increased in intensity again. Emilio succumbed to exhaustion, vomiting and dehydration from motion sickness and had to be rescued and supported by the other two paddlers. Miraculously, they made it to Herschell Island in the dark. Pablo says *"I felt my own demons gazing at me in silence. They were Impatience and Pride, and they nearly killed the three of us."* The men made their way back to Ushuaia via island hops in weather that *"kept teasing us: It would fake sunny and calm whenever we were beached, then put up a gale the minute we took to sea."*[23]

Victoria Jason a Canadian, kayaked through the North-west Passage. The grandmother of four completed the 7500 kilometre adventure over four summers from 1991 through 1994. During the summer of 1991 Victoria and two other paddlers **Fred Reffler** and **Don Starkell** launched from Churchill, Nanitoba, Canada for Tuktoyuktuk, a hamlet in the Northwest Territories, on the Beaufort Sea. When Victoria set out, she had only been kayaking for 12 months and was still recovering from two strokes. During this leg, Fred pulled out due to injury and Victoria suffered serious internal bleeding ulcers. The second year, 1992, Victoria and Don reached Gjoa Haven where she had to pullout suffering from edema (muscle breakdown) caused by excessive fatigue. Don pushed on but, 46 kilometres short of Tuktoyuktuk he had to be rescued suffering from severe frostbite. Over the next two years, Victoria returned alone and completed the journey from west to east. In 1993, starting from Fort Providence on the Mackenzie River, she kayaked to Paulatuk. In 1994, she returned and reached Gjoa Haven. Her story can be found in the book *Kabloona in the Yellow Kayak: One Woman's Journey through the North-west Passage*. Victoria passed away on the 20 May 2000 after battling a brain tumour.

Chris Duff, American adventurer, circumnavigated Ireland in 1996; his account is in his book titled: *On Celtic Tides: One Man's Journey Around Ireland by Sea Kayak*. In 2000, he circumnavigated New Zealand's South Island; with the account of his voyage in his book titled: *Southern Exposure: A Solo Sea Kayaking Journey Around New Zealand's South Island*.

Lonnie Dupre (USA) and **John Hoelscher** (Australia) together circumnavigated the 6,000 mile coastline of Greenland by kayak and dog-sledge between 1997 and 2001. The achievement was completed in three separate expeditions to Greenland. The first expedition titled *The 1997-98 International Greenland Expedition* consisted of three separate legs over 3,000 miles by kayak and dog sledge. The first leg was by single kayaks lashed together as a catamaran. Departing from Paamiut (SSW coast), they paddled 1,250 miles north along the west coast to Kullorsuaq (WNW coast, Baffin Bay) in 84 days. The second leg's first section was by Umiatsiaq (18 foot open fishing boat) to Qaanaaq (Thule). After wintering at Qaanaaq they set off northwards by mid February. By late March near Cape Jefferson, dense impassable ice forced them to return and rethink their strategy to circumnavigate Greenland by non-motorised means.

The third leg saw the men fly SSE across the inland ice cap, to Tasiilaq on the east coast. Departing Tasiilaq on July 9, 1998 they voyaged south on a 980 mile leg back to Paamiut (Frederikshaab). Over the next 43 days, they paddled and hauled their double sea kayak along the coast and around Cape Farewell (the southernmost point of Greenland). By August 21st after traversing 750 miles, and due to the harshness of the weather and the environment, they were forced to stop at Qaqortoq (Julianehaab), 180 miles short of Paamiut. Over 15 months the men traversed 3200 miles of the Greenland coastline. An account of this expedition can be found in Sea Kayaker Magazine, August 1999.

The second expedition called *Thule 2000 Expedition* was an 1,800 mile traverse of northern Greenland. Departing from Illoqqortoormiut (Scorebysund) on the mid-east coast they traversed the coastline in an anti-clockwise direction northward to arrive at Savissivik on the far northeast coast (located below Thule).

The third expedition called *Second Thule* took place between late July and early September, 2001 along the mid south-east Greenland coast. Departing Illoqqortoormiut (Scorebysund) they headed south in a double sea kayak travelling

690 miles in 37 days to Tasiilaq (Ammassalik), the village from where they stated their third leg in 1998. After a total of 22 months in Greenland, between 1997 and 2002, the men had spent 358 days on the trail traversing 6,517 miles around the coastline of which 3,075 miles were by sea kayak. An account of the third expedition can be found in Sea Kayaker Magazine, October 2002.[24]

Tore Sivertsen (Norway) and **Lone Madsen** (Denmark) in August 1998 departed Tasiilaq (Ammassalik) on the southeast coast of Greenland heading south to round Kap Farvel, (Cape Farewell) "The big Kap of Greenland" and up the west coast along the same route as Dupre and Hoelscher, who had departed almost a month earlier. By September 30, 1998, they were camped on an islet inside the mouth of Danell Fjord south of Iluileq Island in far southeast Greenland, not far from Kap Farvel. Deciding to make use of a fine weather window, they set off and rounded the mouth of the fjord near a point called Qasingortoq, where they had agreed to meet up again before heading south in the one metre clean swell. At this point in time, a severe weather change engulfed the two paddlers who were some 200 to 300 metres apart. Strong northerly and north-easterly winds, judged to be of 25 knots steady with 50 knot gusts, hammered the pair. Combined with the strong currents the pair could not turn their kayaks around and run for shelter. Lone Madsen was paddling a "Skerry" by Valley Canoe Products fitted with a skeg and Tore was paddling a Prijon "Seayak" fitted with a rudder. Trapped by cliffs, buffeted by clapotis and with four to five metre breakers driving in, they were struggling in the conditions. Separated, they were soon two kilometres offshore in unprotected waters, with seas rising to between six to seven metres. Working feverishly to keep control of their kayaks and wits, they would surf down the enormous waves while dodging chunks of glacial ice, which would appear in front of them. Briefly meeting up, Tore went in front of Lone to lead the way to safety and was about 50 metres away when he heard Lone scream. Seeing her in the water he tried to stop but the waves drove him further away from Lone. He last saw Lone

separated from her kayak and paddle, calling him for help. After several failed attempts to turn his kayak around he continued in a vain attempt to reach Lone for 45 minutes by paddling in a big half circle but the conditions were unforgiving and unrelenting. After contacting Search and Rescue (SAR) they found Lone's body not far from where her 406 MHz beacon had gone off. It appears she was able to catch her kayak and secure a tether to it and put on her neoprene gloves before succumbing "*to the cold and the awesome power of the North Atlantic storm.*"

Of the tragedy Tore says, "*We both had paddle floats, but we had not practiced assisted rescues together.*" He also reports "*Neither Lone or I were experts at doing Eskimo rolls with our kayaks . . . Lone felt that it would be doubtful that we could manage to do Eskimo rolls under demanding conditions with high seas and a heavy load aboard. Personally, I believe then, as I still do today, that an Eskimo roll might be your only hope.*"[25]

Peter Bray, British adventurer, is the first person to kayak across the Atlantic, solo and unsupported from Canada to Ireland in 2001 taking 76 days. Bray's other achievements are the 1996 Circumnavigation of mainland Britain in a two-man kayak, with a partially sighted friend and no external support. In 1996, he crossed the English Channel and Irish Sea. In 2000, he made his first attempt to cross the Atlantic in a specially designed 27 foot kayak from St Johns, Newfoundland to Ireland. In 2002, he voyaged from Gibraltar to Morocco. In 2003, he circumnavigated Newfoundland alone and unsupported taking 88 days in a standard kayak, encountering Arctic waters, subzero temperatures and atrocious weather conditions. In 2005, he was a member of the British expedition to South Georgia Island. [26]

Magnus Fischer Stockholm, Sweden. Magnus kayaked around Scandinavia in 2001. From Stockholm, via Denmark, and along the entire coast of Norway, and then pulling the kayak 1400 kilometres on a kayak trolley. He then kayaked down through Finland's lake system and across the Baltic Sea back to Stockholm taking 204 days and travelled 5290 kilometres in a kayak. Moreover, that is just one piece of Magnus' kayaking experience.[27]

Justine Curgenven, **Trys Morris** and **Gemma Rawlings** were the first all women team to circumnavigated Tasmania, on one expedition, in November and December 2004. Other expeditions Justine has been involved in are the circumnavigation of New Zealand's South Island in January 2008, with **Barry Shaw**. In 2007, Justine Curgenven, **Shawna Franklin** & **Leon Somme** paddled 500 miles around Haida Gwaii, the Queen Charlotte Islands, in British Columbia. Kayaking and climbing in the Lofoten Islands, Norway, including crossing the Maelstrom tidal race, July 2004. In July 2003, Justine, **Hadas Feldman** and novice Russian paddler **Alexey Sitnokov** successfully completed a 650 kilometre sea kayak journey up the Pacific coast of Kamchatka in remote Siberia. In April 2001, she completed the 75 mile circumnavigation around Anglesey, Wales, in 14.5 hours.[28] In August 2002, she completed a solo sea kayak circumnavigation of Iceland's West Fjords. In June 2002, she completed the first circumnavigation of Wales by sea kayak. Justine is the founder of Crackle TV and the producer of the sea kayaking videos 'This is the Sea' (TITS).[29]

Graham Charles, **Marcus Waters** and **Mark Jones**, New Zealand adventurers who in October and November 2005 became the first to circumnavigate, by sea kayak, South Georgia Island in the Southern Atlantic. Taking 18 days, they covered distance of around 600 kilometres.[30] The story of their adventure can be found in the book *Unclaimed Coast* by Penguin Books.

A British expedition with **Nigel Dennis**, **Peter Bray**, **Hadas Feldman** and **Jeff Allen** were the first successful British expedition to circumnavigate the Island of South Georgia in November and December 2005, setting the fastest time on record in 13 days eight hours.[31]

Freya Hoffmeister from Germany started kayaking in 1997, and has gone on to become one of todays most outstanding sea kayakers. A former gymnast, Freya has become renowned for her mastery of Greenland style rolls. In 2004, she won the open water Arctic Sea Kayak Marathon in Norway. In 2006, she placed second in the 300 kilometre race around the Danish Island Fyn. In June 2007, together with **Greg Stamer**, she circumnavigated Iceland in the record time of 33 days of which, 25 were paddling days. A month later, she set out and became the first woman, and fourth person, to circumnavigate New Zealand's South Island, breaking the old record by more than a week. Freya completed the 1700 kilometre journey on January 2, 2008, in the record time of 70 days, of which 47 were paddling days. During this unsupported trip, she encountered huge seas and crashing surf along the West Coast's remote Fjordlands. This area with no road access for more than 250 miles has few sheltered landing spots. During a surf launch into the Tasman Sea, she broke the stern off her kayak. Another remarkable achievement of this trip was the completion of the final 100 miles (160 km) in a 32.5 hour push.

In 2009, in what she dubbed 'Race Around Australia', Freya has undertook the task of an unsupported circumnavigation of the 9,420 mile (15 166 km) Australian continent. Freya paddled an Epic 18X sea kayak with the Latin phrase of "*Veni—vidi—vici—*I came—I saw—I conquered", which best describes this remarkable paddlers attitude. The kayak is now on display at the Queenscliff Maritime Museum, Victoria along with Paul Caffyn's HM Nordkapp kayak *Lalaguli.*

On January 18, 2009, Freya launched from Caffyn Cove, Queenscliff Victoria, into Bass Straight and the Tasman Sea, heading off anti-clockwise around Australia. By day 70, she had paddled 2,062 miles (3320 km) along the east coast of Australia over the Pacific Ocean. During this time, she was averaging more than 33 miles (54 km) per day.[32] An epic achievement achieve on this voyage was the 350 mile (575 km) direct crossing of the Gulf of Carpentaria. Departing from the mouth of the Jackson River on York Peninsular on the April 24, 2009, she spent seven nights at sea, to land at Nuhlumbuy in the evening of May 1st.[33] Her next destination was Darwin, 817 kilometres away. On June 1st, she set off on stage 8 heading for Broome, Western Australia, 1510 kilometres away. Stages 9 to 12 were completed between July 7th and October 14th. The 3520 kilometres Indian Ocean journey, along the West Australian coast, took her past Onslow, the Zydtorp Cliffs (where she spent a night at sea), Kalbarri, Perth, Cape Leeuwin (Australia's south-western most point) to Esperance in the Southern Ocean.

Stages 13 and 14 during the period 7 November to 2 December, took her along the Great Australian Bight. The 'Bight' extends from Cape Pasley, east of Esperance in Western Australia, to Cape Catastrophe, on the Eyre Peninsula in South Australia.[34] Stage 13 from Esperance to Eucla near the WA–SA border is a distance of 1135 kilometres. During this voyage she spent a night at sea and paddled 165 kilometres across the face of the Baxter Cliffs (near Caiguna in WA).

Stage 14 commenced near Eucla WA and involved paddling 185 kilometres along the Buna Cliffs (aka Nullarbor Cliffs) to the Head of the Bight. (Re WA and SA boarder and the Nullarbor National Park). After traversing the Eyre Peninsula coastline in South Australia, the 820 kilometre voyage took her across the mouth of the Spencer Gulf to the York Peninsula and her stage destination of Victor Harbour.

Stage 15 was the 780 kilometre voyage from Victor Harbour (SA) back to Queenscliff (Victoria) was completed on the December 15, 2010. The 13 790 kilometre voyage over 332 days, involved 245 paddling days at an average of 10.8 hours per day. During this voyage she spent 13 nights afloat.[35]

Fray's current expedition is the circumnavigation of South America. Her expedition is titled 'The Second Continent'. This 24 000 kilometre adventure over 24 months will take her along the coastline of 12 countries. Her plan is to divide her trip into three 8000 kilometre phases (legs, stages). Each phase is over an eight month period, with a four month rest between phases. Phase one starts from Buenos Aires, Argentina, where she will head south along the Southern Atlantic seaboard, to paddle the continent in a clockwise direction. She will round Cape Horn plus the southernmost island of South America, Tierra del Fuego. Heading north along the South Pacific Ocean she will paddle through the beautiful Fjordlands of Patagonia to her destination Valparaiso, Chile.

Phase two is planned to start in September 2012, from Valparaiso, Chile to Georgetown, Guyana. Continuing north along the South American continent's west coast, she will pass the coasts of Peru and Ecuador. While paddling along Ecuador's coast, she will cross the Equator in the Pacific Ocean. Passing Columbia's Pacific coastline, she will cross the isthmus of Panama, via the Panama Canal before rejoining Columbia's coastline in the Caribbean Sea. She will then follow the coastline of Venezuela to end the second phase at Georgetown, Guyana.

Phase three is planned for September 2013, from Georgetown, Guyana back to Buenos Aires, Argentina. She plans to finish on May 10, 2014 on her fiftieth birthday. She will paddle along the Atlantic Ocean coastlines of Surinam, French Guiana. After entering Brazil's coastline, she will cross the Equator for a second time bur in the Atlantic Ocean. From Brazil she will pass Uruguay before entering the Rio de la Plata and returning to her starting point.

At time of writing, Fraya had departed Buenos Aires on August 30, 2011. By day 127 she had circumnavigated Cape Horn. By day 140 and after 90 days of paddling, she was at Caleta Olla, Tierra del Fuego. By day 155 she was eight kilometres north of Cabo San Isidro. Over the 100 paddling days, she had travelled 4597 kilometres (2,855 miles). By November 2012 Freya was paddling along the coast of Peru. By December she had reached Paita, Peru. Through out January to March 2013 she paddled northwards along the Pacific coast past Ecuador and Colombia, to reach Panama City after 417 days of paddling. After crossing through the Panama Canal to the Atlantic side of South America, she traversed the coasts of Panama and Colombia, to reach Venezuela by May after 475 days of paddling. Continuing on again in August, she paddled past the coast of Venezuela to reach Georgetown, Guyana by November 8th, after 560 paddling days. This ended her second leg of her journey around South America. You can follow Freya's exploits on her website.

Patrick Winterton and **Mick Berwick** together in May/June 2009 completed the first successful kayak crossing from Scotland to the Faroe Islands in the North Atlantic Ocean. After a failed attempt in 2008 the pair re-evaluated their plan and made a second successful attempt. Patrick paddled solo from Oban on the Scottish west coast, to Stornoway on the Island of Lewis, off Scotland's north-west coast. With Mick, the pair set off on a 350 kilometre (217 mile) voyage to the Fore Islands, in single kayaks. After two 50 kilometre days of paddling along the coast of the Island of Lewis they made the 80 kilometre crossing to the island of North Rona. He they received a favourable 60 hour weather window in which time they could complete the 300 kilometre (186 mile) crossing to the Faroe Islands. Through careful planning, adhering to a routine, having good communications and being adaptable, the pair spent three nights at sea to reach their destination in 74 hour.

Prior to this successful crossing Patrick had already paddled 1500 kilometres (933 miles) from Aberdovey, on the Welsh coast across to Ireland. He then travelled southwards around the Irish coastline, then northwards along the west coast. Following the Irish coastline he voyaged across the northern coastline and made the crossing over to Scotland. At Oban he had an accident whereby he had to end his adventure. It was then at Oban in 2008 and 2009 that he took up his adventure on the two attempts to paddle to the Faroe Islands. An account of this voyage written by Patrick Winterton can be found in Sea Kayaker Magazine, Issue 133, December 2009.

Sea canoeist of and in Australia

Some of the people featuring below were not born in Australia but they lived here and have contributed to Australian sea kayaking by kayaking in and around Australia.

Reverend Fred C. B. Fairey has been described as "the father of Australian sea kayaking." Born in England, he was a Congregational minister, in St. Kilda, Melbourne. In 1876, after following the exploits of Mr John MacGregor in his Rob Roy canoe, he was inspired to utilise this type of vessel to take the Gospel to the settlers along the remote rivers and coastline of Australia. He ordered his canoe from Messrs. Searle and Co., Lambeth, London. Mr MacGregor himself oversaw the selection and build of the canoe. The model he chose was his Rob Roy model No.5, which had been built as a sea-boat and had successfully, voyaged on the coasts of both

the Orkney and Shetland Islands. Receiving his canoe on June 25, 1877, he describes it as follows:

And now to describe the canoe. She is built of oak, mahogany, and cedar, is copper-fastened, varnished, and has a streak of gold along the upper edge. The name "Evangelist" is painted in blue letters on both bows. Dimensions—12 ft. in length, 12 in. in depth, 28 in. beam, weighing without fittings, about 79 lb. The cedar deck is rounded to throw off the sea. Behind the canoeist's seat there is a bulkhead and a locker-lid, which lifts up—these removed, there is room to lie down and sleep.

By day the provision box, clothes-bag, railway-rug, and cooking apparatus are packed in the locker. The rudder is worked with the feet, by means of lines attached to a bent bar of iron bolted through the centre of the footboard, thus leaving the hands free to handle sail, paddle, or luncheon-locker. The hatch or well is covered with a corded waterproof apron, which is attached to a cedar sliding-board fitting round the body; underneath the forepart of this apron I have fitted a cedar board, which prevents so much water lodging in the waterproof.

The canoe has one mast, which is fitted with a tiny block, and, at the masthead, India-rubber rings, through which is slipped a piece of cane, holding the burgee of the Royal Canoe Club. This mast carries a linen lug-sail, with yard of bamboo, and light boom. The paddle is jointed in the centre, and can be used either as a single or double paddle. The little vessel is a lifeboat, having two India-rubber air-chambers, one being placed aft behind the locker, the other between the footboard and the mast. The cooking apparatus is remarkably compact and ingenious, exciting the admiration of all who examine it. For expedition it cannot be beaten. It will boil water in three and a half minutes. Then there is the provision-box, with its tin canisters for tea, sugar, and biscuits; the waterproof clothes-bag, the railway-rug, water-bottle, and sponge.

On July 12, 1877, he took the *Evangelist* on her maiden voyage from Saint Kilda Pier 40 miles down to Geelong. The journey from Hobson bay to Corio Bay took two days with the *Evangelist* berthing at the Moorobool Street Wharf at about

7 pm, in the dark. On July 16, he ported the canoe onto the Barwon River and by the evening had negotiated the Connewarre Lakes and was in position to reach Bass Strait the next morning. On July 17, he raised his sail for the first time, left the Barwon River bar, and headed east for 11 kilometres and the entrance into Port Phillip. After waiting half-an-hour for slack water, he negotiated his way through 'The Rip' following closely the Lonsdale reef. After successfully negotiating the Heads, he proceeded to Queenscliff where spectators on the wharf greeted him with *a hearty cheer* as his was *the smallest vessel which had ever passed through Port Phillip Heads*. It is not clear how he returned to Melbourne after he visited Drysdale and Geelong but he records his maiden voyage as a 100 mile trip. This being the case, I can only assume he paddled around the Bellarine Peninsula to Drysdale via Clifton Springs, then further down into Corio Bay to Geelong, then back up the western side of Port Phillip to Melbourne.

In November 1877, he had taken up the pastorate of north-west Tasmania and settled, with his family, on the River Forth, not far from Devonport. In early January 1879, he started the planning for his *first Annual Voyage of the Missionary Canoe*. This journey would take him from Hamilton-on-Forth along the central north coast over to the north-east coast, then south along the east coast and west around to Hobart Town; a journey of 300 miles, along *the iron-bound coasts of Tasmania*. From January 27th to February 24, 1877, the Reverend paddled and sailed the *Evangelist* along the Tasmanian coast providing Christian Fellowship to those living in remote stations and towns. While he was *about his Father's business,* he experienced several *exciting times* with the winds and waves which leads him to praise *the wonderful sea-going qualities of the canoe*, Mr MacGregor, the builders in London and God for his safety. After passing Cape Portland and negotiating the current around Swan Island, he proceeded southwards along the east coast past Eddystone point (the southeast boundary marker of Bass Straight) unmolested by the conditions. However, on one occasion, after being warned about the possibility of being shipwrecked if he attempted to land at Falmouth, on the east coast, he was trashed in the surf while coming into land. Breaking only his mast and losing his field glasses, he landed on the beach *panting for breath* but unharmed. Five days later, after visiting the local settlers and having a new mast fashioned, he continued on south. On the day of his departure, he set sail and raced the oncoming deteriorating weather and rising seas for 21 miles down to Long Point Seymour at an average speed of 7.8 knots (14.48 km/h). Due to gale force winds, he portaged 26 miles over to Moulting Lagoon and into Great Oyster bay and the town of Swansea; thereby saving time in delays and avoiding the Freycinet Peninsula and detour around Schouten Island. Delayed for another five days, by foul weather, he set off on February 18th, and reached Buxton (*Buxton Point*) near (*Little*) Christmas Island. February 19th he launched for Blackmans Bay. Passing Cape Bougainville at five miles per hour, he entered the channel (*Mercury Passage*) between Maria Island and Cape Bernier headland. However, at Marion Bay, the swell was rolling in and breaking on the bar at the entrance to Blackmans Bay. Not willing to negotiate the breakers on the bar, he spent a long night sitting off the bar. The next morning he left Marion Bay heading south for the nearest safe landing along the Forestier Peninsula. He soon found a landing spot in the corner of Two Mile Beach Bay (*North Bay*). At 7 am on February 20th, he stepped out of his canoe after 25 hours at sea. With the weather deteriorating further, he portage his canoe over to Blackmans Bay. February 24th, brought good weather and he launched for the quarter mile wide neck of land called East Bay Neck, (*Dunalley, Denison Channel*) which divides Blackmans Bay from Norfolk Bay. The settlers willingly portage his vessel across the narrow strip of land to the beach on Norfolk Bay (*Dunalley Bay*). He sailed across Norfolk Bay and the adjoining Frederick Henry Bay to Ralphs Bay Neck (*Lauderdale*). Finding a farmer and dray, he paid four shillings for his craft to be taken across the neck to Ralphs Bay. Starting his final leg to Hobart Town at 6:30 pm, it soon become dark and by the time he passed Trywork Point and entered the Derwent River, it was quite dark; the Reverend recording *Accustomed to sail along the coast at night, I felt quite comfortable in the river; and as the wind had fallen light, I quietly paddled on . . . At 9 pm on February 24, 1877, he arrived at the wharf of Hobart Town.* [36]

Operation Jaywick was an Australian commando raid, using kayaks, to insert the raiders into Singapore harbour to destroy Japanese shipping. The audacious raid was planned by Special Operations Australia (SOA) with the majority of men coming from Z Special Unit. The team comprised of: two British Army; two Royal Navy; eight Royal Australian Navy; and two Australian Imperial Force (AIF) personnel.

On September 1, 1943, using a previously captured Japanese fishing vessel renamed *MV Krait* the raiders departed Exmouth Harbour heading for the Dutch East Indies (*Indonesia*). To infiltrate Japanese occupied territory unchallenged and unmolested, they flew the Japanese flag from the *Krait*. The men too, in order to disguise themselves as Japanese and Malay fishermen, stained their bodies brown, dyed their hair black and dressed in sarongs. After three-and-a-half weeks, the *Krait* dropped a six man raiding party off on Pandjang Island, 50 kilometres from Singapore, then chugged off towards Borneo until it was time to return and rendezvous with the raiding party.

The three kayaks used by the raiding party were especially flown to Australia from Britain. They were two-man collapsible kayaks; six metres long, less than a metre wide and equipped with a small masts and black silk sails. Having finely tapered ends the hulls were constructed of seven-ply rubber and canvas. The deck covering consisted of three apertures, two for the kayakers and the centre one for supplies and equipment. Each cockpit had a built in skirt.

After narrowly avoiding detection by a Japanese patrol boat, the canoeists left the staging point and island hopped at night towards Singapore. During the day, they would hide out on the islands, until they finally reached Subar Island, 11–12 kilometres from Singapore. From here, they would prep and launched the raid on the Japanese shipping at anchor in Keppel Harbour. The canoes were low in the water, weighed down by their 300 kilogram cargo of kit, weapons, rations and limpet mines. Their first attempt to attack the shipping was foiled by strong currents, so after returning to the island, they were then prevented from attacking due to the weather. September 26, 1943 was their last opportunity to attack. Battling the strong currents, the three kayaks took separate routes into and around Keppel Harbour. After attaching the magnetic limpet mine to the hulls of the targets, then dumping excess equipment, they endeavoured to get as much distance between themselves and Singapore. After reaching their chosen island shortly before dawn, they could hear the explosions in Keppel Harbour. Over the next six nights, they paddled another 80–90 kilometres, avoiding a highly agitated and hostile enemy, to reach their rendezvous with the *Krait*. After midnight on October 2nd, two of the raiders were picked up but the other two kayaks did not show and finally, the *Krait* had to sail. The other four had been on the wrong beach and had seen the *Krait* chug off and resigned themselves to being stranded deep inside enemy territory. However, the crew on board were not about to leave their mates behind, so on the following night, returned to the area and found the missing men. The 21.3 metre long and 3.3 metre wide *Krait*, with a "Gardner" 6LW diesel engine, that was prone to cutting out, provided enough power to propel the escaping *Krait* at a maximum speed of 6.5 knots. On October 19th, the *Krait* anchored off the American base of Potshot in Exmouth Gulf after a voyage 8000 kilometres over 48 days, 33 of which were deep inside occupied territory.

A year later, Lyon organised *Operation Rimau* with a larger team and more complex equipment. Inserted this time by submarine, the raid met with disaster with all of the raiders being killed, captured and executed. Six from Operation Jaywick were a part of Rimau.[37]

Rod Harris, Ian and Peter Richards, are three Australian kayakers, credited with the first kayak crossing of Bass Straight, from Victoria to Tasmania via Flinders Island in 1971. The three friends modified their fibreglass slalom kayaks by adding skegs to them, to increase directional stability. The three men departed Tidal River, on the western side of Wilsons Promontory on March 27, 1971. Navigating with a laminated photocopy of the chart and an orienteering compass, they made their way to the Kent Group of islands. They attempted the next crossing to Flinders on March 30, 1971 but the unfavourable conditions caused the pod to raft-up for a night in Bass Straight. The next morning they returned to Deal Island. Late afternoon, on April 2nd the pod reached Flinders Island. April 6, 1971 the men crossed Banks Straight and landed at Cape Portland on Tasmania's mainland. Rod Harris published an account of this epic trip in Wild Magazine number 118.

Cecily Butorac from Tasmania (born on Flinders Island) in 1978 became the first woman sea kayaker to paddle to Flinders Island. In 1979, she became the first woman to paddle a sea kayak to Maatsuyker Island (Southern Tasmania) and land. In 1981 she circumnavigated Flinders Island. In 1983 she paddled south-west Tasmania from Port Davey on the west to Recherche Bay (south-west of Hobart near South Bruny Island). She has also paddled in Japan (1982), the Greek Islands (1983), and the main Fijian Islands (1984). For her contribution to Tasmanian Sea Kayaking, she was made the first life member of the Maatsuyker Canoe Club in 1998. Information about Cecily Butorac can be found on Laurie Ford's web page.

Earle Bloomfield and **John Brewster** were the first team to circumnavigate Tasmania in 1979. Earle was one of the founding members of the Victorian Sea Kayak Club and its first President.

Peter Carter, **John Hicks**, **Mike Higginson** and **David Nicolson** circumnavigated Kangaroo Island between December 1980 and January 1981.[38]

In January 1981, Peter Carter, John Hicks and **Ray Rowe** (UK) paddled a crossing from Port Lincoln to Adelaide SA.

Paul Caffyn circumnavigated Australia from December 28, 1981 to December 23, 1982, in what he called *Round Australia Kayak Expedition* (RAKE). The Expedition, which was supported by two friends, took 360 days and

covered 9,420 nautical miles (17 446km). See: previous entry.

Laurie Ford, Australian adventurer who paddled and sailed solo across Bass Strait from Tasmania to Victoria via Flinders Island and return in 1982. In 1979–80, Laurie fitted an electric bilge pump to his kayak, a standard fit today in Victoria. In 1981, he developed and fitted the drop down rudder, which was copied by VCP, and is a standard fit today on many kayaks. Laurie Ford's history and views including history of Tasmanian sea canoeing and other interesting information can be accessed on his website.[39]

Larry Grey has paddled extensively. Larry has paddled from Victoria to Papua New Guinea (4500 km), circumnavigated Papua New Guinea (2500 km). Additionally, he has paddled around Singapore through Malaysia to Indonesia as well as having paddled in Arnhem Land and Vanuatu. He has also crossed from Ireland to Brittan and had two expeditions to the Arctic. In 1986, Larry was part of the first Australian expedition to travel 1000 kilometres down the Greenland coast. Within the NSW Sea Kayak Club, he was one of the instigators of their grading system. On the boat builder front, he is the designer of the Pittarak kayak.

Paul Snelgrove is the only Australian and only solo kayaker to paddle around Cape Horn, South America. The trip he under took was a re-enactment of the four man British expedition led by Frank Goodman in 1977.[40]

Dan and **Karen Trotter** a British couple living in Scotland circumnavigated Tasmania on two trips.[41] The first trip from Orford to Strahan via South–East Cape was between the 11th February and 11 April 1991. By day thirteen, Dan's kayak had its stern nearly ripped off when they were both trashed coming in through the surf zone. On other occasions, they were weather bound for eight to ten days before the weather and swell would let them continue. With the weather and swells becoming increasingly unfavourable, the couple decided to continue their adventure the following year. The second trip took place between February 2nd and May 11, 1992, when they kayaked from Strahan to Hobart.

In 1992, **Eric Stiller** (USA) and **Tony Brown** (Australia) paddled from Sydney to Darwin during which they completed a 120 hour crossing of the Gulf of Carpentaria.[42] Their attempt to paddle/sail around Australia in a Klepper Aerius II folding kayak is recorded in the book *Keep Australia on Your Left*.

During April 1998, **Malcolm Hamilton**, **David Williamson**, **Phil Doddridge**, **Gordon Begg**, **Scott Polley**, and **Tim Vogt** paddled to South Neptune Island. South Neptune Island is located on the southern aspect of the Australasian Continental shelf before the Spencer Gulf in South Australia.

Stu Trueman, English born, NSWSKC member. Stu is an Australian Canoeing sea kayaking instructor of instructors and adventurer. Between 30th December 1999 and the 10th January 1999, Stu performed a solo eastern crossing of Bass Straight from Victoria to Tasmania (~309 km). During 2000–2001 he performed a solo crossing from North-west Tasmania to Portsea in Victoria. The journey went via Albatross Island, the western side of King Island and the 55 nautical mile crossing of Western Bass Straight to Apollo Bay. In 2006, along with **Andrew McAuley** and **Lauri Geoghegan,** he under took an expedition to the Antarctic Peninsula, paddling over 800 kilometres to the Antarctic Circle. In 2008, Stu paddled a Mirage 580, solo for 35 hours, from Tidal River (western side of Wilsons Promontory in Victoria), a planned 215 kilometres across Bass Straight to north-west Tasmania.

On April 10, 2010, Stu has set out on a 17 000 kilometres circumnavigation attempt of the Australian continent, paddling a Nadgee Solo kayak. Departing from Broome in WA he spent 16 months paddling the Australian continent. During this time he had to paddle for thirty hours past the Zuytdorp Cliffs before facing the Baxter cliffs then Buna cliffs in the Australian Bight which both required overnight marathon paddling efforts. During his adventure he was knock over in his kayak, knock out of his kayak, had his rudder bitten by a Tiger shark and encounters with territorial salt water crocodiles. Like Paul Caffyn, he paddled around the coastline of the Gulf of Carpentaria from the north-east tip to the north-west tip. After negotiating the six metre tidal ranges of northern Australia and their related tidal streams he arrived in Darwin in mid June 2011. After departing Darwin and negotiating the phenomena of the Joseph Bonaparte Gulf he turned southwards along the Kimberly coast to land back in Broome on July 28, 2011. A log of Stu's adventure can be found on the Nadgee Kayak's website. In 2013 Stu published a book about his adventure around Australia by kayak titled *All the Way Round*. Besides being a great yarn, the book also contains a very useful equipment list.

Dave Winkworth is a well known figure in Australian sea kayaking circles and is known for kayaking expeditions and 100 kilometre distance days. In 1998, while paddling with a group of other NSWSKC members along the Cape York Peninsular, a saltwater crocodile attacked one of the crew. The attack took place at a beach on Macarthur Island. According to Mike Snoad, who was there, the crocodile had Arunus Pilka by the leg and was trying to drag him into deep water. Dave, who was naked nearby, ran and jumped on the crocodile, scaring the reptile away. Arunus, had to be medivaced out by helicopter. In 2005, Dave, undertook a solo Cape York paddle in which he had several 500 metre plus portages due to the large tidal range in North Queensland. In 2008, he paddled from Karumba, on the southeast coast of the Gulf of Carpentaria to Darwin. Dave is also known for being the original builder of the 'Nadgee' sea kayak. Because of the large tidal ranges in Australia's far north (Western Australia to Queensland) Dave modifying his Nadgee (and later Sandy Robinson's Mirage 580) to have removable cantilevered kayak wheels fitted to the hull. When not required the two wheel assemblies are stowed on the aft deck.

Richard Bugg and **Daniel Gardner** between the months of January 16th to February 29, 2000, they paddled anticlockwise around Tasmania. Richard had been a white water kayaker and sea kayaking for 12 years. During this time, he also undertook an 850 kilometre paddle along Cape York Peninsula. Daniel on the other hand, had no previous sea kayaking experience, but was an avid surfer and small-boat sailor. Paddling Dagger Apostle kayaks, they departed from Falmouth on the northeast coast and arrived at Clifton Beach, south of Lauderdale 45 days later. At this stage, they had run out of time and had to return to work. Returning in late July, they departed Clifton Beach and arrived at Falmouth eight days later, thus completing their 650 nautical mile circumnavigation. The account of their voyage can be found in Sea Kayaker Magazine, August 2003.[43]

David Williamson completed a solo crossing to Pearson Island of the Western side of the Eyre Peninsula, SA (South-west of the town of Elliston and the island of Flinders). In January 2001, he completed the first crossing of western Bass Straight from Tasmania to Apollo Bay, Victoria via King Island. David departed Stanley on the January 6, 2001 with two other kayakers, **Jim Townsend** and **Malcolm Hamilton**, who together paddled a double kayak. On the 8th January, the group made the 90 kilometre crossing from Shepherds Bay, on Hunter Island in the Fleurieu Group, to the town of Grassy on King Island. Travelling up the eastern side of King Island to Cape Wickham, the group attempted the second crossing on the 13th January. They intended to kayak the second 55 nautical mile crossing from Disappointment Bay to Apollo Bay in 16 hours but an unfavourable wind shift caused the men to return to King Island.

Departing around midnight, the paddlers experienced the early arrival of the forecasted northeasterly wind shift at 0800 hours, when they were over one third of the way into their journey. As part of their risk management plan, the early arrival of the northeasterly required them to return to King Island. As the wind and seas increased in size, the strong winds and accompanying 'bullets' put the paddlers in a "pretty serious" situation, with the very real possibility of them being swept past King Island; next stop Antarctica. After a harrowing eight and a half hour battle back to King Island they landed around 1620 hours after nearly sixteen and a half hours of paddling. After the ordeal of the first attempt to cross to Victoria, Malcolm and Jim

applied sound judgement and self-awareness and decided not to perform a second attempt.

David felt that with the right conditions he could successfully execute the crossing while having enough reserve strength in case the conditions became unfavourable again. On the January 16th at 0630 hours, he set off for Apollo Bay, taking fourteen and a half hours to complete the 100 km crossing.[44]

Andrew McAuley, 2005 Australian Geographic Adventurer of the year, has several kayaking credits to his name. In 2003, he completed in 35 hours the first solo non-stop 220 kilometre crossing of Bass Straight from Wilsons Promontory in Victoria to Boat Harbour Beach in Tasmania. In 2004, he did the first solo non-stop 530 kilometre crossing of the Gulf of Carpentaria in six and a half days. In 2007, Andrew attempted the first solo 1600 kilometre kayak voyage from Tasmania to New Zealand's Fiordland. Andrew chose to use a more traditional style sea kayak and used a specialised Mirage sea kayak built by Paul Hewitson. For rest and shelter, Andrew would manoeuvre himself down inside the cockpit, with there being only enough room for one arm to be placed along his side while the other arm would have to rest across his chest. When in position he would fit over the cockpit opening a dome capsule that he named *Casper*. With *Casper* in place, Andrew was protected from the fury of the Tasman Sea and the kayak would self-right when capsized. Andrew estimated it would take him 30 days to make the crossing. Departing Fortescue Bay, Tasmania on January 11, 2007 Andrew endured 30 foot swells, storms, 40 knot head winds, rough seas and repetitive capsizing to make his way across the Tasman Sea. On February 9th, the New Zealand Coast Guard received a garbled radio message from 'Kayak One'. Late the following evening after a sea and air search Andrew's empty kayak was discovered 70 to 80 kilometres off Milford Sound on New Zealand's south island west coast.[45]

John Jacoby and **Jarad Kohlar** paddled from Victoria to Tasmania via King Island in November 2004.[46]

Justine Curgenven, **Trys Morris** and **Gemma Rawlings** were the first all women team to circumnavigated Tasmania, in one expedition, in November and December 2004. See: previous entry.

Kate Yeomans from Queensland paddled from Brisbane to Cape York.[47]

Sandy Robinson from Western Australia; in 2006–07, Sandy embarked on what she called *Sandy's Long Australian Paddle* (SLAP). Departing from Caffyn Cove, Queenscliff, Victoria on the December 22, 2006 she reached far North Queensland, paddling a Mirage 580 sea kayak.[48] By Day 157, she was at Cooktown in Far North Queensland. On June 5, 2007, day 166, at Villis Point near Cape Direction, while looking for a campsite after her days paddle, a large territorial male crocodile attacked her kayak. By day 177, Sandy decided to get to Broome in WA and continue her journey south from there, giving the 'Top End' a miss.[49] Continuing from Broome, on day 286, (October 3, 2007), she reached Lancelin, near Geraldton, WA.

Matty Watton, Tasmanian kayaker. Matt in February 2007 set the fastest time for a kayak circumnavigation of Tasmania (1416 km), taking 26 days. To Matt's credit are two other solo circumnavigations of the 'Apple Isle' in November 1999 (1517 km in 34 days) and November 2001 (1462 km in 30 days).[50]

James Castrission and **Justin Jones**, Australian adventurers, planned to paddle form Sydney, Australia to Auckland, New Zealand; a planned distance of 2200 kilometres. They chose to paddle a specially designed two-man ocean-going kayak, called *Lot 41*, which was similar to the ocean-going rowboats with their cabin. Departing Foster in NSW on the 13 November 2007, they spent 62 days at sea and travelled 3318 kilometres to arrive at Nagamotu Beach, New Plymouth on the west coast of New Zealand's North Island. UK marine designer Rob Feloy designed Lot 41 specifically for the crossing. Graham Chapman and the team, at Adventure Marine, constructed the ocean-going kayak at their workshop on the NSW Central Coast.

The name Lot 41 refers to the auction lot of the famous 'big hearted' racehorse Phar Lap, who was sold to his Australian trainer in Lot 41. The duo encountered strong winds and currents, which caused them to paddle around in circles and added more than 1000 kilometres to the trip. The men endured sleep deprivation, lack of vitals, leg muscle atrophy and slow healing sores to be the first duo in a double kayak to complete the longest trans-oceanic expedition.

Julian Smith, English born, Victorian kayaker and VSKC member and former President. In February 2008 Julian had lead his fourth crossing of eastern Bass Straight, but this time he went from south to north. Julian also instructs members of the Australian Defence Forces on sea kayaking as a Unit Adventurous Training Leader Instructor.

Tina Rowley, English born, Victorian kayaker and VSKC member. In March 2007, Tina became the first woman to kayak across western Bass Straight. Departing from Apollo Bay, Victoria, she with two companions **John Evertze** (Tasmanian) and **Greg Murray** (South African) paddled via the western side of King Island to the north-west coast of Tasmania. Greg Murray had previously completed two eastern Bass Straight crossings; one of which was with Hew Kingston. Tina had previously completed two eastern Bass Straight crossings.

Gerrit 'John' Evertze a Tasmanian and VSKC member. John has been kayaking in one form or another since he was 12 years old under the tutelage of Cecily Butorac. In 2007, he completed a solo crossing of western Bass Straight, via eastern King Island, Albatross Island and the Fleurieu Group. In 2008, John led a group for his second western Bass Straight crossing.

Bill Robinson, VSKC member, and marathon kayaker. Bill is a lifelong member of the VSKC and well-known 'brown water' marathon paddler. In 2005, Bill paddled the length of the Murray River from Yarrawonga, Victoria to Goolwa, South Australia; a distance of 1987 km. In 2007, Bill completed a Bass Straight crossing led by Julian Smith.

Mike Snoad, NSWSKC member has participated on several expeditions. In 2009, at age 65, he completed a solo crossing of Eastern Bass Straight.

John Wilde, NSWSKC member and all round nice guy from the Lakes District in the UK. As a young man he was a standby member of the Olympic team for white water kayaking. In Australia, he was a TAFE teacher and kayaking instructor as well as one of the driving forces behind sea kayaking in Australian Canoeing. In 1995, he completed a Bass Straight crossing. While solo kayaking along Tasmania's east coast, John's kayak was bitten in the midsection by an unknown 'big' species shark. After landing and inspecting the damage, he removed bits of teeth and repaired his carbon fibre Nadgee kayak. He continued on the next day.

Hew Kingston, NSWSKC member and owner/operator of the outdoors and adventure racing company 'Wild Horizons' in the Southern Highlands of NSW. Between 1997 and 2004, Huw completed his 25 000 kilometre Australian City2City journey by kayak, bike, ski and foot. The seven stages took 543 days to complete. During this time he travelled 19 051 kilometres in 238 days by mountain bike, 3749 kilometres in 145 days by both river and sea kayak, 1807 kilometres in 119 days on foot and 380 kilometres in 28 days on ski.[51]

Terry Bolland, of Western Australia and operator of Canoeing Down Under. Some of Terry's achievements listed on his website are a 1979 World Record for paddling 220.8 kilometres in 24 hours. Paddling the entire length of the Missouri River (4000 km) and Yukon River (3300 km). Paddled the Mississippi River (4000 km) in 35 days. Paddled the Blackwood River in southwest WA (500 km) and the Murray River Victoria/NSW/South Australia (2500 km) in 21 days. Paddling the entire length of the Athabasca, the Slave and the MacKenzie River (4000 km). Paddled, cycled and walked 24 000 kilometres around Australia. Paddled cycled and walked unassisted for 16 000 kilometres around the USA.

Terry has completed five expeditions by kayak and foot around the isolated Kimberley coast encountering huge tidal streams, crocodiles and sharks. His travels include a solo trek from Broome to Mitchell Plateau in 100 days. A 54 day, solo trek, from Lake Argyle, Wyndham to the Mitchell Plateau. The Drysdale River Expedition, involving travelling from Derby to Prince Regent River and return to Broome in 65 days. The 3500 kilometres 'Around the Kimberley Expedition', by kayak, mountain bike and foot, taking 91 days.

West Australian Kayaking trips include paddling from Perth to Shark Bay (WA), including a 30 hour paddle along the Zuytdorp Cliffs, encountering 30 knot winds. His fellow paddlers on this trip were **Tel Williams** and **John Di Nucci**. Paddling from Geraldton to Kalbarri then walking from Kalbarri along the Zuytdorp cliffs to Steep Point (mainland Australia westernmost point). Paddling from Steep Point to Carnarvon via Dirk Hartog, Dorre and Bernier Islands. Paddling around Peron Peninsular, Francois Peron National Park from Denham to Monkey Mia.[52] On the eastern seaboard, he has paddled from Cooktown to Cape York. He has also paddled around Hinchinbrook Island, Fraser Island and Whitsunday Islands.[53]

Shaan Gresser from Sydney is a member of the NSWSKC. Shaan is the first woman to paddle solo across Eastern Bass Straight. In 2008, Shaan joined the NSWSKC with little prior sea kayaking experience. In her words "I discovered that sea kayaking was a limitless adventure and embraced every aspect of the sport." On February 7, 2011 she launched from Port Welshpool, Victoria. Nineteen days later (February 25) she landed at Little Muscleroe Bay, Tasmania. In describing her trip Shaan says, "I took the Eastern Bass Strait route—via Wilson's Promontory, Hogan, Deal and Flinders Islands. Of the 19 days, 8 were spent paddling—the remainder was spent at various locations along the route waiting for the right weather. My longest day was a 73 kilometre, 10 hour paddle from Winter Cove on Deal Island to Royden Island, which lies 2 kilometres off the north western side of Flinders Island."

Shaan is also a regular paddler of the New South Wales (NSW) coastline with many days spent touring the various wilderness areas. She has also spent time touring in Queensland and the South Island of New Zealand.

Tara Mulvany from Invercargill New Zealand and KASK member, completed a circumnavigation of the New Zealand South Island. Departing on May 18, 2012 from Milford Sound on the west coast with **Sim Grigg**, the duo set about the task of circumnavigating the 3300 kilometre coastlines of both the South Island and Stewart Island (aka Rakirua). For the adventure Tara chose a Q-Kayaks (PE) Suka, which she found to be a marvellous kayak to paddle and stood up superbly to the rigours of the trip. Sim paddled a '*Mission Eco Bezhig, which he had no end of problems with, including nearly folding in half on one surf landing! Not ideal.*' The trip was planned for and conducted during the winter months; a time when the west coast is battered by huge swells (6–9 metres) from the Southern Ocean and gale to storm force winds. Paddling clockwise around the South Island, the pair reached Christchurch on the east coast in early September. At this point Sim retired from the expedition. During his trip he was trashed at Heapy River mouth and finished the trip with a roll count of around 10. Tara continued with the voyage over the next five weeks to paddle solo along the remote Otago and Southland coastline. Leaving the circumnavigation of Rakirua until another time (when she can explore it at leisure), she headed into the isolated Fiordland region. During this section of the trip she paddled up to 15 hours a day in 4 metre swells and strong winds. On October 22nd, 2012 Tara completed the adventure back at Milford Sound.[54] Tara when asked to describe any highlights of the trip replied '*The Fiordland coast! Paddling huge seas in such a wild and remote place, all alone– totally awesome. However brutal the west coast was, it was also really exciting to say the least and a real solid adventure.*'

1 Diana & Michael Preston, A Pirate of Exquisite Mind The Life of William Dampier, (Corgi Books, London, 2005) p.261
2 Ibid, p.266, p.262

3 Fridtjof Nansen, Translated by William Archer, Eskimo Life, (London, Longmans, Green & Co, 1893), pp.51
4 The "Fram", meaning "Forward", was an immensely strong and cunningly designed ship. On September 22, 1893, it was frozen into the pack-ice off Siberia, north of Kotelnoi, to emerge thirty-five months later on August 13, 1896, into open water near Spitzbergen. Nansen and Johansen were reunited with the crew on August 21 at Tromsø, Norway.
5 Fridtjof Nansen, Farthest North, Vol. 1., (New York, Harper & Brothers Publishers, 1897), p.543
6 www.time.com/time/magazine/article/0,9171,731942,00.html, from the article Ships at sea, October 1st 1928, accessed 4May09
7 www.telegraph.co.uk/news/worldnews/australiaandthepacific /australia/1383632/Incredible-journey-of-Nazi-who-canoed-to-Australia.html by Nick Squires in Sydney, 2Feb02 accessed 15Apr09
8 www.anmm.gov.au/site/page.cfm?u=354&c=915, Oskar Speck's 50,000 km voyage to Australia . . . by kayak, 25 October 2006 accessed 15Apr09
9 www.riverbendnelligen.com/dearall27.html, 10Apr05 accessed 20Apr09. Using Oskar Speck's story reprinted in the New South Wales Sea Kayaker magazine issues 50-52 thru the kind permission of Post Magazine.
10 The Orinoco river system originates along the southern borders of Venezuela and Brazil, in the state of Amazonas. It flows west, next north, creating the border with Colombia, and then turns east and bisects Venezuela on its 1290 mile (2150km) way to the Atlantic Ocean. The name Orinoco is derived from a Guarauno words meaning "a place to paddle"
11 Madeira River is a tributary of the Amazon River formed by the junction of the Mamoré and Beni rivers in Bolivia, which flows north along the border between Bolivia and Brazil. It meanders northeast in Brazil to join the Amazon River east of the city of Manaus. Measured from the upper reaches of the Mamoré, it is 2,082 mi (3,352 km) long.
12 Most of Mato Grosso region lays on the western extension of the Brazilian Plateau, across which runs the watershed that separates the Amazon River basin to the north from the basin system of the Río de la Plata to the south. The Mato Grosso Plateau is at an elevation of about 3,000 feet (900m) above sea level. The northern slopes, are drained by the Xingu, Tapajós, and Madeira rivers, which descend into the Amazon Valley. The southern portion of the state drains southward through a multitude of streams emptying into the Paraguay River to the southwest.
13 Paraguay River (Río Paraguay in Spanish, Rio Paraguai in Portuguese) flows for 1,584 miles (2,549km) from its headwaters in the Brazilian state of Mato Grosso to its confluence with the Parana River north of Corrientes, Argentina.
14 www.krugercanoes.com accessed 20Jul09
15 Tien Shan Mountains, Central Asia, bordering Kazakhstan, Kyrgyzstan and Chinese Xinjiang.
16 Jon Turk, Shipwrecked Off Cape Horn, Sea Kayaker Magazine, Vol.15, No.4, October 1998
17 Jon Turk, The Ragged Edge of the Pacific Rim from Japan to Alaska, Sea Kayaker Magazine, Vol.18, No.4, October 2001, pp.32-44.
18 Sea Kayaker Magazine has published a profile on Jon Turk in the June 2005 edition.
19 Paul Caffyn, The Dreamtime Voyage—Around Australia Kayak Odyssey, (1994, Caxton Press, Christchurch), p.21
20 Tideplay, op. cit. Pioneers of Sea Kayaking
21 Wikipedia, Canoe Sailing, accessed 26Apr09
22 www.kokatat.com, Kayaking to Save the Albatross First Solo Kayaking Attempt to Circumnavigate South Georgia dated 2Oct08, accessed 4May09

23 Daniel E Arias, Rounding the Horn, Sea Kayaker Magazine, Vol.21, No.3, August 2004, pp.31-43.

24 Sea Kayaker Magazine has published a profile of Lonie Dupre in the April 2005 edition.

25 Tore Sivertsen, Lone Madsen's Last Journey, Sea Kayaker Magazine, Vol.16, No.2, June 1999, pp.26-31

26 www.peterbrayenterprises.co.uk/profile/index.html, Peter Bray Profile, accessed 4May09.

27 Silva 2008 Catalogue, p.54

28 The Isle of Anglesey (Ynys Môn in Welsh) is situated off the north-west coast of Wales and is separated from the mainland by the Menai Strait.

29 Information about Justine Curgenven and Crackle TV can be found at the website: www.cackletv.com/index.html.

30 www.outside.away.com/outside/destinations/south-georgia-1.html, New Zealand Team Aims for First Sea Kayak Circumnavigation of South Georgia Island by Sara Bask, accessed 4May09. Concerning distance around South Georgia Island different references read have 600 km, nearly 400 miles and approximately 490 nautical miles.

31 www.seakayakingcornwall.com/jeff-allen/south-georgia-kayak-expedtion.html, Around South Georgia, Geoff Allen, accessed 4May09

32 Sea Kayaker Magazine, Vol. 26, No. 2, June 2009, p.23

33 Freya's account of this crossing can be read in Sea Kayaker Magazine, Vol. 26, No. 3, August 2009, pp.14-18

34 Great Australian Bight Marine Park (Commonwealth Waters and State Waters)—A Description of Values and Uses, Australian Government, Director of National Parks, 2005, www.environment.gov.au/coasts/mpa/publications/pubs/gab-values.pdf of 14mar10

35 Freya Hoffmeister, http://qajaqunderground.com/australia-2008/race-around-australia-trip-report/ accessed 14Mar10

36 Laurie Ford, The Voyage of the Evangelist, the Reverend Fred C. B. Fairey or Canoe Travelling upon the rivers and coasts of Australia, 1877-1879, NSW Sea Kayaker Magazine, accessed from www.nswseakayaker.asn.au/magazine/39/fairey.htm

37 The names of the commandos are: Lieutenant Colonel I. Lyon (GH)*, Lieutenant Commander D. Davidson (RNVR)*, Captain R. Page (AIF)**, Lieutenant H. Carse (RANVR), Leading Stoker J. McDowell (RNR), Leading Telegraphist H. Young (RANR), Acting Leading Seaman K. Cain (RANR), Able Seaman W. Falls, (RANVR)**, Able Seaman A.W.G. Huston DSM (RANVR)*, Able Seaman A. Jones (RANVR), Acting Able Seaman F. Marsh (RANVR)*, Acting Able Seaman M. Berryman (RANVR), Corporal R. Morris (RAMC) and Corporal A. Crilley (AIF). * Denotes killed on Operation Rimau, ** Denotes captured and executed by Japanese. Reference: The MV Krait and Operation Jaywick, www.anzacday.org.au/History/ . . . /krait

38 Peter Carter, www.users.on.net/~pcarter/seakayak.html accessed 3Mar10

39 www.laurieford.net/lford.htm accessed 28May09

40 Paul Snelgrove, Cape Horne, VSKC Sea Trek Magazine, Spring 2008, Issue 62, p.26.

41 Dan was born in Tasmania but his parents moved to Scotland when he was six months old.

42 Carter, op. cit.

43 Richard Bugg, Way Down Under Circumnavigating Tasmania, Sea Kayaker Magazine, Vol.20, No.2, July/August 2003, pp.18-29.

44 David Williamson's story can be found at www.laurieford.net or at www.outdooraustralia.com

45 www.andrewmcauley.com accessed 17Aug2007

46 www.laurieford.net

47 Dave Winkworth, The Development of Paddle Wheels, VSKC Sea Trek Magazine, Summer 2009, Issue 63, p.13

48 https://netstorage.penrhos.wa.edu.au/slap/index.html

49 Sandy Robson, Trip Diary, June 2007, https://netstorage.penrhos.wa.edu.au/slap/TripDiary/Jun2007/jun2007.html accessed 18Jun09

50 Accounts of Matt Watton's adventures can be found on his website: http://mwatton.customer.netspace.net.au.

51 Huw Kingston, www.wildhorizons.com.au/city2city of 22 Mar. 2010

52 Information about Shark Bay (WA) can be found at www.sharkbay.org/default.aspx

53 Terry Bolland, www.canoeingdownunder.com.au/who.php#books of 22Mar10

54 Tara's blog can be found at http://winterkayakers.blogspot.co.nz/

Bibliography

American Meteorological Society (AMS). *Glossary of Meteorology.* 2000. http://amsglossary.allenpress.com/glossary (accessed March 17, 2011).

American Plastics Council. *Plastics: The Basics.* n.d. www.americanplasticscouncil.org (accessed October 16, 2003).

Amtmann, John. "Rotator Cuff Injury: Prevention and Recovery." *Sea Kayaker Magazine,* 2008 йил August, 3 ed.: 41-45.

ASAF. *Australian Shark Attack File (ASAF.* 2009. www.taronga.org.au/tcsa/conservation-programs/australian-shark-attack-file.aspx (accessed 2010 йил 6-July).

Attarian, Adam. *Risk Management in Outdoor and Adventure Programs Scenarios of Accidents and Misadventures.* Champaign: Human Kinetics, 2012.

Australian Academy of Science. *Biological Science the web of life.* Edited by David Morgan and et al. Canberra, ACT: Australian Academy of Science, 1979.

Australian Army. *Adventourous Training, Planning & Preparation (LWP-G 7-6-1).* Defence Publications Unit, 2004.

—. *Sea Kayaking (LWP-G 7-6–8).* Defence Publication Unit, 2006.

Australian Broadcasting Corporation (ABC). *Interview with Dr. Nathan Hart, University of Queensland by Suzannah Lyons: 'Can sharks detect colour?'.* 2009. www.abc.net.au/science/articles/2009/11/26/2754146.htm (accessed 2010 йил 12-July).

Australian Broadcasting Corporation (ABC) Radio. *Listening to ABC Radio.* n.d. www.abc.net.au/reception/radio/listen.htm (accessed October 14, 2008).

Australian Canoeing (AC). *Canoe Disiplines.* n.d. www.canoe.org.au (accessed April 24, 2009).

—. *Canoe Marathon Class Distances.* n.d. www.marathon.canoe.org.au (accessed April 26, 2009).

—. "Documents, Policies and Bylaws." *International Canoe Federation Canoe Sprint Competition Rules.* 2009. www.canoe.org.au (accessed April 14, 2009).

—. *Instructors, Guides and Skills.* n.d. www.canoe.org.au (accessed February 1, 2012).

—. "International Canoe Federation Canoe Marathon Competition Rules." *Documents, Policies and Bylaws.* n.d. www.canoe.org.au (accessed April 26, 2009).

—. "Paddle Your Own . . ." *Australian Canoeing.* n.d. www.canoe.org.au/site/canoeing/ac/downloads/Education/ACAS/Resources/Techniques/paddle_your_own.pdf (accessed February 20, 2012).

—. "Paddling A Kayak." *Australian Canoeing.* n.d. www.canoe.org.au/default.asp?ID=2264&MEnuID=Website+Administration%2F17%2F20 (accessed September 22, 2010).

—. *Risk Management and Safety.* n.d. www.canoeing.org.au (accessed February 1, 2012).

Australian Government Department of Environment, Water, Heritage and the Arts (DEWHA). *Three Sharks Listed as Migratory Under the EPBC Act.* n.d. www.environment.gov.au/coasts/species/sharks/publications/fs-three-sharks/index.html (accessed 2010 йил 25-July).

Australian Hydrographic Service. *Seafares Handbook.* Edited by A.R. Coulls. Melbourne: Commonwealth of Australia, 2004.

—. *Tidal Glossary.* n.d. www.hydro.gov.au (accessed September 10, 2004).

Australian Maritime College (AMC). *Marine Radio Operators Handbook Revised.* Launceston, Tasmania: Office of Maritime Communications, Australian Maritime College, 2003.

Australian Maritime Safety Authority. *Safety.* 2004. www.amsa.gov.au (accessed 2004 йил 27-May).

Australian National Maritime Museum (ANMM). n.d. www.anmm.gov.au (accessed January 15, 2010).

Australian Naval Reserve Cadets. "Naval Reserve Cadets Publication." *Cadets Guide (NRC-RS 6) Part 2 Chapters 30 to 57.* Melbourne: Defence Publication Unit, 2000.

—. "Naval Reserve Cadets Publication." *Cadets Guide (NRC-RS 6) Part 1 Chapters 1 to 29.* Melbourne: Defence Publication Unit, 2000.

—. "Naval Reserve Cadets Publication." *Cadets Guide (NRC-RS 6) Part 3 Chapters 58 to 82.* Melbourne: Defence Publication Unit, 2000.

Australian Red Cross. *Australian Red Cross First Aid Responding to Emergencies rev.* Edited by Tom Lochhass. Marrickville: Mosby Lifeline, 2000.

Australian Venom Research Unit (ARVU). *Snake bite.* n.d. www.arvu.org/compendium/biogs/A000084b.htm (accessed August 14, 2012).

Australian Venom Research Unit (AVRU). *AVRU Facts and Figures.* n.d. www.avru.org/general_factfig.html (accessed August 14, 2012).

Bally Ribbon Mills. "Yarns and Fibers Explained." *Bally Ribbon Mills Web site.* 2006. www.ballyribbon.com/fibers_yarns.htm (accessed 2009 йил 16-September).

Barclay-Kerr, H. *Waka—canoes—Waka in New Zealand.* 2 March 2009. www.TeAra.govt.nz (accessed February 10, 2010).

Barrett, David H. (ed.). *Crawford's Mariners Atlas Apollo Bay to Jervis Bay.* Bathurst, 1997.

Barton, Greg. *Use of Rudders.* 2009 йил 20-June. (accessed 2009 йил 15-July).

Bate, James. "Emergency Position Indicating Radio Beacon (EPIRB)." *Victorian Sea Kayak Club Seatrek Magazine,* Autumn 2008: 16–17.

BBC h2g2. *The Great White Shark.* 2006. www.bbc.co.uk/dna/h2g2/A15854952 (accessed 2010 йил 6-July).

Berke, Les. "Sea kayaking—Speed-Drag-HP." *Keelhauler.org.* n.d. www.keelhauler.org/khcc/seakayak.htm (accessed September 1, 2009).

Blue Jacket Boats. *Planning Boat Theory.* n.d. www.bluejacketboats.com (accessed October 17, 2009).

Brandon, John. *Meteorology Section 01a Atmospheric Thermodynamics 1 & 2 and Dynamics.* n.d. www.auf.asn.au/meteorology/section1a.html (accessed October 9, 2004).

—. *Meteorology Section 03 Cloud, Fog and Precipitation.* n.d. www.auf.asn.au/meteorology/section 3.html (accessed October 8, 2004).

—. *Meteorology Section 04 Planetary Scale Systems.* 8 October n.d. www.auf.asn.au/meteorology/section4.html (accessed 2004).

—. *Meteorology Section 05 Synoptic Scale Features.* n.d. www.auf.asn.au/meteorology/section5.html (accessed October 8, 2004).

—. *Meteorology Section 06 Southern Hemisphere Winds.* n.d. www.auf.asn.au/meteorology/section4.hrtml (accessed October 8, 2004).

—. *Meteorology Section 07 Mesoscale Systems.* n.d. www.auf.asn.au/meteorology/section7/.html#density_current (accessed October 8, 2004).

—. *Meteorology Section 09 Microscale Meteorology.* n.d. www.auf.asn.au/groundschool/umodule21.html (accessed October 8, 2004).

—. *Meteorology Section 12.3 Moon Phases.* n.d. www.auf.asn.au/meteorology/section12.html#moonphase (accessed October 8, 2004).

Bray, Peter. *Peter Bray Adventurer.* 2009. www.peterbrayadventurer.com (accessed June 24, 2012).

Brewer, Ted. *Understanding Boat Design.* 4th. Camden: International Marine, 1994.

British Admiralty. *Australia Pilot.* 6th Ed. Vol. 2. London: Hydrographic Department, 1982.

Broze, Matt, and George Gronseth. *Sea Kayaker Deep Trouble True Stories and Their Lessons from Sea Kayaker Magazine.* Edited by Christopher Cunningham. Camden, Maine: Raged Mountain Press, 1997.

Burch, David. *Fundamentals of Kayak Navigation.* Connecticut, 1999.

Bureau of Meteorology (BOM). *Boating Weather Series: Wind Waves Weather Victorian Waters.* Canberra: Bureau of Meteorology, Dept of Administrative Services, 1989.

—. *Marine.* 2008. www.bom.gov.au/info/marine (accessed 2008).

—. *Oceanography.* 2007. www.bom.gov.au/oceanography (accessed 2007 йил 19-February).

—. *Weather.* 2004 йил 9-June. www.bom.gov.auweather/vic (accessed 2004).

Burgess, George H. "How, When and Where Shark Attacks." *Florida Museum of Natural History (FLMNH).* 1995-2012. www.flmnh.ufl.edu/fish/sharks/attacks/howwhen.htm (accessed September 12, 2012).

Burke's Backyard. *Snake Bite Fact Sheet.* 1999. www.burkesbackyard.com (accessed August 14, 2012).

Caffyn, Paul. *Sea Kayaks Techniques Bulletin Board: Rudders.* 2005 йил 5-May. www.kayakforum.com/cgi-bin/Technique/index.cgi/noframes/read/23128 (accessed 2008 йил 9-June).

Campbell MD, FRAC, Earnest. "Sea snakes." *Scubadoc's Diving Medicine.* 10 July 2010. www.scuba-doc.com (accessed August 16, 2012).

Canadian Coast Guard (CCG). *International Association of Marine Aids to Navigation and Lighthouse Authorities Maritime Buoyage System.* 06 June 2012. http://www.ccg-gcc.gc.ca/eng/Ccg/InternationalAssociationofLighthouseAuthoritiesMaritimeBuoyageSystem (accessed June 22, 2012).

—. *The Canadian Aids to Navigation System 2011.* 21 June 2012. www.ccg-gcc.gc.ca/Aids_To_Navigation_System_2011 (accessed June 24, 2012).

Captain Monahan, K. H. *The Chilling Truth About Cold Water.* Shipwrite Productions. 7 February 2009. www.shipwrite.bc.ca?Chilling_truth.htm (accessed June 15, 2009).

Centre for Disease Control & Prevention (CDC). "Crypto—Cryptosporidiosis." *http://www.cdc.gov/crypto/.* 2008 йил 16-April. (accessed 2008 йил 13-October).

—. "Giardiasis Fact Sheet." *http://www.cdc.gov/ncidod/dpd/parasites/Giardiasis/2004_PDF_Giardiasis.pdf.* 2004 йил 3-Sep. (accessed 2008 йил 12-October).

Chargingchargers.com Inc. *Battery Tutorial.* n.d. www.chargingchargers.com/tutorials/batteries.html (accessed June 11, 2009).

Chave, Lynne. *Mal de Mer Who Gets It?* 2008. www.seasickness.co.uk (accessed 2008 йил 16-October).

Clark, Nancy. *Nancy Clark's Sports Nutrition Guidebook.* 4th Ed. Champaign: Human Kinetics, 2008.

Cleveland Clinic. *Spondylolysis.* n.d. http://my.clevelandclinic.org/disorders/Back_Pain/hic_Spondylolysis.aspx (accessed October 27, 2008).

Clinic, Cleveland. "Spondylolysis." *http://my.clevelandclinic.org/disorders/Back_Pain/hic_Spondylolysis.aspx.* (accessed 2008 йил 27-October).

Coastguard New Zealand. *Coastguard New Zealand.* 2012. www.coastguard.co.nz/ (accessed July 1, 2012).

Cogger, Harold G. "General Description and Definition of the Class Reptilia." *Fauna of Australia Vol. 2A.* 1993. www.environment.gov.au/biodiversity/arbs/publications/fauna-of-australia-2a.html (accessed August 10, 2012).

—. "General Description and Definition of the Order Crocodylia." *Fauna of Australia Vol. 2A.* 1993. www.environment.gov.au/biodiversity/arbs/publications/fauna-of-australia-2a.html (accessed August 2, 2010).

—. "General Description and Definition of the Squamata." *Fauna of Australia Vol. 2A.* 1993. www.environment.gov.au/biodiversity/arbs/publications/fauna-of-australia-2a.html (accessed August 10, 2012).

Colfelt, David. *100 Magic Miles of the Great Barrier Reef the Whitsunday Islands Eighth Edition*. Berry, NSW: Windward Publications, 2007.

Colls, Keith, and Whitaker, Richard,. *The Australian Weather Book 2nd ed.* Sydney, 2001.

Commonwealth Department of Transport. *Survival at Sea*. Canberra, ACT: Australian Government Publishing Service, 1978.

Commonwealth Scientific and Industrial Research Organisation (CSIRO-MAR). *CSIRO fact sheet 35, White Sharks Filling the Gaps in Our knowledge*. 1999 йил May.

—. "Facts on Australia's Oceans." *CSIRO Marine*. n.d. www.marine.csiro.au/leafletsFolder/25.html (accessed September 1, 2004).

—. "Ocean Currents Around Tasmania." *CSIRO Marine*. n.d. www.marine.csiro.au/LeafletsFolder/12tas/12.html (accessed September 1, 2004).

—. *Summary of CMAR white shark tagging in Australian waters*. 2008. www.cmar.csiro.au/tagging/whitesharks/taggedsharks.html (accessed 2010 йил 5-July).

—. "The East Australian Current." *CSIRO Marine*. n.d. www.marine.csiro.au/LeafletsFolder/37eac/index.html (accessed September 1, 2004).

—. *White Sharks The Biology of White Sharks*. 2008. www.cmar.csiro.au/whitesharks/biology.html (accessed 2010 йил 5-July).

Conservation Council of South Australia (CCSA). *Great White Shark Information*. n.d. www.ccsa.asn.au/index.php?option=com_content&task=view&id=404&Itemid=594 (accessed 2010 йил 6-July).

Cooper-Preston, Harvey, and Robert W. G. Jenkins. "Natural History of the Crocodylia." *Fauna of Australia Vol. 2A*. 1993. www.environment.gov.au/biodiversity/arbs/publications/fauna-of-australia-2a.html (accessed October 1, 2010).

COSPAS–SARSAT. *COSPAS–SARSAT System Overview*. n.d. www.cospas-sarsat.org/en/system/systemoverview (accessed August 1, 2012).

Crawford's Mariners Atlas. *Apollo Bay to Jervis Bay*. Edited by D. H. Barrett. Bathurst: Crawford Publishing House, 1997.

—. *Jervis Bay to Port Stephens*. Adelaide: Crawford House Publishing, 2008.

—. *Port Stephens to Bundaberg*. Bathurst: Crawford House Publishing, 1996.

Crow, Steve. "A Bit About Boat Building." *Wavelength magazine Dec02/Jan03*, January 2003.

Cruz MD, Luzia S., MPH, Roberto Vargras MD, and MPH, PhD, Antonio, Alberto Lopes MD. "International Society on Toxinology—Global Snakebite Initiative." *The International Society on Hypertension in Blacks (ISHIB)*. 2009. http://www.ishib.orgwww.ishib.org/journal/19-1s1/ethn-19-01s1-42.pdf (accessed 2012).

Department of Environment, Water, Heritage and the Arts (DEWHA). *Great White Shark (Carcharodon carcharias)*. 2007. www.environment.gov.au/coasts/species/sharks/greatwhite/index.html (accessed 2010 йил 5-July).

Department of Military and Emergency Medicine. *The Navy SEAL Fitness Guide*. Edited by Patricia Deuster, Ph.D., M.P.H. Bethesda: Uniformed Services University of the Health Sciences (USU formerly USUHS), August 1997.

Dick, Margret. "Phytophthora Identification." *Frm Forestry New Zealand (FFNZ)*. Oct/Nov 2010. www.nzffa.org.nz/farm-forestry-model/the-essentials/forest-health-pests-and-diseases/diseases/Phytophthora/phytophthora-identification/ (accessed August 9, 2012).

Dick, Margret, and Tod Ramsfield. "Phytophthora Diseases of Trees." *Farm Forestry New Zealand (FFNZ)*. 9 August 2012. www.nzffa.org.nz/farm-forestry-model/the-essentials/forest-health-pests-and-diseases/diseases/Phytophthora/ (accessed August 9, 2012).

Dowd, John,. *Sea Kayaking A Manual for Long Distance Touring, 5th ed.* Vancouver, 2004.

Dr. Ellsworth, Abby. *Pilates Anatomy A Comprehensive Guide.* Heatherton, Victoria: Hinkler Books, 2009.

Dr. Fenner, Peter. *Marine Medic.* 2000. www.marine-medic.com.au/ (accessed June 9, 2005).

Dr. Fry, Bryan Grieg. "Taxonomy and toxinology of Australasian sea snakes." *The Australia & Pacific Science Foundation.* n.d. www.toxinology.com/fusebox.cfm?fuseaction=main.snakes.display&id=SN0606p (accessed August 20, 2012).

Dr. Neme, Laurel A. *Crafting Walrus Skin Boats.* 2008-2009. www.laurelneme.com (accessed February 11, 2010).

DuPont. "Dupont Kevlar Products." *DuPont Website.* 2009. www2.dupont.com/Kevlar/en_US/products/index.html (accessed 2009 йил 14-September).

Ehmann, Harold. "Family Boidae." *Fauna of Australia Vol. 2A.* 1993. www.environment.gov.au/biodiversity/arbs/publications/fauna-of-australia-2a.html (accessed August 9, 2012).

—. "Family Colubridae." *Fauna of Australia Vol. 2A.* 1993. www.environment.gov.au/biodiversity/arbs/publications/fauna-of-australia-2a.html (accessed August 9, 2012).

Eleftheriou, Kyriacos. "Canoing Injuries and Kayaking Injuries." *Sports Injury Bulletin.* n.d. www.sportsinjurybulletin.com/archive/canoeing-kayaking-injuries.html (accessed 2008 йил 8-June).

Epic Kayaks. *Wing-paddle.* www.epickayaks.com/extras/tips/equipment/wing-paddle (accessed 2009 йил 7-August).

Eyres, D.J. *Ship Construction.* 6th. Oxford: Elsevier, 2007.

Ferrero, Franko.,. *Sea Kayak Navigation.* Gwynedd, 1999.

Fisheries and Oceans Canada. *Fisheries & Oceans Canada.* 2012. www.dfo-mpo.gc.ca/index-eng.htm (accessed 2012).

—. *Tides, Currents, and Water Levels.* 2012. www.tides.gc.ca/eng (accessed July 1, 2012).

Fyfe, Peter W.,. *The Paul Hamlyn Instant Metric Reckoner,.* Edited by Judith Dine. Sydney, 1973.

Giancoli, D. C.,. *Physics: Principles with Applications, 5th ed.,.* Upper Saddle River, 1998.

Gillmer, Thomas C.; Johnson, Bruce. *Introduction to Naval Architecture.* Annapolis: Naval Institute Press, 1982.

Golden, Harvey. *Kayaks of Greenland The History and Development of the Greenlandic Hunting Kayak, 1600–2000.* Portland, OR: White House Grocery Press.

Gottfred, J. *Art. 1 On the Condtruction of Birchbark Canoes.* n.d. www.northwestjournal.ca (accessed February 15, 2010).

Graham, John. *Outdoor Leadership Technique, Common Sense & Self-Confidence.* Seattle: The Mountaineers, 2009.

Grigg, Gordon, and Carl Gans. "Morphology & Physiology of the Crocodylia." *Fauna of Australia Vil. 2A.* 1993. www.environment.gov.au/biodiversity/arbs/publications/fauna-of-australia-2a.html (accessed October 1, 2010).

Grinblat, Marcus. "Technical Marine Repeaters, How They Work." *Boatmaster* (Australian Volunteer Coast Guard), no. 4th Ed. (June 2007): 19-20.

Guillemot Kayaks. *Kayak Design.* 2012. www.guilemot-kayaks.com/guillmot/information/kayak_design (accessed August 2, 2012).

Haddock, C. *Managing Risks In Outdoor Activities, Mountain Safety Manual 27.* Edited by P. Wishart. Wellington: New Zealand Mountain Safety Council, 1993.

Harbour Dive. *Dive Sites—Popes Eye.* n.d. www.harbourdive.com.au (accessed October 28, 2004).

Harper, Douglas. *Online Etymology Dictionary.* 2001. www.etymonline.com (accessed 2008).

Harvey, Mark. *The National Outdoor Leadership Shool's Wilderness Guide.* New York: Fireside, 1999.

Headquarters Department of the Army. *Field Manual No. 21-76 Survival.* Washington, DC: Headquarters Department of the Army, 1992.

Heatwole, Harold, and Harold C. Cogger. "Family Hydrophiidae." *Fauna of Australia Vol. 2A.* 1993. www.environment.gov.au/biodiversity/arbs/publications/fauna-of-australia-2a.html (accessed August 9, 2012).

Heatwole, Harold, and Michael L. Guinea. "Family Laticaudidae." *Fauna of Australia Vol. 2A.* 1993. www.environment.gov.au/biodiversity/arbs/publications/fauna-of-australia-2a.html (accessed August 9, 2012).

International Satellite System For Search and Rescue. *International Cospas–Sarsat Programme.* n.d. www.cospas-sarsat.org/Description/satellites.htm (accessed June 22, 2009).

Isbister, Geoffrey K. "Snake bite: a current approach to management." *Australian Prescriber Vol. 29, No. 5.* October 2006. www.australianprescriber.com//magazine//29/5/125/9/# (accessed August 14, 2012).

Jason, Victoria. *Kabloona in the Yellow Kayak: One Woman's Journey Through the Northwest Passage.* Winnipeg, Manitoba: Turnstone Press, 1997.

Johnson, Shelley. *The Complete Sea Kayakers Handbook.* Camden: Ragged Mountain Press/McGraw-Hill, 2002.

Kermode, A. C. *Mechanics Of Flight.* 10th Edition. Harlow: Pearson Prentice Hall, 1996.

Kiwi Association of Sea Kayakers (KASK). *KASK New Zealand's National Sea Kayaking Body.* 2012. www.kask.org.nz/ (accessed June 10, 2012).

—. *The KASK Handbook A Manual For Sea Kayaking In New Zealand (LRB3), 3rd ed.* Edited by Paul Caffyn. Runanga, 2003.

—. *The KASK Handbook A manual for Sea Kayaking in New Zealand.* 4th Ed. Edited by Paul Caffyn. Runanga: Kiwi Association of Sea Kayakers, 2006.

Kosseff, Alex. *AMC Guide to Outdoor Leadership.* 2nd Ed. Boston: Appalachain Mountain Club Books.

Kruger, Verlen, and Frenz Brand. *The Ultimate Canoe Challenge 28 000 Miles Through North America.* New York: iUniverse, Inc., 2005.

Land Information New Zealand (LINZ)—Toitū te whenua. *Charts and Hydrographic Services.* 2011. www.linz.govt.nz/hydro (accessed September 9, 2011).

—. *Maps and Topographic Services.* 2011. www.linz.govt.nz/topography (accessed September 9, 2011).

Langewiesche, Wolfgang. *Stick and Rudder.* New York: McGraw-Hill, 1994.

Laughlin, Greg,. *The Users Guide to the Australian Coast.* Sydney: New Holland, 1997.

Lazaukas, Leo, and John Winters. "Hydrodynamic Drag of Some Small Sprint Kayaks." *www.cyberiad.net/library/kayaks/jwsprint/jwsprint.htm.* Dept Applied Mathematics Technical Report LW9701. 1997 йил 30-October. (accessed 2009 йил 24-April).

Lazauskas, Leo, John Winters, and E. O. Tuck. "Hydrodynamic Drag of Small Sea Kayaks." *Cyberiad.net.* 30 October 1997. www.cyberiad.net/library/kayaks/skmag.htm (accessed April 24, 2009).

Loganbill, J. *Skin Material for Frame and Skin Kayaks.* n.d. www.thewoodshop.20m.com (accessed January 19, 2010).

Lucas, Alan. *Cruising the New South Wales Coast.* 6th Edition. Point Clare, NSW: Alan Lucas Cruising Guides, 2010.

MacRitchie, David. "The Kayak in North-Western Europe." *The Journal of the Royal Anthropological Institute of Great Britain and Ireland* (Royal Anthropological Institute of Great Britain and Ireland) 42 (Jul.—Dec. 1912): 493-510.

Marchaj, C.A. *Sailing Theory and Practice.* New York: Dodd, Mead & Company, 1964.

Marine and Safety Tasmania (MAST). *General Safety.* 2012. www.mast.tas.gov.au/domino/

mast/mastweb.nsf/v-lu-all/General+Safety~Tri p+Preparation?OpenDocument (accessed July 31, 2012).

—. *Marine Communications*. Edited by t. 20. www.mast.tas.gov.au/domino/mast/mastweb. nsf/v-lu-all/Marine+Communications~Mari ne+VHF+Repeater+Network?OpenDocumen (accessed June 9, 2009).

Marine Conservation Branch Environment Australia (MCBEA). "White Shark (Carcharodon carcharias) Recovery Plan." *Marine Conservation Branch Environment Australia (MCBEA)*. 2002 йил July. www.environment. gov.au/coasts/publications/gwshark-plan/ pubs/greatwhiteshark.pdf (accessed 2010 йил 6-July).

Marine Safety Queensland. *Small Ships, Training and Operational Manual, 3rd. Ed.* Brisbane: Queensland Government, 2004.

Marine Safety Victoria (MSV). *Recreational Boating Vic.* 2004. www.marinesafety.vic.gov. au (accessed 2004 йил 1-July).

—. *Victorian Recreational Boating Safety Handbook*. Melbourne: Victorian Government, 2007.

Maritime and Coastguard Agency (MCA). *Leisure and Seaside*. 2012. www.dft.gov.uk/ mca/mcga07-home/leisurenandtheseaside.htm (accessed June 30, 2012).

Maritime New Zealand. *Maritime New Zealand*. 2012. www.maritimenz.govt.nz/default.asp (accessed July 1, 2012).

Maritime Safety Queensland (MSQ). "Queensland Recreational Boating and Fishing Safety Handbook." Vers. 2011-2012. *Maritime Safety Publications*. 2011. www.msq.qld.gov. au?publications.aspx (accessed August 3, 2012).

Marshall, Stuart. "Motion or Sea sickness— Some Suggestions." *www.melbsailing.com.au*. 2005 йил 7-December. (accessed 2008 йил 10-October).

Mather, F. G. "The Evolution of Canoeing." *LA84 Foundation*. 1885. www.la84foundation.

org/SportsLibrary/Outing/Volume_05?outV06b. pdf (accessed September 18, 2010).

Matthews, Clifford. *Engineers' Data Book*. 2nd Edition. London: Professional Engineering Publishing, 2000.

Mattos, Bill. *Kayaking & Advanced Canoeing A Practical Guide to Paddling on White Water, Open Water and the Sea*. London: Anness Publishing Ltd, 2004.

Mattos, Bill, and Jeremy Evans. *The Illustrated Handbook of Kayaking, Canoeing & Sailing*. London: Anness Publishing Ltd, 2007.

McGill Library. *The Birch Bark Canoe*. 2010. www.mcgill.ca/library/ (accessed February 15, 2010).

McGrouther, Mark. *Bull-Shark-Carcharhinus-leucas-Valenciennes-1839*. 2010 йил 27-September. http://australianmuseum.net.au/ Bull-Shark-Carcharhinus-leucas-Valenciennes-1839/ (accessed 1010 йил 4-October).

Meyer, Kathleen. *How to Shit in the Woods An environmentally sound approach to a lost art*. 3rd Ed. Berkely: Ten speed Press, 2011.

Molnar, Ralph E. "Biogeography and Phylogeny of the Crocodylia." *Fauna of Australia Vol. 2A*. 1993. www.environment.gov.au/biodiversity/ arbs/publications/fauna-of-australia-2a.html (accessed October 1, 2010).

Nansen, Fridtjof. *Eskimo Life*. 2nd. London: Longmans, Green and Co., 1894.

—. *Farthest North*. New York: Skyhorse Publishing, Inc., 2008.

National Geographic. *Bull Sharks*. 2010. http:// animals.nationalgeographic.com/animals/fish/ bull-shark/ (accessed 2010 йил 8-July).

National Geospatial-Intelligence Agency (NGA). "American Practical Navigator (Bowditch)." *NGA Marine Safety Information Publications*. n.d. http://msi.nga.mil/NGAPortal/MSI.portal?_ nfpb=true&_pageLabel=msi_portal_page_62 (accessed August 2, 2012).

—. "NGA List of Lights." *NGA Marine Safety Information Publications*. 2012. http://msi.nga. mil (accessed August 2, 2012).

—. "Pub. 175 Sailing Directions (Enroute) North, West, and South Coasts of Australia." *NGA Marine Safety Information Publications.* 2010. http://msi.nga.mil (accessed September 1, 2010).

—. "Sailing Directions Enroute." *NGA Marine Safety Information Publications.* 2012. http://msi.nga.mil (accessed August 2, 2012).

—. "Sailing Directions Planning Guides." *NGA marine Safety Information Publications.* 2012. http://msi.nga.mil (accessed August 2, 2012).

—. "U.S. Chart No. 1." *NGA Marine Safety Information Publications.* 2011. http://msi.nga.mil (accessed August 2, 2012).

National Imagery and Mapping Agency (NIMA). "Ch. 03 Nautical Charts." *The American Practical Navigator.* Bethesda: National Imagery and Mapping Agency (NIMA), 1995. pp.23-50.

—. "Ch. 09 Tides and Currents." *The American Practical Navigator.* Bethesda: National Imagery and Mapping Agency (NIMA), 1995. pp.143-164.

—. "Ch. 10 Radio Waves." *The American Practical Navigator.* Bethesda: National Imagery and Mapping Agency (NIMA), 1995. pp.165-177.

—. "Ch. 31 The Oceans." *The American Practical Navigator.* Bethesda: National Imagery and Mapping Agency (NIMA), 1995. pp.427-453.

—. "Ch. 32 Ocean Currents." *The American Practical Navigator.* Bethesda: National Imagery and Mapping Agency (NIMA), 1995. pp.435-441.

—. "Ch. 33 Waves, Breakers and Surf." *The American Practical Navigator.* Bethesda: National Imagery and Mapping Agency (NIMA), 1995. pp.443-453.

—. "Ch. 35 Weather Elements." *The American Practical Navigator.* Bethesda: National Imagery and Mapping Agency (NIMA), 1995. pp.483-503.

—. "The American Practical Navigator." *I'd Rather Be Sailing (irbs).* 1995. www.irbs.com/bowditch (accessed September 1, 2003).

National Sanitation Foundation (NSF). *About NSF.* n.d. www.nsf.org (accessed October 16, 2008).

National Tidal Facility (NTF). *Tides.* n.d. www.ntf.flinders.edu.au (accessed September 1, 2004).

Nelson, Anold G., and Jouko Kokkonen. *Stretching Anatomy Your Illustrated Guide to Improving Flexibility and Muscular Strength.* Champaign: Human Kinetics, 2007.

New Hampshire Historical Society. *Dugout Canoes.* n.d. www.nhhistory.org (accessed February 10, 2010).

New South Wales (NSW) Government. "NSW Maritime Boating Handbook." Vers. 2011-2012. *NSW Transport Maritime.* 2011. www.maritime.nsw.gov.au (accessed August 2, 2012).

New South Wales (NSW) Government. *NSW Coastline management manual Appendix B3 Storms.* September 1990. www.deh.gov.au/coasts/publications/nswmanual/appendixb3.html (accessed September 9, 2004).

—. *NSW Coastline Management manual Appendix B5 Waves.* September 1990. www.deh.gov.au/coasts/publications/nswmanual/appendixb5.html (accessed September 9, 2004).

—. *NSW Coastline Management Manual Appendix B6 Currents.* September 1990. www.deh.gov.au/coasts/publications/nswmanual/appendixb6.html (accessed September 9, 2004).

New South Wales Department of Industry & Investment, Fishing & Aquaculture (NSW DPI). *Identifying Sharks.* 2005. www.dpi.nsw.gov.au/fisheries/info/sharksmart/identifying-sharks (accessed 2010 йил 5-July).

—. *Identifying Sharks and Rays A Guide for NSW Commercial Fishers.* 2008. www.dpi.nsw.gov.au/fisheries/commercial/fisheries/otl-fishery/identifying-sharks-and-rays (accessed 2010 йил 5-July).

—. "Status of Fisheries Resourses in NSW 2006/07 Tiger Shark (Galeocerdo cuvier)." *New South Wales Department of Industry & Investment, Fishing & Aquaculture.* 2007. www.

dpi.nsw.gov.au/research/areas/systems-research/wild—fisheries/outputs/2008/972/status_short/Tiger-Shark.pdf (accessed 2010 йил 5-July).

New South Wales Sea Kayak Club (NSWSKC). *Key Documents.* 2012. www.nswseakayaker.asn.au/homepage/about-the-club/key-documents (accessed July 31, 2012).

—. "Policy Guidelines and Standard Operating Procedures." Sydney: New South Wales Sea Kayak Club, May 2007.

—. *Trip Leaders Briefing Guide.* n.d. www.nswseakayaker.asn.au (accessed August 2, 2012).

New Zealand Government Department of Conservation (NZDOC). "Great White Shark Identification Guide." *New Zealand Government Department of Conservation (NZDOC).* n.d. www.doc.govt.nz/upload/documents/conservation/native-animals/marine-fish/great-white-shark-identification-guide.pdf (accessed 2010 йил 5-February).

New Zealand Mountain Safety Council. *Managing Risks In Outdoor Activities, Mountain Safety Manual 27.* Edited by Pippa Wishart. Wellington, 1993.

New Zealand's Boating Website. *New Zealand's Boating Website.* 2012. www.boaties.co.nz/ (accessed June 10, 2012).

Northern Territory (NT) Government. "Safety Guide for Pleasure Craft, Edition 8." *NT Transport Group Marine Safety.* n.d. www.marinesafety.nt.gov.au (accessed August 3, 2012).

Our Hiking Blog. "Food to Go." *Our Hiking Blog.* n.d. http://ourhikingblog.com.au (accessed December 8, 2010).

Pacific Aviation. *Standard Aircraft Handbook.* 4th Ed. Edited by Larry Reithmaier. Aero Publishers Inc., 1986.

Paddle Canada. *Paddle Canada.* 2012. www.paddlingcanada.com/ (accessed July 19, 2012).

Parker, Steve, and Jane Parker. *The Encyclopaedia of Sharks.* Rev. London: Burlington Books, 2003.

Peterson, Philip SR. *All Things Are Possible The Verlen Kruger Story: 100,000 Miles by Paddle.* Cambridge, Minnesota: Adventure Publications, 2006.

Port of Melbourne Corporation. *Port of Melbourne Corporation.* n.d. www.portofmelbourne.com (accessed May 19, 2009).

—. *Westernport History.* n.d. www.portofhastings.vic.gov.au/Port-History/Western-Port-History.asp (accessed October 14, 2009).

Priest, Simon, and Michael A Gass. *Effective Leadership in Adventure Programming.* 2nd Ed. Champaign, IL: Human Kinetics, 2005.

Queensland Health. *General First Aid for Bites and Stings.* 30 October 2008. www.health.qld.gov.au/poisonsinformationcentre/bites_stings/bs_general.asp (accessed September 14, 2012).

—. *Pressure Immobilisation Technique.* 31 October 2008. www.health.qld.gov.au/poisonsinformationcentre/bites_stings/bs_pressure.asp (accessed September 14, 2012).

Reader's Digest. *Sharks Silent Hunters of the Deep.* 2nd Rev., 1st. Sydney: Reader's Digest, 1990.

RFSE. *Great White Shark Facts.* n.d. www.rodneyfox.com.au (accessed 2010 йил 7-July).

Robertson, D., and M. Simpson. "Review of Probable Survival Times in the North Sea." *Health and Safety Executive Off-shoreTechnology Report OTO 95 038.* Sheffield: Health and Safety Executive, January 1996.

Rock Island. "Floating Bodies—101." *rockisland.com.* n.d. http://cronus.rockisland.com/~kyak/floatbod.html (accessed June 2, 2009).

Romberg, Megan. "Spotlight on New Species of Phytophtora." *Farm Forestry New Zealand (FFNZ).* April 2010. www.nzffa.org.nz/farm-forestry-model/the-essentials/forest-health-pests-and-diseases/diseases/Phytophthora/spotlight-on-new-species-of-phytophthora/ (accessed August 9, 2012).

Royal Australian Air Force (RAAF). *Combat Survival Training Guide TG1.* Melbourne: Defence Publication Unit, 1997.

—. *Combat Survival Training Manual.* Melbourne: Defence Publication Unit, 1993.

Royal Australian Air Force (RAAF). "RAAF Adventourous Training." In *Ground Training*, by Training Command, 1-12. Melbourne: Defence Pulication Unit, 1995.

Sailing Issues. *Sea Sickness.* n.d. www.sailingissues.com/yachting-guide/seasickness . . . . html (accessed October 10, 2008).

Schade, Nick. *How a Paddle Works.* 2009. www.guillemot-kayaks.com/guillemot/information/kayak_design/how_a_paddle_works (accessed 2009 йил 20-August).

—. *Kayak Stability.* n.d. www.guillemot-kayaks.com/guillemot/information/kayak_design/kayak-stability (accessed 2009 йил 15-April).

Sea Kayaker Magazine. "Kayak Review Information." *Sea Kayaker Magazine.* June 2004. www.seakayakermag.com/PDF/Kayak_Review_Info_0609.pdf (accessed September 1, 2009).

Sea Kayaker Magazine. "Kayak Reviews 18X Sport by Epic Kayaks." Edited by Christopher Cunningham. *Sea Kayaker* 25, no. 126 (October 2008): 12–14.

Sea Kayaker Magazine. "Kayak Reviews Rapier 20 by Valley Kayaks." Edited by Christopher Cunningham. *Sea kayaker* 24, no. 118 (June 2007): 16–18.

Sea Kayaker Magazine. "Roy Grabenauer: Inventor of Sit-on-Top Kayaks." Edited by Christopher Cunningham. *Sea Kayaker* 21, no. 101 (August 2004): 28–29.

Sea Kayaking UK. *Sea Kayaking UK.* n.d. www.amsa.gov.au (accessed August 1, 2012).

Seluga, K. *Design: Requirements & Concepts.* 2009. www.rclandsailing.com/catamaran/design.html#hull (accessed October 17, 2009).

Services, Dept. Health & Human. "Health and Well Being Directory, cryptosporidiosis." *www.dhhs.tas.gov.au/service_information/information/cryptosporidiosis.* (accessed 2008 йил 16-October).

Sevareid, Eric. *Canoeing with the Cree A 2,250-mile voyage from Minneapolis to Hudson Bay.* Dexter, Michigan: Borealis Books, 2004.

Shark Research Institute, Inc. *Tiger Shark (Galeocerdo cuvier).* 2005. www.sharks.org.au/species.html#tiger (accessed 2010 йил 14-July).

Shea, Glenn, Richard Shine, and Jeanette C. Covacevich. "Family Elapidae." *Fauna of Australia Vol. 2A.* 1993. www.environment.gov.au/biodiversity/arbs/publications/fauna-of-australia-2a.html (accessed August 7, 2012).

Shine, Richard, and Darryl Houston. "Family Acrochordidae." *Fauna of Australia Vol. 2A.* 1993. www.environment.gov.au/biodiversity/arbs/publications/fauna-of-australia-2a.html (accessed August 9, 2012).

Short, Andrew D.,. *Beaches of the Victorian Coast & Port Phillip Bay.* Sydney, 1997.

Singh, PH.D., RD, Anita, M.S., Tamara L Bennett, and PH.D., M.P.H., Patricia A Deuster. *Peak Performance Through Nutrition and Exercise.* Bethesda: Department of Military and Emergency Medicine, September 1999.

Singh, PH.D., RD, Anita, Tamara L Bennett, M.S., and Patricia A Deuster, PH.D., M.P.H. *Force Health Protection: Nutrition and Exercise Resource Manual.* PDF. Bethesda: Department of Military and Emergency Medicine, September 1999.

South Australian Government (SAG). "South Australian Recreational Boating Safety Handbook." Vers. 1. *SAG Transport, Travel and Motoring / Boating and Marine.* Energy and Infrastructure (DTEI) SAG Department for Transport. June 2011. www.sa.gov.au/boatingmarine (accessed August 2, 2012).

State Emergency Service, Tasmania. *Map Reading Handbook.* 2nd Ed. Hobart, Tasmania: TASMAP, Dept of Environment and Planning, Tasmania, 1991.

State Government of Victoria. "Bursitis Fact Sheet." *Better Health Channel.* 2010. www.betterhealth.vic.gov.au (accessed September 17, 2010).

—. "Motion Sickness Fact Sheet." 2008. http://www.betterhealth.vic.gov.au/bhcv2/bhcarticles.nsf/pages/Motion_sickness (accessed 2008 йил 16-October).

Steinbright, Jan. "Qayaqs and Canoes: Native Ways of Knowing." *Education Through Cultural & Historical Organizations.* 2008. http://www.echospace.org/articles/273/sections/661 (accessed January 19, 2010).

Stejskal, Vaclav. "Ocean Kayak Built the Cedar Strip Way." *Ocean Kayaks Publication.* Edited by Maria Lane. Massachusetts, 2009.

—. "Stitch & Glue Sea Kayak." *Ocean Kayaks Publication.* Edited by Maria Lane. Massachusetts: One Ocean Kayaks, 2009.

Stormsurf.com. *Wave Basics.* n.d. www.stormsurf.com/page2/tutorials/wavebasics.shtml (accessed January 18, 2005).

Stranard, Kent, interview by Philip Woodhouse. *Information about White Sharks in Victoria* (2010 йил 2-July).

Surfline.com. *Surfology Index.* n.d. www.surfline.com/surfology/surfology_a2z_index.cfm (accessed September 29, 2004).

—. *Surfology Index.* n.d. www.surfline.com/surfology/surfology_index.cfm (accessed January 18, 2005).

Sutherland, Charles A. "The Loss of a Novice Sea Kayaker The Tradjic Consequence of an Unexpected Capsize." *Sea Kayaker*, December 2004: 42–45.

Tahtonka. *Woodland Nations.* n.d. www.tahtonka.com (accessed February 12, 2010).

Tasmanian Department of Primary Industries, Parks, Water and Environment. *Biosecurity Plant Health—Phytophthora.* n.d. http://www.dpiw.tas.gov.au/inter.nsf/ThemeNodes/LBUN-6XP7AY?open (accessed August 9, 2012).

The Canadian Encylopedia. "Inuit." *The Canadian Encylopedia.* Edited by Historica Foundation. n.d. www.thecanadianencylopedia (accessed 2010).

The Scout Association of New Zealand. *New Zealand Scout Handbook.* Wellington: The Scout Association of New Zealand, 1970.

The United Kingdom Hydrographic Office. *Admiralty Leisure Products.* 2012. www.ukho.gov.uk/ProductsandServices/Leisure/Pages/leisure-products.aspx (accessed June 10, 2012).

—. *Admiralty Nautical Paper Publications.* 2012. /www.ukho.gov.uk/ProductsandServices/PaperPublications/Pages/NauticalPubs.aspx (accessed June 10, 2012).

—. *Admiralty Paper Charts.* www.ukho.gov.uk/ProductsandServices/PaperCharts/Pages/Home.aspx.

—. *Maritime Safety Information.* 2012. www.ukho.gov.uk/ProductsandServices/MartimeSafety/Pages/Home.aspx (accessed June 10, 2012).

Transport Canada (TC). "BOATING: Imersion and Trauma Deaths in Canada: 18 Years of Reasearch." *Transport Canada Marine Safety PUBLICATIONS.* 2011. www.tc.gc.ca/eng/marinesafety/debs-obs-resources-publications-menu-696.htm (accessed June 9, 2012).

—. "BOATING: Immersion and Trauma Deaths in Canada: 16 Years of Research." *Transport Canada Marine Safety Publications.* 2010. www.tc.gc.ca/eng/marinesafety/debs-obs-resources-publications-menu-696.htm (accessed June 9, 2012).

—. *Cardinal Buoys and Special Buoys TP14542.* 19 January 2010. Transport Canada Marine Safety Publications (accessed June 9, 2012).

—. *Lateral Buoys and Standard Daybeacons TP14541.* 14 January 2010. Transport Canada Marine Safety Publications (accessed June 9, 2012).

—. "Safe Boating Guide TP 511E (2011)." *Transport Canada Marine Safety Publications.* 29 April 2011. www.tc.gc.ca/eng/marinesafety/tp-tp511-menu-487.htm (accessed June 22, 2012).

—. "Sea kayaking Safety Guide TP 14726." *Transport Canada Marine Safety Publications.* 19

January 2010. www.tc.gc.ca/eng/marinesafety/tp-tp14726-menu-1098.htm (accessed June 22, 2012).

—. "Survival in Cold Waters TP 13822." *Transport Canada Marine Safety Publications.* 2003. www.tc.gc.ca/eng/marinesafety/debs-obs-resources-publications-menu-696.htm (accessed June 9, 2012).

Transport Canada. "Rules of the Road TP 14352." *Transport Canada Marine Safety Publications.* 2009. www.tc.gc.ca/eng/marinesafety/debs-obs-resources-publications-menu-696.htm (accessed June 9, 2012).

Transport Safety Victoria (TSV). *Maritime Safety Recreational Users.* 2012. www.transportsafety.vic.gov.au/maritime-safety (accessed July 31, 2012).

—. "Victorian Recreational Boating Safety Handbook." *TSV Maritime.* November 2011. www.transportsafety.vic.gov.au (accessed February 19, 2012).

Tuck, E. O., and L. Lazauskas. "Low Drag Rowing Shells." *Cyberiad.net.* 2 October 1996. www.cyberiad.net/library/rowing/misbond/misbond.htm (accessed June 1, 2009).

Tudball, L., and R. Lewis. "Ten Canoes Study Guide." *Australian Teachers of Media Inc. (ATOM).* 6 June 2006. www.tencanoes.com.au (accessed April 14, 2009).

Turk, Jon. *Cold Oceans Adventures in Kayak, Rowboat and Dogsled.* Bloomington, IN: iUniverse, 2009.

U.S. Coast Guard (USCG). *U.S. Coast Guard Boating Safety Resource Center.* 13 October 2011. www.uscgboating.org/ (accessed June 24, 2012).

—. *U.S. Coast Guard Navigation Center.* 2012. www.navcen.uscg.gov/index.php (accessed June 24, 2012).

United Kingdom Maritime and Coast Guard Agency (MCA). *Leisure and the Seaside.* n.d. www.dft.gov.uk/mca/mcga07-home/leisurenandtheseaside.htm (accessed June 9, 2012).

—. *Weather and Tides.* n.d. www.dft.gov.uk/mca/mcga07-home/leisurenandtheseaside/mcga-bc-weather.htm (accessed June 9, 2012).

United Satates Navy (USN). *Aerograher's Mate Module 5—Basic Meteorology.* Prod. Rick Krolak. Pensacola: Naval Education and Training Professional Development and Technology Center, June 2001.

United States Marine Corps (USMC). *Land Navigation.* Quantico: USMC Marine Corps University (MCU), September 2001.

United States Navy (USN). "Aerographer's Mate 1 & C." *Meteorology.* Prods. B. J. Bauer and T. Howlett. Pensacola: Naval Education and Training Professional Development and Technology Center, September 1995.

United States Navy (USN). *Aerographer's Mate Module 1—Surface Weather Observations.* Prod. Stephen Volpe. Pensacola: Naval Education and Training Professional Development and Technology Center, April 1999.

United States Navy (USN). *Aerographer's Mate Module 2—Miscellaneous Observations & Codes.* Prods. Stephen M. Volpe and Daniel T. Hoffman. Pensacola: Naval Education and Training Professional Development and Technology Center, April 1999.

United States Navy (USN). "Aviation Weather Student Guide." *Preflight 2003 Student Guide For Preflight Aviation Weather.* Corpus Christi, Texas: USN Naval Air Training Command (NATRACOM), 2003.

Univeristy of Michigan Museum of Zoology (UMMZ). *Animal Diversity Web.* 2008. http://animaldiversity.ummz.umich.edu (accessed August 21, 2012).

University of Southern California (USC). *Deep Oceans.* n.d. http://earth.usc.edu/%7Egeol150/variability/deepocean.html (accessed June 7, 2006).

—. *Deep Water.* n.d. http://earth.usc.edu/~scott/Catalina/Deepwater.html (accessed June 7, 2006).

—. *Oceans.* n.d. http://earth.usc.edu/~scott/Catalina/Oceans.html (accessed June 7, 2006).

Venom Supplies Pty Ltd. *Dangerous Snakes of SA.* 2008. www.venomsupplies.com/dangerous-snakes/ (accessed August 14, 2012).

—. *Relative Toxicity.* 2008. www. venomsupplies.com/toxicity/ (accessed August 14, 2012).

Vikamus. *Virtual Kayak Museum (Virtuelles Kajakmuseum).* January 2011. www.vikamus.de/index_e.htm (accessed June 25, 2012).

Wadsworth, R. "Bush Camping and Code." *Department of Sustainability Victoria.* n.d. www.dse.vic.gov.au (accessed June 9, 2005).

Warring, R.H. *The Glassfibre Handbook.* King's Lynn, Norfolk: Special Interest Model Books Ltd, 2003.

Wavewalk, Inc. "Kayak Speed Basics, the Twinhull Advantages and the Principles of W Kayak Design." *Wavewalk.com.* February 2008. www.wavewalk.com/KAYAK_SPEED-ARTICLE.html (accessed April 1, 2009).

Waymire, J. "Dugout Canoes of the Peruvian Rainforest." *BioBio.com.* n.d. www.biobio.com (accessed February 3, 2010).

Weather Zone. *Glossary.* n.d. www.weatherzone.com.au/misc/glossary.jsp (accessed October 27, 2004).

Weiss, M.D., Eric A, and Michael Jacobs, M.D. *A Comprehensive Guide to Marine Medicine.* Oakland, CA: Adventure Medical Kits, 2005.

Western Australian Government (WAG). n.d. www.transport.wa.gov.au/imarine/15830.asp (accessed August 3, 2012).

White, Julian. "CSL Antivenom Handbook." Vers. 2nd Ed. *Clinical Toxinology Resources.* Commonwealth Serum Laboratories (CSL) Ltd. 2001. www.toxinology.com/generic_static_files/cslb_index.html (accessed August 14, 2012).

Wikipedia. *Great White Shark.* 2010. http://en.wikipedia.org/wiki/Great_white_shark (accessed 2010 йил 8-July).

Wilkie, Kellie. "Injury Prevention and Performance Optimization for Kayaking." *Sea Canoeing, Journal of the Tasmanian Sea canoeing Club*, 2005 йил September: 3-9.

Wilson, Neil. *The SAS Handbook of Tracking & Navigation.* 2002.

Winters, John. "Boat Design [33]." *New South Wales Sea Kayak Club Magazine.* 24 February 1998. www.nswseakayaker.asn.au/magazine/33/design.htm (accessed September 1, 2009).

—. "Controllability." *QCC Kayaks.* n.d. www.qcckayaks.com/resources/controllability.asp (accessed June 1, 2009).

—. *Kayak Design Seaworthiness & Stability.* n.d. www.seakayakers.org/stability.htm (accessed June 1, 2009).

—. *Kayak Design Volume.* n.d. www.seakayakers.org/tenpounds.htm (accessed June 1, 2009).

—. "Speaking Good Boat Part 1." *QCC Kayaks.* n.d. www.qcckayaks.com/resourses (accessed April 20, 2004).

—. "Speaking Good Boat Part 2." *QCC Kayaks.* n.d. www.qcckayaks.com/resources (accessed April 20, 2004).

—. *The Shape of the Canoe (Designing Canoes and Kayaks).* 3rd Ed. Kitchener, Ontario: Green Valley Boat Works, 2005.

—. *The Shape of the Canoe Part 1: Frictional Resistance.* n.d. www.greenval.com/shape_part1.html (accessed October 26, 2003).

—. *The Shape of the Canoe Part 2: Residual Resistance.* n.d. www.greenval.com/shape_part2.html (accessed October 26, 2003).

—. *The Shape of the Canoe Part 3: Applying the Theory.* n.d. www.greenval.com/shape_part3.html (accessed October 26, 2004).

Wiseman, John. *The SAS Survival Handbook.* 1986.

Withers, Philip C., and James E. O'Shea. "Morphology and Physiology of the Squamata." *Fauna of Australia Vol. 2A.* 1993. www.environment.gov.au/biodiversity/arbs/publications/fauna-of-australia-2a.html (accessed August 10, 2012).

Women's & Children's Hospital (WCH), Adelaide, Toxinology Department. *Clinical Toxinology Resources*. 2012. www.toxinology.com (accessed August 10, 2012).

—. "First Aid." *Clinical Toxinology Resources*. 2012. www.toxinology.com/fusebox.cfm?fuseaction=main.first_aid.firstaid&id=FAD-01 (accessed August 20, 2012).

WorkSafe BC. "Cold Water Can Kill." *Work Safe British Columbia*. n.d. www2.worksafebc.com/PDFs/fishing/cold-water-kill.pdf (accessed September 1, 2009).

—. "Cold Water Immersion." *Work Safe British Columbia*. n.d. www2.worksafebc.com/i/posters/2004/WS%2004_01.htm (accessed October 17, 2010).

Zimmerly, David. "An Illustrated Glossary of Kayak Terminology." *Canadian Museums Association Gazette*, 1976.

—. *Form Followed Function—And The Function Was Hunting*. www.arctickayaks.com. www.arctickayaks.com.

Zimmerly, David W. *Hooper Bay Kayak Construction*. Hull, Quebec: Canadian Museum of Civilization, 2000.

—. *Qayaq Kayaks of Alaska and Siberia*. Fairbanks: University of Alaska Press, 2000.

Zoological Museum Hamburg. *The reptile Database*. Edited by Peter Utez and Jakob Hallermann. n.d. www.reptile-database.reptarium.cz (accessed August 21, 2012).

GLOSSARY

General

Bag—Refers to a wide variety of bags used to stow equipment, clothing and supplies. Depending upon the material and or manufacturer they may or may not be waterproof. Types of bags used by sea kayakers are deck bag, dry bag, compression sack (e.g. for sleeping bag) and gear bags for carting equipment and supplies to and from the kayak.

Deck bag—Is a bag that is attached usually to the front foredeck. They are useful for holding items such as cameras, fishing gear and on-water snacks and drinks. Some paddlers are against the use of deck bags and are derogative towards those that do use them; but who cares what small-minded people think.

Compression bag—Is a cylindrical shaped gear bag that has straps sown on to the sides in order for the contents to be crushed down. They are ideal for your sleeping bag and clothing items like down jackets.

Dry bag—Is a sealable gear bag that is supposedly able to keep water out. They come in various sizes and are manufactured from a range of waterproof materials. The thicker plastic types are more ridged and possibly more durable than the softer rubberised/plasticised materials.

Gear bags—Are used for both day and over night kayaking. They need to be crushable so that they can be shoved into the ends of the boat or some space but do not take up valuable room in the holds on over night trips. Using something that has a dual function is ideal. Some people use a tarp (like a Santa sack) that also doubles as a shelter to carry their gear in from the kayak to the campsite. A common and functional cheap gear bag is the plastic strand woven *Raffia* bags—as used for storage—available in various sizes from Discount shops (e.g. Two Dollar shops). Experiment with the sizes but two medium size bags are often easier to carry than one large.

Boat—A vessel used for transport by water. It is constructed to provide buoyancy by excluding water and shaped to give stability and permit propulsion.

Bay paddling—Refers to paddling in enclosed waters for example Port Phillip Bay and Western Port in Victoria; Port Jackson, Sydney Harbour, Botany Bay, Jervis Bay, Brisbane Water, Port Stephens, NSW.

Bilge pump—Is a pump used to clear water from a kayak's cockpit. They may be either: fixed in place or a hand pump. The fitted types may be either: electrically or manually operated. The manually operated types may be either: foot operated or hand operated.

Electric bilge pump—Is typically a 500 GPM 12 volt electric bilge pump wired up to a 12 volt ~2 amp hour battery.

Foot pump—Is a foot operated bilge pump. There are several types of foot pumps used to empty a bilge of water. Some are modified hand bilge pumps while others are specifically designed to be foot operated.

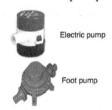

Electric pump

Foot pump

Hand pump—Is a hand operated bilge pump. The pump may be either fixed to the deck behind and to the side of the cockpit, or portable. Even if you have an electric bilge pump, you should carry a hand pump in an accessible place, as a back up.

Hand pump

Bilge pump battery—Is usually a 12 V 2 Ah sealed lead acid batteries but smaller 1.3 Ah (and 1.2 Ah depending upon brand) are used. See chapter on kayak ancillary systems.

Bungee cord—See shock cord.

Canoe—As a word, is a superordinate and therefore used by the author to represents human powered boats that are paddled as opposed to rowed. It includes but not limited to the hyponyms coracles, skis, open-canoes, out-rigger canoes, kayaks and sit-on-top kayaks.

Entomologically canoe is French for the Spanish *canoa*. Columbus introduced canoa to the West, from the Arawakan (Haiti) word *canaoua*, used to describe their dugout canoes. Kayak is from the Danish word *kajak*, which is from the Greenland Inuit word *qayaq*, literally 'small boat of skins' (Harper).

Canoeist—Is one that paddles a canoe. In some countries, namely Britain, it can refer to someone who paddles an open canoe or a kayak. In New Zealand, KASK refer to their club journal as 'The Sea Canoeist Newsletter'. In Tasmania, the 'Tasmanian Sea Canoeing Club' call their journal 'Sea Canoeing'. To remove ambiguity from the type of canoe paddled, many paddlers like to refer to themselves as *canoeists* for open-canoes, *kayaker* for kayaks, or *ski paddler* for skis. The type of environment the boat is paddled in also defines the type of craft; for example a white-water kayaker paddles a kayak designed for paddling through river rapids (white-water).

Canoe classifications terms—Nothing is straight forward.

Canoe freestyle—The type of kayaks used in this white water sport have a flatter hull and different volume displacement from the river runner kayaks allowing the participants more control and creativity in their 'gymnastic' routines.

Canoe marathon—Australian Classes of kayak used are the TK-1 single Touring Kayak, TK-2 double Touring Kayak, TC-1 single Touring Canadian and TC-2 double Touring Canadian. Measurements of the TK-1 are maximum length 4.572 metres and a minimum waterline beam of 0.508 metres; TK-2 maximum length 5.487 metres, minimum waterline beam 0.533 metres; TC-1 and TC-2 maximum length 5.03 metres, minimum waterline beam 0.712 metres.

Canoe polo—Events use small 3 m x 0.6 m kayaks that have a bluff bow to prevent/reduce injury to other players.

Canoe sailing—Events utilise specialised (open) canoes with principle diamensions of 5.18 m x 1.01 m, with a sail area 10 m^2.

Canoe slalom—Events use single kayaks (K1) and both single canoes (C1) and double canoes (C2). Slalom boats are required to meet minimum length and weight requirements with kayaks being restricted to a minimum 3.5 m x 0.6 m and a minimum weight of 9 kilograms.

Canoe sprint (aka *Flat-water racing*)—Events utilise K1, K2, K4 kayaks and C1, C2, and C4 canoes. The ICF recognises 'International Boats' as K1 kayaks measuring a maximum of 5.20 metres and wength 6.5 m, min. Weight 18 kg); and C1 (max. 5.2 m, min. weight 16 kg).

Wild-water canoeing (aka *Down-river racer*)—Utilises both kayaks and canoes. The kayak is a 4.5 m x 0.6 m distinctive 'diamond' shape, unstable rudderless kayak. The solo canoes measure 4.3 m x 0.7 m; the two-person whitewater canoes measure 5.0 m x 0.8 m.

Enclosed kayak—Is a term used to describe traditional style kayaks. It is used to distinguish a sit-on-top (open deck) from a kayak (enclosed deck with aperture).

Open-canoe—Refers to Canadian canoes, Wobbegong canoes, dugouts et cetera.

Ocean-going kayak—A kayak especially designed with a survival module (aka cabin) for undertaking ocean crossings. This is a seaworthy vessel designed to undertake extended voyages away from the coast. They are similar in concept to the ocean-going rowboats used on large crossings. For examples of such vessels see 'Lot 41' used to cross the Tasman Sea in 2007 and Peter Bray's kayak used to cross the Atlantic Ocean.

Ocean-going kayak

Recreational kayak—Means different things to different people. From an advertising perspective, it is a small (less than 4.5 m

OAL) kayak designed for paddling in sheltered waters such as rivers, dams and estuaries.

Wilderness Pungo 120 recreational kayak   Wilderness Tsunami 125 recreational kayak

Sea kayak—Is a boat that has a deck with an enclosed cockpit and is propelled by a person or persons using double or single bladed paddles. The design is based upon the Inuit/ Eskimo people's kayaks of the Artic Circle region. A sea kayak is a 'seaworthy kayak' that is designed to be operated in ocean conditions. It has the minimum features as described in this manual (e.g. greater than 4.5 m OAL) Other terms used to describe this type of kayak are *expedition kayak*, *sit-inside kayak* and *touring kayak*.

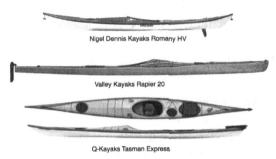

Nigel Dennis Kayaks Romany HV

Valley Kayaks Rapier 20

Q-Kayaks Tasman Express

Sit-in-side kayak—Is a term used to describe a traditional designed kayak as opposed to a sit-on-top kayak.

Sit-on-top kayak (SOT)—According to an article in *Sea Kayaker* magazine Roy Grabenauer, an American, is the inventor of the Sit-on-Top kayak.[1] In the 1950's in order to reach SCUBA diving spots, he fashioned aircraft wing fuel tanks as canoe hulls and put a deck on them with a cavity for his diving gear. By 1968 Roy had developed several versions of his SOT canoe and by 1970 was granted a patent number for his invention a 'self-bailing skin/scuba diver's float'. He then started *Royak Marine* and started to mass produce SOT kayaks known as *Royak*. The SOT is a very popular design of canoe with one retailer telling me that it is through the sale of SOT kayaks and not sea kayaks that he makes a profit. The advertisements for SOT kayaks, class their functions as recreational paddling, surfing, fishing and sea touring. Sit-on-tops have varied forms from wide stable platforms to narrow sleek touring kayaks. There is some comment about SOT kayaks not being a true kayak. Leaving the debate about form aside, the popularity of the SOT kayak has given rise to the term sit-inside-kayak. The possible reason why a SOT is called a kayak and not a canoe is because the paddler uses a double or single blade paddle to propel the craft, as one does in a *traditional* style kayak.

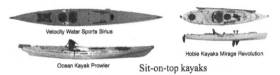

Velocity Water Sports Sirius

Hobie Kayaks Mirage Revolution

Ocean Kayak Prowler   Sit-on-top kayaks

Skis—Can be divided into two main categories of surf/racing/ocean ski and wave ski. The surf ski is also known as a racing ski and is used in Surf Life Saving club events, adventure racing and for general fitness. Racing skis are long and narrow thereby having a smaller wetted surface than a SOT kayak. Wave skis (aka 'goat boats') are used for surfing.

Fenn Mako ocean ski

Wave ski

Finn Endorfin surf ski

Touring kayak—Is a term that means different things to different people. Touring kayaks to some people are not 'sea kayaks' but to others the term includes sea kayaks. One classification of 'touring kayak' is kayaks, which have been generally designed for use on rivers, lakes, estuaries and bays. Like sea kayaks, people can and do camp from 'touring kayaks' and paddle them along the coast.

White-water boat—Play-boat and Rodeo-boats are small kayaks used to paddle white-water (rapids and moving water).

Carbine hooks—See snap hooks.

Cleats—Are used to fasten the running end of cordage. Two common types used on canoes and kayaks are the jamming cleat and the clam cleat.

Jamming & clam cleats

Deck compasses—May be either fixed to the deck or removable. For night time illumination some paddlers wire-up a light source. On removable deck compasses, a small chemical light stick can be inserted under the base for illumination.

Fairlead—A fitting used to guide a cable, rope or line in a particular direction and to prevent chaffing. It is also holds cordage in place though not so tight as to prevent its movement. Fairleads may be either fixed permanently into a structure or are removable. They are found around the deck's sides to hold the deck lines in place.

moulded deckline fairleads

Deckline fairlead styles

Penny washer

Farmer John wetsuit—Is a neoprene rubber wetsuit (aka *wetty*) between 3–5 mm thick. They are sleeveless and have long legs. Other types have short legs. Paddlers often have them modified with a 'relief zipper' at the front for urinating.

Footwear—Varies from wetsuit booties, sandals, 'Crocs', and runners. For people with feet smaller than a UK size 12 there does not seem to be any problem with the type of footwear worn while paddling. For those with big feet, the selection of footwear if worn is of importance in order to have foot clearance inside the cockpit. The surfboard booties do not have excess rubber around the heel and toes, thereby providing some clearance inside the cockpit from the deck underside. The drawback is when you walk on rocks, (especially with soaked feet) you feel the sharp protrusions. When wearing sandals, be aware that they may pose an entrapment problem on some style of foot pegs. In Tasmania, the outdoor guides on the SW coast have chosen to wear 'Crocs'. Sandals tend to trap abrasive particles that cut up the feet, which are continually wet. Wet feet do not heal quickly and the abrasions soon become infected. Crocs allow sand and pebbles to be easily dislodged from inside the shoe and stay on your feet when portaging through shallow water. A problem with Crocs is that they allow sharp long objects like thorns to pass through the sole and lodge there.

To remove sand that has dried and stuck to your feet, rub 'talcum powder' over your feet. This dries any moisture and allows the sand to be easily brushed off before getting fully into your tent.

International Canoe Federation (ICF) **disciplines**—Are Canoe Freestyle (aka Rodeo), Canoe Marathon, Canoe Polo, Canoe Sailing, Canoe Slalom, Canoe Sprint and Wild-water Canoeing (aka Down-river racing, Wild-water racing).

Kayak trolleys—Are useful devices used to portage kayaks. Trolleys usually have removable wheels, which can be stowed inside the kayak on day trips. For travel over soft sand, the pneumatic wheels are better suited than the ridged plastic wheels. Dave Winkworth designed and uses a set of cantilevered struts with wheels that fit into a receptacle on the side of the hull behind the cockpit. When not required, they are stowed on the aft deck. He uses this wheel arrangement on his 'Top End' paddles where there are meso and macro tides, which necessitate long portages to the water over intertidal areas. This type of trolley arrangement is provided by Nadgee Kayaks.

Kayak trolley

Nadgee Kayaks struts & wheels

Kayaker—One who paddles a kayak and the ultimate source of canoe stability.[2]

Munched—Is a metaphor describing a person (or item) being swallowed up by a wave and then being tossed about in a fashion akin to being masticated (chewed).

National Sanitation Foundation (NSF)—Has earned the Collaborating Centre designations by the World Health Organization (WHO) for Food and Water Safety and Indoor Environment. www.nsf.org

Paddle—A device used to propel a boat by a person using manual labour. Unlike oars that are pivoted on the gunwale or such structure, while paddles are kept free of the structure by the handler (paddler). Paddles may either be the single blade type or double bladed. There are many styles and forms of paddles to suit different sports and recreational pursuits. For double bladed paddles, they can vary from the classic Inuit style through to the modern 'Wing' blade style. The shafts can be straight or bent (cranked).

Paddle float—Is a buoyancy device that fits over the blade of a paddle. Paddle floats can be inflatable bags or solid cloth covered foam blocks. Paddle floats are used by many paddlers in North America. Like rudders, there are detractors who think that using a paddle float is anathema. An issue raised is 'what happens if you lose your paddle float?' People who do use a paddle float find them useful during self-rescue and can be used as an aid to performing a re-enter and roll.

Paddle leash—This is used to prevent a paddler from losing their paddle. Some people are against using them for fear of entanglement, in the leash if capsized, particularly in the surf. The leash may be any type of cordage, bungee cord, or a boogie board leash. The boogie board leashes adapted to be paddle leashes have the benefit of having the coiled cordage and therefore, less spare cordage lying around on the deck. The only drawback to a boogie board leash is the incessant noise, the hard plastic makes as it knocks against the deck.

Paddling—In this manual, refers to travelling in a canoe or kayak using either a double or single blade paddle. This is in contrast to propelling a boat with an oar (and oar lock device) i.e. *rowing*.

Paddler—Is a canoeist or kayaker, who uses either a double or single blade paddle. This is in contrast to a person rowing a boat using an oar i.e. a *rower*.

Pee bottle—An appropriately sized necked plastic bottle for peeing in. It is better than peeing in your pants or having to land. For females, there are funnel arrangements that can be employed.

Penny washers—Re washers that (subjectively) have a ¾ inch or greater diameter (e.g. a Grade 316 Imperial flat washer with a 3/16 inch inside diameter hole and available with an outside diameter between ¾–1 ¼ inches. Their greater outside diameter spreads the torque loading of the nut and bolt/screw over a greater area thereby reducing the stress concentration at the fastener.

Personal flotation device (PFD)—Provides additional buoyancy to a person in the water. In Victoria, there are three types of PFDs. PFD Type 1 is a recognised lifejacket. A PFD Type 1 will provide a high level of buoyancy and keep the wearer in a safe floating position. They are made in high visibility colours with retro-reflective patches. PFD Type 2 is a buoyancy vest—not a life jacket. It will provide less buoyancy than a PFD Type 1 but is sufficient to keep your head above water. Like Type 1 PFDs they are manufactured in high visibility colours. Type 3 PFDs are a buoyancy garment—

Type 1 PFD

Type 2 PFD

not a lifejacket. The have similar buoyancy to a Type 2 PFD. Refer to you state government or government marine safety website to ensure you have an appropriate PFD. For Victorians refer to the MSV VRBS handbook for a list of Australian and International PFD Standards.

When wearing your PFD, ensure the buckles are fastened and the straps done up. The reason for this is that if you end up in the water, a loose fitting PFD will ride up and make moving around in the water difficult. In the worst-case scenario, the 'swimmer' could slip out of the PFD. In the surf zone, a PFD makes it difficult to dive under on-coming waves. However, when surfing and an out of control kayak slams into your chest, the PFD does help protect your ribs.

Podded seat—Is a term used to describe the kayak seat backrest that forms the bulkhead behind the cockpit.

Rand—Is the name given to the elastic edging of a spray skirt that is used to hold the skirt in-place around the cockpit coaming.

Rare earth magnets—Feature a rear earth compounds combined with ferrite (anisotropic) to produce a very strong magnetic attraction/repulsion. They are encased in nickel jackets to protect the very brittle internal compounds.

Recreational paddler—Is a person who does not participate in International Canoe Federation canoe disciplines. Australian Canoeing classes sea kayakers as part of the recreational paddler category. Therefore by default a sea kayak becomes a recreational kayak!

Rescuee (aka *swimmer*)—Is a canoeist that has wet exited their kayak and needs assistance to re-enter.

Rescue knife—Is carried on the PFD and is useful to cut cordage and fishing line. Some people like to carry a stainless steel sheath/dive knife fastened to their PFD. If you choose a knife avoid the ones with a sharp point and look for a rescue style round tip. I prefer a folding pocketknife carried inside the PFD pocket.

Shock cord (aka *bungee cord*)—Is elasticised (rubber strands protected by an outer material sheath) cordage. It is used to secure items to the deck of a kayak as well as for paddle leashes and the return spring for rudder pedals on some foot control pedals.

Shock cord hooks (aka *bungee hooks*)—There are different types of hooks with differing means of securing the hook to the bungee cord. One type

(e.g. *quick connect shock cord hooks*) is designed to fit over the running end of bungee cordage, with a locking ring designed to compress the tangs into the cord. As the bungee cord ages and with repeated usage the locking mechanism tends to fail. Using this type of fitting is useful on the paddle leash, as it can be made to fail by pull hard on the paddle. Another type of hook has an eyelet so that you can whip or use a zip-tie to secure the running end of the bungee cord.

Shock cord olive cleats—Are available in different sizes to suit different diameter bungee cord. They are a useful means of securing items to a deck with bungee cord.

Sister clips—Are a useful simple clip used to attach items to your kayak or PFD. You can get them in stainless steel or nylon in various sizes. They are often used to secure flags to the hauling lanyard.

Skirt—See spray skirt.

Snap hooks (aka *carbine hooks*)—There are several varieties of snap hooks and clips available for use by paddlers. Some people do use aluminium climbing carabineers but they corrode. Useful snap hooks and clips are made from stainless steel or nylon and are available from chandleries. Some retailers distinguish carbine hooks from snap hooks and others class carbine hooks as snap hooks. When choosing a snap hook for a towline using thin cordage, be aware that the gates receptacle on carbine hooks can catch and foul the cordage. You are best to choose a snap hook that has a wire gate.

Sponge—Is used to mop up water that the pump cannot scavenge. Commonly used are the types used to wash a car. Often only half of this type of sponge is carried. One method employed to prevent the sponge being lost in event of capsize, is to put it inside a small mesh gear bag.

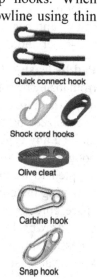

Quick connect hook

Shock cord hooks

Olive cleat

Carbine hook

Snap hook

Sister clips

Spray skirt (aka *spray deck, spray cover, spray apron, skirt*)—Is worn by the paddler and have the function of preventing the cockpit from becoming flooded. They are made from a variety of materials with neoprene rubber being quite common.

Stainless steel—
Used for marine application comes from the *Austenitic* 300 series range. Two series of 300 stainless steel used in hardware (i.e. nuts, bolts and washers) are 304 and 316 stainless steel. The difference between 304 and 316 is Type 304 contains 18 per cent chromium and 8 per cent nickel. Type 316 contains 16 per cent chromium, 10 per cent nickel and two per cent molybdenum. The molybdenum (aka 'moly') is added to help resist corrosion to chlorides such as seawater and de-icing salts. Type 316 possessing excellent corrosion and pitting resistance and is chosen for applications requiring corrosion resistance superior to Type 304.

For stainless steel to be effective, the metal must contain greater than 10.5 per cent chromium (Cr). The chromium reacts with the oxygen in the air and forms an invisible but protective chrome-oxide surface layer. Higher levels of chromium and or the addition of the elements nickel (Ni) enhance the protective surface layer to improve corrosion resistance (oxidation), while adding molybdenum (Mo) increases the metals resistance to pitting corrosion. If you have rust staining on a stainless steel item it is most likely from iron (Fe) particles trapped on the surface. This can be easily removed with a commercial product from a hardware store.

The 'L' suffix (e.g. 304L and 316L) refer to the metals carbon content and the ability for the material to be welded and maintain corrosion resistance at the joint. The old designators for stainless steel were for example: 18/8 and 18/10. The higher the numbers, the higher the corrosion resistance of the steel. These designators referred to the amount of chromium and nickel alloyed with the iron, to make the stainless steel. Type 18/8 is the same as Type 304 and 18/10 refers to Type 316. If you come across products (e.g. a divers knife) be aware that there are different grade of stainless steel. For example, Type 400 series stainless steel does not contain nickel (Ni) and is not as corrosion resistant as the Type 300 series stainless steels. Simplistically, Type 300 contains nickel and is not magnetic, while Type 400 series does not contain nickel and is magnetic.

Swatted—Is a metaphor used to describe someone who has had a large wave collapse on them. It is a metaphor of a fly swatter coming down and hitting a bug.

Swimmer—A person who is out of their boat in the water. Not necessarily a rescuee as they may be capable of self-rescue.

Trangia® cooking set—Is a popular cooking set that can use either gas or methylated spirits. The advantage of just using methylated spirits is there is no issue with foreign bodies damaging seals or blocking jets. However, they are slow to boil water in winter using methylated spirits. To prevent liquid fuel leaking out of the burner when packed up, use a small plastic container to hold the burner.

Trashed—Is a term used to describe a person (or item) being cast aside, treated as 'worthless' and left exhausted by the environment. Possibly happens after being swatted then munched by a large swell set in the surf zone.

Weekend paddler—Is a recreational paddler who predominately paddles sea kayaks on a weekend and or possibly during the week. They are also known as *recreational paddlers*.

Earth Sciences & Navigation Terminology

Amprodromic point—Is the point on a tide chart where the cotidal lines meet.

Atmospheric equilibrium—Is when light air is above heavy air. The weight of air varies with air temperature and moisture content. When comparing two parcels of air, warm air is less dense (lighter) than cold air, and moist air is lighter than dry air. If the air is relatively warmer or moister than its environment, it is forced to rise and is unstable.

Atmospheric instability—Is referred to as unstable air, front or conditions. Unstable air is less dense than the surrounding air in its environment and therefore rises, creating turbulent air. If the rising parcel of air contains enough moisture, condensation will occur and clouds will be formed. The condensation releases heat, which warms the air parcel causing the air to rise further. This process is how cumulonimbus cloud and thunder storms form.

Atmospheric stability—The atmosphere has a tendency to resist vertical motion, which is known as stability. The normal flow of air tends to be horizontal. Normally in the atmosphere, if an air parcel rises, it will be colder and denser than the surrounding air, and will sink back down again. Stable air has a tendency to resist vertical movement and return to equilibrium.

Backing—According to international usage is when the wind changes direction in a counter clockwise direction (e.g. northerly to westerly, westerly to southerly, southerly to south-easterly, or easterly to north-easterly etc.). According to widespread usage among U.S. meteorologists, a change in wind direction in a counter clockwise sense in the Northern Hemisphere, clockwise in the Southern Hemisphere; the opposite of veering (AMS, 2000).

Blue water (aka *open water*)—Refers to paddling in coastal waters (i.e. Pacific Ocean, Tasman Sea, Southern Ocean and Bass Straight).

Bombora—Australian Aboriginal for a dangerous current over a hidden reef. Has come to mean a submerged rock or reef and colloquially known as a *bombie*.

Brown water—Refers to paddling on rivers and inland lakes.

Cable—Refers to one tenth of a nautical mile and equals about 200 metres. This term is still used in The Australian Pilot.

Cardinal points—Refers to the compass points of north, south, west and east. The divisions form four quadrants on a compass circle.

Half cardinal points—Consist of four further divisions to the cardinal points. They are northeast, southeast, northwest and southeast.

Intermediate points—Consist of eight further compass divisions. Two per cardinal point quadrant. For example north-north-east, south-south-west.

By-points—Consist of a further sixteen compass divisions. Four per Cardinal point quadrant. For example, north-by-east, northeast by north. Each by-point represents 11.25 degrees of arc.

Cold water—Is defined by the USCG as water with a monthly mean temperature of 15 degrees Celsius (59 °F) or less. Cold water conditions in Victorian waters in winter can be around 11 degrees Celsius in Port Phillip and 13 degrees Celsius in the ocean.

Cold water breathing rate—Refers to the increase in respiration while exposed to cold water. A person who can hold their breath for 60 seconds in normal circumstances can be reduced down to 25–20 seconds and even 10 seconds. Breathing rate can be four times quicker than normal.

Cospas-Sarsat satellite constellation—Is composed of search and rescue satellites in low Earth orbit (LEOSAR) and geostationary orbit (GEOSAR). LEOSAR Satellite Constellation has a nominal system configuration of four satellites; two Cospas and two Sarsat. Russia supplies two Cospas satellites placed in near-polar orbits at 1000 kilometres altitude and equipped with SAR instrumentation at 406 MHz. The USA supplies two NOAA meteorological satellites placed in sun-synchronous, near-polar orbits at about 850 kilometres altitude, and equipped with SAR instrumentation at 406 MHz supplied by Canada and France. Each satellite makes a complete orbit of the Earth around the poles in about 100 minutes, travelling at a velocity of 7 kilometres per second. The satellite views a 'swath' of the Earth of approximately 6000 kilometres wide as it circles the globe, giving an instantaneous 'field of view' about the size of a continent. When viewed from the Earth, the satellite crosses the sky in about 15 minutes, depending on the maximum levation angle of the particular pass (International Satellite System For Search and Rescue, 2009).

Co-tidal—Refers to tides occurring at the same time.

Downslope winds—Occur on the leeside of mountains and are a common phenomenon around the world. The well known downslope winds are the *fÖhn* in Alpine Europe, the *mistral* of the northern Mediterranean coast, the *zonda* of Argentina and the *Chinook* of North America. In Australia two well known downslope winds are the *Adelaide gully wind* and the *scarp wind* of Perth. These winds can gust to 185 kilometres per hour (99.892 knots) with the Adelaide gully wind recording gusts up to 110 kilometres per hour (59 knots).

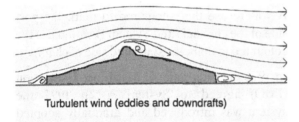

Turbulent wind (eddies and downdrafts)

Downslope winds are similar to katabatic winds in that gravity is the driving force. However it is the synoptic pressure gradient (i.e. a synoptic wind) that is the prime mover to start their movement. There are various theories about downslope winds. One is that an air mass close to the ground, on the weatherside of a range of mountains/hills, is forced up the slopes and over the mountain/hills crest, by a synoptic wind. This cooler and denser air, once over the crest of the ranges, gathers momentum as it flows down the leeside under the force of gravity and rapidly increases speed. Accompanied by the synoptic wind that forced it to move.

Earth axis—Is tilted at 66.5 degrees to the path it tracks around the sun in one year. At midsummer the South Pole is tilted at 23.5 degrees towards the sun. This results in the sun's rays shining perpendicularly on latitude 23.5 degrees south and not the equator. The reverse happens in the Northern Hemisphere's midsummer.

Eddies—In water are counter flowing currents, or whirlpools, near shoals, projecting headlands, near shores of straights and channels, including banks of rivers.

In the atmosphere, the term refers to turbulent counter flowing air currents associated with the wind speed, steepness and roughness of the terrain, cliffs and the leeside of features such as hill/mountain peaks. Onshore winds colliding with a cliff face may develop a reverse flow (aka *separation bubble,* or *eddies*), which extends back approximately half the cliff height. Offshore winds flowing over a cliff may create a reverse flow pattern (i.e. eddies), whose length extends out from the cliff, up to four times the height of the cliff. In both cases strong gusts of wind can travel opposite to the prevailing winds. These gusts may capsize a paddler.

Enclosed waters—Are areas defined by relevant government organisations. For example in Victoria, the Victorian Recreational Boating Safety Handbook, defines Port Phillip Bay and Western Port as enclosed waters.

Ellipsoidone—Is a shape, which bulges around the equator. The circumference of the earth at the equator is 24,901.55 miles (40 075.16 km). But if you measure the earth through the poles the circumference is a bit shorter at 24,859.82 miles (40 008 km). The earth is a slightly wider than it is tall, giving it a slight bulge at the equator. This shape is known as an ellipsoid or more properly, geoid (earth-like).

Equatorial trough (aka *intertropic convergence zone* (ITCZ))—Is a quasi-continuous belt of low-pressure situated between 30° S or 30° N (i.e. subtropical high-pressure belts of Southern and Northern Hemispheres). Described as possessing very homogenous air but high humidity. If the highly humid air experiences slight variations in stability, it causes major variations in weather. The position of the equatorial trough is fairly constant in the eastern portions of the Atlantic and Pacific, but it varies greatly with seasonal changes in the western portions of those oceans and in southern Asia and the Indian Ocean. It migrates into or toward the summer hemisphere (AMS, 2000).

Fathom—Is a measure of six feet. The term can still be seen on old Admiralty charts prior to the advent of metric measures on charts.

Flat water—For sea kayaking is wind conditions less than Beaufort scale Force 3 (less than or equal to 10 knots) producing a calm (mirror sea) to a smooth sea of wavelets.

Freshets—Occur when a river's flow meets tidal water. The outgoing stream will naturally run longer and stronger than the ingoing stream. It is also amplified when the river is swollen with recent rains. When backed by a river's current, the outgoing stream at half-ebb can be very strong, particularly during spring tides.

Furious Fifties—See Roaring Forties.

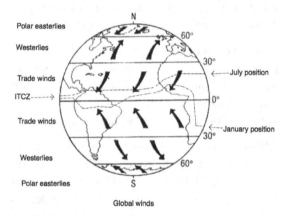

Global winds

Global winds—Consist of Polar highs, Temperate latitude low-pressure systems, Westerlies, Subtropical anticyclones, Trade winds, Intertropical Convergence Zone (ITCZ).

High-latitude—The area between 55° S and the South Pole and 55° N and the North Pole.

High-pressure systems—Generally form in one of two ways: by convergence and decent of upper atmosphere cold dense air; or by movement of cold dense air in to layers of lower relatively warm air creating *highs, or cold highs*. A high-pressure system is also known as an *anticyclone, high*. On a synoptic chart high-pressure systems are annotated by the capital letter H. Depending upon their location they may be referred to as subtropical anticyclones, subtropical highs, mid-latitude highs or highs (located between latitudes 30° S – 40° S and 30° N – 40° N, see mid-latitude), and Polar highs.

Indian springs low water (ISLW) (aka *Indian tide plane*, *harmonic tide plane*)—Is the low water datum, on relevant charts, that include a portion of the spring effect of a semi-diurnal tide and the tropic effect portion of a diurnal tide. It is considered to be about the level of lowest normal low water (aka lowest low water) of mixed tides at the time when the moon's maximum declination coincides with the time of the full or new moon.

International Association of Lighthouse Authorities (IALA)—Was formed in 1957 and was used to address the conflicting and confusing maritime navigation rules. By 1971 it was decided to combine the Lateral and Cardinal rules, and define how the colours red and green were to be used in defining channels. The approach taken was to develop two navigation systems called System A and System B. System A was to use the colour red to mark the port side of the channels and System B would use the colour red to mark the starboard side of channels.

In 1976 the International Maritime Association (IMO) agreed to System A. In 1977 the system was introduced and gradually adopted throughout Europe, Australia, New Zealand, Africa, the Gulf and some Asian countries.

By 1980 the rules for System B were developed and adopted by North, Central and South America, Japan, Republic of Korea and the Philippines. Since the System A and System B rules were so similar, with exception to the marking of channels as either red or green to port, they were combined by the IALA executive committee. In November 1980, they were agreed to by the 50 country members of the IALA. These combined rules are known as 'The IALA Maritime Buoyage System (MBS)'. This single set of rules allows Lighthouse Authorities the choice of using either red to port or red to starboard, on a regional basis. The two regions being known as Region A and Region B. All other aspects (rules for lateral, cardinal, danger, special buoys) of the IALA Maritime Buoyage System are the same in both Regions 'A' and 'B'. In 2010 the MBS rules were revised with the only major changes being the addition of Aids to Navigation.

Intertropic convergence zone (ITCZ)—See equatorial trough.

Ionosphere—Is the part of the Earth's atmosphere that lies approximately 80 to 350 kilometres above the Earth's surface.

Lee shore—The shore on to which the wind is arriving. However, if you are on the weather shore (also termed windward) and sheltered from the wind, you are said to be in the lee. The Bowditch glossary of marine navigation defines lee shore *'as observed from a vessel, the shore towards which the wind is blowing'.* See weather shore.

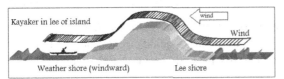

Lightening—Is the electrical discharge produced when voltage differences, between the ground and atmospheric electrical charge, is large enough (i.e. several hundred million volts) to overcome the insulating effect of air. Strikes can occur within the cloud, between clouds, or between clouds and the ground. Thunder is the sound produced by the explosive expansion of air heated by the lightning stroke to temperatures as high as 30 000 °C. lightening bolts on average possess a current of 10 000 to 30 000 amps. World wide there are approximately 6000 lightening strikes every minute. Lightening can and does strike more than one in one place. If struck by lightening the heart and breathing are often affected. Only about 30 per cent of people struck die, with the incidence of long-term disability being considered low.

Low-latitude—Is the area between the equator and 30° S or 30° N.

Lowest normal low water (aka *lowest low water*)—Is a datum that approximates the average heights of monthly lowest low water tides under normal conditions (e.g. data not disturbed by storm action etc.). This is an extremely low datum and conforms generally to the lowest tides observed or even lower.

Low-pressure system (aka *depression, cyclone* or *low*)—Is formed in two ways: cold air or warm air. Cold air low-pressure systems are predominant in high and mid-latitudes. They are referred to as *temperate cyclones, extra-tropical cyclones*. They are also referenced in regard to their latitude: *mid-latitude depressions.* Warm air cyclones are predominantly found in the low latitudes. They are referred to as *tropical cyclones, heat lows, cut-off lows* and *monsoon depressions.* On a synoptic chart low-pressure systems are annotated by the capital letter L.

Mid-latitude—Is the area between latitudes 30° S – 55° S and 30° N – 55° N.

Overfalls—Are most turbulent with steep breaking pressure waves. Tide races and overfalls are more hazardous with the presence of wind and or swell. Tidal stream strength and turbulence will be greatest at spring tides (i.e. at or after new moon and full moon), and minimum at neap tides. New moon tides are often more extreme than full moon tides. If the tidal range is greater than normal (i.e. perigee), the rate will roughly increase proportionally. Some turbulence only occurs on a flood and not the ebb, or vice versa, or only on a weather tide. This is where local knowledge is vital.

Pneumatophores—Are erect roots like those found in mangroves. They form upward appendages or extensions from the underground root system. The soil (mud) in mangroves is anaerobic (oxygen poor) and plants have developed a mechanism whereby the roots can obtain oxygen when the pneumatophore is exposed to the air.

Polar highs (aka *polar easterlies*)—Are situated around 60 degrees latitude in both hemispheres. The prevailing westerlies join with polar easterlies. Sinking very cold air from the troposphere reaches the surface and spreads out resulting in easterly winds around high-pressure systems. Winds are named from the direction they come from; and easterlies turn away to the west, through Coriolis effect.

Reef—A formation with less than 16 fathoms; 30 metres of water covering it.

Roaring Forties and the *Furious Fifties*—Are terms often applied to the strong westerly winds, which are experienced over the mid-latitudes of the Southern Hemisphere (i.e. 40° S and 50° S).

Severe thunderstorms—Are defined by the BOM as ones that produce: *hail, diameter of 2 cm or more ($2 coin size); or wind gusts of 90 km/h* (Storm force winds, Beaufort scale 10, 48.5–55 knots) *or greater; or flash floods; or tornadoes, or any combination of these.* These storms are localised events and usually affect smaller areas the tropical cyclones. These storms are more common than any other natural hazard, and can occur anywhere in Australia. Measured in terms of insurance, they are responsible for more damage than tropical cyclones. They are responsible for between 5 and 10 deaths per year by lightening strike with many more being injured or killed by falling/flying debris, and small boats in open water capsizing. Tornadoes are also associated with thunderstorms.

Storm surge—Is associated with tropical cyclones and can produce coastal flooding. The effect of the bathymetry and shallowness of the water for the waves to 'feel bottom', and the presence of reefs modify the waves and creates differing effect for different locations. Other factors that determine the impact of storm surge are the: intensity of the cyclone, forwards speed of the cyclone, angle at which the cyclone crosses the coast, and local topography such as bays, islands, and headlands, which can amplify the winds, and low lying land. The worst impacts occur when the cyclone arrives with tidal high water. The largest storm surge measured in Australia was seven metres in 1923, from cyclone *Douglas Mawson*. An unofficial record was in 1899, when cyclone *Mahina* produced an estimated 14 metre surge at Bathurst Bay. In Bangladesh 1970, a severe tropical cyclone caused a storm surge killed over 300 000 people.

Storm tide—Is the combination of storm surge and normal tide.

Subtropical anticyclones—Are areas of high pressure located approximately between 30° S – 40° S and 30° N – 40° N. These mean surface winds are light and variable.

Surf—Refers to breaking waves at a beach. In Australia, it is measured from the back of the breaker, which is from behind the waves crest down to the following trough. The face of the breaker is generally estimated to be 1.5 times the height of the back of the wave. In reports, the height expressed is for the average 33 per cent of breakers. However, it is acknowledged that some references estimate the height as high as five times the back of the wave's height, depending upon a multitude of factors (e.g. gradient of sea floor, offshore wind and wave period).

Surface low—Is a low-pressure area whereby the isobars do not enclose the area of low-pressure.

Synoptic scale (aka *Macroscale circulation*)—Refers to the large-scale circulation of air around high-pressure and low-pressure systems.

Temperate low latitude low-pressure systems—Are located around 60° S or 60° N and are regions of variable winds converging into low-pressure areas. They are often 'anchor points' of fronts. (Colls & Whitaker, 2001)

Tide-rip—Refers to an area of swift moving water under tidal influence.

Tide race—Refers to turbulence and white caps within swift moving water under tidal influence.

Tideway—Refers to channels with shoals on each side, created by the action of a tidal stream. The water in between is known as a tideway. Tidal streams run faster in deep or narrow channels.

Toxicology—Is the study of manmade poisons or toxins.

Toxinology—Is the study of natural poisons and toxins.

Topographic winds—Are topographically generated winds called *katabatic winds*, and are the result of temperature differences caused by local topography such as mountains or hilly regions. They are strongest during anticyclonic weather. Katabatic winds develop when the sun heats the sides of mountains/hills and the valley floor/plains below. The air above between the valley walls is cooler than the ascending warm air. The air pressure on the valley floor is greater than the pressure on the slopes, thereby causing the warm air to flow up the slopes. This upslope airflow is called *anabatic wind*. The air flowing up the slopes is replaced by the cooler air above the valley sinking down into the valley, in order to create and maintain a closed flow circulation of raising and sinking air.

Now considering a horizontal aspect, in the Southern Hemisphere the north facing slopes receive more direct sun than south facing slopes. In the afternoon depending upon the steepness of the valley walls, west-facing slopes receive more sun than east facing slopes. The net effect of the above described vertical airflow and topography, results in higher air temperatures within the valley compared to air at the same altitude on a plain or further down a valley. This temperature differential will cause a pressure gradient that will create an up-flow wind along the valley. This is known as a *valley wind*. The up-flowing wind is superimposed on the

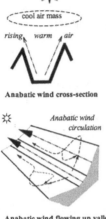

Anabatic wind cross-section

Anabatic wind flowing up valley

Katabtic wind flowing down valley

anabatic wind. To maintain continuity the up-flowing air is replaced and a general circulation cycle is set up.

At night there is a reversal of the above anabatic wind process. At night, when the valley slopes and floor cools, the air descends under its own weight of gravity back down the slopes. The downslope flow is termed a *katabatic wind*. The cooler air above and between the valley walls flows towards the slopes to replace the downslope wind. The downslope wind interacts with the cool valley floor air and both under the influence of gravity flow along the valley/plain. This is referred to as the so-called *mountain wind*. (Colls & Whitaker, 2001)

Katabatic winds are variable in speed and are often less than four kilometres per hour. Much stronger flows occur over snow and ice fields where the cooling effect may take place day and night. In Antarctica the katabatic flows may be 500 metres thick, thereby creating very strong and fast winds in excess of 95 kilometres per hour (i.e. 51 knots). In tropical regions the anabatic winds result in more rain falling on the slopes than the valley floor. Mountains/hills and valleys tend to funnel the general circulation along the axis of the feature rather than across it. If the air has enough moisture vapour and the temperature is below the dew point fog will occur on the valley floors. Frosts may develop if the katabatic winds are blocked or restricted along pockets of the valley floor.

Tornadoes—Occur in Australia and are associated with thunderstorms. They are considered to be the rarest and most violent thunderstorm phenomena. They are rapidly rotating columns of air that descend as a funnel shape from the base of a storm cloud. The tornado vortex, which can range in width from hundreds of metres to a few metres, usually spins clockwise (viewed from above) and contains very damaging winds that may reach more than 450 km/h (243 knots). In Australia 41 people at least, having been killed by tornadoes. A tornado over water is known as a waterspout.

Trade winds—Occupy most of the tropics and blow from the subtropical highs towards the equatorial trough (aka *intertropic convergence zone* (ITCZ)). In terms of latitude they are located between 30° S – 30° N. Since the equator receives the Sun's rays directly the air here heats and rises, creating a low-pressure system behind. Around 30° S – 30° N most of the air sinks back to the equator to become the warm, steady breeze known as trade winds, while the rest of the air flows back to the poles. In the Southern Hemisphere winds blowing out of the subtropical highs are called south-easterlies (aka *south-east trades*) and north-easterlies (aka *north-east trades*) in the Northern Hemisphere. If the equatorial trough is in the Northern Hemisphere the south-east trades turn to the south-west as they cross the equator. If the equatorial trough is in the Southern Hemisphere, the north-east trades turn north-west. These winds do not occur in the northern Indian Ocean.

Tropics—Is defined as the area between the tropic of Cancer in the Northern Hemisphere, and the Tropic of Capricorn in the Southern Hemisphere. Both tropics lies along the 23.5 degree parallel. The earth is tilted from its axis to 23.5 degrees and this is the reason for the positioning of the Tropic of Cancer and the Tropic of Capricorn. The positioning of the two tropics allows the sun to be directly overhead at noon on the two solstices. On June 21st, at noon the sun is directly overhead of the Tropic of Capricorn, which is the beginning of summer in the Northern Hemisphere and winter in the Southern Hemisphere. On December 21st, the sun is directly overhead the Tropic of Capricorn, which is the beginning of summer in the Southern Hemisphere and the beginning of winter in the Northern Hemisphere. The latitude of the tropics results in the sun always being high in the sky, which results in their being little to no seasonal variation like autumn and spring, as there is in the latitudes outside of the Tropics. As a result of the tropics yearly orientation towards the sun, there are different weather pattern experienced.

Different references give different positions for the northern and southern tropic boarders with 30 degrees north and south being used by Colls and Whitaker in *The Australian Weather Book, 2nd Ed., 2001*. Thirty degrees south passes south of Grafton on the NSW north coast; pass the northern end of the Flinders Ranges in South Australia; and between Green Head and Leeman in Western Australia.

Troposphere—Is the lowest layer of the earth's atmosphere. Almost all of the weather occurs in this layer. It contains 75–80 per cent of the atmosphere's mass and 99 per cent of its water vapour, dust particles and aerosols. From the earth's surface, the troposphere has a height from 7–20 kilometres (23,000–65,000 feet). The average depth of the troposphere is 20 kilometres in the tropics, 17 kilometres in the mid-latitudes and 7 kilometres at the poles in summer and almost indistinct in winter. The lowest part of the troposphere is called the 'boundary layer'. Winds in the boundary layer are affect by the roughness of the earth's surface (e.g. mountains, forests, bodies of water). Winds above the boundary layer are not affected to the same extent, by physical features. The depth of the boundary layer varies typically from a few hundred metres to 2 kilometres, depending upon the landforms, seasons and time of day. The troposphere is heated from below by reflected radiation off the earth's surface. As the sun warms the land and seas, the heat is radiated into the air above it. As the air raises it stirs up the troposphere creating a pressure difference and weather.

Turbulence—Refers to the disturbance of the even flow of a current or stream. Causes may include: promontories, islands, pier or jetty, meeting of opposite currents or streams (converging eddies), sudden change in the depth of water (i.e. potholes or sudden shelves in the sea-bed, shoals, reefs, passage constrictions). Turbulence usually occurs on the lee side (opposite side) of an obstruction. Associated names for turbulence include tide-rip, tidal race, overfalls, eddies, tideway, freshets, and weather-going stream.

Veering—Has two definitions depending upon country of usage. According to international usage, it is when the wind changes direction in a clockwise manner (e.g. northerly to easterly, south-westerly to westerly etc.). According to widespread usage among U.S. meteorologists, a change in wind direction in a clockwise sense in the Northern Hemisphere, counter-clockwise in the Southern Hemisphere; the opposite of backing (AMS, 2000). Many if not most American authors use this U.S. interpretation. The Royal Australian Navy and Australian publications use the international interpretations.

Wave-set-up—Refers to wave modification as the wave reaches a water depth along the coast that allows the oscillatory motion to *feel-the-bottom* and modify its height

Weather-going stream (aka *weather tide*)—Is when a wind is blowing against a strong tidal stream.

Westerlies (aka *prevailing* westerlies, *westerly wind belt, countertrades, middle-latitude westerlies, polar westerlies, subtropical westerlies* etc.)—Are regions of belts of predominantly westerly winds usually situated between 40° S – 60° S and 40° N – 60° N (Colls & Whitaker, 2001). Some meteorologist put these wind between 35° S – 65° S and 35° N – 65° N. Others cite 30° S – 60° S and 30° N – 60° N too which they ascribe much of the weather movements in the Northern Hemisphere. Possibly an easier way to look at this, is by the central point of their eastward migration by saying, the westerly wind belt is said to be centred around 45° S or 45° N. In the Southern Hemisphere the westerlies are an almost completely uninterrupted belt of strong ocean winds, which often have fronts embedded in them.

Weather shore—The Bowditch glossary of marine navigation defines weather shore '*as observed from a vessel, the shore lying in the direction from which the wind is blowing*'. See lee shore.

Waterspout—A tornado relative over water; most common over subtropical and tropical areas. They are funnel-shaped columns of rapidly rotating air and water particles reaching down from the base of clouds. They are not necessarily associated with thunderstorms and have been observed at the base of large cumulus clouds often with heavy showers in the region.

Boat Terminology

Abaft—Refers to the rear of: (i.e. behind).

Aft—Meaning at, in or towards the stern; also used as a directional term.

Amidships—Meaning in or towards the middle of the vessel; or part way between the stem and stern.

Asymmetrical hulls—Are hull forms other than symmetrical. Tend to pitch less in waves.[3] See Hull form.

Athwart, Athwartship—Means across a boat's beam (width), at right angles to the keel. The same as *abeam*.

Beam—Is the transverse breadth of the hull (i.e. across the hull). The transverse measurement of a boat is at the widest point; also called breadth.

Bow—Is the forward end of a boat (either side of the stem).

Bow angle of entry (aka *half angle of entry*)—Is determined by a line intersecting the centreline at the bow and tangent to the waterline (Winters). Bow angle of entry is rarely less than seven degrees or larger than twenty-five degrees. Bow angle of entry is another emotive and controversial subject discussed amongst designers and paddlers, about the pros and cons of different styles and angles. Test data shows smaller angles (e.g. *plumb bows)* are efficient as speed increases with high speed Navy ships possessing around seven degrees bow angle of entry (Winters, The Shape of the Canoe Part 2).

Bow rake—Describes the side (sheer) view of the bow.

Bulkhead—A term applied to the vertical partition walls that subdivide the interior of a kayak into separate compartments. They also provide rigidity and strength into the kayak hull and deck structure.

Bulwark—A solid part of the ship's side extending like a fence above the level of the deck.

Camber—Transverse curvature of a boats deck.

Coaming—The raised deck section (usually vertical) around hatchways and other apertures' to keep water out.

Chine—Any corner or angle as opposed to a curve in cross-section; *turn of the bilge*. Also described as the angular intersection between the bottom and side of a boat and may be described as an angular shoulder.

Cutwater—Knee at head of ship, dividing water before it reaches the bow; the forepart of a boat's stem.

Deadrise—The angle between the hull's surface (when looking at it in a cross-section) and a horizontal plane extending laterally from the baseline. An angle greater than 20 degrees is termed: *steep dead-rise*.[4]

Deadwood—The portion of a hull that displaces a volume small in proportion to its weight, but has a function (e.g. structural support). Deadwood has a small effect on frictional resistance. For canoes, John Winters defines it as: *Those portions of a hull that have high surface area relative to their enclosed volume. Typically at the bow and stern.*

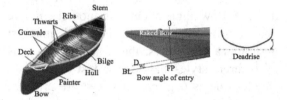

Deck centreline—Is a physical or imaginary line along middle of deck dividing the craft lengthwise into left and right halves.

Deck (well)—Low, inside the craft (e.g. a 'sit-on-top' kayak's deck has a deck well).

Fore—Means at or towards the bow.

Fore body—The portion of a boats body lying forward of amidships.

Foredeck—The portion of deck at or near the bow.

Forefoot—The curvature of the lower stem where it meets the keel (keelson on a kayak). A deep forefoot is one, which extends deep into the water. This is found on most Eastern Canadian Arctic kayaks.[5]

Forward edge—Used interchangeably with leading edge. It refers to the leading edge on some part of an object.

Freeboard (FB)—Is a dynamic measure of the vertical distance from the waterline to sheer. The amount of freeboard decreases as weight increases. **Least freeboard** is the lowest portion of freeboard. See topsides.

Freeboard deck—The uppermost complete deck open to the weather and sea.

Gunwale—The upper side rail of the hull. The upper edge sides of a boat. It is the uppermost *wale* of a ship, next below the *bulwarks*. It got its name from the fact that the guns were set upon it. In kayaks (*skin-on-frame*), it refers to the deep uppermost longitudinal stringer that is the main strength member in the framework.[6]

Hard chine—*See chine.*

Hogback—This refers to an upward arch along the deck profile. Interchangeable with the terms: *humpbacked* and *humped deck*.

Hogging (*aka reverse sheer*)—Refers to both the bow and stern drooping. See hogback and sheer.

Horn—A stern and or stem extension, ranging from almost vertical to near horizontal. For example, found on the Inuit Mackenzie kayaks and on some Caribou kayaks.

Hull form—Shows a plan view of the hulls shape, for kayaks there are three basic types of hull form (plan shape) called, *symmetrical, Swede form* and *Fish form*.

Hull speed (aka *displacement speed, critical speed-length ratio*)—A term used to describe the relationship between a hull and the wave of translation. See: wave making resistance, speed/length ratio.

Keel—The fore and aft backbone of vessel along the hull.

Keelson—Is a beam attached to the top of the floors to add strength to the keel on a wooden boat. In a skin-on-frame kayak, as there is no true keel, the longitudinal centreline stringer along the bilge acts as the strength member.

Midships—The midpoint of the load waterline length (L_{WL}), located halfway from the forward most point on the waterline to the rearmost point.

Monocoque—Meaning 'single shell' in French, is a construction technique that utilises the external skin to support some or most of the external stresses (loads).

Painter—A line (rope/cordage) attached to a boat for the purpose of mooring and or portage.

Pearl—A term used to describe the bow of a boat burying itself in to a wave or trough.

Pintle—The vertical shaft or pin acting as an axis for the rudder.

Plumb bow (aka *straight bow* or *vertical bow*)—As the alternate names describe, is a bow that is vertical and not raked. Used on many racing craft since there is no excess structure to be influenced by wind and water.

Rake—Refers to an angle away from a vertical or horizontal plane (i.e. slope). See bow angle of entry.

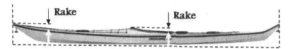

Shell—Refers to the watertight skin, over the hull, which also gives strength to the construction of intermediate parts.

Sheer—The top edge of a hull, fore and aft, where it meets the deck. On canoes that do not have a deck, it refers to the highest points defining the top of the hull (gunwales).

Sheer line—(aka *deck out line, deck edge, deck line*).

Stem—The forward most part of the hull (i.e. the upright, sharp section of the bow right at the front).

Stern—Refers to the after end of the boat (i.e. the rear end of a vessel).

Transom—The backboard of a boats stern. The flat rear end across a boats stern. Some canoes have a transom for the fitment of an electric motor.

Watertight—Refers to the arrangement whereby the structure or fittings prevent the ingress of water under pressure.

Weather-tight—Refers to the arrangement whereby the structure or fittings prevent the passage of water through in ordinary sea and weather conditions.

Position Relative to the Boat

Abeam—At right angles to the centreline.

Aft—Is near or towards the stern.

Ahead—In front of the boat.

Astern—Behind the boat.

Bow—Is the front end of a vessel.

Forward—Near or towards the bow.

Port—Left side of a craft when looking to bow. Colour code: red. Port is so called because it was always the way a craft was berthed (tied up) in harbour to prevent the steer-board being damaged by the quay.

Starboard—Right side of a craft when looking to bow. Colour code: green. Starboard is so called because the right hand side of a boat was the side where the steering oar, or 'steer-board' was set in the days before central, stern-post rudders were used (e.g. Viking longships).

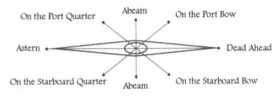

Relative Positions

Quarter—Refers to the portion of a vessel forward of the stern and abaft (behind) of the beam. 'On the port/starboard quarter' applies to a bearing 45° abaft the beam. Every vessel has a starboard and a port quarter.

Boat motions

Surge is the bodily motion of a vessel forward and backward along the longitudinal (x) axis. The force of the sea acting alternately on the bow and stern causes surge. **Heave** is the oscillatory rise and fall due to the entire hull being lifted by the force of the sea. **Sway** is the side-to-side bodily motion, independent of rolling, caused by uniform pressure being exerted entirely along one side of the hull. **Yaw** is the oscillation about a vertical (y) axis approximately through the vessel's centre of gravity. **Roll** is the oscillation about the longitudinal (x) axis. **Pitch** is the oscillatory motion about the transverse (z) axis, due to the bow and stern being raised or lowered on passing through successive crests and troughs of waves.

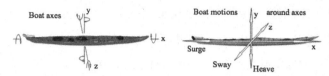

Handling terms

Astern and/or 'to go astern'—Means to go backwards.

Beam sea—Is a sea moving in a direction approximately 90° from the heading.

Beam wind—Wind blowing in a direction approximately 90° from the heading.

Broad on the beam—Is the position of an object that lies off to one side of the vessel.

Broaching—To spin out of control (an involuntary change in heading caused by following and/or quartering seas) and capsize or nearly capsize. The turning of a boat broadside, to the wind or waves, subjecting it to possible capsizing. A turning or swinging of the boat, that puts the beam of the boat against the waves, creating a danger of swamping or capsizing. A knockdown. See: *Pooped.*

Crosswind—Is a wind blowing in a direction approximately 90° from the course.

Feel the bottom (aka *smell the bottom*)—Refers to the effect of shallow water on a vessel while underway. The effect of shallow water tends to reduce boat speed, make her slow in answering the helm, and often make her sheer off course. The speed reduction is largely due to increased wave making resistance resulting from higher pressure differences due to restriction of flow around the hull. The increased velocity of the water flowing past the hull results in an increase in squat.

Following sea—Is a sea in which the waves move in the general direction of the heading. The opposite is Head Sea.

Following wind—Is a wind blowing in the general direction of a vessel's course (i.e. aeronautical term: tail wind).

Forward of the beam—Is any direction between broad on the beam and ahead.

Give way—To slow, stop, go astern, or change course to keep clear of another vessel.

Head wind—Is a wind blowing opposite to a vessels course.

Heading Sea—Is the opposite of a *following sea.*

Heave—Is the oscillatory vertical rise and fall of a vessel, due to the entire hull being lifted by the force of the sea. Movement of a boat, up and down the vertical (y-axis).

Heave to—Steering into the wind and sea making minimum headway.

Heel—Is the lateral inclination of a vessel. As a verb, it means to incline or be inclined to one side. The sideways leaning of a boat, which is caused by the force of the wind, a leaning paddler, a narrow beam, a round bottom or a combination of factors. A boat that heels easily is termed *tender, crank* or *cranky* with those that resist heeling called *stiff.*

Lee-cock, Lee-cocking—Refers to the bow of a boat swing in the direction away from the wind. It is the opposite term to weathercock.

Leeward, (to lee)—Is the side away from the wind's direction. The opposite of windward.

Leeway—The sideways movement of a boat caused by the wind, normally unwanted. In general, keels and other design features help prevent excessive leeway.

Making way—Is when a boat is underway and moving through the water using power, sail and or paddle.

Pooped—Is when a wave comes over the stern; having the wave wash over the stern of the boat. See: Broaching.

Quartering sea—Refers to the sea moving in a direction approximately 45° from the heading (waves striking the vessel on the quarter). Alternatively, it can refer to the relative bearings of approximately 045°, 135°, 225°, and 315°.

Stem the tide—To go forward against the current.

Downwind—To leeward.

Weather side, to weather—See: *windward*.

Under way—Is when a vessel is not at anchor, made fast to the shore, or aground. If you are drifting, you are under way.

Weathercock, weathercocking—Refers to the tendency of a boat to turn its bow into the wind (to windward) without input from the helmsman or paddler. Boats that are said to have a weather helm have been designed to turn slightly into the wind, as it is easier to keep the boat on course with little helm (steering). The opposite term is *lee cock*.

Windward—Is the weather side. The general direction from which the wind blows (upwind); on the weather side. It is the opposite of *leeward*.

Drafting Terms

Axis—The x-axis is the longitudinal axis. A boat rolls (left and right) around the x–axis. The y-axis is the vertical axis. A boat yaws (slews) around the y–axis. A boat also heaves vertically up and down the y–axis. The z–axis is the lateral (transverse) axis. A boat pitches (pivots up and down) around the z–axis. See boat motions.

Base line—Refers to the imaginary straight horizontal line projected through the lowest point of the keel's moulded surface. The base line is used as a reference to measure vertical heights in a horizontal plane (i.e. horizontal distances going up the side of the boat). See waterlines.

Buttock lines—Are the vertical slices running parallel to the keel at a given distance from the centreline of the boat. Shipwrights use a buttock merely as a distance from the centreline. Buttocks are shown in the sheer plan of lines drawing. Note: on the half-breadth plan, do not confuse the buttock lines with the waterlines as seen in the sheer plan and vice versa.

Body plan—Is the view showing the shapes of the frame lines. The body plan is made up of two views (parts) of the portside joined together at the centreline. The right-hand part is an aft-ward looking view (e.g. looking from the bow to the stern). The left-hand part is a forward looking view. This perspective prevents the frame lines

at the aft end from obliterating or interfering with the frame lines at the forward end. This view shows buttock lines and waterlines as straight, while the frame lines appear in their true shape.

Centreline—Is the term for the vertical line extending from the bow to the stern, midway between the sides of a boat. It divides a vessel lengthwise into right (starboard) and left (port). All transverse horizontal dimensions are taken from the centreline.

Cross-section (aka *section*)—Refers to a section made by a plane cutting at right angles. In drafting, a section is an orthographic projection of a three-dimensional object from the position of a plane through the object. This is to say, when cutting an object into slices one gets many parallel cross-sections. A section cuts (slices) through the craft and the location of this 'cut through' is noted on the plan. The slice is rotated 90 degrees to show its profile. The section can be used to describe how the craft will be constructed and discusses how the internal finishes are to look. Sections are used because they explain certain conditions in more detail. See: body sections, station.

Drafts—Ships plans.

Frame line (aka *frames*)—Is a line showing the intersection of the moulded surface with a vertical plane perpendicular to the centreline (i.e. transverse plane). Frame lines are shown in the body plan of the lines drawing. They get their name from the fact that the shell 'frames' or ribs (in other than a monocoque structure) usually are made to this shape and installed transversely (i.e. across) in the boat.

Half-breadth plan (aka *waterline plan*)—Is a view of the portside looking down on the moulded surface. Here the frame lines and buttock lines appear straight, while the waterlines show their true shape.

Isometric drawing—A drawing projection showing vertical lines at 90 degrees and horizontal line at 30 degrees. This is done to show the two sides of an object simultaneously. Isometric drawings combine the two separate projections (plan and elevation) of an orthographic drawing into one three dimensional projection.

Line drawing—Is the name given to the plans showing three views of a boat. The three views are *sheer plan* (*profile view*), *half-breadth plan* and a *body plan*. These views (usually) each show the portside of the ship, since boats are symmetrical about the centreline (i.e. because all dimensions for the port are the same as for starboard).

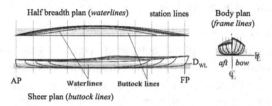

Moulded surface—The inside surface of the skin, planking or plating of a boat/ship. It also refers to the outside surface of frames, bulkheads, ribs and stringers. The moulded surface has no thickness, and is fair and smooth. Actually, when the boat has been built, the thickness of the planking et cetera will extend outside of the moulded surface.

Orthographic projection—A drawing projection representing a three-dimensional object in two dimensions.

Plan view—A plan is an orthographic projection of a three-dimensional object from the position of a horizontal plane through the object. This is to say, looking down on top of the object.

Elevation (aka *profile view, side view* and *sheer plan*)—A drafting term for an orthographic projection of a three-dimensional object. Drawn from the position of a horizontal plane beside an object. That is to say, an elevation is a side-view as viewed from the front, back, left or right. On a line drawing, it is the view looking at the moulded lines from starboard to port (right to left). The waterlines and the frame lines are straight. The deck line (aka sheer curve) shows up clearly in the profile, which is the reason why the profile is sometimes called the sheer plan.

Sectional shape—Refers to an athwartships slice view of a hull design. The drawing shows views of cross sectional shapes (cut-away) from different stations. John Winters in his article titled The Shape of the Canoe, Part 2: Residual Resistance, Fairing and Function, has the following to say about sectional shape:

Much is made of sectional shapes in advertising that attributes or implies some mystical importance to a particular shape or combination of shapes. In fact, subjective evaluations of these features are all we have, and their reliability is highly suspect.

Station lines (aka *section lines*)—Are a position along the centreline or buttock line from where measurements are recorded (i.e. station numbers).

Waterlines—Are lines on a drawing showing the intersection between the moulded surface with a horizontal plane, at a given height above the base line (e.g. on a ship, the seven foot water line is exactly seven feet higher than the base line). These intersections are shown in the half breadth plan in the lines drawing and should not be confused with the load line marked on the outside of a ship when built. Shipwrights use a waterline merely as a height above the base line; and in this sense, waterlines are marked on bulkheads, frames, and other members, for the purpose of properly setting and aligning the structure.

Design Terminology

Acute angle—less than 90°

Approximate bare boat weight—The weight of a craft before it is fitted out with seats, hatches and fittings.[7]

Aquaplaning—In this manual refers to an object skidding across the surface of the water. It is closely related to surfing.

Beam (B) (aka *breath*)—Is the width of the hull. The following terms are used in relation to beam (aka *width in design*):

Beam overall (B$_{OA}$)—Is the width at the widest point of the hull.

Beam at waterline (B$_{WL}$)—Refers to the widest (maximum) part of the kayak's beam, at the waterline.

Coefficients—The multiplier of a variable (a letter that can be replaced by one or more numerical values) or number. Coefficients are useful because there are no units of measurement (e.g. SI or Imperial) and therefore you can make comparisons between different craft readily, since the coefficient, is standard between the two or more craft. For example, a model boat's coefficients determined through SI units are the same as the full-scale boats coefficients that are determined through Imperial units. Coefficients used to compare hull forms are:

Block coefficient (C$_B$)—Is the volumetric ratio between the volume of the immersed hull portion and that of the volume of a solid block. See prismatic coefficient.

Longitudinal coefficient (C$_L$) (aka longitudinal prismatic coefficient), see prismatic coefficient.

Maximum section coefficient (C$_X$)—Is the ratio between the sectional area divided by the square root of the length. It is used as a measure of the relative fullness of a section and allows comparisons to be made between hulls of differing sizes and shapes. See sectional shape.

Mid-ship section coefficient (C$_X$ or C$_M$)—Is the area of the largest hull section (A$_X$) divided by a rectangular section having the same beam (B$_{WL}$) and draft (T) as the underwater section of the hull. It is used to define the fullness of the largest hull section and allows comparisons to be made between hulls of different sizes. The best mid-ship section coefficient lies between 0.94 for fine end hulls and 0.88 for full-end hulls with the difference between the ideal and typical values being around four per cent however, aesthetic and design considerations generally hinder the designer in achieving the ideal (Winters, The Shape of the Canoe Part 1: Frictional Resistance, 2010). Written as:

- $C_X = A_X / B_{WL}$ x T
- See sectional shape.

Prismatic coefficient (C$_p$) (aka *longitudinal coefficient*)—Is a measure of the distribution of volume along a hull's length and is used to evaluate the distribution of the hull's volume. See block coefficient.

Cross-sectional area (A$_X$)—Refers to the area of a particular section in a hull.

Depth (D)—Is the vertical distance from the base line to the lowest part of the freeboard deck.

Design waterline displacement (D$_{WL}$)—Used to determine the total amount of weight the craft is designed to carry.

Displacement (Δ)—The weight of water equivalent to the immersed volume of the hull and is the total weight of a boat. The Greek capital letter delta is the symbol used in equations. A boats displacement has a direct relationship to wetted surface area. For a given length, weight and cross sectional area (displacement/ weight per unit area), one boat builder did some research on different cross-sectional hull shapes, to determine the shapes frictional resistance. His research was into shapes for catamaran hulls. Using eight shapes floating in still water, he determined that the ellipse provided the least wetted surface area and therefore, less frictional resistance (skin friction).

For displacement type hull, which catamarans, canoes and kayaks are, frictional resistance is a major form of drag. A conclusion from this study is that, different shapes having the same variables as described above have different displacements. However, the author pointed out that in real life, he would use a shape that provided a smooth ride; and therefore, handling characteristics is of concern, along with hull shape (Seluga, 2009). With reference to the diagram, the eight hull shapes used in determining the shape that provides the less wetted surface area. The lower the value (inside the shape), the less wetted surface area.

Eight hull displacement types

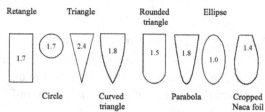

Displacement/Length ratio (D/L)—The ratio between waterline length and displacement. It is determined by the non-dimensional formula: volume of displacement (V) divided by the load waterline (L_{WL}) cubed; $V/(0.1L_{WL})^3$. The resultant number is called the fatness ratio. See Volumetric coefficient). For kayaks, the fatness ratio varies from 0.63 for long, light boats to 1.8 for short heavy boats. Loaded touring kayaks have a fatness ratio around 1.4 (Winters, Speaking Good Boat: Part 1, 2010).

Draught (d or T) (aka *Draft*)—Refers to the depth of water, the hull is displacing, as measured from the keel (base line) to waterline. Draft is related to displacement.

Effective waterline length—A measurement used by Sea Kayaker Magazine as part of the equation in predicting speed/resistance figures. The shape of a hull and particularly the bow affect wave-making resistance (wave making characteristics). The effect different hulls have on wave making is accounted for in the prismatic coefficient but the results are refined by the determination of effective waterline length. The effective waterline length is determined form a plotted curve of areas. The shape of the bow affects the position and formation of the bow wave, which is directly related to the formation of the wave of translation.

Fatness ratio—See: fineness, block coefficient, Displacement/Length ratio (D/L), Volumetric coefficient (C_V).

Fineness—One of several methods used to express the fineness of a hull (e.g. *Displacement/ Length ratio (D/L), Block coefficient (C_B) and Prismatic coefficient (C_P)*). Fineness is closely relates to boat hull resistance, since the manner in which the hull separates the water and draws it back in, as it passes through, can result in either turbulent flow or laminar (smooth) flow. See: flow, Froude number, resistance, wave making resistance, fine-end, and full-end.

Fine-end—Refers to a hull being able to gradually part the water, which requires less energy as opposed to a full-end boat ploughing through the water. For ships, consider a destroyer's bow compared to a super tankers bow and how the water is parted and moves around the vessel. See: full-end, prismatic coefficient.

Flow—The movement of particles. There are two types of flow streamline (laminar flow) and turbulent. In streamline flow, each particle of the fluid follows a smooth path and these paths do not crossover each other. Turbulent flow is characterised by erratic, small, whirlpool-like circles called eddy currents. Eddies absorb a great deal of energy.

Freeboard (F_B)—The difference between depth and draft. Measured at three points along the hull (aft, mid and forward) it is the measure of the vertical distance from the waterline to sheer.

Froude number (F_n)—A dimensionless number comparing inertial forces to gravitational forces. The Froude number is associated with wave making resistance, since the energy in the bow and stern waves depend upon gravity. The Froude number is used in tank testing and for the comparison of wave patterns between different boat shapes and reduces the need to build full-scale models for research and development. From the Froude number is derived the more commonly used *speed/length ratio*. See Speed/ Length ratio (S/L).

Froude 'Law of Comparison'—Froude through his experiments laid down the principles by which full scale resistance may be predicted from said experiments. The law states that the ratio of wave resistance to displacement is the same for geometrically similar hulls, when the speed/length ratios are the same.[8] See: resistance, speed/length ratio (S/L), wave making resistance.

Full-ended—A craft that maintains a fairly wide and uniform beam from stem to stern. See: fine-end, Prismatic coefficient.

Hull categories—There are three categories of hull as described below:

Displacement hulls—Are a hull that is supported exclusively or predominately by buoyancy. Displacement hulls travel through the water at a limited rate, which is defined by their waterline length; and they do not obtain lift from their speed.

Semi-displacement hulls (aka *semi-planing hulls*)—Are hulls that have features of both planing and displacement hulls. The hull form is capable of developing a moderate amount of dynamic lift; however, the craft's weight is still supported through buoyancy.

Planing—Refers to aquaplaning and hulls that have speed/length ratios (knots/feet) over 2.5 up to 10 or higher. True planing hull designs use the concept of hydrodynamic lift developed from its own power-plant, as opposed to surfing on the energy of a wave.

Hydroplaning—Refers to a planing hull under the power of the power-plant, rising up out of the water, thereby reducing the wetted surface area of the hull. The shortened form of hydroplaning is *planing*.

Length/Beam ratio (L/B or **B/L)**—A very useful measure for comparing boats with different hull shapes and dimensions. L/B is waterline length divided by waterline beam. For example, a boat built as having a L_{WL} of 17 feet and a B_{WL} of 21 inches (1.75 ft) has the same L/B of 9.7:1 as a boat that was designed and built using metric units of 5.182 m x 0.533 m.

Length on deck (LD)—The distance on deck from the fore part of the hull to the after part of the hull, measured parallel to the design loaded waterline.

Non-dimensional formulas—Used by naval architects to define quantities as a meaningful measure for definition and comparison purposes.

Planing—In this manual, it refers to hydroplaning as opposed to aquaplaning.

Pounds Per Inch Immersion (PPI)—The additional weight required to sink the vessel one inch further in water. The further a kayak sinks

into the water (displacement), the greater the wetted surface area and the resulting frictional resistance. According to Sea Kayaker Magazine, 2008:

A kayak with flared sides and a raked bow and stern is going to create a larger 'footprint' in the water as it is loaded and will take more weight to sink another inch than a kayak that has more vertical sides and ends.

Prism—See prismatic coefficient.

Resistance—The fluid force acting on a moving body in such a way as to oppose its motion. Resistance is the preferred term in ship hydrodynamics, while drag is generally used in aerodynamics and for submerged bodies:

Frictional resistance (R_F)—Is *skin friction*, which occurs between the hull's skin and the water. Frictional resistance takes into account the total effect of the hulls wetted surface (S_W), load waterline (L_{WL}) length, surface condition (smooth or rough) and speed.

Residual resistance (R_R)—Means the sum of all the resistances caused by the hull except frictional resistance (skin friction resistance, R_F). The resistances include wave making resistance (R_W), induced resistance (R_I) and heeling resistance (R_H) e.g.

$$R_R = R_W + R_I + R_H.$$

Total resistance (R_T)—Is the sum of all sources of resistance taken into account. For example, $R_T = R_F + R_R$. Total resistance is measured experimentally in a wave tank and through Froude's theory, frictional and residual resistance can be analysed and calculated separately. However, it is not clear if skin friction alone affects residual resistance and therefore there is a (not very significant) calculable error.

Wave-making resistance (R_W)—Is a type of drag, which affects the hull of a kayak and reflects the energy required to push the water away from the hull.[9] In small boats, wave-making resistance is the major source of drag. For all displacement type hulls, the system of waves produced by speed becomes an unavoidable trap.

Speed/Length ratio (S/L)—Is a dimensional number and the more commonly used term, used to quantify the resistance of a hull through the water. It varies from the Froude number through the absence of acceleration due to gravity. It is written as $Vs / \sqrt{L_{WL}} = 1.34$ for knots to feet and gives a relationship (between the hull and wave of translation) commonly referred to as *hull speed*. To be of use the units need to be known and therefore the table below has been included.

From the speed/length ratio three general categories of boat can be derived: displacement hull, semi-displacement hull and planing hull. See: Froude number, resistance, wave making resistance (R_W), displacement hull, semi-displacement hull and planing hull.

Speed/Length ratio units	
Knots ≈ $1.34\sqrt{L_{WL}}$ in feet	Knots ≈ $2.5\sqrt{L_{WL}}$ in metres
Mph ≈ $1.55\sqrt{L_{WL}}$ in feet	m/s ≈ $2.25\sqrt{L_{WL}}$ in metres

Topsides—Is the part of the hull below the sheer line (deck edge) and above the load waterline (L_{WL}).

Volumetric coefficient (C_V) (aka *the fatness ratio*)—Used to indicate volume to length. See Displacement/Length ratio (D/L).

Volume (V)—Is the size, measure or amount of anything in three dimensions. Depending upon application, it refers to the volume of water displaced by a hull when talking about displacement and stability or if used in determining the entire volume of a kayak or just a cockpit or compartment. When used to describe a boat in advertising as either high or low volume it is a nebulous advertising ploy as there is no comparison or standard. What some consider important is the Design waterline displacement (D_{WL}), that is, how much was it designed to carry and yet be manageable.

Wetted surface (S_W) (aka *wetted area*)—The area of the hull's surface in contact with the water when loaded to its designed displacement. Simply put, the less the area the less the resistance (drag) and therefore the more efficient

the hull. At low speeds (generally paddled by sea kayakers), the water friction against the hull is the main factor in determining how fast a kayaker will go for a given level of effort.

Waterline beam (B_{WL})—See beam waterline.

Waterline length (L_{WL})—See length.

Waterplane area—The hull area defined by the water outline, being the area of the waterplane.

Wave of translation—See wave making resistance (R_W), resistance.

Stability Terminology

Physics terms

Mass (m)—of an object refers to the amount of matter that is contained by the object. The SI is kg. All mechanical quantities can be defined in terms of mass, length, and time.

Weight—Is the mass of an object subjected to the force of gravity. The weight of an object equals the mass of the object times the acceleration of gravity ($9.8 m/s^2$). W = mg. The SI is the newton (N) since weight is a force.

Mass and weight: A 1 kg object on earth will have a mass of 1 kg on the moon but will weigh one sixth as much.

Density (ρ)—Is defined as mass per unit volume ($\rho = m/V$). The symbol for density is the Greek small letter ρ ('rho'). The SI for density is kilograms per cubic metre (kg/m^3). Outside of SI units, density can be expressed as grams per cubic centimetre (g/cc or g/cm^3).

Specific gravity (SG)—Of a substance is defined as the ratio of the density of that substance to the density of water at 4° C. Abbreviated as SG it is without dimension or units. If a substance has, a SG of one or less, it will float; if greater than one it will sink.

Stability terms

Buoyancy—The upward force exerted by the water in which a vessel is immersed. The weight of the floating object displaces water equal to its weight. The displacement of water by a vessel's weight (W) is termed *displacement*. Therefore it can be said that the force of buoyancy equals displacement.

Buoyancy, positive—Positive buoyancy is one of three buoyancy terms usually associated with submarines and SCUBA divers: positive, neutral and negative. Simplistically, positive buoyancy refers to the ability for an object to float (it is less dense [mass/volume] than the medium it is in.

Buoyancy, neutral—Neutral buoyancy refers to the state where the objects weight equals the amount of water it displaces.

Buoyancy, negative—Negative buoyancy refers to the objects state of sinking (denser than its surrounding medium).

Centreline (CL)—Refers to the line dividing the vessel in to two halves.

Centre of buoyancy (CB, B)—Is an imaginary point along the centreline of a stable vessel *below the waterline*, at which all of the resultant buoyancy forces (*force of buoyancy*), of both forward and aft, are said to act and be in equilibrium. The force of buoyancy acts through the centre of buoyancy and always acts vertically upward.

When a vessel heels/lists, the centre of buoyancy moves to the *geometric centre* (aka *centroid*) of the *underwater* section, in the direction of the heel. The location of the centre of buoyancy depends upon the underwater shape of the vessel. As the underwater shape changes, the centre of buoyancy changes. Besides design, the shape of a hull can change shape through heeling, trim, pitch and when a capable vessel begins or stops planing. Regardless of the action that changes the underwater sections shape (form) the centre of buoyance will move to the vessels underwater geometric centre.

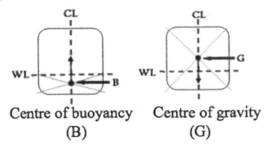

Centre of buoyancy (B)   Centre of gravity (G)

Naval architects give great thought to the underwater section/shape of a hull and the effect the shape will have on the centre of buoyancy. The athwartships (side-to-side) centre of buoyance is considered to be the most important as it effects roll. The centre of buoyancy can move in three dimensions simultaneously through pitch, roll and a combination of both.

Centre of effort (CE)—The centre of sail area. It is usually calculated using 100 per cent of the *foretriangle area* (the sail area bounded between the headstays, mast and foredeck).

Centre of Gravity (CG, G)—Is an imaginary point at which all the weight of an object's mass are considered to act. It can also be considered to be the point at which all the weights of a system or unit concentrate, having the same effect as all of the concentrated parts. Gravity always acts vertically downwards through this point. The force of gravity is considered to act downwards through a vessels centre of gravity along the centreline. In hydrostatics the position of a vessels centre of gravity is said to be fixed and does not move. However in real life, on small vessels like yachts and kayaks, movement of the crew can change the centre of gravity position. Adding weight to a vessel changes the centre of gravity position. Adding weight up high raises the centre of gravity while the opposite is true if you add the weight low down. Depending upon the shape of the vessel (e.g. twin hull), the imaginary centre of gravity may be outside of the vessel, since the centre of gravity of a vessel is the result (sum) of its individual components.

Centre of gravity of a person—Is considered to be located around the naval region of a standing adult. Females standing centre of gravity is around 53–56 per cent. Males are around 54–57 per cent. Depending upon the actions of a person the centre of gravity can move outside of the body. Females tend to have a larger mass around their hips and thighs. Males tend to have a larger mass around their chest and shoulders, though many have a larger mass around their waists. The most stable position for a person in a canoe is when they are kneeling. When seated with the legs extended as in a kayak the centre of gravity can move up and down depending upon the position of the torso and head.

Centre of lateral plane (CLP)—The centre of the underwater area of the hull. CLP is only important for sailboats because it is a guide to the location of the sails and rig.[10] Refer to Centre of effort (CE). (Brewer, 1994).

For a boat to sail a straight course, two opposing lateral forces must be brought into balance. These two primary forces are centred in the sails and the hull. The centre of force or lift, generated as wind flows over the sails is called the *centre of effort* (CE). The pressure of the water against the load waterline length (L_{WL}) (e.g. the hull, rudder, keel or centre-board) resists this pull and balances against it, working with the sails' force to move the boat ahead. The resistance of the hull is focused at the *centre of lateral resistance* (CLR). The relative positions of the two forces CE and CLR (called *lead*) determine whether a boat wants to turn into the wind (*weather helm*), away from the wind (*lee helm*), or sail a straight course when the helm is released.

If the lead is too small a sailboat develops a weather helm requiring the helmsman to turn the tiller to weather; thus weather helm. This action positions the rudder to leeward. A weather helm of 2–4 degrees is considered desirable as the rudder works with the keel to generate lift like a sail or wing allowing to boat to sail faster and a point closer to the wind. In addition, it also provides a safety feature whereby if the helm is released the boat automatically turns into the wind thereby spilling wind pressure from the sails, slows down the boat and then stands upright. For a helmsman, it also provides a feel for the boat.

A lee helm is when the lead is too great creating a dangerous situation for sailors. If the tiller is left unattended the boat will not round up into the wind and spill the wind pressure from the sails. A serious lee helm may make it impossible to bring a yacht about forcing the helmsman to jibe in order to change course.

Centre of lateral resistance (CLR)—A point at the geometrical centre of the submerged hull and fin (keel) when viewed from the side. It does not usually include the rudder area. The CLR does move about as the hull changes its attitude. (Marchaj, 1964). The term is associated with the centre of lateral plane and in one reference (Brewer, 1994) it is synonymous, as the dialogue refers to CLP and the diagrams refer to CLR.

Couple (*moment of couple*)—Refers to a pair of coplanar forces of equal magnitude acting parallel but in opposite directions *capable of producing rotation* (when not inline with each other, but not translation (i.e. a pure moment). For example, the centre of buoyancy (B) and the centre of gravity (G) are coplanar and work opposite each other along a vertical axis keeping a body stable; but when not inline with each other the forces rotate the body. The moment of the couple = force (F) x distance (d).

Directional stability—A measure of a craft's ability to maintain straight-line movement despite cross winds and uneven paddling. A craft with a high degree of directional stability will be less manoeuvrable than one without. Directional stability and manoeuvrability are inversely proportional to each other. See: *stability*.[11]

Equilibrium—For a vessel to remain upright and at rest on the water there must not be any unbalanced forces or moments acting on it. For a vessel that is upright and motionless on the water, at rest, two forces need to be in equilibrium: the *force of gravity* and the *force of buoyancy*. These two forces act in the same vertical plane (line) opposite to each other. For a vessel to float, they must both be exactly numerically equal and be acting in the opposite direction.

The three states of equilibrium

Stable   Neutral   Unstable

Static equilibrium—Is when a body is at rest.

Stable equilibrium—Is when a body is disturbed by an external force but returns to its original position at a state of rest after the force is removed.

Neutral equilibrium—Is when an applied force disturbs a body and moves it, but when removed, the body will rest at any point along the plane it was moved on.

Unstable equilibrium—Is when any slight force causes a body to move from its position of rest.

Free surface effect—Refers to the movement of liquids (e.g. water, fuel in the bilges or on the deck of ships). It can also refer to any loads that can move when a boat is heeled. Water is heavy and its build up and movement in a cockpit and or bilge affect a boat's stability, both longitudinally and laterally, causing it to behave tender or even unstable.

To minimise free surface effect sea kayaks have bulkheads, which prevent water moving longitudinally and affecting trim. In the lateral plane, an accumulation of free water, loose cargo, or incorrectly loaded cargo, will change the righting lever's length. In fair weather conditions, the paddler by shifting their body position and the use of correction strokes can correct this. However depending upon the situation, this can lead to fatigue. In challenging conditions physical and mental fatigue may result in capsize.

To minimize free surface effect: keep bilges/ cockpit dry or at least on long paddles with a leaking spray skirt, monitor the build up of water; ensure cargo is loaded with the weight evenly distributed laterally and longitudinally; and the cargo is secured in the compartments.

Heel—The movement of a boat away from upright through an external force (wind, waves etc.). It is to be distinguished from rolling, which is an oscillatory motion.

Law of Floatation, First—A vessel will float (with freeboard) if it has more than enough watertight volume to displace a weight of water equal to the weight of the vessel.

Law of Floatation, Second—A vessel will float (with freeboard) provided its density is less than the density of the water in which it is placed.

List—Is the movement of a boat away from upright because of an uneven transverse distribution of weight (i.e. centre of gravity is the off centreline).

Loll (aka *angle of loll*)—Is a term used to describe a boat that is unstable when upright and therefore heels to one side. The boat is in a state of unstable equilibrium.

Longitudinal centre of buoyancy (LCB)—Is the longitudinal position for the centre of buoyancy (B) and is often amidships.

Longitudinal centre of gravity (LCG)—Refers to the longitudinal position of gravity (G).

Longitudinal centre of floatation (LCF)—Refers to the centre of the water plane area around which boat trims.

Metacentre (M)—An imaginary point found by extending a line vertically upwards from the centre of buoyancy to cut the centre line. It may be considered as the pivot about which the force of buoyancy swings as a vessel rolls. Note: the metacentre is only valid for angles of inclination of 0° up to a range of 7° to 10° of heel.

Metacentric height (GM)—The vertical distance between the vessels centre of gravity (G) and the metacentre (M). For any given angle of heel there is a definite relationship between GM and GZ (righting lever) as shown by $GZ = GM \sin \theta$. GM is also an indication of whether a vessel is stable or unstable. If the metacentre (M) is above the centre of gravity (G) the metacentric height (GM) is positive. When the vessel is inclined, the moments that are developed will be *righting moments* and the vessel will be stable. If the centre of gravity (G) is above the metacentre (M) the metacentric height is negative and the moments that are developed when the vessel is inclined will be *upsetting moments* making the vessel unstable.

If the metacentric height is large the righting arms that develop at small angles of heel will be large. The vessel will resist rolling and is said to be *stiff*. If the metacentric height is small the developed righting arms will be small and therefore a vessel will roll more readily and is said to be *tender*.

Moment (aka *moment of force*)—A measure of force applied to a lever arm (aka *moment arm*). It is associated with torque. A 'moment' (Nm) = force (Newtons) x length of lever arm (metre). A moment can be said to be the product of a force tending to produce a rotation about an axis multiplied by it distance from the axis. Simplistically a moment is the force generated by both the length of lever and weight of the mass. Technically the force exerted by a weight is a product of mass and the effect of gravity. A moment can be increased by either extending the lever arm or by adding weight.

Reserve buoyancy—Is the volume of a watertight vessel above the waterline. As draft increases and therefore freeboard decreases, reserve buoyancy decreases. The opposite is true if draft is decreased.

Righting arm (GZ) (aka *GZ lever, ship's righting arm*)—The perpendicular (horizontal) distance between two lines of force (e.g. between the forces of gravity and buoyancy), when displaced from each other's vertical plane when a boat is heeled.

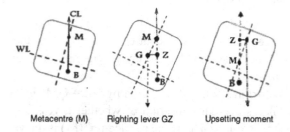

Metacentre (M)   Righting lever GZ   Upsetting moment

Righting moment (RM)—The rotational force (torque) generated by the length of the righting arm (GZ) and a boat's displacement that will return a boat upright (back to stable equilibrium). A vessels righting moment is the result of two intersecting forces: buoyancy acting through the centre of buoyancy and weight (W) acting through the centre of gravity. If these two equal and opposite forces are separated by distance (e.g. GZ) the moment will become a *couple*, which is measured using only one of the opposing forces, times the distance of separation. In a vessel the righting moment is the product of

the force of buoyancy multiplied by length of the righting arm GZ that separates the forces of buoyancy and gravity. Righting moments (Nm) are decreased as a result of decrease in GZ length. Righting moments increased as a result of increased weight (W).

A righting moment (RW) is expressed in newton metre (Nm). RM = W x GZ. Where W is weight (i.e. a force acting on a mass causing displacement) in newton (N) and GZ is the righting lever length in meter (m).

Stability—Refers to a kayak's ability to resist any change in buoyancy and return itself to its former state of equilibrium. It is the ability of a body to maintain equilibrium.

Stability characteristics—Comprise terms like stiff and tender to compare boats of similar type and size. *Stiff* refers to a boat with a short, jerky roll and it is difficult to heel initially. It has a large metacentric height, with the centre of gravity being well below the metacentre; and it has a large righting arm (GZ lever). *Tender* refers to a boat with a weak-righting moment; returns upright slowly and has a long roll period. It has a small metacentric height, with the centre of gravity not being far below the metacentre; and having a small righting arm (GZ lever).

Stability, final—Refers to stability at the swamp point, the point where a heeled boat takes on water. More applicable to open canoes where water can flood the cockpit/bilge.

Stability, primary (aka *initial stability)*—Refers to how a kayak feels (and therefore is subjective to the person describing it) while sitting at rest (without listing) on flat water. It is a subjective measure of the *tippiness* of a kayak when a person gets in and sits on the water.

Stability, secondary (aka *reserve, dynamic* or *ultimate stability*)—The force with which a kayak resists being put on to its edge and or capsize.

Stability, vertical—Refers to the ability of a ship to return to the upright condition when heeled. This ability is primarily governed by the vertical height of a ship's centre of gravity (G).

Stiff—Is a term used to describe a vessel that strongly resists heeling. The opposite is *tender*. Refer to stability characteristics.

Swamp point—Describes the heeled point where the water is level with the sheer line. Applicable to open canoes where water can enter the cockpit/bilge.

Synchronisation—Is a state in which the boat's period of roll coincides with the period of its encounter with waves (causes excessive rolling).

Tender—Is a term used to describe a vessel that heels readily. The opposite is *stiff*. Refer to stability characteristics.

Trim—The difference between the forward and aft draughts.

Upsetting moment—Refers to the rotational force generated by forces that will move the boat further from upright. See metacentric height.

Waterline (WL)—Refers to the vessels designed waterline.

Water plane area—The outline shape of the hull at the waterline.

Yaw—The angle of the hull's centreline relative to the true course of the hull. The Bowditch glossary defines yaw as:

The oscillation of a vessel in a seaway about a vertical axis approximately through the centre of gravity. Depending upon hull shape (e.g. shallow flat hulls) the increase in resistance due to yaw can be as much as five per cent at quite small angles of around six degrees.

Yawing—The angular motion about a vertical axis, through the boat's centre of gravity. The motion is generally described as the result of: poor steering, the orbital motion of water in a seaway and gyroscopic action. Describing the quasi-static forces, generally, the wave profile on the port and starboard sides of a boat are not uniform and as a result, the longitudinal position of the centre of pressure, on one side of the submerged portion of the hull, is offset both longitudinally and vertically, from the other side of the boat. This produces a strong rotation coupled about the vertical axis–a

yawing tendency including a heeling moment. The orbital motion of the water particles in a wave produces a dynamic yawing moment. At the crest of the wave–the water particles are travelling in an orbital motion and in the same direction as the wave–are at the top of their orbital rotation. In the trough, the particles are at the bottom of their orbital rotation and moving in the opposite direction to the waves advance. As a result, a boat moving in a quartering sea or with the sea at an angle to the bow is subject to a yaw couple.

Terms applied to Rudders and Skegs

The basic definitions and terms used to describe the shape and hydrodynamic characteristics of rudders and other boat control surfaces (foils) are the same as those used to describe aerodynamic lifting surfaces.[12]

Angle of attack (α)—The angle between the mean cord line of a foil and the direction of free stream flow (velocity).

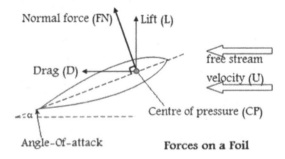

Forces on a Foil

Aspect ratio (AR)—A term used to describe an aerofoil's plan form and is also referred to as the span/chord ratio. Aerofoils can have the same area but are described as being a low, medium or high aspect ratio. In terms of the component of *lift* and the *lift/drag ratio*, there is an advantage in larger span over smaller span aerofoils.

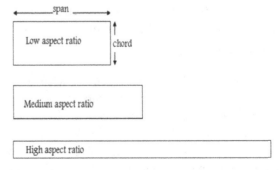

In the associated drawing, the three aerofoils all have an area of 12 m² with the ratio of span to chord determining if the foil (wing, rudder, paddle etc.) is of high, medium or low aspect ratio. The low aspect ratio foil has a span of 6m and a chord of 2m giving it an aspect ratio of 3. The medium aspect ratio foil measures 8 m x 1.5m resulting in an aspect ratio of 5.33. The high aspect ratio foil measures 16 m x 0.75 m resulting in an aspect ratio of 21.33.

Chord line and therefore *mean chord*—Refers to the average fore and aft distance between the forward and trailing edges of a foil.

Camber—On a foil refers to the maximum distance between the chord line and the mean line, which lays half way between the outer surfaces of a foil. Simply it is a measure of the curvature of the foil. Since rudders are required to provide the same amount of force to port as well as starboard, they are generally symmetrical about the chord line and therefore have zero camber. Note: camber is also a term used in paddle design.

Forces on a foil—These forces are said to act from the centre of pressure and are the:

Centre of pressure (CP)—The point on a foil through which the resultant force is said to act. Its position varies along the cord for low aspect ratio foils.

Drag (D)—The component parallel to the direction of flow.

Lift (L)—The component at right angles to the direction of flow.[13]

Normal force (F)—The component of resultant force on a control surface acting perpendicular (at right angles) to a boats longitudinal axis. It can be broken down into the components of lift and drag.

Material Terms

Dynamic Loading—A sudden or rapid force applied to a rope caused by stopping, jerking, swinging, et cetera. In some cases, the force may be two, three, or even more times the normal load involved. For example, picking up a tow on a slack line or stopping a falling object, can cause a dynamic loading of a rope. Working loads do not apply under such conditions.

Materials strength terms—Are used to define the stress forces acting on a material and the plane from which they act:

Compressive strength—Is the opposite of tensile strength and describes a material's ability to withstand or succumb to crushing loads.

Deformation—Of the material is the change in geometry when stress is applied.

Elasticity (*elastic region, limit*)—Is the linear response of materials in terms of stress and strain. It describes the characteristic of the ability of a material to return to its original shape after a force has been removed.

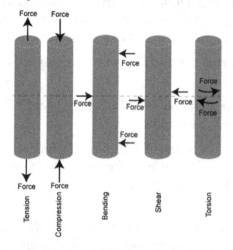

Terminology of forces on materials

Plastic *(region, limit)*—Refers to the state of a material after an external force has been removed and the material cannot return to its original shape but is permanently deformed.

Stress—Is defined as a measure of internal forces per unit area. Stresses are normally resolved into *normal stresses*, which have lines of action acting perpendicular (at right angles) to the area in question. Shear (tangential) stresses have lines of action coplanar, (i.e. in the same plane, e.g. the x-axis, y-axis, z-axis) with the area under consideration. Normal stresses pulling away (apart) from the plane area are called *tensile stresses*. Stress forces acting towards each other are *compressive stresses*. The other type of stress is called *shear stress* (τ) and can be described as parallel or tangential forces opposing each other but apart on the same plane. An object under shear stress has equal and opposite forces applied across its opposite faces producing a sliding failure of a material. Consider a thick book on a table: if you push down on top of the book (exert a force parallel to the top surface) the table exerts an equal and opposite force along the bottom face and the books shape changes as its top surface *slides* in the direction of the force.

Strain—Is the response of a system to an applied stress. When a material is loaded with a force, it produces a stress, which then causes a material to deform.

Tensile strength—Is a measure of the resistance of a material subjected to a stretching load. Materials can withstand some *tensile loading*, but if enough force is applied, they will eventually break apart. In other words, the tensile strength of a material is the maximum amount of tensile stress that can be applied to it before it ceases to be elastic. If too much force is applied to the material, it will break or become plastic, (i.e. once the force exertion is stopped the material will not return to its initial shape).

Specific tensile strength—Is a measure of the tensile strength/weight ratio. *Tensile modulus* may be read as a measure of the materials stiffness. *Specific tensile modulus* is a measure of the materials stiffness/weight ratio. The *ultimate tensile strength* (UTS) of a material is the limit stress where the material cracks grows so that the material continuity is loosened and it breaks into two pieces, with a sudden release of the stored elastic energy. *Yield tensile strength* is the measure of a material under tensile stress

at the point where the material yields and becomes elastic (deforms).

Young Modulus (*E*) (*Modulus of elasticity*)— Is a material property that describes its stiffness and is therefore one of the most important properties in engineering design. It is used to predict the compression or elongation of a material when the applied stress is less than the yield strength.

Denier—Is a unit of measure for the linear mass density (measure of mass per unit of length) of fibres. It is defined as the mass in grams per 9000 meters. A common term most likely to be used in the United States and United Kingdom with Europe using the term *tex*.

1 Jeff Lancaster, Roy Grabenauer: Inventor of Sit-on-Top Kayaks, Sea Kayaker Magazine, Vol.21, No.3, August 2004, pp28-29.
2 Winters, The Shape of the Canoe Part 2: Residual Resistance, Section Shape
3 John Winters, The Shape of the Canoe Part 2: Residual Resistance, Bow and Stern Details.
4 Zimmerly (1976)
5 Zimmerly, (1976)
6 Zimmerly, (1976)
7 Note: some manufactures advertise their boats using the bare boat weight figure (number) where as in fact the boat is heavier than advertised (i.e. with hatches, fittings, seat).
8 C.A. Marchaj, op. cit., p.250
9 Hydrodynamic drag
10 CLP has been included because there is documentation describing kayak stability in terms of CLP and CE!
11 Zimmerly, (1976)
12 The theory and practice around control surfaces (e.g. rudders) is quite involved and I will not make any attempt to expound on the theory but rather provide fundamental information so if the reader reads another article about control surfaces and manoeuvrability they have another reference for consideration.
13 Even in aerodynamics, the term can be misleading; under certain flight conditions, such as a vertical nose dive, lift may act horizontally or in other cases act vertically downwards. Whether a horizontal or vertical foil, it is just a term for this component acting at right angles to the direction of free stream velocity on a foil.

INDEX